OXFORD PRIVATE INTERNATIONAL LAW SERIES

GENERAL EDITOR: JAMES J. FAWCETT
Professor of Law
University of Nottingham

CIVIL JURISDICTION RULES OF THE EU AND THEIR IMPACT ON THIRD STATES

OXFORD PRIVATE INTERNATIONAL LAW SERIES

General Editor: James Fawcett

The aim of this series is to publish works of quality and originality in a number of important areas of private international law. The series is intended for both scholarly and practitioner readers.

CIVIL JURISDICTION RULES OF THE EU AND THEIR IMPACT ON THIRD STATES

THALIA KRUGER

Foreword by
Professor Dr Hans Van Houtte

OXFORD
UNIVERSITY PRESS

OXFORD /oos4424З○
UNIVERSITY PRESS

Great Clarendon Street, Oxford OX2 6DP

Oxford University Press is a department of the University of Oxford.
It furthers the University's objective of excellence in research, scholarship,
and education by publishing worldwide in

Oxford New York

Auckland Cape Town Dar es Salaam Hong Kong Karachi
Kuala Lumpur Madrid Melbourne Mexico City Nairobi
New Delhi Shanghai Taipei Toronto

With offices in

Argentina Austria Brazil Chile Czech Republic France Greece
Guatemala Hungary Italy Japan Poland Portugal Singapore
South Korea Switzerland Thailand Turkey Ukraine Vietnam

Oxford is a registered trade mark of Oxford University Press
in the UK and in certain other countries

Published in the United States
by Oxford University Press Inc., New York

© Thalia Kruger, 2008

British Library Cataloguing in Publication Data

Data available

Library of Congress Cataloging in Publication Data

Data available

Typeset by Cepha Imaging Private Ltd., Bangalore, India
Printed in Great Britain
on acid-free paper by
Biddles Ltd., King's Lynn

ISBN 978-0-19-922857-7

1 3 5 7 9 10 8 6 4 2

General Editor's Preface

The previous monograph in the *Oxford Private International Law Series* was concerned with conflict of laws within the UK. One of its themes was the impact of the Europeanization of private international law on intra-UK cases. The present monograph is also concerned with the impact of the EU private international law rules (in this case civil jurisdiction rules) but now, not on one Member State, but on third States. It looks outwards, whereas its predecessor looked inwards.

Like the previous monograph, this book puts the law in its constitutional context. It contains a very full discussion of the external relations law of the EC and its effect on private international law. For private international lawyers, who must increasingly become EU lawyers, this is especially welcome. The examination of the relationship between the EU and the Hague Conference on Private International Law is particularly timely.

The book is wide in its scope and deep in its analysis. Civil jurisdiction rules of the EU are spreading inexorably into new areas and the book looks not only at the Brussels Convention, Brussels I Regulation, the Insolvency Regulation and Brussels II *bis* but also at the proposed Maintenance Regulation and the Hague Convention on Choice of Court Agreements. The jurisdiction rules are analysed for their impact on third States in terms of cornerstones of jurisdiction: the defendant's domicile, exclusive jurisdiction, choice of forum clauses, and declining jurisdiction. The book concludes with proposals for amending certain EU civil jurisdiction rules so as to improve the position for litigants from third States.

This book combines the discussion of difficult theoretical issues with practical discussion of problems that face the practitioner. It should be of great interest not only to lawyers from third States, who might mistakenly think that EU private international law is of no relevance to them or their clients, but also to lawyers within the EU. Of particular interest to lawyers in the UK is the exhaustive discussion of the topic of declining jurisdiction and conflicting proceedings where the alternative forum is a third State. The full ramifications of *Owusu v Jackson* and *Turner v Grovit* have still to be worked out in the English courts and in the European Court of Justice. In the meantime, Dr Kruger brings to the debate the views of someone trained in the Romano-Dutch and then the civil law tradition but at the same time having a familiarity with the common law.

The stated aim of the *Oxford Private International Law Series* is to publish works of quality and originality in a number of important areas of private international law. *Civil Jurisdiction Rules of the EU and their Impact on Third States* meets these criteria admirably.

James Fawcett
Nottingham
July 2007

Foreword

The European Jurisdiction Convention has been an expanding reality. Initially applicable in six European countries in 1968, it has followed the successive enlargements of the European Community. One hundred and forty preliminary rulings of the European Court of Justice and hundreds of national court decisions have added flesh to the bone. Its successor, the Regulation Brussels I, will have the same destiny. Initially applicable in 14 EU states (the Regulation did not apply in Denmark which stuck to the Jurisdiction Convention), it now also applies in the 12 newer Member States and in Denmark, which concluded a separate agreement with the EC, and it will undoubtedly be shaped by further decisions from the Court of Justice and national courts.

From the outset the Jurisdiction Convention stirred commotion beyond the boundaries of Europe. Not only the nature of some jurisdiction rules, but also the subsequent easy enforcement of a Member State judgment all over the European Community, was disturbing. With time the 'outside world' became more accommodating. The EFTA countries copied the Jurisdiction Convention for use among themselves and in their relations with the European Union. The Hague Conference on International Private Law attempted to draft a worldwide jurisdiction convention that was largely modelled on the European precedent. When this ambition was frustrated it settled for a Convention on Choice of Court Agreements.

The extent to which the Jurisdiction Convention and Brussels I apply to situations with close links outside the EU remained a delicate matter. Recently, in its *Owusu* decision (2005) and in the *Lugano* opinion (2006) the Court of Justice made it clear that the Convention, and thus also the Regulation that contains the same provisions, apply extensively. Although they claim exclusive jurisdiction as soon as the dispute concerns rights *in rem* over immovable property located within the EU (regardless where the defendant is established), they do not admit that a non-EU court would have a similar jurisdiction when the property is located outside the EU but the defendant is established within it. The Court seems to deny any *éffet reflexe* which would admit the jurisdiction of foreign courts for mirror images of situations where EU courts would claim to have sole jurisdiction. Apparently 'what is sauce for the goose is sauce for the gander' does not apply to the jurisdictional appetite of the Member States. Moreover, although the Member States have their own jurisdiction rules for certain disputes outside the territorial scope of the Jurisdiction Convention (now Brussels I) these rules are considered to be part of the all-encompassing

EU jurisdiction system and no longer fall within the purview of the Member States.

Most questions about the jurisdictional ambitions of courts of EU Member States over disputes having some connection with EU countries have been raised in the context of the Jurisdiction Convention. Indeed, the first version of this Convention dates from 1968 and has an extensive material scope. It inevitably provoked extensive discussions on the impact of its jurisdiction rules on third states. In 2000, after the EU acquired the competence to introduce uniform jurisdiction rules, the Council of Ministers introduced jurisdiction rules for insolvency (Insolvency Regulation 1346/2000) and divorce proceedings (Brussels II, Regulation 1347/2000, replaced in 2003 by Brussels II *bis*, Regulation 2201/2003). And new EC legislation on private international law is constantly on the drawing board.

In the present study Dr Thalia Kruger clearly explains the genesis of and philosophy behind the different existing jurisdiction rules. For those less familiar with how the EU has changed domestic procedural law in the Member States, this book is an efficient introduction to a complicated subject. Having studied law in South Africa, she understands very well what to highlight for readers less familiar with the continental European approach to jurisdiction, which largely inspired the Jurisdiction Convention and the later regulations. Familiar with the common law, she points out how the European jurisdiction rules, in which there is no room for *forum non conveniens* and 'anti-suit injunctions' differ from the common law approach.

She addresses the four European cornerstones for jurisdiction (the domicile of the defendant, exclusive jurisdiction over specific matters, forum clauses, and declining jurisdiction and dealing with parallel proceedings) as well as the possibility of issuing provisional and protective measures. She analyses not only the relevant European Court decisions but, thanks to her knowledge of English, French, German, and Dutch, also judgments from national courts and legal writings; her work has thus an exceptional comparative dimension. Moreover, intertwined with the discussion of the European rules are references to the aborted Hague draft for a worldwide jurisdiction convention and to the Hague Convention on Choice of Court Agreements, with which Dr Kruger is particularly familiar as she has been working as recording secretary for the Conference during the negotiations.

Many authors have studied the European jurisdiction rules from the inside. Dr Kruger's work is refreshing and innovative as she submits them to the litmus test to see how they relate to the 'outside' world. The insights obtained are formulated at the end of the book as suggestions for the coming revision of Brussels I.

This book is an updated and amended version of the PhD thesis that Dr Kruger prepared and presented at the Law School of the Katholieke Universiteit Leuven. I have had the pleasure to have Thalia as my assistant for six years and am proud to have been her *directeur de thèse*.

Prof Dr Hans Van Houtte
Leuven, 21 March 2007

Preface

Coming from a third State myself, I was stunned by how much the European Union has achieved, especially in law. At the same time I was a little surprised by the fact that the delimitation of the EU's rules is not always clear. It is from this personal and professional interest that this book was born. I have attempted to look at the EU legislation on civil jurisdiction from the outside; to ask when third States should be aware of all these rules. This starting point has led me to identify changes that should be made to the EU legislation to be better suited for an integrated world community based on respect, comity, and efficiency.

The main focus of this book is the jurisdiction rules contained in Regulation 44/2001 (Brussels I). The jurisdiction rules of Regulation 2201/2003 (Brussels II *bis*) and the Insolvency Regulation (1346/2000) are also covered, as well as a brief look at the proposed Maintenance Regulation. Consideration is given to the international functioning and limitations of various rules of jurisdiction. The place in the EU's system for rules related to jurisdiction, such as *lis pendens*, *forum non conveniens*, and anti-suit injunctions, is examined.

The topic of the book includes the larger picture of the scope for third States to negotiate and conclude treaties with EU Member States. This question is subject to complex issues of EU institutional law and the external competence of the European Community.

This book is a revised version of my PhD thesis, defended at the Katholieke Universiteit Leuven in Belgium. While writing the thesis I was employed as an academic assistant at that university. This made the journey much less lonely. In the first place my supervisor, Professor Hans Van Houtte, with his practical approach and his view that law is an instrument, not a philosophy, has taught me to ask 'so what?' after every sentence. The Institute of Private International Law has always been filled by that rare breed of people who not only know almost everything, but also want to share their knowledge without a hint of arrogance: Marta, Patrick, Ilse, and Karen. Working together with colleagues was enriching: Jos, Johan, Kristof, Hans, Bart, and Iasson. The conversations with the specialists in European Union law— Marlies and Tim—were particularly helpful. Our secretary, Viviane, the staff of the library and of the in-house copying service, and the IT support staff, ensured that researchers had the time and facilities to do what they were there for. The small group of private international law specialists in Belgium has created a forum to share ideas and sometimes to differ from each other in a constructive way. The project on civil judicial cooperation in the relations between European and third

States, in which Arnaud Nuyts invited me to participate, has enabled me to meet private international law specialists from all over the EU and from the USA.

The members of my PhD jury have shared their insights: former First Secretary at the Hague Conference on Private International Law, Doctor Andrea Schulz; Judge of the European Court of Justice, Professor Koen Lenaerts, Professor Christopher Forsyth; and Professor Alain Verbeke. In the course of publication I have received valuable comments from Professor Paul Beaumont and series editor Professor James Fawcett, as well as a few anonymous reviewers. Kirsty Allen of Oxford University Press was amazingly well organized and always ready to help with editing and language issues. My thanks also go to Emma Gould and Keith Comline for the language editing. In the last steps of publication, I appreciate the support and interest of my new colleagues at the University of Cape Town.

Numerous friends have followed the process closely, kept extending unreturned dinner invitations, called me to go cycling or to go on a weekend trip, and offered constant encouragement. Special thanks go to Eric Demeester, Marlies, Peggy, Peter, Leen, Sampie, Pietro, Elsa, Pieter, Bart Kurcz, and Wouter. My parents gave me the opportunity to come to Europe in the first place and have always encouraged me. My mother always believed in the final success of the process. My father has read and reread every word I wrote. He is the intelligent lawyer not specialized in private international law for whom I write. I dedicate this book to him.

During the long days as recording secretary at the Hague Conference on Private International Law I realized how much there is to the topic of civil jurisdiction. And it was there that I learnt from the late Doctor Allan Philip that 'the perfect is the enemy of the good'. This book is certainly not perfect, but I hope that it is good enough to be useful.

I have attempted to state the law not only as I understood it to be on 1 July 2007, but also as I believe it should have been, and as I hope it will become in the near future.

Thalia Kruger
Leuven and Cape Town
July and October 2007

Table of Contents—Summary

Contents

Table of Cases

France

Germany

United States

Table of National Legislation

Table of European Union Legislation

Regulations

Proposed Regulations

Treaties

Table of Conventions

List of Abbreviations

ASEAN	Association of Southeast Asian Nations
Brussels Convention	Convention on Jurisdiction and the Recognition and Enforcement of Judgments in Civil and Commercial Matters
Brussels I	Council Regulation (EC) no 44/2001 on jurisdiction and the recognition and enforcement of judgments in civil and commercial matters
Brussels II	Council Regulation (EC) no 1347/2000 of 29 May 2000 on jurisdiction and the recognition and enforcement of judgments in matrimonial matters and in matters of parental responsibility for children of both spouses, OJ L 160, 30 June 2000
Brussels II *bis*	Council Regulation (EC) no 2201/2003 of 27 November 2003 concerning jurisdiction and the recognition and enforcement of judgments in matrimonial matters and the matters of parental responsibility, repealing Regulation (EC) no 1347/2000, OJ L 338, 23 December 2003
COMI	centre of main interests
EC	European Community; successor to the EEC
EEC	European Economic Community
EU	European Union
EFTA	European Free Trade Association
ERTA	European Agreement on Road Transport
INCOTERMS	International Commercial Terms used in international trade and published under the auspices of the International Chamber of Commerce
Insolvency Regulation	Council Regulation (EC) no 1346/2000 of 29 May 2000
IP(R)	intellectual property (right)
Maintenance Regulation	Proposal for a Council Regulation on Jurisdiction, Applicable Law, Recognition and Enforcement of Decisions and Cooperation in matters relating to

	Maintenance Obligations, 15 December 2005, COM(2005) 649final
MERCOSUR	Southern Common Market: Regional Trade Agreement between Argentina, Brazil, Paraguay, Uruguay, and Venezuela
REIO	Regional Economic Integration Organisation

Introduction

A. THE EU

The European Union (EU), like its main pillar, the European Community **In.01** (EC), and their predecessor, the European Economic Community (EEC), is an important international economic player. It has internal rules regulating its internal market. Very early on, it became apparent that economic integration needed support from legal rules. The European judicial area constitutes the legal (civil and criminal law) framework that facilitates the functioning of the free movement of persons, goods, capital and services; it is the judicial side of the internal market. However, as the EU acts on the international scene, its effects are not limited to its own territory. Some elements to a dispute may be located in the EU while others are in third States (States that are not members of the EU). International contracts, torts and family relations do not stay strictly within or outside the EU.

The fact that legal disputes are not always limited to the well-defined ter- **In.02** ritory of the European judicial area has two consequences that will be examined in this book. First, the EU's internal rules may affect parties or property in third States. Second, the EU and its Member States must coordinate their actions towards the outside world, such as in their negotiations with and taking up of international obligations to third States.

The problems discussed here no doubt also occur in other domains of the **In.03** law.[1] This book, however, focuses on specific pieces of EU legislation, namely those defining civil jurisdiction. It examines the impact of those EU rules on third States.

---

[1] TC Hartley, *The Foundations of European Community Law* (5th edn, Oxford: Oxford University Press, 2003) p 91 stated 'it is not always easy to discern exactly where a legal system begins and ends: the community legal system, like most other legal systems, has fuzzy edges.'

B. CIVIL JURISDICTION

In.04 In 1968 the EEC started its activity in the sphere of civil jurisdiction, by way of the Brussels Convention. The aim of the Convention was to facilitate the recognition and enforcement of judgments throughout the EEC. The recognition and enforcement of judgments were essential for the proper functioning of the EEC market that was taking shape: if cross-border trade is to be efficient, one must be able to enforce a civil judgment against one's debtor in another EEC State where he or she has assets. The negotiators realized that this aim could be achieved more easily if they were able to establish common jurisdiction rules. The basic structure was that the (then) six Member States agreed the bases of jurisdiction to use so that they could recognize and enforce each other's judgments without further ado. This inclusion of jurisdiction rules in a convention on recognition and enforcement was novel at the time. The Convention was seen as a 'double convention', referring to the fact that it included rules both on jurisdiction and on recognition and enforcement.

In.05 As a matter of international law, the Brussels Convention was a multilateral treaty. It did not form part of EEC legislation. The European Court of Justice only had power to interpret the Convention because it had been granted such power by way of a protocol. Every time new Member States joined the EEC the Convention had to be renegotiated. It then had to be signed and ratified by all the Member States, in the manner customary in public international law.

In.06 It was only in 1999, through the entry into force of the Treaty of Amsterdam that the European Community obtained authority to legislate on civil jurisdiction. That brought, among others, the three instruments that are the focus of this book: the regulations Brussels I (jurisdiction and the recognition and enforcement of judgments in civil and commercial matters), Brussels II *bis* (jurisdiction and the recognition and enforcement of judgments on divorce and parental responsibility), and the Insolvency Regulation.[2] It is worth noting that the EC has not exhausted its power—it is continuously in the process of enacting new legislation in this field. In this regard,

---

[2] Council Regulation (EC) no 44/2001 on jurisdiction and the recognition and enforcement of judgments in civil and commercial matters (Brussels I); Council Regulation (EC) no 2201/2003 of 27 November 2003 concerning jurisdiction and the recognition and enforcement of judgments in matrimonial matters and the matters of parental responsibility (Brussels II *bis*), repealing Regulation (EC) no 1347/2000, OJ L 338, 23 December 2003 Brussels II *bis*; Council Regulation (EC) no 1346/2000 of 29 May 2000, Insolvency Regulation.

reference will be made, where appropriate, to the proposed Maintenance Regulation, which will also contain civil jurisdiction rules. There are also regulations, conventions, or proposed legislation dealing solely with enforcement, civil procedure, or applicable law.

Of these regulations Brussels I will receive the greatest attention for two main **In.07** reasons. The first is that it contains the most diverse set of rules. Some of the chapters will deal with issues that arise more frequently under this more general regulation than under the regulations that deal with the specific matters of divorce and parental responsibility, or insolvency. The second reason is that the longer history of the regulation (starting with the 1968 Convention) has established a wealth of case law not only in the European Court of Justice, but also in national courts. The other regulations still have to establish their case law and for the time being must learn from the existing examples.

In the course of the analysis, frequent reference will be made to the **In.08** rules on recognition and enforcement, because the EU's civil jurisdiction rules exist primarily to facilitate recognition and enforcement in the EU. Jurisdiction rules do not constitute a goal in themselves. At the same time, researching only the recognition and enforcement rules is not as useful. It is clear that these rules apply to judgments from courts of other EU Member States and not to judgments from courts of third States. Further discussion seems unnecessary. This explains why the Enforcement Order Regulation (which deals only with the enforcement of uncontested claims within the EU) is not relevant for the purposes of this book.

Other EU regulations concerning civil procedure will not be dealt with either: **In.09** the Service, Evidence, and Small Payments Regulations come to mind. These regulations seek to simplify civil proceedings in the EU. The link between the EU instruments and third States is not directly apparent.[3] Similarly, the Insolvency Regulation's rules on applicable law will not be examined, because they are distinct from the core issues dealt with in this book. Furthermore, the proposed legislation on the laws applicable to contractual and non-contractual obligations, and to divorce, will not be discussed.

---

[3] See, however, JJ Forner, 'Service of judicial documents within Europe and third States', C Besso, 'Taking of evidence abroad: from the 1970 Hague Convention to the 2001 Evidence Regulation', P de Vareilles-Sommières, 'Le règlement communautaire sur l'obtention de preuves à l'étranger et les rapports avec les Etats tiers' in A Nuyts & N Watté, *International civil litigation in Europe and relations with third States* Brussels: Bruylant, 2005).

C. THIRD STATES

In.10 The double nature of the Brussels Convention became its defining feature. Within the EEC it worked well, to such an extent that it was envied by other states, which at various times and with varying degrees of success attempted to copy the Brussels system. Easy recognition based on the underlying agreement on acceptable bases of jurisdiction was a good idea and it worked well.

In.11 On the other hand, this feature has also led to severe criticism of the Brussels Convention, especially from the outside world. It had the result of emphasizing the bad bases for jurisdiction of some of the Member States. These bad bases for jurisdiction would give rise to judgments that would have effects not just in one country but in an entire region. In other EU Member States the judgments would be recognized and enforced without any examination of the basis for jurisdiction. This characteristic of the regulations will be examined in this book and it will be pointed out that the problem lies in the fact that the double nature is incomplete.

In.12 What is so particular about civil jurisdiction that it has such great importance for third States? It is hard to capture in exact words why states might feel more threatened by the jurisdiction rules of other states than by their rules on applicable law. Maybe it is because jurisdiction is part of exercising state sovereignty: it concerns the question of when the judicial arm of a state can act. In this sense jurisdiction rules are most often unilateral: a court can only decide whether or not it has jurisdiction; it has no power to determine the jurisdiction of other courts. In the EU, these unilateral rules have been elaborated to an entire region. That the EU Member States are prepared to give up a part of their sovereignty is of course their decision. But a far-reaching jurisdictional rule is much more threatening to the outside world if it can be applied by 26 states (all EU Member States except Denmark) than if only one state had such a rule. A threat also arises because of the inseparable link that the EU has created between jurisdiction on the one hand and recognition and enforcement on the other. Thus permissible national jurisdiction rules, which might in some cases be exorbitant, will also result in judgments that can be recognized throughout this area.

In.13 Moreover, jurisdiction rules affect litigating parties very directly: issues such as where they have to travel to, how long their proceedings will last, and the form these will take, are at stake.

In.14 Over the years several questions arose regarding the application of the Brussels Convention and the later Regulation when parties from third

States were involved in disputes: where third State courts were chosen; where English courts wanted to decline jurisdiction on the basis of *forum non conveniens;* where English courts wanted to grant anti-suit injunctions, etc. The European Court of Justice has had the opportunity to respond to some of these questions, but not all. Its arguments have frequently been based on the goals of the EU's internal market. Of course there is nothing wrong with such goals, but regarding civil jurisdiction, the approach has at times led to results that are detrimental to third State courts or parties domiciled in third States, or, even worse, to international trade generally.

D. THE DELIMITATION OF THE JURISDICTION RULES

The boundary around the EU's jurisdiction rules is not a perfect circle. **ln.15** Four cornerstones have been identified, making it more accurate to speak of a quadrangle. These cornerstones, varying in size and importance, are discussed in chapters 2 to 5 of the book.

Chapter 1 gives a brief background on the EU in general and the birth and **ln.16** growth of *European* private international law, specifically concerning civil jurisdiction. This chapter is meant to make the technicalities of EU law more comprehensible for readers from third States.

The first cornerstone, the domicile of the defendant, is discussed in chap- **ln.17** ter 2. Broadly speaking, if the defendant is domiciled in the EU, the EU's jurisdiction rules apply and if not, they do not. In this chapter habitual residence and nationality, the Brussels II *bis* alternatives to domicile as grounds for jurisdiction, are included. In the discussion on Brussels II *bis*, the Hague Conventions on Child Abduction and on Protection of Children will also be discussed. These conventions have an important international role to play, and the way in which Brussels II *bis* fits into this international context is key. The Insolvency Regulation has introduced a new variant of domicile: the centre of main interests.

Additional defendants brought to the court of the first defendant's domi- **ln.18** cile (in the same action as against that defendant) are considered. Voluntary appearance is likewise included, as it is argued that this ground for juris- diction requires reference to the domicile of the defendant to determine whether the Regulation's rule applies or not.

Brussels I's alternative rules for jurisdiction in (for instance) contract and **ln.19** tort cases only come into play when the defendant is domiciled in the EU. Similarly, the Regulation's protective rules are applicable to certain 'weaker' parties that are domiciled in the EU. These are also discussed in chapter 2 of this book.

In.20 Chapter 3 addresses the narrower cornerstone of exclusive bases of jurisdiction. Under Brussels I, some cases can only appropriately be heard in one forum, despite the domicile of the defendant, and despite parties concluding a forum clause. Examples are claims regarding immovable property and the validity of legal persons, intellectual property rights, or entries in public registers. Of course, the exclusivity is also important at the time of recognition and enforcement: only the judgment by the court of the EU Member State where exclusive jurisdiction lay can be recognized and enforced in the EU. The presence in the EU of immovable property means that disputes regarding that property will fall under Brussels I. Where the parties come from is irrelevant. The same principle applies to the other bases of exclusive jurisdiction, such as the validity of intellectual property rights. What then about immovable property situated in a third State while the defendant is domiciled in the EU? For this eventuality Brussels I does not provide a rule. Of course the Regulation cannot grant jurisdiction to a court in a third State. However, it does not grant a basis for refusal of jurisdiction by EU courts in such cases. The possible solutions are discussed in chapter 3.

In.21 The next cornerstone is that of forum clauses. Brussels I explicitly states that it applies to forum clauses between parties, at least one of whom is domiciled in the EU, appointing an EU Member State court. (Brussels II *bis* permits forum clauses only in very limited cases.) Chapter 4 deals with forum clauses in favour of courts inside and outside the EU. Regarding the latter, the same difficulty arises as for exclusive jurisdiction: the Regulation is silent. The chapter also briefly deals with the Hague Choice of Court Convention. If the EC becomes party to the Convention, courts in EU Member States will be forced to respect forum clauses in favour of the courts of third States.

In.22 The last cornerstone concerns the hybrid rules of *lis pendens, forum non conveniens,* related actions and anti-suit injunctions. These are not rules granting jurisdiction, but rules of civil procedure that have an undeniable influence on jurisdiction. They establish mechanisms that enable courts to resolve the conflict between parallel proceedings, to decline jurisdiction, or to prevent parties from pursuing litigation in other courts. A discussion of civil jurisdiction without an examination of these rules would be incomplete. Regarding their scope, these rules have more in common with recognition and enforcement than with jurisdiction. This means that their scope is mainly determined by the courts involved, rather than by the domicile of the parties or some other element of the dispute. If the same action is pending in the courts of two EU Member States, the EU rule on *lis pendens* will resolve the situation. If the same action is pending both in a court in an EU Member State and in a third State court, that rule will not apply. However, this is not the complete picture. Since the rules impact on jurisdiction, one also has to examine the jurisdictional bases in order to define their exact scope. This is particularly the case with the rules of *forum non conveniens* and anti-suit injunctions. Chapter 5 deals with some of the most fundamental problems of the interaction between the EU's jurisdiction rules and third States.

Some authors would have made this book a pentagon rather than a quadrangle. This is because of the intangible subject of provisional and protective measures. These are discussed in chapter 6, where it is argued that provisional and protective measures do not merit forming their own cornerstone, or their own rule determining their scope. They are integrated into the system that has been expounded above. **In.23**

E. EXTERNAL RELATIONS OF THE EU

The last chapter takes a few steps back and ponders whether the quadrangle can in any way be seen as a piece of a larger building. This requires delving into EU law again, specifically into the theories and case law on the EU's external relations. Can the EU and/or its Member States contract with third States in order to conclude conventions? The European Court of Justice has ruled in the *Lugano* opinion that the European Community has exclusive external competence over the matters covered by Brussels I. Therefore, no longer can Member States independently conclude conventions on the same matter with third States; third States should deal with the European Union as a whole. The work of the Hague Conference on Private International Law is important in this discussion. Its projects at times are closely related to those of the EU. Moreover, the Conference provides a forum for third States to negotiate and conclude conventions with the EU. **In.24**

F. WHERE DO WE GO FROM HERE?

It will be noticed that the EU's jurisdiction rules have been drawn up from the inside: with the goals and needs of its internal market in mind. As time passed, certain clarifications had to be made regarding exactly how the EU's civil jurisdiction rules impact on third States. It will be argued that the (imperfect) double nature of the regulations causes difficulties for third States. Criticism aside, it is my belief that it is possible to create double rules serving the EU goals, while taking justified account of the rest of the world. Recommendations will be made on the assumption that EU rules can also be fair towards third States. **In.25**

1

Background

Article 220 of the EC Treaty (Rome):

Member States shall, so far as is necessary, enter into negotiations with each other with a view to securing for the benefit of their nationals:

. . .

— *the simplification of formalities governing the reciprocal recognition and enforcement of judgments of courts or tribunals and of arbitration awards.*

Article 65 of the EC Treaty (Nice version):

Measures in the field of judicial cooperation in civil matters having cross-border implications, to be taken in accordance with Article 67 and in so far as necessary for the proper functioning of the internal market shall include:

a) improving and simplifying:
— *the system of cross-border service of judicial and extra-judicial documents,*
— *cooperation in the taking of evidence*
— *the recognition and enforcement of decisions in civil and commercial cases, including decisions in extra-judicial cases;*
b) promoting the compatibility of the rules applicable in the Member States concerning the conflict of laws and of jurisdiction;

c) eliminating obstacles to the good functioning of civil proceedings, if necessary by promoting the compatibility of the rules on civil procedure applicable in the Member States.

Article 67 of the EC Treaty (Nice version):

During a transitional period of five years following the entry into force of the Treaty of Amsterdam, the Council shall act unanimously on a proposal from the Commission or on the initiative of a Member State and after consulting the European Parliament.

After this period of five years:

— *the Council shall act on proposals from the Commission; the Commission shall examine any request made by a Member State that it submit a proposal to the Council,*
— *the Council, acting unanimously after consulting the European Parliament, shall take a decision with a view to providing for all or parts of the areas covered by this title to be governed by the procedure referred to in Article 251 and adapting the provisions relating to the powers of the Court of Justice.*

. . .

By derogation from paragraph 1, the Council shall adopt, in accordance with the procedure referred to in Article 251:

— . . .
— *the measures provided for in Article 65 with the exception of matters relating to family law.*

Article 68 of the EC Treaty (Nice version):

Article 234 shall apply to this title under the following circumstances and conditions: where a question on the interpretation of this title or on the validity or interpretation of acts of the institutions of the Community based on this title is raised in a case pending before a court or a tribunal of a Member State against whose decisions there is no judicial remedy under national law, that court or tribunal shall, if it considers that a decision on the question is necessary to enable it to give judgment, request the Court of Justice to give a ruling thereon.

. . .

A. INTRODUCTION

1.01 Before turning to the substance of this book, it is necessary to examine briefly some general background issues. First, one must bear in mind that the rules discussed emanate from the European Union and are now entrenched in EU legislation. This chapter gives an overview of the

development of European private international law, of which civil jurisdiction is a part, and analyses the general scope of the EU civil jurisdiction
rules. The relationship that these rules have with conventions on specific
matters, and with the Lugano Convention, is of importance for third States
and deserves some attention.

The analysis is critical of the EU's unclear policy towards the outside **1.02**
world. However, it is not my intent to condemn the entire EU and its functioning; the discussion is confined to civil jurisdiction. The concern of this
study is the relationship the EU maintains with third States and the spill-
over effect that EU legislation has on such third States.

Finally, this chapter discusses the Hague Conference on Private Interna- **1.03**
tional Law, which is an important meeting place between the EU and third
States in the sphere of civil jurisdiction.

B. THE EU AND THE DEVELOPMENT OF EUROPEAN PRIVATE INTERNATIONAL LAW, INCLUDING CIVIL JURISDICTION

Background to the European Union

The origins of the European Union go back to the 1950s. The early associa- **1.04**
tion was comprised of three communities:

- the European Coal and Steel Community (ECSC), which entered into
  force in 1952 and ended in 2002 on the expiry of its 50-year shelf life;[1]
- the European Economic Community (EEC), established by the Treaty of
  Rome which entered into force on 1 January 1958;[2] and
- the European Atomic Energy Community (EURATOM), which also
  entered into force in 1958.[3]

The separate treaties created various detached institutional bodies. The
Treaty establishing a Single Council and a Single Commission (commonly

---

[1] Treaty establishing the European Coal and Steal Community, Paris, 18 April 1951.
[2] Treaty establishing the European Economic Community, Rome, 25 March 1957.
[3] Treaty establishing the European Atomic Energy Community, Rome, 25 March 1957.
For an overview of the history of the European Union, see TC Hartley, *The Foundations
of European Community Law* (5th edn, Oxford: Oxford University Press, 2003) 3–9; P Craig &
G de Búrca, *EU Law* (3rd edn, Oxford: Oxford University Press, 2003), 3–53; K Lenaerts &
P Van Nuffel (ed R Bray), *Constitutional Law of the European Union* (2nd edn, London: Sweet
& Maxwell, 2005) 3–75; P-O Lapie, *Les trois communautés* (Paris: Librairie Arthême Fayard,
1960).

known as the Merger Treaty) partially remedied that situation in 1967.[4] This step did not merge the communities, only their institutions.

1.05 The six initial Member States were Belgium, France, (West) Germany, Italy, Luxembourg and the Netherlands. This was an attempt to bind the economies of these States together so that future wars would become impossible. From its establishment, the EEC has evolved, not only by embracing a growing number of Member States (now 27), but also by increasingly integrating their economic and social policies. Civil jurisdiction was only one of the elements of this integration, and its roots are regarded below.

The Brussels Convention

1.06 In 1968 the then-six Member States concluded the Convention on Jurisdiction and the Recognition and Enforcement of Judgments in Civil and Commercial Matters in Brussels, hereafter referred to as the Brussels Convention. This was an international convention and not an EEC instrument. However, it was negotiated in the same forum as EEC legislation.[5] The legal basis was Article 220 of the Rome Treaty. That provision encouraged Member States to cooperate regarding the recognition of judgments, but contained no reference to rules of jurisdiction.[6] It was the drafters of the Brussels Convention that considered the establishment of jurisdiction rules useful for facilitating recognition and enforcement. They argued that if jurisdiction rules were brought into line, recognition and enforcement could be semi-automatic. There would be no possibility of refusing recognition or enforcement on the grounds that the court had taken jurisdiction on an exorbitant basis.

1.07 This idea was quite novel at the time, when most bilateral recognition and enforcement conventions did not contain a unified set of jurisdiction rules.[7] Multilateral recognition and enforcement conventions that existed

---

[4] Signed in Brussels in 1965 and entered into force in 1967.

[5] TC Hartley, *Civil Jurisdiction and Judgments* (London: Sweet & Maxwell, 1984) 2.

[6] On the relationship between that provision and the Brussels Convention, Hartley, ibid, 2 and 6–7; H Duintjer Tebbens, 'De Europese bevoegdheids- en executieverdragen: uitlegging, samenloop en perspektief' in PAM Meijknecht & H Duintjer Tebbens, *Europees bevoegdheids- en executierecht op weg naar de 21ste eeuw* (Deventer: Kluwer, 1992) 53–117 at 63–66; O Remien, 'European Private International Law, the European Community and its emerging area of freedom, security and justice' [2001] CML Rev 53–86 at 55.

[7] Many of these Conventions existed between EU Member States, the oldest dating back to 1899 (between Belgium and France); see Art 69 Brussels I, stating that the Regulation now supersedes these conventions. It is interesting to note here that the USA is not party to any bilateral treaty governing enforcement of its judgments in foreign countries. One was being negotiated with the UK. The reason for its failure in 1980 is said to be British insurers' wariness

then and in the 1970s did not contain unified jurisdiction rules either; they merely contained recognition and enforcement rules. Jurisdiction rules were only indirectly implied: recognition and enforcement could be refused if certain jurisdictional bases were employed. Examples of this kind are the Montevideo Convention of May 1979 on the Extraterritorial Validity of Foreign Judgments and Arbitral Awards, drawn up within the framework of the Organization of American States (OAS) and in force in a number of South American countries,[8] and the Hague Convention of February 1971 on the Recognition and Enforcement of Foreign Judgments in Civil and Commercial Matters.[9]

In this way the distinction between simple and double recognition and **1.08** enforcement conventions came about. The old-style conventions were classified as simple, while the Brussels Convention was double, since it contained jurisdiction rules as well as recognition and enforcement rules. Under double conventions it becomes impossible to test the bases for jurisdiction at the time of recognition and enforcement due to the unification of the jurisdiction rules.[10] Double conventions became more common after the success of the Brussels Convention.[11] In its global jurisdiction Convention (which was never concluded), the Hague Conference has

---

of large American jury verdicts; see PJ Borchers, 'Comparing Personal Jurisdiction in the US and the EC: Lessons for American Reform' [1992] AJCL 121–157.

[8] This Convention can be found at <http://www.oas.org>; reference number: B–41. States Party are Argentina, Bolivia, Brazil, Colombia, Ecuador, Mexico, Paraguay, Peru, Uruguay and Venezuela.

[9] This Convention can be found at the website of the Hague Conference on Private International Law: <http://www.hcch.net>. This Convention was only adopted by Cyprus, the Netherlands (including Aruba), Portugal and Kuwait. Its failure has been attributed to, *inter alia*, its unusual and complex structure and the success of the Brussels and Lugano Conventions. The Convention required bilateralization, which means that, apart from the primary convention, a state would have to conclude a separate agreement with other Contracting States in which it wishes its judgments to be enforced; see Art 21 on supplementary agreements.

[10] See in general, on the distinction between single and double conventions, Hartley, *Civil Jurisdiction and Judgments* , note 5 above, 6–7; P Nygh & F Pocar, Report on the preliminary draft Convention on Jurisdiction and Foreign Judgments in Civil and Commercial Matters (Choice of Court Convention Preliminary Document No 11, 2000), available at <http://www.hcch.net>.

[11] For example the Hague Convention on Jurisdiction, Applicable Law, Recognition, Enforcement and Cooperation in respect of Parental Responsibility and Measures for the Protection of Children (1996), which regulates exhaustively the jurisdiction that authorities of Contracting States may exercise, even regarding children not habitually resident in a Contracting State (available at <http://www.hcch.net>); Report by P Lagarde on the (1996) Hague Convention on Jurisdiction, Applicable Law, Recognition, Enforcement and Cooperation in respect of Parental Responsibility and Measures for the Protection of

attempted a third category: a mixed convention.[12] That convention would not be completely double since it would contain some jurisdiction rules, whereas others would be left to national law.

1.09 However, in the instruments discussed 'double' does not always mean a strict parallelism. A judgment handed down by an EU Member State court, if it falls within the material scope of the Brussels I, Brussels II *bis* or Insolvency Regulations, will be recognized and enforced according to the rules of that instrument. At the recognition stage, the jurisdictional basis is not checked. Thus, even if a domestic rule of jurisdiction was applied (for instance via Article 4 of Brussels I or Article 7 of Brussels II *bis*), in principle the judgment will be recognized. This only partly double nature causes difficulties for third States, as will be indicated in the following chapters.

1.10 In a sense, the Brussels Convention was regarded as community law and thus engendered the requirement that new Member States ratify it.[13] However, being an international convention meant that a new version had to be negotiated and concluded every time more states joined the EU. In this way the Brussels Convention was modified when Denmark, Ireland and the United Kingdom became party to it (1978), when Greece joined in 1982, when Spain and Portugal acceded (significant changes were made at this point in what was called the San Sebastian version, 1989), and lastly when Austria, Finland and Sweden became party (1997).

1.11 The Treaty of Rome was modified in 1992 by the Treaty of Maastricht, which entered into force in 1993.[14] This Treaty, although of significance for EU law, marking not only the transformation of the European Economic Community in the European Community, but also the creation of the European Union, did not herald great changes for the domain of civil jurisdiction. At that time the European Union was installed as the 'roof' to 'the three pillars': the community pillar (which encompassed the European Communities), common foreign and security policy, and intergovernmental cooperation in justice and home affairs.[15] The fact that the first pillar, the communities, was now only a part of the larger Union amounted to an admission that the European club had expanded to more than their communities. The second and third pillars involved sensitive matters, closely connected to state sovereignty. Member States were and remain more

---

Children, [1996] Hague Conference on Private International Law. Proceedings of the Eighteenth Session, vol. II, 'Protection of children', 539–541.

[12] For a brief discussion of this project, see below, para 1.87 and following.
[13] See also Hartley, *Civil Jurisdiction and Judgments*, note 5 above, 3.
[14] Published in OJ C 191, 29 July 1992, p 1.
[15] See Lenaerts & Van Nuffel, note 3 above, 53–57.

reluctant to allow European Community integration or harmonization in these fields. Private international law, named 'judicial cooperation in civil matters', remained an intergovernmental matter and was therefore part of the third pillar. The Brussels Convention and its amending conventions belonged to the third pillar. The legal basis that already existed in the Rome Treaty (Article 220) was retained.

The Treaties of Amsterdam and Nice

In 1997 the Treaty of Amsterdam was concluded and it entered into force **1.12** in 1999.[16] This treaty brought a significant change for the entire body of European private international law, including civil jurisdiction.[17] It transposed judicial cooperation in civil matters to the first pillar (the Community pillar) meaning that the European Union can now adopt the relevant legislation, instead of the Member States continually negotiating and ratifying treaties.

The legal basis for this legislation on private international law is Article 65 **1.13** of the EC Treaty (Amsterdam version). The fact that the Treaty still uses the word 'cooperation' in the first pillar (Article 65) is confusing. Some consider that this terminology should be changed, since first pillar matters are not issues of cooperation, but of Community legislation. Cooperation in this Article means something different, though. It refers to the interaction between Member States that the Treaty wishes to establish. A measure

---

[16] Published in OJ C 340, 10 November 1997. This Treaty repealed the Merger Treaty, which was no longer necessary.

[17] See, in this regard, P Beaumont, 'European Court of Justice and jurisdiction and enforcement of judgments in civil and commercial matters' [1999] ICLQ 223–229; J Basedow, 'The Communitarization of the Conflict of Laws under the Treaty of Amsterdam' [2000] CML Rev 687–708; P Beaumont, 'Interplay of private international law and the European Community' in C Kilpatrick, T Novitz & P Skidmore (eds), *The future of remedies in Europe* (Oxford: Hart Publishing, 2000) 137–190; Remien, note 6 above; W Kennett (ed), 'Current developments: Private International Law. Brussels I' [2001] ICLQ 725–737; H Van Houtte, 'De gewijzigde bevoegdheid van de Europese Unie inzake IPR' in H Van Houtte & M Pertegás Sender (eds), *Het nieuwe Europese IPR: van verdrag naar verordening* (Antwerp: Intersentia Rechtswetenschappen, 2001) 1–10; CA Joustra, 'Naar een communautair international privaatrecht!' in CA Joustra & MV Polak, *Internationaal, communautair en nationaal IPR* (The Hague: TMC Asser Press, 2002) 1–60 at 11–20; A-M Van den Bossche, 'L'espace européen de justice et le (rapprochement du) droit judiciaire' in M Storme & G de Leval (eds), *Het Europees gerechtelijk recht & procesrecht* (Bruges: die Keure, 2003) 1–23; B Nascimbene, 'Community courts in the area of judicial cooperation' [2005] ICLQ 489–497; TC Hartley, 'The EU and the systematic dismantling of the common law conflict of laws' [2005] ICLQ 813–828; A Dickinson, 'European private international law: embracing new horizons or mourning the past?' [2005] *Journal of Private International Law* 197–236.

such as the Evidence Regulation can be seen as cooperation: the Member States cooperate in the sense that they help each other in the quest for evidence in civil proceedings. The same can be said of the Service Regulation: Member States cooperate by ensuring that judicial and extra-judicial documents from other Member States are forwarded in an efficient way. The Brussels I, Brussels II *bis* and Insolvency Regulations, and also the Enforcement Order, provide forms of cooperation regarding jurisdiction, applicable law, and the enforcement of foreign judgments.

1.14 The Treaty of Nice entered into force in February 2003.[18] While allowing for the further enlargement of the EU, the changes brought for civil jurisdiction were restricted to legislative points.[19] They are of limited relevance for the purpose of this book. A Constitutional Treaty for the European Union had been signed in Rome in November 2004.[20] Remaining a Treaty in the international law sense, the Constitution would incorporate the EU's Charter of Fundamental Rights into the text. The establishment of a constitution caused great political turmoil, although the Treaties always performed the same function.[21] Even though the Constitution will not be adopted as such, the elaborate text remains useful for reference. It defines concepts of European Union law and I have used these definitions in this book.

The European Court of Justice and the interpretation of the civil jurisdiction instruments

1.15 The European Court of Justice, seated in Luxembourg, guards over the application of EU law. It does so in many ways: it is competent to review the legality of EU legislation and the acts (or failures to act) of the institutions; it may give preliminary rulings on the interpretation of EU law; it can hear disputes between Member States on EU law; and it may give judgments on the competences of EU institutions.[22] The special capability to interpret EU law includes responding to preliminary questions posed by courts of the Member States. The European Court of Justice will only provide an answer concerning a point of law. It must be provided with the

---

[18] Treaty of Nice published in OJ C 80, 10 March 2001, p 1.0 The consolidated version of the Treaty now in force can be found in OJ C 325, 24 December 2002, p 33.

[19] See Article 67 of the Nice version of the EC Treaty.

[20] Published in OJ C 310, 16 December 2004, p 1.

[21] See also TC Hartley, 'International Law and the Law of the European Union— A Reassessment' [2001] *British Yearbook of International Law* 1–35 at 3–4, arguing that the Treaties really amounted to a constitution.

[22] See Arts 230–239 EC Treaty (Nice version); Arts III–270 to III–280 Constitution.

factual background to enable it to make a ruling, but it will not rule on points of fact. Upon receiving a response, the application of the ruling to the facts is up to the national, referring court. For civil jurisdiction instruments the European Court of Justice derives its power directly from the EC Treaty.[23] Based on a 1971 protocol, the Court also had the power to interpret the Brussels Convention.[24] The judgments interpreting the Brussels Convention continue to be relevant to the extent that Brussels I has not modified the rule in question. That protocol provided that any national court sitting as an appellate body may pose a preliminary question.

In the sphere of some politically sensitive matters (such as visas, asylum, **1.16** and immigration), the EC Treaty reduces the scope for preliminary questions. Civil jurisdiction falls in the same subdivision of the EC Treaty (Title IV of Part Three) and is subject to the same limitations. Only the highest court in a Member State may (and must if uncertainty exists) pose a preliminary question in these matters.[25] The Constitution purported to change this so that the exception concerning preliminary questions would no longer apply to private international law.[26] Even though the Constitution will not be adopted in its orignial form, this point will probably survive. This means that any court will be able to pose a preliminary question. If there are more preliminary questions at an earlier stage, the result will be more uniform interpretation and clarity. On the other hand, preliminary questions can be a way to delay judgment. Arguing about jurisdiction, even under national law, is often a means of delay used by an uncooperative party. If this delay can be extended by a further two years to allow the European Court of Justice to give a preliminary judgment, the final result might not be reached within a reasonable time. This change is therefore greeted with mixed feelings. The terms of the protocol to the Brussels Convention seemed the perfect compromise, adapted to the needs of this field of the law: the first court of appeal could pose a preliminary question.

There is another problem with the capacity of the European Court of **1.17** Justice to interpret instruments in the field of civil jurisdiction. This domain of the law necessarily implies an international element, and may fall within

[23] Art 234 EC Treaty (Amsterdam and Nice versions).
[24] Protocol concerning the interpretation by the Court of Justice of the convention of 27 September 1968 on jurisdiction and the enforcement of judgments in civil and commercial matters, 3 June 1971, OJ L 204, 28–31.
[25] Art 68 EC Treaty (Amsterdam and Nice versions). See Case C–555/03 *Warbecq v Ryanair Ltd* [2004] ECR I–6041, where the European Court of Justice was unable to respond to a question by the Tribunal du travail (Employment Tribunal) of Charleroi. See also case note by T Kruger [2004–2005] *Columbia Journal of European Law* 203–206.
[26] Art I–29(3)(b) Constitution.

the borders of the European Community, but can also reach beyond those borders. One or several Member States and a third State might be involved. The European Court of Justice, though, is supposed to interpret and apply European Union law. Even if other legal problems arose, the Court might not be competent to expose them and deal with them.[27] The European Court of Justice is not like a state's highest national court, which has competence to rule on anything; it is an institution of the European Union and in that sense has a clearly demarcated task. Judgments are often reasoned from the point of view of European Union law.

C. MEMBER STATES AND THEIR PARTICIPATION

General

1.18 As the concern of this study is the position of third States, states that are not Member States of the EU, a precise definition of 'Member States' is necessary. The six original Member States were Belgium, France, (West) Germany,[28] Italy, Luxembourg, and the Netherlands. Since that time the number of Member States has expanded at regular intervals. Denmark, Ireland, and the United Kingdom joined in 1973;[29] Greece in 1981;[30] Portugal and Spain in 1986;[31] Austria, Finland, and Sweden in 1995;[32] Cyprus, the Czech Republic, Estonia, Hungary, Latvia, Lithuania, Malta, Poland, Slovakia, and Slovenia in 2004;[33] Bulgaria and Romania in 2007.[34]

1.19 However, there are a number of territories whose status is less clear. Furthermore, identifying the Member States does not fully clarify the scope of EU law.[35] None of the civil jurisdiction regulations names its exact territorial scope. As they are EU legislation, the determination of territorial scope can only be found in the general rules of EU law, such as the EC Treaty. This was of course different when civil jurisdiction was still organized by means of a convention. The EC Treaty did not define the states and territories party to the Brussels Convention.

---

[27] See in general S Francq, *L'applicabilité du droit communautaire dérivé au regard des méthodes du droit international privé* (Brussels: Bruylant & Paris: LGDJ, 2005).
[28] Upon the reunification of Germany in 1990, East Germany joined alongside West Germany.
[29] Accession Treaty published in OJ L 73, 27 March 1972.
[30] Accession Treaty published in OJ L 291, 19 November 1979.
[31] Accession Treaty published in OJ L 302, 15 November 1985.
[32] Accession Treaty published in OJ L 241, 29 August 1994.
[33] Accession Treaty published in OJ L 236, 23 September 2003.
[34] Accession Treaty published in OJ L 157, 21 June 2005.
[35] See Francq, note 27 above.

The pre-1989 versions of the Brussels Convention contained a provision **1.20** allowing Contracting States to declare it applicable to territories for whose external relations they were responsible. The first version concerned France and the Netherlands and the next version Denmark and the United Kingdom.[36] Whether this possibility remained under public international law despite the deletion of the provision, was uncertain,[37] but the controversy has lost its relevance. Such declarations are not possible in relation to the Regulations, as they are EU law. The Brussels Convention remains in force in the territories where it was applicable but which are excluded from Brussels I.[38] The result is that the Brussels Convention was or is applicable in some territories, while the Brussels I, Brussels II *bis* and Insolvency Regulations are not. This will be discussed below.

Participation of some of the Member States

Some of the EU Member States do not wish to go as far as the others **1.21** in certain matters.[39] For private international law, including civil jurisdiction (Article 65 of the Amsterdam and Nice versions of the EC Treaty), Denmark, Ireland and the United Kingdom have negotiated special terms. These special terms relate not only to judicial cooperation in civil matters, but also to judicial cooperation in criminal matters, police cooperation, visas, asylum and immigration (Title IV of Part Three). Of all these matters judicial cooperation in civil matters is the least politicized. However, it is treated in the same title of the EC Treaty and therefore the same special arrangements apply.[40] The Treaty of Amsterdam by way of protocols

---

[36] Art 60 of the Brussels Convention. The provision for such declarations was deleted by the Treaty on the Accession of Portugal and Spain to the Brussels Convention. It never existed in the Lugano Convention. One of the reasons for its disappearance was the Spanish fear that the United Kingdom would declare the Conventions applicable in Gibraltar. On the other hand, many thought that the possibility to extend the Convention to overseas territories would be useful to prevent debtors placing assets in such territories to which access was easy but enforcement difficult, and so beyond the reach of creditors. It is possible that the rule allowing for declarations survived in the other conventions, despite its deletion, on the basis of general international law; see H Duintjer Tebbens, 'Het toepassingsgebied van de verdragen van Brussel en Lugano naar onderwerp, tijd en ruimte,' in H Van Houtte & M Pertegás Sender (eds), *Europese IPR-Verdragen* (Leuven: Acco, 1997) 37–38.

[37] See GAL Droz, 'La Convention de San Sebastian alignant la Convention de Bruxelles sur la Convention de Lugano' [1990] *Revue critique de droit international privé* 1–21 at 17.

[38] Rec 23 of Brussels I.

[39] For example, regarding the elimination of internal borders, Ireland and the United Kingdom have a special regime and are not parties to the Schengen treaty. For some other matters Denmark has obtained exceptions.

[40] Title IV of Part Three.

introduced the arrangements and the Treaty of Nice reintegrated those protocols without change.

1.22 Protocol 4 on the Position of the United Kingdom and Ireland determines that Title IV does not apply to those states. They do, however, have a right to 'opt in'. They may inform the President of the Council, within three months after a proposal or initiative has been presented to the Council, that they wish to participate in it.[41] They also, after the adoption of the measure, may inform the Council and the Commission that they wish to accept it.[42] Ireland could notify the President of the Council that it no longer wants to be bound by the Protocol, thus cancelling its special regime, with the result that all EU legislation in this field would apply in Ireland.[43] A similar provision does not exist for the United Kingdom. Both Ireland and the United Kingdom have decided to participate in all the regulations that have been adopted in the field of civil jurisdiction thus far. However, this situation seems about to change.[44]

1.23 Protocol 5 on the Position of Denmark is less flexible. It merely states that Denmark does not participate in Title IV. Therefore, no measures taken under Title IV in general, or Article 65 specifically, are applicable in Denmark. Thus the private international law regulations are not applicable there. According to the Protocol Denmark may inform the other Member States that it no longer wishes to avail itself of the Protocol, or a part of it, in which case its special position will be cancelled and all EU legislation in this field will apply to it.[45] Denmark does not have the possibility to 'opt in' to a specific instrument that the United Kingdom and Ireland have.

1.24 Denmark has concluded an agreement with the European Community to the effect that the rules of Brussels I also apply there.[46] This agreement

---

[41] Art 3 of Protocol 4, published with the Treaty establishing the European Community (Amsterdam consolidated version), OJ C 340, 10 November 1997, 173.

[42] Art 4 of Protocol 4.

[43] Art 8 of Protocol 4.

[44] Regarding the Proposal for a Council Regulation on jurisdiction, applicable law, recognition and enforcement of decisions and cooperation in matters relating to maintenance obligations of 15 December 2005, COM(2005) 649 final, the United Kingdom has indicated that it will opt out, while Ireland will opt in. Both will opt out of the Proposal for a Council Regulation amending Regulation (EC) No 2201/2003 as regards jurisdiction and introducing rules concerning applicable law in matrimonial matters of 17 July 2006, COM(2006) 399 final. Both proposals are available at <http://eur-lex.europa.eu>.

[45] Art 7 of Protocol 5, published with the Treaty establishing the European Community (Amsterdam consolidated version), OJ C 340, 10 November 1997, 173.

[46] Council Decision 2006/325/EC of 27 April 2006 concerning the conclusion of the Agreement between the European Community and the Kingdom of Denmark on jurisdiction

entered into force on 1 July 2007. A similar agreement has been concluded regarding the Service Regulation[47] and it is possible that others will follow on other private international law matters where regulations exist. In this way, for private international law including civil jurisdiction, Denmark circumvents the Protocol it has ensured for sensitive matters such as visas, immigration and asylum.

For matters of civil jurisdiction, Denmark (and to the extent that they had **1.25** not opted in, the United Kingdom and Ireland) therefore has special status. They are of course EU Member States, but they are set apart from the other 24. This distinction is of interest in examining the external competence of the European Community. As these states do not, or only partly, recognize the EC's competence over a matter, they will not be fully bound by the external competence of the EC.[48]

Overseas territories, European territories with special status, and specific European territories

Overseas territories, as the name indicates, are not geographically part of **1.26** Europe, but have a special relationship with one of the Member States and therefore with the EU. These territories have varying degrees of independence or connection with the Member States. In the same sense, EU civil jurisdiction rules have different influences in these areas.[49]

Some territories are in actual fact part of the European Member State and **1.27** the civil jurisdiction regulations apply in them to the full extent that they are applicable to the Member States. These are the French overseas *départements* (Guadeloupe, French Guiana, Martinique, and Réunion), the Azores, Madeira, and the Canary Islands.[50]

For the other overseas territories, listed in an annex to the EC Treaty,[51] the **1.28** answer is less simple. EU law applies in varying degrees to them. The EU

---

and the recognition and enforcement of judgments in civil and commercial matters, OJ L 120 of 5 May 2006, p 22.

[47] Council Decision 2006/326/EC of 27 April 2006 concerning the conclusion of the Agreement between the European Community and the Kingdom of Denmark on the service of judicial and extrajudicial documents in civil or commercial matters, OJ L 120 of 5 May 2006, p 23.

[48] This issue will be investigated more closely in chapter 7.

[49] See Lenaerts & van Nuffel, note 3 above, 843–846.

[50] Art 299 EC Treaty (Nice version); Art IV–440 Constitution.

[51] Annex II to the EC Treaty. These are Greenland, New Caledonia and Dependencies, French Polynesia, French Southern and Antarctic Territories, Wallis and Futuna Islands, Mayotte, Saint Pierre and Miquelon, Aruba, Netherlands Antilles (Bonaire, Curaçao, Saba,

Regulations of civil jurisdiction do not apply in these territories. These territories are in an advantaged position because of their association with the EU. The special arrangements include trade, customs duties, investment and the freedom of establishment. These arrangements may be detailed by legislation.[52]

1.29 EU law applies to European territories that are dependent on a Member State for their external relations; strictly speaking, of course, these are not 'overseas'. Gibraltar falls in this category, as it is geographically linked to Spain as a peninsula, but the United Kingdom is responsible for its external relations, and it joined the EU with the United Kingdom. There are however certain exceptions to the application of EU law in Gibraltar.[53] The civil jurisdiction regulations apply if the United Kingdom opts in, so such instruments become applicable there also.[54] It has done so for all EU civil jurisdiction instruments thus far. Before the advent of these regulations, provisions corresponding to those of the Brussels Convention were applicable as between the United Kingdom and Gibraltar.[55] Consequently, if a measure is not applicable in the United Kingdom, it is not applicable in Gibraltar. The United Kingdom has the power to decide not to participate in a regulation on private international law. It has not yet done so, but the possibility exists. In that case, it is likely that if the United Kingdom did not participate in the regulation, and therefore it was not applicable in the United Kingdom, it would not be applicable in Gibraltar.

1.30 Greenland is a special case. It became part of the EU alongside Denmark in 1971, as it was at that time under Danish authority. Regarding the Brussels

---

Sint Eustatius, Sint Maarten), Anguilla, Cayman Islands, Falkland Islands, South Georgia and the South Sandwich Islands, Montserrat, Pitcairn, Saint Helena and Dependencies, British Antarctic Territory, British Indian Ocean Territory, Turks and Caicos Islands, British Virgin Islands, Bermuda. (Annex II of the Constitution text contains the same list.)

[52] Arts 182–188 EC Treaty (Nice version).

[53] The difficult position of Gibraltar, since 1713, has led to many conflicts between Spain and the United Kingdom. One of these disputes provided a part of the reason for the United Kingdom never signing the Insolvency Convention; see P Wautelet, 'De Europese insolventieverordening,' in Van Houtte & Pertegás Sender (eds), *Het Europese IPR* note 17 above, 103–167, at 113–114. It is also delaying the ratification by a number of EU Member States of the Hague Convention of 19 October 1996, note 11 above; see A Schulz, 'Haager Kinderschützbereinkommen von 1996: Im Westen nichts Neues' [2006] *Zeitschrift für das gesamte Familienrecht* 1309–1311.0 The Schengen agreement does not apply to Gibraltar, as it does not apply to the United Kingdom.

[54] See also A Briggs & P Rees, *Civil Jurisdiction and Judgments* (4th edn, London: LLP, 2005) 45.

[55] See P North & JJ Fawcett, *Cheshire and North's Private International Law* (13th edn, London: Butterworths, 1999) 180.

Convention, after acceding to the Convention in 1978 Denmark made a declaration to the effect that it was not applicable in Greenland. This was strange because Article 60 of the recently renegotiated Brussels Convention explicitly stated that it would apply to Greenland, as a European territory of Denmark. It can even be questioned whether the declaration conformed with international law.[56] Greenland obtained home rule in 1979 and stepped out of the EU; it is now treated as an overseas territory.[57] Like other EU legislation, the civil jurisdiction regulations are not applicable in Greenland, and neither is the agreement between Denmark and the European Community regarding Brussels I. If it later becomes possible for Denmark to opt into private international law (including civil jurisdiction) instruments, such opting-in would be irrelevant to Greenland, which would remain outside the scope of EU law.

The Faroe Islands, which are part of the Danish kingdom, are not subject **1.31** to EU law. The islands have had home rule since 1948, before Denmark's accession to the EU. Denmark could have made a declaration to the effect that the Brussels Convention would be applicable in the Faroe Islands, but did not do so and therefore the Convention is not applicable there.[58]

In the Åland Islands, the self-governing province of Finland, EU law is **1.32** applicable with certain derogations, provided for by the Accession Treaty for Austria, Finland, and Sweden. These derogations are justified by the special status of the province under international law and the aim of maintaining a viable local economy.[59] The civil jurisdiction regulations are not part of the derogations and do therefore apply in the Åland Islands.[60]

In the sovereign base areas of the United Kingdom in Cyprus (Akrotiri **1.33** and Dhekelia), the civil jurisdiction regulations and other EU law do not apply.[61] Neither does the Brussels Convention.[62]

---

[56] See Duintjer Tebbens, note 36 above, 38; Droz, note 37 above, at 16.

[57] See Annex II to the EC Treaty; Annex II to the Constitution.

[58] Duintjer Tebbens, note 36 above, 37.

[59] Protocol no 2 to the Accession Treaty for Austria, Finland, and Sweden, published in OJ C 241, 29 August 1994, p 1.

[60] For most areas of civil and criminal law, the Åland Islands fall under the authority of Finland.

[61] There are certain exceptions to this general rule, but those are not relevant for the current topic. See Protocol no 3 to the Accession Treaty of the Czech Republic, Estonia, Cyprus, Latvia, Lithuania, Hungary, Malta, Poland, Slovenia, and Slovakia, published in OJ L 236 of 23 September 2003, p 1.

[62] Droz, note 37 above, 15.

1.34 EU law is applicable in the Channel Islands and the Isle of Man to the extent necessary for the implementation of specific arrangements.[63] Thus the civil jurisdiction regulations are not applicable there. The Brussels Convention was not applicable in these areas either.[64]

1.35 Countries and territories that have special relations with the United Kingdom, but that are not contained in the list in the annex to the EC Treaty, are not subject to EU law, and thus not to the civil jurisdiction regulations.[65]

1.36 The Netherlands declared the Brussels Convention applicable in Aruba, but only the 1978 version. Therefore, that version of the Convention remains applicable for Aruba.[66]

1.37 The independent States of Andorra, Monaco, San Marino, Liechtenstein,[67] and the Vatican are not EU Member States, nor are they associated with the EU in any of the ways described above. No EU legislation applies in those States and they remain third States.

Candidate Member States

1.38 The European Union has been enlarged a number of times and the EU now has three candidate states: Croatia, the former Yugoslav Republic of Macedonia, and Turkey. A candidate state waits to accede whilst taking the measures necessary for entry to the EU. The most important preparatory measure is the acceptance of the *acquis communautaire*. This literally means that the national legal order has to integrate thousands of pages of European Union legislation and adapt accordingly. Whilst waiting the states are not yet subject to EU legislation that does not require conversion, so the regulations of civil jurisdiction are not yet applicable. For the purpose of examining the effect the regulations have on third States, candidate Member States will be considered as third States. Before the accession of ten new Member States in 2004, the idea was that those states

---

[63] Art 299 EC Treaty (Nice version); Art IV–440 Constitution; Protocol 3 to the Accession Treaty, note 61 above; Treaty on the Accession of Denmark, Ireland and the United Kingdom.

[64] See A Briggs & P Rees, *Civil Jurisdiction and Judgments* (2nd edn, London: LLP, 1997) 10.

[65] For a full account of the application of the Brussels and Lugano Conventions in the Overseas Territories, see Droz, note 37 above, at 15–19.

[66] Rec 23 of Brussels I.

[67] Liechtenstein is a member of the European Free Trade Association (EFTA) and can therefore become party to the Lugano Convention according to Arts 60, 62 & 63.

would accede to the Lugano Convention while they were waiting. Poland was the only state to realize this accession.

D. DELIMITING THE EU CIVIL JURISDICTION RULES

Delimitation and principles of EU law

The three Regulations that are the main focus of this book are legislative acts of EU law. They purport to harmonize the civil jurisdiction rules in the EU Member States (to an extent). It is therefore useful to examine EU legislation more generally and to take note of how it is delimited. **1.39**

Civil jurisdiction rules concerned with international trade and international families cannot be restricted to the EU, and cannot ignore the world outside the EU. (The same is true of rules of private international law in general.) The nature of these areas of law is such that they involve private parties who live their lives, and conduct their businesses, in a way that suits them, without necessarily considering political borders. Attempts to divide these civil jurisdiction rules up into two spheres—inside and outside the EU—is a response to political will rather than a human and economic reality. While promoting the EU's internal market might be a sound political goal, care should be taken not to pursue this goal at the expense of solutions that might be more practical on a global level. As international trade opens up, EU rules should not segment it again. **1.40**

The interests of the EU and its internal market often form the main motivation for legislative drafting in the EU. The outside world is not often considered at the time of legislating. One often finds that clear rules of scope are missing from EU legislative acts.[68] The European Union's legislative power is not borderless, however, but limited by the principles of conferral, subsidiarity and proportionality.[69] These principles and their **1.41**

---

[68] See Francq, note 27 above, 46–50.
[69] Art I–11 of the Constitution text usefully defines these concepts of EU law:
  1. The limits of Union competences are governed by the principle of conferral. The use of Union competences is governed by the principles of subsidiarity and proportionality.
  2. Under the principle of conferral, the Union shall act within the limits of the competences conferred upon it by the Member States in the Constitution to attain the objectives

relevance for legislating in the field of civil jurisdiction will be considered in the following paragraphs.

The principle of conferral

1.42 According to this principle, the EU only exists, and only has power, as a result of the willingness of the Member States to confer it. Concerning civil jurisdiction this conferral is found in the EC Treaty: the Member States agreed that there may be EU legislation on private international law 'in so far as necessary for the proper functioning of the internal market'.[70] Interpreting these words it seems that recognition and enforcement of judgments in civil matters are clearly necessary for the proper functioning of the internal market. The same can be said regarding insolvency proceedings. On the other hand, one might wonder whether civil jurisdiction rules in the field of family law were really necessary for the proper functioning of the internal market. However, the protagonists have explained that some steps into this arena are necessary to ensure the free movement of persons within that market.[71]

set out in the Constitution. Competences not conferred upon the Union in the Constitution remain with the Member States.

3. Under the principle of subsidiarity, in areas which do not fall within its exclusive competence, the Union shall act only if and insofar as the objectives of the proposed action cannot be sufficiently achieved by the Member States, either at central level or at regional and local level, but can rather, by reason of the scale or effects of the proposed action, be better achieved at Union level. The institutions of the Union shall apply the principle of subsidiarity as laid down in the Protocol on the application of the principles of subsidiarity and proportionality. National Parliaments shall ensure compliance with that principle in accordance with the procedure set out in that Protocol.

4. Under the principle of proportionality, the content and form of Union action shall not exceed what is necessary to achieve the objectives of the Constitution. The institutions of the Union shall apply the principle of proportionality as laid down in the Protocol on the application of the principles of subsidiarity and proportionality.

[70] Art 65 EC Treaty (Amsterdam and Nice versions).
[71] See, in general, P McEleavy, 'The Brussels II Regulation: How the European Community has moved into Family Law' [2002] ICLQ 883–908; J-Y Carlier, 'La libre circulation des personnes dans l'Union européenne' [2004] *Journal des tribunaux* 74–80; E Caracciolo di Torella & A Masselot, 'Under Construction: EU Family Law' [2004] ELR 32–51; V Van den Eeckhout, 'Communitarization of private international law: Tendencies to 'liberalise' European family law' [2004] *Tijdschrift@ipr.be* vol 3, 52–70; V Van den Eeckhout, 'Communitarization of international family law as seen from a Dutch perspective: what is new? A prospective analysis' in A Nuyts & N Watté (eds), *International civil litigation in Europe and relations with third States* (Brussels: Bruylant, 2005) 509–561. See also Basedow, note 19 above, 687–708, stating at 701 that the requirement of necessity for the internal market would hardly put additional obstacles in the way of legislation. He added that one should bear in mind that all measures

The principle of subsidiarity

This principle has two elements.[72] First, for the EU to take action, it must **1.43** be impossible for the Member States to achieve the objectives of the proposed actions sufficiently. Second, it must be clear that these objectives can be better achieved by the Union. The principle of subsidiarity in effect limits the competences or the intensity of the exercise of competence by the EU. It could even be an instrument used by the Member States to push back a Commission that was too activist.[73] This principle is relevant in the area of civil jurisdiction to the extent that the Union does not have exclusive competence.[74] Where the Community has exclusive internal competence, there is no question of the Member States being able to regulate the matter sufficiently and therefore their competence does not need to be limited, and the purpose of the principle of subsidiarity falls away.

Subsidiarity is of special interest when relations with third States are at **1.44** stake. The questions can arise, why should the EU take responsibility for an issue that has effects outside its borders, and why are the Member States not in a better position to take these measures?[75]

Specifically, it is the elaboration of the EU civil jurisdiction rules on family **1.45** law that raises subsidiarity concerns. Family law is a matter intricately linked to the morals, culture, and usages of a state. Rules on divorce, for instance, differ greatly between legal systems. In some countries (Malta) divorce is not permitted. Some systems have fault as a relevant element in divorce proceedings, others do not; some systems allow divorce on the

---

in civil matters enacted under Title IV were related to the free movement of persons, one of the constituents of the internal market.

[72] Art 5 EC Treaty (Amsterdam and Nice versions) states that 'any action by the Community shall not go beyond what is necessary to achieve the objectives of this Treaty'.

[73] See Hartley, *Foundations of European Community Law*, note 3 above, 114–118; M Wathelet, 'Propos liminaires' in F Delpérée, *Le principe de subsidiarité* (Brussels: Bruylant, 2002) 17 and J Verhoeven 'Analyse du contenu et de la portée du principe de subsidiarité' in ibid, 376–389, making critical observations about the use of the principle of subsidiarity.

[74] See also K Lenaerts, 'De Europese Unie: doel of middel' [1998–1999] *Rechtskundig Weekblad*, 689–710. The external competences of the EU will be discussed in chapter 7 below. P-E Partsch, *Le droit international privé européen: De Rome à Nice* (Brussels: Larcier, 2003) states at 327 that measures in the domain of private international law tend to be more in line with the principle of subsidiarity since it is less upsetting to national systems than the unification of material law. This book does not compare various areas where EU law might have an influence and therefore takes no view on this point.

[75] In general, K Lenaerts, 'The principle of subsidiarity and the environment in the European Union: keeping the balance of federalism' [1993–1994] *Fordham International Law Journal* 846–895 at 848–852.

basis of factual separation, others do not; some legal systems have legal separation as a stopgap between being married and being divorced, in some such separation is a requirement before divorce is possible, while in other Member States the phenomenon is not known at all, or has been abolished. The EU's interference has been justified in terms of the free movement of persons. Free movement of persons traditionally means that persons should be allowed to practise their trade throughout the EU without hindrance. To this end they need to be able to establish themselves in foreign countries without too many formalities such as work permits and visas. The argument is that, if the EU does not assist in the area of family law, the free movement of persons will be hampered. For example, if a trader from Germany wants to open a shop in Austria, he should not only have the opportunity to take his wife along, but should also be able to divorce in Germany and have that divorce easily recognized in Austria (or vice versa) so that he can marry again. One has to admit that this personal misadventure is no longer related to a person's trade in the internal market. Only an attenuated form of subsidiarity would permit EU legislation in this field. This principle requires that the EU should not take measures that are unnecessary for its functioning.[76]

1.46 Necessary or not, the field of family law is being Europeanized. In the Tampere (1999) and Hague (2004) Conclusions of the European Council, provision was made for the elaboration of rules in this area. Both of these conclusions refer explicitly to family law. Extending it even further, the law of succession will also be treated.[77]

1.47 Uniform rules for the law applicable to divorce, or rules for the recognition of divorces, have an impact on third State nationals. A third State spouse of an EU national has certain rights in the EU. If a person is regarded as divorced in one EU Member State, but still married in another, his status will be different in those States.[78]

---

[76] Specifically on the principle of subsidiarity in relation to the Brussels II project, see P Beaumont & G Moir, 'Brussels Convention II: A New Private International Law Instrument in Family Matters for the European Union or the European Community?' [1995] ELR 268–288 at 281–285. See also, more generally, McEleavy, note 71 above, 883–908; Caracciolo di Torella & Masselot, note 71 above, 32–51; Van den Eeckhout, 'Communitarization of Private International Law', note 71 above, 52–70; Van den Eeckhout, 'Communitarization from a Dutch perspective', note 71 above, 509–561.

[77] See Tampere European Council, Presidency Conclusions of 15 and 16 October 1999 (available at <http://www.europarl.eu/summits/tam_en.htm>), especially para 34 and the Hague Programme of the Presidency, Conclusions of 4 and 5 November 2004 (available at <http://www.europarl.eu/summits/pdf/bru1104_en.pdf>), especially p 46–47 of Annex 1.

[78] See Beaumont & Moir, note 76 above at 276.

One might ask whether the principle of subsidiarity is being respected if **1.48**
the EU legislates in an area where well-functioning international conventions such as those of the Hague Conference on Private International Law
already exist.[79] It seems difficult in these cases to indicate that the EU
Member States cannot sufficiently achieve a goal that to an extent has
already been achieved, and that the EU can achieve it more efficiently. In
this sense subsidiarity is of significant interest to third States. Hague
Conventions are open to such states so they would be bound by the same
international rules as the EU Member States.

On the other hand, in the EU the belief is that, in an international organiza- **1.49**
tion where there is mutual trust of each other's legal systems, legislation
is capable of encompassing more, and there can be closer cooperation than
in an international convention. However, this argument still does not
seem to comply with the subsidiarity test. According to P Beaumont and
G Moir, in a larger EU deeper agreement is not possible to the same extent
as it was when there were only six Member States. They wrote this about
an EU of 15 Member States, and today there are 27. They propose that
instead, the EU Member States be part of a larger field (that created by the
Hague Conference) in situations where more intensive cooperation is not
possible.[80]

In some areas a separate EU instrument would probably be less effective **1.50**
than an international convention. For instance, child abduction does not
only occur within the EU. Such acts are not restrained by political borders.
Therefore creating a separate system does not contribute much. Fortunately
Brussels II *bis* does contain references to the Hague Conventions on child
abduction[81] and on the protection of children.[82] It seems that when drawing
up the initial Brussels II Convention, the EU remained in contact with the
Hague Conference.[83] Both Brussels I and Brussels II *bis* contain references

---

[79] See Joustra, note 17 above, 27–34. At p 54 she states, however, that the political will to
continue on the current path of Community private international law seems stronger than a
judicial reference to the principle of subsidiarity. Judging the political will is difficult, but a
proper legal basis to act is essential and the principle of subsidiarity cannot be ignored.

[80] Beaumont & Moir, note 76 above, at 288.

[81] Hague Convention of 25 October 1980 on the Civil Aspects of International Child
Abduction; Arts 11, 42 and 60 of Brussels II *bis*.

[82] Hague Convention of 19 October 1996, note 11 above; Arts 12 and 61 of Brussels II *bis*.
This matter will be discussed in chapter 2 below, para 2.123 and following.

[83] Borrás Report on the Convention, drawn up on the basis of Article K.3 of the Treaty on
the European Union, on Jurisdiction and the Recognition and Enforcement of Judgments in
Matrimonial Matters; OJ C 221, 16 July 1998, 27, at para 9, p 31.

to the Hague Service Convention (1965) for cases to which the Service Regulation[84] does not apply.[85]

The principle of proportionality

1.51 This principle states essentially that the burden a measure imposes must not be disproportionate to the objective. The measure must be reasonably likely to bring about the object envisaged. At the same time, it must not harm the public disproportionately. It has its roots in German law (*Verhältnismässigkeit*, which underlies certain provisions of the German Constitution). It can also be compared to the English concept of reasonableness:[86] Are the means adopted suitable with a view to the end? In the arena of civil jurisdiction, this principle does not often come into play. What the EU has done until now is to promote the cooperation of the judicial organs of Member States. This does not impose a burden on anyone in the EU in the way that specific economic law rules can impose burdens. The burden, the costs, the harm to the public, and the avoidance of creating something excessive refer to elements in the EU. The interests of third States do not influence whether a measure would be proportional.

The EU jurisdiction rules and their interaction with national law

1.52 When should third State domiciliaries adhere to Brussels I and when, if not to other international conventions, to domestic law? The exact point at which the EU Regulations and the national rules on jurisdiction meet, is discussed throughout this book.[87] Before venturing to the specific Regulations, a preliminary question should be posed: do they completely

---

[84] Hague Convention of 15 November 1965 on the Service Abroad of Judicial and Extrajudicial Documents in Civil or Commercial Matters, available at <www.hcch.net>. Council Regulation (EC) No 1348/2000 of 29 May 2000 on the service in the Member States of judicial and extrajudicial documents in civil or commercial matters, OJ L 160, 30 June 2000, p 37–52.

[85] Art 26(4) of Brussels I; Art 18(3) of Brussels II *bis*.

[86] See Hartley, *Foundations of European Community Law*, note 3 above, 151; GA Bermann, 'Proportionality and Subsidiarity' in C Barnard & J Scott (eds), *The Law of the Single European Market* (Oxford: Hart Publishing, 2002) 75–99 at 79: 'in the Community law system, as in so many national law systems, proportionality figures conspicuously among the doctrinal weapons in the general arsenal of weapons that may be levelled at the legality of a legislative measure'.

[87] See also R Fentiman, 'National law and the European jurisdiction regime' in Nuyts & Watté, note 71 above, 83–128; P Grolimund, *Drittstaatenproblematik des europäischen Zivilverfahrensrechts* (Tübingen: Mohr Siebeck, 2000) esp 25–70.

replace national law for the matters that they regulate, or have (some) domestic jurisdiction rules survived?

The first view is that the EU Regulations have completely taken over juris- **1.53** diction in civil and commercial matters.[88] GAL Droz speaks of the '*code judiciaire européen*' (European code of civil procedure).[89] Briggs and Rees, supporting this view, state that it is a misreading of the instruments to interpret them as amending and partly replacing the rules of common law, or to state that common law continues to apply except where the Conventions apply. They state that the Conventions and Regulations are the starting points when there is a question of jurisdiction, recognition, or enforcement in civil and commercial cases.[90] Domestic rules only remain if, and in so far as, they are authorized by these Regulations.[91] Therefore, when a case falls inside the material scope of any of the Regulations, the Regulation is the point of departure. Only when the Regulation states that for the case at hand reference may be made to domestic jurisdiction rules, can those be activated. The foundation of this view is mostly in EU law. The EU aims to create an area of justice, freedom and security and the further the integration reaches, the better. However, there is a conceptual difficulty in justifying broad EU rules by EU interests, where a case has nothing to do with the European judicial area.

The second view is that a Regulation governs international jurisdiction **1.54** between the EU Member States in so far as the European judicial area is concerned. If not, national rules apply as part of the national legal system, independent of the Regulation. Therefore, in every EU Member State there are two sets of rules on civil jurisdiction that exist side by side: the EU

---

[88] For support of this view, see L Pålsson, 'Interim Relief under the Brussels and Lugano Conventions' in J Basedow, I Meier, AK Schnyder, T Einhorn, D Girsberger (eds), *Private Law in the International Arena. Liber Amicorum Kurt Siehr* (The Hague: TMC Asser Press, 2000) 633, who writes about the indirect application of the [Regulation] via Art 4; B Audit, *Droit international privé* (3rd edn, Paris: Economica, 2000) 436; A Saggio, 'The outlook for the System for the Free Movement of Judgments Created by the Brussels Convention' in Court of Justice of the European Communities, *Civil Jurisdiction and Judgments in Europe* (London: Butterworths, 1992) p 201; Briggs & Rees, 4th edn, note 54 above, 3–6; A Briggs, *The Conflict of Laws* (Oxford: Oxford University Press, 2002) 91; D McClean, *Morris: The Conflict of Laws* (5th edn, London: Sweet & Maxwell, 2000) 123.

[89] GAL Droz, 'Les règles du traité CEE sur la compétence judiciaire et l'exécution des décisions en matière civile et commerciale' in P Bourel, U Drobnig, GAL Droz, B Goldman, O Lando, K Lipstein, C Morse, J Pipkorn & F Pocar, *The Influence of the European Community upon Private International Law of the Member States* (Brussels: Larcier, 1981) 49–76, at 51.

[90] Briggs & Rees, 4th edn, note 54 above, 3–6.

[91] The references to national law are found in Art. 4 Brussels I and in Art 7 Brussels II *bis*. For more information on the difficulties that Art 7 has led to, see below, chapter 2, para 2.087 and following.

rules and the national rules. The opinion of Advocate General Darmon in *Brenner and Noller v Dean Witter Reynolds*,[92] although not totally clear, seemed to support this view. The Advocate General stated that the Brussels Convention was not applicable to a case where the defendant was domiciled in a third State. In support of this finding, he called the reference in the Brussels Convention to national law (Article 4) a 'reminder'.[93] The Court did not pay much attention to this point and merely stated that Article 4 (thus national law) governed the case.[94] The essence of this second view is that the reference to national law in the Brussels Convention, which has been taken over in Brussels I, does not make national law applicable. It only reminds the court of the relevant national rules. According to this view, when the national rules apply, such application emanates from the rules themselves and is not the result of their appointment by an EU regulation. The rules have a *raison d'être* independent of the EU rules. This view is appealing because it limits the reach of EU legislation towards the outside world. There are two regimes in EU Member States: one for the Member States and one for everybody else.

1.55 The discussion also arises concerning Brussels II *bis*. This Regulation determines that a spouse who is habitually resident in or a national[95] of a Member State, may be sued in another Member State only in accordance with the jurisdiction rules of the Regulation. This seems to imply that the Regulation is not applicable to a defendant habitually resident in, or a national of a third State.[96] However, the following Article states that where no court in an EU Member State has jurisdiction according to the Regulation's rules, recourse may be had to the domestic rules of jurisdiction.[97] This provision appears to contradict the previous one. It seems that, irrespective of the habitual residence and nationality of the defendant, one should always give preference to the system created by the Regulation. Have these domestic rules now only survived for cases when the Regulation does not appoint any EU Member State court? Or have they survived to regulate matters where the defendant is habitually resident in a third State and has no EU nationality? The contradiction seems to be resolved by the proposed amendments to the Regulation. In the proposal the provision on habitual residence and nationality of defendants is deleted. Therefore the interpretation that the Regulation has replaced the

---

[92] Case C–318/93 [1994] ECR I–4275.
[93] At para 10–20.
[94] At para 16–18.
[95] For Ireland and the United Kingdom 'nationality' is replaced by 'domicile.'
[96] Art 6 of Brussels II *bis*.
[97] Art 7 of Brussels II *bis*.

domestic rules prevails. Only when there is no jurisdiction in any EU Member State court can the domestic rules come into play. It seems, therefore, that the Regulation has imposed a single system in which domestic rules can only be applied when the Regulation so permits.

The European Court of Justice in the *Lugano* opinion seems to have reached the same conclusion regarding Brussels I.[98] It stated that Brussels I contained a complete system of jurisdiction rules. Thus it seems that the reference to national law had the effect of incorporating those rules into the Regulation.[99] **1.56**

This means that the Regulations must always form the starting point in the search for the applicable rule of jurisdiction. Only when these Regulations refer to national rules can those rules be applied. The rules then are not applied independently, but as part of the system of the Regulation. This approach will be taken into account throughout the discussions in this book. **1.57**

Influence of national rules on EU rules

In any event, once it has been determined that an EU civil jurisdiction regulation applies, these rules have precedence over the rules of national law. This principle was enunciated by the European Court of Justice and applied in several cases.[100] Despite the hierarchy just explained, there is a tendency to season the systems of the Regulations with national elements. This seasoning can take various forms, for instance using a national rule, such as *forum non conveniens*, to neutralize a ground for jurisdiction of the Regulation. The European Court of Justice has ruled that this doctrine of English law may not be used to decline jurisdiction that has been based on the domicile of the defendant under Brussels I (Article 2). Courts might wish to add something to the rules, such as rules taking public policy into **1.58**

---

[98] Opinion 1/03 *Opinion of the Court on the competence of the Community to conclude the new Lugano Convention on jurisdiction and the recognition and enforcement of judgments in civil and commercial matters* [2006] ECR I–1145.

[99] At para 148.

[100] Case 25/79, *Sanicentral v René Collin* [1979] ECR 3423, at para 5; Case 288/82, *Duijnstee v Goderbauer* [1983] ECR 3663, at para 13–14; Case C–432/93, *Société d'Informatique Service Réalisation Organization v Ampersand Software BV* [1995] ECR I–2269. See also A Nuyts, 'Questions de procédure: la difficile coexistance des règles conventionelles et nationales' in R Fentiman, A Nuyts, H Tagaras & N Watté (eds), *The European Judicial Area in Civil and Commercial Matters* (Brussels: Bruylant, 1999) 235–250; F Salerno, 'European international civil procedure' in B von Hoffmann (ed), *European Private International Law* (Nijmegen: Ars Aequi Libri, 1998) 151–153.

account or jurisdiction to prevent a denial of justice.[101] This is not permissible, since the European Court of Justice has ruled it impermissible to add criteria for the validity of forum clauses that are not contained in the Brussels Convention.[102]

The limitation of the EU civil jurisdiction rules to international cases

1.59 An issue that has remained unclear for a very long time is whether the EU civil jurisdiction rules also apply to cases that are linked to only one EU Member State and a third State. The case is international, but has no cross-border element within the EU; it seems that the case has no relevance for the European judicial area. The European Court of Justice resolved this controversy in *Owusu*.[103] In this case the defendant was domiciled in England, as was the plaintiff. A number of co-defendants were domiciled in Jamaica, and the facts leading to the dispute took place in this third State as well. No parties from any other EU Member States were involved. Neither was there a basis for exclusive jurisdiction tying the case to another EU Member State, a forum clause in favour of another EU Member State, a contract that had to be performed in, nor a tort committed in another EU Member State. The European Court of Justice found that the link to Jamaica internationalized the case, and this was sufficient for the Brussels Convention to apply if the defendant was domiciled in the EU. The fact that the plaintiff was domiciled in the same EU Member State was irrelevant, as long as the case had some element of internationality (in this case the co-defendants and the place of the facts). That internationality does not have to involve another EU Member State.

E. THE RELATIONSHIP BETWEEN THE EU CIVIL JURISDICTION RULES AND CONVENTIONS ON SPECIFIC MATTERS

1.60 In some instances the EU Member States are obliged under international law to respect other conventions (on various matters) with third States, despite the fact that a conflict might exist with Brussels I or Brussels II *bis*. Conflicts with Brussels I arise frequently, as this Regulation covers a large area of civil and commercial law. For example, the transport treaties: the international

---

[101] See H Born, M Fallon & J-L Van Boxstael, *Droit judiciaire international. Chronique de jurisprudence 1991–1998* (Brussels: Larcier, 2001) 61–62.

[102] Case 150/80, *Elefanten Schuh GmbH v Pierre Jacqmain* [1981] ECR 1671.

[103] Case C–281/02, *Owusu v Jackson* [2005] ECR I–1383.

transport of both passengers and goods is a specialized economic activity often requiring particular legal rules. Many of the conventions on specific matters might contain provisions on jurisdiction and/or on the recognition and enforcement of foreign judgments.

Brussels I explicitly acknowledges that it leaves such Conventions intact.[104] **1.61** For instance, the Convention on the Contract for the International Carriage of Goods by Road (CMR Convention)[105] is applied in the Member States with regard to disputes on transport contracts. If one party is from the EU and another from a third State (CMR Contracting State), a dispute on a transport contract will fall under the CMR Convention. That will be the case even if the parties had chosen, by way of a jurisdiction clause, the courts of an EU Member State. In other words, that jurisdiction clause, because it belongs to the transport sector, will be adjudicated as to its validity on the basis of the CMR Convention and not on the basis of Brussels I. The same will of course apply if the same two parties chose a court in a third State that is party to the CMR Convention. Even if the parties were both from EU Member States and appointed an EU court, by way of a forum clause, the CMR Convention would prevail.[106] The European Court of Justice has confirmed that the jurisdiction rules of the CMR Convention apply even if the criteria for the personal scope of the Brussels Convention are met. In the *Portbridge* case, when the defendant did not appear, the Oberlandesgericht (District Court of Appeal) of Munich posed a preliminary question as to whether it might assume jurisdiction on the basis of the CMR Convention.[107] The Court replied that the jurisdiction rules of the CMR Convention were still in force, and applied to the same extent as those of the Brussels Convention itself. Therefore, the German Court clearly had jurisdiction and could hear the case.[108] Similarly, the Air Carriage Convention[109] is applied regarding disputes over carriage by air, even if both parties are domiciled in EU Member States.[110] Therefore, *a fortiori*, it will apply if only one of the parties

---

[104] Art 71 Brussels I Regulation.

[105] Geneva, 1956.

[106] See Belgian Hof van Cassatie (Court of Cassation), C020250N, 29 April 2004, available at <http://www.juridat.be>; Rechtbank van koophandel (Commercial Court) of Hasselt (Belgium), 24 November 2004 (AR 04/4119), available at <http://www.euprocedure.be> under AR04/4119.

[107] Case C–148/03, *Nürnberger Allgemeine Versicherungs AG v Portbridge Transport International BV* [2004] ECR I–10327.

[108] Art 26 of Brussels I (at the time Art 20 of the Brussels Convention).

[109] Convention for the unification of certain rules relating to international carriage by air (Warsaw, 1929). This Convention has in the meantime been updated by the Montreal Convention of the same name (1999).

[110] *Milor SRL & others v British Airways plc* [1996] QB 702; [1996] ILPr 426, CA.

is from the EU and the other from a third State. The Arrest Convention[111] also takes precedence over Brussels I, as has been recognized by the English Court in *The 'Linda'*,[112] In that case jurisdiction was based on the arrest of ships, in accordance with the Arrest Convention.

1.62 If the convention on a specific matter contains jurisdiction rules, but no rules on *lis pendens* or related actions, Brussels I can be applied to resolve an issue between the courts of two EU Member States. This has been affirmed by the European Court of Justice in *The 'Tatry'*[113] regarding the Arrest Convention[114] and in the *Mærsk Olie* case,[115] concerning the International Convention relating to the Limitation of the Liability of Owners of Sea-Going Ships[116] (although the facts of these cases did not permit the application of the *lis pendens* rule, since respectively the parties and the causes of action were not identical).

1.63 Likewise, the recognition and enforcement of judgments can fall under Brussels I even though jurisdiction has been based upon a convention on a specific matter. The European Court of Justice, in *Mærsk Olie*, ruled that a limitation of liability established by an EU Member State court, according to the Limitation of Liability Convention, was a 'judgment' for the purposes of the Brussels Convention and therefore had to be recognized under the Brussels Convention. It did not take into account the basis of jurisdiction. Therefore, parties from third States could easily give greater effect to the limitation of their liability under the Limitation of Liability Convention by obtaining a declaration from an EU Member State court (provided that such a court has jurisdiction to make one under the Convention). The limitation of liability would automatically be valid throughout the EU.

1.64 The Hague Choice of Court Convention[117] which deals with one of the topics of Brussels I, will be considered in chapter 4 on forum clauses.[118]

---

[111] International Convention for the Unification of Certain Rules relating to the Arrest of Seagoing Ships (Brussels, 1952).

[112] *The 'Linda'* [1988] 1 Lloyd's Rep 175.

[113] Case C–406/92 *The owners of the cargo lately laden on board the ship 'Tatry' v the owners of the ship 'Maciej Rataj'* [1994] ECR I–5439.

[114] See note 111 above.

[115] Case C–39/02 *Mærsk Olie & Gas A/S v Firma M de Haan en W de Boer* [2004] ECR I–9657.

[116] Brussels, 1957.

[117] Hague Convention of 30 June 2005 on Choice of Court Agreements, not yet in force.

[118] See below, chapter 4, para 4.46.

Possible conflicts with Brussels II *bis* also exist, mainly because of the recent **1.65** and successful activities of the Hague Conference on Private International Law. Brussels II *bis* respects the international conventions already in force. However, regarding relations between Member States, the Regulation will supersede these conventions.[119] The Insolvency Regulation is still almost unique, as not many international conventions exist in that field.

F. THE RELATIONSHIP BETWEEN THE EU CIVIL JURISDICTION RULES AND THE LUGANO CONVENTION

The Lugano Convention came into existence in 1988. A number of European **1.66** states that were direct neighbours of the EU had witnessed the benefits of an easy system for recognition and enforcement of judgments. The new Convention was virtually a carbon copy of the Brussels Convention.[120] The current Contracting States are the 15 old EU Member States (Austria, Belgium, Denmark, Finland, France, Germany, Greece, Ireland, Italy, Luxembourg, the Netherlands, Portugal, Spain, Sweden and the United Kingdom), Poland, Switzerland, Iceland and Norway. It is a closed system in the sense that it is not possible for all states to become party to the Lugano Convention. The Contracting States created a system of invitation. It is in this way that Poland (when it was still a candidate EU Member State) joined the Convention in 2002. A new version of the Lugano Convention came into being in 2007. To a large extent this Convention is the same as Brussels I. The 11 remaining new EU Member States (Bulgaria, Czech Republic, Cyprus, Estonia, Hungary, Latvia, Lithuania, Malta, Romania, Slovakia, Slovenia) are not yet party to the Lugano Convention, but they will soon be able to ratify the new version since they are now EU Member States.

---

[119] See H Gaudemet-Tallon, 'Le Règlement no. 1347/2000 du Conseil du 29 mai 2000: 'Compétence, reconnaissance et exécution des décisions en matière matrimoniale et en matière de responsabilité parentale des enfants communs',' [2001] *Journal de droit internatio-nal* 381–430 at 421–426; M Jänterä-Jareborg, 'Marriage dissolution in an integrated Europe: The 1998 European Union Convention on Jurisdiction and the Recognition and Enforcement of Judgments in Matrimonial Matters (Brussels II Convention)' [1999] *Yearbook for Private International Law* 1–36 at 27–31.

[120] Convention on jurisdiction and the enforcement of judgments in civil and commercial matters (Lugano Convention), 16 September 1988, OJ L 319, 9–48. Regarding the history of the Lugano Convention, see PAM Meijknecht, 'The verdrag van Lugano en het toetredings-verdrag van San Sebastian, in onderling verband' in Meijknecht & Duintjer Tebbens, note 6 above, 3–49 at 7–11.

1.67 The rules of the Brussels Convention and of the Lugano Convention were almost identical, so the question which applied was often rather academic. At the same time there were small differences, which might prove pertinent in a particular case. There is one large difference between the two: the interpretative authority of the European Court of Justice. If an appeal court is unsure as to the application of the Brussels Convention, it may refer a preliminary question to the European Court of Justice. This is not possible when the court is applying the Lugano Convention. The ECJ may also give preliminary rulings regarding Brussels I, on the basis of the EC Treaty.[121] The Lugano Convention contains a protocol providing that in the interpretation of the Convention, any such preliminary rulings on the Brussels Convention and Brussels I will be taken into account, as well as national case law.[122]

1.68 With the conversion of the Brussels Convention to Brussels I the parallelism was lost as some of the rules were changed or updated. Negotiations to allow for the updating of the Lugano Convention to bring its rules into line with Brussels I were stalled by a dispute between the EU Member States and the EC (embodied by the Commission) regarding the external competence of the EC, and who might negotiate and sign the new Lugano Convention. After the European Court of Justice ruled that the European Community was exclusively competent in the matter,[123] negotiations were taken up again and the Convention came into being in 2007. With its entry into force, the parallelism will be reinstated. The European Court of Justice will of course remain incompetent to interpret the Lugano Convention, but the protocol encouraging uniform interpretation is retained.

1.69 The relationship between Brussels I and the Lugano Convention manifests itself on different points: rules on jurisdiction, procedural rules related to jurisdiction (such as *lis pendens* and related actions), and rules on recognition and enforcement.

1.70 Turning first to the jurisdiction rules, the Lugano Convention extends the rules of Brussels I to a number of neighbouring states. Therefore it changes the situation for a few specific third States, namely Iceland, Norway and Switzerland. For other third States, its existence will not influence the rules considered in this study. Support for this view can be found in Article 54B of the Lugano Convention, which states that the

---

[121] Arts 234 and 68 EC Treaty. Only the highest court of every Member State may request such a preliminary ruling.

[122] Protocol 2 of the old and of the 2007 Lugano Conventions.

[123] *Lugano* Opinion, note 98 above. This case is discussed in more detail in chapter 7, para 7.27 and following.

Convention shall not prejudice the application of Brussels I in the EU.[124] In the 2007 version of the Lugano Convention Article 64, which is almost exactly the same as the old Article 54B, governs the relationship with Brussels I.

Regarding general bases of jurisdiction, the Lugano Convention is appli- **1.71** cable if the defendant is domiciled in a Lugano Contracting State that is not an EU Member State (i.e. Iceland, Norway or Switzerland). Nationality, as under Brussels I, plays no role. If there are multiple defendants, juris- diction over every defendant is determined according to his or her domi- cile. Therefore if one defendant is domiciled in France, Brussels I will be applied. For his or her co-defendant domiciled in Switzerland, the Lugano Convention will be applied. For a third co-defendant domiciled in South Africa, the domestic rules of the forum will be applicable.[125]

This basic standpoint is important for defendants from Iceland, Norway **1.72** and Switzerland, as a specific category of third States. However, the English courts did not follow this basic rule in *Canada Trust and others v Stolzenberg and others*.[126] One defendant was domiciled in England, others in Switzerland, and yet others in Liechtenstein, Panama and the Netherlands Antilles. The House of Lords, like the courts from which the appeal came, applied the Lugano Convention to the entire case. The rule prescribing jurisdiction to the courts of the place where the defendant is domiciled, is the same in the Brussels Convention and the Lugano Convention, so that at first sight no harm was done to the particular defendants from Switzerland.[127] However, as has been indicated, there are small differences between Brussels I and the Lugano Convention

---

[124] It took the negotiators a long time to reach consensus on this article; Y Donzallaz, *La Convention de Lugano du 16 septembre 1988 concernant la compétence judiciaire et l'exécution des décisions en matière civile et commerciale* (Berne: Editions Stæmpfli + Cie SA Berne, 1996) vol 1, 101–104. See, in general, on the limitation between Brussels I and the Lugano Convention: GAL Droz, 'La convention de Lugano parallèle à la convention de Bruxelles concernant la compétence judiciaire et l'exécution des décisions en matière civile et commerciale' [1989] *Revue critique de droit international privé* 1–51 at 7–9; J Erauw, 'De verdragen van Brussel en Lugano uitmekaar houden' [1996] *Revue de droit commercial belge* 772–782 at 780; Briggs & Rees, 4th edn, note 54 above, 275–287.

[125] For more detail see chapter 2 below, para 2.130 and following. See also M Carpenter, 'Developments in the Law relating to the International Conventions Considered in the Context of the European Judicial Area,' in ECJ, note 88 above, 234; Donzallaz, ibid, vol 1, 104; Duintjer Tebbens in Meijknecht & Duintjer Tebbens, note 6 above, 53–117 at 89–90.

[126] [2002] 1 AC 1 (HL). For a more detailed discussion of this case, see below, chapter 2, para 2.031 and following.

[127] The case was decided before the enactment of Brussels I; of course the rule on the domi- cile of the defendant is the same in that Regulation as well.

(for instance, the first version of the Lugano text, with regard to employees). The Lugano Convention should only have been applied against the defendant domiciled in Switzerland. The Brussels Convention should have been applied against the defendant domiciled in England. With regard to the other defendants, and the question of whether they could be joined to the proceedings, the courts should have applied English domestic law. Furthermore, a difficult point of interpretation surfaced in this case. The House of Lords interpreted this point without reference to the European Court of Justice, since it found that it could not pose preliminary questions of interpretation regarding the Lugano Convention. If it had posed the preliminary question the result of the case might have been different.

1.73 On the jurisdictional level, exclusive bases of jurisdiction can also determine the relationship between Brussels I and the Lugano Convention. The Lugano Convention applies if an exclusive basis of jurisdiction (e.g. immovable property) is situated in a Lugano Contracting State that is not an EU Member State.[128]

1.74 Similarly, if a forum clause appoints the courts of a Lugano Convention Contracting State that is not an EU Member State, while one of the parties is domiciled in any Lugano Convention Contracting State (EU or non-EU), the Lugano Convention will apply.[129] Whether the other party is domiciled in an EU Member State, a non-EU Lugano State, or another third State, is irrelevant.

1.75 Turning to the second point on the relationship between Brussels I and the Lugano Convention, namely *lis pendens* and related actions, the distinction does not lie with the parties involved, but with the courts. If there is a problem of *lis pendens* between two Lugano Contracting States, one of which is an EU Member State and the other not, the Lugano Convention will govern the relation. It makes no difference which court was seised first, nor whether jurisdiction was based on the rules of Brussels I.[130]

---

[128] Art 54B(2)(a) of the old Lugano Convention; Art 64(2)(a) of the 2007 Lugano Convention. Art 16 of the old Lugano Convention and Art 22 of the 2007 Lugano Convention are almost identical to Art 22 of Brussels I (exclusive bases of jurisdiction). For a more detailed discussion of this rule, see chapter 3.

[129] See Art 54B(2)(a) of the old Lugano Convention; Art 64(2)(a) of the 2007 Lugano Convention. Art 17 of the old and Art 23 of the 2007 Lugano Convention are almost identical to Art 23 of Brussels I (forum clauses). For a more detailed discussion of this rule, see chapter 4.

[130] Art 54B(2)(b) of the old Lugano Convention; Art 64(2)(b) of the 2007 Lugano Convention; Carpenter, note 125 above, 234; Donzallaz, note 124 above, vol 1, 105; Droz, 'La convention de Lugano', note 124 above, 9–10.

This solution is in line with the basic rule of Brussels I that its provisions only apply if both courts are EU Member States.[131]

Lastly, concerning recognition and enforcement, the principle is the same **1.76** as for *lis pendens:* if one of the courts (the court that gave the judgment or the recognizing or enforcing court) is in a non-EU Lugano Contracting State, the Lugano Convention will apply.[132] The basis of the initial jurisdiction (whether domestic law, the Lugano Convention or Brussels I) is irrelevant. Jurisdiction will not be tested at the time of recognition or enforcement, unless an exclusive basis of jurisdiction in an EU Member State or Lugano Convention Contracting State is concerned, or a protective basis of jurisdiction with regard to consumers or insured parties.

However, there are authors who do not agree with this straightforward **1.77** construction, even though it seems perfectly compatible with the borders of Brussels I. The argument has been advanced for an extended interpretation of the concept of domicile. The Lugano Convention should then be applied if the defendant has one of the elements of his patrimony in a Lugano Contracting State that is not an EU Member State, even if jurisdiction is not based on that element. For example, a defendant is sued in Germany on the basis of his domicile there. If the defendant has a branch in Switzerland, the Lugano Convention should be applied instead of Brussels I.[133] This seems incorrect and conflicts with the borders of Brussels I regarded in their own right.

G. THE HAGUE CONFERENCE ON PRIVATE INTERNATIONAL LAW AS MEETING PLACE BETWEEN THE EU AND THIRD STATES

General

Established in 1893 in The Hague, the Netherlands, the goal of the Hague **1.78** Conference on Private International Law is the progressive unification of the rules of private international law.[134] Although it was first set up among

---

[131] See chapter 5 for more detail.

[132] See Art 54B(2)(c) of the old Lugano Convention; Art 64(2)(c) of the 2007 Lugano Convention; Donzallaz, note 124 above, vol 1, 105–110; Droz, 'La convention de Lugano', note 124 above, 8.

[133] Donzallaz, note 124 above, vol 1, 104.

[134] See Art 1 of the Statute of the Hague Conference, which entered into force in 15 July 1955 (from 1928 to 1951 the Conference was inactive). See also its website: <http://www.hcch.net>.

solely European States, the Conference currently has 67 Members from all over the world: 66 States[135] and the European Community. Non-Member States may also attend meetings of the Hague Conference as observers.[136] This possibility is likewise available to non-governmental and international organizations. The European Communities, since their early days, observed the work of the Hague Conference, as did the Council of Europe.[137] In this sense the Hague Conference has become a forum for negotiating international conventions of all kinds in the field of private international law. Because of the negotiating opportunities it offers, it has also become a school for comparative private international law in its own right. Arguably nowhere else have the different views that exist in various legal systems on civil jurisdiction given rise to such confrontation, and such search for creative solutions as at the Hague Conference.

The Hague Conference and the EU

1.79 All 27 Member States of the European Union are Members of the Hague Conference. The European Community as an institution has many legislative powers in the domain of private international law, including external competence, and became a Member of the Hague Conference on 3 April 2007.[138] The Hague Conference's 1955 Statute permitted only states to be members, but in June 2005, the Member States of the Hague Conference reached agreement on amending the Statute in order to allow Regional Economic Integration Organizations (REIOs) to join.[139] At the

---

[135] Albania, Argentina, Australia, Austria, Belarus, Belgium, Bosnia and Herzegovina, Brazil, Bulgaria, Canada, Chile, China, Croatia, Cyprus, Czech Republic, Denmark, Egypt, Estonia, Finland, France, Georgia, Germany, Greece, Hungary, Iceland, Ireland, Israel, Italy, Japan, Jordan, Republic of Korea, Latvia, Lithuania, Luxembourg, Malaysia, Malta, Mexico, Monaco, Montenegro, Morocco, the Netherlands, New Zealand, Norway, Panama, Paraguay, Peru, Poland, Portugal, Romania, Russian Federation, Serbia, Slovakia, Slovenia, South Africa, Spain, Sri Lanka, Suriname, Sweden, Switzerland, Turkey, Ukraine, United Kingdom of Great Britain and Northern Ireland, United States of America, Uruguay, Venezuela and the former Yugoslav Republic of Macedonia.

[136] Before it became a Member State in 1964, the United States of America was such an observer; KH Nadelmann & WLM Reese, 'The Tenth Session of the Hague Conference on Private International Law' [1964] AJCL 612–615 at 612. At that point English became the second official language of the Conference (alongside French); specifically on the language issues, see KH Nadelmann & AT von Mehren, 'Equivalences in treaties in the conflicts field' [1966–1967] AJCL 195–203 at 195. Until its admission as a Member on 3 April 2007, the European Community was an observer as well.

[137] See the Documents, Conférence de la Haye de Droit international privé, les 2 avant-projets [1996] *Netherlands International Law Review* 327–336 at 327.

[138] On the external competences of the EU, see chapter 7 below.

[139] The new Statute entered into force on 1 January 2007; see <http://www.hcch.net>.

time of applying for membership, a REIO must declare its competences, and must also inform the Hague Conference of any subsequent changes to its competences.[140] The EC made a declaration of competences.[141] The changes to the Hague Conference's Statute were primarily made to welcome the European Community, although the general wording will allow other international organizations with similar status and competences in the future to join the Hague Conference as full Members.[142] In Africa many regional organizations exist, but are in the early stages of development, such as the African Union (AU), the Southern African Development Community (SADC), the Southern African Customs Union (SACU), the Organization for the Harmonization of Business Law in Africa (known by the French acronym OHADA), the Economic and Monetary Community of Central Africa (CEMAC, French acronym) and the Economic Community of West Africa States (ECOWAS).[143] How far these organizations will integrate remains to be seen. The most activist in this area seems to be OHADA, which has adopted uniform acts. Therefore more general REIO clauses may be able to serve them. The Organization of American States (OAS) is also a regional organization, enhancing cooperation in fields such as human rights, peace, security and trade. However, it does not at the moment seem that it will ever develop to the extent that it will be able to legislate. MERCOSUR, the common market of the southern cone (composed of states in southern America), is on its way to becoming a true REIO.[144] It has a parliament drawn from the Member States' national parliaments and has already adopted a number of protocols in different spheres, including private international law. Some of the former USSR states are associated in the Commonwealth of Independent

---

[140] Art 3(3) and (4) of the Statute.

[141] By letter to the Secretary General of the Hague Conference dated 15 February 2007.

[142] Remien, note 6 above 53–86 at 73 states that Art 65 of the EC Treaty would lead to competition between the European Community and the Hague Conference on Private International Law. He adds: 'For the Community, it will be important to acquire at least the same expertise in conflict of laws as hitherto was found in national circles and the Hague Conference. The goals should be to achieve at least the same quality and even more democratic discourse and legitimacy.'

[143] See, in general, H Van Houtte, *The Law of International Trade* (2nd edn, London: Sweet & Maxwell, 2002) 48–52.

[144] RA Porrata-Doria Jr, 'MERCOSUR: The Common Market of the Twenty-first century?' [2004] Georgia Journal of International and Comparative Law 1–72; T Zamudio, 'MERCOSUR: General Ideas' [2004] International Journal of Legal Information 627–638; ME Carranza, 'MERCOSUR, the Free Trade Area of the Americas, and the future of US hegemony in America' [2003–2004] *Fordham International Law Journal* 1029–1065; Z Kembayev, 'Integration processes in South America and in the post-Soviet area: a comparative analysis,' [2005] *Southwestern Journal of Law and Trade in the Americas* 25–44.

States (CIS). This organization cannot draft legislation, but facilitates cooperation between its Member States by way of treaties and coordinating institutions.[145] Some of the CIS Member States created a customs union in 1995 and this customs union gave birth to the Eurasian Economic Community in 2000,[146] which had the goal of creating a common market and forming a unified position on international trade issues. The Association of Southeast Asian Nations (ASEAN) is a regional organization with political, economic, and socio-cultural objectives; it is, *inter alia*, working towards economic integration and eventually an economic community.[147] These organizations might gradually evolve to REIOs in future.

In practice

1.80 The Hague Conference functions by way of special commissions and diplomatic sessions. A special commission is a negotiation between experts from the Member States. A diplomatic session is the finalizing negotiations and adoption by representatives from the Member States. Member States are not obliged to ratify all conventions, even if they had participated in the negotiations. On the other hand, non-Member States may accede to conventions.

1.81 The Hague Conference has a secretariat, the Permanent Bureau, which is responsible for the preparatory research for conventions, and the preparation and organization of special commissions and diplomatic sessions between the Member States. The Foreign Ministry of the Netherlands has a special role in the Hague Conference: it serves as the depository of the conventions.

1.82 The Hague Conference has to date adopted 43 conventions on various private international law topics concerning jurisdiction, applicable law, recognition and enforcement and international procedure. The most successful of these are the Apostille Convention,[148] the Service Convention,[149]

---

[145] E Gerasimchuk, 'The relationship between the judgments project and certain regional instruments in the arena of the Commonwealth of Independent States' (Choice of Court Convention Preliminary Document No 27), available from <http://www.hcch.net>.

[146] Kembayev, note 144 above, at 36.

[147] R Amoussou-Guénou, 'Perspectives des principes ASEAN (ou Asiatiques) du droit des contrats' [2005] *Revue de droit des affaires* 573–591.

[148] Hague Convention of 5 October 1961 Abolishing the Requirement of Legalisation for Foreign Public Documents.

[149] Hague Convention of 15 November 1965 on the Service Abroad of Judicial and Extrajudicial Documents in Civil or Commercial Matters.

the Evidence Convention,[150] the Child Abduction Convention,[151] and the Adoption Convention.[152] The Child Abduction Convention has gained importance by its partial incorporation into Brussels II *bis*, and is in force in all EU Member States. Instead of creating a new system for international child abduction, Brussels II *bis* (partially) uses the system installed by that Convention.[153] The themes of the recognition and enforcement of foreign judgments, and of civil jurisdiction, have returned several times to the agenda of the Hague Conference.

The 1971 Hague Convention[154]

An early venture at a recognition and enforcement convention in civil **1.83** matters occurred in 1960 when the Council of Europe suggested a general regularization of the issue. A Special Commission studied the subject.[155] The negotiations for this Convention began after the 1964 publication of the Common Market Draft of the Brussels Convention. All of the then-23 Member States of the Hague Conference were present: the meetings provided a forum for discussing the threats that the Draft Brussels Convention posed.[156] The negotiations of this Hague Convention and the Brussels Convention continued simultaneously. It seemed as if there was a race between the two to complete first.[157] Another reason for the project was that many states required reciprocity in the recognition and enforcement of judgments. In others, recognition and enforcement are only possible if a convention to that effect exists.[158] Therefore the best way to allow for recognition and enforcement is the conclusion of conventions, or creation of a framework to that end.

---

[150] Hague Convention of 18 March 1970 on the Taking of Evidence Abroad in Civil or Commercial Matters.

[151] See note 81 above.

[152] Hague Convention of 29 May 1993 on Protection of Children and Co-operation in respect of Intercountry Adoption.

[153] For more detail, see chapter 2, below, para 2.112.

[154] See note 9 above.

[155] Explanatory report by CN Fragistas, published in Conférence de La Haye de droit international privé [1969] Hague Conference on Private International Law Proceedings of the Extraordinary Session 11, 360–388 at 361. See also P Mercier, 'Le projet de convention du marché commun sur la procédure civile internationale et les états tiers' [1967] *Cahier de droit européen* 367–368 and 513–531, especially 515–517.

[156] See BM Landay, 'Another Look at the EEC Judgments Convention: Should Outsiders be Worried?' [1987–1988] *Dickenson Journal of International Law* 25–44 at 33.

[157] [1969] Hague Conference on Private International Law Proceedings of the Extraordinary Session 10.

[158] [1969] Hague Conference on Private International Law Proceedings of the Extraordinary Session 11; Explanatory report by CN Fragistas in the same volume, 360–338 at 360.

1.84 One of the main features of the Convention is that it requires bilateralization. This means that it cannot enter into force between two Contracting
States before they have concluded an extra agreement. These extra agreements can broaden or narrow the scope of the Convention, widen the permitted bases for jurisdiction, define exclusive bases of jurisdiction or alter
the procedure of recognition or enforcement. It allows states to adapt the
Convention to their particular needs.[159] This feature was included in the
Convention because there were differences among the experts on whether
a model for bilateral conventions should be created, or a multilateral convention, where parties remained free to select their partners.[160] Jenard
explains that bilateralization differs from a model law: Contracting States
do not have an unlimited possibility to modify the convention. They now
can only choose their partners. Modifications can only be made to the
extent that they are permitted by the Convention itself.[161] This bilateralization is cumbersome, as it requires more negotiation, more signing and
more ratification. The reason for its introduction was mistrust. Member
States of the Hague Convention did not know in advance which states
would want to accede to the Convention, and therefore included a safety
net. It can be compared with the safety net of the Lugano Convention,
providing that states may only become party to the exclusive club if they
so request and are invited.[162]

1.85 The Convention only indirectly prescribed jurisdiction rules. In other
words it would be a 'simple' convention, as opposed to a 'double' one.[163]
This means that Contracting States would remain free to determine their
own jurisdiction rules; if recognition were sought in another Contracting
State, however, the court might consider the jurisdictional basis of the
judgment. If the jurisdictional basis were not contained in the 'blessed' list

---

[159] Arts 21–23 of the 1971 Convention; see also P Jenard, 'Rapport du Comité restreint
sur la bilateralisation' and Explanatory report by CN Fragistas, both published in [1969]
Hague Conference on Private International Law Proceedings of the Extraordinary Session 11
145–151 and 360–388 at 362–364; GAL Droz, 'Le récent projet de Convention de La Haye sur
la reconnaissance et l'exécution des jugements étrangers en matière civile et commerciale'
[1966] *Netherlands International Law Review* 225–242 at 242. KH Nadelmann & AT von Mehren,
'The extraordinary session of the Hague Conference on Private International Law' [1966]
AJIL 803–806 at 804 state that the feature of bilateralisation was perhaps a first in treaty law;
TC Hartley in AF Lowenfeld & LJ Silberman (eds), *The Hague Convention on Jurisdiction and
Judgments* (USA: Juris Publishing, 2001) 110–115.

[160] Nadelmann & von Mehren, ibid, 803.

[161] Jenard, note 159 above, 145 and 146–147.

[162] Arts 60 and 62 of the old Lugano Convention; Arts 70 and 72 of the 2007 Lugano
Convention.

[163] On the difference between simple and double conventions, see Droz, 'La récent projet
de Convention de La Haye', note 159 above, at 226.

of the Convention, recognition or enforcement might be refused. It was thought that a 'double' convention (as was at the same time being negotiated between the Member States of the European Community) would be too difficult to achieve because of the great number of Member States in the Hague Conference.[164] This is ironic, since the number of Hague Conference Member States at that time was smaller than the number of Member States that the European Union now has. Arguably it was not just the number of Member States that caused a problem, but also their diversity.[165]

The Convention was adopted by the Extraordinary Session of 1966, but **1.86** was eventually ratified or acceded to by only four states: Cyprus, the Netherlands, Portugal and Kuwait. The first three of these states are Member States of the European Union, and thus the Convention does not really have any added value for the relations between them. Kuwait only acceded in 2002. The bilateralization requirement disables this Convention further. States have to conclude extra agreements in any event so that the Convention in itself is not very useful.

A global Hague jurisdiction convention?

In 1992 on the initiative of the United States of America, a fresh attempt **1.87** was made.[166] The Hague Conference started preliminary work on a convention on international jurisdiction and the effects of judgments in civil and commercial matters. One of the reasons for taking the theme up once more was again the fact that the Brussels Convention was so favourable to EU Member States whilst unfavourable to third States. Moreover, in some countries, recognition and enforcement of foreign judgments outside a treaty is difficult, if not impossible.[167] The USA had also come to understand that its liberal approach to recognizing and enforcing foreign judgments was not being reciprocated. If you can't beat them, join them; or rather, if you can't lead by example, join them by the rules of their game.

---

[164] [1969] Hague Conference on Private International Law Proceedings of the Extraordinary Session 10–11.

[165] See also Fragistas, note 155 above, at 362.

[166] In a Letter from the United States Legal Adviser of 5 May 1992; see [1993] Acts & Proceedings of the Seventeenth Session, I, 231.

[167] See A Bucher, 'Vers une convention mondiale sur la compétence et les jugements étrangers' [2000] *La Semaine juridique* 77–133 at 79; G Walter & SP Baumgartner (eds), *Recognition and Enforcement of Foreign Judgments Outside the Scope of the Brussels and Lugano Conventions* (The Hague: Kluwer 2000) at 5; see also the national reports.

1.88 The reasons for choosing the Hague Conference as forum were the Secretariat's interest in the topic, the preparatory and logistical support that the Conference could provide, and the fact that there the USA would not stand alone (as it otherwise would if it were to negotiate only with the EU or Lugano States).[168] Preparatory work was done and at the eighteenth Diplomatic Session in 1996 it was decided to refer the matter to a Special Commission.[169] Five Special Commission meetings between 1997 and 1999 followed. The last text of the Special Commission will be referred to as the 1999 text.[170] The nineteenth Diplomatic Session was spread over two sessions, the first of which took place in June 2001. The text then adopted (the 2001 text) was full of square brackets, the Hague Conference's way of indicating lack of consensus.[171] The text became so complex, that one could not understand it without reading the footnotes indicating the underlying issues. Because of the many remaining difficulties, the work was put on hold while the Conference considered whether the work on this project should proceed and what the alternatives were.

1.89 The negotiations were made more difficult by the fact that the experts and representatives did not vote once; everything had to be agreed by consensus. When there was lack of consensus, even if this concerned only one Member State, square brackets were inserted in the draft text. Another difficulty was that the position of the European Community was unclear: it was not a member of the Hague Conference, but in the course of the negotiations, with the entry into force of the Amsterdam Treaty, it gained external competence in the matters under discussion. Whether or not that competence would become exclusive by the adoption of Brussels I, was uncertain at that point in time.[172] In practice the European Union and its Member States coordinated their points of view.

1.90 The ambitious idea was to negotiate a convention that would include jurisdiction rules and facilitate recognition and enforcement of judgments from other Contracting States. It would be a 'mixed convention' (mixed referring to the fact that it would be neither a simple nor a

---

[168] See AT von Mehren, 'Recognition and Enforcement of foreign Judgments: a New Approach for the Hague Conference?' [1994] *Law and Contemporary Problems*, 271–287 at 273.

[169] Nygh & Pocar, note 10 above, 25.

[170] This text is taken up. See ibid.

[171] 'Summary of the Outcome of the Discussion in Commission II of the First Part of the Diplomatic Conference (2001),' available from <http://www.hcch.net>.

[172] In the meantime the European Court of Justice has ruled that the EC has exclusive external competence in the matter: *Lugano* Opinion, note 98 above. See chapter 7 below for more detail.

double convention).[173] The drafters were of the view that a single conven-tion, dealing only with recognition and enforcement, would not address the needs sufficiently. On the other hand, a double convention unifying jurisdiction rules, as do Brussels I and the Lugano Convention, was seen to be a good goal, but too ambitious. For this reason the Special Commission decided on a 'mixed convention', a structure that has some of the advan-tages of a double convention, yet still retains flexibility.[174]

The proposed Convention never saw the light of day, but its structure is **1.91** nevertheless interesting to examine briefly. It contained a list of required bases for jurisdiction to be used in the Contracting States. This was called the 'white list' and these bases for judgment would suffice for the recogni-tion and enforcement of judgments. An example of uncontroversial white list jurisdiction is the domicile of the defendant. The Convention also had a 'black list' of excluded bases for jurisdiction, which might not be used except with regard to parties from non-Contracting States. This list con-tained rules similar to those outlawed by Article 3 of Brussels I and the Lugano Convention.[175] If used, the judgments resulting from these bases for jurisdiction would not be recognized in other Contracting States. Between these two categories a so-called 'grey zone' was created, explain-ing the 'mixed' nature of the Convention. These were bases for jurisdiction that were neither required nor excluded. Enforcement via the Convention then would not be automatic. However, enforcement would not be pre-vented and would remain possible via national law. This idea came from Professor von Mehren, who had realized that the differences not only in specific rules of national law, but also in approaches to jurisdiction, are so

---

[173] For that distinction, see above, para 1.06 and following.

[174] On the debate between the specialists on the issue of whether the convention should be a double or a mixed one: C Kessedjian, 'International jurisdiction and foreign judgments in civil and commercial matters' (Choice of Court Convention Preliminary Document No 7); Nygh & Pocar, note 10 above.

[175] Although these instruments only outlaw them if the defendant is domiciled in a Member State or Contracting State, and not for defendants from outside the protected zone. This has been severely criticized in the United States of America: see, for example, von Mehren, note 168 above, 280–281; KH Nadelmann, 'Jurisdictionally Improper Fora in Treaties on Recognition of Judgments: The Common Market Draft' [1967] *Columbia Law Review* 995–1023 at 1002–1004 & 1019; F Juenger, 'Judicial Jurisdiction in the United States and in the European Communities: a comparison' [1984] *Michigan Law Review* 1195–1212 at 1210–1212; AT von Mehren, 'Recognition and Enforcement of Sister-State Judgments: Reflection on General Theory and Current Practice in the European Economic Community and the United States' [1981] *Columbia Law Review* 1044–1060 at 1057–1060; Landay, note 156 above, at 28–29 & 40; P Hay, 'The Common Market Preliminary Draft on the Recognition and Enforcement of Judgments—Some Considerations of Policy and Interpretation' [1968] AJCL 149–174 at 172–174.

big that they pose insurmountable problems to unification.[176] Professor Lowenfeld agreed with this idea, referring to green, red and yellow jurisdictional bases.[177] Despite this attempt at flexibility, the differences still proved fundamental. Importantly, the United States of America and the European Union (negotiating as a single block) could not agree on other essential points. Their approaches clashed and agreement could not be reached concerning in what category (white, black, or grey) various rules should be placed.

1.92 Some saw the Brussels and Lugano Conventions as a model for a worldwide convention. It was recognized that the Brussels and Lugano Conventions served their purposes with great efficiency. Determining jurisdiction and the recognition and enforcement of judgments in the EU, and between Lugano States, was easy and the procedures were clear. In case of doubt, there was always the European Court of Justice (for the application of the Brussels Convention, and used as an example for the Lugano Convention). However, that model did not assist the worldwide convention as much as hoped. On the contrary, it enlarged the gap between the European Union and other negotiating states. The systems in force in Europe exhibited a characteristically different procedural law. The United States of America, for example, could not accept many of the rules in those conventions.[178] At the same time those conventions are embedded in closer economic unions, which made them desirable and necessary.[179] Naturally the conventions follow the European habit of enlisting permitted bases for jurisdiction and outlawing exorbitant bases. These would be the white and black lists in the von Mehren model. There is not much room left for a grey zone or discretions. For the United States of America a complete 'cataloguing' of bases for jurisdiction would not be acceptable.[180] In the USA jurisdiction is based on comity and the main test is compatibility with the Due Process Clause of the Constitution.[181] This is very different

---

[176] See von Mehren, note 168 above, especially at 285–287.

[177] See AF Lowenfeld, 'Thoughts about a Multinational Judgments Convention: A Reaction to the von Mehren Report' [1994] *Law & Contemporary Problems* 289–303. See also Lowenfeld & Silberman, note 159 above, viii, referring to the different groups as essential, exorbitant and tolerable.

[178] Von Mehren, note 168 above, at 280–281 states that even if invited, the United States of America would not be able to accede to the Lugano Convention because Art 3 violates US due process standards, and therefore other states' judgments (where jurisdiction had been based on grounds listed in Art 3) could not be enforced in the US.

[179] See Bucher, note 167 above, 78.

[180] See von Mehren, note 168 above, 281.

[181] United States Constitution, Fifth Amendment (1791): 'no person shall . . . be deprived of life, liberty, or property, without due process of law; . . .' and the State-law equivalent in the Fourteenth Amendment (1868): '. . . nor shall any State deprive any person of life, liberty,

from the much stricter civil law approach.[182] Europe opts for certainty and has clear rules on jurisdiction that cannot be interpreted liberally. For the Europeans 'doing business' is too uncertain and almost too arbitrary to be a basis for jurisdiction. These two different points of view can be called the 'Court–Claim Nexus' and the 'Court–Defendant Nexus.' The 'Court–Claim Nexus' is commonly found in civil law countries while the 'Court–Defendant Nexus' is commonly found in common law countries.[183]

Reciprocity is often required for enforcement.[184] The USA is considered to **1.93** be open to the enforcement of foreign judgments because this is done under the common law in the absence of treaties, while other countries often refuse to enforce US judgments because of its broad jurisdiction rules and far-reaching punitive damage awards. One should note here that recognition and enforcement is regulated at state level in the USA.[185]

From the US point of view, the European approach clashes with the due **1.94** process approach since some of the specific rules may lead to assuming jurisdiction in a situation that would be constitutionally unsound. It is, for instance, unthinkable under the American approach to accept jurisdiction in tort solely on the basis of the place of injury, or jurisdiction in contract solely on the basis of the place of performance. On the other hand, for countries that are not familiar with activity as basis for jurisdiction and

---

or property, without due process of law. . . .' See also GB Born & D Westin, *International Civil Litigation in United States Courts* (Deventer/Boston: Kluwer, 1989) 23; P Hay, RJ Weintraub & PJ Borchers, *Conflict of Laws Cases and Materials* (11th edn, New York: Foundation Press, 2000) 35–39.

[182] See also H Gaudemet-Tallon, 'De quelques raisons de la difficulté d'une entente au niveau mondial sur les règles de compétence judiciaire international directe' in JAR Nafziger & SC Symeonides (eds), *Law and Justice in a Multistate World. Essays in Honor of Arthur T von Mehren* (Ardsley: Transnational Publishers, 2002) 55–71 at 62–65; RA Brand, 'Jurisdictional Common Ground: in Search of a Global Convention' in the same book, 11–32.

[183] See M Dogauchi, Professor of Law at the University of Tokyo in his paper 'The Hague Draft Convention from the Perspective of Japan,' submitted to the Seminar on the Draft Convention on Jurisdiction and Foreign Judgments in Civil and Commercial Matters, organised by UIA (Union International des Avocats), on 20–21 April 2001 in Edinburgh. Interestingly, he states that Japan is closer to a civil law system but adheres to the 'Court–Defendant Nexus' principle; LJ Silberman, 'Comparative Jurisdiction in the International Context: will the Proposed Hague Judgments Convention be Stalled?' [2002] *DePaul Law Review* 319–349 at 330–331.

[184] See Walter & Baumgartner, note 167 above, 34–35.

[185] *Erie RR Co v Tompkins*, 304 US 64 (1938). See also L Silberman in Lowenfeld & Silberman, note 159 above, 119–124 especially 122. There are also Uniform Acts, such as the Uniform Foreign Money-Judgments Recognition Act, which has been accepted by many states and the principles of which are followed by other states that have not adopted it.

constitutional tempering, it is difficult to see in which cases jurisdiction would not be allowed.[186]

1.95 Brussels I is only one small lane of a larger common road. It is necessary to ensure the four freedoms of the EU (free movement of persons, goods, capital and services). Some even see it as a fifth freedom: the free movement of judgments. The Regulation states in its preamble:

> [t]he Community has set itself the objective of maintaining and developing an area of freedom, security and justice, in which the free movement of persons is ensured. In order to establish progressively such an area, the Community should adopt, amongst other things, the measures relating to judicial cooperation in civil matters which are necessary for the sound operation of the internal market.[187]

1.96 At the same time, a convention on jurisdiction and the recognition and enforcement of foreign judgments may be experienced as an infringement of state sovereignty, especially if states are not used to giving up a part of their sovereignty as the European Union Member States are.[188] In the absence of such a common road, worldwide cooperation has proved to be very difficult. A convention regulating the recognition and enforcement of judgments in itself will be useful, but the incentive for common rules of jurisdiction was perhaps not great enough to be an adequate reward for the efforts made.[189]

1.97 Furthermore, a worldwide jurisdiction treaty would require trust in foreign legal systems, for example with regard to the notions of *forum non conveniens* and the principle of *lis alibi pendens*, especially if there is no higher court to force a court to stay its proceedings, and the national court knows that its own legal system can provide a judgment before the court of the other legal system will. It is an open question whether it will decline jurisdiction. The rise of the anti-suit injunction has confirmed the existing distrust between legal systems.[190] To dissolve all the fear and distrust with one convention proved very difficult. There would have to be mutual trust that other Contracting States would apply the convention and not assume jurisdiction contrary to it. This is also important for the

---

[186] One of the problems encountered at the Edinburgh Informal Meeting (23–26 April 2001) was the delimitation of activity-based jurisdiction within the white and grey lists. Another problem was whether activity should be defined negatively or positively. In the June 2001 versions of Art 6 (*Contracts*) and Art 10 (*Torts and Delicts*) of the Hague Convention, activity as basis for jurisdiction was included for the first time.

[187] Rec 1.

[188] See Gaudemet-Tallon, 'De quelques raisons de la difficulté', note 182 above, 58–62.

[189] See also AT von Mehren in Lowenfeld & Silberman, note 159 above, 63–64.

[190] For a discussion of anti-suit injunctions, see chapter 5 below, para 5.147 and following.

subsequent enforcement of judgments. The trust should exist to such an extent that a court accepted that another court would use its jurisdiction in accordance with the convention and to merit enforcement. Accordingly, courts would need to trust each other to decline jurisdiction in matters where another court had exclusive jurisdiction, or where there was a choice of court agreement in favour of another court.

Jurisdiction, involving the recognition and enforcement of foreign judg- **1.98** ments, is arguably the area in civil law where politics can play the greatest role. States can impose sanctions by extending their own jurisdiction or express political objections by refusing to recognize judgments of co-signatory states, or by ignoring the jurisdiction of their courts. It is questionable whether the desire for uniform international jurisdiction, as a goal in itself, will be strong enough to trump parochial political considerations.

In the end, the negotiators' ambition could not be tempered. They **1.99** attempted to put almost everything in either the white or the black list. They seemed to have forgotten the grey area, which would have made the project more realistic. A part should have been left uncategorized: agreeing to disagree. The differences between the legal cultures were huge. But even a formidable political will to complete the project might not have sufficed. Apart from legal policies, many interest groups were present and made their concerns known, and these were of course also in conflict. In the end it became impossible to agree on rules that could satisfy all.

However, ten years of effort and money had not been wasted; the project **1.100** produced an enormous source of comparative law and legal understanding of underlying principles and fears.[191] The disputes arising from the inclusion or exclusion of specific bases of jurisdiction that gave rise to difficulties at the negotiations will be referred to throughout the substantive part of this book.

The Hague Convention on Choice of Court Agreements

It was decided to begin with something smaller, to try to reach consensus, **1.101** and, if that worked, build further conventions. The starting point was

---

[191] Lowenfeld and Silberman, note 159 above, at vii: '[w]hether or not the proposed Hague Convention on Jurisdiction and Foreign Judgments enters into effect among a large group of states, the negotiations and successive drafts have provoked fresh thinking throughout the world about international litigation, about one's own and other legal systems, and about what is a matter of custom or taste in the approach to civil procedure, in contrast to what is truly fundamental'. See also the preliminary documents to the Hague Convention on Choice of Court Agreements, available at <http://www.hcch.net>.

choice of court agreements in business-to-business contracts, and this led to the adoption in June 2005 of a Convention.[192] The negotiators realized that this was a field in which consensus should not be too difficult, and at the same time it could become extremely useful. The New York Convention already facilitates the enforcement of foreign arbitral awards.[193] If the same type of rules could be created for choice of court agreements, legal certainty and protection for international trading would be achieved. Businesses would then be more comfortable with choice of court clauses in favour of Contracting States' courts: if they obtain a judgment, at least it will be readily enforceable in other countries and reliance would no longer have to be placed on comity.[194] The specific rules of this new Convention and its disconnection from Brussels I will be considered in chapter 4 on forum clauses.[195]

The 1980 and 1996 Hague Conventions

1.102 The Hague Convention of 25 October 1980 on the Civil Aspects of International Child Abduction is in force in all 27 EU Member States and currently has 77 Contracting States. As one of the most successful conventions of the Hague Conference, its goal is to return children who have been abducted by one of their parents to another state as soon as possible. Its mechanism is simple: in general, children are to be returned and the court of the state where they came from should take care of the rest.

1.103 The Hague Convention of 19 October 1996 on Jurisdiction, Applicable Law, Recognition, Enforcement and Cooperation in respect of Parental Responsibility and Measures for the Protection of Children has been signed by all EU Member States except Malta. It has, however, only been ratified by (or acceded to) and entered into force in eight EU Member States: Bulgaria, the Czech Republic, Estonia, Hungary, Latvia, Lithuania, the Slovak Republic, and Slovenia. It will probably enter into force on the same day for all the other EU Member States because of the EC's external

---

[192] See A Schulz, 'Reflection paper to assist in the preparation of a convention on jurisdiction and recognition and enforcement of foreign judgments in civil and commercial matters' (Choice of Court Convention Preliminary Document No 19), available at <http://www.hcch.net>.

[193] Convention on the Recognition and Enforcement of Foreign Arbitral Awards. This Convention is old (it was signed in 1958), but because of its simplicity and uncontroversial nature, it has proved very successful in international arbitration and currently has 142 Contracting States.

[194] See the research done by the International Chamber of Commerce in this respect: available at <http://www.iccwbo.org/law/jurisdiction/>.

[195] See below, para 4.46 and following.

competence in this field—a political dispute currently delays ratification by the EU Member States.[196]

Brussels II *bis* covers the matters of parental responsibility and parental **1.104** abduction. The difficult relationship between these Hague Conventions and Brussels II *bis* will be discussed in chapter 2.[197]

A future Hague Convention on Maintenance Obligations

The Hague Conference on Private International Law is currently working **1.105** on a Convention on the international recovery of child support and other forms of family maintenance.[198] In this way the older Hague Conventions on maintenance will be updated. This convention will facilitate the recovery of maintenance by creating central authorities. It will focus on administrative cooperation and will not contain any rules on jurisdiction. At the same time legislation on maintenance is underway in the European Community.[199]

H. CONCLUSION

This chapter has provided the necessary background before the substan- **1.106** tive investigation of civil jurisdiction and third States can begin. It has indicated the origins of EU civil jurisdiction that started in 1968 with the Brussels Convention, and was significantly changed by the advent of the Amsterdam version of the EC Treaty.

The chapter has paid some attention to the interaction between the EU **1.107** civil jurisdiction rules and national rules in the area. The scope of the EU civil jurisdiction rules will be examined throughout the book, but two underlying views have been necessarily explained and will be referred to when the need arises.

When dealing with Brussels I, the reader must remain aware of the paral- **1.108** lel Lugano Convention, which makes Iceland, Norway, and Switzerland third States in a particular category: they often have the same civil jurisdiction rules and therefore in practice cannot really be seen as third States

---

[196] This dispute between Spain and the United Kingdom concerns Gibraltar: Schulz, 'Haager Kinderschützbereinkommen', note 53 above. The external competence of the EU in the domain of civil jurisdiction will be discussed in chapter 7 below.

[197] Para 2.111 and following.

[198] See <http://www.hcch.net>, under 'Work in Progress'.

[199] See Proposal of 15 December 2005 COM(2005) 649 final, note 44 above.

in the same way as others can. Some conventions on specific matters exist to which EU Member States and third States are party. Those conventions will be respected and applied, sometimes entailing a carve-out of Brussels I or Brussels II *bis*.

1.109 Lastly, the importance of the Hague Conference on Private International Law, as a meeting place between the EU and third States, has been explained, and its efforts will also be referred to during the following discussions.

2

First cornerstone: the defendant, general jurisdiction and its alternatives

A. GENERAL

Article 59 of Brussels I:

In order to determine whether a party is domiciled in the Member State whose courts are seised of a matter, the court shall apply its internal law.

If a party is not domiciled in the Member State whose courts are seised of the matter, then, in order to determine whether the party is domiciled in another Member State, the court shall apply the law of that Member State.

Article 60 of Brussels I:

For the purposes of this Regulation, a company or other legal person or association of natural or legal persons is domiciled at the place where it has its:

a) statutory seat, or
b) central administration, or
c) principal place of business.

For the purposes of the United Kingdom and Ireland 'statutory seat' means the registered office or, where there is no such office anywhere, the place under the law of which the formation took place.

In order to determine whether a trust is domiciled in the Member State whose courts are seised of the matter, the court shall apply its rules of private international law.

Recital 13 of the Insolvency Regulation:

The 'centre of main interests' should correspond to the place where the debtor conducts the administration of his interests on a regular basis and is therefore ascertainable by third parties.

Recital 14 of the Insolvency Regulation:

This Regulation applies only to proceedings where the centre of the debtor's main interests is located in the Community.

Article 3 of the Insolvency Regulation:

The courts of the Member State within the territory of which the centre of a debtor's main interests is situated shall have jurisdiction to open insolvency proceedings. In the case of a company or legal person, the place of the registered office shall be presumed to be the centre of its main interests in the absence of proof to the contrary.

Where the centre of a debtor's main interests is situated within the territory of a Member State, the courts of another Member State shall have jurisdiction to open insolvency proceedings against that debtor only if he possesses an establishment within the territory of the latter Member State. The effects of those proceedings shall be restricted to the assets of the debtor situated in the territory of the latter Member State.

. . .

INTRODUCTION

The best place to start the substantive part of this book is with the general **2.01** rule of jurisdiction: the domicile (under Brussels I), habitual residence, nationality or domicile in the common law sense (under Brussels II *bis*) of the defendant, or the centre of the debtor's main interests (under the Insolvency Regulation), can grant jurisdiction. This rule also provides the first general delimitation of the scope of these Regulations.

Brussels I applies to defendants domiciled in the EU.[1] The reverse side of **2.02** the coin is that, in general, the national bases of jurisdiction are applied when defendants are domiciled in third States.[2] The rule of the domicile of

---

[1] Jenard Report on the 1968 version of the Brussels Convention; OJ C 59, 5 March 1979, 1 (Jenard Report) 13; A Saggio, 'The outlook for the System for the Free Movement of Judgments Created by the Brussels Convention' in Court of Justice of the European Communities, *Civil Jurisdiction and Judgments in Europe* (London: Butterworths, 1992) 201; GAL Droz, *Pratique de la convention de Bruxelles du 27 Septembre 1968* (Paris: Dalloz, 1973) 17 & 39; P Gothot & D Holleaux, *La Convention de Bruxelles du 27.9.1968. Compétence judiciaire et effets des jugements dans la CEE* (Paris: Editions Jupiter, 1985) 19; H Born, M Fallon & J-L Van Boxstael, *Droit judiciaire international. Chronique de jurisprudence 1991–1998* (Brussels: Larcier, 2001) 25; B Audit & GA Bermann, 'The application of private international norms to 'third countries': the jurisdiction and judgments example' in A Nuyts & N Watté (eds), *International Civil Litigation in Europe and Relations with Third States* (Brussels: Bruylant, 2005) 55–82 at 66–68.

[2] Art 4 of Brussels I.

the defendant is the first of three main rules on the scope of Brussels I. As will be seen in the following chapters, the other two rules cover the existence of exclusive bases of jurisdiction,[3] and forum clauses in favour of an EU Member State court if one of the parties is domiciled in the EU.[4]

2.03 Habitual residence and nationality perform the same function for Brussels II *bis*. Habitual residence will also be the relevant criterion for the proposed Maintenance Regulation.[5] The centre of a debtor's main interests provides the focus for the applicability of the Insolvency Regulation.

2.04 In this chapter, after a brief overview of general jurisdiction, the term 'domicile' will be discussed, as compared to 'habitual residence' and 'centre of main interests'. These concepts must be examined in regard to both natural and legal persons. Next, the positions of plaintiffs and defendants inside and outside the EU will be investigated. Attention will be paid to the particular way of determining the scope of Brussels II *bis* and this instrument's relation to two Hague Conventions on the same matters. By way of comparison, the proposed Maintenance Regulation will also be addressed briefly. Then the chapter will turn to those issues that arise when there are multiple defendants, actions on warranties and guarantees, or counterclaims. It also deals with special bases for jurisdiction (such as contractual and non-contractual obligations) and with protective bases for jurisdiction (over consumers, employees, and insured parties).

WHAT IS GENERAL JURISDICTION?

2.05 General jurisdiction refers to the basis upon which a court can always assume jurisdiction with regard to a particular defendant, irrespective of the legal nature of the action, i.e. whether it is based in tort, maintenance, divorce, or the non-performance of a contractual obligation. General jurisdiction is based on a link between the court and the defendant, while special jurisdiction is based on a link between the court and the facts of the case.[6]

---

[3] See chapter 3 below.

[4] See chapter 4 below.

[5] Proposal for a Council Regulation on jurisdiction, applicable law, recognition and enforcement of decisions and cooperation in matters relating to Maintenance Obligations of 15 December 2005, COM(2005) 649 final, available at <http://eur-lex.europa.eu>. Note that this Regulation, like the other regulations on civil and commercial matters, will not apply in Denmark (rec 27 and Art 1). The United Kingdom has indicated that it would not opt into this Regulation, and thus would not be bound by it (unless it decides later to opt in). Ireland would opt in, so that the Regulation would apply there.

[6] TC Hartley, *Civil Jurisdiction and Judgments* (London: Sweet & Maxwell, 1984) 23.

The basis of the rule lies in Roman law: *actor sequitur forum rei*. At first this **2.06** was a principle of domestic law, but later it was transposed to international disputes.[7] The historical concept of jurisdiction was based on the sovereign's relationship with the defendant or his or her property, not the character of the dispute. The exercise of power over the defendant was important, and in a sense was seen as a confirmation of sovereignty over him or her, so that he or she could be brought before the courts. This exercise of power extended in strange ways. In the nineteenth century, in most cases the parties could be found where the dispute arose. All claims, except those regarding immovable property, could be decided in any forum where the defendant was found.

Different legal systems developed the concept differently. Service (of a **2.07** writ) was seen as a form of physical power, because it entailed getting hold of the defendant.[8] In the USA, a defendant who was regularly found in a jurisdiction, because he conducted business there, could be subjected to the US courts. A distinction developed in the USA between general and specific jurisdiction. Whereas general jurisdiction meant that a court had jurisdiction over a defendant, whatever the claim, specific jurisdiction was issue-related.[9] A court then had jurisdiction only over the specific matter concerned with the defendant's business in that area. The distinction in the EU between jurisdiction based on the domicile of the defendant and jurisdiction based on the performance of a contract or the committing of a tort, is very similar to that between general and specific jurisdiction.

Another underlying thought in civil jurisdiction is that if the plaintiff **2.08** wants to trouble the defendant by suing him or her, the plaintiff should go to the place where the defendant is. The plaintiff controls the institution of the proceedings and many are of the view that the plaintiff could abuse this power and that the defendant should therefore be protected.[10] In theory a defendant is also in a stronger position when litigating in his or her own court, where he or she knows the procedural law. Whether these

---

[7] AT von Mehren & DTT Trautman, 'Jurisdiction to Adjudicate: A Suggested Analysis' [1966] *Harvard Law Review* 1121–1179 at 1127–1128.

[8] M Twitchell, 'The Myth of General Jurisdiction' [1988] *Harvard Law Review* 610–681 at 614–622; *McDonald v Mabee*, 243 US 90, 37 S Ct 343 (1917); *Michigan Trust Co v Ferry*, 228 US 346, 33 S Ct 550 (1913); JJ Fawcett, 'A new Approach to Jurisdiction over Companies in Private International law' [1988] ICLQ 645–667 at 648.

[9] Borchers makes the distinction that general bases of jurisdiction are independent of the dispute while specific bases are dependent on the dispute; PJ Borchers, 'Comparing Personal Jurisdiction in the US and the EC: Lessons for American Reform' [1992] AJCL 121–157 at 133.

[10] See ER Sunderland, 'The provisions relating to trial practice in the new Illinois Civil Practice Act' [1933–1934] *University of Chicago Law Review* 188–223 at 192.

ideas still hold true is questionable. Von Mehren and Trautman stated—as early as 1966—that the emerging bases of jurisdiction founded upon activity resulted in a movement away from the bias favouring the defendant towards permitting the plaintiff to insist that the defendant come to him or her.[11] After all, if the plaintiff finds him- or herself in a situation where there is no choice but to start court proceedings in order to obtain what legally belongs to him or her, he or she cannot reasonably be labelled a 'troublemaker.' The plaintiff might have acted completely within the bounds of his or her rights and obligations whilst being confronted by a defaulting contracting party, or could be the victim of a delict or tort. In such a case, one could question the emphasis on the protection of the defendant, as opposed to the 'troublemaking' plaintiff.

2.09 On many occasions the European Court of Justice (ECJ) has confirmed the general nature of this rule of jurisdiction based on the domicile of the defendant.[12] On the other hand, in the EU one also sees jurisdiction based on the place of the performance of a contract, or on the place of the commission of a tort. These places often coincide with the domicile or residence of the plaintiff.[13]

---

[11] Von Mehren & Trautman, note 7 above, 1128. It was in this article that the concepts of 'general' and 'specific' jurisdiction were first used; it was then taken over by the courts; see PJ Borchers, 'Jurisdiction to Adjudicate Revisited' in JAR Nafziger & SC Symeonides (eds), *Law and Justice in a Multistate World. Essays in Honour of Arthur T von Mehren* (Ardsley: Transnational Publishers Inc, 2002) 4.

[12] Case 24/76 *Estasis Salotti di Colzani Aimo et Gianmario Colzani v Rüwa Polstereimaschinen GmbH* [1976] ECR 1831, at para 7; Case 73/77 *Sanders v van der Putte* [1977] ECR 2383, at para 8–9; Case 23/78 *Meeth v Glacetal* [1978] ECR 2133, at para 5; Case 33/78 *Somafer SA v Saar-Ferngas AG* [1978] ECR 2183, at para 7 & 11; Case 56/79 *Zelger v Salinitri* (No 1) [1980] ECR 89 at para 3; Case 220/84 *AS–Autoteile Service GmbH v Pierre Malhé* [1985] ECR 2267 at para 15–16; Case C–261/90 *Mario Reichert, Hans-Heinz Reichert and Ingeborg Kockler v Dresdner Bank AG* (No 2) [1992] ECR I–2149, at para 10; Case C–26/91 *Jakob Handte & Co GmbH v Traitements Mécano-chimiques des Surfaces SA* [1992] ECR I–3967 at para 14; Case C–89/91 *Shearson Lehmann Hutton Inc v TVB Treuhandgesellschaft für Vermögensverwaltung und Beteiligungen mbH* [1993] ECR I–139 at para 14–15; Case C–288/92 *Custom Made Commercial Ltd v Stawa Metallbau GmbH* [1994] ECR I–2913 at para 12; Case C–364/93 *Antonio Marinari v Lloyds Bank plc and Zubaidi Trading Company* [1995] ECR I–2719 at para 13; Case C–106/95 *Mainschiffahrts–Genossenschaft eG (MSG) v Les Gravières Rhénanes SARL* [1997] ECR I–911 at para 14; Case C–269/95 *Benincasa v Dentalkit* [1997] ECR I–3767, at para 13; Case C–51/97 *Réunion européenne SA and others v Spliethoff's Bevrachtingskantoor BV and the Master of the vessel 'Alblasgracht V002'* [1998] ECR I–6511 at para 16; Case C–256/00 *Besix SA v WABAG GmbH & Co KG & Plafog GmbH & Co KG* [2002] ECR I–1699 at para 26 & 50. See also K Hertz, *Jurisdiction in Contract and Tort under the Brussels Convention* (Copenhagen: Jurist-og Økonomforbundets Forlag, 1998) 47.

[13] See P Nygh, 'The criteria for judicial jurisdiction' in AF Lowenfeld & LJ Silberman (eds), *The Hague Convention on Jurisdiction and Judgments* (USA: Juris Publishing, 2001) 13; E Jayme,

The criterion of the domicile of the defendant seems relatively clear and **2.10** easy to apply, but it will be suggested in what follows that it is not always as straightforward as at first appears.[14]

The Concepts of Domicile, Habitual Residence, and Centre of Main Interests

Domicile of natural persons

The term 'domicile' is used throughout Brussels I and usually refers to the **2.11** domicile of the defendant; but in cases of maintenance and protective bases for jurisdiction, it also refers to the domicile of the plaintiff.[15] However, no clear and binding definition exists in the Regulation. It was thought, at the time the first version of the Brussels Convention was negotiated, that a definition of 'domicile' would go beyond the Convention and would amount to a uniform law.[16] The drafters worried that a multiplicity of definitions would lead to incoherence, and the evolution of national law might have rendered the definition outdated.[17]

The first version of the Brussels Convention contained a separate rule for **2.12** determining the domicile of dependent persons:

The domicile of a party shall, however, be determined in accordance with his national law if, by that law, his domicile depends on that of another person or on the seat of an authority.

This provision was deleted from the San Sebastian version (1989) of the Convention. The reasoning given in the Almeida/Cruz/Jenard Report is that the provision was no longer necessary with regard to women, as the domestic laws of the states had changed. In deciding whether someone is a minor, a court must apply its own conflict of law rules.[18]

'The role of Article 5 in the scheme of the Convention. Jurisdiction in matters relating to contract' in ECJ, *Civil Jurisdiction*, note 1 above, 74.

[14] See Fawcett, note 8 above, 648.

[15] Arts 5(2), 8(1)(b), and 16(1) of Brussels I. Note that Art 5(2) will be replaced on the advent of a separate Regulation on Maintenance: Proposed Maintenance Regulation, note 5 above. However, these provisions will probably survive with regard to the United Kingdom, which has decided to opt out of the Maintenance Regulation.

[16] Y Donzallaz, *La Convention de Lugano du 16 septembre 1988 concernant la compétence judiciaire et l'exécution des décisions en matière civile et commerciale* (Berne: Editions Stæmpfli + Cie SA Berne, 1996) vol 1, 394.

[17] Jenard Report, note 1 above, 15.

[18] See de Almeida Cruz,Desantes Real & Jenard Report on the San Sebastian (1989) version of the Brussels Convention, C 189 of 28 July 1990, 80–81. See also PAM Meijknecht, 'Het verdrag van Lugano en het toetredingsverdrag van San Sebastian, in onderling verband' in

2.13   In the civil law European countries, 'domicile' and 'residence' are in principle the same. They generally mean the place where a person has his or her main residence and (in some countries) is enrolled on public registers.[19]

2.14   In English and Irish law, 'domicile' has a different meaning, encompassing both a mental and a physical element. Living in a place does not in itself provide a domicile; one must also have the intention of staying there for an undetermined period. Every person is ascribed a domicile of origin. That domicile is retained until the person decides to move somewhere else for an indefinite period of time, and thus obtains a domicile of choice. Lord Cranworth, in *Wicker v Hume*, made the following remark on domicile:

> By domicile we mean home, the permanent home. And if you do not understand your permanent home, I'm afraid that no illustration drawn from foreign writers or foreign languages will very much help you.[20]

Such a flexible concept does not fit into the civil law systems of the European continent; thus this concept of English law never played any role in the Brussels Convention or Brussels I. In English and Irish private international law, domicile as a connecting factor is rather more comparable with nationality than with the concept of domicile found in civil law systems. In that sense nationality as such is not an important connecting factor in those systems. Accordingly, Brussels II *bis*, which attributes a limited role to nationality, replaces 'nationality' with 'domicile' for Ireland and the United Kingdom.[21]

2.15   Consequently, in English and Irish law two meanings of 'domicile' now exist side by side. For the purposes of Brussels I, 'domicile' is given the European

---

PAM Meijknecht & H Duintjer Tebbens, *Europees bevoegdheids- en executierecht op weg naar de 21ste eeuw* (Deventer: Kluwer, 1992) 3–49 at 35.

[19] See, for instance Art 4 of the Belgian Code de droit international privé (Private International Law Code), Act of 16 July 2004, published in *Belgisch Staatsblad* of 27 July 2004; for France: B Audit, *Droit international privé* (3rd edn, Paris: Economica, 2000) 303.

[20] *Wicker v Hume* (1858) 7 HLC 124. The importance of this notion of domicile has decreased for purposes of jurisdiction, but is still used for conflicts of law. On this concept of English law, see J O'Brien, *Smith's Conflict of Laws* (2nd edn, London: Cavendish Publishing Ltd, 1999) 65–88; L Collins (ed), *Dicey, Morris and Collins on the Conflict of Laws* (14th edn, London: Sweet & Maxwell, 2006) vol I, 122–174; PM North & JJ Fawcett, *Cheshire and North's Private International Law* (13th edn, London: Butterworths, 1999) 133–176; CMV Clarkson & J Hill, *Jaffey on the Conflict of Laws* (2nd edn, London: Butterworths, 2002) 21–49; P Kaye, 'The Meaning of domicile under United Kingdom Law for the Purposes of the 1968 Brussels Convention on Jurisdiction and the enforcement of Judgments in Civil and Commercial Matters' [1988] *Netherlands International Law Review* 181–195.

[21] Art 3(2) of Brussels II *bis*.

civil law meaning.[22] In most cases this equates to residence in combination with a substantial connection.[23] For English common law purposes, the concept stays as it was. The exact delimitation between Brussels I and national rules is thus important, since a person from a third State can be domiciled in the EU (in particular in England) but have the intention to return to his or her country after a certain period. This person would be domiciled in the EU for the purposes of Brussels I, although he or she is domiciled in a third State for the purposes of English national law.

To find some guidance on the interpretation of the concept of domicile **2.16** given in Brussels I, one has to turn to its general provisions. National law should determine the domicile of a natural person. In order to determine whether a person is domiciled in an EU Member State, one has to apply the national law of that state.[24] (For Ireland and the United Kingdom, domicile is meant in the sense of European civil law, as explained.) For instance, if a case is brought before a judge in Austria, he has to determine according to Austrian law whether the defendant is domiciled in Austria. If he finds that the defendant is not domiciled in Austria, he has to apply French law to determine whether the defendant is domiciled in France. In the English case *Haji-Ioannou and others v Frangos and others*,[25] the defendant had a private residence in Monaco, but he conducted his business from Greece. The question was whether he had to be considered domiciled in Monaco, or whether he had a special domicile in Greece on the basis of the

---

[22] Sec 41 of the Civil Jurisdiction and Judgments Act 1982 states:
(2) An individual is domiciled in the United Kingdom if and only if—a) he is resident in the United Kingdom; and b) the nature and circumstances of his residence indicate that he has a substantial connection with the United Kingdom . . . (6) In the case of an individual who—a) is resident in the United Kingdom, or in a particular part of the United Kingdom; and b) has been so resident for the last three months or more, the requirements of subsection (2)b) . . . shall be presumed to be fulfilled unless the contrary is proved.
See also A Briggs & P Rees, *Civil Jurisdiction and Judgments* (4th edn, London: LLP, 2005) 136–144. Hartley *Civil Jurisdiction and Judgments*, note 6 above, 31 states that it might have been better if the word 'domicile' had not been used in the English text of the Brussels Convention.

[23] See *Bank of Dubai Ltd v Abbas* [1997] I L Pr 308, CA at 309. See also North & Fawcett, note 20 above, 188; Collins, note 20 above, vol I, 333–339.

[24] Art 59 of Brussels I. See also *Bank of Credit and Commerce International SA (in liquidation) and Another v Wajih Sirri Al-Kaylani and Others* [1991] I L Pr 278 (CA), where the defendant contended that he was domiciled in Tunisia and not in France so that the jurisdiction rules of Brussels I could not be applied to him. The English court applied French law to determine whether he was domiciled in France (at 379–380 and 285).

[25] [1999] 2 Lloyd's Rep 337 (CA). This case is discussed in more detail (regarding *forum non conveniens*) in chapter 5 below, para 5.113.

Greek civil code.[26] If that had been the case, the Brussels Convention would have been applicable, since a domicile in the EU would exist. The court of first instance found that the defendant had no special domicile in Greece, but the Court of Appeal overturned that judgment and found that he did, with the result that the Brussels Convention and its rules on parallel proceedings became applicable. This indicates the relevance of an interpretation of 'domicile' according to the law of another EU Member State.

2.17   It also indicates that under the Brussels Convention and Brussels I, a person might have more than one domicile. This is different to the approach of English law, which provides that English law determines where a person is domiciled. A person can have only one domicile under English law.[27] Under the EU rule, for instance, a person can simultaneously be domiciled in Germany and in Austria. In a German court the person would probably be regarded as domiciled in Germany, while in Austria he would be regarded as domiciled in Austria. This is because every court would start by checking whether the person is domiciled within its own state (in accordance with the way in which the provision is worded). It is unclear, however, how the English court should resolve the situation of a person simultaneously domiciled in Germany and in Austria. Would it be able to revert to principles of English law? This was possibly not the intention of the drafters, yet this seems to be the only plausible solution. If the courts of two EU Member States consider a defendant domiciled in their territory, the *lis pendens* rule may come into effect.

2.18   Hartley pointed out that the advantage of the EU rule is that a person considered by English law as domiciled in England for purposes of the EU regulations, will be so domiciled, irrespective of the view of Italian law on the matter. On the other hand, this approach might lead to the negative result that a person is domiciled nowhere. English law traditionally states that everyone must be domiciled somewhere. This rule, however, does not apply under Brussels I.[28] If one finds no domicile under the application of the EU rule, the result will be that the person is not domiciled in the EU and Brussels I does not apply (unless there is an exclusive basis of jurisdiction or a forum clause).[29]

---

[26]   Article 51 of the Greek civil code states: 'The person has as domicile the place of his main and permanent establishment. No one can have simultaneously more than one domicile. For matters which relate to the exercise of business, the place where the person exercises that business is considered as special domicile.' (Translation in judgment, ibid, at 344.)

[27]   See Hartley *Civil Jurisdiction and Judgments*, note 6 above, 25–26.

[28]   Ibid at 26.

[29]   See chapters 3 and 4.

However, nothing is said of the determination of domicile outside the EU. **2.19**
If a person were indeed domiciled in a third State, Brussels I would not apply
(unless under exclusive bases of jurisdiction or forum clauses). Brussels I can-
not grant jurisdiction to the courts of a third State. For the purposes of
Brussels I it is irrelevant in which third State a party may be domiciled; an
EU court will only consider whether or not there is a domicile in the EU.

The framework of the Regulation is broad so as to draw defendants into **2.20**
its sphere of application. For instance, it might happen that a person could
be considered domiciled both in an EU Member State under the national
law of that Member State (in accordance with the test set by Brussels I), and
at the same time in a third State according to the law of that third State.
In such event, if they adhere to the letter of Brussels I, the EU courts will
give preference to the domicile in the EU. The courts may not investigate
further to determine whether there is indeed a second domicile in a third
State; a domicile in the EU suffices for jurisdiction.

The Cour d'appel (Court of Appeal) of Paris was confronted with such a **2.21**
case.[30] It considered whether French law or the law of Saudi Arabia had to
be applied to determine the domicile of the defendant, a Saudi Arabian
prince. Contrary to the finding of the court of first instance, the Cour
d'appel came to the conclusion that French law could not be applied, and
consequently that the courts of Saudi Arabia had exclusive jurisdiction.[31]
According to Audit, debating which law to apply became irrelevant on the
advent of the Brussels Convention.[32] The Convention is applicable if the
defendant is domiciled in an EU Member State. In order to determine
whether a defendant is domiciled in an EU Member State, the Convention
states that the court should apply its own law.[33] Therefore the Brussels
Convention should have been applied first to determine whether the
defendant had a domicile in France. If the answer were yes, the court would
have had jurisdiction and the other domicile would not be taken into
account. If the answer were no, the court would be able to rely on other
national bases of jurisdiction (such as the nationality of the plaintiff) in
order to assume jurisdiction. If there are no bases of jurisdiction in national
law, as in this case, the court must find that it lacks jurisdiction. The court
cannot conclude that a third State court has jurisdiction; only the courts of
that third State can make such a ruling.

---

[30] 18 February 1994 [1994] Recueil Dalloz 351 (summary and case note by B Audit).
[31] Although of course a French court cannot rule on the jurisdiction of the courts of another
state; see Audit, ibid, 351.
[32] Ibid 351; Born *et al*, note 1 above, 75.
[33] Art 59 of Brussels I (at the time Art 52 of the Brussels Convention).

2.22 Moreover, the EU rules of civil jurisdiction are sometimes incorrectly expanded. This happened, for instance, in another judgment of the Cour d'appel of Paris. The Court applied the Brussels Convention, but based its jurisdiction on the defendant's residence in Paris, while ignoring his Brazilian domicile.[34] It was uncontested in the case that the residence in Paris was no domicile. The case has been criticized.[35] One cannot apply the EU rules and broaden them further so as to base jurisdiction on residence.

2.23 While using 'habitual residence' and not 'domicile,' the draft Hague convention on jurisdiction and foreign judgments in civil and commercial matters (which was never concluded) did foresee a rule for the situation where a person is habitually resident in more than one state. One then had to look at his or her principal residence. If that could not be found, the person could be sued in any of the Contracting States in which he or she was resident.

Domicile of legal persons

2.24 First, it must be pointed out that in private international law there are two main theories on the domicile of a legal person. The first is that a legal person is domiciled at the place where it is incorporated. This is the incorporation theory. The supporters of this theory are drawn by the legal certainty it grants. The United Kingdom,[36] Ireland, The Netherlands, Denmark, Finland and Sweden apply this theory to determine the domicile of a legal person. The opposite theory, called the real seat theory, determines the domicile of a legal person by reference to where it truly operates. Incorporation is a relevant factor in the process of seeking the true seat, but it is not decisive. One may also consider the central administration and the management of the legal person. Belgium, France, Germany, Greece, Luxembourg and Spain apply this theory to varying degrees.[37]

---

[34] Judgment of 30 November 1990 [1992] *Journal de droit international* 192–195.

[35] Note by A Huet [1992] *Journal de droit international* 192–195.

[36] Traditionally common law legal systems adhere to the incorporation theory; see Hartley *Civil Jurisdiction and Judgments*, note 6 above, 35. In the United Kingdom, the Civil Jurisdiction and Judgments Act now explicitly mentions the different possibilities; see s 42(3): '[a] corporation or association has its seat in the United Kingdom if and only if—a) it was incorporated or formed under the law of a part of the United Kingdom and has its registered office or some other official address in the United Kingdom; or b) its central management and control is exercised in the United Kingdom'.

[37] For a thorough study on and comparison of these theories, see J Meeusen, 'De werkelijke zetel-leer en de communautaire vestigingsvrijheid van vennootschappen' [2003] *Tijdschrift voor rechtspersoon en vennootschap* 95–127. See also Born *et al*, note 1 above, 73 and following;

The rule contained in the Brussels Convention for the determination of the **2.25** domicile of legal persons was similar, but not identical, to the test used for natural persons, as it referred to the national laws of the EU Member States. However, it did not refer to the rules of the EU Member State where the legal person was presumed to be domiciled but only to the private international law of the forum.[38] The explicit reference to the private international law of the forum probably served the purpose of making clear that EU Member States could adhere to their own preference between the two main views discussed above. The Brussels Convention did not compel them either way.

Brussels I introduced an autonomous definition of the domicile of legal **2.26** persons. A legal person is domiciled where it has its statutory seat, central administration or principal place of business.[39] While it is true that the Regulation refrained from choosing between the two main theories, the seemingly innocent amendment of Brussels I might have broadened its personal scope. Setting the criteria as alternatives for the determination of the domicile of legal persons has the result that an EU Member State does not necessarily have to apply the criterion for domicile that it would apply according to its domestic private international law.

In other words, a court under the Brussels Convention applied only **2.27** one criterion for domicile (although that rule might not be the same in different EU Member States, as explained above). Conversely, under Brussels I, the different possibilities pose alternatives for every court to pick and choose from. Let us take the example of a company incorporated

regarding English law: North & Fawcett, note 20 above, 188–189. This debate has caused endless trouble in private international law and can lead to the application of the doctrine of *renvoi*. The European Court of Justice has ruled that legal persons incorporated in one EU Member State have to be recognized in the other EU Member States; see Case C–212/97 *Centros Ltd v Erhvervs- og Selskabsstyrelsen* [1999] ECR I–1459; Case C–208/00 *Überseering BV v Nordic Construction Company Baumanagement GmbH* [2002] ECR I–9919; Case C–167/01 *Kamer van Koophandel en Fabrieken voor Amsterdam v Inspire Art Ltd* [2003] ECR I–10155. I will not discuss these judgments in detail, as they are a good example of interaction between the legal systems within the EU, but have little relevance for third States. The European Court of Justice has not prohibited either of the theories (incorporation or real seat), but has emphasized that neither theory may be applied so as to hamper the free movement of (legal) persons in the EU.

[38] The English Court of Appeal nevertheless applied the rule in the same way as the rule for natural persons: see *The 'Deichland'* [1990] 1 QB 361 (CA) at 375, where it was found that a company incorporated in Panama, but having its central management and control in Germany, was domiciled in Germany. The English Court of Appeal relied on German law, which would view the company as domiciled in Germany.

[39] Art 60 of Brussels I.

in India, but having its activities exclusively in England. Under the Brussels Convention the English court, according to its rules of private international law, would regard this company as domiciled in India. Now the English court will have to consider the alternatives. According to at least one of the alternatives (the principal place of business), the company is domiciled in England, and thus in the EU. A similar example can be given of a company incorporated in Spain, but having its principal place of business in Mexico. Under the Brussels Convention, the Spanish courts would consider the company domiciled in a third State. The Regulation, on the other hand, providing a list of alternative criteria, might draw that company into its sphere of application.

2.28 The same amendment was not made in the Regulation provision regarding the exclusive basis of jurisdiction for the validity of legal persons. For these matters exclusive jurisdiction is retained by the courts of the place of the seat of the legal person. To determine the seat of a legal person, the provision states that a court shall apply its rules of private international law.[40] This makes sense, because a court would be in a predicament if it were required to declare a legal person invalid because its own law did not view that legal person as having its seat on the territory of the court's state.

2.29 In some instances legal persons are presumed to be domiciled at the place in the EU where they have a branch or other establishment. This is particularly the case when protective bases of jurisdiction exist. For instance, if a consumer buys something from a Canadian company which has a branch in France, the company might be presumed to be domiciled in France for jurisdictional purposes. These examples will be treated later in this chapter.[41] In other matters, suing a defendant at the place of its branch or establishment is only possible if the defendant is also domiciled in the EU and the dispute has arisen from the operations of the establishment. This rule will also be examined later in this chapter.[42]

2.30 The draft Hague convention on jurisdiction and foreign judgments in civil and commercial matters used 'habitual residence' instead of 'domicile' and contained four alternatives for legal persons: where it had its statutory seat, the law under which it was incorporated, its central administration, or its principal place of business. These alternatives took sufficient

---

[40] Art 22(2) of Brussels I; para 3.33 below; P Vlas, case note on *Coreck* [2001] *Nederlandse jurisprudentie. Uitspraken in burgerlijke en strafzaken* no 599, 4442–4445.

[41] Para 2.276 below.

[42] Art 5(5) Brussels I; see para 2.234 and following for a more detailed discussion of this provision.

account of the difference between the legal systems and all could accept the provision at the time of the negotiations. An extension to this general jurisdiction rule caused more disagreement. It could be extended to the place where a defendant had a branch, agency or establishment.[43] The existence of a subsidiary would not necessarily amount to a branch for purposes of jurisdiction. Another option was the extension to places where the defendant had carried on regular commercial activity by other means. Both these grounds would only apply if the dispute arose from the activity of the branch or of the particular regular commercial activity.

The time of domicile

The point in time at which the domicile must be determined may be **2.31** important. A party might, for example, move to a different state. This issue arose before the English court in the case of *Canada Trust and others v Stolzenberg and others*.[44] In this case jurisdiction was based on the domicile in England of Mr Stolzenberg, despite the fact that he was moving to Germany. There were many interim measures at the beginning of the proceedings to prevent assets from being moved and this delayed the issue of the writ. The question before the House of Lords was what the relevant time of the defendant's domicile was for purposes of the Lugano Convention (although it seems that the Brussels Convention should have been applied).[45] The writ was issued when Mr Stolzenberg was still domiciled in England. When the writ was served, he was not found in England and there was uncertainty as to his domicile. The House of Lords, dismissing the appeal against the judgment of the Court of Appeal, found that the relevant time for determining domicile was the time of the issue of the writ.[46] It stated that this provided certainty for the plaintiff and prevented defendants from changing their domicile for the purpose of circumventing the jurisdiction of a court. Mr Stolzenberg's domicile was of particular importance in this case, because he was only one of a number of defendants.

---

[43] 'Summary of the Outcome of the Discussion in Commission II of the First Part of the Diplomatic Conference (2001),' Art 9, available at <http://www.hcch.net> under the preliminary documents related to the Hague Convention on Choice of Court Agreements.

[44] [2002] 1 AC 1 (HL).

[45] On that issue: chapter 1, above, para 1.066. Case C–412/98 *Group Josi Reinsurance Company SA v Universal General Insurance Company (UGIC)* [2000] ECR I–5925, made it clear that the domicile of the defendant in a Contracting State is sufficient to make the Convention applicable. (For a more detailed discussion of this case, see below, para 2.067 and following.) The Lugano Convention does not change this; see Art 54B. However, the rule under discussion here is identical under Brussels I and the Lugano Convention so that the practical impact of the mistake is small.

[46] *The Canada Trust Company v Stolzenberg* [1998] 1 WLR 547.

None of the other defendants was domiciled in England, but in Switzerland, Liechtenstein, Panama and the Netherlands Antilles. They could all be hooked onto the procedure in England on the basis of the Lugano Convention and English national law.[47] The House of Lords noted that other provisions, such as the ones on *lis pendens* and related actions, referred to a different moment for the institution of the proceedings, but that other factors were relevant for the application of those provisions.[48]

2.32 Of course one should avoid the possibility of parties evading the jurisdiction of the courts, but if this could be done while applying consistent criteria, such a solution should be promoted. At the time of *Stolzenberg*, the Brussels Convention contained no unified rule on the time a court becomes seised. This had to be determined according to national law. However, Brussels I brought a specific rule (while taking the different systems in the Member States into account): a court is deemed to be seised at the moment the document instituting the proceedings or an equivalent document is lodged with the court (provided that the plaintiff subsequently took the steps required to effect service on the defendant), *or* if the document has to be served before lodging with the court, at the time when it is received by the authority responsible for service (provided that the plaintiff subsequently took the steps required to have the document lodged at the court).[49] With this more harmonized approach, one might wonder whether that date should not also be the relevant one for determining domicile, or whether the House of Lords would still have found that the purpose of the provision is different and that it therefore could not be used in this case.

Habitual residence

2.33 Brussels I does not, and the Convention did not, employ the concept of 'habitual residence', because the notion of 'habitual' was not the same in all the Member States.[50] A combination of the two terms, domicile and habitual residence, did not seem like a good and clear alternative either. This would have led to a multiplication of courts with jurisdiction.[51] The Regulation does use the notion of habitual residence with regard to maintenance claims.[52] Apart from that provision, domicile is the criterion, rather

---

[47] See the discussion on multiple defendants below, para 2.136.
[48] Note 44 above, at p 10–11.
[49] Art 30 of Brussels I. Similar rules exist in Brussels II *bis*, Art 16, and in the proposed Maintenance Regulation: note 5 above, Art 9, available at <http://eur-lex.europa.eu>.
[50] Jenard Report, note 1 above, 15; Donzallaz, note 16 above, vol 1, 395.
[51] Jenard Report, note 1 above, 16.
[52] Art 5(2) of Brussels I.

than habitual residence. The term 'habitual residence' was used in that provision to avoid clashes with the 1958 and 1973 Hague Maintenance Conventions, which also use 'habitual residence'.[53] It should be noted that this provision will soon be replaced by the new Regulation specifically on maintenance.[54] That Regulation uses 'habitual residence' as its criterion.

For the purposes of Brussels II *bis*, domicile (in the civil law sense) is not **2.34** important, but to a large extent the jurisdiction rules are based on habitual residence.[55] In family law matters, the concept of habitual residence has become more and more popular in modern legal texts.[56] It is preferred over domicile because of the flexibility it permits, especially in matters affecting persons in a time of personal crisis, where they often move from one country to another. A habitual residence does not necessarily coincide with the place where a person is registered as living.

Brussels II *bis* does not define 'habitual residence,' and neither does the **2.35** Borrás Report. The best available definition is a type of justification in the preamble of the Regulation:

The grounds of jurisdiction accepted in this Regulation are based on the rule that there must be a real link between the party concerned and the Member State exercising jurisdiction; the decision to include certain grounds corresponds to the fact that they exist in different national legal systems and are accepted by the other Member States. [57]

Although flexibility should be welcomed in this area of the law, it does **2.36** cause difficulties in drawing the borderline for applicability. While domicile in the civil law sense is relatively easy to determine (it is sometimes written in a register), the question where exactly a person is habitually resident may be more difficult. This concept tries to take account of reality. However, this is not always an easy task: various facts may be relevant, such as where a person lives or works. His or her intentions might also be relevant. If a person moves to a new country, the issue arises as to how

---

[53] Hague Convention of 15 April 1958 concerning the recognition and enforcement of decisions relating to maintenance obligations towards children and Hague Convention of 2 October 1973 on the Recognition and Enforcement of Decisions relating to Maintenance Obligations; available at <http://www.hcch.net>. See also Hartley *Civil Jurisdiction and Judgments*, note 6 above, 49.

[54] Proposed Maintenance Regulation, note 5 above.

[55] Arts 3(1) and 8 of Brussels II *bis*; para 2. 83 and following below.

[56] See also P Rogerson, 'Habitual residence: the new domicile?' [2000] ICLQ 86–107.

[57] Rec 12 of Brussels II *bis*. Borrás Report on the Convention, drawn up on the basis of Article K.3 of the Treaty on the European Union, on Jurisdiction and the Recognition and Enforcement of Judgments in Matrimonial Matters; OJ C 221, 16 July 1998, 27.

soon a new habitual residence can be established. This question is not resolved in the same way in all legal systems.

2.37 It is interesting to note that many Hague Conventions use 'habitual residence' instead of 'domicile'.[58] The Draft Hague Convention on jurisdiction and foreign judgments in civil and commercial matters, which was never concluded, also used the term 'habitual residence', whilst the Hague Convention on Choice of Court Agreements uses only 'residence'.

Centre of main interests

2.38 This weird and wonderful phrase, unlike its peers discussed above, is a new concept, introduced in civil jurisdiction by the Insolvency Regulation. The negotiation of an insolvency convention between the EU Member States (before a Regulation in this matter was possible)[59] proved very difficult because of the difference between the legal systems of EU Member States regarding the issue of the domicile of legal persons.

2.39 It seemed impossible that the Insolvency Regulation would choose between the incorporation and real seat theories (discussed above).[60] At the same time, a clear criterion had to be found. The structure of the Regulation is such that, from the moment they are opened in an EU Member State, insolvency proceedings are recognized throughout the EU. If different Member States have opposing views on where the insolvent person is domiciled, this would cripple the working of the Regulation to such an extent that it would become a dead letter.

2.40 A compromise was found in the 'centre of main interests' (COMI). Fortunately the Insolvency Regulation provides aid in the interpretation of this new notion it introduces: for legal persons, the registered office is presumed to be the COMI. The starting point therefore coincides with the incorporation theory. It is, however, only a presumption and may be rebutted. If, for instance, a company is incorporated in Canada, but has almost all its activities in Sweden and is managed there, the Swedish court may reasonably come to the conclusion that the COMI is situated in Sweden,

---

[58] Notably the Hague 1958 and 1973 Maintenance Conventions, note 53 above; Hague Convention of 29 May 1993 on Protection of Children and Co-operation in respect of Intercountry Adoption; Hague Convention of 19 October 1996 on Jurisdiction, Applicable Law, Recognition, Enforcement and Co-operation in respect of Parental Responsibility and Measures for the Protection of Children; Hague Convention of 13 January 2000 on the International Protection of Adults etc.

[59] See chapter 1, para 1.12 and following for an explanation of the framework of EU legislation.

[60] See the discussion on the domicile of legal persons above, para 2. 24 and following.

so that the Swedish courts will be able to open insolvency proceedings. It is also problematic that the concept of COMI exists only within the EU. One is not comparing domicile with domicile, or habitual residence with habitual residence, but totally different things.

COMI could be interpreted very broadly. The fear is that as soon as either **2.41** the statutory seat or the central administration is established in the EU, the COMI will be found to be in the EU, even though other elements are outside.

The European Court of Justice has already had its first opportunity to rule **2.42** on the meaning of this concept.[61] In the Parmalat insolvency a difference of interpretation arose between the Irish and Italian courts. Eurofood IFCS Ltd, incorporated in Ireland, was a wholly-owned subsidiary of Parmalat SpA, incorporated in Italy. The High Court of Ireland had appointed a provisional liquidator for Eurofood on 27 January 2004. That was the first step towards insolvency. On 23 March 2004 the High Court found that the appointment of the provisional liquidator in January had in fact amounted to the opening of insolvency proceedings on that date. However, a court at Parma in Italy had opened insolvency proceedings for the entire Parmalat group between those two dates, on 20 February 2004. It considered Eurofood part of this group. The High Court of Ireland did not recognize the decision of the court in Parma on the basis that it was contrary to public policy. An appeal was brought to the Supreme Court against the decision of the Irish High Court. The Supreme Court referred several questions of interpretation to the European Court of Justice. One of those questions concerned the location of the COMI. The ECJ found that the presumption that the COMI was at the place of registration could be rebutted only if factors, which were objective and ascertainable by third parties, indicated a different actual situation. The mere existence of a parent company which could control the economic choices of the company, was not sufficient to rebut the presumption.[62]

The Regulation has brought about a compromise, but it is not free of flaws. **2.43** Even within the EU, disputes have arisen with regard to the location of

---

[61] Case C–341/04 *Eurofood IFSC Ltd* [2006] ECR I–3813; case notes: T Bachner, 'The Battle over Jurisdiction in European Insolvency Law' [2006] *European Company and Financial Law Review* 310–329; AJ Berends, 'The Eurofood Case: One Company, Two Main Insolvency Proceedings: Which One is the Real One?' [2006] *Netherlands International Law Review* 331–361; A Wittwer, 'Zuständigkeit, Anerkennung und ordre public im internationalen Insolvenzrecht—ein wegweisendes Urteil' [2006] *European Law Reporter* 221–224. See also *French Republic v Klempka (administrator of ISA Daisytek SAS)*, Court of Cassation (Commercial, Economic and Financial Chamber), Paris [2006] BCC 841.

[62] Paras 34–37; also Opinion of Advocate General Jacobs, paras 123–126.

the COMI. The Rechtbank van koophandel (Commercial Court) of Tongeren in Belgium incorrectly opened secondary insolvency proceedings against a debtor for which a main insolvency had been opened in Luxembourg.[63] Normally a secondary insolvency proceeding is opened if a separate establishment exists in another EU Member State. However, that was not the case here. The debtor had its statutory seat in Luxembourg, but its factual seat in Belgium. A correct interpretation of the Insolvency Regulation would have denied the Commercial Court of Tongeren jurisdiction after the opening of the insolvency proceedings in Luxembourg. It seems that the Belgian court launched the secondary insolvency because it did not agree with the Luxembourg court's interpretation of the COMI.

2.44 Certainly similar questions will arise when it is unclear whether the COMI is situated in the EU, or when the registered office or principal place of business is located in a third State.[64]

Nationality and dual nationality

2.45 It is important to note at this stage that Brussels I attaches no importance to the notion of nationality. The domestic jurisdiction rules that are based on the nationality of one of the parties have been listed in Article 3, among the exorbitant bases of jurisdiction. These have been abolished for defendants domiciled in the EU. The most often quoted examples are the French rules that a French national may always bring proceedings in France[65] and that a French national may always be sued in the courts in France.[66] Because nationality is irrelevant, a dispute between an Irishman and a German both domiciled in France will not fall under Brussels I, but under French national rules on jurisdiction.[67] The flip side is that the Regulation

---

[63] Judgment of 20 February 2003 [2004] *Revue de droit commercial belge* 70–71; case note by T Kruger, 71–74; see also <http://www.euprocedure.be>.

[64] This book deals only with jurisdiction rules and their impact on third States. Therefore the rights, privileges, and disadvantages of creditors in third States, and the effects of rights *in rem* in property situated in third States, have not been addressed. The reader is referred to C Barbé & V Marquette, 'Council Regulation (EC) No 1346/2000. Insolvency Proceedings in Europe and Third Countries. Status and Prospects' in Nuyts & Watté, note 1 above, 419–507. On trans-border proceedings and cooperation, see also V Marquette & C Barbé, 'Les procédures d'insolvabilité extracommunautaire' [2006] *Journal de droit international* 511–562.

[65] Art 14 of the French code civil (Civil Code).

[66] Art 15 of the French code civil. This rule also existed in Belgium, but was deleted in 2004, with the entry into force of the Belgian Code de droit international privé, note 19 above.

[67] Born *et al*, note 1 above, 70; see also Cour d'appel of Paris, judgment of 27 March 1987 with case note by A Huet, [1988] *Journal de droit international* 140–143, finding that the Ivorian nationality of the defendant was irrelevant since he was domiciled in France.

will apply between two French nationals, one domiciled in France and the other in Ireland. If a French national, domiciled in France, wants to bring action in the EU against an Irish national domiciled in Hawaii, he or she would have to search for a basis of jurisdiction not in the Regulation, but in the relevant national systems. That is because the defendant is not domiciled in the EU; the Irish nationality of the defendant is irrelevant.

In the Insolvency Regulation, as in Brussels I, nationality plays no role.   **2.46**

However, nationality does play a role in the jurisdiction rules of Brussels **2.47** II *bis*.[68] The nationality of one party is never sufficient to grant jurisdiction, but nationality plus habitual residence, or the common nationality of the parties, can do so.[69] Furthermore, if no court in the EU has jurisdiction according to the Regulation's rules, there is a reference to domestic bases for jurisdiction. If those domestic rules are based on nationality, they have to be made available to all EU nationals with habitual residence in that EU Member State.[70] The EU principle that there should be no distinction between EU nationalities has a far-reaching effect in broadening exorbitant bases of jurisdiction. For instance, not only is a French national able to bring an action in the French court, but so are all EU nationals habitually resident in France.[71] The proposed amendments to Brussels II *bis* will change that provision, deleting the reference to domestic bases of jurisdiction, but elaborating jurisdiction on the basis of nationality.[72] Where neither spouse is habitually resident in the EU, and they do not have a common EU nationality, the court of the nationality of one spouse has jurisdiction.[73] For both the current and the proposed Regulations, 'nationality' is replaced by 'domicile' for Ireland and the United Kingdom. Under the proposed Maintenance Regulation, the common nationality of the parties may also grant jurisdiction if no court in an EU Member State has jurisdiction according to the other rules.[74]

---

[68] One can debate whether a distinction on the basis of nationality is justified in EU law, where all EU citizens are supposed to be treated equally and discrimination on the basis of nationality is not permitted (Art 12 EC Treaty). That fine-tuning of EU law falls beyond the ambit of this book. Note that for Ireland and the United Kingdom, nationality is not important, but rather domicile in its common law sense.

[69] Art 3(1) of Brussels II *bis*.

[70] Art 7.

[71] On the basis of Art 14 of the French *code civil* and the elaboration by the Brussels II *bis*.

[72] See Proposal for a Council Regulation amending Regulation (EC) No 2201/2003 as regards jurisdiction and introducing rules concerning applicable law in matrimonial matters of 17 July 2006, COM(2006) 399 final, available at <http://eur-lex.europa.eu>.

[73] Proposed amendment to Art 7.

[74] Art 6. The United Kingdom has indicated that it would not opt in and the Regulation thus would not apply there. On the other hand, it would apply in Ireland, which would opt in.

2.48 Determining the nationality is clearly an issue for each EU Member State and needs no further elaboration. The more difficult issue is that of dual nationality, on which the Borrás Report states only the following:

> The [Regulation] is silent on the consequences of dual nationality, so the judicial bodies of each State will apply their national rules within the framework of general Community rules on the matter. [75]

These general rules are found for example in the principles of the free movement of persons. Accordingly case law of the European Court of Justice can also be important when interpreting Brussels II *bis* with regard to dual nationality.

2.49 Some EU Member States are party to the Hague Convention on Certain Questions relating to the Conflict of Nationality Laws of 1930.[76] Brussels II *bis* does not contain a reference to this Convention. According to the Convention, when a person has two nationalities, one should look at the state with which he or she has the closest link.[77] However, if one of the nationalities is that of the state where the proceeding is taking place, that state will be able to give preference to the forum nationality.[78]

2.50 However, distinguishing between EU nationalities has become an evil. This seems to raise two difficulties: the first is the treatment of a person with two EU nationalities (and its effects on a party from a third State), and the second is that of a person who has both a third State nationality and nationality of an EU Member State other than the one of the state where the proceeding is taking place.

2.51 First, if a person has two EU nationalities, no distinction should be made between these nationalities. This principle was emphasized in the *Garcia Avello* case.[79] A Spanish father (Garcia Avello) and a Belgian mother (Weber)

The current version of Art 6 does not replace 'nationality' by 'domicile' for those states, but it can be imagined that this might change if they do join.

[75] Borrás Report, note 57 above, para 33, p 39.

[76] Of the EU Member States Belgium, Cyprus, Malta, The Netherlands, Poland, Sweden, and the United Kingdom are party. Others, namely Austria, Czechoslovakia (as it then was), Denmark, Estonia, France, Germany, Greece, Hungary, Ireland, Italy, Latvia, Luxembourg, Portugal, Spain, and Yugoslavia (as it then was), have signed but not ratified the Convention: Convention on Certain Questions relating to the Conflict of Nationality Laws (The Hague, 1930).

[77] Art 5.

[78] Art 3.

[79] Case C–148/02 *Carlos Garcia Avello v the Belgian State* [2003] ECR I–11613; P Lagarde, case note on *Garcia Avello* [2004] *Revue critique de droit international privé* 192–202; G-R de Groot & S Rutten, 'Op weg naar een Europees IPR op het gebied van het personen- en familierecht' [2004] *Nederlands Internationaal Privaatrecht* 273–282.

had two children. In Belgium they had been registered as Garcia Avello, according to the Belgian law that children get the surnames of their fathers. In Spain these children had the names Garcia Weber, according to the Spanish law that children get the first surname of their father and the first surname of their mother. The parents wanted to have the Belgian surnames of the children changed to Garcia Weber, so that they would have the same name in both countries, and therefore throughout the EU. The Belgian authorities refused to change the names because the children also had Belgian nationality which meant, certainly according to the Hague Convention, that in Belgium they could be regarded as Belgian citizens and Belgian law would be applicable to their names. Finally a preliminary question was referred to the European Court of Justice. The Court found that this distinction could not be made and that the Belgian authorities were under an obligation to change the names of the children if they (or their parents) chose to have the law of another EU Member State (of which they also had nationality) applied to their name. In this sense the effect of the 1930 Hague Convention was reduced to be subordinate to that of the equality of all EU nationalities.

The *Garcia Avello* judgment has even led some authors to conclude that **2.52** family rules of private international law should be harmonized by the European Union, simply because this will be more efficient.[80] The spirit of the judgment probably goes further than just change of name. If one recognizes the precedent system, the judgment could be seen as an interpretation of the concept of dual EU nationality. Thus, when a person has two EU nationalities, no distinction should be made between those nationalities. A party from a third State would have to take both nationalities of the other party into account.

The second question that can arise concerns simultaneous nationality of **2.53** an EU Member State and a third State. An example is someone with Russian and Polish nationality, who is resident in Russia and has a much closer link to Russia than to Poland. In applying the 1930 Hague Convention on Conflict of Nationality Laws, the English court (assuming that it has jurisdiction) would be able to state that the Russian nationality was the relevant one. However, could the person argue that, since he also has Polish nationality (even if he has no link with Poland), this EU nationality would have to be preferred? A Polish court would consider the EU nationality more important than the third State nationality. Should the English court do the same? In other words, should all EU Member State courts give

---

[80] De Groot & Rutten, ibid at 282. For a critical view of this far-reaching influence and the difficulties the case introduces, see P Lagarde, ibid, especially 195–197 and 200–201.

preference to the EU nationality of parties, even if the nationality of the forum is not concerned?

2.54 A person qualifies to benefit from the free movement rules as soon as he or she has any EU nationality. The fact that it is a person's second nationality and that he or she has no link with a specific EU Member State is irrelevant. The extent to which this principle can be transposed to jurisdiction rules is unclear. One cannot avoid wondering about the effect of the fact that all EU nationalities are equal. If the treatment of dual nationality is such that any EU nationality should be seen as equal to the EU nationality of the court where the proceeding is, Brussels II *bis* will be extended even further.

2.55 Furthermore, these examples show that nationality is not a suitable criterion for jurisdiction rules in an EU where all nationalities are equal and no distinction on the basis of nationality is tolerated. This ground for jurisdiction, in conjunction with the principle of non-discrimination on the basis of nationality, will probably only draw more and more people into the sphere of Brussels II *bis*, especially those with dual nationality.

B. JURISDICTION BASED ON THE DOMICILE OF THE DEFENDANT

Article 2 of Brussels I:

1. *Subject to this Regulation, persons domiciled in a Member State shall, whatever their nationality, be sued in the courts of that Member State.*
2. *Persons who are not nationals of the Member State in which they are domiciled shall be governed by the rules of jurisdiction applicable to nationals of that State.*

Article 3 of Brussels I:

1. *Persons domiciled in a Member State may be sued in the courts of another Member State only by virtue of the rules set out in Section 2 to 7 of this Chapter.*
2. *In particular the rules of national jurisdiction set out in Annex I shall not be applicable as against them.*

Article 4 of Brussels I:

1. *If the defendant is not domiciled in a Member State, the jurisdiction of the courts of each Member State shall, subject to Articles 22 and 23, be determined by the law of that Member State.*
2. *As against such a defendant, any person domiciled in a Member State may, whatever his nationality, avail himself in that State of the rules of jurisdiction there in force, and in particular those specified in Annex I, in the same way as the nationals of that State.*

DEFENDANTS DOMICILED IN THIRD STATES

General

As has been pointed out, domicile as the criterion for applicability is of **2.56** importance for Brussels I. The basic principle is that its jurisdiction rules apply if the defendant is domiciled in the EU. On the other hand, if the defendant is domiciled in a third State, a court in an EU Member State need not follow the jurisdiction rules of Brussels I, but will base its jurisdiction on its domestic rules. Some states' domestic rules allow jurisdiction in cases where the court has a very tenuous link with the dispute or the parties. These rules are outlawed when the defendant is domiciled in the EU, but still apply if the defendant is domiciled in a third State.[81]

As explained in chapter 1,[82] there are two possible ways to understand **2.57** Article 4. The first is that the provision appoints the national rules and in this way incorporates them into the scheme of Brussels I. The second is that the provision merely confirms that national rules of jurisdiction have survived to a certain extent, and that in certain cases they are applicable in their own right. In the *Lugano* opinion the European Court of Justice followed the first of these approaches. It found that Brussels I has established a coherent system of jurisdiction rules.[83]

At this stage one notices a severe distinction between defendants who are **2.58** domiciled in the EU and those who are not. The discrepancy does not end here. When one turns to the rules of recognition and enforcement of judgments, one finds the true source of concern for parties from third States. A judgment granted by any EU court must be recognized and enforced throughout the EU. At the stage of recognition and enforcement, the identities of the parties, and to a large extent the jurisdictional bases, become irrelevant.[84] Therefore, a judgment in which jurisdiction was based on an exorbitant ground in (say) France, does not have effects just in France, but throughout the EU. In other words, the worst habits of every EU Member State are exported to all the others. Consequently since the entry into force of the first version of the Brussels Convention this result has been heavily criticized by authors from outside the EU, even going so

---

[81] Arts 3 and 4 of Brussels I.
[82] Para 1. 52 and following.
[83] Opinion 1/03 *Competence of the Community to conclude the new Lugano Convention on jurisdiction and the recognition and enforcement of judgments in civil and commercial matters* [2006] ECR I–1145, especially para 148.
[84] Except for the rules on exclusive jurisdiction and some of the protective bases of jurisdiction: see chapter 3.

far as accusing the EU States of chauvinism.[85] The effect has also been highlighted by case law.[86]

2.59 The draft Hague convention on jurisdiction and foreign judgments also dealt with the matter in a different way: this Convention would have been applicable in the courts of the Contracting States, unless both parties were domiciled in the same Contracting State.[87] In itself, the domicile of the defendant would not be relevant for the determination of scope. In this

---

[85] See Y Donzallaz, *La Convention de Lugano du 16 septembre 1988 concernant la compétence judiciaire et l'exécution des décisions en matière civile et commerciale* (Berne: Editions Stæmpfli + Cie SA Berne, 1996) vol 1 22; PJ Borchers, 'Comparing Personal Jurisdiction in the US and the EC: Lessons for American Reform' [1992] AJCL 121–157 at 132–133, stating that '[t]he Brussels Convention overtly discriminates against outsiders'; KH Nadelmann, 'Jurisdictionally improper fora in treaties on recognition and enforcement of judgments: the Common Market draft' [1967] *Columbia Law Review* 995–1023; P Mercier, 'Le projet de convention du marché commun sur la procédure civile internationale et les états tiers' [1967] *Cahiers de droit européen* 367–368 and 513–531 (from a Swiss point of view); BM Landay, 'Another look at the EEC Judgments Convention: should outsiders be worried?' [1987–1988] *Dickenson Journal of International Law* 25–44; FK Juenger, 'La Convention de Bruxelles du 27 septembre 1968 et la courtoisie internationale, Réflexions d'un américain' [1983] *Revue critique de droit international privé* 37–51. AT von Mehren, 'Recognition and enforcement of sister-state judgments: reflection on general theory and current practice in the European Economic Community and the United States' [1981] *Columbia Law Review* 1044–1060 states at 1060:
> Unless and until [modified], this aspect of the Brussels Convention will remain the single most regressive step that has occurred in international recognition and enforcement practice in this century. If not corrected, the example set by the Convention may well set in motion forces that will undermine much of what theory and practice have done during our century to create, with respect to recognition and enforcement of judgments, a decent and workable international order.

Conversely, the US jurisdictional principles are even-handed: the same jurisdictional bases apply to Americans from different states and to foreigners; *Helicopteros Nacionales de Colombia SA v Hall*, 466 US 408, 104 S Ct 1868 (1984); *Insurance Corp of Ireland, Ltd v Compagnie des Bauxites de Guinée*, 456 US 694, 102 S Ct 2099 (1982); *Asahi Metal Industry Co v Superior Court*, 480 US 102, 107 S Ct 1026 (1987). Regarding jurisdiction rules in the USA, see also F Juenger, 'Judicial Jurisdiction in the United States and in the European Communities: a comparison' [1984] *Michigan Law Review* 1195–1212; HS Lewis Jr, 'A brave new world for personal jurisdiction: flexible tests under uniform standards' [1984] *Vanderbilt Law Review* 1–66. AT von Mehren, 'Recognition and Enforcement of Foreign Judgments: a new approach for the Hague Conference?' [1994] *Law and Contemporary Problems* 271–287 states at 280–281 that the USA would not be able to accede to the Lugano Convention (with the same provisions as the Brussels Convention), even if it were invited, because the Convention's Art 3 violates due process standards under US law.

[86] See Cour d'appel (Court of Appeal) Paris 17 November 1993 [1994] *Journal de droit international* 671–676, note by A Huet, 676–678; also published in [1994] *Revue critique de droit international privé* 115–117, note by H Gaudemet-Tallon, 117–120, admitting Juenger's criticism.

[87] 'Summary of the Outcome of the Discussion in Commission II of the First Part of the Diplomatic Conference (2001),' Art 2, available at <http://www.hcch.net>. See also B Audit & GA Berman, 'The application of private international norms to 'third countries': the

way Contracting States would vow true comity to each other and not create an 'exclusive club', as the EU is sometimes perceived.

On the other hand, according to Gaudemet-Tallon the EU Member States **2.60** have committed each other to excluding these exorbitant bases for jurisdiction because they trust the other judges of the EU, and also because this commitment is mutual. If the EU Member States agreed to abandon their exorbitant bases for jurisdiction with regard to all defendants, this would be a unilateral gesture and not a mutual arrangement.[88]

To understand this difference in viewpoints, one has to turn back to the **2.61** nature of double conventions (or regulations).[89] The jurisdiction rules are linked to recognition and enforcement in such a way that recognition becomes automatic because of the unified rules of jurisdiction. However, leaving the defendants from outside the EU out of the Regulation's jurisdiction rules, but including the recognition and enforcement of subsequent judgments in the scope of the Regulation, gives rise to concerns. The structure of Brussels I should be balanced. Either it is a double Regulation, linking jurisdiction completely to recognition and enforcement, or it is not. In other words, if the Regulation does not apply to defendants from outside the EU, neither should the resulting judgments be permitted to fall under its scope. Conversely, if the EU truly wants to create a European judicial area where all judgments can travel freely, the jurisdiction rules must be equitable in all the judgments that are included in this zone of free movement. The Regulation should then contain universal rules on jurisdiction, and any exorbitant bases of jurisdiction should disappear entirely from the EU.

It has to be borne in mind that Article 4, dealing with defendants from **2.62** outside the EU, gives precedence to the exclusive bases of jurisdiction,[90] and forum clauses specifying EU courts if one of the parties is domiciled in the EU.[91] As regards the rules on *lis pendens* and related actions, the domicile of the defendant is irrelevant.[92]

---

jurisdiction and judgments example' in A Nuyts & N Watté (eds), *International Civil Litigation in Europe and Relations with Third States* (Brussels: Bruylant, 2005) 55–82 at 68.

[88] H Gaudemet-Tallon, 'Les frontières extérieures de l'espace judiciaire européen: quelques repères' in A Borrás, A Bucher, AVM Struycken, M Verwilghen, *E Pluribus unum. Liber Amicorum Georges AL Droz* (The Hague: Martinus Nijhoff Publishers, 1996) 85–104, 94.

[89] Explained in chapter 1, para 1. 08 and following.

[90] Art 22; these bases of jurisdiction and their personal scope are discussed in chapter 3.

[91] Art 23; forum clauses and their personal scope are discussed in chapter 4.

[92] Arts 27 and 28; these procedural rules related to jurisdiction are discussed in chapter 5.

Exceptions

2.63 Some defendants from outside the EU can become subject to Brussels I, for instance, refugees and stateless persons.[93] According to the Convention on the Status of Refugees, a refugee or stateless person should be treated as a national/domiciliary.[94] Accordingly, the Regulations are extended to these persons through a fiction of domicile (Brussels I), or of nationality (Brussels II *bis*). The situation regarding candidate refugees is unclear. It has been suggested that the same should apply to these persons, since determining otherwise would practically deny them justice.[95] The Court of Brussels has followed this point of view.[96]

Who is the defendant?

2.64 It is not always clear in a specific matter who the defendant is. A first example is claims *in rem*. By definition there is no clear defendant if an action is *in rem*. In Admiralty claims *in rem*, the ship owner can be seen as the defendant, but so can other interested parties. In these cases one needs to consider the 'reality of the matter' to determine who the defendant is. The English Court of Appeal has admitted that, even if formally speaking there is no defendant, the ship owners were interested in the outcome of the case and wished to contest the merits of the plaintiffs' claim.[97]

2.65 Subrogation may also make it difficult to know who the true defendant is. The applicable domestic law determines the extent to which a party takes over the rights and obligations of another party.[98] A judgment of the Rechtbank (Court of First Instance) of Rotterdam illustrates the point.[99] The contract concerned the transport of oil from Algeria to the United States of America on board the 'Orembae', a ship belonging to Ananias, domiciled in Cyprus. The bill of lading contained a clause for arbitration in London and a choice of English law. However, the plaintiffs claimed

---

[93] H Born, M Fallon & J-L Van Boxstael, *Droit judiciaire international. Chronique de jurisprudence 1991–1998* (Brussels: Larcier, 2001) 35.

[94] Geneva, 1951.

[95] Born *et al*, note 93 above, 35.

[96] Brussels, 25 September 1996 [1997] *Jurisprudence de Liège, Mons et Bruxelles* 100, referring to Art 6 of the European Convention on Human Rights (Rome, 1950).

[97] See *The 'Deichland'* [1990] 1 QB 361 (CA), at 374.

[98] This has been decided by the European Court of Justice with regard to the provision on forum clauses: Case 71/83 *Tilly Russ & Ernest Russ v NV Haven- & Vervoerbedrijf Nova & NV Goeminne Hout* [1984] ECR 2417 at para 26; Case C–387/98 *Coreck Maritime GmbH v Handelsveem BV & others* [2000] ECR I–9337, at para 23–24.

[99] Judgment of 16 September 1988 [1990] *Nederlands Internationaal Privaatrecht* 366–369.

damages from Ananias before the Rechtbank of Rotterdam because the oil showed shortcomings when it arrived in New York. The defendant, Ananias, claimed that the Dutch court lacked jurisdiction and stated that the dispute did not have any connection with the Netherlands. Only the insurer and one of the plaintiffs were domiciled in the Netherlands, while all other parties were domiciled outside the Netherlands. One of Ananias's arguments was that if the insurance contract was valid, that contract would be subject to English law. According to English law a subrogated insurer (since it had already paid to the insured) cannot institute a claim in its own name, but should do so in the name of the indemnified insured party. Since the defendant was domiciled in a third State,[100] the Dutch court could base its jurisdiction on the domicile of the plaintiff.[101] The issue of subrogation was not further at issue. The case does, however, illustrate the point that domestic substantive law can influence the identity of the litigating parties.

What About the Plaintiff?

'Plaintiffs deserve as much protection as defendants.'[102]   **2.66**

If the plaintiff is domiciled in a third State and the defendant in the EU, the plaintiff is drawn into the system of Brussels I. At first sight, and especially with the rule *actor sequitur forum rei* in mind, this is not unsettling. The plaintiff can now sue other defendants in the same forum.[103] Alternatively, he or she can make use of the other bases of jurisdiction provided for by the Regulation, such as the contract's place of performance, or the place of damage.[104] On the other hand, other jurisdictional grounds that might exist in national law are denied to this plaintiff. The exorbitant bases for jurisdiction are outlawed as regards to defendants domiciled in the EU. At issue is not the advantage or disadvantage of the plaintiff, but the requirements of justice and equity.[105] This does not mean that plaintiffs

---

[100] Brussels I only became applicable in Cyprus on 1 May 2004.

[101] At the time Art 126(3) and (5) of the Wetboek van burgerlijke rechtsvordering (Code of Civil Procedure).

[102] A Bucher in AF Lowenfeld & LJ Silberman (eds), *The Hague Convention on Jurisdiction and Judgments* (USA: Juris Publishing, 2001), 24.

[103] Art 6(1) of Brussels I.

[104] Art 5 of Brussels I.

[105] See H Gaudemet-Tallon, 'Les frontières extérieures de l'espace judiciaire européen: quelques repères' in A Borrás, A Bucher, AVM Struycken, M Verwilghen, *E Pluribus unum. Liber Amicorum Georges AL Droz* (The Hague: Martinus Nijhoff Publishers, 1996), 85–104 at 89.

should receive special protection, but merely that their rights of access to justice and procedural fairness should not be infringed.

2.67 The *Josi* judgment provides a fine example of a plaintiff domiciled in a third State that was prohibited from using domestic French rules of jurisdiction.[106] The case investigated the degree of connection with the European judicial area sufficient to make the EU jurisdiction rules applicable. Universal General Insurance Company (UGIC) was an insurance company, incorporated in British Columbia in Canada. It instructed its agent, Euromepa, a company incorporated under French law, to find a reinsurer for certain home occupiers' insurance policies based in Canada. This led to the conclusion of a reinsurance contract between UGIC and Group Josi Reinsurance Company SA (Josi), a company incorporated under Belgian law. UGIC, in liquidation, claimed a sum of money from Josi pursuant to this contract. However, Josi refused to pay as it had been induced to enter into the contract on the basis of information that turned out to be false. Subsequently, UGIC brought an action before the Tribunal de commerce at Nanterre in France for payment of this sum. Josi contested the Tribunal's jurisdiction on the basis that, according to the Brussels Convention Article 2, UGIC would have to sue Josi in the country of its domicile, i.e. Belgium.

2.68 The Tribunal de commerce at Nanterre ruled that it had jurisdiction according to French law and ordered Josi to pay the claimed sum to UGIC. Josi appealed against this judgment to the Cour d'appel in Versailles. The Cour d'appel in Versailles referred a preliminary question to the European Court of Justice concerning the application of the Brussels Convention not only to intra-Community disputes but also to disputes that are integrated into the Community. More particularly, it asked whether a defendant established in a Member State could rely on the specific rules on jurisdiction set out in that Convention if the plaintiff was domiciled in Canada.

2.69 The European Court of Justice found that the EU jurisdiction rules did apply in this case. If one regards the question merely from the point of view of Brussels I, the position seems to be that defendants in the EU fall within the scope of the Regulation, irrespective of the domicile of the plaintiff. For this reason the judgment was accepted without much criticism.

2.70 However, the reasoning of both the Advocate General and the European Court of Justice was rather one-sided. For instance, the Advocate General relied on the Jenard Report's statement that a Convention conveying direct

---

[106] Case C–412/98 *Group Josi Reinsurance Company SA v Universal General Insurance Company* [2000] ECR I–5925.

jurisdiction ensures legal certainty more effectively. While this statement might be true, the justification for enacting a double convention (also containing jurisdiction rules) and the concern for legal certainty within the European Union, can hardly be seen as authority for determining its scope of application when parties from third States are involved. Moreover, the Advocate General stated that the application of Article 2 without consideration of the plaintiff's domicile would increase legal certainty since the uncertainties of national private international law rules would not come into play.[107] However, the reverse argument might also hold true—if the domicile of the plaintiff were relevant, local private international law could be applied and the foreigner has to consider only the local rules of the forum that he chooses, and does not have to take into account the possible application of a technical Convention which is not part of the legal system of his or her home country. Some might say that searching for national legal rules on civil jurisdiction is more difficult than applying Brussels I, but that probably depends on the particular plaintiff. Some parties might be active only in one EU Member State and know the private international law rules of that state, so that the application of the Regulation would add a difficulty for them.

The Advocate General also stated that the Convention provided a com- **2.71** prehensive scheme encompassing all defendants. If plaintiffs domiciled outside the European Community were not included in the scope of the Brussels Convention, this would be an illogical gap in its scheme and would jeopardize the working of the provisions on *lis pendens* and related actions.[108] The argument goes on to state that, if there were nothing specific on foreign plaintiffs in the Convention, they must be included in its scope in order to make the scheme complete, rather than leaving them out of the picture. Once again the arguments determining the scope of civil jurisdiction rules were based solely on EU principles. Furthermore, the scope of application of the provisions on *lis pendens* and related actions is determined independently of the domiciles of the parties, as will be pointed out in chapter 5 of this book. Therefore those phenomena cannot influence the scope of the jurisdiction rule that Brussels I applies if the defendant is domiciled in the EU. The *Owusu* judgment has confirmed that the Brussels Convention (and thus Brussels I) has established a complete scheme of jurisdiction rules.[109] Therefore the result of *Josi* can no longer be contested.

---

[107] Ibid, para 15.
[108] Ibid; see paras 19 and 20 of the Advocate General's opinion.
[109] Case C–281/02 *Owusu v Jackson* [2005] ECR I–1383.

2.72 Even before this line was taken by the European Court of Justice, the English court had come to the same conclusion. In the case of *Sameon co SA v NV Petrofina SA & another*, the plaintiff, Sameon, was a Panama company managed in Hong Kong.[110] It sued two Belgian companies in England. The court did not question the applicability of the Brussels Convention and used it to determine jurisdiction.

2.73 Similarly, in another English case, *Re Harrods (Buenos Aires) Ltd*, the plaintiff was Swiss and the defendant was incorporated in the UK, but conducting business exclusively in Argentina.[111] Jurisdiction was based on the Brussels Convention even though Switzerland was not Party to it and the plaintiff was Swiss. (At that time the Lugano Convention was not yet in force, so Switzerland could be seen as a normal third State.)

WHAT IF THE PLAINTIFF AND THE DEFENDANT ARE DOMICILED IN THE SAME EU MEMBER STATE?

2.74 Determining this is important for relations with third States, since it is an indication of the exact boundary between Brussels I and national rules on civil jurisdiction. As has been pointed out, the nationalities of the parties are irrelevant for Brussels I.[112] Accordingly a Canadian and an Australian who live in London would be concerned with this delimitation.

2.75 In principle a case where the plaintiff and the defendant are domiciled in the same EU Member State is purely internal. Lacking internationality, Brussels I does not apply.[113] The Jenard Report states that the Brussels regime 'alters the rules of jurisdiction in force in each Contracting State only where an international element is involved.'[114] A cross-border link was necessary to trigger the Convention, and later the Regulation.

2.76 However, the matter does not end there. A case before an EU Member State court may become international if a second defendant is domiciled in another state. The case then being international, Brussels I would apply. Whether the second defendant is domiciled in another EU Member State

---

[110] QBCMI 96/0476/B, judgment of 30 April 1997 (England), Court of Appeal (Civil Division), unreported.

[111] [1992] Ch 72. This case is also discussed in chapter 5 below, para 5. 77 and following, with regard to the compatibility of the doctrine of *forum non conveniens* with EU jurisdiction rules.

[112] Para 2.045 above.

[113] See also the discussion on the limitation of the EU civil jurisdiction rules to international cases in chapter 1 above, para 1.59.

[114] Jenard Report on the 1968 version of the Brussels Convention; OJ C 59, 5 March 1979, 1 (Jenard Report), 8.

or a third State does not influence the international nature of the dispute. This means that the basis of jurisdiction, being the domicile of the first defendant, would be Brussels I instead of national law. The European Court of Justice clarified this rule in *Owusu*, where both the plaintiff and the defendant were domiciled in England and the action was brought in the High Court there.[115] The facts of the case took place in Jamaica and the co-defendants were domiciled in that country. The question arose whether the Brussels Convention applied to this case. The European Court of Justice had little difficulty in finding that the Brussels Convention governed the situation. How a case became international was of less importance to the court. What was important was the fact that it was international, which made the Brussels Convention and its rule on the domicile of the defendant applicable.[116]

CONCLUSION

A primary delimitation of Brussels I is that it provides jurisdiction rules **2.77** for cases where the defendant is domiciled in the EU. If the defendant is domiciled in a third State, Brussels I does not prescribe a separate set of rules, but refers to the national rules on jurisdiction of the Member States. This reference to national law has the effect of incorporating those rules into the system of the Regulation. Such rules obtain an EU blessing. If a defendant from a third State is subjected to such jurisdiction rule in one of the EU Member States, the resulting judgment will take effect not only in that state, but in all other EU Member States. This effect of Brussels I is seen as unfair towards defendants from third States.

---

[115] *Owusu*, note 109 above; commentary: E Peel, 'Forum non conveniens and European ideals' [2005] LMCLQ 363–377; A Briggs, 'Forum non conveniens and ideal Europeans' [2005] LMCLQ 378–382; A Briggs, 'The Death of Harrods: Forum non conveniens and the European Court' [2005] LQR 535–540; R Fentiman, 'Civil jurisdiction and third States: Owusu and after' [2006] CML Rev 705–734; BJ Rodger, 'Forum non conveniens Post-Owusu' [2006] Journal of Private International Law 71–97; C Chalas, case note in [2005] Revue critique de droit international privé 708–722; G Cuniberti, 'Forum non conveniens and the Brussels Convention' [2006] ICLQ 973–981; H Duintjer Tebbens, 'From Jamaica with pain' in P van der Grinten & T Heukels (eds), Cross Borders. Essays in European and Private International Law, Nationality Law and Islamic Law in honour of Frans van der Velden (Deventer: Kluwer, 2006) 95–103; C Thiele, 'Forum non conveniens im Lichte europäischen Gemeinschaftsrechts' [2002] Recht der Internationalen Wirtschaft 696–700 at 689–699; H Tagaras, 'Chronique de jurisprudence de la Cour de justice relative à la Convention de Bruxelles' [2006] Cahiers de droit européen 483–553, 507–514.

[116] The question of additional defendants domiciled outside the EU will be discussed later in this chapter: para 2.131 and following.

2.78 The domicile of the plaintiff is irrelevant, although this rule might in some instances lead to inequitable results. The reasoning behind this choice is that the rules are supposed to protect defendants domiciled in the EU. This basic cornerstone has further specifications, as will be indicated in the remainder of this chapter. It also has to give way when other cornerstones, discussed in the following chapters, regulate the matter.

C. THE JURISDICTION RULES OF BRUSSELS II *BIS*

Article 3 of Brussels II *bis*:

1. *In matters relating to divorce, legal separation or marriage annulment, jurisdiction shall lie with the courts of the Member State*
   a) *in whose territory:*
      the spouses are habitually resident, or
      the spouses were last habitually resident, insofar as one of them still resides there, or
      the respondent is habitually resident, or
      in the event of a joint application, either of the spouses is habitually resident, or
      the applicant is habitually resident if he or she resided there for at least a year immediately before the application was made, or
      the applicant is habitually resident if he or she resided there for at least six months immediately before the application was made and is either a national of the Member State in question or, in the case of the United Kingdom and Ireland, has his or her 'domicile' there;
   b) *of the nationality of both spouses or, in the case of the United Kingdom and Ireland, of the domicile of both spouses.*
2. *For the purpose of this Regulation, 'domicile' shall have the same meaning as it has under the legal systems of the United Kingdom and Ireland.*

Article 5 of Brussels II *bis*:

Without prejudice to Article 3, a court of a Member State that has given a judgment on a legal separation shall also have jurisdiction for converting that judgment into a divorce, if the law of that Member State so provides.

Article 6 of Brussels II *bis*:

A spouse who:
   (a) is habitually resident in the territory of a Member State; or
   (b) is a national of a Member State, or, in the case of the United Kingdom and Ireland, has his or her 'domicile' in the territory of one of the latter Member States,
may be sued in another Member State only in accordance with Articles 3, 4 and 5.

Article 7 of Brussels II *bis*:

1. *Where no court of a Member State has jurisdiction pursuant to Articles 3, 4 and 5, jurisdiction shall be determined, in each Member State, by the laws of that State.*
2. *As against a respondent who is not habitually resident and is not either a national of a Member State or, in the case of the United Kingdom and Ireland, does not have his 'domicile' within the territory of one of the latter Member States, any national of a Member State who is habitually resident within the territory of another Member State may, like the nationals of that State, avail himself of the rules of jurisdiction applicable in that State.*

Article 8 of Brussels II *bis*:

1. *The courts of a Member State shall have jurisdiction in matters of parental responsibility over a child who is habitually resident in that Member State at the time the court is seised.*
. . .

Article 12 of Brussels II *bis*:

1. *The courts of a Member State exercising jurisdiction by virtue of Article 3 on an application for divorce, legal separation or marriage annulment shall have jurisdiction in any matter relating to parental responsibility connected with that application where:*
   a) at least one of the spouses has parental responsibility in relation to the child; and
   b) the jurisdiction of the courts has been accepted expressly or otherwise in an unequivocal manner by the spouses and by the holders of parental responsibility, at the time the court is seised, and is in the superior interests of the child.

. . .

4. *Where the child has his or her habitual residence in the territory of a third State which is not a contracting party to the Hague Convention of 19 October 1996 on jurisdiction, applicable law, recognition, enforcement and cooperation in respect of parental responsibility and measures for the protection of children, jurisdiction under the Article shall be deemed to be in the child's interest, in particular if it is found impossible to hold proceedings in the third State in question.*

Article 14 of Brussels II *bis*:

Where no court of a Member State has jurisdiction pursuant to Articles 8 to 13, jurisdiction shall be determined, in each Member State, by the laws of that State.

INTRODUCTION

2.79 This section deals mainly with Brussels II *bis*. It also refers to the proposed Maintenance Regulation[117] and proposed amendments to Brussels II *bis*.[118] The reason for treating these Regulations alongside Brussels I is twofold. First, the Brussels II *bis* and Maintenance Regulations provide a natural extension of Brussels I and an examination of the one necessarily leads to comparison with the other. Second, Brussels II *bis* provides a fine example of one-sided EU rules that are difficult to understand from the point of view of third States. The proposed Maintenance Regulation's rules are also drawn up with EU litigating parties in mind, but they seem more balanced and equitable.

2.80 I will use the numbering of the articles as in Brussels II *bis* (which became applicable on 1 March 2005), although reference will be made to Brussels II, its predecessor, for the sake of completeness and history.[119]

2.81 The new family law Regulations (Brussels II and II *bis*) of the EU and their scope of application caused, and still cause, a great deal of discussion.[120]

---

[117] Proposal for a Council Regulation on Jurisdiction, Applicable law, Recognition and Enforcement of Decisions and Cooperation in Matters relating to Maintenance Obligations of 15 December 2005, COM(2005) 649 final. This Regulation will apply neither in Denmark nor in the United Kingdom (except if it decides later to opt in), but it will apply in Ireland.

[118] Proposal for a Council Regulation amending Regulation (EC) No 2201/2003 as regards jurisdiction and introducing rules concerning applicable law in matrimonial matters of 17 July 2006, COM(2006) 399 final. This Regulation will not apply in Denmark and it seems that the United Kingdom and Ireland would not opt in, so that it would not apply in those states either.

[119] Art 72 of Brussels II *bis*.

[120] For instance P Beaumont & G Moir, 'Brussels Convention II: A New Private International Law Instrument in Family Matters for the European Union or the European Community' [1995] ELR 268–288; J Meeusen, 'Nieuw internationaal procesrecht op komst in Europa: het EEX II-verdrag' [1998–1999] *Rechtskundig Weekblad* 755–758; M Jänterä-Jareborg, 'Marriage dissolution in an integrated Europe: The 1998 European Union Convention on Jurisdiction and the Recognition and Enforcement of Judgments in Matrimonial Matters (Brussels II Convention)' [1999] *Yearbook for Private International Law* 1–36; S Drouet, 'La communautarisation de "Bruxelles II". Chronique d'une mutation juridique' [2001] *Revue du Marché commun et de l'Union européenne* 247–257; V Van den Eeckhout, ''Europees' echtscheiden. Bevoegdheid en erkenning van beslissingen op basis van de EG Verordening 1347/2000 van 29 mei 2000' in H Van Houtte & M Pertegás Sender (eds), *Het nieuwe Europese IPR: van verdrag naar verordening* (Antwerp: Intersentia, 2001) 69–101 at 76–82; J-Y Carlier, S Francq & J-L Van Boxstael, 'Le règlement de Bruxelles II Compétence, reconnaissance et exécution en matière matrimoniale et en matière de responsabilité parentale' [2001] *Journal des tribunaux* 73–90, at 77–79; N Watté & H Boularbah, 'Les nouvelles règles de conflit de jurisdictions en matière de désunion des époux. Le règlement dit "Bruxelles II"' [2001] *Journal des tribunaux* 369–378 at 374; P McEleavy, 'The Brussels II Regulation: How the European Community has moved into

The basic problem lies in two contradictory provisions, which seem crucial for any attempt at finding the borders of the Regulation. At the same time Brussels II *bis* does not contain a clear structure with three main rules indicating its outer limits, as does Brussels I (with some nuances). Brussels II *bis* granted great importance to the availability of fora for separating couples and parents seeking custody of or access rights to their children. In this preoccupation, which is doubtless an important one for those concerned, a consideration of the exact extent of the Regulation seem to have been pushed to the background. This goal is further pursued in the proposed amendments to the Regulation.[121]

The resulting confusion is best dealt with under two sub-headings: first **2.82** divorce, legal separation, and marriage annulment, and second parental responsibility. Reference will then be made to the interaction between Brussels II *bis* and the Hague Conventions on Child Abduction[122] and the Protection of Children.[123]

SCOPE FOR DIVORCE, LEGAL SEPARATION, AND MARRIAGE ANNULMENT

The jurisdiction rules

The jurisdiction rules of Brussels II *bis* differ greatly from those of Brussels **2.83** I. Instead of a hierarchy of rules, the Regulation just creates alternative bases of jurisdiction. The idea was to create many possible routes to court in a situation of family difficulty. When international families fall apart, people often move, whether it is back to the country of their nationality or to another country. These people must have easy access to justice.

The Borrás Report summarizes four elements that have to be taken into **2.84** consideration before assigning jurisdiction in family law matters: the interests of the parties, flexible rules to deal with mobility, individual

---

Family Law' [2002] ICLQ 883–908 at 886–887; ThM de Boer, 'Jurisdiction and Enforcement in International Family Law: A Labyrinth of European and International Legislation' [2002] *Netherlands International Law Review* 307–345 at 313–314 and 327–328; P McEleavy, 'The Communitarization of Divorce Rules: What Impact for English and Scottish Law?' [2004] ICLQ 605–642 at 610–617; E Caracciolo di Torella & A Masselot, 'Under Construction: EU family law' [2004] ELR 32–51.

[121] Proposed amendments to Brussels II *bis*, note 118 above, Explanatory Memorandum, 8–9.

[122] Hague Convention of 25 October 1980 on the Civil Aspects of International Child Abduction, available at <http://www.hcch.net>.

[123] Hague Convention of 19 October 1996 on Jurisdiction, Applicable Law, Recognition, Enforcement and Co-operation in respect of Parental Responsibility and Measures for the Protection of Children, <http://www.hcch.net>.

needs, and legal certainty.[124] These are all important considerations worthy to pursue in an international instrument. However, if that international instrument is only applicable in a certain area, there are additional elements that should be considered: the borders of the instrument, subsidiarity, and the concerns of non-EU parties. Family ties, like international trade, do not stay within the EU borders. International families that are linked to both the EU and a third State seem to have been left steeped in uncertainty.

2.85 Seven alternative bases of jurisdiction are provided:

(a) the habitual residence of both spouses;
(b) the last habitual residence of both spouses if one of them still resides there;
(c) the habitual residence of the respondent;
(d) in the case of a joint application, the habitual residence of either of the spouses;
(e) the habitual residence of the applicant if he or she resided there for at least a year immediately before the application;
(f) the habitual residence of the applicant if he or she has resided there for at least six months immediately before the application and has the nationality of that state, or, in the case of Ireland or the United Kingdom, is domiciled there; and
(g) the state of the nationality of both spouses or, in the case of Ireland or the United Kingdom, the domicile of both spouses.[125]

The court that has jurisdiction to hear the case also subsequently has jurisdiction to convert a legal separation that it granted into a divorce.[126] This basis for jurisdiction is necessary because not all legal systems know the phenomenon of legal separation.

The proposal for an amendment to Brussels II *bis* includes a limited possibility for spouses to select a forum to hear their dispute.[127]

Scope: habitual residence and nationality

2.86 On the one hand, Brussels II *bis* states that a spouse who is habitually resident in the territory of an EU Member State or is an EU national (or a

---

[124] Borrás Report on the Convention, drawn up on the basis of Article K.3 of the Treaty on the European Union, on Jurisdiction and the Recognition and Enforcement of Judgments in Matrimonial Matters; OJ C 221 of 16 July 1998, para 27, p 37.

[125] Art 3 of Brussels II *bis*.

[126] Art 5 of Brussels II *bis*.

[127] Art 3a of Brussels II *bis*.

domiciliary of Ireland or the United Kingdom) may only be sued in another EU Member State court on one of the Regulation's bases for jurisdiction.[128] This rule seems similar to that of Brussels I.

Scope: EU jurisdiction in the first place

The next provision of the Regulation promptly states that where no court **2.87** in an EU Member State has jurisdiction under the rules of Brussels II *bis*, the national laws of the Member States shall determine jurisdiction.[129] This provision also seems to be drawing a borderline for the Regulation. That borderline would be where each basis for jurisdiction lies. In other words, an EU court first has to determine whether there is any EU court that could have jurisdiction according to the Regulation. If so, the Regulation applies. The jurisdiction rules of the Regulation, one could say, always impose themselves.

This taking charge by the rules themselves is also seen in the proposed **2.88** Maintenance Regulation. This Regulation clearly states that it is not limited to defendants domiciled or habitually resident in the EU.[130] After the coming into force of the Regulation, a court in an EU Member State seised of a maintenance action will always have to start by looking for a basis for jurisdiction in the Regulation. It should not consider the habitual residences, domiciles or nationalities of the parties before it.

Two examples

To understand the problem of Brussels II *bis*, one has to consider national **2.89** bases of jurisdiction that are wider, on the one hand, and others that are narrower, on the other hand, than those of the Regulation.

For example, under French national law, a French court has jurisdiction **2.90** if the plaintiff is a French national.[131] A French woman could marry a Mexican and they could stay for their entire married lives in Mexico. When the woman returns to the EU to live in Belgium and wants to file for divorce, should she rely on Brussels II *bis*, or could she file immediately under the French national rule just mentioned? Reading only Article 6 of the Regulation, one would conclude that since the defendant is habitually resident in a third State and has the nationality of a third State, the

---

[128] Art 6 of Brussels II *bis*.
[129] Art 7 of Brussels II *bis*.
[130] Rec 10 of the proposed Maintenance Regulation.
[131] Art 14 of the French code civil (Civil Code).

Regulation should not be applied. Thus the French plaintiff could always rely on the French national rule (jurisdiction because of her French nationality). Reading only Article 7 of the Regulation, one would first ask whether there is jurisdiction on the basis of the Regulation. Since there is none for the first year after the plaintiff moved to Belgium, the French courts would have jurisdiction on the basis of French national law. However, if she stayed in Belgium for more than one year, the Belgian courts would have jurisdiction on the basis of the Regulation.[132]

2.91 The second example regards the converse problem: a legal system that has narrower rules than the Regulation. For instance, the Belgian legislator used Brussels II *bis* as a model when drawing up the similar provisions for the Code de droit international privé (Private International Law Code).[133] The legislator, however, did not go quite as far as the Regulation. Therefore Belgium now has narrower bases of jurisdiction on this matter than the Regulation provides. For instance, this new Belgian code does not claim jurisdiction for a plaintiff who has lived in an EU Member State for six months and has the nationality of that state. Changing the example slightly, suppose that a Belgian woman marries a Mexican man and they live in Mexico for their entire married lives. The Belgian spouse returns to Belgium and wants to file for divorce there. Reading only Article 6, one would once again conclude that the Regulation is not applicable. In this example, however, the Belgian woman would only have Belgian national law to base her claim on, and so would only be able to institute proceedings after one year's residence. Reading Article 7, one would first check whether there were a basis of jurisdiction under Brussels II *bis*. This being the case after six months,[134] the Belgian national law provision would never apply. Narrower rules on the matters regulated by Brussels II *bis* are therefore senseless.

Solution?

2.92 Trying to find a solution by juxtaposing the two conflicting provisions remains difficult.[135] The Swedish Högsta Domstolen (Supreme Court) has

---

[132] Art 3(1)(a) of Brussels II *bis*, a fifth possibility.

[133] Belgian Code de droit international privé, Act of 16 July 2004, *Belgisch Staatsblad* of 27 July 2004. For the position in the Netherlands, see PMM Mostermans, 'Nieuw Europees scheidingsprocesrecht onder de loep. De rechtsmacht bij echtscheiding' [2001] *Netherlands International Law Review* 293–305 at 302–304.

[134] Art 3(1)(a) of Brussels II *bis*, sixth possibility.

[135] Following this route, see Meeusen, 'Nieuw internationaal procesrecht', note 120 above, at 756; J-Y Carlier *et al*, note 120 above, at 77–79; M Traest, *De verhouding van de Europese*

requested the European Court of Justice for a preliminary ruling on the issue:

The respondent in a case concerning divorce is neither resident in a Member State nor a citizen of a Member State. May the case be heard by a court in a Member State which does not have jurisdiction under Article 3 [of the Brussels II Regulation], even though a court in another Member State may have jurisdiction by application of one of the rules on jurisdiction set out in Article 3? [136]

Many authors propose reading the two provisions together in the following way: Article 7 determines the scope of the Regulation. Article 6 is not relevant for the scope, but merely states that, as against EU defendants (defendants that are habitually resident in the EU, or that have an EU nationality), national bases of jurisdiction may no longer be used.[137] This interpretation could make sense, but it solicits an objection on grounds of subsidiarity. The EU can legislate on family law only to the extent that the rules are necessary for the proper functioning of the internal market. If the matter has no or a very weak link with the European judicial area, whether or not an EU Member State court has jurisdiction to hear a divorce probably cannot be regulated more effectively by EU legislation. The examples discussed above have no bearing on the internal market. Recognition in another EU Member State is only a future possibility. If all possible future recognitions of divorces were taken into account, however, it would have been simpler to replace all national bases of jurisdiction. Furthermore, the view of these authors prompts the question: what does Article 6 mean by the 'exclusive nature of jurisdiction under Articles 3, 4 and 5'? How can the provision make the jurisdictional bases exclusive without specifying *something* that they exclude? Is not that *something* the national bases for jurisdiction? If so, then the provision seems to demarcate the border between the Regulation and national rules and is in this sense a scope rule.

Others are of the view that Article 6 should be granted preference.[138] One **2.93** may then revert to the national bases of jurisdiction only if a defendant is not habitually resident in the EU and does not have EU nationality, or is

gemeenschap tot de Conferentie van Den Haag voor het Internationaal Privaatrecht (Antwerp: Maklu, 2003) 234–235.

[136] Case C-68/07 *Kerstin Sundelind Lopez v Miquel Enrique Lopez Lizazo*, reference for a preliminary ruling on 12 February 2007, pending.

[137] See, for example, Meeusen, 'Nieuw internationaal procesrecht', note 120 above; B Ancel & H Muir Watt, 'La désunion européenne: le Règlement dit "Bruxelles II"' [2001] *Revue critique de droit international privé* 403–457, at 412–413; Carlier *et al*, note 120 above, at 77–79; V Van den Eeckhout, note 120 above, 78–82.

[138] See McEleavy, 'Brussels II', note 120 above, 886; McEleavy, 'Communitarization of Divorce Rules', note 120 above, 614.

not domiciled in Ireland or the United Kingdom. This approach limits the Regulation to its goals: within the EU.

2.94 In a proposal to amend Brussels II *bis*, the European Commission might have admitted what it had actually meant.[139] The proposal deletes Article 6. The explanatory memorandum states that the provision caused confusion and was superfluous.[140] This probably means that it has always been the intention of the legislator that Article 7 should determine the scope of the Regulation's jurisdiction rules. Thus, to the extent that it has been indicated above that the two provisions contradict each other, Article 7 should prevail. The applicability of the Regulation's jurisdiction rules can then be described in three steps.

2.95 A court in an EU Member State must always take the Regulation as a starting point. In this context, the domiciles, habitual residences, and nationalities of the parties are irrelevant. The court has to go straight to the jurisdiction rules and seek a basis upon which it could assume jurisdiction. If it finds such a basis for jurisdiction, the court can hear the case and there is no need to proceed to steps two and three.

2.96 If it finds none, the second step is to consider whether courts in other EU Member States have Regulation-based jurisdiction. Of course, in this step the court takes into account the same rules as in the first step, but with a different mindset. Now, it is not concerned with its own jurisdiction, but considers where in the EU there might be jurisdiction. If it finds that the rules in Brussels II *bis* grant jurisdiction to the courts of some other EU Member State, the investigation stops here.

2.97 The court turns to the third step only if the Regulation provides for jurisdiction neither in its own EU Member State, nor in any other. This step leads to the national rules on jurisdiction and the court can now apply them. If these rules are based on nationality, they must also be made available to any EU national habitually resident in the EU Member State of the court, in cases where the defendant is not habitually resident in an EU Member State and does not have an EU nationality (or in the case of Ireland and the United Kingdom, is not domiciled there).[141] Thus, any EU national habitually resident in France would be able to use these provisions if neither the French courts nor the courts of any other EU Member

---

[139] Proposed amendments to Brussels II *bis*, note 118 above.

[140] Ibid, Explanatory Memorandum, 8.

[141] Art 7(2) of Brussels II *bis*. For instance, this will be the case for Arts 14 and 15 of the French code civil (civil code), which always give French plaintiffs and French defendants access to the French courts.

State have jurisdiction on the basis of the Regulation (the first and second steps).[142] This will be the case, for instance, for a Maltese woman moving to France and wishing to divorce her Californian husband, who lives in California. However, reference is only made to rules based on nationality and no mention is made of the rules based on domicile. If the Maltese woman moves to England instead of France, she will not be able to rely on the English provisions granting immediate jurisdiction to divorce if she is not domiciled there herself: the rule is only valid for domiciliaries of England and is not extended to all other EU nationals habitually resident in England.[143] This extension goes quite far in discriminating against defendants from outside the EU. Not only can they be subjected to exorbitant bases for jurisdiction, but also these bases are elaborated. The EU's concern is probably that there should be no discrimination between different EU nationalities, but the effect seems completely disproportionate. To make matters worse, these judgments will be recognized throughout the EU.

The proposal to amend Brussels II *bis*, however, will modify the provision **2.98** on residual jurisdiction so that the three-step procedure will change. The residual bases of jurisdiction will no longer come into play where no court in an EU Member State has jurisdiction, but neither of the spouses is habitually resident in the EU, and they do not share a common EU nationality. Thus the distinction between defendants will return. In this situation the Regulation will contain two autonomous bases of jurisdiction and there will be no reference any more to the national bases. This will strengthen the double character of the Regulation since there will be complete harmonization of jurisdiction rules. However, these defendants will be triable in fora of a past habitual residence (of at least three years, but without specification of how long ago it might have been), or of the nationality of one of the spouses. It is relevant to note here that jurisdiction based on the nationality of one of the parties has been seen as exorbitant since the first version of the Brussels Convention (1968). How has it managed to find its way into an EU instrument now? In its Explanatory Memorandum the Commission states that, in the application of the current rules, there might be situations where no court in the EU, nor in a third State, has jurisdiction.[144] No examples are mentioned and it is hard to think of any. The EU's rules are broad already and in most other legal systems there would at least be jurisdiction at the place of the domicile or habitual residence of the defendant. Furthermore, the Commission states that third State judgments

---

[142] On the basis of Art 14 of the French code civil (civil code).

[143] See McEleavy, 'Communitarization of Divorce Rules', note 120 above, 614–615.

[144] Proposed amendments to Brussels II *bis*, note 118 above, Explanatory Memorandum, 8.

cannot be recognized on the basis of the Regulation. This is of course true, but it can hardly be a justification for jurisdiction rules that might be exorbitant in some situations.

2.99 The proposed Maintenance Regulation contains a structure similar to the three steps of the current Brussels II *bis*. First a court must consider the main jurisdiction rules of the Regulation, including the rules of a forum clause and on the voluntary appearance of the defendant.[145] If it does not have jurisdiction, the court must consider whether a court in another EU Member State has jurisdiction according to any of those rules. The third step differs, in that the provision on the residual bases of jurisdiction does not contain a reference to national law. The Regulation itself stipulates two residual bases: a court of the EU Member State of the common nationality or, in the case of maintenance claims between spouses or ex-spouses, the last common habitual residence no longer than a year previously.[146]

The double nature of Brussels II *bis*

2.100 Brussels II *bis* contains the same flaw as Brussels I. These are supposed to be double instruments, but the parallel between the jurisdictional rules and the rules on recognition and enforcement is incomplete.[147] All judgments can be recognized, irrespective of whether jurisdiction had been based on the Regulation or on national rules. This can bring about unfair results for parties habitually resident in third States, since exorbitant bases of jurisdiction used against them can lead to a judgment that has effects not only in the EU Member State where it was granted, but also in all other EU Member States. Brussels II *bis* further prejudices defendants from third States by the elaboration of national bases for jurisdiction against them. These judgments can then be recognized and enforced throughout the EU, even though the jurisdictional grounds have not been completely harmonized and exorbitant national rules are even extended. A possible solution could be to harmonize all jurisdiction rules, as is done in the proposed Maintenance Regulation, but this will again pose problems of subsidiarity. If all jurisdiction rules are harmonized, there should be no differentiation between various groups of defendants, as is the case in the current proposal to amend Brussels II *bis*.

---

[145] Arts 3–5 of the proposed Maintenance Regulation.
[146] Art 6 of the proposed Maintenance Regulation.
[147] See the general discussion on single and double instruments in chapter 1 above, para 1.08.

SCOPE FOR PARENTAL RESPONSIBILITY

The jurisdiction rules

The basic rule in cases of parental responsibility is that jurisdiction is given **2.101**
to the court where the child has habitual residence.[148] For four other cases
the Regulation creates special rules that derogate from the general basis of
jurisdiction. These are the (limited) continuing jurisdiction if the child
moves, prorogation of jurisdiction, jurisdiction in cases of child abduction,
and jurisdiction regarding the return of the child.

If the child legally moves to a different EU Member State, while a person **2.102**
that has rights of access stays in the first EU Member State, and a court in
that first Member State had given a judgment on rights of access, the courts
of the same Member State retain jurisdiction to amend that order for a
period of three months, unless the person who has rights accepts the jurisdiction of the courts of the state where the child now resides.[149] This rule
does not seem to extend jurisdiction in the EU if the child moves to a third
State.

The court of the state where a child had habitual residence just before **2.103**
being abducted will maintain jurisdiction until all persons and institutions
with rights of custody have acquiesced in the removal or retention, or the
child has resided in the new state for at least a year and return is no longer
possible or sought (by persons or institutions that have custody rights).[150]

Where a child's habitual residence cannot be determined and there can be **2.104**
no jurisdiction on the basis of prorogation, the courts of the Member State
where the child is present shall have jurisdiction. This rule particularly
applies to refugee children, or children internationally displaced because
of disturbances in their country.

If it is in the best interests of the child, the following courts can be chosen: **2.105**

- the court that has jurisdiction to grant a divorce, legal separation, or annulment of marriage in the same proceedings, if at least one of the spouses
  has parental responsibility over the child; or
- the courts of an EU Member State with which the child has a substantial
  connection (for instance the child's nationality, or the habitual residence
  of one of the holders of parental responsibility).[151]

---

[148] Art 8 of Brussels II *bis*.
[149] Art 9 of Brussels II *bis*.
[150] Art 10 of Brussels II *bis*.
[151] Art 12 of Brussels II *bis*.

2.106 Lastly, Brussels II *bis* provides the same rule on residual jurisdiction as it does for divorce. If no EU Member State court has jurisdiction according to the rules mentioned, the national rules of the Member States will determine jurisdiction.[152]

Habitual residence of the child

2.107 The basic criterion for the scope of Brussels II *bis* over parental responsibility is the habitual residence of the child: if the child resides in the EU the Regulation will apply, otherwise it will not.[153] However, this rule is not without exception. In some instances the mere presence of the child can convey jurisdiction. This is specifically so if the habitual residence of a child cannot be established.[154] This rule can be useful in the case of refugee children or children displaced internationally because of disturbances in their country. The provision should not, however, become an easy way to apply the Regulation instead of genuinely trying to ascertain the true habitual residence of a child, especially if this is probably in a third State. Similarly, 'disturbances' should be given a strict interpretation, and always with the best interests of the child in mind.

Chosen forum

2.108 If an EU court has jurisdiction in an action for divorce, legal separation or marriage annulment, and parental responsibility for the children is at issue, the spouses may choose that court to hear the case on parental responsibility if it is in the superior interests of the child.[155] These children might be third State nationals and have a habitual residence in a third State.

2.109 In the same fashion, a court in a state with which a child has a substantial connection may also be chosen. This provision can influence the personal scope of the Regulation: the child in question does not have to be habitually resident in the EU.[156] The Regulation can be applied in cases where a child lives in a third State that is not a Party to the Hague Child Protection Convention. This application enters through the back door of a presumption: when choice of forum is a possibility, the requirement is that the jurisdiction must be in the best interests of the child. If the child lives in a third State that is not Party to the Hague Child Protection

---

[152] Art 14 of Brussels II *bis*.
[153] See also de Boer, note 120 above, 328.
[154] Art 13 of Brussels II *bis*.
[155] Art 12(1) of Brussels II *bis*.
[156] Art 12(3) of Brussels II *bis*.

Convention, the jurisdiction in an EU Member State is presumed to be in his or her best interests.[157] This is not a hard and fast rule, but a possibility. The best interests of the child should of course always be the main consideration.

Abduction from one EU Member State to another

For cases of child abduction, the Regulation contains a specific rule governing when it applies. The Regulation deals with unlawful removals of children from one EU Member State to another and with the unlawful retention of children in an EU Member State other than that of their habitual residence.[158] When children are abducted from the EU to a third State or from a third State to the EU, the Regulation refers to the Hague Child Abduction Convention.   **2.110**

Residual jurisdiction

The section on jurisdiction with regard to parental responsibility includes a rule stating that if no court in an EU Member State has jurisdiction under the Regulation, jurisdiction may be based on the national rules of an EU Member State.[159] This provision is similar to the one for divorce, described above. The three-step approach that has been explained must also be followed in the application of this rule.[160] Thus a court in an EU Member State will first check its own jurisdiction. If it has none, it would examine whether a court in another EU Member State has jurisdiction under the Regulation. Only if that search also yields no result may the court revert to its national rules on jurisdiction. The proposal to amend Brussels II *bis* will not change this approach for parental responsibility cases.   **2.111**

INTERACTION WITH THE HAGUE CONVENTIONS ON CHILD
ABDUCTION AND CHILD PROTECTION

Brussels II *bis* operates in a field in which there are two recent Hague Conventions: one concerning Child Abduction[161] and one on the Protection of Children.[162] These Conventions, which are relevant in the context   **2.112**

---

[157] Art 12(4) of Brussels II *bis*.
[158] Arts 10 and 11 of Brussels II *bis*.
[159] Art 14 of Brussels II *bis*.
[160] See above paras 2.95–2.97.
[161] Child Abduction Convention, note 122 above.
[162] Hague Convention of 19 October 1996 on Jurisdiction, Applicable Law, Recognition, Enforcement and Co-operation in respect of Parental Responsibility and Measures for the

of parental responsibility and not those of divorce, legal separation, or marriage annulment, will briefly be discussed in turn.[163]

The Hague Convention on Child Abduction (1980)

2.113 All 27 EU Member States are Party to the Hague Child Abduction Convention, which currently has 80 Contracting States.[164] This Convention establishes mechanisms for the prompt return of abducted children and facilitates administrative cooperation for that purpose. The discussion here will be limited to the topics dealt with by Brussels II *bis*. In this regard, recognition and enforcement will also be briefly explained.

2.114 The relation between Brussels II *bis* and the Hague Child Abduction Convention is a complicated one.[165] On the one hand, the Regulation states in Recital no 17:

[i]n cases of wrongful removal or retention of a child, the return of the child should be obtained without delay, and to this end the Hague Convention of 25 October 1980 would continue to apply as complemented by the provisions of this Regulation . . .

On the other hand, Article 60 states:

[i]n relations between Member States, this Regulation shall take precedence over the following Conventions in so far as they concern matters governed by this

---

Protection of Children, <http://www.hcch.net>.

[163] See also PR Beaumont & PE McEleavy, *The Hague Convention on International Child Abduction* (Oxford: Oxford University Press, 1999); C Gonzalez Beilfuss, 'EC legislation in matters of parental responsibility and third States' in A Nuyts & N Watté, *International Civil Litigation in Europe and Relations with Third States* (Brussels: Bruylant, 2005) 493–507; A Schulz, 'Internationale Regelungen zum Sorge- und Umgangsrecht' [2003] *Zeitschrift für das gesamte Familienrecht* 336–348; A Schulz, 'Die Zeichnung des Haager Kinderschutz-Übereinkommens von 1996 und der Kompromiss zur Brüssel-IIa Verordnung' [2003] *Zeitschrift für das gesamte Familienrecht* 1351–1354; P McEleavy, 'The New Child Abduction regime in the European Union: Symbiotic Relationship or Forced Partnership?' [2005] *Journal of Private International Law* 5–34; S Armstrong, 'L'articulation du règlement "Bruxelles II *bis*" et des Conventions de La Haye de 1980 et 1996' (2005) 139 *Droit & Patrimoine* 46–51.

[164] Apart from the EU Member States these are Albania, Argentina, Armenia, Australia, Bahamas, Belarus, Belize, Bosnia and Herzegovina, Brazil, Burkina Faso, Canada, Chile, China, Columbia, Costa Rica, Croatia, Dominican Republic, Ecuador, El Salvador, Fiji, Georgia, Guatemala, Honduras, Iceland, Israel, Mauritius, Mexico, Moldova, Monaco, Montenegro, New Zealand, Nicaragua, Norway, Panama, Paraguay, Peru, Saint Kitts and Nevis, San Marino, Serbia, South Africa, Sri Lanka, Switzerland, Thailand, Trinidad and Tobago, the former Yugoslav Republic of Macedonia, Turkey, Turmenistan, Ukraine, United States of America, Uruguay, Uzbekistan, Venezuela and Zimbabwe; see <http://www.hcch.net>.

[165] See also McEleavy, 'The New Child Abduction regime', note 163 above.

Regulation . . . (e) the Hague Convention of 25 October 1980 on the Civil Aspects of international Child Abduction.

This seems to be a contradiction; the truth lies somewhere between the two **2.115** provisions. In fact the final text of the Regulation contains a compromise between EU Member States that wanted to replace the Hague Convention entirely and those that wanted to keep it and not impose a separate set of EU rules in the field of child abduction.[166] Thus the Regulation refers to the Hague Convention, but modifies a few of its rules as between the EU Member States.[167]

It is important to note at the outset that the modified rules apply only if **2.116** the child is to be returned from one EU Member State to another. This is perhaps the weakest point of Brussels II *bis*: it has created two different regimes for child abductions. The Hague Convention has attempted to establish uniform principles in this field, as an expression of the rather broadly phrased children's rights under the UN Convention on the Rights of the Child (1989). A certain degree of success can be ascribed to the Hague Convention, based on its large number of States Party and on the case law the Convention has produced.[168] Even more importantly, it is said that the Hague Convention has an important deterrent effect on parents contemplating unlawful removal or retention.[169] While the EU harmoniously formed part of this regime, Brussels II *bis* creates a distinction so that there are now different rules on child abduction. In reality the rules are not substantially different. However lawyers, and particularly judges, are confronted with different criteria in similar situations, depending on whether a child has been abducted within the EU on the one hand, or from a third State to the EU or from the EU to a third State on the other hand. The existence of different regimes is not a positive development: children are abducted within, to, and from EU Member States.[170]

In essence the adapted rules of Brussels II *bis* indicate more trust between **2.117** EU Member State courts. For example, the Hague Convention provides that an authority is not bound to order the return of a child if there is a grave risk that the return would expose the child to physical or psychological harm

---

[166] For a detailed analysis of the negotiation process, see McEleavy, 'The New Child Abduction regime', note 163 above, 6–16.

[167] Arts 11 and 42 of Brussels II *bis*.

[168] See the Hague Conference on Private International Law's database containing case law: <http://www.incadat.com>.

[169] See Beaumont & McEleavy, note 163 above, 4 & 155.

[170] See Armstrong, note 163 above, 49.

or otherwise place him or her in an intolerable situation.[171] Brussels II *bis* states that EU Member State courts may not refuse the return of a child on that basis if adequate arrangements have been made to secure the protection of the child after return.[172] Thus, within the EU, refusals of immediate return have to be limited to a minimum. Whether this rule, testimonial of EU trust, is justified and will work fairly in practice remains to be seen.[173]

2.118 Brussels II *bis* furthermore inserts the obligation that the child must be heard in the return proceedings, unless this would be inappropriate given the age or degree of maturity of the child (Article 11 of Brussels II *bis*, referring to Articles 12 and 13 of the Hague Child Abduction Convention). However, this provision is not entirely new. The UN Convention on the Rights of the Child imposes the obligation on Contracting States to ensure that a child capable of forming his or her own views has the right to express those views freely in all matters affecting him or her, and to ensure that these views be given due weight in accordance with the age and maturity of the child. In this regard the Convention explicitly refers to the child's opportunity to be heard in any judicial or administrative proceedings affecting him or her.[174] The way in which Article 11 of Brussels II *bis* formulates the obligation does not differ fundamentally from the interpretation of a rule which already existed before the advent of the Regulation. However courts could see the different formulation as the introduction of different standards for EU abductions and other abductions. Such a result would serve neither the purposes of justice, nor the best interests of the abducted children.

2.119 It is sometimes difficult to distinguish between the operation of child abduction rules and provisional measures. The principle is that an abducted child must be returned immediately. Jurisdiction in cases of parental responsibility remains with the court where the child habitually

---

[171] Art 13(b) of the Hague Child Abduction Convention, note 122 above. This provision has been strictly interpreted; see Armstrong, note 163 above, 48.

[172] Art 11(4) of Brussels II *bis*. See also the practice guide for the application of the Regulation, drawn up by the European Commission in consultation with the European Judicial Network in civil and commercial matters; available at the European Judicial Network website of the European Commission: <http://ec.europa.eu/civiljustice> at p 32–33.

[173] Schulz, 'Die Zeichnung und der Kompromiss', note 163 above, 1353 discusses this modification in relation to common law systems, where judges have a greater discretion. See also Armstrong, note 163 above, 49, expressing the hope that better cooperation channels within the EU will also be used to increase cooperation with third States, and the efficiency of the Convention as a whole.

[174] Art 12 of the UN Convention on the Rights of the Child. This Convention is in force in 193 States: for details, see <http://www.ohchr.org>.

resided prior to the abduction. Technically the abduction starts at the moment when the parental responsibility arrangement (by operation of law, judgment or agreement) is not or no longer respected. For instance, a parent can legally take a child to another state for a vacation. When that parent prevents the child from returning on the set date, this amounts to abduction. If the parent then approaches the court of the EU Member State where the child is physically present, in general that court has jurisdiction to grant provisional measures on the basis that the child is on the territory of that state. However, since the child's presence is in fact in contravention of the parental responsibility, the qualification of the case as *child abduction* should receive the foremost attention. This will not remove jurisdiction; Article 20 remains applicable. However, once an abduction has occurred, it should be more difficult for the abducting parent to alter the parental responsibility arrangement quickly. If Article 20 of Brussels II *bis* were used to alter parental responsibility arrangements in such a case, the strict rule of returning abducted children forthwith would be thwarted.

The situation might be different if the abducting parent had requested **2.120** provisional measures before the abduction, i.e. before the wrongful retention, while the child's stay with that parent was still in line with the parental responsibility arrangement. In such a case, Article 20 might provide the court with the possibility of granting provisional measures. The moment at which the measures are requested seems crucial. Judges should use their discretion wisely where they notice that proceedings are initiated shortly before a situation might tip over into abduction (i.e. shortly before the child should be returned to another country). The principle of loyalty between EU Member State courts would require them to leave the jurisdiction regarding parental responsibility to the court of the child's habitual residence and not to sanction a circumvention of this rule by way of provisional measures. More important than the principle of loyalty between EU Member State courts are the best interests of the child.

The Hague Child Protection Convention's approach to provisional mea- **2.121** sures is different: courts may take measures of protection in urgent cases, but other provisional measures are excluded when the case concerns abducted children.[175]

---

[175] Arts 11 and 12; Explanatory Report by P Lagarde, [1996] Hague Conference on Private International Law. Proceedings of the Eighteenth Session, vol II, *Protection of children* at 569.

2.122 On the recognition side, the Regulation imports the EU semi-automatic regime for Hague Convention judgments. If a third State court had delivered a judgment of non-return of a child under the Hague Abduction Convention (1980), and subsequently an EU Member State court delivered a judgment requiring the return of the child, the latter judgment will be enforced according to the procedure set out in Brussels II *bis*.[176]

2.123 Judgments from EU Member State courts regarding the return of abducted children are automatically recognized and enforced, without the need for enforcement proceedings.[177] The Hague Convention explicitly permits its Contracting States to alter the grounds for refusal as between themselves.[178]

The Hague Convention on Protection of Children (1996)

2.124 All EU Member States except Malta have signed the 1996 Convention, but it has only been ratified by (or acceded to) and entered into force in eight of them: Bulgaria, the Czech Republic, Estonia, Hungary, Latvia, Lithuania, the Slovak Republic, and Slovenia.[179] It will probably enter into force on the same day for all the other EU Member States as the EC has obtained external competence in this field by the adoption of Brussels II.[180] This Convention contains rules not only on jurisdiction and the recognition and enforcement of judgments, but also on applicable law and administrative cooperation. While a brief analysis of the rules on recognition and enforcement is useful, the last two topics will not be discussed here, as they fall beyond the scope of this book.

2.125 This Convention is broader than the Hague Child Abduction Convention. For instance, where the best interests of a child have to be determined for purposes of jurisdiction under Brussels II *bis*, there is a presumption that EU Member State jurisdiction is in his or her best interests if he or she is habitually resident in a third State that is not party to the Hague Child Protection Convention.

---

[176] Arts 11(8) and 40–45 of Brussels II *bis*.

[177] Art 42 of Brussels II *bis*. See also Practice Guide, note 172 above, 28 and 38–39.

[178] Child Abduction Convention, note 122 above, Art 36. See also Schulz, 'Die Zeichnung und der Kompromiss', note 163 above, 1352.

[179] The other Contracting States to the Convention are currently Albania, Australia, Ecuador, Monaco and Morocco; see <http://www.hcch.net>.

[180] See A Schulz, 'Haager Kinderschutzübereinkommen von 1996: Im Westen nichts neues' [2006] *Zeitschrift für das gesamte Familienrecht* 1309–1311; and chapter 7 on the external relations of the EU.

The rules of jurisdiction of Brussels II *bis* and of the Hague Convention are **2.126**
similar. The main rule is that the courts of the habitual residence of the
child have jurisdiction. Brussels II *bis*, however, contains a rule continuing the jurisdiction of the child's former habitual residence for three
months after a (legal) move to alter the parental responsibility order.[181]
The Hague Convention does not contain a similar provision. This Article
thus can only be used when the child moves from one EU Member State
to another. If the child moves from an EU Member State to a Hague
Convention Contracting State that is not an EU Member State, the Hague
Convention will apply for the determination of jurisdiction. The EU Member
State of the former habitual residence will thus lose its jurisdiction upon
the move.

The most important point on which the relation between the Hague **2.127**
Convention and the Regulation has to be investigated, is the chapter on
the recognition and enforcement of judgments. All judgments given by
EU Member State courts must be recognized and enforced in all other EU
Member States, irrespective of the basis for jurisdiction. One could imagine a situation in which a court in Argentina has jurisdiction as the child in
issue habitually resides there. A Spanish judgment concerning the child
(for whatever reason the court had jurisdiction) is automatically effective
in the entire EU, while the situation under the Hague Convention might
be different: one of the grounds for the refusal of recognition or enforcement is that jurisdiction had not been based on the rules of the Convention.[182]
On first sight it seems positive that the Hague Convention gives wider
effect to judgments. However, in this field of the law, there are sensitive
concerns on more than one front. If this ground for refusal is no longer
available in any part of the EU, this weakens the position of Argentina,
where the child is habitually resident.[183] Such a situation probably will not
occur frequently, as the jurisdiction rules in Brussels II *bis* and the Hague
Convention are to a large extent similar. However, the possibility exists
that third States could be adversely affected.

There is also a point of principle, namely the international law obligations **2.128**
of the EU Member States, and of the EC in the areas where it has external
competence. Being party to an international convention gives rise to obligations towards other parties. It is not generally permitted to change these
engagements.

---

[181] Art 9 of Brussels II *bis*.
[182] Art 23(2)(a) of the Hague Child Protection Convention.
[183] See Gonzalez Beilfuss, note 163 above, 506.

CONCLUSION

2.129 Brussels II *bis* has brought about a new way of determining the application of its jurisdiction rules. First, a court within the EU must consider whether it has jurisdiction according to the rules in the Regulation. If it does not, it has to examine whether a court in another EU Member State may have jurisdiction according to those same rules. Only if that is not the case can the court turn to its national rules on jurisdiction. In this inquiry, the domicile, habitual residence, and nationality of the parties are irrelevant. However, when a court in an EU Member State applies a rule of national law that grants jurisdiction on the basis of nationality, all persons habitually resident in that state should be able to benefit from the rule as against defendants neither habitually resident in the EU, nor EU nationals (domiciled in Ireland or the United Kingdom for these two states). This enlarges the unfair effect of the use of exorbitant bases of jurisdiction against these defendants, especially since the judgments can be recognized and enforced across the entire EU.

2.130 Brussels II *bis* has amended the Hague Child Abduction Convention for intra-European cases. While trust between EU Member States is undoubtedly important, there is a risk of establishing different rules in a field where all children should be protected. The Regulation has the same effect with regard to the Hague Child Protection Convention, changing its rules slightly. The effect of these amendments in practice will have to be reviewed once a body of case law has accumulated.

D. ADDITIONAL DEFENDANTS

Article 6 of Brussels I:

A person domiciled in a Member State may also be sued:

1. *where he is one of a number of defendants, in the courts for the place where any one of them is domiciled, provided the claims are so closely connected that it is expedient to hear and determine them together to avoid the risk of irreconcilable judgments from separate proceedings;*
2. *as a third party in an action on a warranty or guarantee or in any other third party proceedings, in the court seised of the original proceedings, unless these were instituted solely with the object of removing him from the jurisdiction of the court which would be competent in his case;*
3. *on a counter-claim arising from the same contract or facts on which the original claim was based, in the court in which the original claim is pending; . . .*

Article 4 of Brussels II *bis*:

The court in which proceedings are pending on the basis of Article 3 shall also have jurisdiction to examine a counterclaim, insofar as the latter comes within the scope of this Regulation.

INTRODUCTION

In international disputes it often happens that there are more than two **2.131** parties. Additional defendants can have various capacities. They can be co-defendants (defendants to the main claim). Another possibility is that the first defendant calls a third party in an action on a warranty or guarantee. It is also possible that a defendant might bring counter-claims (regarding the counter-claim, the original plaintiff becomes a defendant). Brussels I contains rules for these three types of defendant if they are domiciled in the EU. One sees that these are a special type of defendant. They are not the first or only defendants in a proceeding. An interaction between Brussels I and national rules is possible in these cases. For instance, jurisdiction over the original proceedings can be conferred by national rules because the first defendant was domiciled in a third State. Jurisdiction over the additional defendants can then be based on Brussels I's rules.

Brussels II *bis* contains a rule concerning only counter-claims. One might **2.132** wonder why there is no rule on co-defendants. Regarding divorce, the answer seems straightforward: there could only be two parties, i.e. one plaintiff and one defendant. Regarding parental responsibility and the abduction of children, one might envisage situations in which there is more than one defendant.[184]

The Insolvency Regulation, dealing with the insolvency of a specific **2.133** debtor, does not need rules on additional defendants either.

CO-DEFENDANTS

General

Under Brussels I, a plaintiff may bring an action where a defendant is **2.134** domiciled, not only against that defendant, but also against co-defendants in the same case.[185] The provision permitting joinder of such defendants

---

[184] The question why the drafters did not create rules for such a situation falls beyond the scope of this book.
[185] Art 6(1) of Brussels I.

states clearly that it deals with defendants domiciled in the EU. The rule does not apply to co-defendants domiciled outside the EU. The order for service of the defendants is of no importance. In the English case *Canada Trust & others v Stolzenberg & others*[186] the defendant domiciled in England was served only after the co-defendants domiciled in Switzerland (on application of Article 6(1) of the Lugano Convention). The court found that this was not material with regard to its jurisdiction over the defendants domiciled in Switzerland.

2.135 The European Court of Justice has ruled that the provision must be interpreted restrictively: one can only apply the co-defendants rule if one of the defendants is domiciled at the place of the forum, and not if jurisdiction is based on the place of the performance of a contract or the place of the commission of a tort.[187]

To each his or her own rule

2.136 Only other defendants domiciled in the EU may be sued in the same court on the basis of the provision under discussion. That means that in a single case one might see Brussels I applicable to some defendants and domestic rules to other defendants.

2.137 In *Stolzenberg*,[188] for example, the first defendant was domiciled in England, others in Switzerland (party to the Lugano Convention), and yet others in Panama, Liechtenstein, and the Netherlands Antilles (third States). The Lugano Convention was applied to the defendant domiciled in England, although it seems that the Brussels Convention should have been applied.[189] Regarding the parties domiciled in Switzerland, the House of Lords also relied on the Lugano Convention, which contains the same pro-

---

[186] [1998] ILPr 290 (CA) at, 568. This point was not overturned by the House of Lords: see [2002] 1 AC 1 (HL).

[187] Case C–51/97 *Réunion européenne SA and Others v Spliethoff's Bevrachtingskantoor BV and the Master of the vessel Alblasgracht V002* [1998] ECR I–6511.

[188] See note 186 above (HL).

[189] Convention on jurisdiction and the enforcement of judgments in civil and commercial matters (Lugano Convention), 16 September 1988, OJ L 319, 25.11.1988, 9–48. The domicile of the defendant in a Contracting State is sufficient to make the Brussels Convention applicable: Case C–412/98 *Group Josi Reinsurance Company SA v Universal General Insurance Company (UGIC)* [2000] ECR I–5925. The Lugano Convention does not adjust the sphere of application of the Brussels Convention (or now of Brussels I); see Art 54B Lugano Convention. On this issue in *Stolzenberg*, see chapter 1 above, para 1.72.

vision as Article 6(1) of Brussels I.[190] For jurisdiction over the other parties, the House of Lords applied English domestic law.[191]

In the more recent English case of *Konkola*, the Queen's Bench Division **2.138** (Commercial Court) stated that Brussels I's Article 6 applied to a co-defendant domiciled in Switzerland.[192] While Brussels I was the correct instrument for the English-domiciled defendant, it seems that the Lugano Convention should have been applied regarding the Swiss-domiciled co-defendant. The Court of Appeal did distinguish between the Regulation and the Lugano Convention (although the point concerning the Regulation and Lugano Convention was not at issue in the appeal, but only briefly mentioned).[193]

Of course, the result of applying the Brussels I Regulation/Convention **2.139** or the Lugano Convention would be the same in these cases. However, attention should be paid to applying the correct instrument. The Belgian Hof van Cassatie (Court of Cassation) correctly applied domestic law regarding the joining of a defendant domiciled in the Congo.[194]

However, the European Court of Justice, in *Réunion européenne*[195] did not **2.140** distinguish clearly between EU-domiciled defendants and defendants from third States either. The case concerned actions in tort and contract against transporters of fruit. Some of the defendants were domiciled in Australia and others in the Netherlands. In responding to the questions of the French Cour de cassation (Court of Cassation), the European Court of Justice was silent on the fact that the co-defendants were from a third State. It gave an elaborate interpretation of the interaction of the provision on multiple defendants with the jurisdiction rules based on contract and tort. The European Court of Justice should have stated plainly that co-defendants from third States do not fall under the EU jurisdiction rules, but under domestic law.

Further difficulties may arise where one defendant is domiciled in an EU **2.141** Member State and another in a third State while jurisdiction is based on contract or tort. Let us assume that the national court in question has juris-diction over the party domiciled in another EU Member State on the basis of Article 5 (for instance a contract to be performed at the place where the

---

[190] Art 6(1) of the Lugano Convention.
[191] RSC Ord 11, r 1(1)(c).
[192] [2005] EWHC 898 (Comm); para 49.
[193] [2006] 1 Lloyd's Rep 410.
[194] Judgment of 2 November 2001 [2004] *Tijdschrift@ipr.be* vol 1, 73–75.
[195] *Réunion européenne*, note 187 above; note by H Gaudemet-Tallon [1999] *Revue critique de droit international privé* 333–340.

court is situated). On the basis of some national procedural rules, it is possible to join cases that are narrowly connected.[196] Under Brussels I, it is possible to join two connected cases only if they are pending before the courts of different EU Member States. This is a procedural rule dealing with pending cases, and not a jurisdiction rule that can allow joining the cases in the first place.[197] Therefore, defendants from the EU can only be joined in limited cases, while defendants from third States might be joined on the basis of wider criteria, found in national law.

2.142 Once a judgment is obtained in a court in the EU, the judgment can move freely throughout the EU. Thus enforcement is possible against the foreign defendant in all other EU Member States. The basis for jurisdiction, and whether this was found in Brussels I, in the Lugano Convention, or in national law, become irrelevant. This is once again an indication of the imperfect double nature of Brussels I: at the jurisdiction stage defendants are treated differently based on their domicile, but all judgments are within the ambit of the Regulation's recognition and enforcement rules.

Different rules to one defendant?

2.143 On the other hand, some domestic systems, such as the English, require investigation for each defendant separately whether he is a necessary or proper party. In *Mölnlycke AB and Another v Procter & Gamble Ltd and others*[198] the court combined the Brussels Convention rule with this requirement of English law. The reason was that it was clear in this case that the additional defendant (a subsidiary domiciled in Germany) was only sued in order to get hold of documents that would not otherwise be available during discovery proceedings. In considering whether the German company could be joined to the proceedings on the basis of the Brussels Convention's rule on co-defendants, the Court of Appeal took account of the fact that evidence could be obtained in Germany by way of the Hague Evidence Convention.[199] However, that argument was not pursued further, since the court found that it also had jurisdiction over the German company on the basis of the fact that the tort was committed in England (Article 5(3) Brussels Convention).

---

[196] For example, Art 9 of the Belgian *Code de droit international privé* (Private International Law Code), Act of 16 July 2004, published in *Belgisch Staatsblad* of 27 July 2004.

[197] Art 28 of Brussels I, discussed in chapter 5 below, para 5.133 and following.

[198] [1992] 4 All ER 47.

[199] Hague Convention of 18 March 1970 on the Taking of Evidence Abroad in Civil or Commercial Matters, available at <http://www.hcch.net>.

This combination of the Brussels rule and domestic law seems incorrect. **2.144**
The only consideration that Brussels I permits, is whether the claims are so
closely connected that it is expedient to hear them together in order to
avoid irreconcilable judgments.[200] The Brussels and domestic rules cannot
be combined with regard to the same defendant, especially not after the
European Court of Justice's rejection of the doctrine of *forum non conveniens*
in conjunction with Article 2 of Brussels I.[201]

A bad rule?

English law is not the only system where stricter rules apply for the **2.145**
joining of additional defendants. Under US law, a jurisdiction rule such as
that of Brussels I would not pass the due process test, as this test has
to be applied separately to each defendant.[202] The 1999 text of the Draft
Hague Convention on Jurisdiction and Foreign Judgments in Civil and
Commercial Matters contained a provision to join defendants at the place
of the residence of one defendant, on condition that there was a substantial link between the state and the dispute involving every defendant
not resident in that state.[203] It had subsequently been agreed between the
negotiators to delete the multiple defendants jurisdictional basis from
the Convention.[204] One should keep in mind that the negotiations took
place on the understanding that decisions always had to be taken by consensus. In order to succeed, compromises were necessary. Even taking that
into account, it is interesting that the European negotiators could be con-
vinced to delete this provision. Apart from the fact that the rule in itself
should be improved, the distinction between EU-domiciled and third State-
domiciled defendants should disappear if Brussels I is to be a true double
instrument.

---

[200] Art 6(1) of Brussels I. This provision is identical to that in the Brussels Convention,
upon which *Mölnlycke* was determined.

[201] Case C–281/02 *Owusu v Jackson* [2005] ECR I–1383, also discussed in chapter 5 below,
para 5.86 and following. See also JJ Fawcett, 'Multi-party litigation in private international
law' [1995] ICLQ 744–770 at 754.

[202] The rule might be pushed back if the *forum non conveniens* doctrine were applied by the
courts of the European Union, but that is not the case. The anomaly has been well illustrated
by *Owusu*, note 201 above.

[203] 'Preliminary Draft Convention on Jurisdiction and Foreign Judgments in Civil and
Commercial Matters adopted by the Special Commission and Report by Peter Nygh and
Fausto Pocar' (Preliminary Document No 11), Art 14, available at <http://www.hcch.net>.

[204] 'Summary of the Discussion in Commission II of the First Part of the Diplomatic
Conference (2001),' Art 14, available at <http://www.hcch.net>.

PARTIES IN WARRANTY OR GUARANTEE

2.146 Jurisdiction can also be extended to third parties in an action on a warranty or guarantee or in other third party proceedings.[205]

Combination with national rules

2.147 This basis for jurisdiction can be combined with national rules. Two types of interaction can be envisaged. First, the first defendant could be from outside the EU, so that national bases of jurisdiction are applied to his or her case. EU parties in an action on a warranty or guarantee could then be sued before the same court on the basis of this rule. A case of the French Cour de cassation provides an example.[206] The court based its jurisdiction on Article 14 of the French code civil (civil code), i.e. the fact that the plaintiff was a French national. The defendant was Saudi-Arabian and the EU jurisdiction rules were therefore not applicable. The Court then used Article 6(2) against a third party domiciled in the Netherlands in the action on a guarantee.[207]

2.148 Second, jurisdiction over the main claim can be based on Brussels I, while the party in an action on a warranty is sued on the basis of national rules, because he or she is from a third State. This happened in a case before the Rechtbank van koophandel (Commercial Court) of Veurne (Belgium).[208] In that case the question arose with regard to a party joining a pending dispute voluntarily—without being sued by one of the parties. The plaintiff was domiciled in Belgium and the defendant in France. Brussels I was therefore clearly applicable. A party domiciled in Costa Rica then joined the proceedings, claiming damage from the plaintiff. An intricate dispute on jurisdiction arose. The main action was one in contract and tort. The court ruled that it lacked jurisdiction, because the forum clause was not valid and the places where the contract had been performed and the tort committed were not in Belgium. The defendant, as stated, was domiciled in France. After having found that it lacked jurisdiction as to the main claim, the court considered its jurisdiction regarding the claim by the

---

[205] Art 6(2) of Brussels I.

[206] Cass civ 1re ch, 14 May 1992, approving note by A Huet [1993] *Journal de droit international* 151–2.

[207] See H Born, M Fallon & J-L Van Boxstael, *Droit judiciaire international. Chronique de jurisprudence 1991–1998* (Brussels: Larcier, 2001) 26.

[208] Judgment of 21 April 2004, AR A/02/00464, unpublished.

Costa Rican party, who voluntarily joined the proceedings. The court pointed out that this was an incidence of 'aggressive' joining, because the party sought to protect its own interests. The admissibility of the claim was adjudicated according to Belgian law. With regard to jurisdiction, the court found that the defendant of the voluntary claim was domiciled in Belgium (the original plaintiff). The court therefore found that it had jurisdiction over this claim on the basis of Article 2 of Brussels I.

This result is strange and difficult to justify. In the first place, if a court has **2.149** found that it lacks jurisdiction as to the main claim, it seems that this is the end of the story. The court cannot then take on a claim that had been hooked onto the main claim, which it has refused to hear. Furthermore, parties from outside the EU that voluntarily join proceedings pending in the EU, can hardly be seen as plaintiffs. EU plaintiffs failing to establish jurisdiction can hardly be seen as defendants for the purposes of determining the scope of Brussels I.

It is relevant to recall at this point that all judgments of EU Member State **2.150** courts can be recognized and enforced in all other EU Member State courts, independent of the domiciles of the parties to the dispute. Therefore, in this case the effect on the party from a third State is broader than only in Belgium.

A bad rule?

This basis for jurisdiction was also found to be problematic at the negotia- **2.151** tions of the draft Hague convention on jurisdiction and foreign judgments in civil and commercial matters. Joinder of parties in warranty or guarantee is not always fair and may lead to strange results concerning parties from other States. As regards the co-defendants issue, the negotiators had decided to delete the rule.[209] That the rule itself, within the EU, can be improved is one issue. The other concern is that the rule, applying only to defendants domiciled in the EU, again evinces an imperfect double instrument.

COUNTER-CLAIMS

Brussels I and II *bis* also allow parties to bring counter-claims arising from **2.152** the same contract or facts as the main claim.

---

[209] 'Summary of the Discussion Outcome', note 204 above, 15.

Combination with national rules

2.153 In Brussels I the provision deals with a counter-claim against a person domiciled in the EU. In the application of the provision one might once again see an interaction between Brussels I and the national rules of jurisdiction. If a plaintiff from a third State brings an action in an EU court where the defendant is domiciled, the provision of Brussels I on counter-claims will not be applicable. If the defendant wishes to bring a counter-claim against the plaintiff domiciled in a third State, the possibility will have to be adjudicated under domestic law. The German Bundesgerichtshof (Federal Supreme Court) followed this analysis in proceedings between a plaintiff domiciled in Finland and a defendant domiciled in Germany before Finland joined the EC, so that it can be considered as a third State.[210] The jurisdiction over the counter-claim by the German-domiciled defendant was adjudicated according to German national law.

2.154 Conversely, if a plaintiff from the EU brings an action in an EU court against a party from a third State, the national rules of jurisdiction will apply. It seems in line with this approach that if the party from the third State then wishes to bring a counter-claim, he or she may do so on the basis of Brussels I.

Brussels II *bis*

2.155 In Brussels II *bis*, the applicability of the provision is different. The starting point of the provision seems not to be the defendant on counter-claim, but the court. The rule states that the court that has jurisdiction also has jurisdiction to hear the counter-claim. A plaintiff habitually resident in a third State and with third-State nationality bringing proceedings against a defendant habitually resident in the EU, may then be subjected to the rules of Brussels II *bis* regarding counter-claims. The counter-claim against him may be based on the Regulation.

2.156 One notes that Brussels II *bis* is broader at this point than Brussels I. However, the broad nature of Brussels II *bis* can be explained with reference to the different way of determining application of its jurisdiction rules. As has been explained, a court in an EU Member State must always use the

---

[210] Judgment of 8 July 1981 [1981] *Neue Juristische Wochenschrift* 2644–2646. See also P Grolimund, *Drittstaatenproblematik des europäischen Zivilverfahrensrechts* (Tübingen: Mohr Siebeck, 2000) 57–58.

Regulation's jurisdiction rules as a starting point.[211] If the Regulation does not grant jurisdiction to the courts of that state nor to the courts of any other EU Member State, only then can one revert to national bases of jurisdiction. For this reason, and because of the broad nature of the Regulation's jurisdiction rules, the national bases of jurisdiction will probably be used infrequently. However, if a court uses the national rules for jurisdiction, the counter-claim will fall under the Regulation without further ado.

Tying the rule on counter-claims to the court instead of the defendant has **2.157** the procedural advantage that jurisdiction for all the claims will more often be adjudicated under the same instrument, rather than the chopping-up that will occur under Brussels I. It is also in line with a true double instrument: jurisdiction rules are harmonized.

CONCLUSION

Suing more defendants in the same court often requires combining **2.158** Brussels I's rules with those of national law. This respects the rights of each defendant individually. However, the rules of Brussels I sometimes lead to inequitable results, especially since the judgments can be recognized and enforced in the entire EU, irrespective of the bases for jurisdiction used.

Brussels II *bis* has a different approach: if a court has jurisdiction, the **2.159** Regulation grants it jurisdiction to hear the counter-claim. This is more in line with the double nature of the instrument. However, for co-defendants (under Brussels I), if this rule is introduced and the distinction between defendants disappears, care should be taken to avoid abuse and to ensure that proceedings do not take place in courts that have almost no connection with most of the defendants or the dispute.

E. VOLUNTARY APPEARANCE

Article 24 of Brussels I:

Apart from jurisdiction derived from other provisions of this Regulation, a court of a Member State before which a defendant enters an appearance shall have jurisdiction. This rule shall not apply where appearance was entered to contest the jurisdiction, or where another court has exclusive jurisdiction by virtue of Article 22.

---

[211] See above, paras 2.95–2.97.

Introduction

2.160 Is voluntary appearance a form of tacit jurisdiction clause? One could say that the defendant tacitly agreed with the forum chosen by the plaintiff, and therefore did not contest jurisdiction.[212] This argument is supported by the fact that voluntary appearance will only be accepted in areas where parties may choose a court. Where there is an exclusive basis of jurisdiction, another court seised of an action must of its own motion declare that it has no jurisdiction.[213] Similarly, in the sphere of Brussels II *bis*, which concerns family law, voluntary appearance is not a basis for jurisdiction and the court has to investigate its jurisdiction of its own motion.[214] Even with the limited possibility for choice of forum that is inserted by the proposed amendment to that Regulation, no provision on voluntary appearance is added.[215] Under the Insolvency Regulation, due to the nature of insolvency, the rule on voluntary appearance does not exist.

2.161 On the other hand, some are of the opinion that voluntary appearance cannot be likened to a choice under a forum clause. They argue that voluntary appearance is a matter between the defendant and the court and has nothing to do with the plaintiff. It is rather seen as submission by the defendant, which must be distinguished from submission by way of consent between the parties in some common law states.[216]

Parties from Third States

2.162 What are the boundaries of this provision? Which voluntarily appearing defendants will be bound by the jurisdiction of the court? To answer these questions, one has to enter into the technicalities of Brussels I. The often-quoted Article 4 determines that, as against defendants not domiciled in the EU, jurisdiction shall not be determined by the rules of the Regulation, but according to the national bases for jurisdiction of the Member States.

---

[212] Jenard Report on the 1968 version of the Brussels Convention; OJ C 59, 5 March 1979, 1 (Jenard Report), 36–38, supports the view that voluntary appearance amounts to a tacit choice of forum.

[213] Art 25 of Brussels I.

[214] Art 17 of Brussels II *bis*.

[215] See Proposal for a Council Regulation amending Regulation (EC) No 2201/2003 as regards jurisdiction and introducing rules concerning applicable law in matrimonial matters of 17 July 2006, COM(2006) 399 final, especially Art 3a.

[216] On the different forms submission can take and how they function as basis of jurisdiction, see CF Forsyth, *Private International Law* (4th edn, Lansdowne, South Africa: Juta, 2003) 202–205.

Article 4 provides an exception for Articles 22 and 23; those are the provisions on exclusive jurisdiction and forum clauses. Article 24 is not mentioned. According to the letter of the rule in Article 4, only defendants domiciled in the EU will thus be subjected to the jurisdiction of a court in front of which they have voluntarily appeared.

How the exact scope of the provision on voluntary appearance should be **2.163** determined is not clear. The European Court of Justice in *Josi* stated obiter that this provision applies irrespective of the domiciles of the defendant or the plaintiff.[217] As an obiter dictum, this finding binds neither the European Court of Justice nor the national courts when interpreting the provision in future. Moreover, the interpretation is unclear. Does it mean that one of the parties may be from outside the EU, but the other must be from within the EU for this provision to apply (although it does not matter which party is from where)? Did the European Court of Justice perhaps mean that neither party has to be domiciled in the EU?

If the provision is in fact a tacit choice of forum agreement one might think **2.164** that the same limits would apply as those of the provision on forum clauses (Article 23). That means that the provision will apply if one of the parties (it does not matter whether it is the plaintiff or the defendant) is domiciled in the EU.[218] This would be in line with the first possible reading of what the European Court of Justice meant in *Josi*. Of course, the court before which the voluntary appearance takes place would have to be an EU court, otherwise the question of the application of Brussels I will not arise. According to this logic, a party from outside the EU that inadvertently appears voluntarily before an EU court can be drawn into the system of Brussels I.

The second possible reading would permit the provision to go even **2.165** further. If a party from a third State tried his luck and sued another party from (the same or a different) third State in the EU and the defendant did not immediately contest jurisdiction, the court would assume jurisdiction.[219] This broad reading does not require either party to be domiciled in

---

[217] Case C–412/98 *Group Josi Reinsurance Company SA v Universal General Insurance Company* [2000] ECR I–5625, para 44–45; case notes: F Leclerc [2002] *Journal de droit international* 623–628; P Vlas [2003] *Nederlandse jurisprudentie. Uitspraken in burgerlijke en strafzaken* no 597, p 4584–4586; A Staudinger [2000] *Praxis des internationalen Privat- und Verfahrensrechts*.

[218] For support of this view, see J Kropholler, *Europäisches Zivilprozeßrecht. Kommentar zu EuGVO und Lugano-Übereinkommen* (7th edn, Heidelberg: Verlag Recht und Wirtschaft GmbH, 2002) 318–319; Staudinger, ibid, 485.

[219] For support for the view that the provision applies even when the defendant is domiciled in a third State, see Droz, *Pratique de la convention de Bruxelles*, note 1 above, 38–39; P Gothot & D Holleaux, *La Convention de Bruxelles du 27.9.1968. Compétence judiciaire et effets*

the EU. It does not seem that Brussels I should regulate this matter. Not all legal systems accept voluntary appearance as a basis for jurisdiction in all areas of law (for instance tort).[220]

2.166   In his report Jenard shares the view that the letter of Article 4 should be followed. He states that the rule only applies if a defendant domiciled in the EU is sued in the courts of another EU Member State.[221] The German Bundesgerichtshof (Federal Supreme Court) also came to this conclusion.[222] The plaintiff in this case was domiciled in Germany while the defendant was domiciled in Switzerland. The Lugano Convention was not yet in force at that time, so Switzerland should be seen as a third State under the Brussels Convention. The court found that the Brussels Convention's provision on voluntary appearance was not relevant if the defendant was domiciled in a third State.

2.167   According to the rule in Article 24, when the defendant first begins to defend him- or herself as to the substance of the claim, he or she loses the right to contest jurisdiction.[223] This non-contesting of jurisdiction might be due to a lack of knowledge of the jurisdiction rules of the European Union, rather than a true agreement.[224] Furthermore, the rule might differ in different states. Under some legal systems, for instance, it might not be possible to assume jurisdiction in this way over claims in delict or tort.

2.168   It is important to note here the fundamental difference between the provisions on voluntary appearance and forum clauses—a forum clause can, and usually does, come into existence before a dispute arises between the parties. At that stage it is unknown in what capacity (plaintiff or defendant) future litigants will appear. Therefore legal certainty requires that a clause be respected if one of the parties is domiciled in the EU, and not just if the defendant is domiciled in the EU. This argument does not hold for voluntary appearance: at that stage, it is inevitably clear which party is the

---

des jugements dans la CEE, (Paris: Editions Jupiter, 1985), 111; Advocate General Darmon in Case C–318/93 *Brenner & Noller v Dean Witter Reynolds Inc* [1994] ECR I–4275 at paras 13 and 15 (this view was not essential to the decision in the case).

[220] This had been pointed out at the negotiations of the Hague Convention of 30 June 2005 on Choice of Court Agreements; see *Procès verbal* No 7, p 8.

[221] Jenard Report, note 212 above, 38.

[222] Judgment of 21 November 1996 (1998) 134 *Entscheidungen des Bundesgerichtshofes in Zivilsachen* 127–137. See also P Grolimund, *Drittstaatenproblematik des europäischen Zivilverfahrensrechts* (Tübingen: Mohr Siebeck, 2000), 55.

[223] Except if he or she contests jurisdiction and in the alternative brings an argument on the substance: Case 150/80 *Elefanten Schuh GmbH v Pierre Jacqmain* [1981] ECR 1671.

[224] See H Gaudemet-Tallon, *Compétence et exécution des jugements en Europe* (3rd edn, Paris: LGDJ, 2002) 119–120.

plaintiff and which the defendant.[225] At the same time, the structure of Brussels I seems to support this analysis. Section 7 contains only two provisions, that on forum clauses (Article 23) and that on voluntary appearance (Article 24). If the drafters had intended the same rule on scope to apply to both provisions, they could have stated so at the beginning of the section, as was done for the protective bases of jurisdiction.[226] Alternatively both rules could have been inserted in the same article. In line with this view, the Jenard Report in its explanation on the provision clearly refers to 'a defendant domiciled in a Contracting State'.[227] Advocating this as the correct view on the current version of Brussels I does not mean accepting that it is the best possible rule. As has been stated, it would be better if the Regulation did not distinguish between various types of defendants. That would mean that the Regulation would contain an autonomous rule on a defendant which voluntarily appears in a court of an EU Member State. This would be in line with the pursued double nature of the instrument: recognition and enforcement would be facilitated because the jurisdiction rules were uniform.

RENUNCIATION OF WRITTEN FORUM CLAUSES

Voluntary appearance can amount to a tacit renunciation of a valid, written **2.169** forum clause. In the cases of *Elefanten Schuh GmbH v Pierre Jacqmain*[228] and *Spitzley v Sommer Exploitation*[229] the European Court of Justice stated that, where a court has jurisdiction pursuant to a jurisdiction clause and the case is brought before another court, but the defendant does not contest jurisdiction, that court will have jurisdiction. In both these cases the appointed court was in the EU. The cases therefore deal with the interaction between certain provisions of Brussels I, rather than truly examining relations with third States.

Transposing the facts to relations with third States, a party from India and **2.170** one from Ireland, for instance, conclude a forum clause for a court in London. Subsequently the Indian party brings suit in a court in Ireland. If the Irish domiciled party appears without contesting jurisdiction, the legal construction is that the parties have implicitly agreed that the court

---

[225] See Kropholler, note 218 above, 318–319.

[226] Sections 3, 4, and 5 of Brussels I.

[227] Jenard Report, note 212 above, 38.

[228] Note 223 above; case notes: H Gaudemet-Tallon [1982] *Revue critique de droit international privé* 152–161; TC Hartley [1982] ELR 237–239.

[229] Case 48/84 [1985] ECR 787; case notes: H Gaudemet-Tallon [1985] *Revue critique de droit international privé* 687–688; TC Hartley [1986] ELR 98.

in Ireland should hear their dispute. To this effect they have implicitly renounced their first choice of the London court. Difficult to make, but easy to renounce, is the nature of these forum clauses.

2.171 If one reverses the roles of the parties so that the Irish domiciled party is the plaintiff and the Indian party the defendant, the points of view discussed above recur. According to the first view, which maintains the same scope rules as for forum clauses, Brussels I would regulate the matter, since one of the parties is domiciled in the EU. The second view also holds that Brussels I would regulate the matter, because the proceedings are in an EU court. However, according to the third view, Brussels I would not regulate the matter. Since the defendant is domiciled in a third State, the national rules on jurisdiction would have to be applied.

2.172 It might happen that a court outside the EU is appointed and that an action is subsequently brought in an EU Member State court. If one accepts that that an EU court can have jurisdiction on the basis of the voluntary appearance of the defendant, it will probably assume jurisdiction. It will probably not have to consider the jurisdiction clause in favour of the third State court, since the parties had renounced that former choice by a later consent. If consent is clear and the defendant does not wish to contest jurisdiction, there is no reason to hold the parties to an old forum clause. Neither would they have been held to the forum clause if it had stipulated an EU court.

Counter-claims

2.173 The provision on voluntary appearance also applies to counter-claims. The plaintiff, who had now become the defendant on the counter-claim, is bound by the jurisdiction of the court if he voluntarily appeared, i.e. did not contest jurisdiction. This rule was established by the European Court of Justice in *Spitzley*, where the counter-claim did not relate to the same contract as the original claim. In the contract from which the counter-claim arose, a forum clause existed in favour of another EU court. However, the European Court of Justice stated that even in those circumstances the provision on voluntary appearance could be applied.

Voluntary Appearance under the Proposed Maintenance Regulation

2.174 The proposed Maintenance Regulation determines that a court in an EU Member State before which a defendant enters an appearance (without contesting jurisdiction) shall have jurisdiction.[230] This provision differs from that of Brussels I in the sense that it does not apply if the parties had concluded an exclusive forum agreement. As explained above, under Brussels I a forum agreement can be amended by a plaintiff bringing suit in a court other than the chosen court if the defendant does not contest jurisdiction. This will thus be impossible under the Maintenance Regulation. It seems a bit strange to force parties to stick to a rule that they had freely chosen: why should they not be permitted to change their minds? If they wish to change their minds, they will have to do so in a new agreement in writing.

For parties domiciled or habitually resident in third States, the rule is **2.175** the same: the Regulation will not distinguish between different defendants.[231] There is thus no requirement that the defendant who appears voluntarily must be habitually resident in the EU. This goes much further than Brussels I. As has been explained, the Maintenance Regulation will completely harmonize the jurisdiction rules of the Member States and they will be applied no more—not even residually.[232] Even though subsidiarity issues might arise, the advantage of this approach is fairness and clarity.

CONCLUSION

Although the phenomenon of voluntary appearance has some similarities **2.176** to forum clauses, assuming jurisdiction in such a case touches the defendant more severely than the plaintiff, who has made the decision to go to a specific EU court. This rule of Brussels I should only apply if the defendant appearing voluntarily is domiciled in the EU. If the defendant is domiciled in a third State, the national rules on voluntary appearance should regulate the matter. However, under the proposed Maintenance Regulation, a court may have jurisdiction if the defendant appears without contesting jurisdiction, even if that defendant is domiciled or habitually resident in a third State. This rule has the advantage of respecting the strict double nature of the instrument: uniform jurisdiction rules lead to recognition and enforcement.

---

[230] Proposal for a Council Regulation on Jurisdiction, Applicable law, Recognition and Enforcement of Decisions and Cooperation in Matters relating to Maintenance Obligations of 15 December 2005, COM (2005) 649 final, Art 5.

[231] Rec 10.

[232] Para 2.99 above.

F. SPECIAL BASES FOR JURISDICTION

Article 5 of Brussels I:

A person domiciled in a Member State may, in another Member State, be sued:

1. *(a) in matters relating to contract, in the courts for the place of performance of the obligation in question;*
   (b) for the purpose of this provision and unless otherwise agreed, the place of performance of the obligation in question shall be:
      —in the case of the sale of goods, the place in a Member State where, under the contract, the goods were delivered or should have been delivered,
      —in the case of the provision of services, the place in a Member State where, under the contract, the services were provided or should have been provided,
   (c) if subparagraph (b) does not apply then subparagraph (a) applies;
2. *in matters relating to maintenance, in the courts for the place where the maintenance creditor is domiciled or habitually resident or, if the matter is ancillary to proceedings concerning the status of a person, in the court which, according to its own law, has jurisdiction to entertain those proceedings, unless that jurisdiction is based solely on the nationality of the parties;*
3. *in matters relating to tort,* delict or quasi-delict, *in the courts for the place where the harmful event occurred or may occur;*
4. *as regards a civil claim for damages or restitution which is based on an act giving rise to criminal proceedings, in the court seised of those proceedings, to the extent that that court has jurisdiction under its own law to entertain civil proceedings;*
5. *as regards a dispute arising out of the operations of a branch, agency or other establishment, in the courts for the place in which the branch, agency or other establishment is situated;*
6. *as settlor, trustee or beneficiary of a trust created by the operation of a statute, or by a written instrument, or created orally and evidenced in writing, in the courts of the Member State in which the trust is domiciled;*
7. *as regards a dispute concerning the payment of remuneration claimed in respect of the salvage of a cargo or freight, in the court under the authority of which the cargo or freight in question:*
   (a) has been arrested to secure such payment, or
   (b) could have been so arrested, but bail or other security has been given;
   provided that this provision shall apply only if it is claimed that the defendant has an interest in the cargo or freight or had such an interest at the time of salvage.

Article 6 of Brussels I:

A person domiciled in a Member State may also be sued:

. . .

4. *in matters relating to a contract, if the action may be combined with an action against the same defendant in matters relating to rights in rem in immovable property, in the court of the Member State in which the property is situated.*

INTRODUCTION

First it is necessary to situate this provision in the scheme of Brussels I. **2.177** This rule can only come into play when there is neither exclusive jurisdiction[233] nor protective jurisdiction for a weaker party.[234] Article 5 is also subordinate to a forum clause, in matters such as contract where choice of forum is permitted.[235] In essence this provision is on the same level, in the form of an alternative, as the general basis of jurisdiction, namely the domicile of the defendant. This means that the plaintiff can choose whether to sue the defendant at the domicile of the defendant, or at this alternative forum.

Regarding its scope, this provision falls in the same category as the juris- **2.178** diction rule on the domicile of the defendant. In other words, Article 5 applies to defendants domiciled in the EU. Thus, although these provisions are often used, the impact on third States is smaller than some of the other provisions. It is the impact on third States that will receive the main focus here.

The existence of the rules in this provision is justified by a link between the **2.179** facts and the forum.[236] Granting jurisdiction to the courts of a place connected to a dispute seems reasonable. However, the facts of international civil disputes are not always straightforward and the link therefore is not

---

[233] Discussed in chapter 3.
[234] Discussed in the next section of this chapter, para 2.248 and following.
[235] Discussed in chapter 4.
[236] According to the Jenard Report on the 1968 version of the Brussels Convention; OJ C 59, 5 March 1979, 1 (Jenard Report), 22: '[a]doption of the "special" rules of jurisdiction is also justified by the fact that there must be a close connecting factor between the dispute and the court with jurisdiction to resolve it'. See also Gaudemet-Tallon, *Compétence et exécution*, note 224 above, 125.

always direct and visible. Some authors, specifically from outside the EU, have criticized this rule as inherently exorbitant.[237]

2.180 A particularity of Article 5 is that it does not refer only to the EU Member State that has jurisdiction, but directly to a specific court. For most of the other provisions, Brussels I only indicates in which EU Member State the competent court will be found. The internal rules of that Member State then have to determine which court has jurisdiction. On the other hand, because of its direct link to the facts, Article 5 appoints a court directly.

2.181 Because the provision under discussion derogates from the defendant's natural forum, the European Court of Justice has emphasized that it should be interpreted strictly, in order to promote foreseeability.[238] For instance, an EU defendant may not be sued as a co-defendant in the place where the contract was performed. In other words, jurisdiction for each defendant needs to be established separately if the plaintiff pursues on the basis of Article 5.[239]

2.182 Advocate General Léger in his opinion in *Owusu* made a distinction between the sphere of application of Articles 2 and 5.[240] According to him, Article 5 is applicable only if the dispute or the situation of the parties is connected with two or more EU Member States. That, in his view, is different from Article 2, which applies regardless of the domicile of the plaintiff, so even if the plaintiff and the defendant are domiciled in the same EU Member State. (The European Court of Justice subsequently found in *Owusu* that a case must be international for the Convention to be applicable.[241]) For Article 5 he states that a cross-border element is required.[242]

2.183 However, it is submitted that the cross-border element is not a separate requirement for the application of Article 5, but rather a logical consequence of its mechanics. The provision states that a defendant domiciled

---

[237] For instance, AT von Mehren, 'Theory and Practice of Adjudicatory Authority in Private International Law: a comparative study of the doctrine, policies and practices of common- and civil-law systems. General course on Private International Law' (2002) 295 Collected Courses of the Hague Academy for International Law, 72.

[238] Case 189/87 *Kalfelis v Bankhaus Schröder, Münchmeyer, Hengst and Co and others* [1988] ECR 5565, para 19; Case C–220/88 *Dumez France v Hessische Landesbank* [1990] ECR I–49 para 17; Case C–26/91 *Handte & Co GmbH v Traitements Mécano-chimiques des Surfaces SA* [1992] ECR I–3967 para 18; Case C–440/97 *GIE Groupe Concorde and Others v The Master of the vessel 'Suhadiwarno Panjan' and Others* [1999] ECR I–6307, para 24; Case C–256/00 *Besix SA v WABAG and Plafog* [2002] ECR I–1699, paras 26 and 53.

[239] Case C–51/97 *Réunion européenne SA and Others v Spliethoff's Bevrachtingskantoor BV and the Master of the vessel Alblasgracht V002* [1998] ECR I–6511.

[240] Case C–281/02 *Owusu v Jackson* [2005] ECR I–1383.

[241] Ibid, paras 25–26 of the judgment. This issue was discussed above, para 2.76.

[242] Ibid, para 126 of the Advocate General's opinion.

in *one* EU Member State may be sued in *another* EU Member State on several grounds. Often the alternative forum provided by Article 5 would be popular since it will coincide with the domicile of the plaintiff.[243] This interpretation makes the provision seem largely irrelevant to parties from third States: the defendant has to be domiciled in the EU for the provision to apply; the plaintiff, also domiciled in the EU, then goes to his own court, which is conveniently also the court of the place where the contract was due to be performed or the tort committed. The matter ends there with two parties from the EU, two EU courts that have jurisdiction, and no link with third States. However, the domicile of the defendant is a broad notion, as has been indicated.[244] The defendant company might have two domiciles, only one of which is in the EU. Furthermore, there might be more than one defendant drawn in by this rule. The place of performance of the contract or of commission of the tort might be (partly) outside the EU.

The special rules of jurisdiction will be discussed in the sequence that they **2.184** appear in the Regulation, namely contracts, maintenance, torts, criminal proceedings, agency, trusts, and salvage of ships or cargo. Although an explanation of the provisions and the existing perplexity is necessary, not all the confusion to which Article 5 has led will be discussed in detail. It might happen that both (or all) parties are domiciled in the EU, but that a contract is to be performed in a third State, or that a tort had been committed (or damage occurred) in a third State. This situation, and the effects that recent case law of the European Court of Justice have had on it, will be discussed.

CONTRACTS

Brief historical overview: under the Brussels Convention

Contracts jurisdiction under the Brussels Convention has been severely **2.185** complicated by the European Court of Justice; beginning with the first judgments it gave on the interpretation of the Convention.[245] The rule

---

[243] P Nygh, 'The criteria for judicial jurisdiction' in AF Lowenfeld & LJ Silberman (eds), *The Hague Convention on Jurisdiction and Judgments* (USA: Juris Publishing, 2001) 13; E Jayme, 'The role of Article 5 in the scheme of the convention. Jurisdiction in matters relating to contract' in Court of Justice of the European Communities, *Civil Jurisdiction and Judgments in Europe* (London: Butterworths, 1992), 74. This was even more so under the old rule of the Brussels Convention that gave jurisdiction to the court of the place of payment, under many legal systems the residence of the creditor, thus the plaintiff; see A Briggs & P Rees, *Civil Jurisdiction and Judgments* (4th edn, London: LLP, 2005) 146–147.

[244] Paras 2.11 and following, especially para 2.20.

[245] See, in general, K Hertz, *Jurisdiction in Contract and Tort under the Brussels Convention* (Copenhagen: DJØF Publishing, 1998); W Kennett, 'Place of Performance and Predictability'

states that one may sue the defendant in the place of the performance of the obligation at stake.

Article 5 of the Brussels Convention merely stated:

A person domiciled in a Contracting State may, in another Contracting State, be sued:

1. in matters relating to a contract, in the courts for the place of performance of the obligation in question; . . .

No presumptions existed to find the 'place of performance'. Two questions soon arose: (1) which obligation, and (2) according to which law should the place of performance be determined?

2.186 The European Court of Justice found that one had to look at the obligation that gave rise to the dispute.[246] If the litigation concerned the payment, suit could be brought at the place where payment had to be made. If the dispute was about (faulty or non-) delivery, the case could be brought at the place where the delivery took place or should have taken place. This did not simplify matters, since it often meant that different courts would have jurisdiction depending on which action was brought first. Often the buyer does not pay because of non-conform delivery. If the seller sued first for payment, the court of the place of payment would have jurisdiction. If the buyer sued first for damages or reparation, the court of the place of performance would have jurisdiction. However, if the seller sued first, the buyer might of course bring a counter-action for damages against the seller in the same court.[247] This dichotomy led to a proliferation of the available fora, and to confusion and legal uncertainty, and even encouraged a race to the courtroom.

2.187 The question of which law to apply in order to determine the place of performance was also solved in a rather cumbersome manner. The European Court of Justice ruled that the EU Member State courts had to use their conflict of law rules to find the applicable law and use that to determine where the obligation in question had to be performed.[248]

2.188 The practical inequity with this application of the Brussels Convention was particularly apparent when the seller sued the buyer for payment,

---

[1995] *Yearbook of European Law* 193–218; J Hill, 'Jurisdiction in Matters relating to a Contract under the Brussels Convention' [1995] ICLQ 591–619; P Kaye, *Law of the European Judgments Convention* (Chichester: Barry Rose, 1999) vol 2.

[246] Case 14/76 *A De Bloos, SPRL v Société en commandite par actions Bouyer* [1976] ECR 1497.
[247] According to Art 6(3) of Brussels I.
[248] Case 12/76 *Industrie Tessili Italiana Como v Dunlop AG* [1976] ECR 1473.

which, of course, is not a rare event. One would then have to determine, in accordance with the applicable law, where the place of performance had been. According to some legal systems of the EU, the place of payment is the domicile of the debtor, and according to others, the domicile of the creditor.[249] Fortunately, with regard to business-to-business sales contracts, a degree of uniformity had been attained by the frequent application of the Vienna Sales Convention (CISG).[250] According to the Convention, the place of payment for an international sales contract is the place of business of the seller.[251] The CISG is in force in 23 of the 27 EU Member States; the abstainers are Ireland, Malta, Portugal, and the United Kingdom. The Convention does not regulate all sales contracts, but a large number. When the place of performance is the domicile of the seller, this amounts to the court of the domicile of the plaintiff having jurisdiction, even in cases where the facts had a very tenuous link, or none at all, with that forum. In cases where the defendant is domiciled in the EU, while the rest of the dispute has little bearing on the EU, jurisdiction may be founded on the basis of the place of payment.

Did Brussels I simplify matters?

Brussels I attempted to simplify the maze the European Court of Justice **2.189** has created in contracts jurisdiction. Whether or not the drafters were successful remains to be seen. Brussels I has created specific rules to determine the 'place of performance of the obligation in question' for two types of contract: sales and services. These two types embrace the largest number of contracts. For contracts that cannot be categorized as sales or services, the old rule remains in force. The new rule is that sales contracts are to be performed at the place for delivery of the goods under the contract, unless otherwise agreed. The rule for service contracts is that the place of performance is where the services had to be provided under the contract, unless otherwise agreed. Only if neither of the rules applies can one fall back on the general rule, which is the same as the old provision.[252]

---

[249] Briggs & Rees, note 243 above, 172–173.

[250] United Nations Convention on Contracts for the International Sale of Goods (CISG) (Vienna 1980). This Convention currently has 70 Contracting States; see <http://www.uncitral.org>; <http://www.cisg.law.pace.edu>.

[251] Art 57(1) of the CISG.

[252] For instance, for contracts of rent, see Rechtbank van koophandel (Commercial Court) of Hasselt, Belgium, judgment of 11 December 2002 (AR 02/03167), unpublished, or for contracts for the lease of movables, see Rechtbank van koophandel of Hasselt, judgment of 22 January 2003 (AR 03/0196), unpublished and Rechtbank van koophandel of Hasselt, judgment of 24 September 2003 (AR 03/3011), unpublished, or for a tiling contract, Rechtbank

2.190 The new rule has caused great confusion amongst legal writers.[253] The first question is what 'under the contract' means. If the contract did not specify where the goods had to be delivered, can one then assume that the court of the place of actual delivery has jurisdiction? Or should one, in the absence of specification in the contract, return to the general rule? Contracts are not always in writing and proving what the parties exactly agreed, might be very difficult.[254]

2.191 The next question regards the phrase 'unless otherwise agreed.'[255] What does this mean? It is clear that this phrase does not refer to a forum clause, because that is dealt with in a separate provision, with different conditions. The European Court of Justice confirmed long ago that fixing the place of performance in a contract is not the same as concluding a forum agreement.[256] The ECJ has ruled further that, if parties appoint a fictitious place of delivery in order to circumvent the formalities for forum clauses, that agreement will not be given effect with respect to jurisdiction.[257]

---

van koophandel of Hasselt, judgment of 11 February 2004 (AR 03/4286), unpublished; all available at <http://www.euprocedure.be>.

[253] For instance, Briggs & Rees, note 243 above, 159–162; J Fawcett, J Harris & M Bridge, *International Sale of Goods in the Conflict of Laws* (Oxford: Oxford University Press, 2005) 83–123; Gaudemet-Tallon, *Compétence et exécution*, note 236 above, 158–164; A Nuyts, 'La communautarisation de la convention de Bruxelles. Le règlement 44/2001 sur la compétence judiciaire et l'effet des décisions en matière civile et commerciale' [2001] *Journal des tribunaux* 913–922 at 916; P Vlas, 'Herziening EEX: van verdrag naar verordening' [2000] *Weekblad voor Privaatrecht, Notariaat en Registratie* 745–753; I Couwenberg & M Pertegás Sender, 'Recente ontwikkelingen in het Europees bevoegdheids- en executierecht' in H Van Houtte en M Pertegás Sender (eds) *Het nieuwe Europese IPR: van verdrag naar verordening* (Antwerp: Intersentia, 2001), 45–50; GAL Droz & H Gaudemet-Tallon, 'La transformation de la convention de Bruxelles du 27 septembre 1968 en Règlement du Conseil concernant la compétence judiciaire, la reconnaissance et l'exécution des décisions en matière civile et commerciale' [2001] *Revue critique de droit international privé* 601–652; C Bruneau, 'Les règles européennes de compétence en matière civile et commerciale' [2001] *La Semaine juridique* 533–541; JJ van Haersolte-van Hof, 'EEX-verordening treedt in werking per 1 maart 2002' [2001] *Nederlands Internationaal Privaatrecht* 244–248; P Vlas, 'Stoeien met verbintenissen, worstelen met Art 5 sub 1 EEX-Verordening' [2002] *Weekblad voor Privaatrecht, Notariaat en Registratie* 301–302.

[254] The Rechtbank van koophandel (Commercial Court) of Kortrijk in Belgium, expressed the lack of clarity in its judgment of 4 December 2003 (AR 04279/03, unpublished, see <http://www.euprocedure.be>) and regretted that it, as court of first instance, could not pose a preliminary question to the European Court of Justice (on the basis of Art 68 of the EC Treaty).

[255] See also Briggs & Rees, note 243 above, 159–160, calling the words 'unintelligible' and stating further '[t]hey can be forgotten until an imaginative court is able to breathe intelligent life into them'.

[256] Case 56/79 *Zelger v Salinitri* [1980] ECR 89.

[257] Case C–106/95 *Mainschiffahrts–Genossenschaft eG v Les Gravières Rhénanes SARL* [1997] ECR I–911, para 31–35.

This 'otherwise' agreement must have something to do with the place of **2.192** performance. However, a place of performance can always be agreed: this is contract law. The point is that in a sales contract there are two main performances: delivery by the seller and payment by the buyer. This provision indicates that it is the delivery which is the relevant factor of the two. Where exactly delivery should take place can of course be agreed by the parties (and most likely will be). Does the phrase 'otherwise agreed' now mean that the contracting parties can agree that delivery is not the relevant performance? What if the parties do not agree on a place of delivery, but only on the place of payment: have they now 'agreed otherwise'? It is uncertain whether or not parties can indicate a place of payment outside the EU in order to annul the jurisdiction that the EU court of the place of delivery would have had.

Will the European Court of Justice come up with yet another autonomous **2.193** definition? It might be difficult for legal systems to have one definition of service contracts for purposes of jurisdiction (prescribed by the European Court of Justice) and another for purposes of substantive law (the old national one). Therefore, EU Member States might transpose the European Court of Justice's definition to their national substantive rules. Parties from third States should then realize that this classification of their contract with an EU party might have unforeseen implications for jurisdiction. The European Court of Justice might provide a broader definition of 'services' than the definition of the particular EU Member State in which a party from a third State carries on commercial activities. Such parties might be surprised, for various reasons not least of which is jurisdiction, at the new classification of their contracts.

Another uncertainty that has arisen was whether one had to take account **2.194** of the legal place of delivery (for instance referring to the INCOTERMS[258]) or whether it is the actual destination of the goods that is important. Some argue that one has to refer to the place of factual delivery. They state that some legal forms of delivery, such as FOB (free on board), present no real link with the place in question. If a German contracting party sells the goods FOB Antwerp to an Irish buyer, for example, there seems to be no reason why the court in Antwerp should have jurisdiction.[259]

---

[258] INCOTERMS is an acronym for International Commercial Terms. These are standard terms used in international trade and published under the auspices of the International Chamber of Commerce. Since there is a common understanding, with a few letters, an entire clause is in fact written, including rules on the transfer of property and risk. See H Van Houtte, *The Law of International Trade* (2nd edn, London: Sweet & Maxwell, 2002) 171–175.

[259] S Rutten, 'IPR-aspecten met betrekking tot de betaling van de koopprijs—art 5, 1° b) EEX-Verordening,' noot onder Hb Gent 31 januari 2002 [2002–2003] *Rechtskundig Weekblad*

These authors find authority for their proposition in the Explanatory Memorandum of the European Commission that accompanied the proposal for the Regulation.[260] The problem with this authority, though, is that not all language versions contain the reference to 'factual'. The English version only refers to a 'pragmatic' approach, although the Dutch, German, French, Italian, and Spanish versions contain the adjective 'factual'. Probably it was not the intention of the European legislator to make a distinction between a legal and a factual delivery. The word 'factual' was probably merely used to describe delivery as a more appropriate indicator of jurisdiction.

2.195 Factual delivery as the new criterion would lead to tremendous uncertainty. In the first place it is often difficult to prove where the goods were eventually delivered—more so for international sales than for service contracts. Legal delivery is something lawyers know. Moreover, legal delivery presents the passing of the risk. This is often a place where important evidence will have to be gathered: were the goods damaged before or after the passing of the risk? It is hard to see, therefore, why a different and unknown criterion of factual delivery should now be used.

2.196 It is submitted that the place of delivery has to be ascertained in a legal sense. Delivery has always been a term with a specific legal meaning and it would lead only to confusion to strip the term now of that well-known meaning. This argument was followed by the Rechtbank van koophandel of Hasselt in Belgium.[261] If the place of delivery were not determined in the contract, it would have to be ascertained with reference to the law applicable on the contract.[262] In this case some of the factual places of delivery were outside the EU, while the legal delivery was in the EU.

2.197 Linked to this problem is the question of what happens when the goods were delivered to a different place than contractually agreed.

2.198 To conclude: many hoped that revision would bring improvement, but one wonders whether the new rule is better than the old one.[263]

664–669 and [2002–2003] *Rechtskundig Weekblad* 1637–1639; Nuyts, note 253 above, at 916.

[260] Explanatory Memorandum of 14 July 1999, COM(1999) 348 final, available at <http://europa.eu/eur-lex/lex/LexUriServ/site/en/com/1999/com1999_0348en01.pdf>.

[261] Two judgments of 16 April 2003 (AR 03/211 and AR 03/592), unpublished, available at <http://www.euprocedure.be>.

[262] In support of this view, see Briggs & Rees, note 243 above, 171–172.

[263] See, for instance, A Bucher, 'Vers une convention mondiale sur la compétence et les jugements étrangers' [2000] *La Semaine juridique* 77–133 at 85; B Audit, 'A view from France' in AF Lowenfeld & L Silberman (eds), *The Hague Convention on Jurisdiction and Judgments* (USA: Juris Publishing, 2001) 124–129 at 125; PM North & JJ Fawcett, *Cheshire*

Various solutions are possible. Maybe the European Court of Justice will have to create as complex a set of interpretation rules as they had done for the old provision. Maybe it will have to refer to the rules on applicable law.

Performance or eventual delivery outside the EU

If the performance of a contract took place or should have taken place in a **2.199** third State while the defendant was domiciled in the EU, the jurisdiction of the court in the EU Member State where the defendant is domiciled is compulsory. That court may not decline jurisdiction in favour of the third State court that might be more appropriate to hear the case. The European Court of Justice specified this in *Owusu*.[264] The defendants, only one of whom was domiciled in England, were sued there by the English-domiciled plaintiff. The action was partly based on a contract that had to be performed in Jamaica. The English court had jurisdiction according to Article 2 of the Brussels Convention (which was identical to Article 2 of Brussels I). Yet the court wanted to decline jurisdiction by applying the *forum non conveniens* rule. Before doing so, the Court of Appeal posed a preliminary question to the European Court of Justice. That court found that Article 2 jurisdiction was mandatory so that the English court was not permitted to decline jurisdiction on the basis of *forum non conveniens*. The reasoning of the European Court of Justice was based on considerations of European Union law and the fact that not all national legal systems know the doctrine of *forum non conveniens*.

Brussels I also contains an exception if Article 5 appoints the courts of a **2.200** third State. The Explanatory Memorandum of the European Commission that accompanied their proposal for Brussels I states:

Where the effect of the autonomous definition is to designate a court in a non-member country, rule (a) will apply rather than rule (b). Jurisdiction will lie with the court designated by the rules of private international law of the State seised as the court for the place of performance of the obligation in question (c).[265]

In other words, the drafters of Brussels I troubled themselves to bend the rule in such a way that performance should be located inside rather than outside the EU. Effectively, the presumptions are rebutted if they point

---

and North's Private International Law (13th edn, London: Butterworths, 1999), 210; Jayme, note 243 above, 79–80.

[264] *Owusu*, note 240 above; the case is discussed in more detail in chapter 5 below, paras 5.86 and following.

[265] At p 14. See also Couwenberg & Pertegás Sender, note 253 above, 49; Vlas, 'Herziening EEX', note 253 above, 750.

to performance outside the EU. Then one should fall back on the old, complicated rule of looking at the performance that lies at the centre of the dispute and determining its location by reference to the conflict of law rules and without the help of the new presumptions. The rule does not have any logic beyond drawing more disputes into the legal sphere of the EU. Its approach is one-sided. If the rule aims to grant jurisdiction to courts within the EU, it should do so in an objective and neutral way, so as to avoid exorbitant jurisdiction. Objective connections should not be bent so as to draw more cases into the EU courts.

The location of contractual performances inside and outside the EU

2.201 Of course not all contractual performances can be clearly located. For instance, parties might agree *not to do something*. Where is the place of performance for such a contract? The contract is then not limited to the European judicial area. The breach can as easily take place outside the EU as inside. Should one then regard the place of contracting, the place of the eventual breach, or the place of the primary obligation to which the obligation not to do something is linked (in cases where there is such primary obligation)? Another question is what happens if the defendant is domiciled in the EU, but the contract was actually to be performed outside the EU.

2.202 Both these questions arose before the European Court of Justice in the case *Besix SA v WABAG and Plafog*.[266] Besix was a company incorporated and domiciled in Belgium. WABAG and Plafog, both members of the Deutsche Babcock group, were companies incorporated in Germany and domiciled at Kulmbach in Germany. None of the parties had a link to third States. However, the facts were at least partly located outside the EU. Besix and WABAG agreed to submit a joint tender for a project of the Ministry of Mines and Energy of Cameroon to supply water in eleven urban centres in Cameroon. In this agreement they committed themselves to cooperate exclusively with each other and not to join other partners for tenders. It later turned out that Plafog had submitted a tender together with a Finnish firm. They were awarded a part of the contract, while Besix and WABAG were awarded nothing. Besix subsequently sued WABAG and Plafog for damages before the Rechtbank van koophandel (Commercial Court) of Brussels. The question was where this contract's place of performance was. The judge of first instance found that he had jurisdiction

---

[266] *Besix*, note 238 above; case notes: P Vlas [2004] *Nederlandse jurisprudentie. Uitspraken in burgerlijke en strafzaken* 1283–1297; JJ Van Haersolte-Van Hof [2002] *Nederlands Tijdschrift voor Europees recht* 226–229; J Verlinden [2002] *Columbia Journal of European Law* 493–497.

because the exclusivity agreement had to be performed in Belgium, and the exclusivity agreement was really a corollary to the preparation of the joint tender. On the substance Besix did not succeed and therefore appealed to the Hof van beroep (Appeal Court) of Brussels. By way of cross-appeal WABAG argued that the German courts had exclusive jurisdiction. The Hof van beroep posed a preliminary question to the European Court of Justice:

Must Article 5(1) of the [Brussels] Convention . . . be interpreted as meaning that a defendant domiciled in a Contracting State may, in another Contracting State, be sued, in matters relating to a contract, in the courts for any of the places of performance of the obligation in question, in particular where, consisting in an obligation not to do something—such as, in the present case, an undertaking to act exclusively with another party to a contract with a view to submitting a joint bid for a public contract and not to enter into a commitment with another partner— that obligation is to be performed in any place whatever in the world?

If not, may that defendant be sued specifically in the courts for one of the places of performance of the obligation and, if so, by reference to what criterion must that place be determined?

The reasoning of the European Court of Justice was based on concerns for **2.203** protecting EU defendants and ensuring clarity for plaintiffs as to where they might sue. The Court also considered it important to avoid a multi-plication of fora with jurisdiction. These are of course important consider-ations, but one might think that the impact outside the EU received too little attention. The European Court of Justice found that basing jurisdic-tion on the place of performance, in a case where the performance has to take place everywhere, could not be permitted.[267] Moreover, the Court found that the place of performance could not be deduced from the facts of the particular case, as the Rechtbank van koophandel of Brussels had done, so that one would be able to state that a particular case had a close connection to a particular forum.[268] Referring to the place where the breach occurred, as that could be located even if the place where one had to perform the obligation could not, was not a satisfactory solution to the Court; this would amount to a reversal of its judgments that have always connected contracts to the place of their performance.[269] A last option was to let the obligation to refrain from doing something follow the primary obligation, namely submitting the tender. This argument was based on the decision in *Shenavai*, in which a corollary performance was ruled to follow

---

[267] *Besix*, note 238 above, para 34–35.
[268] Ibid, para 37.
[269] Ibid, para 41; see *Industrie Tessili v Dunlop*, note 248 above.

the primary one.[270] The *Shenavai* construction, although based on good sense and useful in practice, had not often been followed. Where there are no clearly distinguishable main and subsidiary obligations, the European Court of Justice has held that a court only had jurisdiction over the claim on the obligation that had to be performed in its territory.[271] In *Besix* too the Court did not accept the argument of primary and corollary obligations; it found that, upon a strict reading of the provision, one had to look at the place of performance of the obligation *in question*.[272] Therefore the Court came to the conclusion that Article 5(1) could not be applied to grant jurisdiction in this dispute. The plaintiff could only sue at the domicile of the defendant.

2.204 One cannot help but wonder whether the outcome would have been different if the tender had been for a project somewhere in the EU. Would the Court then have had less difficulty in letting the obligation not to do something follow the main obligation of the tender? The other point about which one wonders, is what the outcome of the case would have been if the dispute had arisen at a later stage. What would the Court have said if Besix and WABAG had been awarded part of the contract, and in executing their contractual duties a dispute had arisen? It is clear that the EU instruments can only grant jurisdiction to courts in the EU. However, in finding connections between cases and courts the criteria should be objective. If the ECJ is of the view that an obligation not to do something does not follow the main obligation and one can sue only at the domicile of the defendant, this rule should apply, whether the main obligation is inside or outside the EU. The most important point is that the basis of jurisdiction must be formulated in such a way that it ensures a true connection between the court and the defendant, or between the court and the dispute, and that it does not lead to exorbitant jurisdiction.

Other viewpoints on this rule of Brussels I

2.205 The draft Hague convention on jurisdiction and foreign judgments in civil and commercial matters (which was never completed) again offers an interesting lesson in comparative law and the criticism that can be made of the European approach. Regarding contracts two broad ideas were represented in the 2001 text.[273]

---

[270] Case 266/85 *Shenavai v Kreischer* [1987] ECR 239.
[271] Case C–420–97 *Leathertex Divisione Sintetici SpA v Bodetex BVBA* [1999] ECR I–6747.
[272] *Besix*, note 238 above, para 44.
[273] Art 6.

The European view endorsed a provision similar to Brussels I: a well-defined   **2.206**
but stringent rule granting jurisdiction to the courts of the place of the
contract's performance. This was further specified as the place of the supply of goods or services, or, where both goods and services were involved,
the place of the principal obligation. This rule was subject to criticism on
various points. The first problem was the detour via applicable law in order
to find the court that had jurisdiction. While conflict of law rules have
been unified in the EU,[274] this is not the case globally, and the reference to
the applicable law would lead to divergent results.[275] This indicates the
complex nature of the European rule. Second, the rule was criticized for its
inflexible nature.[276] It could be exorbitant to grant jurisdiction to the court
of a state where the defendant had never even been, but just sent someone
to deliver goods. One should also realize that this 'place of performance'
is frequently, if not almost always, the residence of the other party, i.e. the
plaintiff. For the US, the rule even posed constitutional concerns.[277]

On the other side stood the American idea of doing business. This concept   **2.207**
relies on the presence of a defendant in the forum's territory. If a company
consistently trades in a certain area, and has become part of that market, it
should not be surprised that it can be sued in the courts of that area or that
market. This rule caused much discord between the negotiators. However,
it is interesting to note that even those concerns did not lead to accepting
the European alternative. The European rule is not one that is accepted
internationally as always leading to a just result.

MAINTENANCE

The current rule contained in Brussels I

The fact that this provision is present in Brussels I is surprising from a   **2.208**
material scope point of view. The Regulation is supposed to be on civil
and commercial matters, but the largest part of family law has been
excluded from its scope.[278] Maintenance obligations are civil matters and

---

[274] By the Convention on the law applicable to contractual obligations, signed in Rome in
1980; consolidated version published in OJ C 27 of 26 January 1998, p 34–46. This Convention
is being converted into a regulation: Proposal for a Regulation of the European Parliament
and the Council on the law applicable to contractual obligations (Rome I) of 15 December
2005, COM/2005/0650 final—COD 2005/0261; available at <http://eur-lex.europa.eu>.

[275] Bucher, note 263 above, 85.

[276] For instance Audit in Lowenfeld & Silberman, note 263 above, 127; Bucher, note 263
above, 84–87.

[277] Bucher, note 263 above, 84.

[278] Art 1(2)(a) of Brussels I.

concern money judgments, but they are, in the first place, part of family law.[279] At the time of drawing up the Brussels Convention, the argument was that a Convention that did not include a forum for maintenance actions would be of limited value.[280] In the meantime, the European Commission has made a proposal for a separate Regulation on maintenance obligations.[281] This Regulation will take maintenance out of the scope of Brussels I altogether. The proposed Regulation will be discussed after Article 5(2).

2.209 Let us now turn to the existing Article 5(2). Like the entire Article 5, this provision can only come into play when the defendant is domiciled in the EU. The provision grants an alternative basis for jurisdiction: the domicile or habitual residence of the maintenance creditor. The normal criterion used by Brussels I is domicile (in the civil law sense) and not habitual residence.[282] The result of having the two concepts as alternatives in one provision might be an expansion of its scope. An example is provided by a couple domiciled in Morocco. After a divorce, one spouse moves to France to live there. The other spouse remains domiciled in Morocco, but assumes a habitual residence in Belgium. Whereas jurisdiction in the EU would normally be based only on domicile, in this situation the Regulation creates an extra jurisdictional basis. At the same time habitual residence might be a more appropriate connection in family law matters.

2.210 Furthermore, the second part of Article 5(2) creates a link to the Member States' 'own law' of jurisdiction for actions concerning a person's status. In such cases, the court that has jurisdiction may also grant an order for maintenance. There is only one limitation: jurisdiction may not have been founded only on the basis of the nationality of the parties. This maintenance order will be recognized and enforced throughout the EU under Brussels I. Before the enactment of Brussels II *bis*, this provision might have referred to more different bases of jurisdiction than it does now. That Regulation created EU jurisdiction rules for divorce and marriage

---

[279] Briggs & Rees, note 243 above, 177, explain that the inclusion of this part of family law has its origins in Roman Law.

[280] See Jenard Report on the 1968 version of the Brussels Convention; OJ C 59, 5 March 1979, 1 (Jenard Report), 25.

[281] Proposal for a Council Regulation on Jurisdiction, Applicable law, Recognition and Enforcement of Decisions and Cooperation in Matters relating to Maintenance Obligations of 15 December 2005, COM(2005) 649 final. This Regulation, like the other regulations on civil and commercial matters, will not apply in Denmark (rec 27 and Art 1). The United Kingdom has indicated that it would not opt in, so that the Regulation would not apply there (unless it decides later to opt in). Ireland would opt in so that the Regulation would apply there.

[282] Above, paras 2.11 and following.

annulment. Divorce is probably the action concerning status to which a maintenance claim is most often connected. Other possibilities might exist, such as an action for the establishment of parenthood, or for maintenance.

One might wonder why Brussels I does not refer to Brussels II *bis* in this **2.211** provision, in addition to the national law of the Member States. The latter Regulation has created a coherent scheme of jurisdiction rules and the national rules may only be applied in as far as they are authorized by Brussels II *bis*, at least for the matters that fall within its material scope (such as divorce).

The proposed Maintenance Regulation

The proposed Maintenance Regulation will be broader than Brussels I. **2.212** Apart from rules on jurisdiction and the recognition and enforcement of judgments, the Regulation will also contain provisions on applicable law, common procedures, and cooperation between central authorities of the EU Member States.

Most notably, the Regulation will not be limited to defendants habitually **2.213** resident in an EU Member State.[283] It seems that, as soon that there is a rule that grants jurisdiction to a court in an EU Member State, that court will have jurisdiction. The scope of the Regulation is thus determined by its jurisdiction rules.[284] The Regulation grants jurisdiction to the EU Member State court of the habitual residence of the defendant, or of the habitual residence of the creditor.[285] Furthermore, the EU Member State court that has jurisdiction over an action concerning the status of a person may also rule on a maintenance claim which is ancillary to it, unless the jurisdiction is based solely on the nationality of one of the parties. Here again, Brussels II *bis* will determine jurisdiction over divorce proceedings, while national law will determine jurisdiction over an action on parenthood. This provision contains no explicit reference to Brussels II *bis*.[286] The next provision states that an EU Member State court which has jurisdiction over an action concerning parental responsibility will also have jurisdiction over

---

[283] Rec 10 states '[t]he fact that the defendant is habitualy resident in a non-member State of the European Union should no longer be a reason for non-application of Community rules and for reference to national law.'

[284] Above, para 2.99.

[285] Art 3(a) and (b).

[286] Art 3(c).

an ancillary maintenance claim. This provision does refer to the jurisdiction rules of Brussels II *bis*.[287]

2.214 The Regulation also contains rules on the prorogation of jurisdiction[288] and on the voluntary appearance of the defendant.[289]

2.215 Lastly the Regulation also contains a provision on 'residual jurisdiction'. When none of the rules discussed in the previous paragraphs grants jurisdiction to any court in an EU Member State, then the courts of the Member State of the common nationality of the creditor and debtor will have jurisdiction. If the maintenance obligation concerns spouses or ex-spouses, and none of the rules discussed in the previous paragraphs grants jurisdiction to a court in an EU Member State, the courts of the Member State of the last common habitual residence (not more than a year before the institution of the proceedings) will have jurisdiction.[290] This provision has the same title and function in the Regulation as Article 7 of Brussels II *bis*. However, that provision refers, residually, to the Member States' national jurisdiction rules. The Maintenance Regulation will leave no residual place for national jurisdiction rules.

2.216 This approach has two advantages. First, it does not discriminate against defendants domiciled or habitually resident outside the EU; different jurisdiction rules do not apply to them leading to judgments that can be recognized and enforced throughout the EU in the same way as those against defendants domiciled or habitually resident in the EU. Second, it is clear. It sets out all the rules and there are no rules hiding in national law that parties from third States should be wary of. The disadvantage is of course one of subsidiarity: should the EU really regulate jurisdiction over people domiciled or habitually resident in third States? Or should the national laws of the Member States regulate such matters? Perhaps the choice of a coordinated approach should be appreciated, despite the far-reaching effect this attributes to EU law. Indeed, EU law is far-reaching in any event, on the basis of the recent interpretations given by the European Court of Justice. Furthermore, the recognition and enforcement rules apply to all judgments from EU courts in all cases.

---

[287] Art 3(d). Brussels II *bis* states in its Rec 11 that a court having jurisdiction under that Regulation will generally have jurisdiction to rule on maintenance obligations by application of Art 5(2) of Brussels I. This explicit rule in the proposed Maintenance Regulation seems to complete the system. The rule is also included in Art 5(2)(c) of the 2007 Lugano Convention (without reference to Brussels II *bis*).

[288] Art 4. This issue is discussed in chapter 4 of this book.

[289] Art 5. This issue has been discussed above, paras 2.160 and following; specifically regarding the proposed Maintenance Regulation, paras 2.174–2.175.

[290] Art 6.

Thus harmonizing the jurisdiction rules that lead to judgments that can be recognized and enforced might comply with the principle of subsidiarity after all.

TORTS, *DELICTS*, AND *QUASI-DELICTS*

General

Actions with regard to non-contractual obligations can also be brought at the court of the place where they were committed. For the provision to come into play, the defendant once again must be domiciled in the EU. The main application of the provision is therefore that a party domiciled in one EU Member State can be sued in the courts of another Member State. **2.217**

Torts, *delicts* and *quasi-delicts* can vary in different legal systems and the European Court of Justice has not really provided an autonomous definition of what exactly these entail. It has held that the provision 'covers all actions which seek to establish the liability of a defendant and which are not related to a "contract" within the meaning of Article 5(1)'.[291] That is a very broad definition, if it deserves being termed a definition at all. Whether or not an act is a tort or *delict* under the law of a specific EU Member State, it might be so considered for purposes of jurisdiction of the courts of that state. Pre-contractual liability, also a matter that is not always easy to qualify, equally falls within the scope of the provision on tort.[292] **2.218**

Not only torts, etc already committed but also the threat of unlawful acts falls in the scope of the provision. That change in wording was brought by Brussels I. The extension to acts not yet committed did not exist explicitly under the Brussels Convention, although some contended that it was included in any event.[293] **2.219**

---

[291] *Kalfelis*, note 238 above, para 17.

[292] Case C–334/00 *Fonderie Officine Meccaniche Tacconi SpA v Heinrich Wagner Sinto Maschinenfabrik GmbH (HWS)* [2002] ECR I–7357.

[293] Schlosser Report on the 1978 version of the Brussels Convention; OJ C 59, 5 March 1979, 71, para 134, p 111 states '[t]here is much to be said for the proposition that the courts specified in Article 5(3) should also have jurisdiction in proceedings whose main object is to prevent the imminent commission of a tort'. See also Gaudemet-Tallon, *Compétence et exécution*, note 236 above, 167–168. H Duintjer Tebbens, 'Jurisdiction in Matters relating to Tort or Delict and to the Operations of a Branch, Agency or Other Establishment,' in Court of Justice of the European Communities, *Civil Jurisdiction and Judgments in Europe* (London: Butterworths, 1992) 87–98 at 90–91 and 92 mentions the possibility that actions aimed at preventing torts might be included under the old provision; he also states that such explicit extension of the

2.220 The European Court of Justice has found that the place where the harmful event occurred has to be defined autonomously, rather than permitting a link to the applicable law in order to find that place, or the place of the damage.[294]

Damage in a third State

2.221 How would Article 5(3) be applied if the damage occurred in a third State while the defendant was domiciled in the EU? In such a case Article 5(3) would not be applicable. Of course, Brussels I can only grant jurisdiction to EU courts, in this case if damage occurred inside the EU. Conversely, if damage arises in a third State so that the case is closely linked with that State, there is no mechanism in Brussels I for declining jurisdiction on the basis of the domicile of the defendant in the EU. This became clear in *Owusu*, where the plaintiff had based his action on both contract and tort. The European Court of Justice found that the English courts were compelled to assume jurisdiction on the basis that the defendant was domiciled in England, despite the fact that the damage occurred entirely in Jamaica.[295]

Financial loss

2.222 For determining the place of the harm, the European Court of Justice has held that the mere creation of financial loss for an indirect victim is irrelevant.[296] The same holds true for financial loss as a result of wrongful conduct by sellers of call options relating to shares.[297] In these cases it will be the courts of the place where the initial harm occurred that would have jurisdiction, and not the courts of the place where the loss was felt in the estate of the plaintiff.

2.223 If the financial loss were suffered in a third State, Article 5(3) would not be applicable. In *Marinari v Lloyds Bank plc and Zubaidi Trading Company*,[298]

Brussels Convention might not be necessary because an action to prevent a tort might be brought at the domicile of the defendant (Art 2), or under the provision allowing provisional and protective measures (Art 31 Brussels I). Briggs & Rees, note 243 above, 196–197 did not exclude the possibility that future torts were included under the rule, but they took a more cautious stance.

[294] Case C–364/93 *Marinari v Lloyds Bank plc and Zubaidi Trading Company* [1995] ECR I–3719, paras 18–19.
[295] *Owusu*, note 240 above.
[296] *Dumez France*, note 238 above.
[297] Case C–168/02 *Kronhofer v Maier and others* [2004] ECR I–6009.
[298] Note 294 above.

the facts took place both inside and outside the EU. Mr Marinari lodged promissory notes with the Manchester branch of Lloyds Bank. These notes had been issued by the Negros Oriental province of the Republic of the Philippines in favour of Zubaidi Trading Company of Beirut. The bank refused to return the notes and informed the police that they were of dubious origin. Mr Marinari was subsequently arrested and the promissory notes sequestered. Mr Marinari sued Lloyds Bank in Italy, stating that he had incurred damage there (where he was domiciled). The European Court of Justice found that the place where the victim suffered financial damage was not the place where the harmful event occurred. That certainly cannot be contested. However, the Court did not consider the facts that at least part of the damage occurred outside the EU, and that one of the defendants (possibly instrumental in the damage) was domiciled in a third State (Lebanon).

Quasi-contractual obligations?

Quasi-contractual liability (such as *negotiorum gestio* and unjustified **2.224** enrichment) may fall under the broad definition of torts, *delicts* and *quasi-delicts* as well, if one interprets the requirement of obligation *other than a contractual obligation* literally. If unjustified enrichment falls under the provision on tort, then the occurrence of the facts in a third State will not be taken into account, so that only the domicile of the defendant in the EU will confer Regulation-based jurisdiction. That jurisdiction will be compulsory, so that the facts in a third State will not be able to lead to the declining of jurisdiction.

Some authors argue that jurisdiction for quasi-contractual liability will **2.225** lie only with the court of the defendant's domicile (Article 2).[299] They rely on the *Kalfelis* judgment[300] to support their argument. It does not seem, however, that the judgment contains authority for this. The action in question concerned claims in contract, tort and quasi-contract (unjustified enrichment). The European Court of Justice stated that, if jurisdiction over a part of the action could be based on Article 5(3), that jurisdiction could not be elaborated to parts of the action that did not fall under the provision. The Court did not specify whether it was referring to both the contractual and quasi-contractual parts of the action. It was referring to something other than the tort part of the action. If it had been referring to the contract and unjustified enrichment actions, then it would seem that unjustified

---

[299] See Gaudemet-Tallon, *Compétence et exécution*, note 236 above, 138–139.
[300] Note 238 above.

enrichment falls only under the general basis of jurisdiction. If, however, it had been referring only to the contractual obligation, it could have implied that unjustified enrichment did fall under Article 5(3). The House of Lords has found (three Lord Justices concurring, two dissenting) that a claim for restitution of moneys paid under a void contract did not fall under the jurisdiction rules on contract or those on tort.[301] It was found not to be contractual in nature, because it was clear that the contract was void from the start; there had never been a valid contract and the parties did not dispute this fact. However, the dissenting Lord Justices argued that it would not make sense to include cases where the argument that a contract is void is posed by a litigating party as an alternative argument, while excluding claims where the nullity of the contract is not disputed.[302] All the Lord Justices agreed that the claim of restitution was not tort, because there was no question of a harmful act or a threatened wrong. The House of Lords added that it was a misreading of *Kalfelis* to see it as meaning that a claim for unjust enrichment falls under the tort rule.[303]

2.226 If quasi-contractual obligations do not fall within the contract or tort provisions, then probably only Article 2 on the domicile of the defendant will apply to them. In any event, there will be jurisdiction in the EU according to the Regulation only if the defendant is domiciled in the EU. If he or she were not, one would fall back on national bases for jurisdiction, appointed by Article 4 of the Regulation.

The influence of this provision on national rules of jurisdiction as regards third States

2.227 The case law on the Brussels Convention also has an influence on the national legal systems of the Member State courts. The English judgment *Berezovsky v Michaels and Others and Glouchkov v Michaels and Others* considered jurisdiction in a libel case.[304] *Forbes*, an American fortnightly

---

[301] *Kleinwort Benson Ltd v City of Glasgow District Council* [1997] CLC 1609 HL. This case was not based directly on Brussels I, but on Arts 16 and 17 and Schedule 4 of the Civil Jurisdiction and Judgments Act 1982, which incorporates the rules of Brussels I for the allocation of jurisdiction between the parts of the United Kingdom, in this case between England and Scotland. For this reason the ECJ, when asked for a preliminary ruling by the Court of Appeal, found that it lacked jurisdiction to give such ruling: Case C–346/93 *Kleinwort Benson Ltd v City of Glasgow District Council* [1995] ECR I–615.

[302] [1997] WLR 923. See the dissenting judgment written by Lord Nicholls of Birkenhead, paras 28–47.

[303] Ibid, at para 24.

[304] [2000] WL 544123.

magazine, published an allegedly defamatory article about two influential Russian men, Berezovsky (businessman and politician) and Glouchkov (First Deputy Manager and later Managing Director of Aeroflot, Russian airline). The magazine was circulated in various places: most readers were in the US, an estimated 6,000 in the UK and only about 13 in Russia. The magazine was also available on the internet. The plaintiffs brought action in an English court against Forbes Inc (publisher of the magazine) and Michaels (editor), both based in the United States of America. The question arose as to whether this court had jurisdiction. The plaintiffs contended that they had extensive contacts with England (business and in the case of Mr Bezezovsky, family). Both of them also spoke English well.

At first instance, the court granted a stay on the basis of *forum non conven-* **2.228** *iens* and directed the defendants to submit to the jurisdiction of the Russian courts, which it considered to be the more appropriate forum. When new evidence on the detrimental effect of the articles on the reputation of the plaintiffs in England was brought before the Court of Appeal, that court reversed the decision and found that the English court did in fact have jurisdiction.[305] Counsel for *Forbes* contended that 'the correct approach is to treat multi-jurisdiction cases like the present as giving rise to a single cause of action and then to ascertain where the global cause of action arose'. He relied *inter alia* on the US Uniform Single Publication Act which provides that for a single publication only one action for damages is possible. In the House of Lords, Lord Steyn (giving the leading part of the majority judgment) disagreed and made reference to English law and to the case law of the European Court of Justice, specifically *Shevill*.[306] According to this case, separate actions in every relevant jurisdiction would be permissible. Lord Steyn admitted that *Shevill* dealt with the Brussels Convention, while the case before him did not. Yet he used the argument of *Shevill* as part of his reasoning and the appeal was dismissed. This shows the subtle way in which case law on the EU legislation has an effect on parties established outside the EU. None of the parties in this case was from the EU.

The Belgian legislator has also taken up the European Court of Justice rul- **2.229** ing that one could cut the action into pieces. The new Code de droit international privé (Private International Law Code) states that the Belgian courts have jurisdiction if, or *in so far as*, the damage has occurred or might

---

[305] [1999] ILPr 358; [1999] EMLR 278.
[306] Case C–68/93 *Fiona Shevill and others v Presse Alliance SA* [1995] ECR I–415.

occur in Belgium.[307] This partial jurisdiction does not seem to sit well in national law. Having it in Brussels I seems more logical because there is a group of friendly states dividing jurisdiction between their courts and they do not want to tread on each other's territories. In a unilateral system, such as national rules on jurisdiction, a chopped-up rule on jurisdiction does not seem useful, nor does it incite legal certainty and foreseeablility in international disputes.

2.230 The splitting of cases often arises, as in *Shevill* and *Berezovsky*, in those concerning libel. With internet publications the dividing up becomes more and more difficult. Such a chopped-up and old-fashioned rule should not exist any more, and should not be copied into national legal systems. Jurisdiction should lie with a court that has a proper link to the case, and a proper link should be more than a small part of the damage. Effort should be made to find a place where the *delict* was committed, caused, or most greatly felt. If no such proper link exists, a court plainly lacks jurisdiction, and should not get an opportunity to hear a tiny part of the case. Moreover, outside the framework of Brussels I there is no guarantee that, if the action were chopped up, the other courts would assume jurisdiction on the basis of their national rules.

Other viewpoints on this provision of Brussels I

2.231 This rule was also discussed at negotiations of the draft Hague convention on jurisdiction and foreign judgments in civil and commercial matters. The European rule formed the first alternative: the courts of the place where the act was committed or where the injury arose have jurisdiction. The US approach was to look at the direction of activity (as for contracts): if the defendant had engaged in frequent and significant activity, or directed activity into a state, and the injury resulted from that activity, the court of that place would have jurisdiction. Attempts to limit this basis of jurisdiction include requiring the link between the defendant and the court to be reasonable; that it would not apply if the defendant had taken all reasonable steps to avoid directing activity into that state; and that the court would have jurisdiction with regard to the injury resulting from the tort and nothing else. No consensus could be reached between the negotiators. These discussions once again indicated the different views on jurisdiction and that the European approach is far from globally accepted. One can either

---

[307] Act of 16 July 2004, published in *Belgisch Staatsblad* 27 July 2004, Art 96(2). According to the Parliamentary documents, the provision was inspired by the case law of the European Court of Justice.

link the dispute, such as the tort, to the court, or one can link the defendant to the court. The argument is that if a corporation enters into a market, it implicitly subjects itself to that entire market, including its courts.[308]

CRIMINAL PROCEEDINGS

Article 5(4) permits EU Member States to retain such a rule where civil **2.232** proceedings can be linked to criminal proceedings.[309] In effect one hooks one's claim for damage or restitution onto the already pending criminal action, rather than bringing a separate action. In other legal systems, one may bring civil claims against administrative actors or people vested with public authority in civil or in criminal courts.[310] The civil law part of the resulting judgment would thus be recognized and enforced under Brussels I, even though in the first place jurisdiction had been founded on a law of criminal procedure.

One can think of a situation in which a person domiciled in a third State **2.233** is accused of a criminal act in an EU Member State. In some EU Member States, it would be possible for victims to hook civil actions against this person onto the criminal proceedings. The judgment on the civil actions will be recognizable and enforceable against the third State domiciliary throughout the EU. This is another example of the imperfect double nature of Brussels I. Jurisdiction is based on national rules of criminal procedure, but the civil law part of the action has effects throughout the EU. In a truly double instrument such a rule should be deleted. However, that might have the result that some victims of crimes could not easily have their civil law actions recognized in other EU Member States, merely because of procedural specificities of the legal system in an EU Member State. Another victim, who had to institute a separate civil law action, would be able to benefit from the system. The solution is probably to permit the rule, but to give it an autonomous EU flavour: inserting conditions which will make recognition in other EU Member States possible. These conditions should be based on finding a connection between the court and the defendant or between the court and the facts.

---

[308] See RA Brand, 'Jurisdictional Common Ground: in Search for a Global Convention,' in JAR Nafziger & SC Symeonides (eds), *Essays in Honor of Arthur T von Mehren, Law and Justice in a Multistate World. Essays in Honour of Arthur T von Mehren* (Ardsley: Transnational Publishers Inc, 2002) 11–32 at 19–20.

[309] See Case C–172/91 *Sonntag v Waidmann* [1983] ECR I–1963; Case C–7/98 *Krombach v Bamberski* [2000] ECR I–1935.

[310] For a thorough legal comparative analysis, see the opinion of Advocate General Darmon in *Sonntag v Waidmann*, ibid.

BRANCH, AGENCY OR OTHER ESTABLISHMENT

General

2.234 This rule grants jurisdiction to the courts where a branch, agency or other establishment is located when the dispute arises out of the operations of that establishment. As throughout Article 5, this basis of jurisdiction only exists if the legal person-defendant is domiciled in the EU.[311] If one considers the EU's internal market where goods, services, capital, and persons are supposed to move freely, this basis of jurisdiction makes sense: if corporations are permitted to operate easily throughout the EU, they should also be easy to sue in the EU at the places where they are active.

2.235 The European Court of Justice has explained the terms used in this provision.[312] The concept of branch, agency, or other establishment means that there is a place of business with the appearance of permanency, with a management, and which is materially equipped to negotiate business with third parties so that they do not have to deal directly with the head office. The concept of 'operations' encompasses contractual and non-contractual obligations concerning the management of the branch in itself. It also comprises contractual and non-contractual obligations undertaken in the name of the parent legal person at the business place of the branch, agency, or establishment and performed at that place.

2.236 Furthermore, the European Court of Justice has extended the reach of this provision to situations where two separate but identical legal persons exist. In the *Schotte* case[313] there were two separate legal persons, one incorporated in France and the other in Germany. They had the same name and identical management. The German entity negotiated and conducted business in the name of the French entity and the French entity used the German entity as an extension of itself. The European Court of Justice found that the German courts had jurisdiction in a dispute between the French entity and another party because of the establishment in Germany, despite the fact that it was legally a separate entity. The true test seems to be whether or not the establishment acts on behalf of, or for the defendant, and not whether the establishment has a separate legal personality.[314]

---

[311] Regarding the domicile of a legal person-defendant: paras 2.24 and following; TC Hartley, *Civil Jurisdiction and Judgments* (London: Sweet & Maxwell, 1984) at 53.

[312] Case 33/78 *Somafer SA v Saar-Ferngas AG* [1978] ECR 2183, para 13; see also Duintjer Tebbens, 'Jurisdiction in Tort or Delict', note 293 above, 96–98; Hartley, *Civil Jurisdiction and Judgments*, ibid, 54.

[313] Case 218/86 *SAR Schotte v Parfums Rothschild SARL* [1987] ECR 4905.

[314] See also North & Fawcett, note 263 above, 220–222.

Third State corporations?

It has been stated that this provision is supposed to come into play only if **2.237**
the defendant-corporation is domiciled in the EU. That corporation can
then be sued in other EU Member States where it has a branch. This basis
for jurisdiction, unlike the protective bases of jurisdiction, is not a fiction
that a legal person domiciled in a third State is deemed to be domiciled in
the EU at the place of its branch, agency or other establishment.[315]

However, it should be recalled here that the definition of domicile for cor- **2.238**
porations (Article 60) is a broad one.[316] A company with statutory seat in
Texas and real seat in France will be domiciled in the EU for purposes of
Brussels I. Actions relating to the operations of that company's branch in
London would then also fall under Brussels I. One could also change the
example slightly: would a company with statutory seat in Texas and real
seat in London be domiciled in the EU for purposes of Brussels I? England
(like the United States of America) adheres to and applies the incorporation theory. Therefore, according to English law (and US law) the company
would be seen as domiciled in Texas. However, Brussels I states in Article 60
that there are three alternatives an EU Member State court might apply
when determining the domicile of a legal person. Every EU Member State
court might thus decide to see a company as domiciled at the place of its
statutory seat, its central administration, or its principal place of business.
Although an English court would not have done so under its own law, it
would be able to regard the Texas company as domiciled in London. The
as yet unanswered question is whether the English court might be compelled to see the Texan company as domiciled in the EU, since the EU
jurisdiction rules are compulsory (as had been found in *Owusu*). Disputes
regarding the operations of the French branch would fall under the jurisdiction rules of Brussels I if the corporation were domiciled in the EU.
French law adheres to the real seat theory and a French judge would probably be inclined to see the company as domiciled in London, by which it
would fall under the rules of Brussels I and the French court would have
jurisdiction over the operations of the branch.

The Cour d'appel (Court of Appeal) of Versailles in France has arrived at **2.239**
a rather strange construction in a case concerning a branch in France.
It assumed jurisdiction over a French branch of Citibank, domiciled in
New York.[317] The operations that gave rise to the dispute in this situation

---

[315] Para 2.276 below.
[316] Paras 2.24 and following above.
[317] Judgment of 26 September 1991 [1992] *Revue critique de droit international privé*
333–336.

were not even based on the operations of the bank's French branch (in Nanterre), but of its branch in Monaco. No specific reference was made in the judgment to Article 5(5), but, strangely, jurisdiction was asserted on the general basis of jurisdiction, the domicile of the defendant in France (Article 2) in combination with French national rules on jurisdiction. Gaudemet-Tallon has severely criticized this judgment, stating that, as regards a defendant domiciled in a third State, Article 5(5) could not be applied.[318] Furthermore, since the dispute did not even arise from operations of the French branch, another requirement for the application of Article 5(5) was unmet. This case therefore seems incorrect, and one can only hope that it was a lone, stray case.

The irrelevance of the place of the obligation

2.240 For the application of this provision on branches, the place of performance of a contract is irrelevant. That separate basis of jurisdiction has no connection with this provision. The European Court of Justice confirmed this in *Lloyd's Register of Shipping v Société Campenon Bernard*.[319] In that case the contract covered the testing of concrete-reinforcing steel for the construction of a motorway in Kuwait. Société Campenon Bernard had contracted with Lloyd's through its French branch. According to the contract, the steel would be tested by another of Lloyd's branches in Spain (to determine whether it complied with a US technical standard). At the time both of the facts, and of the proceedings, Spain had not yet become Party to the Brussels Convention, so was a third State in this matter. After the testing (which found that the steel did comply with the standard) the Kuwait Ministry of Public Works refused to accept the steel, which in its view did not comply with the specified standard. This prompted Société Campenon Bernard's action against Lloyd's in France, the location of the branch through which it had contracted. The French Cour de cassation posed a preliminary question to the European Court of Justice, citing the fact that performance of the contract did not take place at the branch and whether this affected jurisdiction on the basis of the operations of the branch. The European Court of Justice ruled that the place of performance of the contract was irrelevant. It stated that to require that the contract must be performed in the EU Member State where the branch was situated would be to make Article 5(5) redundant.

---

[318] Case notes by H Gaudemet-Tallon [1992] *Revue critique de droit international privé* 336–340; A Huet [1993] *Journal de droit international* 51–53.
[319] Case C–439/93 [1995] ECR I–961.

While this argument does not show a lack of logic, it has to be pointed **2.241**
out that it opens the door to legal constructions aimed at manipulating
jurisdiction within the EU, when the contract is to be performed outside
the EU. The provision can only come into play when the defendant is
established in the EU, so the manipulation would have a limited effect.
If Brussels I were to be changed so as to apply to all defendants in the
same fashion (and become a truly double instrument), this provision
would be applied to all defendants, no matter where they are domiciled,
that have a branch in the EU. Such a rule might be acceptable (instead of
applying the national rules of the EU Member States) if a true connection
exists between the activities of the branch and the dispute.

Trusts

In addition to the general basis for jurisdiction in Article 2, jurisdiction **2.242**
over matters relating to trust lies with the court of the state where the trust
is domiciled. This provision is only effected when the defendant is domiciled in a EU Member State different to the one in which the trust is situated.
However, it is conceivable that the trustee-defendant might be domiciled
in the EU while the beneficiary was domiciled in a third State or vice versa.
In such a case the provision might provide a useful alternative for parties
from third States that want to bring actions.

A rule referring to the domicile of the trust is the only reasonable solution **2.243**
for a legal instrument that exists in some of the legal systems of the EU, but
not in all.[320] Granting jurisdiction to the place where the trust is domiciled
creates legal certainty, both within the EU and for parties from outside the
EU who want to create a trust under the law of, for example, England. If
Brussels I were changed so that it applied to all defendants, this provision
would also be extended. This probably would not have much effect in
practice, since the rule is in line with bases for jurisdiction that exist in
states that have the trust as part of their legal system (hence the rules currently applicable if the defendant is domiciled in a third State).

Salvage of Ship or Cargo

Salvaging ships is an internationally acknowledged practice. Therefore **2.244**
Brussels I grants jurisdiction to the courts of the EU Member State where the
cargo or freight has or could have been arrested, but bail or other security

---

[320] It exists in Ireland and the United Kingdom. Article 5(6) was added to the Convention
at the accession of these states, since it was thought that the Convention needed such a rule
to cover such legal entities without legal personality; see Schlosser Report, note 293 above,
105–108, paras 109–120.

had been given. This basis for jurisdiction can certainly affect parties from third States. Also, ships sailing under the flags of third States can be the subjects of this basis for jurisdiction. However, the defendant must be domiciled in another EU Member State if this basis for jurisdiction is to be triggered. It is also required that the defendant has an interest in the cargo or freight, or had such an interest at the time of the salvage.[321]

CONTRACTS RELATED TO RIGHTS *IN REM*

2.245 There is one more provision on contracts that should briefly be mentioned. Tucked away at the end of Article 6 there is a rule providing that in matters relating to contract, if the action can be combined with an action regarding rights *in rem* in immovable property, the contractual action may be brought in the EU Member State court where the property is located. The actions must be against the same defendant. The provision specifically states that it applies to defendants domiciled in the EU. In this sense the rule seems entirely reasonable.

2.246 As indicated in chapter 3, if immovable property is situated in the EU, the EU Member State court of its location has jurisdiction on the basis of Brussels I, irrespective of the domicile of the parties. The hooking-on provision under discussion here, however, can only come into play if the defendant is domiciled in the EU. If the immovable property action is pending in an EU Member State court against a defendant from a third State, the current provisions of Brussels I cannot allow this extension. One would have to look at domestic law to determine whether a contract claim could be brought in the same court against the defendant.

CONCLUSION

2.247 Article 5 provides alternative jurisdiction. 'Alternative' should be understood in relation to the general basis for jurisdiction of the domicile of the defendant (Article 2). Article 5 limits its own application to cases where the defendant is domiciled in an EU Member State; bases are provided for suing these EU defendants in other EU Member States. Even though the provisions of Article 5, especially the bases for jurisdiction relating to contract and tort, are often used in practice, these provisions only occasionally affect parties from third States.[322] It has been pointed out, however, that

---

[321] See Hartley, *Civil Jurisdiction and Judgments*, note 311 above, 56.

[322] This is clear from the case law of the European Court of Justice. For the Article's application in Belgium, see <http://www.euprocedure.be>.

concerns might arise where contracts are to be performed in a third State, or where torts had been committed in a third State. At the same time, these provisions emphasize the distinction between defendants based on their domicile. For Brussels I to become a truly double instrument, where recognition and enforcement were facilitated because jurisdiction rules are unified, the provisions discussed in this section would have to be extended to parties from third States. Accordingly their drafting, and interpretation by the European Court of Justice, should always seek a connection between court and defendant, or between court and facts, so as to avoid exorbitant jurisdiction.

G. PROTECTIVE BASES FOR JURISDICTION

Section 3 of Brussels I: Jurisdiction relating to matters of insurance:

Article 8:

In matters relating to insurance, jurisdiction shall be determined by this Section, without prejudice to Article 4 and point 5 of Article 5.

Article 9:

1. *An insurer domiciled in a Member State may be sued:*
   a) *in the courts of the Member State where he is domiciled, or*
   b) *in another Member State, in the case of actions brought by the policyholder, the insured or a beneficiary, in the courts for the place where the plaintiff is domiciled,*
   c) *if he is a co-insurer, in the courts of a Member State in which proceedings are brought against the leading insurer.*
2. *An insurer who is not domiciled in a Member State but has a branch, agency or other establishment in one of the Member States shall, in disputes arising out of the operations of the branch, agency or establishment, be deemed to be domiciled in that Member State.*

Article 12:

1. *Without prejudice to Article 11(3)* [direct actions], *an insurer may bring proceedings only in the courts of the Member State in which the defendant is domiciled, irrespective of whether he is the policyholder, the insured or a beneficiary.*
2. *The provisions of this Section shall not affect the right to bring a counter-claim in the court in which, in accordance with this Section, the original claim is pending.*

Article 13:

The provisions of this Section may be departed from only by an agreement:

1. *which is entered into after the dispute has arisen, or*
2. *which allows the policyholder, the insured or a beneficiary to bring proceedings in courts other than those indicated in this Section, or*
3. *which is concluded between a policyholder and an insurer, both of whom are at the time of the conclusion of the contract domiciled or habitually resident in the same Member State, and which has the effect of conferring jurisdiction on the courts of that State even if the harmful event were to occur abroad, provided that such an agreement is not contrary to the law of that State, or*
4. *which is concluded with a policyholder who is not domiciled in a Member State, except in so far as the insurance is compulsory or relates to immovable property in a Member State, or*
5. *which relates to a contract of insurance in so far as it covers one or more of the risks set out in Article 14.*

Section 4 of Brussels I: Jurisdiction over consumer contracts:

Article 15:

1. *In matters relating to a contract concluded by a person, the consumer, for a purpose which can be regarded as being outside his trade or profession, jurisdiction shall be determined by this Section, without prejudice to Article 4 and point 5 of Article 5, if:*
   a) *it is a contract for the sale of goods on instalment credit terms; or*
   b) *it is a contract for a loan repayable by instalments, or for any other form of credit, made to finance the sale of goods; or*
   c) *in all other cases, the contract has been concluded with a person who pursues commercial or professional activities in the Member State of the consumer's domicile or, by any means, directs such activities to that Member State or to several States including that Member State, and the contract falls within the scope of such activities.*
2. *Where a consumer enters into a contract with a party who is not domiciled in the Member State but has a branch, agency or other establishment in one of the Member States, that party shall, in disputes arising out of the operations of the branch, agency or establishment, be deemed to be domiciled in that State.*
3. *This Section shall not apply to a contract of transport other than a contract which, for an inclusive price, provides for a combination of travel and accommodation.*

Article 16:

1. *A consumer may bring proceedings against the other party to a contract either in the courts of the Member State in which that party is domiciled or in the courts for the place where the consumer is domiciled.*

2. *Proceedings may be brought against a consumer by the other party to the contract only in the courts of the Member State in which the consumer is domiciled.*
3. *This Article shall not affect the right to bring a counter-claim in the court in which, in accordance with this Section, the original claim is pending.*

Article 17:

The provisions of this Section may be departed from only by an agreement:

1. *which is entered into after the dispute has arisen; or*
2. *which allows the consumer to bring proceedings in courts other than those indicated in this Section; or*
3. *which is entered into by the consumer and the other party to the contract, both of whom are at the time of the conclusion of the contract domiciled or habitually resident in the same Member State, and which confers jurisdiction on the courts of that Member State, provided that such an agreement is not contrary to the law of that Member State.*

Section 5 of Brussels I: Jurisdiction over individual contracts of employment:

Article 18

1. *In matters relating to individual contracts of employment, jurisdiction shall be determined by this Section, without prejudice to Article 4 and point 5 of Article 5.*
2. *Where an employee enters into an individual contract of employment with an employer who is not domiciled in a Member State but has a branch, agency or other establishment in one of the Member States, the employer shall, in disputes arising out of the operations of that branch, agency or establishment, be deemed to be domiciled in that Member State.*

Article 19:

An employer domiciled in a Member State may be sued:

1. *in the courts of the Member State where he is domiciled; or*
2. *in another Member State:*
   a) *in the courts for the place where the employee habitually carries out his work or in the courts for the last place where he did so, or*
   b) *if the employee does not or did not habitually carry out his work in any one country, in the courts for the place where the business which engaged the employee is or was situated.*

Article 20:

1. *An employer may bring proceedings only in the courts of the Member State in which the employee is domiciled.*

2. *The provisions of this Section shall not affect the right to bring a counter-claim in the court in which, in accordance with this Section, the original claim is pending.*

Article 21:

The provisions of this Section may be departed from only by an agreement on jurisdiction:

1. *which is entered into after the dispute has arisen; or*
2. *which allows the employee to bring proceedings in courts other than those indicated in this Section.*

Article 35 of Brussels I:

1. *Moreover, a judgment shall not be recognised if it conflicts with Sections 3, 4 or 6 of Chapter II, or in a case provided for in Article 72.*
2. *. . .*

INTRODUCTION

2.248 The rules for the protection of certain weaker parties have many similarities to the alternative rules discussed above. They also derogate from the general rule. However, they have a degree of priority over the rules of Article 5 instead of simply providing an alternative to jurisdiction of the court of the defendant's domicile (Article 2). They must be applied when one of the parties meets the criteria of a party needing protection. Moreover, the application of these specific rules does not necessarily presuppose that the defendant should genuinely be domiciled in an EU Member State. There is also a rule that deems a party to be domiciled in the EU even though it is not, while it has an agency or branch there.

2.249 So-called 'weaker' parties are defined as those who lack the bargaining power that their stronger contracting partners have. For instance, consumers that receive order forms in the post and fill them in have no say in the contractual terms, often already printed as general conditions on the reverse of the order form. The advent of internet purchases only aggravated the situation. The European Union has always regulated in such a way as to provide protection for weaker parties so that they are not trapped by contractual terms to which they never really agreed, but against which they could not protest.[323] The underlying philosophy is equity; one should

---

[323] See P Nygh, 'Arthur's Baby: The Hague Negotiations for a World-Wide Judgments Convention' in JAR Nafziger & SC Symeonides (eds), *Law and Justice in a Multistate World.*

rectify the lack of party autonomy by not holding the weaker parties to contracts they did not really agree to. On the other hand, these protective bases for jurisdiction might hamper international trade. Sellers and providers of services must be able to contract quickly, and with the assurance that their contractual terms will be respected. If market operators cannot rely on this certainty, the economy will be hampered and the result (whether direct or indirect) will often be that the products or services become more expensive for the consumer.[324]

This difference in policy could be clearly seen at the negotiations of the **2.250** failed draft Hague convention on jurisdiction and foreign judgments in civil and commercial matters.[325] E-commerce had blown up the importance of this problem during the negotiations. In the 2001 text there were various alternatives regarding the consumer contracts provision. Consumers would be protected in the same way as under Brussels I: a consumer could sue the business (stronger party) in the state where that consumer was habitually resident, if the business had directed its activity into that state, and the consumer was not in another state when taking the steps necessary for the conclusion of the contract, or when the goods or services were delivered. Neither was it clear whether or not a choice of forum would be permitted nor under what conditions. A possibility of a system permitting states to make declarations was left open. Another alternative was removing business-to-consumer contracts from the scope of the Convention altogether.

The Draft Hague Convention's provision regarding employment contracts, **2.251** which was equally controversial, contained four proposals. Three of these were more or less the European approach, namely the rule in Brussels I: employees could be sued at their habitual residence or at the place where they usually worked, while they could sue an employer at their habitual residence, at the place where they habitually worked, or at the location of the establishment that engaged them. A choice of court agreement would only be valid if entered into after the dispute had arisen, if it allowed more possible fora to the employee, or if it was permitted under the law of the state where the employee performed the work. The fourth proposal permitted states to make reservations at ratification with regard to

---

Essays in Honour of Arthur T von Mehren (Ardsley: Transnational Publishers Inc, 2002) 151–172 at 169–170.

[324] This debate took place at the negotiations for the conversion of the Brussels Convention into a Regulation; see C Bruneau, 'Les règles européennes de competence en matière civile et commerciale' [2001] *La Semaine juridique* 533–541 at 538.

[325] 'Summary of the Outcome of the Discussion in Commission II of the First Part of the Diplomatic Conference (2001)', Arts 7 and 8, available at <http://www.hcch.net>.

this provision. Another option was to allow declarations that a state will not recognize or enforce judgments concerning employment contracts, or that it will only recognize and enforce these judgments under certain conditions.

STRUCTURE OF THE PROVISIONS

2.252 The Regulation protects three categories of weaker party: insured parties, consumers, and employees. This protection is afforded both to plaintiffs and defendants. The sections containing the protective bases for jurisdiction have precedence over the general basis for jurisdiction (domicile of the defendant, Article 2) and the alternative bases (place of performance of a contract, place of tort or *delict*, etc, Article 5). For protected parties there are also specific rules that regulate the validity of forum clauses. The normal rules on forum clauses (Article 23) are not applicable.

2.253 Weaker plaintiffs are protected by granting jurisdiction to the forum of the weaker party's domicile, thus a *forum actoris,* which is usually seen as exorbitant jurisdiction. These plaintiffs may also bring action at the defendant's domicile.

2.254 The strength of the protection afforded to the weaker parties lies in the rules on recognition and enforcement in the EU. If the rules regarding jurisdiction in consumer and insurance contracts were not respected by an EU Member State this would provide a ground for the refusal of recognition and enforcement of the resulting judgment in other EU Member States.[326] However, such an exception from the obligation to recognize and enforce does not exist for employment.[327]

WHO QUALIFIES AS A PROTECTED PARTY?

2.255 Brussels I should be autonomously interpreted and legal terms will not necessarily have the same meaning as they have in the national legal systems of the EU Member States. Some terms are explicitly defined in

---

[326] According to Art 35(1) of Brussels I.

[327] It is unclear why this lack of parallel exists. It was suggested in the Commission's Explanatory Memorandum that the employee (weaker party) will almost always be the plaintiff so that controlling jurisdiction would prejudice, rather than help that party (p 23). Whether this argument should be different for employees than for insured parties or consumers, lacks justification; see C Bruneau, 'La reconnaissance et l'exécution des décisions rendues dans l'union européenne' [2001] *La Semaine juridique* 801–808 at 805; H Gaudemet-Tallon, *Compétence et exécution des jugements en Europe* (3rd edn, Paris: LGDJ, 2002) 312–313.

Brussels I, and for others one has to rely on the interpretation given by the European Court of Justice.

Protection is granted on the basis of an unequal bargaining power.[328] **2.256** Therefore a contract between two consumers does not fall within the scope of the provision.[329] For example, the individual sale of a second-hand car would not give rise to jurisdiction under the protective bases of jurisdiction discussed in this chapter, but would fall under the normal terms of the Regulation. On the other hand, a business tycoon buying a chair for his house from a small furniture shop would be defined as a consumer and the protective bases of jurisdiction would apply (if he were domiciled in the EU). It seems that drafting rules to provide protection precisely to those who need it, without providing unnecessary protection to economically strong parties is difficult, if not impossible.

'Weaker' parties are widely protected in litigation under Brussels I and **2.257** can be plaintiffs or defendants. Weaker plaintiffs may of course still bring proceedings in the normal forum, i.e. the court of the state where the defendant is domiciled. Additionally, they may bring proceedings in the courts of their own domicile if the contract falls in one of the definitions discussed below. For weaker defendants the bases for jurisdiction are limited. The stronger party may only bring proceedings in the courts of the weaker party's domicile.

Insured parties

Talking about 'insured parties' is too narrow. In fact, Brussels I protects **2.258** not only insured parties, but also policyholders and beneficiaries.[330] It is particularly difficult to distinguish insured parties that deserve special protection from those that do not. Of course big economic operators also insure their losses. They are, therefore, also insured parties, but may not need any special protection as they might be economically stronger than their insurers and do not lack the necessary bargaining power.

The European Court of Justice has had occasion to adjudicate whether or **2.259** not reinsurance contracts fall within the scope of the protective bases for jurisdiction. *Josi* has already been discussed as one of the few European

---

[328] Case 201/82 *Gerling and Others v Amministrazione del Tesoro dello Stato* [1983] ECR 2503, para 17; C–412/98 *Group Josi Reinsurance Company SA v Universal General Insurance Company* [2000] ECR I–5625, para 64.
[329] Art 15(1)(c).
[330] Art 9(1)(b).

Court of Justice cases that deals directly with the question of third States.[331] The plaintiff, an insurance company domiciled in Canada, sued a Belgian reinsurance company in the Tribunal de commerce (Commercial Court) of Nanterre in France. Eventually the Cour d'appel (Court of Appeal) of Versailles referred two preliminary questions to the European Court of Justice. One of these was whether reinsurance contracts fall under the protective bases for jurisdiction provided by the Brussels Convention for insurance contracts. The European Court of Justice found that these contracts do not fall within the ambit of the protection granted to insured parties.[332] Insurance companies could not be seen as economically weak when dealing with or litigating against reinsurance companies.

2.260 A similar question arises when one thinks of insurers of large risks. Sometimes the insured risk is so big that one cannot by any stretch of the imagination contend that the insured owner of the risk is economically weak and needy of special procedural protection. However, the distinction is difficult to draw. For some big contracts the limitation on forum clauses is alleviated.[333]

Consumers

2.261 Brussels I contains an explicit definition of 'consumer'. A consumer is a person who concludes a contract 'which can be regarded as being outside his trade or profession'. This definition has also been used in other European Union instruments, such as the Consumer Credit Directive.[334] The active consumer, who crosses the border to go shopping, or who orders a suit while he is on holiday, cannot invoke the protective bases

---

[331] *Josi*, note 328 above; case notes: F Leclerc [2002] *Journal de droit international* 623–628; P, Vlas [2003] *Nederlandse Jurisprudentie* no 597, 4584–4586; A Staudinger [2000] *Praxis des internationalen Privat- und Verfahrensrechts* 483–488; C Van Schoubroeck [2001] *Revue de droit commercial belge* 146–148.

[332] Paras 66–67. This is also in line with the Schlosser Report on the 1978 version of the Brussels Convention; OJ C 59, 5 March 1979, 71, para 151, p 117. The English court had already reached this conclusion in 1997; see *Agnew v Lansförsäkringsbĺlagens AB* [1997] 4 All ER 937, confirmed by the House of Lords, [2001] 1 AC 223 (HL).

[333] This issue also gave rise to difficult discussions at the time that the United Kingdom and Ireland joined the Brussels Convention; see Schlosser Report, ibid, paras 136–147, p 112–116. It was eventually decided to allow forum clauses for some risks, which entailed contracts that were important for the London insurance market (Art 12 *bis* Brussels Convention; Art 14 Brussels I). See also the discussion of this subject in *New Hampshire Insurance v Strabag Bau* [1992] 1 Lloyd's Rep 361 (CA).

[334] Art 1(2)(a) of Council Directive 87/102/EEC of 22 December 1986 for the approximation of the laws, regulations and administrative provisions of the Member States concerning consumer credit, OJ L 42 of 12 February 1987, p 48–53.

for jurisdiction. The business must have directed its activities to the EU Member State where the consumer is domiciled. This provision remains the same for consumer contracts concluded via the internet.[335]

Sometimes, by way of aggressive marketing, traders promise prizes or **2.262** gifts to consumers in order to attract new customers. The European Court of Justice has had two occasions to rule on the applicability to the resulting contracts of the protective bases for jurisdiction.[336] The Court has introduced a nuanced rule: if the consumer bought goods in order to obtain his or her prize, a consumer contract has come into existence and the protective bases for jurisdiction apply (that was the case for Mr Gabriel). If, on the other hand, the consumer sues for a prize that was supposed to be available without any obligation to buy, there is no consumer contract. Mrs Engler, who was party to such a contract, could not use the protective bases for jurisdiction but had to sue either at the place of the defendant's domicile (Article 2) or at the place where the contract had to be performed (Article 5).

It might happen that a party concludes a single contract that is partly **2.263** related to his or her trade and partly for personal purposes. Whether such a party can be considered a consumer (entitled to procedural protection) was referred to the European Court of Justice in *Gruber v Bay Wa AG*.[337] The case concerned an Austrian farmer, Mr Gruber, who bought roof tiles from a German seller, Bay Wa, after receiving an advertisement. These tiles were to cover his pigsty and storage room as well as part of the farm which Mr Gruber and his family lived in. The residential part comprised approximately 60 per cent of the floor space. Mr Gruber was not satisfied with the quality of the tiles and brought an action against Bay Wa on the basis of the warranty. The Oberster Gerichtshof (Supreme Court) of Austria referred a number of questions to the European Court of Justice. Some of the questions concerned the way the contract was established (including telephone calls), but those are not relevant for the current study. The European Court of Justice ruled that a contract that entails partly professional and partly personal activities is not a consumer contract for purposes of the EU jurisdiction rules granting protection to consumers. Only when the professional part of the contract is negligible can the buyer rely on the protective jurisdictional bases for consumers.

---

[335] See C Bruneau, 'Les règles européennes de competence en matière civile et commerciale' [2001] *La Semaine juridique* 533–541 at 537–538.

[336] Case C–96/00 *Gabriel* [2002] ECR I–6367; Case C–27/02 *Engler v Janus Versand GmbH* [2005] ECR I–481.

[337] Case C–464/01 [2005] ECR I–439.

Employees

2.264 Only employees with individual contracts of employment can rely on the protective bases for jurisdiction; collective employment contracts do not fall under these provisions. Here again one sees the requirement for unequal bargaining power before the protection can be granted. An individual employee has much less power to determine the terms of a contract than the employer. On the other hand, in the case of collective agreements, trade unions are strong and are able to have a substantial impact at the negotiating table and influence the terms of the contract.

2.265 Employees customarily working on the continental shelf can be considered to be habitually working on the territory of the particular EU Member State. That was decided by the European Court of Justice in a case where a cook worked first on the Netherlands' part and subsequently on the Danish part of the continental shelf.[338] Extending the EU jurisdiction rules to work performed on the continental shelf of an EU Member State seems reasonable. Not applying the EU rules would probably lead to a lacuna.

WEAKER PARTIES FROM THIRD STATES

Third State insured parties

2.266 In *Josi*, referred to above, the European Court of Justice found that contracts between insurance and reinsurance companies fall outside the scope of the protective bases for jurisdiction.[339] It is interesting that the Court considered this question at all and did not find it inadmissible. Universal General Insurance Company, the insurance company that would have been able to rely on the protective bases for jurisdiction, was domiciled in Canada, while the reinsurance company was domiciled in Belgium. One could presume for a moment that the Court had found that reinsurance contracts did fall within the ambit of the protective jurisdictional bases for insurance contracts. That would mean that Universal General Insurance Company would have been able to rely on this protection. However, the protective bases for jurisdiction provide that the insured party may bring proceedings at the place of its domicile, which in this case was outside the EU. Of course, the Brussels Convention could not (and Brussels I cannot) grant jurisdiction to the Canadian courts. Therefore, the protection has no sense. The insurer is also permitted to bring an action at

---

[338] Case C–37/00 *Weber v Universal Ogden Services Ltd* [2002] ECR I–2013.
[339] Para 2.259 above.

the courts of the place where the defendant is domiciled. That basis of jurisdiction exists whether a protected party is involved or not.

In the French case *Ben Lassin v Payne*,[340] a French businessman domiciled **2.267** in Geneva contracted with an insurance broker in Liechtenstein. The broker insured the risks with Lloyd's of London via a London broker. The Frenchman sued Lloyd's (and another insurer in subsidiary order). The Cour d'appel (Court of Appeal) of Paris found that the Brussels Convention could not grant jurisdiction to the French courts in this case because the insured party plaintiff was domiciled in a third State and the agents were domiciled in Liechtenstein or in Great Britain, not in France.[341] The Lugano Convention had not come into force when the proceedings were brought, so neither could this Convention have been used to base jurisdiction. The French nationality of the businessman was irrelevant. Neither was there any basis for jurisdiction under French national law, so that the French courts lacked jurisdiction. (The French court found that it had jurisdiction over the subsidiary claim, but temporarily stayed this because it could only be examined after judgment in the main claim.)

Third State consumers

The *ICS Computing Ltd & Fargell Ltd v Capital One Services Inc* case pointed **2.268** out that third State consumers do not receive protection under the Brussels regime, even though upon the facts of this case the defendant was found not to be a consumer at all.[342] The defendant was a company incorporated in the state of Delaware and had a branch at Nottingham in England. The two plaintiffs, established respectively in Northern Ireland and in England, had contracted with the defendant to set up a computer system for payroll and personnel services for the defendant. The plaintiffs subsequently brought an action in Northern Ireland for breach of contract on the basis of non-payment. The question was whether the contract had to be performed in Northern Ireland, so that the court there had jurisdiction. The defendant further contested the jurisdiction of the court in Northern Ireland by contending that it was a consumer and consequently that the

---

[340] An English translation of the case was published in [1995] ILPr 17.

[341] P Kaye, *Law of the European Judgments Convention* (Chichester: Barry Rose, 1999) vol 3, 1798–1799 states that a plainer solution would simply have been to regard an insurance broker as not an insurer for purposes of Art 8, except that a defendant insurer might be deemed to be domiciled in a Contracting State in which its branch, agency, or establishment operated according to Art 8(2).

[342] High Court of Justice in Northern Ireland, unpublished case WEAC3561, judgment of 11 January 2002; available at <http://www.courtsni.gov.uk/en-gb/judicial+decisions/judgments/j_j_weac3561.htm>.

court in England, where its branch was situated, had exclusive jurisdiction, since it should be deemed to be domiciled there.[343] The judge did not accept the argument that the defendant was a consumer. He added that even if it were a consumer, jurisdiction could not lie with the English courts on that basis. The provision deeming a party from a third State to be domiciled at the place of its branch in the EU applies to the business in a consumer contract, and not to the consumer.

2.269 The outcome of the case seems correct according to the rules of the Brussels Convention. One has to admit that contending to be a consumer while one has a branch abroad is a bit far-fetched and the result of the case is probably equitable. The Court also stated that being economically weaker than the other party in itself did not make one a consumer. The case clearly indicates two borders of the Brussels regime: first, that of parties deemed to be domiciled in the EU, and second, the line determining which parties are granted protection by the EU jurisdiction rules.

Employees in third States, or employment in third States

2.270 The case *Mulox IBC Ltd v Geels,* concerned employment in various states, some of which were EU Member States and some of which were not.[344] Mulox was a company incorporated under English law and had its registered office in London. Mr Geels, a Dutch national residing in France, was employed as its international marketing director. He was employed in 1988 and he established his office at Aix-les-Bains in France and sold Mulox products initially in Belgium, the Netherlands, Germany, and the Scandinavian countries. He travelled frequently to these countries. As of 1990, he worked in France. Upon termination of his contract, Mr Geels sued Mulox before the Conseil de prud' hommes (Labour Conciliation Tribunal) of Aix-les-Bains for compensation in lieu of notice and for damages. The tribunal held that it had jurisdiction. Mulox appealed to the Cour d'appel (Court of Appeal) of Chambéry in France contesting jurisdiction. The court referred a preliminary question to the European Court of Justice asking whether it was necessary that the obligation characterizing the employment

---

[343] The Civil Jurisdiction and Judgments Act 1982 of the United Kingdom specifies that the Brussels Convention/Regulation is also used for the allocation of jurisdiction within the United Kingdom (Art 16).

[344] Case C–125/92 [1993] ECR I–4075; case notes: M Fallon [1993] *Journal des tribunaux. Droit européen* 37; N Watté [1993] *Revue de droit commercial belge* 1117; A Briggs [1993] *Yearbook of European Law* 520–525; A Kohl [1994] *Jurisprudence de Liège, Mons et Bruxelles* 463–465; A Huet [1994] *Journal de droit international* 539–546; P Lagarde [1994] *Revue critique de droit international privé* 574–577; TC Hartley [1994] ELR 540–545; H Tagaras [1995] *Cahiers de droit européen* 188–191.

contract be wholly in the state where jurisdiction was sought, or whether it was sufficient that a part (maybe the principal part) was performed there. The European Court of Justice responded that jurisdiction could not be shared between all the places where the employee performed his work. It is necessary to define the place of performance as the place where or from which the employee principally discharges his obligations towards the employer.[345]

When this case was decided, Denmark was the only Scandinavian country **2.271** that was part of the EC and Member to the Brussels Convention. The ECJ did not consider the fact that some of the obligations were performed in third States as an impediment to the Convention's application. The Scandinavian countries (except Iceland) were at that stage parties to the Lugano Convention, but probably not yet at the start of the proceedings. The national court should probably have examined the applicable Conventions or national rules for each defendant as a first step.

The case *Rutten v Cross Medical Ltd* concerned an employee, Mr Rutten, **2.272** who also worked in many different places and who was domiciled in the Netherlands.[346] His employment contract was concluded with Cross Medical BV, established in the Netherlands, a subsidiary of Cross Medical Ltd, established in London. After a year, Mr Rutten's contract with Cross Medical BV was terminated and Cross Medical Ltd then employed him. The first contract contained a jurisdiction clause in favour of the Kanton-rechter (Cantonal Court) of Amsterdam, but the second contract contained no jurisdiction clause. Under both contracts, two-thirds of the employment duties were performed in the Netherlands, and the rest in other places including Belgium, Germany, the United Kingdom, and the United States of America. Mr Rutten's contract was terminated and he brought action against his former employer before the Kantonrechter of Amsterdam, claiming salary arrears and interest.

The case went all the way up to the Netherlands' Hoge Raad (Supreme **2.273** Court), which posed three related preliminary questions to the European Court of Justice regarding the place where the employment was habitually carried out. The Court responded that one had to look at the place where the employee had established the effective centre of his working activities. One had to consider whether the employee spent most of his working

---

[345] Ibid, para 26.
[346] Case C–383/95 [1997] ECR I–57; case notes: Ph Antonmattei [1997] *La Semaine juridique* (ed enterprise II) no 659; H Gaudemet-Tallon [1997] *Revue critique de droit international privé* 341–346; M Pertegás Sender [1997] *Columbia Journal of European Law* 292–298.

time in one of the EU Member States in which he had an office, where he organized his work, and to which he returned after each business trip.

2.274 At first sight, one cannot contest the conclusion of the case. However, it is a bit disturbing that neither the ECJ nor the Advocate General took cognizance of the fact that one of the places where the employee worked was outside the EU, namely the United States of America. It seems clear from the facts that Mr Rutten spent more time inside the EU than outside: only a fraction of the third not spent in the Netherlands was spent in the United States of America. Therefore in this case ignoring the employment outside the EU did not amount to any excessive or exorbitant exercise of jurisdiction. Yet one can imagine a situation where an employee is employed by a company in the Netherlands, but performs only one-third of his work in the EU, and the remaining two-thirds in the United States of America. In such a case, the employee would be permitted to bring proceedings in the Netherlands in any event, because that is the domicile of the employer (defendant). The question arises whether there would in this case be an alternative court in an EU Member State that would have jurisdiction on the basis that the employee habitually performed his employment there. One can assume for a moment that, of the one-third of his employment time in the EU, the employee spends the majority in England. Would the English court have jurisdiction? The issue is whether only the employment in the EU has to be taken into account when determining where the employee habitually works. If so, then the English courts could have jurisdiction on the basis that the employee habitually works there. However, if one looks at the complete picture, one would have to find that there is no place of habitual employment in the EU. That finding could then lead to one of two conclusions. The first considers the next step of the rule: where the employee does not habitually work in one EU Member State, the courts of the Member State of the establishment that employed the employee have jurisdiction. One could possibly equate not customarily working in the EU to not habitually working in one specific EU Member State. This seems to go further than the intention of the rule: it was merely drafted for situations in which the employee travelled so much within the EU that it was impossible to say where he habitually worked. The other possibility, which seems to be the correct one, would be that, if there is no place in the EU where the employee customarily worked, one simply cannot use that basis of jurisdiction. The employee would have to bring his action at the courts of the domicile of the employer (defendant) if he wanted to proceed in the EU.

General

The sections providing special protection for weaker parties explicitly state **2.275**
that they apply without prejudice to Articles 4 and 5(5) of the Regulation.[347]
If a defendant is domiciled in a third State, Article 4 refers to the national
rules on jurisdiction of each EU Member State. Therefore, if the defendant
in a dispute concerning an insurance, consumer, or employment contract
is domiciled in a third State, the national rules on jurisdiction will apply.
Article 5(5) grants jurisdiction to EU courts where a branch, agency, or other
establishment of a legal person is situated in a different EU Member State
to the one in which it is itself domiciled.[348] The provision deals with defendants from the EU and in this sense has a limited influence for parties from
third States.

However, there are exceptions. Stronger party defendants that are domi- **2.276**
ciled outside the EU may be considered to be domiciled in the EU Member
State where they have a branch, agency, or other establishment. An independent operator, such as an insurance broker, would not be regarded as a
branch or agency of the insurer.[349] The qualification is that the dispute must
have arisen out of the operations between that branch, agency, or establishment on the one hand, and the insured, consumer, or employee on the other
hand.[350] This of course means that insurers, sellers (or providers of services) to consumers, and employers domiciled in third States should pay
particular attention. Opening a branch in the EU may have the result of
creating a second domicile for jurisdiction purposes. At that point, having a
forum in the EU might lead to the application of EU protective rules, which
are particularly concerned with the protection of a party with less bargaining power. To take the example of insurance law, the EU has adopted a number
of directives to protect EU insured parties if the risks are situated in the
EU.[351] In principle these directives only apply if the insurer is domiciled in

---

[347] Arts 8(1), 15(1) and 18(1).
[348] Discussed in paras 2.233 and following above.
[349] See Schlosser Report, note 332 above, para 150; TC Hartley, *Civil Jurisdiciton and Judgments* (London: Sweet & Maxwell, 1984) 59.
[350] Arts 9(2), 15(2), and 18(2).
[351] For instance Directive 2002/83/EC of the European Parliament and of the Council of 5 November 2002 concerning life assurance, OJ L 345 of 19 December 2002, p 1–51; Second Council Directive 88/357/EEC of 22 June 1988 on the coordination of laws, regulations and administrative provisions relating to direct insurance other than life assurance and laying down provisions to facilitate the effective exercise of freedom to provide services and amend-ing Directive 73/239/EEC, OJ L 172 of 4 July 1988, p 1–14, as amended by Council Directive

one EU Member State and the risk is situated in another. However, directives only provide frameworks and they need to be transposed into the
national law of the Member States. In transposing directives into national
law, Member States might choose to extend the applicability of the rules.[352]
The same difficulty might arise with regard to the EU directives concerning
material rules for the protection of consumers.[353] Also, in the field of employment law the influence of EU legislation should not be underestimated.[354]

92/49/EEC of 18 June 1992 on the coordination of laws, regulations and administrative
provisions relating to direct insurance other than life assurance and amending Directives
73/239/EEC and 88/357/EEC (third non-life insurance Directive), OJ L 228 of 11 August 1992,
p 1–23. Note that these directives are in force throughout the European Economic Area, i.e.
the EU and Iceland, Liechtenstein, and Norway.

[352] In Belgium, for instance, it is unclear whether the legislator intended an extension of
the EU directives to the effect that the rules also to apply to third State insurers of risks in
Belgium; see C Van Schoubroeck & H Cousy, 'Internationale verzekeringsovereenkomsten'
in H Van Houtte & M Pertegás Sender (eds), *Europese IPR-verdragen* (Leuven: Acco, 1997)
281–309 at 287.

[353] For instance, Council Directive 84/450/EC of 10 September 1984 relating to the approx-
imations of laws, regulations and administrative provisions of the Member States concerning misleading advertisements, OJ L 250 of 19 September 1984, p 17–20; Directive 97/55/EC
of European Parliament and of the Council of 6 October 1997 amending Directive 84/450/
EEC concerning misleading advertising so as to include comparative advertising, OJ L 290 of
23 October 1997, p 18–23; Directive 97/7/EC of the European Parliament and of the Council
of 20 May 1997 on the protection of consumers in respect of distance contracts, OJ L 144 of
4 June 1997, p 19–27; Directive 2005/29/EC of the European Parliament and of the Council
of 11 May 2005 concerning unfair business-to-consumer commercial practices in the internal
market and amending Council Directive 84/450/EEC, Directives 97/7/EC, 98/27/EC
and 2002/65/EC of the European Parliament and of the Council and Regulation (EC) No
2006/2004 of the European Parliament and of the Council ('Unfair Commercial Practices
Directive'), OJ L 149 of 11 June 2005, p 22–39; Directive 87/102/EEC, note 334 above, 48–53;
Council Directive 93/13/EEC of 5 April 1993 on unfair terms in consumer contracts, OJ L 95
of 21 April 1993, p 29–34; Commission's Proposal for a Directive of the European Parliament
and of the Council on the harmonisation of the laws, regulations and administrative provisions of the Member States concerning credit for consumers repealing Directive 87/102/EC
and modifying Directive 93/13/EC, document of 28 October 2004, COM(2004) 747
final, available at <http://www.europa.eu.int/comm/consumers/cons_int/fina_serv/cons_
directive/credit_cons_en.pdf>; Directive 1999/44/EC of the European Parliament and of the
Council of 25 May 1999 on certain aspects of the sale of consumer goods and associated guarantees, OJ L 171 of 7 July 1999, p 12–15; Council Directive 85/577/EEC of 20 December 1985
to protect the consumer in respect of contracts negotiated away from business premises -
'door to door selling,' OJ L 372 of 31 December 1985, p 31–33. See also J Stuyck, 'Internationale
Consumentenovereenkomsten,' in Van Houtte & Pertegás Sender, *Europese IPR-verdragen*,
ibid, 259–280; J Basedow, 'Consumer Contracts and Insurance Contracts in a Future Rome
I-Regulation,' in J Meeusen, M Pertegás Sender & G Straetmans (eds), *Enforcement
of International Contracts in the European Union* (Antwerp:Intersentia, 2004) 269–294;
G Straetmans, 'The Consumer Concept in EC Law' in the same book, 295–322.

[354] In general: H Storme & S Bouzoumita, 'Arbeidsovereenkomsten in internationaal
privaatrecht' [2005] *Nieuw Juridisch Weekblad* 290–314; C Engels, 'Arbeidsovereenkomsten

Insurers

In the English case of *New Hampshire Insurance v Strabag Bau*,[355] the Court of **2.277**
Appeal found that an action by an American insurance company against
insured parties domiciled in Germany and Austria fell under the protective
bases for jurisdiction of the Brussels Convention, and the English courts
therefore lacked jurisdiction. Once again the domicile of the plaintiff was
irrelevant for purposes of the application of the Brussels Convention. This
reasoning is in line with the *Josi* judgment of the European Court of
Justice.[356] In that judgment the European Court of Justice made it clear that
the rules of the Brussels Convention applied regardless of the domicile of
the plaintiff; the important factor was the domicile of the defendant.

The facts in *Jordan Grand Prix Ld v Baltic Insurance Group & others* are com- **2.278**
plicated, but the case provides a good example of insurance contracts
between insured parties in the EU and insurers in third States.[357] Jordan,
an English company engaged in Formula 1 racing, promised its employees a bonus payment if their team finished among the first six in the
Constructors' Formula One World Championships. This exposure to contractual liability was insured with Baltic, a Lithuanian company, through
Baltic's Belgian agent, Compagnie d'Investissements Universelle (CIU),
and with the intervention of another Belgian company, Special Risks
Insurance (SRI). (At the time Lithuania was not an EU Member State.)
Moreover, Jordan contracted with Quay Financial Software, an Irish company, to the effect that Jordan would promote its products and Quay
would pay Jordan a sum if the team finished in the first seven places in the
championships. It was in dispute whether Baltic also covered this liability
through the intervention of SRI. Jordan's team finished fifth. Baltic refused
to pay and alleged conspiracy by Jordan, Quay, and others.

Jordan then brought an action before the English courts against Baltic and **2.279**
two Belgian reinsurers. Baltic brought a counter-claim for damages against
Jordan, Quay, the two intermediaries, the two reinsurers, and various
directors of these companies (altogether twelve defendants to the counter-
claim). Three of the defendants on the counter-claim (Quay and its two
directors) were not plaintiffs in the original claim, but were joined by Baltic
on the counter-claim. The case went all the way up to the House of Lords.

met een internationaal aspect,' in Van Houtte & Pertegás Sender, *Europese IPR-verdragen*,
ibid, 235–257; MV Polak, '"*Laborum dulce lenimen*"? Jurisdiction and Choice-of-law aspects of
employment contracts', in Meeusen, Pertegás Sender & Straetmans, ibid, 323–342.

[355] [1992] 1 Lloyd's Rep 361 (CA); [1992] ILPr 478 CA.
[356] *Josi*, note 328 above; paras 2.67 and following above.
[357] [1999] 2 AC 127 (HL). Judgment of the Court of Appeal: [1998] 3 All ER 418 (CA).

There were two main issues: whether Baltic, as plaintiff on the counter-claim, had to bring proceedings on the basis of the Brussels Convention rules; and whether a counter-claim could be brought against parties not involved in the initial proceedings.

2.280 The House of Lords first considered whether an insurer-plaintiff (on counter-claim) domiciled outside the EU was held to the rule in the Brussels Convention that an insurer may sue a defendant only in the courts of the defendant's domicile.[358] The House of Lords found that this rule also bound insurer-plaintiffs from outside the EU. This conclusion is again in line with the general rule of the later *Josi* judgment. The House of Lords further stated that a contrary conclusion would undermine the purpose of the provision, which is the protection of weaker parties.[359] The argument is that the protection is necessary as against plaintiffs both from inside and outside the EU. While, based on *Josi*, the argument must be correct, the goal of protecting weaker parties in the EU does not seem a sufficient reason for extending the rules to parties from third States.

2.281 The following question concerned the parties to the counter-claim: could Baltic bring a counter-claim in which they sued parties that were not involved in the original claim? Those parties were domiciled in Ireland. The House of Lords found that extending the counter-claim to these parties was not possible. It relied on the structure of the Brussels Convention, arguing that this dictates a strict interpretation of the possibility of bringing counter-claims. Second, the House of Lords referred to the fact that a plaintiff was not allowed to join co-defendants under the jurisdiction rules on insurance contracts. Therefore, permitting a defendant to do so would create an asymmetry. Third, the House of Lords emphasized that the section on insurance contracts comprised an 'independent code'.[360] The resulting conclusion was that Baltic, an insurer domiciled in Lithuania, could not bring a counter-claim in the English courts against its Irish-domiciled insured, which was not party to the original proceedings. The conclusion does not lead to efficient and cost-effective litigation. However, in light of the structure and wording of the provisions on insurance contracts, the House of Lords probably could not have come to a different conclusion. The situation might have been resolved by the provision on related actions, but then proceedings would first have to be made pending in the courts of two different EU Member States.[361]

---

[358] Art 12 of Brussels I (at the time Art 11 of the Brussels Convention).
[359] See note 357 above, at 133.
[360] Ibid, 135.
[361] Art 28 of Brussels I. For a discussion of this provision, see chapter 5 below, paras 5.133 and following.

Stronger parties in consumer contracts

In *Shearson Lehman Hutton v TVB mbh,* the European Court of Justice had **2.282**
to clarify the ambit of the provisions on consumer protection.[362] A German,
who happened to be a judge, had instructed the brokers EF Hutton & Co
Inc to carry out certain transactions under an agency contract. EF Hutton
was later taken over by Shearson Lehman Inc. Both EF Hutton and
Shearson Lehman Hutton were companies incorporated in New York. EF
Hutton had offered its services through press advertisement in Germany.
The business relationships were arranged through EF Hutton & Co GmbH,
a company with its registered office in Germany and dependent on EF
Hutton Inc: its shares belonged to EF Hutton International Inc, a wholly-
owned subsidiary of EF Hutton Inc. In addition, many people having
managerial responsibilities within EF Hutton Inc also had like responsibilities within EF Hutton & Co GmbH. The German assignor lost almost
all his investments. Instead of bringing suit himself, he assigned his rights
to TVB Treuhandgesellschaft für Vermögensverwaltung und Beteiligungen
mbH, incorporated in Munich. TVB instituted an action in the Landgericht
(Regional Court) of Munich claiming from EF Hutton Inc the return of the
sums lost by the assignor. This court held that it did not have jurisdiction.
The Oberlandesgericht (District Court of Appeal) of Munich overturned
that decision. EF Hutton Inc appealed to the Bundesgerichtshof (Federal
Supreme Court), which referred several preliminary questions to the
European Court of Justice.

The first question was whether the protection extended to a case where **2.283**
the business (stronger party) was established in a third State (the United
States of America in this case) because it had an intermediary in the EU
Member State where the consumer was domiciled. Before answering the
questions, the European Court of Justice stated that it had to pay attention
to a preliminary question, namely whether the protective bases for jurisdiction still applied if the consumer had assigned his rights to a third party
so that the consumer was not the litigant. The Court emphasized that
the protective bases for jurisdiction derogated from the general rules of
Brussels I. Therefore the protective bases had to be interpreted strictly so
as not to grant protection in cases where such protection was not justified.[363] The fact that the original contracting party was a consumer could

---

[362] Case C–89/91 *Shearson Lehmann Hutton Inc v TVB Treuhandgesellschaft für
Vermögensverwaltung und Beteiligungen mbH* [1993] ECR I–139; case notes: H Van Houtte
[1993] *Tijdschrift voor Rechtsdocumentatie* 153–154; H Gaudemet-Tallon [1993] *Revue critique de
droit international privé* 325–332; A Briggs [1993] *Yearbook of European Law* 511–517; A Kohl
[1994] *Jurisprudence de Liège, Mons et Bruxelles* 457–459; TC Hartley [1994] ELR 537–538.
[363] Ibid, para 15–19.

not extend procedural protection to a party to whom the consumer had subrogated his rights. Therefore if a corporation from a third State trades through a branch in the EU with a consumer, and that consumer then assigns his rights, he will lose the protective bases for jurisdiction.

2.284 The European Court of Justice therefore did not respond to the specific questions put by the Bundesgerichtshof. However, there seems to be an argument that the first question, concerning the applicability of protection to the intermediary domiciled in the EU, despite the defendant being established in a third State, should actually have been dealt with first. It concerns the applicability of the EU rules altogether, even before one comes to the question which rule (general or protective) should be applied.

2.285 According to Advocate General Darmon, even if the answer were that the third State corporation could be considered domiciled at the place of the independent intermediary, Germany, the jurisdiction rules of the Brussels Convention would have lacked applicability, since all the parties (consumer, corporation, and party to whom the rights had been subrogated) were domiciled in Germany, so that German national rules on jurisdiction would have to be applied.[364]

2.286 Turning to consider the unanswered question, can acting through an independent intermediary, with separate legal personality, draw a third State corporation into the scope of Brussels I? Advocate General Darmon, in his opinion, stated that Brussels I did not apply to a defendant from a third State acting through an independent intermediary. According to him the key question was whether the establishment could conclude contracts to bind the principal.[365] Gaudemet-Tallon agrees with this conclusion, stating that the presumption of domicile in the EU at the location of a branch has to be interpreted restrictively, because it draws defendants from outside the EU into EU courts.[366] The situation could of course be different if there is a case for piercing of the corporate veil and the 'independent' company in the EU was not independent at all, but a mere scheme to circumvent the EU rules.

2.287 The following year the European Court of Justice had the opportunity to consider a similar case. *Brenner and Noller v Dean Witter Reynolds Inc*[367] also

---

[364] Ibid, Opinion of the Advocate General, paras 58–69.
[365] Ibid, paras 36–57.
[366] Gaudemet-Tallon, note 362 above, 330.
[367] Case C–318/93 [1994] ECR I–4275; Kaye, note 341 above, vol 1, 664 and vol 3, 1879–1889; case note by R Libschaber [1995] *Revue critique de droit international privé* 758–769.

concerned the commissioning by German consumers of the defendant, a US investment corporation (commodity futures transactions in this case). In this case the advertisement had been placed through Dean Witter Reynolds GmbH, a German company based in Frankfurt, while the contracts were mediated by Metzler Wirtschafts- und Boersenberatungsg esellschaft mbH, also based in Frankfurt. As in the case discussed above, there was no branch in the EU through which Dean Witter Reynolds Inc contracted. The consumers lost their money and sued the defendant for damages due to a breach of contractual and pre-contractual obligations, and on the bases of tort and unjust enrichment.

The Bundesgerichtshof (Federal Supreme Court) of Germany referred **2.288** four preliminary questions to the European Court of Justice. Two of those were relevant for third States. They concerned the fact that the defendant was domiciled in a third State and the effect of the advertisement in the EU. The ECJ found that there could be no jurisdiction on the protective bases of the Brussels Convention if the defendant were domiciled outside the EU. Only if the defendant had a branch in the EU could it be considered domiciled in the EU so as to fall within the scope of these bases for jurisdiction. The Court considered it unnecessary to respond to the other questions posed by the Bundesgerichtshof. [368] This conclusion seems correct since the provisions apply to defendants domiciled in the EU.

Employers

The case *Six Constructions v P Humbert* demonstrated the effect that the Brussels **2.289** regime can have on employers from outside the EU.[369] Mr Humbert, domiciled in France, was employed by Six Constructions, incorporated under the law of Sharjah, one of the United Arab Emirates. Six Constructions had a branch in Brussels. Under the employment contract Mr Humbert conducted work in Libya, Congo (then Zaire) and Abu Dhabi (another of the United Arab Emirates). After being dismissed, he sued the employer before the Conseil de prud' hommes (Labour Conciliation Tribunal) at Bordeaux in France for payment in lieu of notice, damages, gratuities, and various amounts by way of compensation and arrears of salary.

---

[368] Ibid; see also the Opinion of Advocate General Darmon, para 22, referring to Art 4 and its place in the Brussels Convention.

[369] Case 32/88 [1989] ECR 341; case notes: A Huet [1989] *Journal de droit international* 461–465; TC Hartley [1989] ELR 236–238; P Rodière [1989] *Revue critique de droit international privé* 560–567; A Briggs [1989] *Yearbook of European Law* 323–328; T Rauscher [1990] *Praxis des internationalen Privat- und Verfahrensrechts* 152–157; H Tagaras [1990] *Cahiers de droit européen* 676–681.

2.290 The French Cour de cassation (Court of Cassation) eventually referred two preliminary questions to the European Court of Justice regarding jurisdiction in a dispute arising from an employment contract. The ECJ stated that, where the employment was to be performed outside the EU, jurisdiction could not be founded on the protective bases for jurisdiction. Only the general rule (namely the domicile of the defendant) could apply. Six Constructions was at first thought to be domiciled in Belgium, and the case proceeded on that basis. The Court did not consider Brussels, to which Mr Humbert regularly returned to make reports, as the place that the employment contract was performed.[370]

2.291 It is important to note that this case was decided on a version of the Brussels Convention that did not contain the option to sue the employer in the place where the business that engaged the employee is situated, if the employment is not customarily carried out in one country. (The current Regulation contains such an option.)[371] Would this facility have made a difference? It can only be triggered if the employee does not customarily carry out his employment in one country. The facts given in this case do not permit us to identify the place of performance with certainty. If Mr Humbert had usually carried out his employment in Abu Dhabi, for instance, and only occasionally gone to the other countries, the rule could not be triggered. The outcome of the case should be the same: the employee does not customarily carry out his work in one country and therefore the protective bases for jurisdiction are inapplicable. If, however, it had been impossible to determine the place of habitual employment, under the new rule, Mr Humbert would probably have been able to sue Six Constructions in a court in Belgium. That is the location of the business that concluded the employment contract. Six Constructions, domiciled outside the EU, will be considered, for the protective bases of jurisdiction, to be domiciled in the EU at the place of its branch, i.e. Brussels.

FORUM CLAUSES

General

2.292 The respect for forum clauses is part of the fundamental principle of party autonomy. Therefore Brussels I contains rules on the validity of such clauses.[372] However, the protection of 'weaker parties' would not make much sense if stronger parties could impose on them standard contract

---

[370] Ibid, para 11; for criticism on this conclusion, see A Briggs, ibid, 324–235.
[371] For the current rule, see Art 19(2)(b) of Brussels I.
[372] Discussed below in chapter 4.

terms containing forum clauses. In such a way economically strong parties would be able to negate the protection granted to weaker parties and force them to go to far-off courts (whether as plaintiffs or as defendants). For this reason Brussels I also extended protection of weaker parties to the conclusion of forum clauses.[373] Forum clauses are only permitted under certain conditions. Either they have to be concluded after the dispute has arisen, or they have to make more fora available to weaker party plaintiffs. The European Court of Justice has ruled that an insured party other than the policyholder may also rely on a favourable forum clause between the insurer and the policyholder, even though he was not originally party to it.[374] An exception to this general rule exists for insurance contracts covering specific risks relating to seagoing ships and certain transport contracts. Furthermore, parties insuring certain large risks do not enjoy procedural protection, as they cannot really be considered 'weak' in the sense of unequal bargaining power.[375]

Protected parties from third States

The provisions limiting forum clauses pose themselves not as exceptions **2.293** to the general rule on forum clauses (Article 23), but as exceptions to the limited bases for jurisdiction contained in the protective sections. As has been explained, those entire sections are exceptions to the general rules on jurisdiction contained in the Regulation. The protection is aimed at weaker parties domiciled in the EU. Such parties can only be deprived of their protection by way of a forum clause that meets the stricter requirements.

Weaker parties from third States do not enjoy the protection granted by **2.294** these sections. Therefore, there is nothing to provide an exception for. Weaker parties from third States will be bound by forum clauses under the normal rules:

- if the stronger party is domiciled in an EU Member State, and
- a court of an EU Member State is appointed, and
- the validity requirements of Article 23 are met.

This is explicitly confirmed in Brussels I for insurance contracts: forum clauses issued to policyholders not domiciled in a Member State may derogate from the general protective rules.[376] No similar provisions are to

---

[373] See Arts 13, 17, and 21 of Brussels I.
[374] *Gerling*, note 328 above.
[375] Art 14 of Brussels I.
[376] Art 13(4) of Brussels I. This provision was inserted at the request of the United Kingdom. The reason for its insertion was that British insurers felt that they would otherwise be unable

be found for consumer or employment contracts. This might provoke one to think that consumers and employees from third States fall within the protective rules on forum clauses. However, following the logic set out above, this is not the case and one might think that the explicit statement regarding policyholders from outside the EU is superfluous.

2.295 How would an EU Member State court respond to the argument by the consumer that he must be sued in a third State because of a protective basis for jurisdiction that exists there? Let us assume that the EU court has jurisdiction on the basis of a forum clause that would not have been valid had the consumer been domiciled in the EU. Brussels I does not contain a mechanism to decline jurisdiction in such a case. Such a possibility might exist if the theory of the *effet réflexe* (reflexive effect), established by Droz, were accepted. However, as will be explained in the following chapters, this theory has come under strain after recent cases of the European Court of Justice.[377] If accepted, that theory might be applied to protected parties in this case. An EU Member State court would then decline to take jurisdiction under the forum clause, because a third State court actually afforded protection to the weaker party. Another possibility is to permit EU Member State courts to decline jurisdiction on the basis of national law, such as the English rule of *forum non conveniens*. The European Court of Justice, however, has outlawed that rule in a case where the events took place in a third State while the defendant was domiciled in England.[378] The case did not deal with a protective basis for jurisdiction in a third State, so the operation of the rule in such a situation cannot be excluded with absolute certainty.

2.296 Furthermore, the explicit rule for policyholders from outside the EU was at least partly intended to introduce an exception. The provision states 'except in so far as the insurance is compulsory or relates to immovable property in a Member State'. Therefore, a close link to an EU Member State will draw the case back into the sphere of the EU jurisdiction rules. A question arises with regard to the term '*compulsory*'. Under which law must this be determined? The intention was probably to refer to a law of an EU Member State that requires a type of insurance, and to give the courts of that EU Member State jurisdiction. The national law requiring

---

to compete on equal terms with non-EC insurers in foreign markets; see Hartley, *Civil Jurisdiction and Judgments*, note 349 above, 62.

[377] Chapter 3 below, paras 3.10 and following.
[378] Case C–281/02 *Owusu v Jackson* [2005] ECR I–1383.

the insurance would probably grant that jurisdiction.[379] Brussels I does not prevent jurisdiction over a policyholder domiciled outside the EU. The same applies with regard to the insurance of immovable property in a Member State. The fact that the immovable property belongs to a person domiciled in a third State does not put the contract entirely outside the EU and beyond the EU jurisdictional scope.

Stronger parties from third States

Third State plaintiffs are subjected to the protective rules. In line with this, **2.297** they cannot circumvent these rules by forum clauses. This would negate their protective purpose for weaker parties. Third State defendants fall outside the scope of the rules, because the entire sections on protective jurisdiction were made subject to the rule that defendants domiciled in third States do not fall under Brussels I, but under the national jurisdiction rules of the Member States.[380] Third State insurers, traders, and employers should be particularly careful when contracting with weaker parties from the EU. Forum clauses will be of no use when one wants to sue the weaker party. EU courts will refer to the protective bases for jurisdiction that were created for these weaker parties. On the other hand, the weaker parties will be permitted to rely on those forum clauses if they point to an EU court.

CONCLUSION

The idea of granting procedural protection to weaker parties is acceptable **2.298** in itself. However, the provisions on the protective bases for jurisdiction in Brussels I have been drawn up with only European weaker parties in mind, resulting in a confusion of rules. Furthermore, parties from outside the EU contracting with EU weaker parties are put in an adverse position: not only can they easily be drawn into EU courts, but it is also difficult to work out when they can rely on contractual terms (such as forum clauses), and when those terms would be invalid. And as always, judgments against them can be recognized and enforced in all EU Member States. If Brussels I were to be truly double, these rules would apply to all defendants. However, the rules would then have to be drawn up more carefully so as not to make life unnecessarily difficult for traders, insurers, and employers, and to ensure that the court granted jurisdiction has a sufficient connection with the defendant or facts of the case.

---

[379] See B Audit, *Droit international privé* (3rd edn, Paris: Economica, 2000) 459.
[380] Art 4 of Brussels I.

H. GENERAL CONCLUSION

2.299 This chapter has discussed a great number of rules: those on general jurisdiction, those rules that provide for alternative jurisdiction, protective
bases of jurisdiction, rules on additional defendants, counter-claims, and
the position of defendants that appear voluntarily without contesting
jurisdiction. In the context of Brussels I it can be generally stated that these
rules apply when the defendant is domiciled in the EU. This generaliza-
tion, however, has many exceptions where parties domiciled in third
States can be subjected to Brussels I's jurisdiction rules. In other cases,
if the defendant is domiciled in a third State, the Regulation generally
refers to the national bases for jurisdiction. These national bases have been
incorporated into the scheme of the Regulation by reference. All judgments by courts of EU Member States can be recognized and enforced
in all other EU Member States. As a result the application of exorbitant
national bases of jurisdiction is particularly detrimental to parties from
third States.

2.300 Brussels II *bis* has a different approach to determining the application of
its jurisdiction rules and to completing its scheme with national jurisdiction rules. The Regulation only refers to those rules if neither the court
seised, nor the courts of any other EU Member State, has jurisdiction under
the Regulation's rules. They are only residual. Because of the wide scope
of the Regulation's own rules, the national rules will not often be given
effect. However, where they are given effect, their exorbitant nature is
strengthened by the Regulation. A court in an EU Member State must
make those rules based on nationality available to all EU nationals habitually resident in that Member State if the defendant is not habitually resident in the EU and is not an EU national, or in the case of Ireland and the
United Kingdom, domiciled there. Once again, the resulting judgments
can be recognized and enforced in all other EU Member States.

2.301 The Insolvency Regulation contains only one basis for jurisdiction in the
opening of main insolvency proceedings: the centre of the debtor's main
interests. There are no residual bases of jurisdiction and no reference to
national bases. In order to determine if one can open main insolvency
proceedings in the EU, the pertinent question is whether or not this centre
of main interests is in the EU.

2.302 Under the proposed Maintenance Regulation the habitual residence, domicile, and nationality of the defendant are all irrelevant. The Regulation's
rules on jurisdiction will always apply. This means that the Regulation
will have a truly double nature: every judgment granted by a court in an

EU Member State and capable of being recognized or enforced in other Member States, will have been granted on EU jurisdiction rules. No national exorbitant rules will be applied. One has to admit that totally harmonizing the jurisdiction rules goes quite far, but the advantage is a fair and equitable system for all defendants.

3

Second cornerstone: exclusive jurisdiction

Article 22 of the Brussels I Regulation:

The following courts shall have exclusive jurisdiction, regardless of domicile:

1. *in proceedings which have as their object rights* in rem *in immovable property or tenancies of immovable property, the courts of the Member States in which the property is situated.*
   However, in proceedings which have as their object tenancies of immovable property concluded for temporary use for a maximum period of six consecutive months, the courts of the Member State in which the defendant is domiciled shall also have jurisdiction, provided that the tenant is a natural person and that the landlord and the tenant are domiciled in the same Member State;
2. *in proceedings which have as their object the validity of the constitution, the nullity or the dissolution of companies or other legal persons or associations of natural persons, or of the validity of the decisions of their organs, the courts of the Member State in which the company, legal person or association has its seat. In order to determine the seat, the court shall apply its rules of private international law;*
3. *in proceedings which have as their object the validity of entries in public registers, the courts of the Member State in which the register is kept;*

4. *in proceedings concerned with the registration or validity of patents, trade marks, designs, or other similar rights required to be deposited or registered, the courts of the Member State in which the deposit or registration has been applied for, has taken place or is under the terms of a Community instrument or an international convention deemed to have taken place.*

   Without prejudice to the jurisdiction of the European Patent Office under the Convention on the Grant of European Patents, signed at Munich on 5 October 1973, the courts of each Member State shall have exclusive jurisdiction, regardless of domicile, in proceedings concerned with the registration or validity of any European patent granted for that State;

5. *in proceedings concerned with the enforcement of judgments, the courts of the Member State in which the judgment has been or is to be enforced.*

Article 25 of the Brussels I Regulation:

Where a court of a Member State is seised of a claim which is principally concerned with a matter over which the courts of another Member State have exclusive jurisdiction by virtue of Article 22, it shall declare of its own motion that it has no jurisdiction.

Article 29 of the Brussels I Regulation:

Where actions come within the exclusive jurisdiction of several courts, any court other than the court first seised shall decline jurisdiction in favour of that court.

Article 35 of the Brussels I Regulation:

1. *Moreover, a judgment shall not be recognised if it conflicts with Sections 3, 4 or 6 of Chapter II, or in a case provided for in Article 72.*
2. *. . .*

A. INTRODUCTION

3.01 Some matters have a particularly close link with a specific territory, and therefore Brussels I grants exclusive jurisdiction to the courts of that EU Member State. Brussels II *bis* and the Insolvency Regulation do not cover such matters and will not be discussed in this chapter.[1]

---

[1] Brussels II *bis* provides in Art 6 that certain defendants may only be sued in accordance with Arts 3, 4, and 5. This rule is sometimes described as the exclusive nature of the Regulation's bases for jurisdiction. The term 'exclusive' has a different meaning here: it indicates that only the Regulation's jurisdiction rules may be used and not national ones; it says nothing about the relation between the Regulation's bases for jurisdiction and which of them should be preferred.

Brussels I provides for five fields in which such a close link might exist: **3.02** immovable property, the validity of legal persons, the validity of entries in public registers, the validity or registration of intellectual property rights, and the enforcement of judgments. Exclusive jurisdiction is topmost in the hierarchy of the jurisdiction rules of Brussels I. It applies irrespective of the domiciles of the parties.[2] This provision is the only limitation that is placed on the ability of parties to choose a forum.[3] Where a defendant appears voluntarily without contesting jurisdiction, jurisdiction would not thereby be granted if the case concerned a matter in which a court of another EU Member State has exclusive jurisdiction.[4]

The other side of the coin is the obligation on EU courts to decline jurisdic- **3.03** tion if the courts of another EU Member State have exclusive jurisdiction according to the Regulation.[5]

Further proof of the importance in Brussels I of the exclusive bases for **3.04** jurisdiction is found in the grounds for refusal of recognition or enforcement. A judgment granted by an EU court in a case in which the courts of another EU Member State in fact had exclusive jurisdiction will not be recognized or enforced.[6] This is an exception to the general rule of Brussels I that EU Member States recognize and enforce each other's judgments without evaluating the basis for jurisdiction.[7]

In this chapter, regard must be had both to the situation where an EU court **3.05** has exclusive jurisdiction, and to the situation where exclusive jurisdiction lies with a court outside the EU. One has to consider in which cases EU courts will decline jurisdiction in favour of courts in third States. The theory of the *effet réflexe*, or reflexive effect, will be the starting point. The five bases for exclusive jurisdiction will be discussed in the order that they appear in Article 22 of Brussels I. The issue of simultaneous exclusive jurisdiction in different states can also impact on third States and will be discussed next. Thereafter one turns to the remaining issues regarding

---

[2] P Jenard, 'Rapport du Comité restreint sur la bilateralisation' [1969] Hague Conference on Private International Law. Proceedings of the Extraordinary Session 11, 145–151 (Jenard Report), 34.

[3] See F Salerno, 'European International civil procedure' in B von Hoffmann (ed), *European Private International Law* (Nijmegen: Ars Aequi Libri, 1998) 155.

[4] See Art 24 of Brussels I, which specifically provides an exception for Art 22. Art 24 and the voluntary appearance of defendants is discussed in chapter 2 above, paras 2.160 and following.

[5] Art 25 of Brussels I.

[6] See Art 35(1) of Brussels I.

[7] The exception exists only in two other cases, insurance and consumer contracts (not even employment contracts); see above para 2.254.

exclusive jurisdiction and third States: where a forum clause exists in favour of an EU court while exclusive jurisdiction should lie with the courts of a third State, and the incidental question. Lastly, the situation where a case is connected to only one EU Member State and to a third State will be considered (i.e. the situation where there is no link with the European judicial area).

B. EXCLUSIVE JURISDICTION OUTSIDE THE EU

General

3.06 A defendant might be domiciled in the EU, while the dispute concerned immovable property situated in a third State. Is there any way in which one can respect such third State jurisdiction? The Regulation does not contain an express rule for this situation; for example, it does not expressly authorize Member State courts to decline their Regulation-based jurisdiction. The silence of the Regulation on this matter has given rise to the question whether Regulation-based jurisdiction is compulsory, or may be declined in favour of third State courts. What happens if a dispute concerns immovable property in a third State, while the defendant is domiciled in Spain? What if the parties had included a forum clause in their lease agreement in favour of a court in New York and one of them subsequently brings suit in London, where the defendant is domiciled?[8]

The compulsory nature of the Regulation's jurisdiction rules

3.07 Brussels I states in Article 2(1) '[s]ubject to this Regulation, persons in a Member State shall, whatever their nationality, be sued in the courts of that Member State'. This wording seems to suggest that the Regulation's rules are mandatory. Derogation seems possible only where the Regulation itself provides for an exception.[9] The Reports of de Almeida Cruz, Desantes Real & Jenard, and Jenard & Möller both state that Article 2 (or Article 4, if the defendant is domiciled in a third State) prevails if immovable

---

[8] On this question, see L Barnich, 'Les droits réels immobiliers et les locations de vacances' in R Fentiman, A Nuyts, H Tagaras & N Watté, *The European Judicial Area in Civil and Commercial Matters* (Brussels: Bruylant, 1999) 85–101 at 86–87.

[9] See TC Hartley, *Civil Jurisdiction and Judgments* (London: Sweet & Maxwell, 1984) 66; H Born, M Fallon & J-L van Boxstael, *Droit judiciaire international. Chronique de jurisprudence 1991–1998* (Brussels: Larcier, 2001) 289.

property is situated outside the EU.[10] This seems to support the view that such jurisdiction is compulsory.

The European Court of Justice in the *Owusu* case also followed the inter- **3.08** pretation that Article 2 jurisdiction is compulsory.[11] Acting on a question from the English Court of Appeal, the European Court of Justice replied that the basis for jurisdiction of the domicile of the defendant (Article 2) was compulsory. The English court was not permitted to decline its Regulation-based jurisdiction in favour of the courts in a third State (in this case Jamaica) by applying the rule of *forum non conveniens*. The European Court of Justice added that this was so even if the dispute did not have any connection with another EU Member State. The rules, according to the Court, were compulsory, even when the EU judicial space was unaffected. In *Owusu* the courts of Jamaica did not have exclusive jurisdiction. The judgment thus confirms that Article 2 jurisdiction is compulsory, with no account taken of the nature of the third State court's jurisdiction. The case did not concern the precise point of Article 2 jurisdiction in a case where a court in a third State has exclusive jurisdiction.

The European Court of Justice confirmed its view in the *Lugano* opinion.[12] **3.09** This case concerned the European Community's external competence to negotiate and conclude an updated version of the Lugano Convention.[13] In order to examine this external competence the European Court of Justice had to consider the nature of Brussels I's jurisdiction rules. It stated that, whenever the defendant is domiciled in an EU Member State, jurisdiction lies with the courts of that State (according to Article 2).[14] The ECJ did not explicitly state that Article 2 jurisdiction was compulsory. However, it explained that, if there were no other conventions, the courts in that EU Member State would be the appropriate fora. The Lugano Convention would have the effect that those fora would no longer be appropriate. Interpreting this statement of the ECJ, one sees that if a third State court

---

[10] De Almeida Cruz, Desantes Real & Jenard Report on the San Sebastian (1989) version of the Brussels Convention, p 47; Jenard & Möller Report on the Lugano Convention, 76; para 54 (both published in C 189 of 28 July 1990). The older Jenard (note 2 above) and Schlosser Reports do not seem to contain such statements: Schlosser Report on the 1978 version of the Brussels Convention; OJ C 59, 5 March 1979, 71.

[11] Case C–281/02 *Owusu v Jackson and others* [2005] ECR I–1383. For a more detailed discussion of this judgment and the relationship between the theory of *forum non conveniens* and Brussels I, see chapter 5 below, paras 5.86 and following.

[12] Opinion C–1/03 *Competence of the Community to conclude the new Lugano Convention on jurisdiction and the recognition and enforcement of judgments in civil and commercial matters* [2006] ECR I–1145.

[13] For a more detailed discussion of this external competence, see chapter 7 below.

[14] At para 153.

has exclusive jurisdiction, the Article 2 court in the EU will still have jurisdiction, unless there is a convention to the contrary.

The theory of the reflexive effect

3.10 The theory of the *effet réflexe* (reflexive effect) was developed by Droz in the early days of the Brussels Convention and seeks to provide an escape from the imperative nature of Article 2.[15] While Droz supported the idea that jurisdiction was imperative, he stated that it may be refused in certain cases.[16] The theory asserts that, if EU courts are to assume exclusive jurisdiction in certain cases, they also have to allow third State courts to exercise jurisdiction in similar cases. EU courts must respect such jurisdiction by declining their own jurisdiction. This should be done even if their own jurisdiction is based directly on Brussels I, for instance the domicile of the defendant (Article 2).

3.11 The theory of the reflexive effect is based on reciprocity, self-restraint, and comity. Indeed, it is illogical that a French court could be clearly incompetent as to property situated in Germany, but competent as to property situated in Japan.[17] As regards the property situated in Germany, the French court would have to declare that it lacks jurisdiction.[18] If the dispute concerns immovable property outside the EU, the courts of an EU Member State might be considered to have jurisdiction on the basis of the domicile in the EU of the defendant, performance of the contract in the EU, a forum clause in favour of, or the voluntary appearance in an EU court. All these bases for jurisdiction are lower in the internal hierarchy of Brussels I when jurisdiction in the EU is concerned. The theory of the reflexive effect seeks to extrapolate this internal hierarchy to third States. If Brussels I acknowledges that some bases for jurisdiction are stronger than others, the same

---

[15] See GAL Droz, 'Entrée en vigueur de la Convention de Bruxelles révisée sur la compétence judiciaire et l'exécution des jugements' [1987] *Revue critique de droit international privé* 251–303 at 260–261; GAL Droz, 'La Convention de San Sebastian alignant la Convention de Bruxelles sur la Convention de Lugano' [1990] *Revue critique de droit international privé* 1–21 at 14. See also P Gothot & D Holleaux, *La Convention de Bruxelles du 27 septembre 1968* (Paris: Jupiter, 1985) 84; A Nuyts, 'La théorie de l'effet réflexe' in M Storme & G de Leval (eds), *Le droit processuel et judiciaire européen* (Brussels: die Keure, 2003) 73–89. Specifically with regard to intellectual property, see M Pertegás Sender, *Cross-border Enforcement of Patent Rights* (Oxford: Oxford University Press, 2002) 157–161.

[16] Droz, 'Entrée en vigueur', ibid, 260–261.

[17] See H Gaudemet-Tallon, 'Les frontières extérieures de l'espace judiciaire européen: quelques repères' in A Borrás, A Bucher, AVM Struycken & M Verwilghen (eds), *E Pluribus unum. Liber Amicorum Georges AL Droz* (The Hague: Martinus Nijhoff Publishers, 1996) 95.

[18] According to Art 25 of Brussels I.

standard would have to be applied to jurisdictional bases situated outside the EU. Moreover, if the EU courts refused to take into account such incontestably reasonable jurisdiction rules of third States (which are in accordance with the EU rules themselves), the resulting judgments from the EU courts might lack effectiveness: where the judgment attempted to regulate a dispute on immovable property situated in a third State, this judgment would often need recognition or enforcement in that particular third State. If the third State were to have rules as logical as those of Brussels I, recognition and enforcement would be refused if the judgment concerned immovable property situated in its own territory. The EU rules would have been stringently respected, but would have led to a completely useless judgment: a beached whale.

The theory of the reflexive effect actually means that EU courts should **3.12** decline jurisdiction that they theoretically have under Brussels I, where there exists a stronger or hierarchically higher basis for jurisdiction in a third State. Of course, Brussels I cannot grant jurisdiction to a court in a third State, but the national jurisdiction rules of the third State would probably provide a basis for jurisdiction in these cases. The fact that a state considers a jurisdictional rule to be exclusive is not always directly visible, but often found in the refusal to recognize judgments where the state addressed would have had jurisdiction on a basis such as the location of immovable property. The EU courts should decline jurisdiction in order for the third State court to exercise its jurisdiction. In that sense, the theory of the reflexive effect does not create a jurisdictional basis, but a rule for declining jurisdiction.[19]

The *Lugano* opinion did not recognize the existence of the reflexive effect. **3.13** However, the issue did not concern immovable property situated in a third State while the defendant was domiciled in the EU. The ECJ had only to consider the nature of Article 2 of the Regulation on the way to determining the external competence of the European Community in this matter. Its conclusion might thus be categorized as incidental. Furthermore, the ECJ merely concluded that Regulation-based jurisdiction was compulsory. The theory of the reflexive effect does not deny that fact; it seeks an equitable exception to it.

The ground for refusing jurisdiction in the context of the reflexive effect

In the application of the theory of the reflexive effect, uncertainty has **3.14** arisen with regard to the ground for refusing jurisdiction. Is the ground

---

[19] See Nuyts, note 15 above, 75–76.

something embedded in the Regulation, although it is not explicitly there? Or is the ground for declining jurisdiction to be found in national law? This question goes to the very heart of the nature of Brussels I.

3.15 According to the first point of view, Brussels I should have explicitly stated that EU courts should decline Regulation-based jurisdiction if the dispute concerns immovable property in a third State.[20] For the advocates of this interpretation this is a logical and coherent extension of the rules of Brussels I.[21] Briggs and Rees even go as far as speaking of a 'textual omission'.[22] This first viewpoint follows the principle that the Regulation contains a universal set of rules.[23] The Regulation always applies and its rules must be followed, except in cases where the Regulation itself allows the rules to be set aside, as by the theory of the reflexive effect. The practical advantage of this expounding of the reflexive effect is that the result will be the same in all EU Member States. One would not have to deal with differences in national rules on declining jurisdiction. The theoretical strength of this argument lies in the fact that it can be consistent with the latest case law of the European Court of Justice. The ECJ found in its *Lugano* opinion that Brussels I contains a complete system of jurisdiction rules.[24] Thus the reflexive effect should be part of this coherent system.

3.16 The second point of view is that one would have to revert to the national laws of the Member States to find the basis for declining jurisdiction, as Brussels I did not attempt to solve the situation.[25] This analysis allows for two different sets of rules, namely the Regulation rules when the European judicial area is at stake, and national rules when relations with third States are concerned. This approach has the advantage that it leaves outside the European judicial sphere what should be left out. A dispute on immovable property outside the EU will not, in all likelihood, have much connection with the European judicial area. Later issues of recognition and enforcement of the resulting judgment in the EU (if necessary) would have to be solved under the national law of the EU Member State involved.

---

[20] Some use the name *effet réflexe* only for this first, more limited, interpretation. However, that difference in terminology is not material for the discussion.

[21] See Gaudemet-Tallon, note 17 above, 99.

[22] See A Briggs & P Rees, *Civil Jurisdiction and Judgments* (4th edn, London: LLP, 2005) 90 and 228–230.

[23] Ibid, 3–4; also discussed in chapter 1 above, paras 1.52 and following.

[24] *Lugano* Opinion, note 12 above, para 151–153.

[25] Y Donzallaz, *La Convention de Lugano du 16 septembre 1988 concernant la compétence judiciaire et l'exécution des décisions en matière civile et commerciale* (Berne: Editions Stæmpfli + Cie SA Berne, 1996) vol 1, 423; Gothot & Holleaux, note 15 above, 84. See also R Fentiman, 'Civil jurisdiction and third States: *Owusu* and after', [2006] CML Rev, 705–734 at 722.

Therefore, it is best to refer to the national rules (at the time of jurisdiction, or the declining of it). That way one will prevent the handing down of judgments that follow the EU rules but are not recognizable or enforceable. This solution would have created a harmonious interaction between Brussels I, the Lugano Convention, and national rules of jurisdiction. If the property were situated in the EU, Brussels I would be applicable. If the property were situated in a non-EU Lugano Contracting State, the Lugano Convention would be applicable. If the property were situated in a third State, neither the Regulation nor the Convention would be applicable, but the domestic rules of the forum state. Those domestic rules could then be used to decline jurisdiction. An example of such a domestic rule is *forum non conveniens*, but other rules can be envisaged.[26]

The judgment of the European Court of Justice in the *Coreck Maritime* case **3.17** is also relevant to the debate on the reflexive effect.[27] Dealing with the question of a forum clause in favour of the courts of a third State, the European Court of Justice stated that the validity of such a clause had to be determined according to national law of the forum, including the conflict of law rules.[28] Although the Court did not explicitly state that the domicile of the defendant in the EU was irrelevant, the judgment acknowledges a possibility of declining Regulation-based jurisdiction (in line with the reflexive effect) if a third State court would have exclusive jurisdiction, or if a forum clause appointed the courts of a third State.

The English court declined jurisdiction on the basis of national rules in the **3.18** case *Polly Peck International plc*,[29] dealing with property situated in Northern Cyprus (this case dates from before Cyprus joined the EU). The defendant was a company incorporated in the UK. An old English rule, established in the *Mozambique* case, established that an English court could not decide an action concerning the title to or rights of possession of immovable property situated outside England.[30] The rule was later tempered, however, so that the English courts may rule on torts relating to immovable property situated outside England, unless the proceedings are principally concerned with a question of title or right of possession of

---

[26] The doctrine of *forum non conveniens* is discussed in chapter 5 below, paras 5.51 and following.
[27] Case C–387/98 *Coreck Maritime GmbH v Handelsveem BV and others* [2000] ECR I–9337.
[28] Para 19.
[29] *Polly Peck International Plc (in administration) (No 2)* [1998] 3 All ER 812.
[30] Formulated in the case *British South Africa Company v The Companhia de Moçambique* [1893] AC 602. See also L Collins (ed), *Dicey, Morris and Collins on the Conflict of Laws* (14th edn, London: Sweet & Maxwell, 2006) vol II, 1142–1154, especially 1148–1154.

that property.[31] In this case the judge on appeal found that the question to the title of the property was not merely incidental. Therefore, the court lacked jurisdiction. The judge further found that the general basis for jurisdiction in the Brussels Convention did not prevent the English court from applying its national rule and refusing jurisdiction. He relied on the judgment in *Re Harrods*, an English case that permitted the application of the rule of *forum non conveniens* in conjunction with the EU jurisdiction rules.[32]

3.19 However, finding that Regulation-based jurisdiction can be declined on the basis of national rules seems hard to defend after recent judgments by the European Court of Justice. The Court ruled (as explained above) that a single system of jurisdiction rules has been created. It also ruled that jurisdiction of an EU court on the basis of the domicile of the defendant is compulsory. Therefore, if the reflexive effect has survived these rulings, which only time will tell, then declining jurisdiction must probably be founded on Brussels I itself.

C. IMMOVABLE PROPERTY

General

3.20 Brussels I states that if the dispute concerns immovable property, exclusive jurisdiction lies with the EU Member State where the property is situated. Other EU courts must decline jurisdiction. The rule that a claim with regard to real property located outside the forum could not be decided by a court, even if the defendant was served locally, developed as long ago as the fourteenth century, arguably in England.[33]

3.21 Thus, the rule itself is not surprising. On the other hand, the wide scope of Brussels I's rule is not self-evident. Granting jurisdiction to the court at the location of the immovable property makes sense if the dispute concerns real rights, such as who the owner is, or whether a valid *usufruct* exists. The local judge is indeed in the best position to adjudicate the matter and evaluate evidence where necessary.[34] The European Court of Justice limited the reach of the provision when it ruled in *Land Oberösterreich v ČEZ* that nuisance caused to immovable property (or an application for an

---

[31] Sec 30 of the Civil Jurisdiction and Judgments Act 1982.
[32] [1992] Ch 72.
[33] M Twitchell, 'The Myth of General Jurisdiction' [1988] *Harvard Law Review*, 610–681 at 615–616.
[34] See Gaudemet-Tallon, note 17 above, 88.

interdict to end such nuisance) did not fall within the scope of the exclusive jurisdiction of the court of the place where the property is situated.[35] An Austrian province sought an order against ČEZ, a Czech energy-supply undertaking in which the Czech State had 70 per cent ownership, to end damage to its territory caused by ionizing radiation (claimed to be above normal levels). At the time the proceedings started, the Czech Republic was not yet a Member of the EU. Consequently the defendant was domiciled in a third State. The European Court of Justice started its judgment by stating that the domicile of the defendant was irrelevant when exclusive jurisdiction in the EU on the basis of immovable property was at stake.[36] It then concluded that the nuisance did not fall within the rule on exclusive jurisdiction and that the court where the plant was situated was in a better position to assess the radiation.[37]

The rule in Brussels I does not encompass only disputes relating to real **3.22** rights, but also those concerning tenancies of immovable property. This means that no effect will be given to a forum clause in a lease agreement. For instance, a Canadian company renting a building as business premises in Paris might sublet a floor to a US company. If a dispute arises between those companies, the courts in Paris will have exclusive jurisdiction. Even if the contract contained a forum clause prescribing a Canadian court, the court in Paris will ignore it and assume jurisdiction over the case. If the lessee (for example) thinks that a French court would provide him with a better deal, that court is open to him, irrespective of the forum clause, and even irrespective of a possible earlier action brought in a Canadian court.[38] If one of the parties brings suit in a Canadian court, that court might hear the case and give judgment. As far as enforcement of that judgment in Canada and the US is concerned, there might be no problem. However, if the judgment creditor wishes to enforce the judgment in France, where the debtor might have property, the French courts might refuse enforcement, arguing that the litigation should have taken place in France.

Thus, parties from third States must be wary of the consequences of **3.23** Brussels I. It seems that only an amendment of the Regulation itself will be

---

[35] Case C–343/04 [2006] ECR I–04557. See also H Tagaras, 'Chronique de jurisprudence de la Cour de justice relative à la Convention de Bruxelles' [2006] *Cahiers de droit européen* 483–553, 538–541.

[36] Ibid, para 21.

[37] Ibid, para 39.

[38] For a more detailed analysis of the rules on parallel proceedings, see chapter 5 below.

able to resolve the current situation. The Hague Choice of Court Convention excludes tenancies in immovable property from its scope.[39]

Immovable property situated outside the EU

3.24 On the other hand, if immovable property is situated outside the EU, while the defendant is domiciled in an EU Member State, the courts of that State will have jurisdiction. The possible exceptions, or lack thereof, have been discussed above.[40] If the theory of the reflexive effect were accepted, it would apply only if a third State court has exclusive jurisdiction on the basis of its domestic rules. If its legal system does not grant exclusive jurisdiction over tenancies, no reflexive effect would come into play.

Short-term tenancies

3.25 The Article on exclusive jurisdiction in matters of immovable property explicitly provides an exception for short-term tenancies, and was added after the judgment in the case *Rösler v Rottwinkel*.[41] The dispute arose between two parties domiciled in Germany regarding the three-week lease of a holiday villa in Italy. The European Court of Justice upheld a strict interpretation of the exclusive jurisdiction of the courts of the EU Member State where the immovable property is situated. The judgment, although correct to the letter of the Brussels Convention (of the time) gave rise to criticism on the grounds of equity to the parties and some advocated that the Convention should be amended.[42]

3.26 How does this provision affect third States? For example, two persons domiciled in the same third State conclude a short-term tenancy contract with regard to property in the EU. The tenancy contract covers immovable property in the EU, so that on first sight Brussels I applies and provides exclusive jurisdiction. The exception states that, if the two parties are domiciled in the same EU Member State, the courts of that Member State also have jurisdiction. Thus, the exclusive nature of the jurisdiction is tempered: parties might litigate in the courts of the EU Member State where the property is situated, or in that of their domicile. The question arises

---

[39] Hague Convention of 30 June 2005 on Choice of Court Agreements, Art 2(2)(l). This Convention is not yet in force.

[40] See above, paras 3.07 and following.

[41] Case 241/83 [1985] ECR 99.

[42] See, for instance case notes by FA Mann [1985] LQR 329–330; TC Hartley [1985] ELR, 361–363; GAL Droz, [1986] *Revue critique de droit international privé* 135–142; K Kreuzer [1986] *Praxis des internationalen Privat- und Verfahrensrechts* 75–80.

what the response of the court would be if the defendant states that he or she prefers to be sued in the third State where he or she and the plaintiff are domiciled. The exception to the exclusive jurisdiction seems only to apply if the parties are domiciled in the EU.

The third State court of the domicile of the parties might assume jurisdic- **3.27** tion in such a case. The problem will then arise again at the stage of recognition and enforcement in the EU Member State where the property is situated. That court will probably refuse recognition and enforcement on the basis that it had exclusive jurisdiction. It would be more consistent if Brussels I also permitted an exception to the exclusive jurisdiction in such cases.

Conversely, two parties domiciled in the EU might conclude a short-term **3.28** contract with regard to immovable property in a third State. In this case, the EU court of the domicile of the defendant will hear the case, because of the compulsory nature of Article 2 (as explained above).[43] Even if a reflexive effect were recognized, it probably would not often operate in this case, as few legal systems grant exclusive jurisdiction over tenancy cases.

Time-share

Time-share does not fall within the scope of the exclusive jurisdiction. This **3.29** has recently been clarified by the European Court of Justice in response to a preliminary question posed by the Oberlandesgericht (District Court of Appeal) of Hamm.[44] In this case the defendant, a company managing the time-share, was established in the Isle of Man, a third State for purposes of Brussels I.[45] Thus, if time-share qualified for exclusive jurisdiction, the Regulation would have become applicable. Time-share not being subject to exclusive jurisdiction had the result that the national bases for jurisdiction were applied in this case.[46]

Classifying time-share is not easy. On the one hand, the use of immovable **3.30** property is at stake (to an extent comparable with tenancy). On the other hand, the construction of time-share is such that one pays for membership to a club and in exchange receives a right to use a holiday house or apartment on a part-time basis, for instance one week per year for 20 years. Besides, the European Court of Justice pointed out that this might not

---

[43] Paras 3.07 and following.
[44] Case C–73/04 *Klein & Klein v Rhodos Management Ltd* [2005] ECR I–8667. See also Tagaras, note 35 above, 526–531.
[45] Art 299(6)(c) EC Treaty (Nice version); see chapter 1 above.
[46] Note 44 above, para 14 of the judgment.

even be the same apartment every year so that the right of use is not connected to a single piece of property.[47] At a policy level, the Court emphasized that the provision on exclusive jurisdiction should not be given a broader interpretation than necessary.[48] Some authors have stated that time-share should fall under the protective bases for jurisdiction.[49] Advocate General Geelhoed in his opinion observed that the content and legal nature of time-share arrangements vary greatly in the EU Member States. In some Member States these fall under the law of obligations, in others under company law, and in yet others under property law.[50]

3.31 The result reached by the European Court of Justice was that time-share does not fall within the rule on exclusive jurisdiction. Such a result seems equitable; parties from third States administering time-shares would not be unpleasantly surprised by exclusive jurisdiction in a court with which their contract has a tenuous link. Leaving time-share out of the exclusive jurisdiction provision permits the parties to rely on the legal arrangement they had used, for example, under contract or company law. Also, choice of court agreements would be respected and parties would not be forced to litigate in an EU court in a place where they set foot only one week per year. Moreover, not all possible disputes giving rise to litigation would necessarily be related to the immovable property itself. Other contractual issues might also lead to litigation. In fact, the dispute in *Klein* concerned the payment of the fee and had nothing to do with the property itself.

D. VALIDITY OF LEGAL PERSONS

3.32 Article 22(2) grants exclusive jurisdiction in matters relating to the validity, nullity, or dissolution of legal persons, or the validity of the decisions of their organs to the courts of an EU Member State in which a legal person has its seat. The board of directors of a company has been stated to be an 'organ' of a company.[51]

3.33 To determine the seat, the court should apply its private international law rules. This provision differs from that applicable to jurisdiction based on the domicile of the defendant (Article 2). The domicile of a legal person is

---

[47] Ibid, para 24.

[48] Ibid, para 15.

[49] See C Bruneau, 'Les règles européennes de compétence en matière civile et commerciale' [2001] *La Semaine juridique* 533–541 at 537.

[50] Note 44 above, para 20.

[51] See *Grupo Torras SA and Torras Hostench London Ltd v Sheikh Fahad* [1996] 1 Lloyd's Rep 7 at p 15; *Speed Investment Ltd, SLEC Holdings Ltd v Formula One* [2004] WL 1640302 at para 29.

for that purpose determined autonomously by Article 60. As has been pointed out, that provision might extend the application of Brussels I.[52] It is conceivable that a company might be incorporated in an EU Member State while it has its real seat in a third State or vice versa. In both situations an EU Member State court would be able to find that the company is domiciled in the EU, notwithstanding the court's own private international law rules.

The advent of the Regulation did not bring about an autonomous defini- **3.34** tion for domicile under the provision on validity of legal persons. (It did do so for purposes of the general basis for jurisdiction of the defendant's domicile.) In order to determine which court has exclusive jurisdiction over the validity of a legal person, the rule refers to the 'seat', and states that the court must apply its own rules of private international law to determine such seat.[53] This rule has the advantage that it does not extend the exclusive bases for jurisdiction beyond what would be in line with the national laws of the EU Member States. In other words, an EU Member State which, under its own private international law rules, views a legal person to have its seat at the place of its incorporation, would not find itself having exclusive jurisdiction over a legal person incorporated elsewhere but with its real seat in that State's territory.

However, the rule does not always provide a foreseeable result. While **3.35** one can determine whether a specific EU Member State supports the incorporation or the real seat doctrine, the outcome will not always be clear. One can imagine a company with a statutory seat in the United States of America and with its principal place of business in France. According to the third State (USA), applying the incorporation theory, the corporation would have its seat there, while under French law, applying the real seat doctrine, the corporation would have its seat in France. In such a situation the French courts would assume (exclusive) jurisdiction because France would consider the corporation's seat to be in its territory. Moreover, in states adhering to the real seat theory, confusion might arise as to the point at which a legal person had moved its principal place of business from within the EU to a third State or vice versa. National law will determine exactly when the moving of the legal person takes effect.

The question arises how this determination of exclusive jurisdiction, by **3.36** reference to national law, relates to the obligation of other EU Member State courts to decline jurisdiction. If a case is brought before the courts of

---

[52] Paras 2.26 and following.
[53] Compare this rule of Art 22(2) to Art 60; see also P Vlas, case note on *Coreck* [2001] *Nederlandse jurisprudentie. Uitspraken in burgerlijke en strafzaken*, no 599, p 4442–5 at 4444–5.

one EU Member State, while the courts of another EU Member State have exclusive jurisdiction, the court seised must of its own motion declare that it has no jurisdiction to hear the case.[54] This declining should be carried out in line with Article 22, where the exclusive bases for jurisdiction are set out. Therefore, when a court questions whether it can assume jurisdiction, knowing of the possibility of exclusive jurisdiction in the courts of another EU Member State, it must consider the same rules that the courts that might have exclusive jurisdiction would apply. A court therefore must consider whether a legal person is domiciled in another EU Member State according to the private international law of that State. For example, a company incorporated in some exotic island (third State) has its administration and main activities in England. According to the private international law of England, that company has its seat in the exotic island. It is irrelevant that the private international law rules of some EU Member States will determine the seat to be in England, where the so-called 'real seat' is. The courts of other EU Member States would not have to decline jurisdiction in favour of the courts of England. If a dispute concerns a company with its seat in a third State, while the defendant is domiciled in an EU Member State, the courts of that Member State will have jurisdiction on the basis of Article 2, which is compulsory. Whether or not such jurisdiction can be declined has been discussed above.[55]

E. VALIDITY OF ENTRIES IN PUBLIC REGISTERS

3.37 Public registers may contain civil matters, which in general fall within the scope of Brussels I. If civil matters are recorded in public registers and those registers need to be corrected, the disputes will be heard by the courts of the EU Member State in which the registers are situated. In these actions, the domiciles of the parties are irrelevant for the purposes of jurisdiction.

3.38 A case may fall simultaneously within the rules on public registers and on immovable property.[56] In the majority of cases, this will not pose problems, as a land registry is most often in the country where the land is

---

[54] According to Art 25 of Brussels I.

[55] Paras 3.07 and following.

[56] See, for instance, *In re Hayward* [1997] Ch 45; *Bradley v Halsall and others* [2002] WL 1654856.

located. The English courts have held that registers held by companies may also be considered 'public registers' as they are open to the public.[57] Such registers would most often be kept at the seat of the company. If not, one might have conflicting exclusive jurisdictions at the location of the registers and at the company the seat, if the dispute concerned actions by the company or its organs as well as its registers. The issue of simultaneous exclusive jurisdiction will be discussed later.[58]

As for registers in third States, if the defendant is domiciled in an EU **3.39** Member State, the courts of that State will assume jurisdiction on the basis of Article 2. The possibilities of declining such jurisdiction have been discussed.[59]

F. VALIDITY AND REGISTRATION OF INTELLECTUAL PROPERTY RIGHTS

General

Brussels I grants exclusive jurisdiction in matters concerning the validity **3.40** or registration of 'patents, trade marks, designs, or other similar rights required to be deposited or registered'. The open-ended phrase permits for the further development of the law in this area.[60] Moreover, the rules

---

[57] See *Re Fagin's Bookshop plc* [1992] Butterworth's Company Law Cases, p 118, (short case note in 1992 *Comp Law* 117) concerning the register of shareholders and *Speed Investment*, note 51 above, para 31 concerning the register of directors. See also Briggs & Rees, note 22 above, 84. Note, however, that GAL Droz, *Pratique de la convention de Bruxelles du 27 septembre 1968* (Paris: Dalloz, 1973) 32 and Gothot & Holleaux, note 15 above, 88, state that the justification for the exclusive jurisdiction over public registers is that they affect the functioning of public services. If that is so, one might question whether registers of shareholders and registers of directors should fall under the rule on exclusive jurisdiction.

[58] Paras 3.49 and following below.

[59] Paras 3.07 and following above.

[60] In areas such as geographical indications, plant variety rights, utility models, traditional knowledge, and folklore rights. Attempting to find an exact definition for different intellectual property rights has posed grave difficulties in the negotiations at the Hague Conference, because the rights that exist in national legal systems, and the registration required, vary significantly. Copyright, for instance, must be registered in some legal systems, may be registered in others (although registration is not required), and comprises unregistered rights in yet others. See 'Report of the experts meeting on the intellectual property aspects of the future convention on jurisdiction and foreign judgments in civil and commercial matters', Preliminary Document No 13 of the Judgments Project of the Hague Conference on Private International Law (2001) (available at <http://www.hcch.net>).

on which rights need to be registered are not the same in all EU Member States.[61]

3.41 Advocate General Rozès in her opinion on the case *Duijnstee v Goderbauer*,[62] seemed to support the reflexive effect for patents registered in third States. The case concerned patents registered in 22 countries, some of which were EEC Member States. The dispute between the liquidator of a company and one of the former employees of that company concerned the ownership of and entitlement to use the patents. The European Court of Justice ruled that the exclusive basis for jurisdiction did not apply to such a case, since the validity of the rights was not in dispute. Advocate General Rozès, however, stated that after the dispute in the case at hand had been solved, the issue of the transfer of the rights might arise in the other EEC Member States, and in the countries that were not party to the Convention.[63] Although this statement was by no means relevant to the questions in the case, it is interesting to note that the Advocate General seemed to acknowledge that there must be a mechanism for EU Member State courts to decline jurisdiction if patents registered in a third State are at stake.

How far does exclusive jurisdiction go?

3.42 The provision granting exclusive jurisdiction explicitly states that it only applies if the case deals with validity or registration. A dispute on the infringement of intellectual property rights does not fall within the scope of the exclusive basis for jurisdiction, but may be brought before the court of the defendant's domicile, or before the courts of the country where infringement occurred.[64] However, it often happens that the defendant raises non-validity of the intellectual property right as a defence to an infringement claim. The question then arises whether the court should declare that it lacks jurisdiction, so that the court with exclusive jurisdiction

---

[61] The provision also makes reference to the Convention on the Grant of European Patents (Munich, 1973). That Convention falls beyond the scope of this book, as do other developments in intellectual property law in the EU, such as the Regulation on the Community Trademark (Council Regulation 40/94 of 20 December 1993, published in OJ L 11, 14 January 1994, 1–36). For further information on these issues, see, in general, JJ Fawcett & P Torremans, *Intellectual Property and Private international Law* (Oxford: Clarendon Press, 1998); Pertegás Sender, note 15 above.

[62] Case 288/82 [1983] ECR 3663. See case notes by G Bonet [1984] *Revue critique de droit international privé*, 366–372; D Staunder [1985] *Praxis des internationalen Privat- und Verfahrensrechts* 76–79; TC Hartley [1984] ELR 64–66.

[63] Ibid, at 3683.

[64] Arts 2 and 5(3) Brussels I respectively. See M Pertegás Sender, note 15 above, 83–127; *Pearce v Ove Arup Partnership Ltd* [2000] Ch 403.

over the validity issue can hear the case. The European Court of Justice has ruled that, in such a situation, the exclusive jurisdiction prevails.[65] The reasoning of the ECJ was that exclusive jurisdiction was granted to ensure that the court of the place with a real link to the registration hears the case. Such jurisdiction should not be circumvented if parties bring proceedings on breach rather than on validity.[66] The ECJ also commented on the importance of avoiding conflicting judgments.[67] The result reached in this judgment is not uncontroversial; it permits a party to cancel the effect of a forum clause by including the validity of the intellectual property right in the dispute.[68] The ECJ found that even if validity were added to the litigation by way of defence, the rule on exclusive jurisdiction would still come into play. This issue will be further dealt with later in this chapter, when the issue of incidental questions is discussed.[69]

The possibility for courts to grant provisional and protective measures, **3.43** even if they do not have jurisdiction over the main claim, provides a useful tool for litigation on intellectual property.[70] The provision on provisional and protective measures, as argued later, only becomes applicable if Brussels I is already applicable on some other basis.[71] In that sense, its impact on third States is limited.

That the issue of the reach of the exclusive jurisdictional basis for intellec- **3.44** tual property is controversial has been proved beyond doubt in the negotiations at the Hague: first, for the broader draft convention on jurisdiction and foreign judgments, and second for the Convention on Choice of Court Agreements.[72] The first tough issue at the Hague was whether just the

---

[65] Case C–4/03, *Gesellschaft für Antriebstechnik mbH & Co KG v Lamellen und Kupplungsbau Beteiligungs KG* [2006] ECR I–6509. This conclusion was confirmed in another ECJ judgment of the same day: Case C–539/03, *Roche Nederland BV and Others v Frederick Primus & Milton Goldenburg* [2006] ECR I–6535.

[66] *GAT*, ibid, para 28.

[67] Ibid, para 29.

[68] A Briggs, 'Jurisdiction over defences and connected claims' [2006] LMCLQ 447–452; M Pertegás Sender, news item on the *GAT* and *Roche* judgments [2006] EIPR N193–194. On the discussions before the judgments: Pertegás Sender, note 15 above, 154–157 & 161–174; Fawcett & Torremans, note 61 above, 175–176; M Pertegás Sender & B Strowel, 'Grensoverschrijdende octrooigeschillen: Spannend afwachten op de arresten van het Europees Hof van Justitie' [2004] *Revue de droit commercial belge* 755–763.

[69] Paras 3.54 and following below.

[70] Art 31 of Brussels I. See Pertegás Sender, *Cross-Border Enforcement*, note 15 above, 127–150; W von Meibom & J Pitz, 'The reach and limitations of European transborder jurisdiction' [1999] *Journal of World Intellectual Property* 593–605.

[71] See chapter 6.

[72] In February 2001 a special meeting was organized in Geneva to discuss intellectual property; see 'Report of the experts', note 60 above.

validity of patents, trademarks, and other intellectual property should enjoy exclusive jurisdiction, or also their infringement (the route recently chosen by the European Court of Justice). Exclusive jurisdiction would belong to the court of the place of registration or, in the case of unregistered rights, where those rights arose. If infringement did not give rise to exclusive jurisdiction, would it at least give rise to alternative jurisdiction? In other words, can infringement cases be heard in the courts where the rights are registered, in addition to the other grounds for jurisdiction? This would widen the scope of exclusive jurisdiction so that many defendants would be drawn to a faraway court. On the other hand, infringement and validity disputes are so intertwined that it is difficult to treat them separately. Different results on the two issues might be incompatible so that recognition and enforcement became impossible. Another possible solution would be for the court faced with infringement proceedings to stay them so as to give the court that has exclusive jurisdiction the opportunity to rule on validity.

3.45 The Hague Choice of Court Convention, by its nature, deals only with contracts. It has explicitly excluded from its scope the validity of intellectual property rights, other than copyright and related rights.[73] However, the Convention contains a specific rule on matters that arise incidentally in a case where jurisdiction had been based on a choice of court agreement. This will be discussed later in this chapter.[74]

G. ENFORCEMENT OF JUDGMENTS

General

3.46 Article 22 states that the court of the place of enforcement has exclusive jurisdiction to declare a judgment enforceable. This principle makes sense: if a person wants to attach goods in Germany, on the basis of a judgment from elsewhere, the only place to seek enforcement of the judgment is a German court.[75] The provision applies, in the words of the Jenard Report, only to proceedings that arise from 'recourse to force, constraint or distraint on movable or immovable property in order to ensure the effective implementation of judgments and authentic instruments'.[76] The European Court of Justice followed this principle in its judgment in *Reichert–Kockler v*

---

[73] Art 2(2)(n).
[74] Paras 3.54 and following below.
[75] The Jenard Report (note 2 above) refers to national law rules with the same effect: 36.
[76] Ibid.

Dresdner Bank AG (II),[77] where they decided that an action to preserve the interests of the creditor with a view to subsequent enforcement of the obligation did not fall within the scope of the provision.[78]

Third State judgments

Article 22 encompasses only judgments from EU Member State courts and **3.47** not judgments from third State courts. This conforms with the definition of 'judgment' in Brussels I as 'any judgment given by a court or tribunal of a Member State'.[79]

A judgment from a third State can only be recognized in an EU Member **3.48** State under the national law of that EU Member State. Having a judgment recognized in one EU Member State does not automatically provide a visa for that judgment to travel through the entire EU. If the judgment creditor of a third State judgment seeks enforcement in several EU Member States, he or she will have to apply in each State separately. The European Court of Justice made that clear in *Owens Bank Ltd v Bracco and Bracco Industria Chemica SpA*.[80] Owens Bank had obtained a court order from the High Court of Justice of Saint Vincent and the Grenadines against Bracco for the repayment of a loan. Owens Bank then applied in both Italy and England for the enforcement of the order. The House of Lords posed a preliminary question to the European Court of Justice regarding the applicability of the rules on *lis pendens*.[81] The Court stated that the Brussels Convention's exclusive basis for jurisdiction of the court where enforcement is sought was inapplicable to judgments from third States.[82] In the same vein, the *lis pendens* rule of the Brussels Convention was held to be inapplicable if the enforcement in different EU Member States of a third State judgment were at stake. The rule on *lis pendens* cannot apply to such proceedings: the third State judgment might have to be enforced in different EU Member States, and each enforcement order would be valid only in the State where granted. The enforcement of a third State judgment cannot in itself be

---

[77] Case C–261/90 [1992] ECR I–2149.

[78] Ibid, para 28. The case concerned the French *action paulienne*.

[79] Art 32 Brussels I. See also Briggs & Rees, note 22 above, 89.

[80] Case C–129/92 [1994] ECR I–117. See case notes by A Huet [1994] *Journal de droit international* 546–550; R Fentiman [1994] CLJ, 239–241; E Peel [1994] LQR 386–390; H Gaudemet-Tallon [1994] *Revue critique de droit international privé* 382–387; TC Hartley [1994] ELR 545–547; P Kaye [1995] *Praxis des internationalen Privat- und Verfahrensrechts* 214–217.

[81] This judgment in discussed in more detail regarding *lis pendens* in chapter 5 below, paras 5.29 and following.

[82] Note 80 above, para 24.

required of another EU Member State. Therefore the *lis pendens* rule loses its effect: conflicting rulings will not harm the European judicial area.

H. SIMULTANEOUS EXCLUSIVE JURISDICTION

3.49 It may occur that a court in the EU and another outside the EU simultaneously have exclusive jurisdiction.[83] A company can, for instance, be established in one country according to its private international law rules and in another country according to the latter country's private international law rules. If both these countries are EU Member States, the case is settled by the *lis pendens* rule under the Regulation, determining that where there are two courts that are simultaneously competent, the court where the case was first brought should hear it.[84] This provision cannot be applied where a case is simultaneously pending in an EU court and in a third State court. The issue of declining Regulation-based jurisdiction then arises. The Regulation provides no mechanism for the EU court to decline jurisdiction. Even if the theory of the reflexive effect were accepted, one doubts whether it will be applied in a case where there is also exclusive jurisdiction in the EU. The theory seems only to seek to respect exclusive bases for jurisdiction in third States if the basis for jurisdiction that the Regulation contains is weaker, or more general, such as the domicile of the defendant.

I. EXCLUSIVE JURISDICTION *VS* FORUM CLAUSES

3.50 There might be a forum clause in favour of a court in one state, while the courts of another state in fact have exclusive jurisdiction. If both courts are in EU Member States, the provision on exclusive jurisdiction will prevail. For example, a Canadian company rents office space in London to a French company. Their contract contains a forum clause in favour of the French courts. Such forum clause will have no effect. Brussels I is clear that the rules of exclusive jurisdiction are topmost in the hierarchy of jurisdiction rules. If the French court assumes jurisdiction on the basis of the forum clause, its resulting judgment will not be recognized in the EU.[85]

---

[83] Gaudemet-Tallon, note 17 above, 96.
[84] Art 27 of Brussels I.
[85] According to Art 35(1) of Brussels I.

On the other hand, the forum clause might be in favour of the Canadian **3.51** courts, while the office space is in London. In this example, Brussels I is applicable because an exclusive basis for jurisdiction exists in the EU. If one party brings the case to a court in London, that court will assume jurisdiction irrespective of the forum clause. A party from outside the EU might be unpleasantly surprised to have to travel to London for a dispute regarding a tenancy, even despite the forum clause. If the Canadian court, on the other hand, assumes jurisdiction, the resulting judgment will not fall under Brussels I for purposes of recognition and enforcement, since it is not a judgment from an EU court. Recognition and enforcement would take place via national law (and possibly be refused). Such a conflict arose in *Speed Investment*.[86] The dispute regarded the validity of the appointment of certain directors of a company incorporated in England. With respect to one of the defendants, domiciled in Switzerland, there was a forum clause in favour of the courts of Geneva. The company had its seat in England, so the English courts had exclusive jurisdiction under Brussels I. However, as one of the defendants was domiciled in Switzerland, the court applied the Lugano Convention to him. The court then considered the relationship between the bases for exclusive jurisdiction and the rules on forum clauses in the Lugano Convention. The simple conclusion was that the exclusive bases for jurisdiction prevail over the forum clause.[87] The result is probably correct, although Brussels I should have been applied together with the Lugano Convention. Then the relationship between Brussels I and the Lugano Convention would have been at issue.[88] One would have to evaluate the exclusive basis for jurisdiction according to Brussels I, independent of the domiciles of the parties. The forum clause, on the other hand, had to be evaluated under the Lugano Convention, since the courts of a Lugano Contracting State (Switzerland) had been chosen and one of the parties was domiciled in that State. In this case it seems that the English court would still have to give preference to the exclusive basis for jurisdiction. These bases for jurisdiction are elevated above forum clauses both in Brussels I and the Lugano Convention.

---

[86] Note 51 above.

[87] Ibid, para 36.

[88] The Lugano Convention provides in Art 54B (old) and 64 (2007 version) that it shall not prejudice the application by the Member States of the Brussels Convention or Regulation. It specifically states that, if immovable property is situated in a Lugano State that is not an EU Member State (i.e. Iceland, Norway or Switzerland), or a forum clause appoints such a State, the Lugano Convention is applicable. In this case the property was situated in an EU Member State, but the forum clause was in favour of a Lugano State that was not an EU Member State.

Therefore, combining these two instruments, it seems that the same hierarchy should have been maintained.

3.52 The reverse conflict might also occur: the office block is in Canada and the tenancy contract between the Canadian and French companies contains a forum clause in favour of the courts in England. If the dispute is brought to the courts in England, the question arises whether that court will decline jurisdiction on the basis that a court in a third State might have exclusive jurisdiction. For disputes regarding tenancy, an exclusive basis for jurisdiction might not exist in third States. However, in many states other disputes regarding real rights in immovable property will be a basis for exclusive jurisdiction. If the theory of the reflexive effect were accepted, the English court should consider to whether or not the third State court had jurisdiction and if so, whether it regarded such jurisdiction as exclusive.

3.53 The recognition of the judgment from Canada will not fall under Brussels I. If, however, there is a judgment from an English court, on the basis of the forum clause, that judgment would be recognized and enforced under the Regulation. An exception exists if the judgment conflicts with an earlier judgment from a third State involving the same cause of action and between the same parties, provided that judgment can be recognized or enforced in the EU Member State where recognition or enforcement is sought.[89]

J. THE INCIDENTAL QUESTION OR COUNTER-CLAIM

3.54 Disputes, especially international ones, are not always simple and often deal with multiple issues, where the exclusive jurisdiction of one specific court is unclear. A dispute might relate to a matter for which there is no exclusive basis for jurisdiction, while the defendant might bring a counter-claim that does fall under an exclusive basis for jurisdiction. In the same way it is possible that the court needs to investigate a matter for which an exclusive basis for jurisdiction exists in the course of a case on a different matter. For example, in order to rule on a specific personal right in immovable property, a court might have to determine the ownership of the property, which is a real right and can only be determined by the courts of the place where the immovable property is situated. In intellectual property cases, an infringement action can be brought at the place of the infringement. A defence of non-validity of the intellectual property right

---

[89] Art 34(4) of Brussels I.

is quite common; however, exclusive jurisdiction exists for validity issues and only the court of the place of registration may hear such actions.

Several solutions to the problem of the incidental question have been sug- **3.55** gested.[90] The first is absolute respect for exclusive bases for jurisdiction. The consequence of this is that whenever an incidental question arises, or a defence is brought, which falls under the exclusive jurisdiction of another EU Member State court, the court where the action was being heard should decline jurisdiction to allow the court with exclusive jurisdiction to deal with the entire issue. This solution strictly respects the rules and is conducive to legal certainty. On the flip side, it can bring about great delays and possibilities for abuse. Whenever a defendant wished to transfer the entire case to another forum, all he would have to do is bring up an issue that falls within the exclusive jurisdiction of that court.

If this solution is chosen, the question is whether the reflexive effect will **3.56** be respected likewise. For instance, an action for the infringement of a patent registered in Mexico is brought in Germany against a defendant domiciled in Germany. The defendant questions the validity of the Mexican patent. If one argues that the court of the place of registration should now hear the entire case, the reflexive effect will prescribe that this should apply if that court happens to be outside the EU. However, the European Court of Justice has ruled that Article 2 is mandatory.[91] As has been stated above, this ruling was formulated generally and did not deal with the issue of exclusive jurisdiction in a third State. The Court confirmed this view in the *Lugano* opinion,[92] but that case concerned the external competence of the EU and the finding is incidental. In our example there is an obvious link with the European judicial area: an EU court clearly has jurisdiction over the main part of the claim. One wonders whether the entire case could be stayed in favour of a third State court.

The second solution is much bolder and leads to the opposite result: inci- **3.57** dental questions should be ignored for jurisdictional purposes. Once a court has jurisdiction over a case, it cannot lose that jurisdiction because of an incidental issue or counter-claim. It may rule on the incidental issue or counter-claim if this is necessary in order to reach a result in the case.

---

[90] See, for a more detailed discussion, Pertegás Sender, note 15 above, 161–174. This discussion also arose during the negotiations of the Hague Convention on Choice of Court Agreements (2005): Explanatory Report to the Convention of 30 June 2005 on Choice of Court Agreements by TC Hartley and M Dogauchi at 56–8; available at <http://www.hcch.net>.

[91] *Owusu*, note 11 above.

[92] *Lugano* Opinion, note 12 above, 153.

The effect of the judgment on the incidental issue then provokes further questions. The most common argument is that the ruling on the incidental issue would not bind other courts in future. For instance, if a court has found that an intellectual property right has not been infringed because the right was not valid, future courts are not bound by a decision of invalidity by a court that did not have exclusive jurisdiction to make such a ruling. Such a construction is practical and time-efficient, though it provides no legal certainty as between the EU courts, nor in relations with third States. An issue that should be determined by only one court can end up being thoroughly examined by several. At least this solution will bring about equilibrium in- and outside the EU and the problems discussed in the previous paragraph would not arise.

3.58 The third solution to incidental questions is for the court that has been hearing the dispute to postpone the case so as to permit the court with exclusive jurisdiction to rule on the issue. After the ruling by the appropriate court, the first court can continue with its action. This solution respects the rules, but again can cause delays. It also assumes efficient cooperation and coordination between courts in different EU Member States, which does not always correspond with reality. This solution is difficult in relations with third States. There is no framework for the same level of interaction between an EU court and a third State court. If an action is stayed to permit a third State court to rule first on the matter, that must happen according to the national rules of the Member State granting the stay. Once again, the situation differs from the reflexive effect, because there is a part of the action over which an EU court clearly has jurisdiction and only the incidental question or counter-claim should actually be adjudicated by the third State court.

3.59 The European Court of Justice examined the question in a case on intellectual property.[93] In *GAT*, the plaintiff sought an order declaring that it was not infringing the defendant's patent, arguing that it was invalid. The Landgericht (Regional Court) of Düsseldorf took jurisdiction over the case, even though the patents were registered in France. After an appeal, the Oberlandesgericht (District Court of Appeal) of Düsseldorf posed a question of interpretation of the Brussels Convention to the European Court of Justice. The ECJ, following the opinion of Advocate General Geelhoed, found that whenever the question of validity of a patent arises, it has to be determined by the court with exclusive jurisdiction. Whether the entire case, including the infringement action, has to be transferred to that court (first solution discussed above), or whether a stay should be

---

[93] *GAT*, note 65 above. The ruling was confirmed in *Roche*, note 65 above. Criticism: Briggs, note 68 above; Pertegás Sender, news item, note 68 above.

granted so that the competent court can decide the validity issue before the first court continues with the rest of the case (third solution above), is not stated in the judgment.[94]

The issue of incidental questions also arose in the negotiations of the draft **3.60** Hague convention on jurisdiction and foreign judgments and the Hague Convention on Choice of Court Agreements. Not all disputes concerning intellectual property rights should be able to be drawn to the court where the right was registered, as that would amount to abuse and manipulation of forum. The fact that the reach of an incidental question varies in different legal systems did not make the negotiations any easier.[95] The solution chosen in The Hague is different from that supported by the European Court of Justice. The Hague Choice of Court Convention, to be sure, only contains rules on jurisdiction under choice of court agreements. It does not contain rules on exclusive jurisdiction. According to the Convention, when validity is raised as an incidental (or preliminary) matter by either of the parties, the chosen court will not lose its jurisdiction. It may rule on the incidental question, but that ruling will not be recognizable or enforceable under the Convention. Recognition and enforcement might be possible under national law; the Convention is not applicable to such recognition and enforcement. For instance, a party might sue in the chosen court for damages for the infringement of an intellectual property right. The defendant could now claim that the intellectual property right was invalid. The chosen court might then consider validity incidentally and find that the intellectual property right was valid. The damages granted would be recognizable and enforceable under the Convention, but not the ruling on validity. If validity was later challenged in the court of the place where the right was registered, (assuming this is also in a Hague Contracting State), that court would be able to consider validity without taking into account what the other court had found.[96]

It is a pity that the European Court of Justice chose a different route and **3.61** did not consider the rule of the Hague Convention.

K. NO LINK WITH THE EUROPEAN JUDICIAL AREA

If a case has a link with a single EU Member State and a third State, but no **3.62** connection with the European judicial area, the question arises as to whether Brussels I governs the matter. A discussion has arisen with regard

---

[94] *GAT*, ibid. See also para 46 of the Advocate General's opinion.
[95] 'Report of the experts', note 60 above, 6.
[96] See the Hartley and Dogauchi Report, note 90 above, 56.

to forum clauses: if a German and Canadian party contractually agree that the German courts are to have jurisdiction, the matter seems to have no link with the European judicial area. While there is case law to the contrary, most authors view the situation to fall within the scope of Brussels I.[97]

3.63 This discussion cannot be likened completely to the rule on exclusive bases for jurisdiction. The exclusive bases for jurisdiction apply irrespective of the domiciles of the parties, while the domicile of one of the parties is relevant for the determination of the scope of the forum clause rule. The exclusive bases for jurisdiction would come into play even if the case had a link with a third State and only one EU Member State. For example, if a dispute over immovable property situated in the Netherlands arises between a party domiciled in South Africa and one domiciled in the Netherlands, it is Brussels I, rather than national law, that will determine the jurisdiction of the courts of the Netherlands.

3.64 However, the English courts decided otherwise in a case regarding a company incorporated in England, Newtherapeutics.[98] The company sued two of its former directors regarding the validity of their actions. One of the directors was domiciled in France; the court applied the Brussels Convention to him and found that it had jurisdiction over his acts, on the basis of the exclusive jurisdiction rule. But, since there was no serious case to be made against this director and the action was bound to fail, the court set aside the service of writ against him.[99] The second director, domiciled in the United States of America, was then viewed by the court as the sole defendant. Interestingly, the court did not consider service to the US director outside England as permitted under the Brussels Convention. Under English law, one needs permission from a court to serve outside England, but where Brussels I (previously the Brussels Convention) or the Lugano Convention grants jurisdiction to the court, service is possible as of right.[100] The court ruled on this defendant under national law. It seems, however, that an exclusive basis for jurisdiction in the Brussels Convention exists regardless of the domiciles of the parties. Therefore, the English court could have applied the Brussels Convention to the US director, even though he was not domiciled in the EU.

3.65 The later English judgment in *Speed Investment*[101] follows the same reasoning. The dispute in this case concerned the appointment of certain directors

---

[97] See also the discussion in chapter 4 below, paras 4.79 and following.
[98] *Newtherapeutics Ltd v Katz and another* [1991] Ch 226.
[99] Ibid, at 251.
[100] See Briggs & Rees, note 22 above, 291.
[101] Note 51 above.

of a company incorporated in England. The court made a distinction on the basis of the domiciles of the defendants, applying the Lugano Convention to those domiciled in Switzerland and Brussels I to those domiciled in the EU. If the scope of the rule on exclusive jurisdiction is blind as to the parties, one should apply Brussels I if the company has its seat in the EU, irrespective of some defendants being domiciled in Switzerland. The rule at hand is the same in Brussels I and the Lugano Convention, but in principle it seems that only Brussels I should have been applied in this case.[102]

L. CONCLUSION

The rule seems simple: for immovable property in the EU, Brussels I pro- **3.66** vides that the court of the Member State where it is situated has jurisdiction, irrespective of the domiciles of the parties. Similarly, if the action concerns the validity of a company that has its seat in the EU, or the validity of entries in registers in the EU, or the validity of intellectual property rights registered in the EU, Brussels I determines jurisdiction, irrespective of where the parties are domiciled. The same applies to the enforcement in the EU of EU judgments: Brussels I determines that the courts of the place of enforcement have exclusive jurisdiction, while the domiciles of the parties are irrelevant.

Raising an incidental question complicates the rules on exclusive juris- **3.67** diction. If a court, in the course of proceedings over which it has jurisdiction, has to decide an issue over which another court has exclusive jurisdiction, difficulties arise. Various ways to solve the problem have been discussed in this chapter. The European Court of Justice has chosen a solution that is theoretically correct, but that can open the door to abuse in practice, especially in intellectual property cases. It remained faithful to the idea of exclusive jurisdiction, ruling that a court in the EU may not decide an issue over which another EU court has exclusive jurisdiction. The solution adopted in the Hague Choice of Court Convention is different. More divergent rules on a global level should not be encouraged. A rigorous interpretation by the ECJ of the EU rules, with insufficient regard to the rest of the world and to practice, does not aid international trade.

---

[102] Art 54B of the old Lugano Convention; Art 64 of the 2007 version of the Lugano Convention.

3.68 The most difficult question remains the lack of clarity regarding exclusive jurisdiction of third States while the defendant is domiciled in the EU. The theory of the reflexive effect provides an equitable solution, but has not yet been explicitly accepted by the European Court of Justice. In fact, the latest judgments at the ECJ might suggest that the theory does not exist at all. The last words have not been spoken.

4

Third cornerstone: forum clauses

Article 23 of Brussels I:

1. *If the parties, one or more of whom is domiciled in a Member State, have agreed
   that a court or the courts of a Member State are to have jurisdiction to settle
   any disputes which have arisen or which may arise in connection with a particular legal relationship, that court or those courts shall have jurisdiction.
   Such jurisdiction shall be exclusive unless the parties have agreed otherwise.
   Such an agreement conferring jurisdiction shall be either:*
   a) *in writing or evidenced in writing; or*
   b) *in a form which accords with practices which the parties have established
      between themselves; or*
   c) *in international trade or commerce, in a form which accords with a usage
      of which the parties are or ought to have been aware and which in such
      trade or commerce is widely known to, and regularly observed by, parties
      to contracts of the type involved in the particular trade or commerce
      concerned.*

2. *Any communication by electronic means which provides a durable record of the agreement shall be equivalent to 'writing.'*

3. *Where such an agreement is concluded by parties, none of whom is domiciled in a Member State, the courts of other Member States shall have no jurisdiction over their disputes unless the court or courts chosen have declined jurisdiction.*

4. *The court or courts of a Member State on which a trust instrument has conferred jurisdiction shall have exclusive jurisdiction in any proceedings brought against a settlor, trustee or beneficiary, if relations between these persons or their rights or obligations under the trust are involved.*

5. *Agreements or provisions of a trust instrument conferring jurisdiction shall have no legal force if they are contrary to Articles 13, 17 or 21, or if the courts whose jurisdiction they purport to exclude have exclusive jurisdiction by virtue of Article 22.*

Article 12(3) of Brussels II *bis*:

The courts of a Member State shall also have jurisdiction in relation to parental responsibility in proceedings other than those referred to in paragraph 1 where:

a) *the child has a substantial connection with that Member State, in particular by virtue of the fact that one of the holders of parental responsibility is habitually resident in that Member State or that the child is a national of that Member State;*

and

b) *the jurisdiction of the courts has been accepted expressly or otherwise in an unequivocal manner by all the parties to the proceedings at the time the court is seised and is in the best interests of the child.*

A. INTRODUCTION

4.01 The definition of prorogation is that parties agree a certain court will hear a dispute or disputes between them and in this way they grant jurisdiction to that court. Derogation is the flip side of the coin, meaning that other courts are deprived of their jurisdiction by the fact that a specific court or specific courts had been chosen. In this chapter the term 'derogated court' will be used to refer to a court that would have had jurisdiction under the applicable rules, but that has lost its jurisdiction as the result of a forum clause.

4.02 A forum clause can be one provision of an agreement or can comprise a contract in its own right. A provision might refer to disputes arising from 'a particular legal relationship', and more than just contractual matters may be covered. For instance, in the common law legal systems a trust may contain a choice of forum in favour of an EU court; Article 23 of Brussels I ensures that such a clause will be respected.[1]

In this chapter the test for the applicability of the rule on forum clauses **4.03** will be looked at first, and thereafter the requirements for validity and the exclusivity of forum clauses will be considered. The difficult relationship between forum clauses and parallel proceedings can cause unpleasant surprises for parties from third States and therefore also deserves attention. The overlap between Brussels I and the Hague Convention on Choice of Court Agreements will be discussed, as well as the situation when courts outside the EU are appointed while the Hague Convention does not (yet) apply. The application of forum clauses to parties that have taken over the rights and/or obligations of a contracting party will be examined. The situation where a forum clause falls under the rules of Brussels I, but has no link with the European judicial area, will also be addressed.

Forum clauses are not possible under the Insolvency Regulation. There is **4.04** a limited possibility to choose a forum under Brussels II *bis* and such limitation is addressed in the proposed Maintenance Regulation. Before concluding this chapter, I will address the possible influence that this may have on the sphere of application of that Regulation.

B. TEST OF APPLICATION OF BRUSSELS I TO FORUM CLAUSES

General

Whether a forum clause falls within the scope of Brussels I is the subject of **4.05** a specific rule and is not determined by the general rules in Articles 2 and 4; Article 4 states that the national rules are to apply if the defendant is domiciled in a third State. However, it also explicitly states that Articles 22 (exclusive jurisdiction) and 23 (forum clauses) are excluded from this rule. Article 23 grants jurisdiction when one of the parties is domiciled in a Member State and the courts of a Member State are appointed.

It is important to know exactly when Brussels I's rules on forum clauses **4.06** apply, as opposed to those in national law, because the conditions for validity might differ. If parties conclude their agreement in conformity

---

[1] The wording was adapted to allow this at the accession of Ireland and the United Kingdom; see Schlosser Report on the 1978 version of the Brussels Convention; OJ C 59, 5 March 1979, 71, at para 178, p 124.

with the law in one state, they might be surprised by a different set of rules imposed by the Regulation. The Regulation is concerned with preventing conflicting judgments within the EU and therefore contains a provision to compel non-chosen courts in the EU to respect the choice of the parties.[2] For example, a party domiciled in the USA and one in Canada conclude a forum clause in favour of the courts in London (as often happens in certain branches of international trade), but it is possible that a French court also has jurisdiction according to its national rules (for instance if one of the parties were a French national). The French court is prohibited from exercising its jurisdiction and must respect the clause in favour of London, and the London court will assess the validity of the clause according to its national rules and not under the rules of Brussels I.[3]

4.07 If the chosen court declines jurisdiction, for instance on the basis of *forum non conveniens*, or because the clause is invalid under its national law, the other EU court (in this example the French court) may hear the case.

4.08 Although their validity is not determined by the Regulation, forum clauses have wide protection and a party can keep his or her case out of all other EU courts simply by choosing one competent court in the EU. Recognition and enforcement of this judgment in the EU will take place via Brussels I. In this sense the Regulation can have a wide effect, for parties from third States as well as EU parties.

EU court chosen; one of the parties domiciled in the EU

4.09 The rule in Article 23 of Brussels I states that an EU court appointed by contracting parties, one of whom is domiciled in an EU Member State, has exclusive jurisdiction, unless the parties did not wish that jurisdiction to be exclusive.[4]

4.10 One of the parties must be domiciled in the EU, but it is not necessary that this is the defendant. Indeed, it would not make much sense to require that the defendant be domiciled in an EU Member State, since it is not known at the time of contracting who will be the plaintiff and who the defendant.[5] Thus, a defendant from outside the EU can be drawn into the sphere

---

[2] Art 23(3) of Brussels I.

[3] See B Audit, *Droit international privé* (3rd edn, Paris: Economica, 2000) 468.

[4] See also P Jenard, 'Rapport du Comité restreint sur la bilateralisation' [1969] Hague Conference on Private International Law. Proceedings of Extraordinary Session 11, 145–151 (Jenard Report), 38.

[5] See A Philip, 'The scope of Article 17' in Court of Justice of the European Communities, *Civil Jurisdiction and Judgments in Europe* (London: Butterworths, 1992) 151–152. (Art 23 of Brussels I is virtually the same as Art 17 of the Brussels Convention.)

of application of Brussels I. Why broaden the scope to include parties from outside the EU? Brussels I could have provided that both parties had to be domiciled in the EU. This would have limited the number of forum clauses that would fall under the Regulation and would have minimized the impact on parties from third States. On the other hand, stating that the Regulation would apply as soon as two parties appoint an EU court, no matter where they are domiciled, would have enlarged the scope to include cases to which the EU's link is tenuous. This is the solution that the Hague Convention on Choice of Court Agreements has opted for, because a broader scope would ensure the enforcement of more judgments under the Convention.[6]

To understand the different choices made by the drafters of Brussels I and **4.11** the Hague Convention, one needs to revert to the goals of the instruments: Brussels I seeks to advance the European internal market and judicial area, and to establish jurisdiction rules that would lead to easy recognition and enforcement in that area. The Hague Conference on Private International Law seeks to aid international trade by creating an instrument that will ensure the respect of forum clauses in as many countries as possible, and that will encourage the recognition and enforcement of as many judgments as possible. The instrument is not limited to a particular region or group of states, and any state could join.

EU court chosen; none of the parties domiciled in the EU

Brussels I does contain a rule for the situation where two contracting par- **4.12** ties from third States conclude a forum clause in favour of an EU Member State court: courts in other EU Member States may not take jurisdiction in such a situation unless the chosen court has declined jurisdiction.[7] The jurisdiction of the chosen court in this case is not considered to be mandatory: it 'may' take jurisdiction.[8] Thus the rule differs from the one where one or both of the parties are domiciled in the EU.

Third State court chosen

Brussels I rules on forum clauses do not apply when parties choose **4.13** the courts of a third State. This has been confirmed by the German Bundesgerichtshof (Federal Supreme Court) in *Re Exchange Control and a Greek Guarantor*, where it found that the Brussels Convention did not

---

[6] Art 3 of the Hague Convention of 30 June 2005 on Choice of Court Agreements.
[7] Art 23(3). This paragraph was added in 1978.
[8] TC Hartley, *Civil Jurisdiction and Judgments* (London: Sweet & Maxwell, 1984) 73.

govern a forum clause in favour of a court in Greece because Greece was not a Contracting State at the initiation of the action.[9] In *Aectra Refining and Marketing Inc v Exmar NV (The 'New Vanguard')*[10] the Court of Appeal stated obiter that where a forum clause existed in favour of a non-EU State, the English court had discretion 'under its inherent jurisdiction'.[11] This is in line with the view that the court should apply its national rules when adjudicating a forum clause.

EU court chosen; both parties domiciled in that EU Member State

4.14 If two parties domiciled in the same EU Member State conclude a forum clause in favour of a court in that Member State, Brussels I does not apply to this internal attribution of jurisdiction. The result is not changed by the fact that one of the parties has the nationality of a third State. This occurred in a case before the Cour d'appel (Court of Appeal) of Paris, where all parties involved were domiciled in France. The fact that the defendant was Ivorian (referring to his nationality) was deemed irrelevant.[12]

The time of domicile

4.15 The previous paragraph explained the relevance of the domicile of the parties when determining the application of Brussels I. However, when parties move, the question arises: at which point should one consider their domiciles? For instance, if none of them is domiciled in the EU at the time of contracting, but one or both subsequently move to the EU. The opposite situation may also pose difficulties: when one of the parties is domiciled in the EU at the time of contracting but subsequently moves away. Should this be determined, as under Article 2, at the time the action is brought? Or rather, should one look at the time when the forum clause was concluded? A third possibility is to apply a cumulative test: Brussels I would then apply only if the domicile requirement were met both at the time of contracting and at the time of litigation. Lastly, an alternative test could be applied: the rule in Brussels I would be applicable if one of the parties

---

[9] [1993] ILPr 298 Bundesgerichtshof (German Supreme Court).

[10] [1995] 1 Lloyd's Rep 191 (CA). See also P Kaye, *Law of the European Judgments Convention* (Chichester: Barry Rose Law Publishers, 1999) vol 3, 2510–2511.

[11] *The 'New Vanguard'*, ibid, at 200. See also P North & JJ Fawcett, *Cheshire and North's Private International Law*, (13th edn, London: Butterworths, 1999) stating at 236 that courts might have discretion to decline jurisdiction in such a case.

[12] Cour d'appel (Court of Appeal) of Paris, judgment of 27 March 1987 with case note by A Huet [1988] *Journal de droit international* 140–143.

were domiciled in the EU either at the time of contracting or at the time of litigation.

The argument in support of determining the party's domicile at the time **4.16** of bringing the action is that it is in line with the other provisions of Brussels I (again an EU-perspective argument). Also, one has to admit that this perspective on the time of domicile ensures a link with the EU at the time the court actually takes jurisdiction.[13] Some might read support for this viewpoint in the opinion of the Advocate General in the *Sanicentral* case, but one should be careful in doing so since the case in fact dealt with the temporal applicability of the first version of the Brussels Convention.[14] This solution leads to difficulty regarding legal certainty. At the time of contracting, parties cannot possibly know where their counter-parties will be domiciled at the time of a later dispute. Diamond refers, by way of con-trast, to the European Contracts Convention.[15] Article 4(2) states that the relevant time for determining the habitual residence of a party is the time the contract is concluded. Since that Convention deals with substantive law, it adopted a different solution than a procedural convention should have, he states.[16] This argument does not seem convincing. It purposefully establishes two different times for adjudicating the residence of the con-tracting parties. Parties might be resident in different places during the same dispute, and sometimes even when determining the validity of dif-ferent provisions of the same contract (forum clause and applicable law). This does not contribute in any way to legal certainty.

The second solution, determining domicile at the time of contracting, has **4.17** the benefit that it ensures legal certainty and predictability. It is also in line with the good faith that should exist between contracting parties. The sup-porters of this proposition consider the wording of Article 23 to be in their favour. One has to read it with a bit of a bias to come to this conclusion, although a bias that deserves enthusiastic support. The text states '[i]f the parties, one or more of whom is domiciled in a Member State, have agreed . . .' The supporters of this view say that 'one or more of whom is domiciled' is (clearly) a quality of the contracting parties and they have to

---

[13] In support of this perspective: AL Diamond 'Jurisdiction Clauses' in ECJ, *Civil Jurisdiction and Judgments*, note 5 above, 141.

[14] Case 25/79 *Sanicentral v René Collin* [1979] ECR 3423 at 3436.

[15] Convention on the law applicable to contractual obligations (Rome, 1980), consolidated version published in OJ C 27 of 26 January 1998, p 34–46. The Convention is in the process of being converted into a regulation: Proposal for a Regulation of the European Parliament and the Council on the law applicable to contractual obligations (Rome I) of 15 December 2005, COM/2005/0650 final—COD 2005/0261; available at <http://eur-lex.europa.eu>.

[16] Diamond 'Jurisdiction Clauses', note 13 above, at 141–142.

possess that quality at the moment that they conclude the forum clause.[17] The downside of this solution is that it means that an EU court can test the validity of a forum clause on the basis of Brussels I rules at a point (possibly, long) after the contract's conclusion, when none of the parties has a connection with the EU. That, some admit, would be contrary to Article 4, which states that any defendants from outside the EU should be left out of the scope of the Regulation.[18]

4.18 The third solution limits Brussels I the most. If one requires that at least one party be domiciled in the EU both at the time of contracting and at the time of litigating, one is ensuring a proper link with the EU in order to justify the application of EU rules. This solution also ensures legal certainty.

4.19 The fourth solution broadens the scope of Brussels I as far as possible. Under this one it would suffice that one of the parties be domiciled in the EU either at the time of contracting or at the time that the action is brought.[19] Such an elaboration is confusing and nobody will be able to tell when he or she will be absorbed by the EU rules. National law will then be applied only if none of the parties is or was domiciled in an EU Member State at either of the two moments in time.

4.20 When exactly a court is seised was unclear under the Brussels Convention and national law was to determine whether an action were pending.[20] Brussels I changed this: Article 30 determines the time that a court is seised for purposes of Section 9, on *lis pendens* and related actions. However, this rule can probably also be used in other cases when one needs to determine when a court is seised. This is also the criterion used by Brussels II *bis* (Art 16).[21] Article 30 determines when an action is pending and gives two possibilities, to allow for differences in national procedural rules: an action

---

[17] See P Gothot & D Holleaux, *La Convention de Bruxelles du 27 septembre 1968* (Paris: Editions Jupiter, 1985) 94–95; F Schockweiler, 'Jurisdiction Clauses' in ECJ, *Civil Jurisdiction and Judgments*, note 5 above, 119–128; H Gaudemet-Tallon, 'Jurisdiction Clauses' in the same book, 129–140 at 130–131; Audit, note 3 above, 468; H Gaudemet-Tallon, *Compétence et exécution des jugements en Europe* (3rd edn, Paris: LGDJ, 2002) 93; A Layton & H Mercer, *European Civil Practice* (2nd edn, London: Sweet & Maxwell, 2004) 695–696.

[18] Gothot & Holleaux, ibid, 95.

[19] L Collins (ed), *Dicey, Morris and Collins on the Conflict of Laws* (14th edn, London: Sweet & Maxwell, 2006) vol I, 525; GAL Droz, *Pratique de la convention de Bruxelles du 27 septembre 1968* (Paris: Librairie Dalloz, 1973) 35–36; Philip, note 5 above, 153.

[20] Case 129/83 *Siegfried Zelger v Sebastiano Salinitri* [1984] ECR 2397.

[21] Council Regulation (EC) no 2201/2003 of 27 November 2003 concerning jurisdiction and the recognition and enforcement of judgments in matrimonial matters and the matters of parental responsibility, repealing Regulation (EC) no 1347/2000, OJ L 338, 23 December 2003, p 1–29. Its predecessor, Brussels II, contained the same rule in its Art 11; Council Regulation (EC) no 1347/2000 of 29 May 2000 on jurisdiction and the recognition and

is pending either at the time when the document instituting the proceedings is lodged with the court, or when the document is received by the defendant if he has to be served before the lodging at court.

C. REQUIREMENTS FOR VALIDITY OF THE CLAUSE

As Brussels I determines validity, and parties from third States might be **4.21** subjected to these rules, an evaluation is necessary.

Writing/practice/usage

The requirement for a written clause is contained in Brussels I. Brussels II **4.22** *bis* does not require writing and will not be discussed in this paragraph.

Brussels I provides three forms of validity of a forum clause. The agree- **4.23** ment must be:

- in writing, or evidenced in writing;
- in a form which accords with the practices between the parties; or
- in a form which accords with a usage in the particular branch of international trade which the parties belong to and of which they were aware, or ought to have been aware.

The purpose of the writing requirement is to prove the existence of consensus between the parties; therefore a forum clause in the general conditions on the back of a contract is only valid if there is an explicit reference to it on the front.[22] If the parties had agreed on a forum orally, and this had been confirmed in writing and was not contested by the other party, the clause is valid. Brussels I explicitly states that electronic means that provide a durable record of the agreement satisfy the writing requirement. This probably includes e-mail, which can be saved or printed off.[23]

---

enforcement of judgments in matrimonial matters and in matters of parental responsibility for children of both spouses, OJ L 160 of 30 June 2000, p 19–36.

[22] Case 24/76 *Estasis Salotti di Colzani Aimo et Gianmario Colzani v Rüwa Polstereimaschinen GmbH* [1976] ECR 1831, para 10.

[23] Whether or not voice mail could be included in this definition is unclear. In principle a voice message is not in writing and, before the insertion of the elaboration to electronic forms of communication, it would clearly not have fallen within the definition. It does not seem to have been the intention to also include electronic forms of communication that can provide a durable record, even though they are not a form of 'writing'. On the other hand, if one reads the definition strictly, such messages could be included. Probably the intention should be followed rather than the literal meaning of the words. See also A Briggs & P Rees,

4.24 The second and third possibilities were inserted by the 1978 version of the Brussels Convention. This was the version for the accession of Denmark, Ireland, and the United Kingdom. The amendments were aimed at catering for the specific needs of international trade.[24] The second form for validity can relax the requirement of writing. If a practice has been established, between parties who often trade with each other, of including forum clauses on the back of invoices, they can be accepted as valid. This extension does not apply if the final place for delivery of the goods or provision of the services is in Luxembourg. Luxembourg accepts only agreements in writing or evidenced in writing, an exception valid until 1 March 2008.[25] An example of a usage in a specific branch of trade under the third form is maritime law and the bill of lading, which tends to live a life of its own. Everybody active in maritime transport knows this, and the practice is therefore accepted under Brussels I. The European Court of Justice has ruled that this kind of forum clause does not necessarily mean that consent between the parties is lacking. It does mean, however, that consent is presumed to exist when the parties have acted in accordance with a usage in their branch of international trade that they knew or ought to have known.[26] This extension applies to Luxembourg only as of 1 March 2008.

4.25 The European Court of Justice has ruled that the validity of a forum agreement is a separate issue from that of the validity of the entire contract. Therefore a party cannot invoke the invalidity of the entire contract to circumvent the forum clause.[27]

4.26 Why are these rules of validity relevant for parties from third States? As indicated above, third State parties can sometimes be subjected to the rules of Brussels I, with the result that the validity of their clause will be adjudicated according to the rules of Brussels I. The importance of these rules of validity also lies in the fact that EU courts may not take other formal requirements into account when determining the validity of a forum clause. In this way, according to the European Court of Justice, the Regulation ensures legal certainty. The courts of all Member States should subject the clause to the same test of validity: for instance, the court may not take into

---

Civil Jurisdiction and Judgments (4th edn, London: LLP, 2005) 119, stating that e-mail should be valid but voice mail and text messages not.

[24] See the explanation by the European Court of Justice in Case C–159/97 *Transporti Castelletti Spedizioni Internazionali SpA v Hugo Trumpy SpA* [1999] ECR I–1597 para 18.

[25] Art 63 of Brussels I.

[26] Case C–106/95 *Mainschiffahrts–Genossenschaft eG (MSG) v Les Gravières Rhénanes SARL* [1997] ECR I–911 para 17–19 and *Castelletti*, note 24 above, para 19–21.

[27] Case 269/95 *Benincasa v Dentalkit Srl* [1997] ECR I–3767, para 24–29.

account the language in which the clause is written, even if national law requires the agreement to be in a specific language.[28] Accordingly, the formal validity requirements of Brussels I are all-encompassing.

Substantive validity

Brussels I contains nothing on the questions raised by fraud, mistake, **4.27** duress, misrepresentation, incapacity, etc. How should these substantial elements of validity be determined? Different solutions are possible: one can refer to the law of the forum, or the law of the court seised, which may or may not be the chosen court. One can look for the answer in the law of (one of) the derogated courts. One can refer to the law of the chosen court. Alternatively, one can use the governing law, in other words the law applicable to the contract. A final possibility is that the European Court of Justice will autonomously determine the substantial validity of the agreement. The European Contracts Convention[29] (which contains conflict of law rules for contracts) excludes the validity of forum clauses from its scope.[30] No solutions are to be found there.

The Schlosser Report refers to the law of the forum for the validity of **4.28** forum clauses in favour of third States.[31] Whether this can be understood as including substantial validity is not certain. It is obviously a simple solution for the court seised—check according to your own law whether the clause is valid or not. Applying the law of the forum does not seem totally equitable, however. It allows for the possibility of forum shopping, and a party would be aware of which court to go to in order to get the clause declared invalid.

The substantive law of the derogated court is not necessarily the same as **4.29** the forum, although it often will be. To use the law of the derogated court, if it is not the forum, does not seem to provide a satisfactory solution, as there can be many derogated courts. Should one refer only to the courts that would have had jurisdiction on the basis of Brussels I but for the forum clause, or to any court that would have jurisdiction according to its own rules? Should the rules of these courts be applied cumulatively?

The law of the chosen court seems an equitable solution. It is not random, **4.30** as is the law of the forum. Advocate General Slynn has advanced this as

---

[28] Case C–150/80 *Elefanten Schuh GmbH v Pierre Jacqmain* [1981] ECR 1671, para 26–29.
[29] Note 15 above, 34–46. This Convention is in the process of being converted to a Regulation: also note 15 above.
[30] Art 1(2)(d).
[31] Note 1 above, para 176.

the preferable solution in his opinion on *Elefanten Schuh*.[32] This solution has also been retained in the Hague Convention on Choice of Court Agreements for the determination of substantive validity. The Convention also allows the chosen court to use its own law when wanting to decline jurisdiction.[33] Additionally this rule applies for a seised but not chosen court that wants to hear the case,[34] as well as for a court requested to recognize or enforce a judgment.[35] It should be noted that the reference to the law of the chosen court is not absolute. First, it includes its private international law rules.[36] This means that if the private international law rules of that state refer to the law of another state, the rules of that second state will be applied. Second, the court seised but not chosen may also hear the case if it finds that one of the parties lacked capacity under its own law (including private international law rules).[37] Thus incapacity may be evaluated both according to the law of the chosen court (under the general rule of 'null and void') and according to the law of the court seised.[38] While these two points can be seen as good compromise solutions, they are somewhat complicated. It would facilitate international trade considerably if the European Court of Justice were to take the Hague Convention into consideration when they decide this point. Whether or not the Convention is in force at the time the question reaches the European Court of Justice, it does document a viewpoint by experts in the field. In the past, regrettably, the European Court of Justice has not been keen to take account of these types of international activity.[39]

4.31 Looking to the governing law poses a rather circular argument: the validity of an agreement has to be determined by the law applicable to it, but if the agreement is invalid then there is no law to regulate it. However, it points at a law that has a close connection to the agreement and therefore it is submitted that this remains a better approach than that of the law of the forum, or an autonomous EU concept.[40]

4.32 An autonomous test established by the European Court of Justice would complement the strict interpretation of the formal requirements and the

---

[32] See note 28 above, 1697–1698.
[33] Art 5(1).
[34] Art 6(a).
[35] Art 9(a).
[36] Explanatory Report to the Convention of 30 June 2005 on Choice of Court Agreements by TC Hartley and M Dogauchi, p 43; available at <http://www.hcch.net>.
[37] Art 6(b).
[38] Explanatory Report, note 36 above, 47–48.
[39] For instance Case C–116/02 *Erich Gasser GmbH v MISAT Srl* [2003] ECR I–14693.
[40] JJ Fawcett, JM Harris & M Bridge prefer this solution: *International Sale of Goods in the Conflict of Laws* (Oxford: Oxford University Press, 2005) 37.

fact that EU Member States cannot impose other requirements for formal validity.[41] However, an autonomous interpretation of this type would take a long time to establish, while existing legal systems already contain such a test. Moreover, another set of rules would make things even more difficult and unclear from the point of view of parties from third States.

Jurisdictional *renvoi*: different rulings on validity

It might happen that the prorogated court finds that the prorogation is **4.33** invalid, resulting in the activation of the remaining rules of Brussels I. The judge at the domicile of the defendant, or the judge at the place where the contract was performed (or should be performed) or the place where the tort was committed will be competent. But this judge might decline jurisdiction because of a forum clause pointing to another court. The opposite might also happen: one of the parties could try his luck at a court other than the chosen one. He would then argue invalidity and, if he won on that point, this 'un-chosen' court would be able to base its jurisdiction on a different ground, such as the defendant's domicile or the place of performance of the contract. What if the court named in the forum clause then found that it did have jurisdiction because the clause was in fact valid? In this situation a problem arises because of the varying conclusions on validity reached by the two courts.

If both courts are in the EU, it seems that the European Court of Justice **4.34** will solve the question with the strict rule of *lis pendens* at the time that the two actions are pending.[42] If there is a judgment by one court, that judgment will have to be recognized in all other EU courts. The first court is right and has to be followed.

However, how would a solution be found if this question arose in relation **4.35** to third States? Let us take an example where an EU court was appointed in a forum clause while one of the parties was domiciled in the EU. According to the letter of Article 23 Brussels I would be applicable. If the prorogated court found that the clause was invalid and it therefore did not have jurisdiction, the plaintiff might try to bring the action in a court outside the EU. This court might refuse to assume jurisdiction since there is a forum clause in favour of another court. It might reach this conclusion on the basis of a convention, or on the basis of its national law. It might even evaluate the validity of that clause according to its own rules and find it to

---

[41] *Elefanten Schuh*, note 28 above. See also, in support of this view, Briggs & Rees, note 23 above, 132.
[42] *Gasser*, note 39 above.

be valid. In this interaction between the Regulation and a national legal system, a lacuna has arisen. If the sequence of events is slightly altered and one of the parties went to a third State court first, in violation of an existing forum clause that he claimed to be invalid, the third State court might then refuse to assume jurisdiction on the basis that there was a valid forum clause in favour of another court. That court might subsequently find the forum clause invalid. One is faced with the same lacuna and, if no solution is found, a denial of justice.

4.36 A solution to this issue must be found on two levels. First, one needs a unified manner in which to determine validity. Second, there must be clarity concerning which court's ruling on validity should prevail. The first level has been discussed in the previous paragraphs, where reference was made to the Hague Convention on Choice of Court Agreements. That Convention also (partially) tackles the second level, and might provide a useful example for Brussels I. The Convention gives preference to the chosen court (i.e. the one named in the forum clause). The chosen court should not await the decision of the court seised but not chosen, even if that court was seised first. If both courts hear the case and give judgment, only the chosen court's judgment will be recognizable and enforceable under the Convention. A court asked to recognize or enforce the judgment may refuse to do so if the agreement is 'null and void' under the law of the chosen court. However, the Convention explicitly states that if the chosen court had already ruled on the validity of the agreement, the recognizing court may not make this assessment.[43] In the absence of a convention, there is no certainty.

D. EXCLUSIVITY OF FORUM CLAUSES

4.37 Brussels I gives effect to various forms of choice of court agreements: whether they are exclusive (granting jurisdiction to the court or courts of one state, to the exclusion of all other courts), or non-exclusive (providing an alternative jurisdiction, without taking away the jurisdiction of the courts that would have had it, had there been no clause). The Regulation states that jurisdiction of a court in an EU Member State derived from a forum clause will be exclusive unless the parties have agreed otherwise.[44] This indicates the intention of the Regulation to cover both exclusive and non-exclusive forum clauses.[45] The Hague Convention on Choice of Court

---

[43] Art 9(a).
[44] Art 23(1).
[45] JJ Fawcett, 'Non-exclusive jurisdiction agreements in private international law' [2001] LMCLQ 234–260 at 258.

Agreements deals mainly with exclusive choice of court agreements, although it contains the possibility of reciprocal declarations by Contracting States that their courts would recognize and enforce judgments given by courts of other Contracting States (on the basis of non-exclusive choice of court agreements).[46] Non-exclusive choice of court agreements are frequent in some business sectors and take various forms. A clause can provide that party A may bring proceedings in the courts of state A while party B may bring proceedings in the courts of state B. Another example of a non-exclusive choice of court agreement is a clause giving one party the option of a wide range of courts while compelling the other party to go to a specific court. This type of clause is common in the banking sector and is sometimes called an asymmetrical forum clause.[47]

The reason why Brussels I includes these clauses and the Hague Convention **4.38** does not, is the difficulty of *lis pendens,* for which Brussels I contains a strict and precise rule. If two courts simultaneously have jurisdiction on the basis of the same choice of court agreement and actions are brought in both courts, the conflict will be resolved by the normal *lis pendens* rule: the court first seised will be able to hear the case. The provision on choice of court agreements does not explicitly so provide, but this is in line with, and inferred from the other rules of the Regulation. This logic is contained in Article 29 of Brussels I, dealing with the situation where actions come within the exclusive jurisdiction of several courts: then any court other than the court first seised shall decline jurisdiction in favour of that court. The Hague Convention, on the other hand, does not contain a rule on *lis pendens.* The larger project, the draft convention on jurisdiction and foreign judgments, included a rule on *lis pendens.* For fear of opening up too many contentious issues, and in an attempt to avoid long and complex provisions, the negotiators decided to limit the convention to exclusive clauses. This decision met some criticism by experts who stated that the rule on *lis pendens* had been broadly accepted in the larger project so that including it would not raise grave difficulties.[48] However, the majority of the experts at The Hague thought it sensible not to reopen Pandora's box.

---

[46] Art 22.

[47] An example of such a clause is found in the English case *Continental Bank NA v Aeakos Compania Naviera SA and others* [1994] 1 WLR 588: '[e]ach of the Borrowers... hereby irrevocably submits to the jurisdiction of the English Courts... but the Bank reserves the right to proceed under this Agreement in the Courts of any other country claiming or having jurisdiction in respect thereof.' This case is discussed in further detail in chapter 5 below, paras 5.157 and following.

[48] See the comment made by the expert from Switzerland at the negotiations for the Hague Convention; Minutes no 3 of December 2003, 6.

4.39 The Hague Convention contains a presumption that a choice of court agreement is exclusive. In other words, if parties had included a (valid) choice of court clause in their agreement, the interpretation that these instruments give the clause is that the parties wished only the chosen court to hear their dispute. The jurisdiction of other courts is thus excluded, even if they would otherwise have had jurisdiction on the basis of the domicile of the defendant, or the place of the performance of the contract. This excluded jurisdiction could be based either on Brussels I or on national rules. For instance, a French national, domiciled in New York and a Canadian party domiciled in Canada conclude a choice of forum clause in favour of a court in England. If the French party brings action in France, on the basis of his own French nationality (Article 14 of the French code civil), that jurisdiction would be excluded by the forum clause. Similarly assuming now that the Canadian party were domiciled in Belgium, the jurisdiction that a Belgian court would have had on the basis of the domicile of the defendant (Article 2 of Brussels I) would also be excluded. Only the English court would have jurisdiction to hear the case. The presumption of exclusivity is not the rule in all legal systems. In some common law countries, a choice of court clause is seen as granting jurisdiction to an extra court while the courts that have jurisdiction on other bases retain such jurisdiction. Brussels I does not state that the choice of court agreement is presumed to be exclusive, but its rule might have a similar effect. It stipulates that jurisdiction is exclusive unless the parties agreed otherwise.[49] The first step is thus to determine what the parties intended. This is probably done with reference to national law, just as are issues of capacity to contract.[50] If it is not clear that the parties intended jurisdiction to be non-exclusive, jurisdiction will be exclusive when a case is brought in the chosen EU Member State court. The parties are then prevented from bringing proceedings in a court in another EU Member State.

4.40 The question arises for third State courts whether 'exclusivity' covers only the EU, or the entire world. This point was dealt with by the English courts in exceedingly complex procedures, which will be discussed without entering into unnecessary details.[51] Bouygues, a French company, had contracted with Ultisol, a Bermudan company managed from the Netherlands (and here the complications already start) for the hire of a tug to tow its

---

[49] Art 23(1); Fawcett, note 45 above.

[50] See discussion above, paras 4.27 and following.

[51] See *Bouygues Offshore SA v Caspian Shipping Co and Others* (Nos. 1, 3, 4 and 5), [1998] 2 Lloyd's Rep 461 (CA) and the various first instance decisions relating to the different parties: [1996] 2 Lloyd's Rep 140; [1997] 2 Lloyd's Rep 493; [1997] 2 Lloyd's Rep 533; [1997] 2 Lloyd's Rep 507.

barge from Pointe Noir in the Congo to Cape Town in South Africa. This agreement contained a forum clause for the High Court of Justice in London. Ultisol had time-chartered the tug from Caspian Basu Emergency Salvage Department, a former Azerbaijan government body. Who the owners of the tug were at the time of the accident was uncertain (and here the complications continue). In the South African waters, the towline parted, and the barge was consequently stranded and destroyed. Bouygues brought actions in South Africa against Ultisol, Caspian, and Portnet, the South African authorities who allowed the tug to enter despite bad weather conditions. Ultisol sought an anti-suit injunction in England on the basis of the forum clause for the court in London. When considering whether or not to grant this injunction, the court considered the meaning of 'exclusive jurisdiction'. It acknowledged that the provision of the Brussels Convention on choice of forum was applicable. The requirements were clearly met: one party was domiciled in the EU (France) and an EU court (in England) was appointed. However, the court gave a limiting interpretation to the words 'exclusive jurisdiction' in that provision. It stated, quite creatively, that the exclusiveness related to the EU. In other words, the forum clause in favour of the London court excluded the jurisdiction of all other EU courts. However, that provision did not make the forum clause exclusive of third State courts. The court stated:

In my judgment art 17 was not intended to exclude the jurisdiction of the Courts of non-Contracting States in any circumstances. So for example, where two parties to a contract both domiciled in a Contracting State agree that the Courts of say England and New York are each to have non-exclusive jurisdiction, art 17 does not exclude the jurisdiction of the Courts of New York. The effect of the article is simply to exclude the jurisdictions of other Contracting States. Thus where in the first paragraph it says that . . . that court or those courts shall have exclusive jurisdiction . . . it means exclusive jurisdiction as between the Courts in Contracting States. [52]

For this statement the judge relied on *Re Harrods (Buenos Aires) Ltd*, a judg- **4.41**
ment in which there was no forum clause at issue.[53] The court considered the limits of Brussels I more generally, and how far it should be permitted to impact on third States. It also referred to the Schlosser Report and stated that this approach was in line with the Report. It does not deal with the exact situation that was before the judge; instead it dealt with the limited scope of the Brussels Convention when two parties from outside the EU

---

[52] Ibid, at 146–147.
[53] [1992] Ch 72; discussed in more detail in chapter 5 below, paras 5.77 and following.

appoint an EU court, and the non-application of the Convention when a court outside the EU is appointed. The judge granted the anti-suit injunction and leave to appeal in this case was granted by the Court of Appeal.[54] In considering the leave to appeal, that Court found that the forum clause did not necessarily have to be protected by an anti-suit injunction, although it did not question the ruling on the Brussels Convention by the court at first instance. In fact, it did not even refer to the Brussels Convention in its judgment. It found that the South African court was the better forum.

4.42 While it seems like a good solution that the related disputes should be heard in the same court, and preferably the court of the place where the events took place, the fascinating point of these judgments is that factors such as the evidence, the natural forum for the other parties, and the interest in avoiding contradicting judgments, outweighed a simple forum clause, valid according to the Brussels Convention: the forum clause was not seen as essential.

4.43 Under the new Hague Convention on Choice of Court Agreements the solution reached in this case might have been different. Let us presume that the Convention had entered into force in the EU Member States and in South Africa. If one of the parties is domiciled outside the EU, and a court in a Hague Convention Contracting State is chosen, the Hague Convention will prevail.[55] Thus, the matter at hand would be governed by that Convention. Under the Hague Convention the presumption of exclusivity would apply, irrespective of which other states were connected to the dispute. The argument in the case discussed above could not be relied upon and so the forum agreement would have to be respected.

E. FORUM CLAUSES AND PARALLEL PROCEEDINGS

4.44 In *Gasser* the European Court of Justice reduced the value of forum clauses by finding that the *lis pendens* rule has precedence over the forum clause.[56] In this case an Italian and an Austrian party had concluded a forum agreement

---

[54] [1998] 2 Lloyd's Rep 461 (CA). Under the common law legal tradition, one has to ask permission of the court that gave a judgment before appealing it. Leave to appeal is granted if the court acknowledges that there is a reasonable possibility that another court would decide the matter differently. If the court that gave the judgment refuses leave to appeal, one can request the appeal court to grant leave to appeal (this is called a petition).

[55] See below, paras 4.46 and following.

[56] *Gasser*, note 39 above. Case notes: R Fentiman, 'Access to Justice and Parallel Proceedings in Europe' [2004] CLJ 312–314; A Huet, 'Chronique de jurisprudence du Tribunal et de la Cour de justice des Communautés européennes' [2004] *Journal du droit international* 641–645;

in favour of the court at Innsbruck (in Austria). One of the parties brought action in a court in Italy. The other subsequently initiated proceedings in the chosen court, arguing that the chosen court did not have to stay proceedings according to the *lis pendens* rule. The Court of Innsbruck posed a preliminary question to the European Court of Justice on that point. The Court of Justice ruled that the fact that there was a forum clause in favour of the court seised second did not give that court the right to go ahead with the action in spite of an earlier action pending in a court of another Member State. The court seised second, even being the chosen court, still has to suspend the action to allow the court seised first to rule on its jurisdiction. If there is indeed a valid forum clause, the first court will come to that conclusion and decline jurisdiction. However, this deprives the chosen court of the possibility of adjudicating the forum clause itself. The underlying thought is that the two courts have to determine the validity of the forum clause on the basis of the same rules (of Brussels I) and will come to the same conclusion. Furthermore, the mutual trust between the EU Member States requires that they trust each other to make the correct decision on the validity of a forum clause. However, not all courts will necessarily interpret Article 23 in the same manner. When there is a written contract with a clear choice of forum clause, the chances are good that both courts will come to the conclusion that it is valid. On the other hand, the interpretation of a practice between the parties, or a particular trade practice, might lead to different conclusions. It seems that the chosen court is in the best position to determine the validity of the forum clause. Possibly a trade that is particularly common in that country is involved and the chosen court would better be placed to judge validity.

This solution of the European Court of Justice differs from the direction **4.45** taken by the Hague Convention on Choice of Court Agreements; this Convention always gives preference to the chosen court. Maybe the reason for this is again to be found in the different purposes of the Convention and Brussels I. However, the European Court of Justice, at the time of the project, should perhaps have been more willing to follow international trends and to respect choice of court clauses, rather than solely considering the European judicial area.

Y Baatz, 'Who Decides on Forum clauses?' [2004] LMCLQ 25–29; J Mance, 'Exclusive Jurisdiction Agreements and European Ideals' [2004] LQR 357–365; A Wittwer, 'Auch bei italienischer Prozessdauer gilt Art 21 EuGVÜ' [2004] *European Law Reporter* 48–50; H Muir Watt [2004] *Revue critique de droit international privé* 459–464; P Wautelet [2004] *Revue de droit commercial belge* 794–799; R Fentiman [2005] CML Rev 241–259. On this discussion, see also below, paras 5.38 and following.

F. DELIMITATION BETWEEN BRUSSELS I
AND THE HAGUE CONVENTION ON CHOICE
OF COURT AGREEMENTS

Regarding jurisdiction

4.46 The Hague Convention enjoys precedence over Brussels I if an EU court is chosen by a party domiciled in the EU and a party domiciled in a third State (i.e. non-EU Member State).[57] This is also the case when the party domiciled in the third State is at the same time also domiciled in the EU. It is irrelevant whether the third State in which one of the parties is domiciled is a Contracting State to the Hague Convention: the Convention will prevail, since the Convention does not set any domicile requirement for its application. This means that the validity of the clause will be subjected to the conditions of the Hague Convention and not to those of Brussels I. At the same time, it means that not only the EU courts will be obliged to respect the forum clause and refrain from taking jurisdiction, but the courts of all Contracting States to the Hague Convention will also have this duty. Thus, assuming that all EU Member States become Contracting States to the Hague Convention, if a contracting party domiciled in Germany and one resident in China concluded a forum clause in favour of the English courts, the Hague Convention would apply instead of Brussels I (even though the requirements for the application of Brussels I were met, and even if the Chinese resident is also domiciled in an EU Member State).

4.47 The same solution was not adopted for the Lugano Convention.[58] Let us assume that the Hague Convention is in force in China and in the United Kingdom, but not (yet) in Switzerland. In the situation of the Lugano Convention, if a party domiciled in Switzerland and one domiciled in China concluded a forum clause in favour of the English courts, the Lugano Convention would apply insofar as the application of the Hague Convention would be inconsistent with the UK's obligations under the Lugano Convention. The reason for this is that all the EU Member States

---

[57] Art 26(6)(a); Explanatory Report, note 36 above, 75–79, especially 76–77.

[58] Convention on jurisdiction and the enforcement of judgments in civil and commercial matters (Lugano Convention), 16 September 1988, OJ L 319, 9–48. Art 26(3) of the Hague Convention gives precedence to the Lugano Convention but only where applying the Choice of Court Convention would be inconsistent with the Lugano Contracting State's obligations to any other Lugano Contracting State that is not a party to the Hague Convention. The provision will also apply to updated versions of the Lugano Convention.

will become party to the Hague Convention simultaneously, since the EC now has external competence in this field.[59] The same is not necessarily true for the Lugano Convention Contracting States. Therefore, one might find oneself in a situation where, as in this example, the United Kingdom is party to the Hague Convention, but Switzerland is not (yet). If one of the contracting parties brings an action in a Swiss court and, while the case is pending, the other party brings an action in an English court, the English court would find itself in a predicament. According to the Hague Convention it would be compelled to assume jurisdiction (if the clause was valid), but according to the Lugano Convention's *lis pendens* provision, it may not assume jurisdiction until the Swiss court had declined jurisdiction. This is dictated by the European Court of Justice's interpretation of Brussels I in *Gasser* (valid for the Lugano Convention as well) under which the *lis pendens* rule should receive precedence over a forum clause.[60] With the solution adopted by the Hague Convention, the English court would simply have to adhere to the Lugano Convention and not the Hague Convention. This example indicates how a finding by the European Court of Justice, taking only the European judicial area into consideration, can impact on third States.

If a court of an EU Member State has been appointed by two parties from **4.48** outside the EU, the case will also fall under the Hague Convention. The chosen court, as well as the court seised but not chosen, will have to evaluate the validity of the forum clause according to the rules of the Hague Convention. This goes further than Brussels I, which merely leaves the chosen court in this case to evaluate the validity according to its national law. Brussels I also places the courts of other Member States under an obligation not to hear the case. This obligation will be extended to all Contracting States of the Hague Convention. However, while the duty under Brussels I is absolute, that under the Hague Convention is not. The Hague Convention contains a number of exceptions. A court seised but not chosen may hear the case if the agreement is null and void under the law of the chosen court, if one of the parties lacked capacity under its own law, if giving effect to the agreement would lead to manifest injustice or would be manifestly contrary to public policy, or if the agreement cannot reasonably be performed.[61]

---

[59] On the external competence of the EC, see chapter 7 below.
[60] *Gasser*, note 39 above; see also the discussion above, para 4.44.
[61] Art 6.

Regarding recognition and enforcement

4.49 If jurisdiction is based on a forum clause, the resulting judgment by an EU
Member State court will be able to be recognized or enforced according to
the simplified procedure of Brussels I throughout the EU.[62] The domiciles
of the parties and the instrument on which jurisdiction was based (or according to which the forum clause was evaluated) are irrelevant. Similarly, if a
Lugano Convention Contracting State has given a judgment on the basis
of a forum clause, that judgment will be recognized and enforced in other
Lugano Convention Contracting States according to that Convention.[63]
This is irrespective of the domiciles of the contracting parties and the
instrument on which jurisdiction has been based. The Hague Convention
does specify that the judgment may not be enforced to a lesser extent
than it would be under the Hague Convention. In other Hague Conven-
tion Contracting States which are not EU Member States or Lugano
Convention Contracting States, enforcement will be regulated by the Hague
Convention, if the judgment was given by a court of a Hague Convention
Contracting State, unless a Convention on a specific matter applies.[64]

4.50 This manner in which Brussels I and the Lugano Convention interact with
the Hague Convention ensures the most favourable treatment, and the
greatest possible respect to forum agreements, to the extent possible under
international law.

G. COURT OUTSIDE THE EU APPOINTED: THE REFLEXIVE EFFECT

General

4.51 Brussels I does not contain an explicit provision on forum clauses in favour
of third States. The discussion that follows deals with third States that are
not (or will not be) linked to the EU by way of the Hague Convention, discussed in the previous section of this chapter. This discussion follows on
from the discussion on the reflexive effect in chapter 3.[65]

---

[62] Art 26(6)(b) of the Hague Convention.
[63] Art 26(4) of the Hague Convention. This provision will also apply to subsequent versions of the Lugano Convention.
[64] Art 26(5) of the Hague Convention and Art 71 of Brussels I. This matter is not dealt with
here. For a general discussion on relations between the EU civil jurisdiction rules and conventions on specific matters, see above, paras 1.60 and following.
[65] Paras 3.10 and following.

Obviously Brussels I cannot grant jurisdiction to a court outside the EU. **4.52**
However, what Brussels I could have done, is to state that the rules it
establishes may be set aside if there is a forum clause in favour of a third
State court. This does not in any way affect the sovereignty of any EU
Member State or third State. To the contrary, it is in line with international
comity, respecting the jurisdiction of other courts. At the same time it
respects the important private law principle of party autonomy. Parties
from third States, and even parties from EU States, would be better served
if they knew that their choice, whether in favour of an EU court, or a third
State court, would be respected.

In view of Brussels I's silence on the issue, a strict interpretation means **4.53**
that an EU Member State court must assume jurisdiction it may have on
another ground (such as the domicile of the defendant or the place of performance of the contract). The forum clause in favour of a court outside
the EU would be ignored. This does not seem at all equitable, nor is it in
the interests of international commerce.

The Jenard Report suggests that the Convention would not be applicable **4.54**
where a court outside the EU is appointed.[66] After the *Josi* judgment that
view is probably no longer tenable: the domicile of the defendant in an EU
Member State is seemingly sufficient to lead to the applicability of the EU
civil jurisdiction rules.[67] The German Bundesgerichtshof (Federal Supreme
Court) has also found that the Brussels Convention was inapplicable in
a case where there was a forum clause in favour of a third State court.
It considered forum clauses in favour of courts in Switzerland and Austria,
before the existence of the Lugano Convention and before Austria became
an EU Member State.[68] One can therefore see Switzerland and Austria as
third States in these cases. The Court then considered the clauses on the
basis of German domestic law. Interestingly, the provision is very similar
to that of Brussels I: it only deals with the prorogation of the German
courts, and not with derogation.[69] Yet the German courts use that provision to recognize forum clauses in favour of foreign courts. This practice
provides a good example of the interpretation of Brussels I. It is in fact a

---

[66] Jenard Report, note 4 above; see also H Gaudemet-Tallon, 'Les frontières extérieures
de l'espace judiciaire européen: quelques repères' in A Borrás, A Bucher, AVM Struycken &
M Verwilghen, *E Pluribus unum. Liber Amicorum Georges AL Droz* (The Hague: Martinus
Nijhoff Publishers, 1996) 99.

[67] Case C–412/98 *Group Josi Reinsurance Company SA v Universal General Insurance Company
(UGIC)* [2000] ECR I–5925.

[68] Judgments of 20 January 1986 [1986] *Neue Juristische Wochenschrift* 1438–1439 and of
4 November 1988 [1989] *Neue Juristische Wochenschrift* 1431–1432.

[69] §§ 38 & 40 Zivilprozessordnung (Code of Civil Procedure).

reflexive effect on a small scale. In a note on the first of these judgments, Geimer wrote that the Brussels Convention should in fact have been applied. He stated that the Bundesgerichtshof should have posed a preliminary question to the European Court of Justice on the interaction between the domicile of the defendant in the EU and a forum clause in favour of a third State court.[70] Now, more than 20 years later, the European Court of Justice has given only limited guidance on the point.

4.55 The European Court of Justice has confirmed that clauses referring to the courts of a third State do not fall within the scope of the rule for forum clauses in Brussels I.[71] In the *Coreck Maritime* case the forum clause was formulated in a general way, stating that the courts of the country where the carrier has his principal place of business will have jurisdiction. Upon an interpretation of the facts (which the European Court of Justice did not do, as that is not its function), jurisdiction might have lain with a Russian court in that case. The European Court of Justice stated that if a court in a third State were chosen, the EU Member State court that had been seised must assess the validity of the clause according to the applicable law, found by its private international law rules.[72]

4.56 It is the silence of Brussels I that has led authors to construe the theory of the reflexive effect, which would function in the same way as in cases where there is an exclusive basis of jurisdiction in a third State.

4.57 The Schlosser Report states that there is nothing in the Convention to prevent an EU court from declining jurisdiction.[73] This statement is better than nothing, but does not go the full distance. The Report does not state how the declining of jurisdiction should take place, bringing us back to the reflexive effect, discussed above with regard to exclusive jurisdiction.[74]

How to derogate: on the basis of the Regulation or according to national rules?

4.58 In the discussion of the reflexive effect with regard to exclusive jurisdiction, it has been pointed out that jurisdiction can be declined on the basis of an

---

[70] [1986] *Neue Juristische Wochenschrift* 1439–1440.

[71] Case C–387/98 *Coreck Maritime GmbH v Handelsveem BV and others* [2000] ECR I–9337, para 19; case notes: F Bernard-Fertier [2001] *Revue critique de droit international privé* 367–375; J-M Bischoff [2001] *Journal de droit international* 701–704; P Vlas [2001] *Nederlandse jurisprudentie. Uitspraken in burgerlijke en strafzaken.* no 599, p 4442–4445.

[72] Ibid, at rec 19.

[73] Schlosser report, note 1 above, para 176.

[74] Paras 3.10 and following.

implicit clause in the Regulation itself, or on the basis of national rules for declining jurisdiction, such as *forum non conveniens*. Recent cases of the European Court of Justice have pushed the discussion towards the solution that declining can take place only on the basis of the Regulation itself.

Interestingly, the European Court of Justice has stated previously that the **4.59** validity of a forum clause in favour of a third State must be evaluated according to the law of the forum, including the forum's conflict of law rules. In *Coreck Maritime*,[75] the forum clause stated '[a]ny dispute arising under this Bill of Lading shall be decided in the country where the carrier has his principal place of business...'. Upon a construction of the facts, that could amount to a Russian court, but this was not completely clear. The European Court of Justice's referral to national law is both interesting and encouraging. The Court did not qualify the statement by concerns such as the domicile of the defendant in the EU. It clearly viewed the EU jurisdiction rules to be inapplicable in such a case. The Court said nothing explicitly of derogation of jurisdiction, but allowing the national courts to determine the validity of the clause does imply that the clause will be given effect. The Oberlandesgericht (Regional Court of Appeal) of Bamberg also evaluated a forum clause in favour of a third State according to national German law.[76] In that case the plaintiff was domiciled in Switzerland and the defendant in Germany. Since the Lugano Convention had not entered into force between these states at the relevant time, Switzerland could be seen as a third State. The English courts have a ready-made solution for declining jurisdiction, namely the doctrine of *forum non conveniens*. This doctrine has the effect that a court that has jurisdiction declines it in favour of another court that also has jurisdiction and that is better suited to hear the dispute.[77] The court's own jurisdiction may be based on its national rules or on the rules of Brussels I. When considering whether or not to decline jurisdiction in favour of the other court, the English court will take various factors into account. An important factor is the existence of a forum clause in favour of that court.[78]

---

[75] Note 71 above, para 19; case notes: Bernard–Fertier; Bischoff; Vlas, all note 71 above.

[76] Judgment of 22 September 1988 [1990] *Praxis des internationalen Privat- und Verfahrensrechts* 105–108. See also P Grolimund, *Drittstaatenproblematik des europäischen Zivilverfahrensrechts* (Tübingen: Mohr Siebeck, 2000) 66–67.

[77] The rule of *forum non conveniens* is discussed in more detail in chapter 5 below, paras 5.51 and following.

[78] See *Baghlaf Al Zafer Factory Co v Pakistan National Shipping* [1998] 2 Lloyd's Rep 229 (CA) at 235 and *Aratra Potato Co Ltd and Another v Egyptian Navigation Co, The 'El Amria'* [1981] 2 Lloyds Rep 119 at 123.

4.60 For the purposes of declining jurisdiction in favour of a third State in order to respect a forum clause, the doctrine of *forum non conveniens* provides a workable solution. Unfortunately the doctrine is not always known and/or well received in other states.[79] The use of this doctrine has come under strain since the judgment of the European Court of Justice in the *Owusu* case.[80] The English courts had jurisdiction on the basis of the domicile of the defendant in England (Article 2 of Brussels I). The competing forum, where the facts (contract and tort) took place was Jamaica. The European Court of Justice found that the English court could not decline to hear the case by applying the *forum non conveniens* rule. There was no forum clause involved and so the judgment does not definitely rule out the use of *forum non conveniens* when there is a forum clause in favour of a third State court.

4.61 Let us now turn to the incidences where *forum non conveniens* has been used, and has effected the desired result. The case of *The 'Nile Rhapsody'* before the English Court of Appeal concerned a dispute between Hamed El Chiaty & Co, an Egyptian tourist company specializing in Nile cruises, and the Thomas Cook Group, an international holiday and travel company.[81] The contract contained a clear choice of Egyptian law. There was no written forum clause and there was a dispute between the parties as to whether or not there had been an agreement at the stages of negotiation on the Egyptian courts. Hamed brought proceedings in London for breach of contract. Thomas Cook applied for a stay of the proceedings on the basis that there was an exclusive choice of court agreement in favour of the courts in Egypt. The court accepted that there was an oral choice of court agreement. Thomas Cook was domiciled in England, so that the English courts would have had jurisdiction on the basis of the Brussels Convention (the domicile of the defendant) if one ignored the forum agreement. The Court of Appeal, like the Queen's Bench Division in first instance,[82] stayed the proceedings in favour of the courts in Egypt. The Court did not refer a preliminary question to the European Court of Justice, not because it found the situation absolutely clear, but because there had already been excessive delays in the case. It remains of interest that the Court of Appeal considered it correct to stay the action in favour of a third State court, even though it had jurisdiction on the basis of the Brussels Convention. The court applied the English law doctrine of *forum non conveniens* to stay the proceedings based on the discretion of the English judge.

---

[79] See Gaudemet-Tallon, *Compétence et exécution des jugements en Europe*, note 17 above, 57–58.
[80] Case C–281/02 *Owusu v Jackson and others* [2005] ECR I–1383; discussed in more detail in chapter 5 below, paras 5.86 and following.
[81] [1994] 1 Lloyd's Rep 382 (CA).
[82] [1992] 2 Lloyd's Rep 399 QBD.

When there is a forum clause in favour of a foreign court, the English judge retains discretion as to the staying of proceedings. However, the fact that there is a forum clause, based on the will of the parties, should carry considerable weight.

The English Court of Appeal reached a similar conclusion in *Baghlaf* **4.62** *Al Zafer Factory Co v Pakistan National Shipping.*[83] In this case coils of steel were carried from Bilbão and damaged when they arrived in Damman. The bill of lading contained a forum clause in favour of the court of the principal place of business of the carrier. The ship owners had their principal place of business in Pakistan. The cargo owners instituted action in an English court. They argued in the first place that there had been an oral agreement in favour of the English courts. In the alternative they averred that the acceptance by the respondent's (ship owners') solicitors of the writ, conferred jurisdiction on the English courts according to domestic rules. The question was whether the proceedings should be stayed in favour of a Pakistani court. The argument was based solely on English law. Under English law, even if there is a forum clause in favour of a foreign court, an English court may hear the dispute under certain circumstances. Factors considered included the location of evidence, the applicable law, the countries with which the parties were (closely) connected, whether the defendants genuinely desired trial in the foreign court or were only seeking procedural advantages, and whether the plaintiffs would be prejudiced by having to sue in the foreign court for reasons such as enforcement, time bars, or politics.[84] The English Court of Appeal stayed proceedings in favour of a Pakistani court. These factors show the willingness of the English courts to respect forum clauses in favour of third State courts. This practice should be upheld rather than invalidated by Brussels I. No mention was made in this case of the Brussels Convention and it seems from the facts that the court would not have had jurisdiction under the Convention. It would have had jurisdiction on the basis of the English rule of service of process. It seems that, whatever the basis of jurisdiction, the court should be able to stay proceedings in this type of case. The judgment was subsequently overturned because of a time bar that applied in Pakistan and that could not be waived.[85] However, the relevant point remains that it is possible to stay proceedings in favour of a third State court appointed by a forum clause.

---

[83] Note 78 above.
[84] Ibid, 235.
[85] [2000] 1 Lloyd's Rep 1 (CA).

4.63 Even after *Owusu* the English courts have upheld their position. In *Konkola Copper Mines Plc v Coromin* the Queens Bench Division of the High Court of Justice (Commercial court) considered a forum clause in favour of a court in Zambia.[86] In this case the court carefully analysed *Owusu* and *Coreck*, as well as the Schlosser Report, and previous English case law in point. The court came to the conclusion that an EU Member State court, which has jurisdiction on the basis of the domicile of the defendant, may grant a stay on the basis that a court in a third State had been chosen by the parties. It held that the decision in *Owusu* (preventing the declining of jurisdiction when the third State court would have jurisdiction on the basis of the place of performance of the contract) did not make it impossible to decline jurisdiction when a third State court had been chosen in a forum clause. The Brussels Convention (and Regulation) attached greater importance to a forum clause than to other bases of jurisdiction. On the facts of the case the court did not grant the stay, but its conclusion that a stay was possible remains important. The Court of Appeal confirmed the judgment in *Konkola*.[87] The court of first instance's conclusion regarding the possibility of a stay was not at issue in the appeal.

4.64 The French courts' solutions have been less coherent. The Cour d'appel (Court of Appeal) of Versailles refused to give effect to a forum clause in favour of the courts of Monaco.[88] It found that the Convention only regulated forum clauses in favour of the courts of Contracting States. Therefore there was no ground to derogate from the rules contained in Article 2 of the Convention. Gaudemet-Tallon has criticized this judgment, stating that Article 2 does not create a 'privilege of jurisdiction' that cannot even be derogated from by a forum clause in favour of a third State court.[89] On the other hand, the French Cour de cassation (Court of Cassation), Commercial division, had to consider the jurisdiction of the French courts in an action brought by a German company against a French company, situated in Paris. It was clear that the court had jurisdiction on the basis of Article 2 of the Brussels Convention (domicile of the defendant).

---

[86] [2005] EWHC 898 (Comm). See also R Fentiman, 'Civil jurisdiction and third States: *Owusu* and after' [2006] CML Rev 705–734; H Muir Watt, case note on *Konkola* [2005] *Revue critique de droit international privé* 725–731.

[87] [2006] 1 Lloyd's Rep 410.

[88] Judgment of 26 September 1991, published in [1992] *Revue critique de droit international privé* 333–336, see also D Alexandres, *Encycl. Dalloz, Droit communautaire*, 'Convention de Bruxelles (Compétence)' no 239; chapter 2 above, para 2.239, where the other anomaly in this case is discussed, namely that the defendant is domiciled in a third State, while it had a branch at Nanterre in France.

[89] Case note by H Gaudemet-Tallon [1992] *Revue critique de droit international privé* 336–340.

However, there was a forum clause in favour of the commercial tribunal of Zurich. This was before the existence of the Lugano Convention, so that Switzerland must be regarded as a third State.[90] The Cour de cassation declined jurisdiction, not on the basis of the Brussels Convention, but on the basis of French and Swiss national law. The rules in the two systems were the same on this point, so that the court did not have to choose between them.[91]

The *Lugano* opinion of the European Court of Justice included an inci- **4.65** dental ruling that, even where there is a forum agreement in favour of a court in a third State, while the defendant is domiciled in the EU the EU court would have jurisdiction.[92] It did not mention the possibility that the court could decline such jurisdiction. While the judgment is discouraging for the theory of the reflexive effect, it is not fatal. First, the conclusion on that point is obiter, since the case at hand did not deal with a forum clause in favour of a third State court. Second, the theory of the reflexive effect does not deny that jurisdiction exists in the EU on the basis of the domicile of the defendant; it just goes a step further in seeking a way to decline such jurisdiction.[93]

According to which rules should validity be determined?

The validity of a forum clause in favour of a third State court cannot be **4.66** determined according to Brussels I; regarding neither form nor substance. The jurisdiction of courts outside the EU is a matter that cannot be regulated by Brussels I. Each state determines when it has jurisdiction and when not. However, the nature of the problem at hand is different: according to which rules must a court determine the validity of a clause *depriving* it of jurisdiction? This issue seems to be removed from the sphere of application, but also the sphere of interest, of Brussels I. An important factor is the later recognition and enforcement of a resulting judgment. The recognition and enforcement of a judgment from a third State will not fall under Brussels I.

---

[90] The Lugano Convention was only signed in 1988.

[91] Cour de cassation, 19 December 1978, published in [1979] *Revue critique de droit international privé* 617–624, with case note by A Huet. The judgment has been approved by Gothot & Holleaux, note 17 above, 98.

[92] Opinion 1/03 *Competence of the Community to conclude the new Lugano Convention on jurisdiction and the recognition and enforcement of judgments in civil and commercial matters* [2006] ECR I–1145, para 153.

[93] Fentiman, '*Owusu* and after', note 86 above, 720; G Cuniberti, '*Forum non conveniens* and the Brussels Convention' [2006] ICLQ 973–981 at 974–976.

4.67 In the EU the European Contracts Convention contains the conflict of law rules for contracts.[94] The rules of the Convention are of universal application, meaning that they always apply, irrespective of the law that they point to. The Convention in fact unifies the conflict of law rules of the EU. It comes as no surprise that the validity of forum clauses is excluded from the scope of the Convention.[95] In this way, of course, the Convention does not clash with the determination for validity of forum clauses in favour of EU courts as determined by Brussels I. However, it leaves the lacuna of the adjudication of validity of forum clauses in favour of third State courts, in the event that a party brings proceedings, in contravention of the clause, to an EU court. The non-existence of a rule, while the EU has unified conflict of law rules in the field of contracts, indicates yet again that the drafters of EU legislation seem to have forgotten the outside world. Accordingly the validity would have to be investigated with reference to national law. The European Court of Justice has stated (obiter) that the validity of a clause pointing to a third State should indeed be adjudicated according to national law. It indicated for this purpose the national law of the forum, including its conflict of law rules.[96] Although the European Court of Justice's reference to national law should be appreciated, it is still unclear exactly what the appropriate conflict of law rule is in this case. The validity could be determined according to several national laws. Four possibilities deserve our attention: the law of the forum, the law of the state in which the prorogated court is based, the law of the state in which the derogated court is based, and the law applicable to the agreement.

4.68 The forum law does not appear to be the best solution. It is not conducive to legal certainty as the forum could be anywhere. The parties at the time of contracting have no possibility of knowing where the subsequent plaintiff will choose to bring proceedings (in breach of the forum clause). At the same time, the forum court might be a court that an opportunistic plaintiff chose, perhaps because of its reputation for strict interpretation of forum clauses; it might have no connection with the dispute. The Hague Convention on Choice of Court Agreements adopted this solution with regard to incapacity. For that issue, a chosen and seised court will apply its own law (including its private international law rules); a seised but not chosen court will apply its own law (including its private international law rules). This solution for the seised but not chosen court was preferred because

---

[94] Note 15 above, 34–46. This Convention will soon be replaced by a regulation: also note 15 above.

[95] Art 1(2)(d).

[96] *Coreck*, note 71 above, para 19.

it was considered too ambitious to lay down uniform choice of law rules for the issue.[97]

The law of the prorogated court, on the other hand, provides a clear and **4.69** predictable answer. If the parties had chosen a court, they can have no objection to the validity of the clause being subject to the law of that court. The prorogated court will probably in any event utilize that law, when the case comes before it and it has to determine whether the prorogation was valid. Therefore, if an EU court uses the same law to adjudicate the validity of the clause, the solution will be uniform and the chances that parties are left with a negative accumulation (so that no court seems to have jurisdiction) will be reduced. This seems the most equitable solution. It is also the solution adopted by the Hague Convention on Choice of Court Agreements. The chosen court, the seised but not chosen court, and the recognizing or enforcing court have to apply the law of the chosen court if they evaluate (substantive) validity.[98] Under that Convention the private international law rules of the chosen court are also considered.[99] However, as stated above, when evaluating incapacity the seised but not chosen court will apply its own law, including its private international law rules.[100]

Determining validity according to the law of the derogated court has one **4.70** serious advantage, namely with regard to recognition and enforcement. The derogated court will often be situated where the defendant is domiciled, or where a section of the facts took place. Therefore, chances are that there are assets within the territory of that state and that enforcement would be sought there. One should attempt to avoid the risk of that court subsequently refusing recognition or enforcement, because according to its own law the forum clause was invalid and it should have adjudicated the case. The German Bundesgerichtshof (Federal Supreme Court) has also opted for this solution, although it found that the Brussels Convention was not applicable in the first place. It found that the German provision on prorogation of jurisdiction could also be used for derogation, if the German courts would have had jurisdiction had there been no forum clause.[101] In a later, similar, case, the Bundesgerichtshof applied German law to evaluate the derogation of the German courts, but also considered the law of the prorogated court.[102] The disadvantage of this solution is that there may be

---

[97] Arts 5 and 6(b); Explanatory Report, note 36 above, 47–48.
[98] Arts 5(1), 6(a) & 9(a) of the Hague Choice of Court Convention.
[99] Explanatory Report, note 36 above, 43 and 47–48.
[100] Art 6(b); Explanatory Report, ibid, 47–48.
[101] Judgment of 20 January 1986, note 68 above.
[102] Judgment of 4 November 1988, note 68 above. In this case the prorogated court was in Austria, but before it became a Member of the EU, so that it can be seen as a third State.

more than one derogated court, and one would have to consider a number of legal systems in order to find all the courts that possibly have jurisdiction in absence of a forum clause.

4.71 The law chosen by the parties is plausible because it respects the notion of party autonomy, which is important in contract law. However, there is an inequality of result between contracts containing a choice of court clause and contracts that do not. The solution might also pose problems if the validity of the entire agreement is in dispute. At the same time, it does not have the other practical advantages of the two abovementioned solutions.[103] However, it might be encompassed in the approach of reverting to the law of the prorogated court in the Hague Choice of Court Convention solution. That Convention states that one regards the conflict of law rules of the chosen court. The chosen court may of course refer to the law chosen by the parties.

When not to derogate

4.72 In the internal hierarchy of Brussels I, there are rules that demand respect, even despite a forum clause. If the Brussels system does not permit forum clauses in favour of EU Member State courts, forum clauses in favour of third State courts will probably not be respected either in the same situations. When an EU Member State court is seised in contravention of the forum clause, the court seised will not take account of the forum clause and take the case in any event. The two clear cases where forum clauses in favour of third State courts will probably be ignored, are exclusive jurisdiction and protective jurisdiction in the EU.[104] It seems that a high level of respect is required for exclusive bases of jurisdiction so that one cannot circumvent them by appointing a court in a third State. Moreover, if there is an exclusive basis of jurisdiction for one of the EU Member State courts, that means that there is a real link between the dispute and the EU court. Forum clauses binding weaker parties, i.e. insured parties, consumers and employees (Articles 13, 17, 21) and requiring them to go to third State courts, probably will not be tolerated either. These parties need protection and are often more disadvantaged by a clause prescribing the courts of a third State than those of another EU Member State[105]—even if the difference is only geographical.

---

[103] Gaudemet-Tallon, case note, note 89 above, states that the validity should be determined according to the law of the chosen or derogated court, and in the last instance according to the chosen law.

[104] See Gaudemet-Tallon, 'Les frontières extérieures', note 66 above, 99–100.

[105] Ibid, 100.

If a judgment based on the forum clause is given by a third State court in **4.73**
these situations, recognition and enforcement in the EU might be difficult.
The EU Member States will probably want to ensure the protection Brussels
I grants, and therefore would not be favourable to judgments obtained
from third States when one of these bases of jurisdiction lay in the EU.

H. FURTHER APPLICATION OF THE FORUM CLAUSE
IF PARTIES DOMICILED IN A THIRD STATE

Relevant parties for determination of Brussels I's application

It often happens in the field of maritime law that bills of lading are passed **4.74**
from one party to another, especially where goods are first transported by
sea and then by rail or road by a different party. It is conceivable that some
of these parties are not EU domiciliaries. If one of the initial parties were
an EU domiciliary, and an EU court were chosen, the forum clause would
be governed by Brussels I.

The validity of the forum clause would then also be evaluated as between **4.75**
the original contracting parties. The European Court of Justice confirmed
this in the *Castelletti* case.[106] In this case 22 bills of lading were issued in
respect of goods from several Argentine shippers that were put on board
a vessel operated by Lauritzen. The vessel was bound for Savona in Italy.
There the goods were to be delivered to Castelletti. Problems arose when
unloading the goods and Castelletti brought proceedings against Trumpy,
the agent for the vessel and for the carrier. Both Castelletti and Trumpy
were domiciled in Italy. When considering the forum clause on the back of
the bill of lading, the European Court of Justice found that the validity had
to be determined as between the original contracting parties.[107] In this case
one of the original contracting parties was from a third State (Argentina).
In the end it was not involved in the dispute.

Succeeding in rights and obligations

In the *Tilly Russ* case the third party, domiciled in Belgium, tried to avoid a **4.76**
forum clause by suing in Belgium while the courts of Hamburg were
appointed in the original contract.[108] The European Court of Justice

---

[106] *Castelletti*, note 24 above.
[107] Ibid, para 42.
[108] Case 71/83 *Partenreederei Ms Tilly Russ and Ernest Russ v NV Haven- & Vervoerbedrijf
Nova and NV Goeminne Hout* [1984] ECR 2417.

neverthless held that this party was bound by the forum clause if he succeeded to the rights and obligations of the original contracting party.
Gaudemet-Tallon supports this verdict, stating that it is in line with contract law in general that contractual provisions are binding not only on the
parties to the contract but also on third parties who have particularly close
links to the contract.[109]

4.77 The case *Dresser v Falcongate*[110] concerns the carriage of goods by the
defendants between the places of business of the plaintiffs in Germany
and England. Falcongate sub-contracted with Norfolk for the transport by
sea from Scheveningen (the Netherlands) to Great Yarmouth (United
Kingdom). The bill of lading contained a forum clause in favour of the
court at Rotterdam in the Netherlands. The goods were lost at sea and the
plaintiffs instituted an action in England against all the carriers. The question was whether the forum clause prevented them from suing in England,
even though Norfolk was domiciled in England so that Article 2 of the
Brussels Convention would grant jurisdiction to the English court. The
other defendant, a sister company of Norfolk, could then be sued in
England on the basis of the domicile of Norfolk (Article 6 of the Brussels
Convention). The judge at first instance refused a stay of the proceedings
and the defendants appealed. The Court of Appeal dismissed this limb of
the appeal, finding that the plaintiffs were not bound as against Norfolk
by the forum clause since there had not been a transfer of rights in the
sense of the *Tilly Russ* judgment.[111] Bingham LJ expressed his regret at the
state of the law (regarding the forum clauses provision of the Brussels
Convention) since he believed a pragmatic legal recognition of the commercial reality would have been better.[112]

Impact on parties from third States

4.78 The case law discussed above might affect parties from third States. If a party
domiciled in an EU State and a party domiciled in a third State conclude a
contract containing a forum clause in favour of a court in the EU, the clause
will be adjudicated according to Article 23 of Brussels I. If the EU party is
succeeded by a non-EU party, the reason for the application of the Regulation
to the parties in the litigation no longer exists. This leaves the door open
for potential abuse. A party wanting the regime of Brussels I to apply to his
contract would be able to find a party domiciled in the EU and add his name

---

[109] Gaudemet-Tallon, 'Forum clauses', note 17 above, 132–133.
[110] [1992] QB 502.
[111] Ibid, 511; see *Tilly Russ* , note 108 above.
[112] Ibid.

to the contract, just to make sure that Article 23 of the Regulation would apply. Furthermore, parties that have nothing to do with the European judicial area would be subjected to forum clauses for EU Member State courts, the validity of which will be evaluated according to Brussels I. Succeeding in the rights of parties domiciled in the EU requires caution.

I. NO LINK WITH THE EUROPEAN JUDICIAL AREA

In the case where a party from an EU Member State and a party from a **4.79** third State agree on a forum clause in favour of the EU Member State where the first party is domiciled, the two conditions for the application of Article 23 are met. Is it, however, correct and equitable to apply Brussels I to test the validity of the clause, instead of the national law of the EU Member State in question?

It is relevant here to consider the expectations of the parties. This situation **4.80** came before the Oberlandesgericht (District Court of Appeal) of Munich in 1989.[113] A German and a Canadian party (from British Columbia) concluded various agreements. The German order confirmations contained forum clauses in favour of a German court on their reverse sides. After a dispute arose, the German seller sued the Canadian buyer before the Landgericht (Regional court) at Memmingen in Germany. The case reached the Oberlandesgericht of Munich, which considered whether the validity of the forum clause had to be determined according to the Brussels Convention (1968 version) or according to the German rules on international jurisdiction. The court took note of the wording of the Convention, which stated that one of the parties had to be domiciled in an EU Member State and a court in a Contracting State had to be appointed for the provision to be applicable. It stated that different Contracting States should be concerned: the domicile of one of the parties had to be in a different EU Member State than the chosen court, or that the chosen court and the derogated court had to be situated in different EU Member States. In the case before it, no Contracting State other than Germany was concerned. The derogated court was situated in Canada, and therefore had nothing to do with the Brussels Convention, which had been created for Europe. The Oberlandesgericht also considered the purpose of the Brussels Convention.

---

[113] Oberlandesgericht Munich, 28 September 1989 [1991] *Praxis des internationalen Privat-und Verfahrensrechts* 46–51. See also ER Sachpekidou, 'Substantive requirements and effects of jurisdiction agreements' in R Fentiman, A Nuyts, H Tagaras & N Watté (eds), *The European Judicial Area in Civil and Commercial Matters* (Brussels: Bruylant, 1999) 69–83; Grolimund, note 25 above, 51–55.

It stated that if one considered the origin and the system, the Convention did not create an all-encompassing set of international rules on jurisdiction. It envisaged the legal protection of parties from the EU Member States and the facilitation of recognition and enforcement of judgments between these states. None of these ideals was at stake in the case before it. The protection of the Canadian party was not the interest of the Brussels Convention. When solely the relationship between a Contracting State and a third State was at stake, the court considered that its national rules should apply.[114] According to German national law the forum clause was valid while it might not have been under the requirements of the Brussels Convention. In this case, it was the Canadian party who wanted to get rid of the clause. However, the specific interests of the third State party in this case aside, the legal point remains interesting. The fact that the case had no link with the European judicial area was decisively important. However, on a strict reading of the provision on forum clauses, the rule should have been held to be applicable: one party was domiciled in the EU and an EU Member State court was chosen.

4.81 After *Owusu* the solution adopted by the court might no longer be tenable.[115] The European Court of Justice stated in this judgment that the Brussels Convention applies when the case is international, i.e. more than one state is involved, even if that is one EU Member State and one third State. In *Owusu* the parties were both domiciled in England, but some of the co-defendants were domiciled in Jamaica and the facts took place in Jamaica. According to the European Court of Justice that case fell under the Brussels Convention. Although the case did not deal with a forum clause, the determination of the sphere of application of the Brussels Convention will probably be the same for forum clauses. This means that if a party domiciled in a third State and a party domiciled in the EU conclude a forum clause in favour of the courts of the EU State of the second party's domicile, that clause will fall under Brussels I, even though the European judicial area is not concerned.

4.82 The case of the Oberlandesgericht of Munich has nevertheless been followed in Germany by the Bundesgerichtshof (Federal Supreme Court)[116]

---

[114] B Piltz, 'Die Zuständigkeitsordnung nach dem EWG-Gerichtsstands- und Vollstreckungsübereinkommen' [1979] *Neue Juristische Wochenschrift* 1071–1075 at 1072 supports such an interpretation of the Brussels Convention.

[115] Note 80 above.

[116] Judgment of 14 November 1991 [1992] *Praxis des internationalen Privat- und Verfahrensrechts* 377–380. In this case the defendant was domiciled in Greece, but since at that time Greece was not yet party to the Brussels Convention, Greece can be seen as a third State.

and by the Oberlandesgericht (District Court of Appeal) of Düsseldorf.[117] In these two cases the application of the provision of the Brussels Convention and the rule in German domestic law, would have led to the same result.

The English Court of Appeal came to a similar conclusion as the **4.83** Oberlandesgericht Munich upon similar facts, albeit the procedural history of the case was more complex. In the case *Eli Lilly and Company v Novo Nordisk A/S* a dispute arose concerning patent infringement. Eli Lilly was an Indiana company while Novo Nordisk was from Denmark.[118] The parties had concluded licence agreements regarding the use of Nordisk's patents on certain processes to synthesize human growth hormones (called 'enzyme cleavage'). The agreement at issue contained a forum clause in favour of the courts of London. The forum clause complied with the rules for validity put forward by the Brussels Convention. Novo Nordisk subsequently brought action against Eli Lilly (and other parties) in New Jersey for the infringement of its patents. Nine months later Eli Lilly issued a writ in England for the rectification of the licence agreement between the parties. One of the parties was domiciled in an EU Member State, and a court in another EU Member State was appointed. It seems obvious that the Brussels Convention should have been applied to determine the validity of the forum clause. However, the court seems to have been confused by the other issue in this case; that of *lis pendens*. Concerning the problem of the parallel proceedings, the Brussels Convention could not have been applicable as one of the courts was in the EU while the other was not. For the *lis pendens* rule of the Brussels Convention to come into play, both courts where proceedings are pending would have to have been in EU Member States.[119] Therefore the court rightly found that the Brussels Convention could not be used to solve the problem of the parallel proceedings. However, the court deduced that the Brussels Convention was not applicable at all, instead of distinguishing the issue of the forum clause from that of the parallel proceedings. The court should have applied the Brussels Convention to the forum clause, even if it could not apply the Convention to the different question of the parallel proceedings. The English Court of Appeal did assume jurisdiction, but not on the basis of the Brussels Convention. It considered the forum clause and national rules of jurisdiction. Applying national law, the Court considered the causes of

---

[117] Judgment of 2 October 1997 [1999] *Praxis des internationalen Privat- und Verfahrensrechts* 38–41.
[118] [2000] 1 L Pr 73.
[119] Para 5.17 below.

action of the two cases to be different. Therefore it did not grant a stay on the basis of the earlier New Jersey proceedings.

4.84 These cases indicate the difficult interaction between Brussels I and national rules on jurisdiction when a third State is concerned. Not every element of the case can be considered in the same light. It is possible that the Regulation seeks to be applicable to the basis of jurisdiction, but not to the parallel proceedings issue. However, in most cases the wording of the provision is strictly followed.[120] As soon as it is established that one party is from an EU Member State and an EU court is appointed, the scheme of Brussels I is triggered. Whether or not the problem of parallel proceedings falls under national law should not influence that conclusion on the application of Brussels I on forum clauses.

J. CHOICE OF FORUM UNDER BRUSSELS II *BIS*

4.85 Prorogation of jurisdiction under Brussels II *bis* exists only in cases of parental responsibility and not for divorce, legal separation, or marriage annulment. In a proposed amendment to Brussels II *bis* a limited possibility to choose a forum for divorce will be introduced.[121] The provision differs from the rule in Brussels I; the choice is limited and the choice need not necessarily be in writing, but must be express or unequivocal. There is a possibility that parties may choose to bring proceedings regarding parental responsibility in a court with which the child has substantial connection. The Regulation gives examples of such substantial connection, such as the habitual residence of the holders of parental responsibility or the nationality of the child. These factors, as well as others that might indicate a substantial connection, are elaborations of the scope of application of Brussels II *bis*.

---

[120] See, for instance, Handelsgericht (Commercial Court) of Zurich, judgment of 9 January 1996 [1997] *Schweizerische Zeitschrift für internationals und europäisches Recht* 373–384 and case note by P Volken at 384–386. The forum clause between a party domiciled in Switzerland and one domiciled in Belgium appointed the Swiss courts. At the relevant time the Lugano Convention had not entered into force in Belgium, so that Belgium could be seen as a third State. Therefore, there was only one Contracting State of the Lugano Convention involved. The court applied the Lugano Convention as basis for its jurisdiction. See also Grolimund, note 25 above, 53–54.

[121] Proposal for a Council Regulation amending Regulation (EC) No 2201/2003 as regards jurisdiction and introducing rules concerning applicable law in matrimonial matters of 17 July 2006, COM(2006) 399 final, Art 3a; available at <http://eur-lex.europa.eu>.

A similar rule exists in the 1996 Hague Convention on Jurisdiction, **4.86**
Applicable Law, Recognition, Enforcement and Co-operation in respect of
Parental Responsibility and Measures for the Protection of Children.[122]
This provision was inserted upon request by the negotiators of the EU
Member States, who wanted to bring the text more into line with the
Brussels II text.[123]

The basic idea behind this rule is to create flexibility at a time of family **4.87**
turmoil, and to concentrate divorce and related proceedings in a single
court where possible.[124] This is, of course, positive; however, as has been
explained, the scope of Brussels II *bis* is determined by its jurisdiction rules
collectively. A wider jurisdiction rule means that a court which would not
otherwise have had jurisdiction now obtains it. The habitual residences
and nationalities of the parties are irrelevant. This provision would thus
influence a third State party as it would any other. This should not cause
too big a problem, since parties agreed to the forum.

K. CHOICE OF FORUM UNDER THE PROPOSED MAINTENANCE REGULATION

The European Community is in the process of adopting a separate **4.88**
Regulation on maintenance: the Commission has proposed a Council
Regulation on jurisdiction, applicable law, recognition and enforcement
of decisions and cooperation in matters relating to maintenance obligations.[125] Among other rules, this Regulation will contain provisions
on jurisdiction and will replace the present rules on maintenance in
Brussels I.[126] As will be indicated, the rule is similar to that of Brussels I.
Therefore, the analysis made above will stay valid for choices made in
maintenance disputes, before and after the entry into force of this new
Regulation. As is the case in Brussels I, the Maintenance Regulation will
permit parties to maintenance disputes to choose a forum to hear their

---

[122] Art 10.
[123] Report by P Lagarde on the (1996) Hague Convention on Jurisdiction, Applicable Law,
Recognition, Enforcement and Co-operation in Respect of Parental Responsibility and
Measures for the Protection of Children, [1996] Hague Conference on Private International
Law. Proceedings of the Eighteenth Session, vol. II, *Protection of children*, 534–604 at 563.
[124] Ibid, 563–565.
[125] Dated 15 December 2005, COM(2005) 649 final; available at <http://eur-lex.europa.
eu>. Note that this Regulation will not bind Denmark (rec 27). The United Kingdom has
indicated that it would not opt into this Regulation, so that it would not apply there (unless
the UK decides to opt in later). Ireland would opt in, so that it would apply there.
[126] See Art 48 of the proposed Regulation.

disputes.[127] The criterion for the application of the rule is that a court in the EU must be chosen and that at least one of the parties must have a habitual residence in an EU Member State. This rule is the same as Brussels I, except that habitual residence is used here instead of domicile. As under Brussels I, the jurisdiction will be exclusive unless the parties agree otherwise. The agreement has to be in writing in order to be valid. The new provision will create an exception: a choice of forum may not be made in disputes regarding maintenance obligations towards children under the age of 18.

4.89 If two parties who are habitually resident in third States conclude a forum clause in favour of a court in an EU Member State, the other EU Member States may not assume jurisdiction unless the chosen court has declined jurisdiction.

4.90 Thus, in general the same difficulties regarding parties from third States might arise as discussed throughout this chapter.

L. CONCLUSION

4.91 Forum clauses stand alone in the scheme of Brussels I. They have separate rules regarding their scope, and even if the defendant is domiciled outside the EU, he can be held to a forum clause in favour of an EU court.

4.92 The value of a forum choice in favour of a third State court, while the defendant is domiciled in the EU, has long been unclear. Some authors supported the reflexive effect of the Regulation, under which forum clauses in favour of third States should be respected. According to the recent *Owusu* case, an EU Member State court that has jurisdiction on the basis of the domicile of the defendant may not decline such jurisdiction in favour of a third State court. However, this case did not deal with the situation of a forum clause in favour of the third State court. The English court has subsequently ruled, in *Konkola*, that it could still decline jurisdiction based on the domicile of the defendant if the parties had agreed to the jurisdiction of a third State court.

4.93 In the *Lugano* opinion, the European Court of Justice found incidentally that it is impossible for an EU Member State court to decline regulation-based jurisdiction; irrespective of the nature of the third State court's jurisdiction. This conclusion by the ECJ is based on a formalistic reading of the Regulation. It causes great concern for international comity and respect for third State courts. Furthermore, it has the potential of jeopardizing

---

[127] Art 4 of the proposed Regulation.

party autonomy and rewarding parties that do not respect their contractual obligations. Hopefully the result can be remedied by a preliminary question to the ECJ on exactly this point. Alternatively, third States will be forced to conclude conventions with the EU in order to see forum clauses in favour of their courts respected. Maybe an amendment to the Regulation itself could bring a more equitable solution.

5

Fourth cornerstone: declining jurisdiction and conflicting proceedings

A. INTRODUCTION

Overview of the rules

5.01 In international litigation a plaintiff will seek out a court that he believes is the most favourable to his cause. A defendant, on the other hand, will try to avoid appearing in a court that he believes is unfavourable to his cause, and seek to have the case heard in a court which he perceives as more advantageous to his interests. Such quests could lead to parallel proceedings: the same action pending before courts in different states. In turn this might lead to conflicting judgments and difficulty in getting (one of) the judgments recognized or enforced in other states. In some cases courts attempt to resolve the situation when the proceedings are pending, so that they continue in only one of the two courts and there will be only one judgment. In some instances courts try to find a solution at an earlier stage, in order to avoid the situation of parallel proceedings occurring.

5.02 This chapter deals with different ways that a court can decline jurisdiction (before or after proceedings are pending in another court), avoid conflicting judgments, or even force parties to discontinue proceedings in other courts. The EU's civil jurisdiction regulations contain rules on *lis pendens* and related actions. In common law systems other mechanisms exist, such as *forum non conveniens* and the anti-suit injunction. All of these procedural rules are related to jurisdiction: they determine whether or not the court will decline its jurisdiction, or whether a court will force parties to discontinue proceedings in another court. Their hybrid nature causes difficulties in determining when they should be applied (in the case of those rules in the Regulations) and when they are permitted (in the case of the common law rules).

5.03 In this chapter, after briefly discussing the nature of the rules, the *lis pendens* rule as employed in Brussels I will receive attention. I will then discuss the English doctrine of *forum non conveniens* before turning back to Brussels I and its rule on related actions. The reason for this order is that the discussion of related actions, especially when referring to English case law, makes more sense when it is compared with *forum non conveniens*. In the last instance the anti-suit injunction will be addressed.

Classification of the rules

5.04 The rules discussed in this chapter are hard to classify.[1] On the one hand they seem like jurisdiction rules; on the other they are a class of civil procedure

---

[1] See A Nuyts, *L'exception de* forum non conveniens. *Etude de droit international privé comparé* (Brussels: Bruylant & Paris: LGDJ, 2003) 241–243.

rules, but not jurisdiction rules. The distinction is important for a determination of the scope of the rules, the question that concerns third States. Therefore a brief analysis of the difference between jurisdiction rules and other procedural rules will follow.

Jurisdiction rules make a specific court competent to hear a case on the **5.05** basis of a certain connection, such as the domicile of the defendant. Rules on *lis pendens, forum non conveniens,* related actions, and anti-suit injunctions do not grant jurisdiction. They should only be seen as jurisdictional in the sense that they can take jurisdiction away.

The European Court of Justice has distinguished jurisdiction rules (con- **5.06** tained in the Regulations) from procedural ones (regulated by national law).[2] Rules of civil procedure determine elements of the process, but do not influence jurisdiction as such. Typical examples are prescription, time bars, and the ways of introducing evidence. The European Court of Justice has found on several occasions that the purpose of the Brussels Convention was not to unify procedural rules in the EU Member States; it only established common rules of jurisdiction and facilitated the recognition and enforcement of judgments.[3] However, the European Court of Justice has also found that national rules of civil procedure could not be permitted to impair the functioning of the EU rules on civil jurisdiction.[4] Neither should they convey disloyalty or mistrust between the courts of the EU Member States. Therefore, even though unregulated, these rules do influence the functioning of the rules of jurisdiction. These concerns for the proper functioning of the EU's rules on civil jurisdiction, loyalty, and trust indicate the hybrid nature of the rules on *lis pendens, forum non conveniens,* related actions, and anti-suit injunctions: they cannot be viewed as pure procedural rules. Their impact on jurisdiction is inevitable.[5]

---

[2] Case C–365/88 *Kongress Agentur Hagen GmbH v Zeehaghe BV* [1990] ECR I–1845, para 17: 'It should be stressed that the object of the Convention is not to unify procedural rules but to determine which court has jurisdiction in disputes relating to civil and commercial matters in intra-Community relations and to facilitate the enforcement of judgments'.

[3] Ibid, paras 17–19. See also Case 148/84 *Deutsche Genossenschaftsbank v SA Brasserie du Pêcheur* [1985] ECR 1981 and Case 145/86 *Hoffmann v Krieg* [1988] ECR 645 on the distinction between Convention rules and national rules in the context of enforcement; AR Schwartz, '*In Re Harrods Ltd*: The Brussels Convention and the Proper Application of *Forum Non Conveniens* to Non-Contracting States' [1991–92] *Fordham International Law Journal* 174–206 at 200, using that case as analogous to *Re Harrods*.

[4] *Kongress Agentur Hagen*, ibid, para 20.

[5] See in this sense also R Geimer, 'The Right to Access to the Courts under the Brussels Convention' in Court of Justice of the European Communities, *Civil Jurisdiction and Judgments in Europe* (London: Butterworths, 1992) 39; P North & JJ Fawcett, *Cheshire and North's Private International Law* (13th edn, London: Butterworths, 1999) 266.

5.07 The rules on *lis pendens* and on related actions are covered by the jurisdiction chapter of Brussels I.[6] However, the European Court of Justice has indicated, at least implicitly, that these rules are not entirely jurisdictional, in any case not for determining when they apply and when not. In *Overseas Union Insurance v New Hampshire Insurance* the European Court of Justice found that the provision on *lis pendens* was applicable whenever two courts of EU Member States were involved.[7] The bases of jurisdiction were irrelevant. So too were the domiciles of the parties. This determination of applicability brings the rules of *lis pendens* and related actions in line with the rules on recognition and enforcement of judgments. In order to determine the scope of the EU rules, one no longer looks at the domicile of the parties, the existence of an exclusive basis of jurisdiction, or a forum clause. Instead, one refers to whether the courts concerned are situated in the EU or not. This supports the argument that the rules under discussion are not purely jurisdictional in nature. They are *sui generis* rules very narrowly attached to jurisdiction. They have been called procedural rules related to jurisdiction.

5.08 The scope of the rules on *forum non conveniens* and anti-suit injunctions seems different. These are also procedural rules and they are also related to jurisdiction. However, the basis of jurisdiction may play a more important role in their application than in the application of the *lis pendens* and related actions rules. This is especially true when jurisdiction is based on a national rule (for instance via the application of Article 4 of Brussels I); a wide national rule might have to be limited by the national rule on *forum non conveniens*.

B. *LIS PENDENS*

Article 27 of Brussels I:

1. *Where proceedings involving the same cause of action and between the same parties are brought in the courts of different Member States, any court other than the court first seised shall of its own motion stay its proceedings until such time as the jurisdiction of the court first seised is established.*
2. *Where the jurisdiction of the court first seised is established, any court other than the court first seised shall decline jurisdiction in favour of that court.*

---

[6] The rule is mirrored in the title on recognition and enforcement: where two irreconcilable judgments on the same issue exist, involving the same parties, recognition and enforcement of the second judgment may be refused; Art 34(3) & (4) of Brussels I.
[7] Case C–351/89 [1991] ECR I–3317.

Article 29 of Brussels I:

Where actions come within the exclusive jurisdiction of several courts, any court other than the court first seised shall decline jurisdiction in favour of that court.

Article 19 of Brussels II *bis*:

1. *Where proceedings relating to divorce, legal separation or marriage annulment between the same parties are brought before courts of different Member States, the court second seised shall of its own motion stay its proceedings until such time as the jurisdiction of the court first seised is established.*
2. *Where proceedings relating to parental responsibility relating to the same child and involving the same cause of action are brought before courts of different Member States, the court second seised shall of its own motion stay its proceedings until such time as the jurisdiction of the court first seised is established.*
3. *Where the jurisdiction of the court first seised is established, the court second seised shall decline jurisdiction in favour of that court. In that case, the party who brought the relevant action before the court second seised may bring that action before the court first seised.*

Introduction

The *lis pendens* rule is a common approach only used in bilateral or **5.09** multilateral treaties. It existed as early as 1899 in conventions between European states.[8] It is a kind of politeness that says: 'You first; I am sure that you can do the job as well as I can.' Thus the court second seised stays its proceedings in order for the first court to examine its jurisdiction. If the court first seised finds that it has jurisdiction, the court second seised declines jurisdiction. The rule is mechanical and there is neither discretion nor consideration of which court is more appropriate to hear the case. This indicates an essential underlying precept of the rule: it does not really matter which court hears the case, as the solution should be more or less the same. Such trust in partner legal systems is essential for the proper functioning of the European judicial area. Another notion underlying the rule is that conflicting judgments should be prevented in the European judicial space, as these might pose a difficulty for recognition and enforcement.

---

[8] See, for example the bilateral conventions between Belgium and France on Jurisdiction and the Validity and Enforcement of Judgments, Arbitration Awards and Authentic Instruments (Paris, 1899), Art 4(1); between Belgium and the Netherlands on Jurisdiction, Bankruptcy, and the Validity and Enforcement of Judgments, Arbitration Awards and Authentic Instruments (Brussels, 1925), Art 6(1).

Accordingly, the European Court of Justice has ruled on several occasions that the provision had to be interpreted broadly.[9]

5.10 This section on *lis pendens* will start with a look at the rule in Brussels I, Brussels II *bis* and the Insolvency Regulation. The proposed Maintenance Regulation contains a provision identical to that of Brussels I and will not be discussed separately.[10] In later sections of this chapter *lis pendens* will be regarded in the light of different bases of jurisdiction. *Lis pendens* and third State courts will also be considered. This discussion will include reference to the national *lis pendens* rules of the EU Member States. The permissible and impermissible exceptions to *lis pendens* will be examined. Finally, a brief assessment of the rule will be made.

THE *LIS PENDENS* RULE IN THE CIVIL JURISDICTION REGULATIONS

Lis pendens in Brussels I

5.11 Brussels I's response to parallel proceedings encompasses a strict rule of priority: the court first seised may try the case.[11] The court second seised must stay the proceedings until the court first seised has ruled on whether or not it has jurisdiction. If the first court finds that it has jurisdiction, the second court must declare itself incompetent and let the matter go. Only when the court first seised finds that it has no jurisdiction, can the court second seised continue with the case. There is no discretion in the application of the rule.

5.12 Application of the rule requires the presence of three elements: the same parties, the same dispute, and the same cause of action. The European Court of Justice in *The 'Tatry'* has clarified the requirement for the parties to

---

[9] Case C–351/89 *Overseas Union Insurance v New Hampshire Insurance* [1991] ECR I–3317; Case C–116/02 *Erich Gasser GmbH v MISAT Srl* [2003] ECR I–14693, para 41; Case C–39/02 *Mærsk Olie & Gas AS v Firma M de Haan en W de Boer* [2004] ECR I–9657, para 32.

[10] Proposal for a Council Regulation on Jurisdiction, Applicable law, Recognition and Enforcement of Decisions and Cooperation in Matters relating to Maintenance Obligations of 15 December 2005, COM(2005) 649 final, Art 7; available at <http://eur-lex.europa.eu>. Note that, like the other regulations on civil and commercial matters, this Regulation will not apply in Denmark (rec 27 and Art 1). Whether it will apply in Ireland and the United Kingdom is as yet uncertain (rec 26 and Art 1).

[11] P Wautelet, *Les conflits de procédures. Etude de droit international privé comparé* (unpublished doctoral thesis, Katholieke Universiteit Leuven, 2002) examines different ways of dealing with parallel procedures and at the end pleads for a less rigid priority rule. This means that the priority rule contained in Brussels I should be tempered with an exception of the *forum non conveniens* type: if the second court clearly is better placed to hear the case, it should be allowed to do so. The *lis pendens* rule of the Brussels regime being strict, the Courts of the EU Member States seem to interpret the rule restrictively: H Born, M Fallon & J-L Van Boxstael, *Droit judiciaire international. Chronique de jurisprudence 1991–1998* (Brussels: Larcier, 2001) 418.

be the same.[12] One party was involved only in the proceedings in Rotterdam (the Netherlands) and not in London, where all the others were involved as well. The ECJ found that the plaintiff in the one action might be the defendant in the other. However, the rule on *lis pendens* could only apply to the extent that the parties were identical. In this case that would mean that both actions could continue.[13] The rule has since been slightly relaxed in the *Drouot* case, where the European Court of Justice admitted that an insurer and the insured parties could be regarded as the same parties for the purposes of *lis pendens* if their interests were identical and inextricable.[14]

Lis pendens in Brussels II *bis*

The principle of *lis pendens* (as well as the underlying ideas of politeness and **5.13** mutual trust) in Brussels II *bis* is the same as that of Brussels I.[15] In actions concerning parental responsibility, the rule is the same in all its elements. However, in those concerning divorce, legal separation, and marriage annulment the rule differs, in that it poses only two of the three requirements: the same parties and the same dispute. It is not required that the causes of action in the two cases be identical. If an action for legal separation is pending in a court of one EU Member State and an action for divorce in a court of another EU Member State, the situation will fall within the ambit of the *lis pendens* rule. This flexibility was necessary because the institution of legal separation (as something different from divorce) does not exist in all EU legal systems. Moreover, not all EU Member States have the same legal grounds for divorce, so the causes of action will often be different.[16]

The rule is just as stringent as that of Brussels I. There is no way to guaran- **5.14** tee that the court first seised has a closer connection to the case or is in a better position to consider the facts. Unfortunately the strict priority rule might lead parties to rush to court before they can be sued. Legislation should not create such an incentive to litigate, especially not in the delicate branch of family law, where people need time to assess their situations. The court granting the divorce might also be adjudicating guardianship

---

[12] Case C–406/92 *The owners of the cargo lately laden on board the ship 'Tatry' v The owners of the ship 'Maciej Rataj'* [1994] ECR I–5439.

[13] The correct way to solve this problem would be by way of the rule on related actions, although that rule places no obligation on the courts, but only creates the possibility of allowing the actions to be combined.

[14] Case C–351/96 *Drouot Assurances v Consolidated Metallurgical Industries and others* [1998] ECR I–3075.

[15] Art 19 of Brussels II *bis*.

[16] Malta is the only EU Member State in which divorce is impossible, but even before Malta's accession to the EU, it was possible to have a foreign divorce recognized there.

over children, or financial consequences. Therefore being in a specific court could make an important difference to the parties.[17] Legal traditions and social thinking differ over issues such as custody of children and maintenance between former spouses.

Lis pendens in the Insolvency Regulation

5.15 The Insolvency Regulation, unlike the two other Regulations, does not contain an explicit rule on *lis pendens*. According to the Virgos/Schmit Report, a conflict of parallel proceedings would not often arise.[18] As soon as insolvency proceedings have been opened in one EU Member State, those proceedings must be recognized throughout the EU.[19] Secondary insolvency proceedings may be opened in an EU Member State after the opening of the main insolvency proceedings in another EU Member State. Those secondary proceedings, though, would be complementary to the main proceedings: there would be no conflict between them, and the main proceedings would have universal effect, while the secondary proceedings would be limited to the territory of the Member State in which they were opened. The liquidators would have a duty to cooperate with each other.

5.16 Recognition thus comes at an earlier stage than under the other Regulations. In the *Eurofood* case questions arose as to when exactly insolvency proceedings are opened, and from what point the proceedings have effect in other EU Member States.[20] Eurofood was registered in Dublin, but was a wholly owned subsidiary of Parmalat, incorporated in Italy. Extraordinary administration proceedings were opened in Italy for Parmalat. Thereafter a provisional liquidator was appointed for Eurofood in Ireland. Eurofood was then admitted to the proceedings in Italy. The European Court of Justice pointed

---

[17] See P McEleavy, 'The Brussels II Regulation: How the European Community has moved into Family Law' [2002] ICLQ 883–908 at 887.

[18] Virgos/Schmit Report on the Convention on Insolvency Proceedings (unpublished), para 79. On this issue see also P Wautelet, 'De Europese insolventieverordening' in H Van Houtte & M Pertegás Sender (eds), *Het nieuwe Europese IPR: van verdrag naar verordening* (Antwerp: Intersentia, 2001) 103–167 at 138–139.

[19] Art 16 of Council Regulation (EC) no 1346/2000 of 29 May 2000, Insolvency Regulation; rec 22 states that immediate recognition is also the basis on which a dispute should be resolved where the courts of two EU Member States both claim competence to open the insolvency proceedings; rec 29 states that if the liquidator so requests, the opening of the proceedings should be published in another EU Member State.

[20] Case C–341/04 [2006] ECR I–3813; see also case notes: T Bachner, 'The Battle over Jurisdiction in European Insolvency Law' [2006] *European Company and Financial Law Review* 310–329; AJ Berends, 'The Eurofood Case: One Company, Two Main Insolvency Proceedings: Which One is the Real One?' [2006] *Netherlands International Law Review* 331–361; A Wittwer, 'Zuständigkeit, Anerkennung und *ordre public* im internationalen Insolvenzrecht—ein wegweisendes Urteil' [2006] *European Law Reporter* 221–224.

out that the conditions and formalities for opening insolvency proceedings vary broadly in the EU Member States: in some Member States insolvency proceedings are opened quickly, while in others proceedings are provisional for a period, in order to permit the court to make certain findings first.[21] The ECJ therefore found that the way in which the proceedings were described was irrelevant, and the divestment of the debtor and appointment of a liquidator, even if it is a provisional liquidator, are the key issues. The result of this finding is that the recognition of insolvency proceedings in other EU Member States should take place at the earliest possible moment. Parallel proceedings would be impossible as from that early stage.

LIS PENDENS AND THE BASIS FOR JURISDICTION

General

First, it should be noted that the basis for jurisdiction is irrelevant in the **5.17** application of the *lis pendens* rule. The criterion for its application is that the courts of two EU Member States must be involved. Different bases for jurisdiction will be regarded to illustrate the point.

Defendant from outside the EU

The application of the *lis pendens* rule does not depend on the domicile **5.18** of the defendant, but on the involvement of two EU Member State courts. The European Court of Justice has confirmed this in *Overseas Union*.[22] New Hampshire Insurance was a company established under the law of New Hampshire, USA, while it was registered in the United Kingdom as an overseas company, and in France as a foreign company. It issued a policy of insurance for certain costs of Société Française des Nouvelles Galeries Réunies, a company incorporated in France with its registered office in Paris. It then reinsured a portion of the risk with Overseas Union Insurance (OUI), a Singapore company registered in the United Kingdom as an overseas company, and with Deutsche Ruck and Pine Top, companies incorporated in England with their registered offices in London. A dispute arose on the basis of non-disclosure, misrepresentation, and breach of duty on the side of New Hampshire Insurance. The three reinsurers ceased payment and subsequently purported to avoid the contracts. New Hampshire instituted an action in the Tribunal de commerce (Commercial Court) in Paris against Deutsche Ruck and Pine Top, and a few months later it instituted a similar action against OUI in the same court. Deutsche Ruck and

---

[21] Ibid, para 51.
[22] Case C–351/89 [1991] ECR I–3317; case note by H Gaudemet-Tallon [1991] *Revue critique de droit international privé* 769–777; Born, Fallon & Van Boxstael, note 11 above, 26.

Pine Top contested the jurisdiction of this court and OUI stated that it intended to do the same. These three parties then instituted an action against New Hampshire Insurance in the Queen's Bench Division (Commercial Court) seeking a declaration. This court granted a stay of the proceedings pursuant to the *lis pendens* rule until the French court had established its jurisdiction. The three parties appealed to the Court of Appeal. That Court referred preliminary questions to the European Court of Justice in which it asked whether the rule on *lis pendens* could be applied where some of the parties were not domiciled in the EU.

5.19 The European Court of Justice examined the wording of the *lis pendens* provision and drew attention to the fact that it did not refer to the domicile of the parties. It stated that the purpose of the rule was to facilitate the recognition of judgments and therefore to avoid conflicting judgments in the EU. For this reason, it had to be interpreted broadly.

5.20 The three parties purported to argue that the Brussels Convention contained a rule on conflicting judgments.[23] According to them, the mere existence of this provision implied that conflicting judgments could come about and that the rule on *lis pendens* could not cover all situations. The court rejected this argument and referred to *Gubisch Machinenfabriek v Palumbo* where it was stated that the rule on *lis pendens* aimed to avoid conflicting judgments.[24] The conclusion was therefore that the *lis pendens* rule could be applied, even where the parties were not domiciled in the EU.

5.21 The consequence of these interpretations by the European Court of Justice is that even if an EU Member State court's jurisdiction is based on domestic law, the rule of *lis pendens* can be applied. The rule comes into play when a case is pending in the courts of two different EU Member State courts, irrespective of why the cases are so pending.[25] If, for instance, a defendant is domiciled in a third State and is sued in one EU Member State on the basis of its national rules (via the application of Article 4 of Brussels I), and then in another EU Member State according to its national rules, the first court will be able to hear the case. No determination will be made on the appropriateness of the jurisdiction of the courts.

---

[23] Art 34(3) of Brussels I (at the time Art 27(3) of the Brussels Convention).

[24] Case 144/86 [1987] ECR 4861; case note by A Huet [1988] *Journal de droit international* 537–544.

[25] See also Jenard Report on the 1968 version of the Brussels Convention; OJ C 59, 5 March 1979 (Jenard Report) 20–21; P North & JJ Fawcett, *Cheshire and North's Private International Law* (13th edn, London: Butterworths, 1999) 251.

Lis pendens while jurisdiction based on another convention

The logical consequence of the rule established in the previous paragraph **5.22** is that *lis pendens* can also be applied if jurisdiction had been based on an international convention instead of on domestic law. Brussels I defers to conventions on specific matters.[26] Some of these conventions specify bases for jurisdiction, but do not contain rules on *lis pendens*. As between the EU Member States, the problems of parallel proceedings may be solved by Brussels I rules.

In *The 'Linda'*[27] for example, jurisdiction was based on the Arrest **5.23** Convention.[28] An action was pending before the English Queen's Bench Division (Admiralty Court) as well as before the District Court of Middelburg (the Netherlands). The proceedings concerned a collision in international waters. Two ships had been arrested in this case; therefore both courts had jurisdiction on the basis of the Arrest Convention, which allows the arrest of ships in respect of maritime claims and makes that a basis for jurisdiction.[29] However, the Convention does not contain rules to resolve such a situation of two courts having jurisdiction. The Queen's Bench Division found that the conflict between these proceedings could be solved by the *lis pendens* rules of the Brussels Convention.[30]

Lis Pendens and a Third State Court

General

If the same action is pending in an EU Member State and a third State, the **5.24** civil jurisdiction regulations' *lis pendens* rules do not apply. Whether or not a court in an EU Member State, which is seised of an action already pending in a third State court, can decline jurisdiction, is not explicitly regulated. In some instances there are (bilateral or multilateral) conventions with third States to regulate the declining of jurisdiction.[31] The *lis pendens* rule does not exist only in conventions or international instruments, but also in some of the EU Member States' national legal systems. French law, for example, contains a strict rule that provides little discretion

---

[26] Art 71 of Brussels I.

[27] [1988] 1 Lloyd's Rep 175.

[28] International Convention for the Unification of Certain Rules relating to the Arrest of Seagoing Ships (1952).

[29] Art 7 of the Arrest Convention.

[30] *The 'Linda'*, note 27 above, 178–179. The judge went further to discuss the provision in the Brussels Convention on related actions, in case the finding on *lis pendens* was wrong.

[31] See the references to other conventions in Arts 67–72 of Brussels I and Arts 59–62 of Brussels II *bis*.

for the judge.[32] Dutch authors are of the opinion that the *lis pendens* rule can be applied on the basis of Dutch private international law as an exception that the parties can invoke. The Dutch judge can then declare the case inadmissible (*onontvankelijk*) or stay the proceedings.[33] The new Belgian Code de droit international privé (Private International Law Code) contains a similar provision, stating that a Belgian court may stay proceedings if a foreign court had previously been seised in the same matter between the same parties. Considerations of justice and the possibility of recognizing the foreign judgment are taken into account.[34] As the above-mentioned examples indicate, a *lis pendens* rule in national law does not contain an obligation as stringent as such a rule in a convention. The reason is that the rule is not based on a reciprocal duty and the provision is not part of a framework of sister-courts or trusted friends. Therefore, if not contained within a convention, the rule allows some form of discretion to the national judge.

5.25 The question now is whether such national rules allow courts to decline jurisdiction in favour of a court in a third State that has been seised before the court in the EU. Some have always held the view that declining jurisdiction was impossible. In *van der Eist v Pierson, Helding Pierson NV*[35] the Dutch Hoge Raad (Supreme Court) found that it had no power to stay proceedings between two Dutch domiciliaries in favour of proceedings pending between them in Switzerland (which was a third State like any other at that time since the Lugano Convention had not entered into force).[36] The Advocate General in the case explained that there was no obligation on the Dutch courts to stay proceedings; a reference to a foreign court in which the proceedings were already pending was only possible if an international convention existed between the two states. Since no such convention existed between the Netherlands and Switzerland at

---

[32] Nouveau Code de Procédure Civile (New Code of Civil Procedure) (2002 Dalloz, Paris), Art 100: '[s]i le même litige est pendant devant deux juridictions de même degré également compétentes pour en connaître, la juridiction saisi en second lieu doit se dessaisir au profit de l'autre si l'une des parties le demande. A défaut, elle peut le faire d'office.' See H Gaudemet-Tallon, author of the French report in JJ Fawcett, *Declining Jurisdiction in Private International Law* (Oxford: Clarendon Press, 1995) 175–187 at 180.

[33] See JP Vanheul & MWC Feteris, *Rechtsmacht in het Nederlandse internationaal privaatrecht deel 2* (TMC Asser Instituut, Apeldoorn: Maklu, 1986) 252–255.

[34] Code de droit international privé (Private International Law Code), Act of 16 July 2004, *Belgisch Staatsblad*, 27 July 2004, Art 14.

[35] Hoge Raad, 22 December 1989 [1990] *Nederlands Internationaal Privaatrecht* 338–641.

[36] Convention on jurisdiction and the enforcement of judgments in civil and commercial matters (Lugano Convention), 16 September 1988, OJ L 319, 25.11.1988, 9–48. Now, of course, the Netherlands and Switzerland are mutually bound by the Lugano Convention and the case would have been solved by the Convention's rule on *lis pendens* (Art 21 of the old Convention; Art 27 of the 2007 version).

that stage, the court ignored the proceedings in Switzerland. The Advocate General acknowledged that irreconcilable judgments should be avoided, but added that this was not always possible.

On the other hand, the silence of the regulations has led some to the inter- **5.26** pretation that national law should determine whether declining jurisdiction is possible.[37] This seemingly reasonable point of view has been blurred by the judgment in the *Owusu* case. The European Court of Justice stated that jurisdiction of an EU Member State court on the basis of the domicile of the defendant is compulsory: the court may not refuse to exercise that jurisdiction by applying the *forum non conveniens* rule. The Court said nothing on declining jurisdiction in another way that amounts to international comity. Fentiman argues that the ECJ should not only have considered the question of *asserting* jurisdiction on the basis of Article 2, but also the question of *declining* it.[38] The ECJ's argument was straightforward: jurisdiction based on Article 2 of Brussels I is compulsory. The fact that having jurisdiction might sometimes not be the end of the matter, and that there are other worthwhile considerations, was not discussed. To make matters worse, in its *Lugano* opinion, the ECJ implied that in that case the jurisdiction of an EU Member State court, based on for instance the domicile of the defendant, cannot be declined. This point was incidental. This problem will be considered in more detail in the section on *forum non conveniens* below.[39] Suffice it to note here that if an English court cannot decline Article 2 jurisdiction in favour of a third State court on the basis of *forum non conveniens*, the unfortunate, but logical conclusion is that a continental European court would also be unable to decline jurisdiction on the basis of its national rule on *lis pendens*.

It is submitted that the regulations should at least contain the possibility **5.27** for courts in EU Member States to decline jurisdiction in favour of courts in third States where proceedings are pending in such courts, or where such a court is clearly more appropriate to hear the case (or both).

The *lis pendens* rule in the Lugano Convention

The Lugano Convention contains the same rule on *lis pendens* as Brussels I. **5.28** Problems of parallel proceedings in an EU Member State court and

---

[37] North & Fawcett, note 25 above, 255; P Gothot & D Holleaux, *La convention de Bruxelles du 27.9.1968* (Paris: Jupiter, 1985) 123.

[38] R Fentiman, 'Civil jurisdiction and third States: *Owusu* and after' [2006] CML Rev 705–734 at 714–715.

[39] Opinion 1/03 *Competence of the Community to conclude the new Lugano Convention on jurisdiction and the recognition and enforcement of judgments in civil and commercial matters* [2006] ECR I–1145, para 158. See paras 5.51 and following below.

a non-EU Lugano Contracting State court are regulated by the Lugano Convention.[40] It is not relevant whether jurisdiction was based on the Lugano Convention or Brussels I. When the conflict is between an EU Member State court and a Lugano Convention Contracting State court, this Convention will resolve the matter. This approach is in line with the general rule that the relevant points of reference are the courts where the proceedings are pending.

Enforcement of a third State judgment in the EU

5.29 The European Court of Justice has found that the EU rule on *lis pendens* does not apply when the enforcement of a judgment from a third State is at issue.[41] Owens Bank Ltd was a company domiciled in the independent Caribbean state of Saint Vincent and the Grenadines. Bracco Industria Chimica SpA and its managing director, Fulvio Bracco, were domiciled in Italy. Owens Bank claimed that it had lent a sum of money to Fulvio Bracco in 1979. According to the documentation of the loan, the High Court of Justice of Saint Vincent was to have jurisdiction in any dispute arising from the loan. In January 1988, Owens Bank obtained a court order from a court in Saint Vincent against Fulvio Bracco for the repayment of the loan. An appeal was dismissed. Owens Bank subsequently applied in Italy to enforce the order there. Fulvio Bracco and Bracco SpA claimed that Owens Bank had obtained the Saint Vincent judgment by fraud. While the proceedings for enforcement were still pending before the Italian court, Owens also applied to an English court to have the same Saint Vincent judgment enforced there under English national law.[42] Fulvio Bracco again claimed that the judgment should not be declared enforceable as it was obtained by fraud. That party also relied on the Brussels Convention's rules on *lis pendens* and related actions to request the court to decline

---

[40] Article 54B(2)(b) of the old Lugano Convention, note 36 above; Art 64 of the 2007 Lugano Convention.

[41] Case C–129/92 *Owens Bank Ltd v Fulvio Bracco and Bracco Industria Chemica SpA* [1994] ECR I–117; Born, Fallon & Van Boxstael, note 11 above, 27; case notes by M Looyens [1994] *Tijdschrift voor het Notariaat* 343–347; A Huet [1994] *Journal de droit international* 546–550; H Gaudemet-Tallon [1994] *Revue critique de droit international privé* 382–387; P Kaye [1995] *Praxis des internationalen Privat- und Verfahrensrechts* 214–217 at 216 describing the judgment as 'extremely economical and textual'; I Couwenberg [1993–94] *Rechtskundig Weekblad* 1403; JC Schultsz [1994] *Nederlandse jurisprudentie. Uitspraken in burgerlijke en strafzaken* no 351, p 1627–1646; E Peel [1994] LQR 386–390; TC Hartley [1994] ELR 545–547; P Vlas [1994] *Netherlands International Law Review* 355–359; H Tagaras [1995] *Cahiers de droit européen* 195–199.

[42] Sec 9 of the Administration of Justice Act 1920.

jurisdiction or stay proceedings pending the outcome of the Italian proceedings.

The case reached the House of Lords, which referred a preliminary ques- **5.30** tion to the European Court of Justice: were the Brussels Convention's provisions on *lis pendens* and related actions applicable where the enforcement of a third State judgment was pending in the courts of two EU States? The European Court of Justice replied in the negative. It stated that the Brussels Convention only regulated the enforcement of judgments given in the EU. For purposes of the Convention 'judgment' meant any judgment given by a court or tribunal in the EU.[43] It also cited the purpose of the Convention, which was to simplify procedures of recognition in the EU and to see to the legal protection of persons established therein.

The Court pointed out that the recognition in this case would vary from **5.31** one EU Member State to another, so that a different result would not prejudice the principle of judicial security. The decisions will not really conflict. This is explained by the fact that a decision of enforcement cannot be enforced in another EU Member State (*exequatur sur exequatur ne vaut*).[44] If a party desires to give effect to the same judgment of a third State in another Contracting State he or she will have to seek enforcement of the original judgment. This, again, will happen according to the national enforcement rules of that Contracting State. This means that a third State judgment creditor domiciled in a country that has a bilateral enforcement treaty with an EU Member State cannot use this bilateral treaty for easy, or automatic, enforcement of its judgment in all EU Member States. This conclusion is in line with the objective of Brussels I to facilitate cooperation in civil and commercial matters and recognition and enforcement in the European Union.[45]

Fulvio Bracco and Bracco SpA also relied on the *Overseas Union* case, in **5.32** which it was found that the rules on *lis pendens* and related actions were applicable even if the EU court based its jurisdiction on national law and

---

[43] Art 32 of Brussels I (at the time Art 25 of the Brussels Convention).

[44] *Owens Bank*, note 41 above, see the Opinion of Advocate General Lenz, para 22:

This means, in particular, that the decision of Contracting State A by which the judgment of the non-contracting State is declared enforceable in that Contracting State cannot be enforced in Contracting State B pursuant to Article 31 and following of the Convention. To permit such 'double execution' would. . . create the danger that a judgment creditor could circumvent the conditions laid down by a Contracting State for the recognition of judgments of the courts of the non-contracting State in question.

See also case notes (all note 41 above): Gaudemet-Tallon, 383 and 386; Schultsz, 1631–1632; Tagaras, 196.

[45] Recs 1, 6, and 10 of the Regulation.

not on the Convention.[46] However, the Court stated that, in that case, the subject matter had fallen within the scope of the Brussels Convention. The enforcement of judgments from third States, on the other hand, falls outside the scope of the Convention, and not just outside its jurisdiction rules.

EXCEPTIONS TO LIS PENDENS

General

5.33 There are not many permissible exceptions to the strict rule of *lis pendens*. The rule is based on the principle of mutual trust between the courts of the EU Member States. Arguments, such as the fact that legal proceedings take longer in some EU Member States than in others, may not be used to set the *lis pendens* rule aside.[47]

5.34 Exclusive jurisdiction (based on the rules of Brussels I itself) of the court second seised seems to be the only one. It is submitted that the existence of a forum clause in favour of the court second seised should become a second exception. Another exception that should be added explicitly is provisional measures. It will be argued in the next chapter that these rules form an exception to *lis pendens*: even if proceedings as to the substance are pending in the courts of an EU Member State, a court in another Member State may grant provisional measures. This should be explicitly stated in the Regulations.

Lis pendens **and exclusive jurisdiction**

5.35 The question may arise whether the EU court second seised also has to stay its proceedings if its jurisdiction is exclusive under Brussels I. The rule in the text of the Regulation is not clear on this point, but the European Court of Justice made an obiter statement, in *Overseas Union,* that the *lis pendens* rule of priority to the court first seised was established without prejudice to the case where the court second seised has exclusive jurisdiction, 'in particular' for the exclusive heads of jurisdiction of the Brussels Convention.[48] This seems to have the effect that, if the court second seised has exclusive jurisdiction, it may go ahead without staying its proceedings in favour of the court first seised. The words 'in particular' could give rise

---

[46] *Overseas Union,* note 9 above,.

[47] *Gasser,* note 9 above, para 70–73. See also A Wittwer, 'Auch bei italienischer Prozessdauer gilt Art. 21 EuGVÜ' [2004] *European Law Reporter* 48–50.

[48] *Overseas Union,* note 9 above, para 26.

to confusion: can other grounds of exclusive jurisdiction also be granted precedence over the *lis pendens* rule? In any case, (at this stage) choice of court agreements do not share this privileged position.[49] May the words 'in particular' then be understood in such a way that exclusive jurisdiction might also be founded on a domestic rule if the defendant is domiciled in a third State?

For example, X, domiciled in Germany, brings an action against Y, domi- **5.36** ciled in Australia, in a German court and subsequently in a French court. The German and French courts may base their jurisdiction on their national rules.[50] Both courts are situated in the EU so that the Brussels I provision on *lis pendens* is applicable.[51] Let us suppose that there is an exclusive basis for jurisdiction in French domestic law that is relevant in the dispute, and that this exclusive basis for jurisdiction does not exist under Brussels I.[52] The question is whether the French court might raise the domestic exclusive basis for jurisdiction as reason not to apply the *lis pendens* rule with regard to the proceedings in Germany. It should be borne in mind that jurisdiction in this case is in fact based on Article 4 of Brussels I, which refers to national law. The bases for jurisdiction in national law have been incorporated into the system of the Regulation by that reference. Permitting Article 4 jurisdiction as an exception to *lis pendens* will probably lead to uncertainty and conflicting judgments. Courts in EU Member States can examine whether a court in another EU Member State has exclusive jurisdiction on the basis of the Regulation's direct rule (Article 22). Examining whether a court in another EU Member State considers its Article 4 jurisdiction as exclusive is more difficult. Furthermore, in light of the European Court of Justice's continual emphasis on the mutual trust between EU Member State courts, the French court would probably be obliged to adhere to the *lis pendens* rule, despite its domestic exclusive bases for jurisdiction.[53]

The Regulation contains a specific provision for cases in which more than **5.37** one court has exclusive jurisdiction according to its rules (a situation that

---

[49] *Gasser*, note 9 above.

[50] Art 4 of Brussels I.

[51] *Overseas Union*, note 9 above.

[52] It is often difficult to determine whether the jurisdiction rules in national law are exclusive. The question of the exclusiveness of the jurisdiction often only comes into play at the recognition or enforcement stage: a court will refuse to recognise or enforce a judgment if it considers that the courts of its own state had exclusive jurisdiction. See, for example, the Belgian Code de droit international privé (Private International Law Code), Art 25(7).

[53] For instance, *Gasser*, note 9 above, para 72 and Case C–159/02 *Turner v Grovit* [2004] ECR I–3565, para 24.

will not occur frequently): all courts other than the court first seised shall decline jurisdiction.[54] This provision is in line with the normal rule of *lis pendens*; preference is given to the court first seised without any margin of appreciation as to which court would be better placed to hear the case. It is unclear whether this rule will also apply with regard to more than one EU Member State court having exclusive jurisdiction according to their national rules, when Brussels I is not applicable.

Lis pendens and forum clauses?

5.38 Whether the *lis pendens* rule applied between two EU Member State courts if there was a forum clause in favour of the EU Member State court second seised, was uncertain until recently. The practice in English courts was for the EU Member State court in favour of which there was a forum clause to continue its proceedings, even when another EU Member State court had been seised first. Thus, the forum clause was granted preference over the *lis pendens* rule. The English Court of Appeal, for instance, decided this in *Continental Bank*, stating that the existence of a choice of forum clause was more important.[55] The English court even granted an anti-suit injunction to prevent the borrowers from pursuing the Greek action further. Interestingly, the lawyer for the borrowers (respondents in the English application; plaintiffs in a Greek action) proposed submitting the question of the relationship between the provisions on *lis pendens* and forum clauses to the European Court of Justice as there was no authority directly in point. The Court of Appeal's response was '[t]he more obvious the answer to a question is the less authority there sometimes is on it'. The Court had no doubt as to the fact that the provision on forum clauses should enjoy preference and refrained from referring the question. If it had done so, it would have been surprised by the answer that the European Court of Justice later gave in the *Gasser* judgment.

5.39 After the *Continental Bank* judgment the English court reached the same result in *OT Africa Line Ltd v Hijazy and Others (The 'Kribi')*. [56] The English court, the court chosen in a forum clause, was not bound to stay its proceedings on the basis that the proceedings in Antwerp had been brought first.

---

[54] Art 29 of Brussels I.

[55] *Continental Bank NA v Aekos Compania Naviera SA and Others* [1994] 1 WLR 577. The case will also be discussed in the framework of anti-suit injunctions, para 5.158 and following, below.

[56] [2001] 1 Lloyd's Rep 76 at 88.

However, in 2003 the European Court of Justice ruled in *Gasser* that the *lis* **5.40** *pendens* rule does not bend when there is a forum clause.[57] The parties had concluded a forum clause in favour of a court in Austria. One party brought the case to court in Italy. The other party subsequently brought proceedings in the chosen court in Austria, arguing that the existence of a forum clause has preference over the *lis pendens* rule. In other words, if there is a forum clause in favour of the court second seised, that court is not under the *lis pendens* obligation to stay proceedings. Advocate General Jacobs in his opinion followed that line of reasoning.

The European Court of Justice, however, found that the *lis pendens* rule is **5.41** not subordinate to a forum clause. The defendant in the Italian court should have invoked the forum clause there in order for the Italian court to decline jurisdiction. If the clause were valid, the Italian court would have declined jurisdiction. The Regulation itself gives the requirements for validity of a forum clause, and a Member State may not impose stricter requirements.[58] The principle is that all courts in the EU should come to the same conclusion when confronted with a forum clause, because they all apply the same test. Therefore, all things being equal, there is no reason to give preference to the forum clause above the strict rule of *lis pendens.*

However, this approach does not always correspond with reality. Applying **5.42** the same provision one court may conclude that there is a valid choice of forum agreement, while another may come to the opposite conclusion: the notions of 'practices . . . established between [the parties]' and 'in international trade or commerce. . . a usage of which the parties are or ought to have been aware' are not free of some appreciation by national judges. Moreover, the rules on the substantive validity of forum clauses (issues such as duress, capacity, etc) are not harmonized and different courts might come to different conclusions. It seems strange that a court other than the chosen court should have the facility to adjudicate the validity of the forum agreement, and not the chosen court.

---

[57] *Gasser*, note 9 above. Case notes: R Fentiman, 'Access to Justice and Parallel Proceedings in Europe' [2004] CLJ 312–314; A Huet, 'Chronique de jurisprudence du Tribunal et de la Cour de justice des Communautés européennes' [2004] *Journal de droit international* 641–645; Y Baatz, 'Who Decides on Jurisdiction Clauses?' [2004] LMCLQ 25–29; J Mance, 'Exclusive Jurisdiction Agreements and European Ideals' [2004] LQR 357–365; Wittwer, 'Italienischer Prozessdauer', note 47 above, 49–50; H Muir Watt [2004] *Revue critique de droit international privé* 459–464; P Wautelet [2004] *Revue de droit commercial belge* 794–799; R Fentiman [2005] CML Rev 241–259. See also M-L Niboyet, 'La globalisation du procès civil international dans l'éspace judiciaire européen et mondial' [2006] *Journal de droit international* 937–954 at 944–945.

[58] Art 23; see Case 150/80 *Elefanten Schuh v Pierre Jacqmain* [1981] ECR 1671, para 25–26.

5.43 Furthermore, if one is prepared to accept the fiction that all courts in the EU would reach the same conclusion as to the validity of a particular forum clause, one might as well apply the fiction in the opposite direction: if all courts would reach the same result, one could leave the decision to the chosen court instead of the court first seised but not chosen. If there were a valid forum clause, the court first seised would not be able to continue with the action.[59] If, on the other hand, the chosen court were to find that the forum clause was invalid, it would decline jurisdiction and the court first seised would be able to continue the proceedings. This seems like a more logical approach, and one that respects party autonomy and procedural economy rather than over-emphasizing mutual trust in the EU.

5.44 The line taken by the ECJ may also play against parties from third States. If they are not aware that they should rush to the chosen court first, their forum agreement might be interpreted by a court with a different tradition than the court they have actually envisaged. Thus, the value of a forum clause may be reduced because the determination of its validity is subjected to another court, not chosen by them.

5.45 It also seems strange that the ECJ found the opposite concerning exclusive bases for jurisdiction: these are exceptions to the rule of *lis pendens*, but forum clauses are not.

5.46 In the last instance it should be noted that the approach goes against the recent Hague Choice of Court Convention, respecting choice of court agreements to a high degree.[60] It certainly deserves respect in a situation where one party brings proceedings in a court other than the prorogated one: the court seised but not chosen has to suspend or dismiss the proceedings.[61] It is a pity that the European Court of Justice did not take a broader view. By the time this judgment was given a preliminary draft version of the Hague Convention already existed.

Lis pendens **and provisional measures**

5.47 The *lis pendens* rule does not explicitly refer to provisional measures. However, on a logical construction of the texts of the regulations, the possibility

---

[59] This point was made by the English Queen's Bench Division (Commercial Court) in *IP Metal Ltd v Ruote OZ SpA* [1993] 2 Lloyd's Rep 60 at 67, although the question in that case regarded related actions and not *lis pendens*; see below, para 5.137.

[60] Hague Convention of 30 June 2005 on Choice of Court Agreements; available at <http://www.hcch.net>.

[61] Art 6; there are certain exceptions to this rule, for instance if the agreement is null and void under the law of the state of the chosen court, or the chosen court had decided not to hear the case.

of granting provisional measures encompasses an exception to *lis pendens.* Provisional measures may be granted *even if* a court in another EU Member State has jurisdiction over the substance of the case. This also applies, it seems, when the court that has jurisdiction over the substance has already been seised. One of the parties can then request provisional relief from a court in another EU Member State. Most often this will not be a true occurrence of *lis pendens,* because what is asked of the two courts will probably not be identical. However, it might be that an injunction is sought, for instance provisionally to stop the marketing of a specific product, while the same is asked as a substantive (permanent) measure in a court in another EU Member State.[62]

ASSESSMENT OF THE *LIS PENDENS* RULE

The *lis pendens* rule is based on strict priority. The choice between the two **5.48** courts is arbitrary, or may depend on careful litigational planning by cunning lawyers. There is no guarantee that the court first seised is in a better position to assess the facts and evidence, or that it is the most convenient forum for all involved parties. Furthermore, at least in some legal traditions, it is seen as courteous to write a letter before suing. The civil jurisdiction regulations discourage this practice, as it could give the other party a head start in the race to the courtroom.[63] The *lis pendens* rule may also discourage out-of-court settlement in the same manner. Sue quickly seems to be the moral of the story.

It is important in this field to bear in mind that the first version of the **5.49** Brussels Convention was negotiated by the six initial EEC Member States (Belgium, France, (West) Germany, Italy, Luxembourg, and the Netherlands). These states all belong to the continental civil law tradition. Regarding jurisdiction, the tradition is known for its strict approach of rules rather than principles.

From a common law stance, the *lis pendens* rule stays too rigid to really **5.50** make sense. However, it has been accepted. As Sheen J stated:

Policy was a matter for those who agreed the Convention. The policy of this Convention appears to be to avoid the risks of irreconcilable judgments and to have a simple rule that litigation will be conducted in the Court first seised of the matter. Under arts 21 and 22 [27 and 28 of the Regulation] the Court which must decline jurisdiction or stay its proceedings is 'any court other than the court

---

[62] The question of provisional measures is treated in more detail in chapter 6.

[63] See A Briggs, 'Anti-European teeth for choice of court clauses' [1994] LMCLQ 158–163 at 158.

first seised'. The question: 'Which court would be the more convenient or the more appropriate?' does not arise.[64]

C. FORUM NON CONVENIENS

Article 15 of Brussels II *bis*:

1. *By way of exception, the courts of a Member State having jurisdiction as to the substance of the matter may, if they consider that a court of another Member State, with which the child has a particular connection, would be better placed to hear the case, or a specific part thereof, and where this is in the best interests of the child:*
   (a) *stay the case or the part thereof in question and invite the parties to introduce a request before the court of that other Member State in accordance with paragraph 4; or*
   (b) *request a court of another Member State to assume jurisdiction in accordance with paragraph 5.*

2. *Paragraph 1 shall apply:*
   (a) *upon application from a party; or*
   (b) *of the court's own motion; or*
   (c) *upon application from a court of another Member State with which the child has a particular connection, in accordance with paragraph 3.*
   A transfer made of the court's own motion or by application of a court of another Member State must be accepted by at least one of the parties.

3. *The child shall be considered to have a particular connection to a Member State as mentioned in paragraph 1, if that Member State:*
   (a) *has become the habitual residence of the child after the court referred to in paragraph 1 was seised; or*
   (b) *is the former habitual residence of the child; or*
   (c) *is the place of the child's nationality; or*
   (d) *is the habitual residence of a holder of parental responsibility; or*
   (e) *is the place where property of the child is located and the case concerns measures for the protection of the child relating to the administration, conservation or disposal of this property.*

4. *The court of the Member State having jurisdiction as to the substance of the matter shall set a time limit by which the courts of that Member State shall be seised in accordance with paragraph 1.*

---

[64] *The 'Linda'*, note 27 above, 179.

If the courts are not seised by that time, the court which has been seised shall continue to exercise jurisdiction in accordance with Articles 8 to 14.

5. *The courts of that other Member State may, where due to the specific circumstances of the case, this is in the best interests of the child, accept jurisdiction within six weeks of their seisure in accordance with paragraph 1(a) or 1(b). In this case, the court first seised shall decline jurisdiction. Otherwise, the court first seised shall continue to exercise jurisdiction in accordance with Articles 8 to 14.*

6. *The courts shall cooperate for the purposes of this Article, either directly or through the central authorities designated pursuant to Article 53.*

INTRODUCTION

The plea of *forum non conveniens* is raised where a defendant accepts that **5.51** the court has jurisdiction, but alleges that the case can more conveniently or more appropriately be heard by another court, and that the court in which the plea is raised should therefore decline to hear the case. When successful, the court grants a stay on the basis of *forum non conveniens.* That means that if the other forum, for some reason or other does not take jurisdiction, the parties can return to the court that granted the stay and it will hear the case.

The approach to jurisdiction outside continental Europe is different to the **5.52** continental understanding. In continental Europe jurisdiction rules are precisely defined. In common law the rules that grant jurisdiction might seem broader, but the view is that they might be pushed back in specific situations, with regards to the facts of the particular case. This is done by *forum non conveniens.* [65]

The rule gives the judge discretion not to exercise jurisdiction, even though **5.53** it is uncontested that it exists; common law lawyers see it as courteous and based on self-restraint.[66] Civil law lawyers on the other hand have difficulty with this broad discretion. Gaudemet-Tallon expresses the unease of the civil lawyer when he or she encounters the notion of *forum non conveniens:* it is unclear and includes vague principles such as injustice to

---

[65] See AA Ehrenzweig, 'The Transient Rule of Personal Jurisdiction. The "Power" Myth and *Forum Non Conveniens'* [1955–56] *Yale Law Journal* 289–314 at 312.

[66] Lord Goff of Chieveley stated in a postscript to the judgment in *Airbus Industrie GIE v Patel and Others* [1999] 1 AC 119: 'The principle is now so widespread that it may come to be accepted throughout the common law world; indeed, since it is founded upon the exercise of self restraint by independent jurisdictions, it can be regarded as one of the most civilized of legal principles. Whether it will become acceptable in civil law jurisdictions remains however to be seen.'

the plaintiff. These vague principles are left to the discretion of the judge. They are not inspired by the same source as Brussels I, which imposes a system of jurisdiction based on strict and precise rules.[67]

5.54 Furthermore, in the continental European countries, recognition and enforcement conventions have existed since 1899.[68] Some of these conventions contained rules on *lis pendens*, solving the problem of parallel procedures by granting jurisdiction to the court first seised. In the common law countries, on the other hand, such bilateral conventions are rather rare. One was in the process of negotiation between the United States of America and the United Kingdom at a certain point, but nothing came of it.[69] The result is that the rule of priority is not really known; conflicts of procedure are solved on a unilateral basis. Therefore other ways of dealing with parallel proceedings came about, such as *forum non conveniens* and anti-suit injunctions. In our current study the focus will be on these rules of the United Kingdom and their interaction with the European judicial area, especially in cases where third States are concerned.[70]

---

[67] H Gaudemet-Tallon, 'Le *forum non conveniens*, une menace pour la convention de Bruxelles? (A propos de trois arrêts anglais récents)' [1991] *Revue critique de droit international privé* 491–524 at 496.

[68] The Convention between Belgium and France on Jurisdiction and the Validity and Enforcement of Judgments, Arbitration Awards and Authentic Instruments (Paris, 1899).

[69] See AT von Mehren, 'Recognition and Enforcement of Foreign Judgments: a New Approach for the Hague Conference?' [1994] *Law and Contemporary Problems* 271–287 at 274, stating that the reasons for the failure of the US–UK treaty, the negotiations for which broke down in 1980, were the concerns respecting product liability and the UK insurance industry. Von Mehren added that the negotiators 'preferred the devil they knew to the one they did not'. He also stated that it was more in the European tradition to conclude conventions on recognition and enforcement of foreign judgments. In the USA the law relating to the recognition and enforcement of foreign judgments was developed through case law. See also BM Landay, 'Another Look at the EEC Judgments Convention: Should Outsiders be worried?' [1987–1988] *Dickenson Journal of International Law* 25–44 at 41, naming the UK's fear of US money judgments and the UK's wish to exclude anti-trust from the bilateral treaty as the reasons for its failure. He adds (at 42) that the USA's liberal approach in the recognition of foreign judgments weakened its bargaining power.

[70] For thorough comparative studies of these rules in the United States of America, see JJ Fawcett, *Declining Jurisdiction in Private International Law* (Oxford: Clarendon Press, 1995), where national reporters were asked to deal with (*inter alia*) *forum non conveniens* in their legal systems; A Nuyts, *L'exception de forum non conveniens. Etude de droit international privé comparé* (Brussels: Bruylant & Paris: LGDJ, 2003) and P Wautelet, *Les conflits de procédures. Etude de droit international privé comparé* (unpublished doctoral thesis, Katholieke Universiteit Leuven, 2002). For England: A Briggs & P Rees, *Civil Jurisdiction and Judgments* (4th edn, London: LLP, 2005) at 248–268; L Collins (ed), *Dicey, Morris and Collins on the Conflict of Laws* (14th edn, London: Sweet & Maxwell, 2006) vol I, 461–488. For Ireland: P Huber, '*Forum non conveniens*—The Other Way Round' [1996] *Praxis des internationalen Privat- und Verfahrensrechts*

It does not seem that the question 'is the English rule of *forum non conven-* **5.55**
iens compatible with Brussels I?' has one simple answer. If that were so,
one would have to be satisfied with the *Owusu* judgment and that would
be the end of it. After giving a brief background and definition of *forum
non conveniens* (with reference to civil law systems), the rule will be examined in the context of Brussels I. Through an analysis of the case law, it will
be pointed out that one can divide the question into several issues. In each
case the *forum non conveniens* rule must be examined in light of the basis
for jurisdiction. Jurisdiction on the basis of the domicile of the defendant,
jurisdiction on the basis of national rules (as referred to by Brussels I),
exclusive jurisdiction, and forum clauses will be discussed separately. The
Jenard Report draws a clear and fundamental distinction between the
position of the Community-based defendant and the defendant domiciled
elsewhere.[71] Whether one applies the strict jurisdiction rule of Brussels I,
or the ones of English national law, is relevant for the application of *forum
non conveniens*. Throughout this analysis the distinction will always be
made between the positions for other courts in an EU Member State or in
a third State, a distinction also made by authors.[72] For *lis pendens* the mere
fact that two courts from EU Member States are involved triggers the
rule.[73] The application of the *lis pendens* rule in these cases has an influence
on the extent of the *forum non conveniens* rule. The proposed analysis
remains relevant, even after *Owusu*. While the discussions will focus on
Brussels I and the case law it has produced, in the last part of this section,
the *forum non conveniens*-like rule in Brussels II *bis* will be considered. In
conclusion, there will be a short assessment of the rule.

48–52. For the USA: ML Ultsch, 'Die Forum-non-Conveniens-Lehre im Recht der USA
(inbesondere Floridas)' [1997] *Recht der Internationalen Wirtschaft* 26–31; AA Ehrenzweig,
'The Transient Rule of Personal Jurisdiction. The 'Power Myth' and Forum non Conveniens'
[1955–1956] The Yale Law Journal 289–314 at 312.

[71] See Jenard Report on the 1968 version of the Brussels Convention; OJ C 59, 5 March 1979
(Jenard Report), 13.

[72] H Gaudemet-Tallon, 'Les frontières extérieures de l'espace judiciaire européen: quelques repères' in A Borrás, A Bucher, AVM Struycken & M Verwilghen (eds), *E Pluribus
unum. Liber Amicorum Georges AL Droz* (The Hague: Martinus Nijhoff Publishers, 1996) 85–
104 at 97. See also P North & JJ Fawcett, *Cheshire and North's Private International Law* (13th
edn, London: Butterworths, 1999) 180; Collins, note 70 above, Vol I, 469–474; K Hertz,
Jurisdiction in Contract and Tort under the Brussels Convention (Copenhagen: Jurist-og
Økonomforbundets Forlag, 1998) 48; L Collins, 'Forum Non Conveniens and the Brussels
Convention' [1990] LQR 535–539. P Huber, 'Forum Non Conveniens und EuGVÜ' [1993] *Recht
der Internationalen Wirschaft* 977–983 at 978 makes the distinction between simple *forum non
conveniens* and *forum non conveniens* where there are also parallel proceedings.

[73] Case C–351/89 *Overseas Union Insurance v New Hampshire Insurance* [1991] ECR I–3317.

BRIEF BACKGROUND AND DEFINITION

5.56 The doctrine of *forum non conveniens* originated in Scotland. The effect of the doctrine is that a judge declines to hear an action, despite the fact that he has jurisdiction to hear it, on the basis that his court is not the most appropriate one to do so. The doctrine can only be applied if there is another court that has jurisdiction. Otherwise it would amount to a denial of justice. As early as 1892, the court stated in *Sim v Robinow:*

> . . . the plea can never be sustained unless the court is satisfied that there is some other tribunal, having competent jurisdiction, in which the case may be tried more suitably for the interests of all parties and for the ends of justice.[74]

5.57 The basis upon which the other forum has jurisdiction is not an all-important factor. Instead, the English court looks at the connection between the case and that forum. In the *Lubbe* case,[75] for example, the jurisdiction of the alternative forum, a South African court, was based on submission of the defendant. The Court of Appeal found that this alone would not be a reason not to grant a stay on the basis of *forum non conveniens*, but that it would be a factor to consider when applying the discretion.[76] Other factors taken into account when considering a stay on the basis of *forum non conveniens* include the applicable law, *lis pendens*, the convenience of witnesses, the convenience of the parties, the existence of a real and close connection between the forum and the dispute, actions on related matters already pending in England, in the case of multiple defendants, whether they can all be sued in England, public policy, expense, and time. If the other action were for a negative declaration and in fact amounted to forum shopping, the English court would take that into account as well.[77]

5.58 The doctrine of *forum non conveniens* is based on the principle of appropriateness and the discretionary power often given to judges in common

---

[74] [1892] 19 R 665. See doctoral thesis A Nuyts, *L'exception de forum non conveniens. Etude de droit international privé comparé* (Brussels: Bruylant & Paris: LGDJ, 2003); P Nygh, 'Forum Non Conveniens and Lis Alibi Pendens: the Australian Experience' in J Basedow, I Meier, AK Schnyder, T Einhorn & D Girsberger (eds), *Private Law in the International Arena. Liber Amicorum Kurt Siehr* (The Hague: TMC Asser Press, 2000) 511–526.

[75] [2000] 1 Lloyd's Rep 139. The stay was subsequently lifted by the House of Lords: [2000] 2 Lloyd's Rep 383 at 394. In that judgment the issue of the Brussels Convention was not considered. For a more detailed discussion of the *Lubbe* cases, see below, paras 5.82 and following.

[76] Ibid; see the concurring judgment of Tuckey LJ at 168.

[77] P Beaumont's report on Great Britain in Fawcett, note 70 above, 207–233 at 212–220.

law systems.[78] The advantage of the doctrine is that it breaks away from the rigidity of jurisdiction rules and moves towards a more flexible approach, so the inflexibility of jurisdiction rules can be tempered in order to prevent injustice.[79]

This doctrine should not be confused with that of the *improper forum*. The **5.59** latter refers to a basis for jurisdiction that is in itself objectionable, while *forum non conveniens* deals with the application of certain bases for jurisdiction to a particular set of facts: it is not the basis for jurisdiction in itself that is objectionable, but its use in a particular case.[80]

In English law an action could previously only be stayed if the defendant **5.60** proved that it was vexatious and abusive towards him and no injustice to the plaintiff would result.[81] This differed from the Scottish and American law in the sense that they also allowed a stay on the basis that there was a more appropriate forum to adjudicate the case.[82] The English courts relaxed the strictness of their test over the past 30 years and recognized that an action can also be stayed if another forum is clearly more appropriate. However, it is a precondition that another forum is available to the parties.[83]

The doctrine of *forum non conveniens* is not accepted in most civil law sys- **5.61** tems.[84] In the Netherlands a form of *forum non conveniens* existed, but it

---

[78] Y Donzallaz, *La Convention de Lugano du 16 septembre 1988 concernant la compétence judiciaire et l'exécution des décisions en matière civile et commerciale* (Berne: Editions Stæmpfli + Cie SA Berne, 1996) vol 3, 74–75.

[79] See D Gwynn Morgan, 'Discretion to stay jurisdiction' [1982] ICLQ 582–587 at 582; G Hogan, 'The Brussels Convention, *Forum non conveniens* and the Connecting Factors Problem' [1995] ELR 471–493 at 473.

[80] Donzallaz, note 78 above, vol 3, 74.

[81] See Gaudemet-Tallon, 'Une menace pour la convention de Bruxelles?', note 67 above.

[82] In general, AG Slater, '*Forum non conveniens*, A View from the Shopfloor' [1988] LQR 554–575.

[83] *Spiliada Maritime Corp v Cansulex Ltd* [1987] 1 Lloyd's Rep 1 at 10; *Intermetal Group Limited & Trans-World (Steel) Limited v Worslade Trading Limited* [1998] ILPr 765 at 775 (Irish Supreme Court).

[84] Schlosser Report on the 1978 version of the Brussels Convention; OJ C 59, 5 March 1979, 71, para 76, p 97; North & Fawcett, note 72 above, 262; Fawcett, note 70 above, 21–27 and the national reports. F Juenger, 'Judicial Jurisdiction in the United States and in the European Communities: a comparison' [1985] *Michigan Law Review* 1195–1212 at 1205 mentions German and French and other exorbitant bases of jurisdiction and then states '[t]o make matters worse, continental European countries do not recognize the *forum non conveniens* doctrine, so that their courts cannot decline jurisdiction even if a suit is brought solely to harass the defendant.' This indicates the extent of the opposing views that exist on the two sides of the Atlantic.

was much more limited than the common law concept.[85] According to the Wetboek van Burgerlijke rechtsvordering (Code of Civil Procedure) the application of the doctrine was only possible in proceedings initiated by petition instead of a writ (*verzoekschriftprocedures*). It could only be used in international disputes.[86] The exact relation between a lack of jurisdiction and *forum non conveniens* was not always clear in the case law and it was even extended to cases where a writ had been issued.[87] The courts have described *forum non conveniens* as the judge declaring that he does not have jurisdiction since the case has insufficient links with the legal order of the forum state.[88] The doctrine was subsequently excluded by the legislator when amending the Wetboek van Burgerlijke rechtsvordering, the reason being that the heads of jurisdiction were limited and the rule was unnecessary.[89]

5.62 In Germany *forum non conveniens* does not exist and the taking up of jurisdiction is mandatory. However there has been an interesting evolution with regard to property and the archetypal solution of civil law. The German Zivilprozessordnung (Code of Civil Procedure) attempts to prevent judgments that will obviously not be recognized in other countries.[90] §23 of the Zivilprozessordnung grants jurisdiction to the German courts on the basis of the location of property of the defendant in Germany—a basis for jurisdiction that is widely seen as exorbitant and outlawed by Brussels I. One might argue that this rule goes too far and necessitates a moderation such as *forum non conveniens*. However, the German Bundesgerichtshof (Federal Supreme Court) reached a similar outcome in a different way: it found that the provision had to be interpreted in a limited way, so as to be in conformity with international law. The court used considerations such as the (weak) connection with Germany, the forum from which the defendant was barred, the fact that foreign law would have to be applied,

[85] Art 429c(15) of the Old Code of Civil Procedure. See also JP Verheul, 'The *forum (non) conveniens* in English and Dutch law and under some international conventions' [1986] ICLQ 413–423 at 416–419.

[86] Donzallaz, note 78 above, vol 3, 77.

[87] For instance, Rechtbank (Court of First Instance) the Hague, judgments of 3 October 1990 and 28 January 1991 and Rechtbank Alkmaar, judgment of 24 January 1991 [1991] *Nederlands Internationaal Privaatrecht* 99–100.

[88] See Rechtbank (Court of First Instance) of Arnhem, judgment of 13 July 1989 [1990] *Nederlands Internationaal Privaatrecht* 317–320.

[89] See CJJC van Nispen, AIM van Mierlo & MV Polak, *Burgerlijke rechtsvordering. Tekst & Commentaar* (Deventer: Kluwer, 2002) 4–5 & 12; K Boele-Woelki, 'Kodifikation des niederländischen Internationalen Privat- und Verfahrensrechts' [1995] *Praxis des internationalen Privat- und Verfahrensrechts* 264–271 at 270.

[90] Art 606a, para 4.

and forum shopping to find a reason not to base its jurisdiction on §23.[91]
The result is the same as *forum non conveniens:* the court has jurisdiction on
the basis of the rules but does not exercise it for reasons of comity.

The Institute of International Law adopted a resolution recognizing that **5.63**
the doctrine of *forum non conveniens* can sometimes be in the interests of
justice.[92] It stated that the following factors should be taken into account
when a stay is granted in favour of another court with jurisdiction:

a) the adequacy of the alternative forum;
b) the residence of the parties;
c) the location of the evidence (witnesses and documents) and the procedures for
   obtaining such evidence;
d) the law applicable to the issues;
e) the effect of applicable limitation or prescription periods;
f) the effectiveness and enforceability of any resulting judgment. [93]

It further stated that parallel proceedings should be avoided and emphasized the preference that the court first seised should have.[94]

FORUM NON CONVENIENS IN THE CONTEXT OF BRUSSELS I

During negotiations regarding the accession of Denmark, Ireland, and the **5.64**
United Kingdom to it, the Brussels Convention was changed on several
points. However, the doctrine of *forum non conveniens* was not introduced.
On the other hand it was not explicitly excluded either.[95] The Schlosser
Report states that the courts of the United Kingdom will no longer be able
to apply the doctrine of *forum non conveniens* since the jurisdiction granted
by the rules of the Convention are mandatory.[96] Some authors infer from

---

[91] Judgment of 2 July 1991; (115) [1992] *Entscheidungen des Bundesgerichtshofes in Zivilsachen*
90–99.
[92] At their session at Bruges in Belgium in 2003; [2004] Institute of International Law.
Yearbook, Part II, 81–112; available at <http://www.idi-iil.org>.
[93] Ibid, Art 2.
[94] Ibid, Arts 3–4
[95] An explicit exclusion is seen more and more frequently, e.g. the Hague Convention of
30 June 2005 on Choice of Court Agreements, Art 5(2).
[96] Schlosser Report, note 84 above,81, para 22, 97, para 78 and 125 para 181. See *Re Harrods*
[1992] Ch 72, para 29, where Dillon J found that the Reports (Jenard and Schlosser) did not
constitute authority since the Reporters did not contemplate the question, and since the doctrine was not as developed at the time of the negotiation of the Convention as it later became.
See TC Hartley, *Civil Jurisdiction and Judgments* (London: Sweet & Maxwell, 1984) 78–80;
R Geimer, 'The Right to Access to the Courts under the Brussels Convention' in Court of
Justice on the European Communities, *Civil Jurisdiction and Judgments in Europe* (London:
Butterworths, 1992) 39–40. Hogan, note 79 above, 475, stated the Schlosser Report did not

the absence of reference to the doctrine that it cannot be combined with the Regulation.[97] Others rightly point out that this silence cannot be interpreted either way: it could neither be said that the doctrine is definitely included, nor that it is definitely excluded.[98]

5.65 It is worth noting at this point that the doctrine of *forum non conveniens* was not as widely accepted in English law in 1978 (at the time of the negotiations and subsequent accession of the UK to the Brussels Convention) as it is today. The doctrine was already part of Scottish law, but not beyond doubt part of English law. The introduction into English law was gradual, but became definite in the *Spiliada* judgment of the House of Lords in 1987.[99]

5.66 Hartley stated as early as 1984:

as the European Court consists mainly of Continental lawyers, it is by no means certain that the English courts will be allowed to retain their discretion to stay.[100]

5.67 On the other side of the Channel in 1986, shortly after the Brussels Convention was extended to the UK, Droz wrote that the common law countries had compromised: they had abandoned the doctrine of *forum non conveniens*. [101] He stated that one could neither add to nor take away from the list in the treaty.[102] The doctrine of *forum non conveniens* had no place in the Convention.

---

address the problem that arose subsequently in *Re Harrods*. PA Stone, 'The Civil Jurisdiction and Judgments Acts 1982: Some Comments' [1983] ICLQ 477–499 at 496 states that it is still possible for an English court to grant a *forum non conveniens* stay in favour of a Scottish court. Those internal rules and the effect that the advent of the Brussels Convention had on them, will not be examined in this book.

[97] According to A Briggs, *The Conflict of Laws* (Oxford: Oxford University Press, 2002) 71, Art 5 of the Regulation shows an indirect awareness of *forum conveniens*. That provision grants jurisdiction to a forum that seems linked to the action and is therefore appropriate. However, the Regulation does not go further to accept what for English law is the other side of the coin, namely *forum non conveniens*.

[98] Nuyts, note 74 above, 214.

[99] *Spiliada*, note 83 above. See also the Court of Appeal judgment: [1987] 1 AC 460. See also *Atlantic Star v Bona Spes* [1936] 1 KB 382; *MacShannon v Rockware Glass Ltd* [1978] AC 795; F Salerno, 'European International civil procedure' in B von Hoffmann, *European Private International Law* (Nijmegen: Ars Aequi Libri, 1998) 153–156; Hogan, note 79 above, 473 on the principles laid down in the judgment.

[100] Hartley, note 96 above, 80.

[101] GAL Droz, 'Entrée en vigueur de la Convention de Bruxelles révisée sur la compétence judiciaire et l'exécution des jugements' [1987] *Revue critique de droit international privé* 251–303 at 255.

[102] Ibid, 258.

This might have been a bit over-optimistic. Instead, the UK has become **5.68** the personification of the clash between civil and common law, being constantly confronted with the differences between the two legal traditions and having to find bridges (or tunnels). The clash is nowhere more clearly visible than in the matter under discussion. The UK, together with Ireland, was faced with becoming part of an already-installed jurisdictional regime of civil law origin at the time of their accession to the European Communities. The Brussels Convention was originally negotiated by six civil law countries, and therefore did not contain a discretionary ground for refusing jurisdiction.[103]

When adopting the Brussels Convention into English law, the question of **5.69** *forum non conveniens* was not completely forgotten. The Civil Jurisdiction and Judgments Act 1982 (the 1982 Act), as amended by the Civil Jurisdiction and Judgments Act 1991, which enacted the Convention, provides:

> Nothing in this Act shall prevent any court in the United Kingdom from staying, sisting, striking out or dismissing any proceedings before it, on the ground of *forum non conveniens* or otherwise, where to do so is not inconsistent with the 1968 Convention [the Brussels Convention] or, as the case may be, the Lugano Convention.[104]

Although this provision has often been quoted in literature as well as case law, it has failed to give guidance.[105] It can be read as allowing or disallowing the use of *forum non conveniens*. In fact, it says nothing at all. Stating that the doctrine cannot be used if inconsistent with the Brussels Convention does not solve the problem of deciding when it is inconsistent with the Convention.

The first step towards answering that question is to determine who may **5.70** answer it. According to some English cases it was unnecessary to pose a preliminary question to the European Court of Justice since this was not a matter of the interpretation of European Union law. Rather, it was a matter

---

[103] Belgium, France, (West) Germany, Italy, Luxembourg, and the Netherlands.

[104] Sec 49.

[105] See the case law discussed below, paras 5.75 and following. In *Arkwright Mutual Insurance Co v Bryanston Insurance Co Ltd and Others*, [1990] 2 QB 649 at 653 Potter J commented as follows on this provision:

The section does not in itself assist in any way in deciding whether or not the exercise by the court of its hitherto undoubtedly wide discretion to stay proceedings on the grounds of *forum non conveniens* is, following incorporation of the Convention into English law, to be regarded as inconsistent with the Convention, either generally or in particular categories of case. For that, it is necessary to turn to the terms of the Convention. Further, when considering those terms, it is necessary to approach them unconstrained by the traditional rules of statutory construction previously applied by English courts, but guided by reference to wider sources that [*sic*] the wording of the Convention itself.

of the interpretation of English law. Therefore it took some time before the question reached the European Court of Justice. This first happened in *Re Harrods*, when the House of Lords finally disagreed with the Court of Appeal and referred a preliminary question to the European Court.[106] The case, however, was settled before the Court could deal with the question.[107]

5.71   The next prejudicial question came to the European Court of Justice in 2002 in *Owusu*.[108] The Court outlawed the doctrine (in its judgment of 2005) under the Brussels Convention in cases where jurisdiction is based on the domicile of the defendant in the EU. However, as indicated below, this judgment must not be interpreted more broadly than pure precedent law requires.

JURISDICTION BASED ON THE DOMICILE OF THE DEFENDANT IN THE EU

Other court in EU while jurisdiction based on the domicile of the defendant

5.72   Jurisdiction based on Article 2 is mandatory. A defendant has the right to be sued before the court of his domicile. Brussels I provides for another possibility, namely the place where a contract has been performed or where a tort was committed.[109] The structure of the Regulation makes it clear that this is an alternative jurisdiction and the plaintiff may choose. He may not be hampered in his choice by the fact that one of the courts sees itself unfit to hear the case.

5.73   The Rechtbank (Court of First Instance) of Arnhem (the Netherlands) considered a matter where proceedings were also pending in Germany.[110] It found it inappropriate in the closed system of the Brussels Convention for the judge to rule that he does not have jurisdiction for lack of sufficient connecting factors with the legal system of the forum state. In the case of proceedings pending in the Netherlands and in Germany, the Brussels Convention rule on *lis pendens* could be applied. This rule is based on strict priority, as explained. That was a policy choice and Brussels I does not permit declining jurisdiction for other reasons.

---

[106]   Case C–314/92 *Landinimor v Intercomfinanz*.

[107]   The case was removed from the roll. See OJ C 103 of 11 April 1994, 9.

[108]   Case C–281/02 *Owusu v Jackson* [2005] ECR I–1383; referring judgment of the Court of Appeal [2002] EWCA Civ 877.

[109]   Art 5, discussed in chapter 2 above.

[110]   Judgment of 13 July 1989, note 88 above; see also the following judgments in the matter, 1 March 1990 and 1 November 1990 [1990] *Nederlands Internationaal Privaatrecht* 317–320, no 227.

Other court in third State while jurisdiction based on the domicile of the defendant

This hypothesis has been much discussed and has given rise to different **5.74** opinions, in both case law and literature. It concerns several issues, such as whether Article 2 jurisdiction is mandatory, and whether Regulation-based jurisdiction can be declined. This is also the point on which the European Court of Justice has recently provided an answer in *Owusu*, stating that a stay on the basis of *forum non conveniens* could not be granted when the defendant was domiciled in England and the competing court was in Jamaica. Before discussing that case in further detail, it is worthwhile first to look into previous English judgments on the issue.

In *S & W Berisford plc and Another v New Hampshire Insurance Co* [111] juris- **5.75** diction was not based on the domicile of the defendant in the EU, but on an insurer's branch in the EU (thus presumed domicile).[112] The plaintiffs were a company based in London and its New York subsidiary. They brought an action against their insurer established in New Hampshire. The insurance contract was between the first plaintiff, Berisford, and the defendant, New Hampshire Insurance Co, through its London branch. It concerned theft of jewellery from the shop of the second plaintiff in New York. The Brussels Convention could be applied because of New Hampshire Insurance Co's establishment in England: an insurer with seat in a third State can be sued in the EU Member State where it has an establishment. The court found the forum clause to be non-exclusive and that it thus had jurisdiction on the basis of the establishment in England. The defendants applied for a stay on the basis of *forum non conveniens* since the relevant parties and facts were all located in New York. The English court considered whether it was possible to grant such a stay in the light of the Brussels Convention. It found that it was not. Jurisdiction under the Convention was mandatory and the court could not stay in favour of another court. The judge went on to state that, on the facts of the case, he would not have granted a stay in any event.

Arkwright Mutual Insurance Co v Bryanston Insurance Co Ltd and Others, like **5.76** *Berisford*, concerned insurance contracts, but this time reinsurance.[113] Some of the defendants were domiciled in England, so that jurisdiction over

---

[111] [1990] 2 QB 631.

[112] Art 9(2) of Brussels I (at that time Art 8(3) of the Brussels Convention).

[113] Note 105 above; see also Collins, '*Forum Non Conveniens* and the Brussels Convention', note 72 above. A Briggs, '*Spiliada* and the Brussels Convention' [1991] LMCLQ 10–15 concluded that the decisions in *Berisford* and *Arkwright* were probably wrong.

all the defendants could be based on that domicile.[114] In this case the proceedings in London were second to the proceedings in New York. There was no forum clause between the parties. The court, after considering the opposite views, followed the decision in *Berisford*. It found that the doctrine of *forum non conveniens* was inconsistent with the Brussels Convention. However, it explained that the result of these two cases would be limited in practice since:

a) as between the Member States of the European Community, many situations are catered for by the detailed rules on jurisdiction, which are founded on the notion of 'closest and most real connection' (for instance the rules on exclusive jurisdiction);

b) in relations with third States, the English court would retain the discretion to stay proceedings in cases of exclusive grounds of jurisdiction or forum clauses in favour of third States;

c) in cases that fall outside the scope of application of the Convention, the discretion to grant a stay, would remain, e.g. on applications by nationals of third States served with process on the basis of temporary presence in England.

The judge concluded by stating that, even if he were wrong, on the facts of the case he would not have granted the stay since he viewed London as the more appropriate forum.

5.77 Then came the controversial Appeal Court judgment in *Re Harrods (Buenos Aires) Ltd*, which conflicted with previous English jurisprudence, such as *Berisford* and *Arkwright*.[115] The House of Lords referred a preliminary question to the European Court of Justice, but before these questions could be responded to, the case was settled.[116]

---

[114] Arts 2 and 6 of Brussels I (at the time the same Arts of the Brussels Convention).

[115] Note 96 above. See North & Fawcett, note 72 above, 264–266; A Briggs & P Rees, *Civil Jurisdiction and Judgments* (3rd edn, London: LLP, 2002) p 225–226; A Briggs, 'Forum non conveniens and the Brussels Convention Again [1991] LQR 180–182; TC Hartley, 'The Brussels Convention and *forum non conveniens*' [1992] ELR 553–555; R Fentiman, 'Jurisdiction, discretion and the Brussels Convention' [1993] *Cornell International Law Journal* 59–99; Stone, note 96 above; Gaudemet-Tallon, 'Une menace pour la convention de Bruxelles?', note 67 above; Beaumont, note 77 above, 213–214; AR Schwartz, 'In Re Harrods Ltd: The Brussels Convention and the Proper Application of Forum Non Conveniens to Non-Contracting States' [1991–92] Fordham International Law Journal 174–206; P Kaye, 'The EEC Judgments Convention and the Outer World: Goodbye to Forum non conveniens?' [1992] *Journal of Business Law* 47–76, especially at 70–75, where the author prefers the solution of *Re Harrods* to the earlier judgments, although he admits that 'a very strong case indeed' should be required before a stay on the basis of *forum non conveniens* can be granted.

[116] Notes 106 and 107 above. A ruling in a case of mere theoretical importance is not permitted; see K Lenaerts & D Arts, *Europees Procesrecht* (3rd edn, Antwerp: Maklu, 2003) 77–82.

Harrods (Buenos Aires) Ltd was incorporated in England, but its business **5.78** was carried on exclusively in Argentina. Its central management and control was also in Argentina. Its two shareholders, Intercomfinanz SA (51 per cent) and Landinimor (49 per cent), were both domiciled in Switzerland. Landinimor brought proceedings against Intercomfinanz and Harrods in England. Intercomfinanz argued that Argentina was the competent forum and that a stay should be granted on the basis of *forum non conveniens*. The court of first instance refused the stay, although there was a strong case in favour of a stay on the basis of *forum non conveniens*. The court admitted that the defendant was *also* domiciled in Argentina. However, it held that the Brussels Convention removed the possibility of granting a stay on the basis of *forum non conveniens* since the defendant was domiciled in England.

The Appeal Court was of the opinion that the rule as to domicile in Article 2 **5.79** of the Brussels Convention was not so 'overwhelming and all-pervading' as to preclude a stay not explicitly required or permitted by the Convention. In support of this view, the Appeal Court referred to other exceptions to the rule of jurisdiction based on the domicile of the defendant, such as the rules on jurisdiction of the court of the place of performance of a contract, on multiple defendants, on exclusive jurisdiction, and on forum clauses.

It added that the *forum non conveniens* rule should not be too easily **5.80** discarded:

Any English Court should be slow to construe the Convention as to inhibit the valuable and important jurisdiction of stay on grounds of *forum non conveniens*, which is designed to promote comity, to encourage efficiency in the resolution of disputes, to prevent duplication of time and cost in litigation, and to avoid inconsistent judgments in two jurisdictions.[117]

Dillon LJ found it difficult to give much weight to the Jenard and Schlosser Reports regarding this question: he did not think that the reporters had contemplated the issue. He returned to the basis in the EC Treaty on which the Brussels Convention had been concluded.[118] Referring to the Schlosser Report, he stated that the desideratum was not achieved when the defendant was not domiciled in the EU. He stated that Schlosser was only concerned with defendants domiciled in Contracting States and choices between the courts of several Contracting States.[119] This was in line with the Jenard Report, which stated that the Convention aimed to create an

---

[117] *Re Harrods* , note 96 above, 94.
[118] Art 220 of the EC Treaty.
[119] *Re Harrods* , note 96 above, para 31 of the judgment.

autonomous system of jurisdiction rules between the Member States, in order to create legal certainty in relations between them.[120]

5.81 The Court found that to decline jurisdiction in favour of a court in a third State would not impair these goals of the Convention. In fact the result would be that there is no judgment in the EU, and nothing to be enforced under the Convention. Furthermore, the framework of the Convention would not be destroyed if English courts had the discretion to refuse jurisdiction on the basis that the courts of a non-Contracting State were the appropriate forum, in a case with which no other Contracting State was concerned. It did not agree that Article 2 had a wide mandatory effect, as contended by Hobhouse J in *Berisford*. As a result the Court found that it could grant a stay, applying the *forum non conveniens* rule.

5.82 The judgments in *Lubbe and Others v Cape Plc; Afrika and Others v Same* followed *Re Harrods*.[121] The case concerned more than 3,000 plaintiffs bringing proceedings in England claiming damages for personal injuries or death caused by exposure to asbestos in South Africa (by working or living in certain areas where the defendant was conducting asbestos-related activities). The question was whether the case should rather be tried in South Africa, where the harm was caused, where most of the plaintiffs lived, of which most of the plaintiffs were citizens, and where the evidence was situated. The defendant, a company incorporated in England, was in the business of mining, processing, and selling asbestos. It obtained companies in the same business incorporated in South Africa and eventually transferred these companies to a South African holding company, which was wholly owned by the defendant. Those companies were later sold, but the defendant kept an interest in them until 1989. At the date of service, however, the defendant had no assets in South Africa.

5.83 The defendants applied for a stay on the ground that a court in South Africa was clearly a more appropriate forum. The judge at first instance granted the stay, finding that South Africa was the natural forum for the trial. The plaintiffs appealed that decision and the Court of Appeal lifted the stay.[122] An intricate set of proceedings followed, including joining various actions into a group action. A judge at first instance again concluded that South Africa was a more appropriate forum and ordered a stay.

---

[120] Jenard Report, note 71 above, 7 & 15.
[121] Note 75 above.
[122] [1998] CLC 1559.

The Court of Appeal refused the appeal without considering Article 2 of **5.84**
the Brussels Convention.[123] In order to avoid a further delay, the plaintiffs
had not pursued their initial submission that a stay on the basis of *forum
non conveniens* was contrary to the Brussels Convention and that a preliminary question had to be posed to the European Court of Justice.[124] After
the appeal was refused by the Court of Appeal, the plaintiffs appealed to
the House of Lords, where the main issues in the case were the possibility
of continuing the action in the form of a group action in South Africa and
the availability of legal aid for the plaintiffs.[125] On the basis of those considerations the House of Lords removed the stay in order that the English
courts could hear the action. For that reason their Lordships did not consider whether the stay of an action on the ground of *forum non conveniens*
was in conflict with the Brussels Convention.[126]

At this stage, there were contradictory judgments in England. It was **5.85**
unclear whether, if the English court had jurisdiction on the basis of the
domicile of the defendant, it could decline such jurisdiction in favour of a
court in a third State. The latest view, it seemed, was that Article 2 of
Brussels I did not grant mandatory jurisdiction to the EU Member State
court when another court in a third State also has jurisdiction. Therefore
the *forum non conveniens* rule could be applied.

Owusu finally showed the red light.[127] Mr Owusu, domiciled in England, **5.86**
went on holiday to Jamaica, where he rented a flat from another domiciliary of England (Mr Jackson). Mr Owusu went into the sea from a private
beach. Diving into the water, he hit his head on a sandbank and broke the

---

[123] [2000] 1 Lloyd's Rep 139.
[124] Ibid, 165
[125] [2000] 2 Lloyd's Rep 383.
[126] Ibid, 394.
[127] *Owusu*, note 108 above. See also E Peel, '*Forum non conveniens* and European ideals'
[2005] LMCLQ 363–377; A Briggs, '*Forum non conveniens* and ideal Europeans' [2005] LMCLQ
378–382; A Briggs, 'The Death of Harrods: *Forum non conveniens* and the European Court'
[2005] LQR 535–540; TC Hartley, 'The EU and the systematic dismantling of the common law
conflict of laws' [2005] ICLQ 813–828 at 824–828; J Harris, 'Stays of proceedings and the
Brussels Convention' [2005] ICLQ 933–950; R Fentiman, 'Civil jurisdiction and third States:
Owusu and after' [2006] CML Rev 705–734; BJ Rodger, '*Forum non conveniens* Post-*Owusu*'
[2006] *Journal of Private International Law* 71–97; G Cuniberti, '*Forum non conveniens* and the
Brussels Convention' [2006] ICLQ 973–981; H Duintjer Tebbens, 'From Jamaica with pain' in
P van der Grinten & T Heukels (eds), *Cross Borders. Essays in European and Private International
Law, Nationality Law and Islamic Law in honour of Frans van der Velden* (Deventer: Kluwer, 2006)
95–103; C Chalas [2005] *Revue critique de droit international privé* 708–722; C Thiele, '*Forum non
conveniens* im Lichte europäischen Gemeinschaftsrechts' [2002] *Recht der Internationalen
Wirtschaft* 696–700 at 689–699; H Tagaras, 'Chronique de jurisprudence de la Cour de justice
relative à la Convention de Bruxelles' [2006] *Cahiers de droit européen* 483–553, 507–514.

fifth cervical vertebra in his spine. He became quadriplegic. He then brought a claim for damages in England against Mr Jackson, the owner of the villa, in contract. He added damages claims in tort against Jamaican-domiciled parties as the owners, occupiers, or persons who might have had responsibility for the management and upkeep of the beach.

5.87 The defendants domiciled in Jamaica stated various reasons in support of their argument that the courts of Jamaica were in a better position to hear the case: that most of the defendants were domiciled there, the facts happened there, possible witnesses were there, and investigations could take place there. The first defendant (Mr Jackson), although domiciled in England, also argued that the matter was most closely connected to Jamaica. His insurance policy was such that it would not pay out for damages awarded by courts of first instance outside Jamaica.

5.88 The judge found that no Brussels Convention point arose with regard to the defendants domiciled in Jamaica. He stated that, but for the Brussels Convention, he would have had no hesitation in holding that Jamaica was a more appropriate forum than England. Since the Brussels Convention made a stay as to the first defendant impossible, he found that the entire case should be tried in England. It would not be opportune to grant a stay for some defendants, and not others; that would only result in duplication, and possibly different conclusions.

5.89 On appeal, the Court of Appeal stayed the proceedings and referred two preliminary questions to the European Court of Justice:

1. Is it inconsistent with the Brussels Convention on Jurisdiction and Enforcement of Judgments 1968, where a claimant contends that jurisdiction is founded on Article 2, for a Court of a Contracting State to exercise a discretionary power, available under its national law, to decline to hear proceedings brought against a person domiciled in that State in favour of the courts of a non-Contracting State:
   (a) if the jurisdiction of no other Contracting State under the 1968 Convention is in issue;
   (b) if the proceedings have no connecting factors to any other Contracting State?
2. If the answer to question 1(a) or (b) is yes, is it inconsistent in all circumstances or only in some and if so which?[128]

The Court of Appeal explained that no other EU Member State Court was involved and that the competing jurisdictions were England and Jamaica. If the language of Article 2 were mandatory in this context, no alternative

---

[128] [2002] EWCA Civ 877; Thiele, note 126 above, 696–700.

jurisdiction under Article 5 would exist, since the places of performance and damage were in Jamaica, a third State.

The Court of Appeal emphasized that *Owusu* concerned *forum non conven-* **5.90** *iens*, but that the question with regard to discretionary *versus* mandatory exceptions was broader: it also affected the doctrine of *lis pendens*, prorogation of jurisdiction, or immovable property where third States were concerned. If Article 2 were mandatory, a defendant domiciled in England had to be sued in England in all those cases, even if the Convention would allow or require the action to be brought in another Member State if a domiciliary of another Member State was involved.

The Court of Appeal further explained that, if Article 4 applied, the plain- **5.91** tiff could not be sure which court had jurisdiction. For the English court to refuse jurisdiction in favour of the courts of a third State on the basis of *forum non conveniens* would not impair the object of the Convention. There could then be no judgment of an English court for enforcement in the EU.

The judgment of the Court of Appeal in *Owusu* highlights an important **5.92** problem in Brussels I and its interaction with national law: that of multiple defendants. Suing one defendant in England because he is domiciled there does not seem completely unjust. What does not seem fair is dragging a group of other defendants, who have no connection with England, to the English court on such a tenuous link as the domicile of a person who is not the central figure in the litigation. The other defendants will be sued on the basis of Brussels I if they are domiciled in the EU, and on the basis of national law if they are domiciled in third States. However, it is Brussels I that has opened the door, because of the domicile of any one of the defendants, without regard to whether such a defendant is central to the dispute.

Advocate General Léger found that Article 2 was mandatory except when **5.93** derogations were permitted by the Convention, for instance the provisions on exclusive jurisdiction, forum clauses, *lis pendens*, and related actions. In relations with EU Member States, Article 2 could also be derogated from by the provisions on special jurisdiction (e.g. contracts or torts) and protective jurisdiction (e.g. insurance, consumer, and employment contracts).[129] He further found that Article 2 should be applied even if both original parties (the plaintiff and first defendant) were domiciled in the same EU Member State.[130]

---

[129] *Owusu*, note 108 above, paras 241–257.
[130] Ibid, paras 112–115, 125, and 163–169.

5.94 The Advocate General was of the opinion that *forum non conveniens* was difficult to reconcile with the objectives of the Convention/Regulation, which had largely been inspired by civil law rules. He stated that *forum non conveniens* undermined legal certainty and detracted from the effectiveness of the Convention/Regulation. In this line of thought he considered the intentions of the states at the time of negotiation. However, it must be said that the doctrine of *forum non conveniens* has evolved since the negotiation of the 1978 version of the Brussels Convention, which was the version by which the United Kingdom became Party.[131] Even at that time the doctrine had not been explicitly excluded.

5.95 Furthermore the Advocate General stated that only two EU Member States had the rule of *forum non conveniens* enshrined in their legal systems, and permitting it would result in discrimination. It was irrelevant, in his view, whether the competing court was in an EU Member State or in a third State. While the discrimination argument has merit, it does make the world of difference whether the competing court is in a Member State or in a third State: if the dispute has no connection with the EU and recognition in the EU is not at issue, why then should the strict EU interpretation of Brussels I preclude the staying of an action in favour of a third State court?

5.96 In his view the English Court's second question was broad and sought to ascertain when the doctrine of *forum non conveniens* could be applied. According to him that question was inadmissible since it was hypothetical, and the European Court of Justice should only respond to what is strictly necessary to assist the administration of justice.[132]

5.97 The European Court of Justice's judgment was short: declining Convention-based jurisdiction in favour of a third State court was not permitted. This holds true, *even if* the jurisdiction of no other EU Member State court were at issue. The motivation of the European Court of Justice was again solidly grounded in principles of EU law. The Court recalled the fact that Article 2 was of a mandatory nature and that the authors of the Convention did not include an exception for *forum non conveniens*. Then the Court emphasized the importance of legal certainty and the legal protection of persons in the EU by common rules on jurisdiction which were designed to provide certainty as to the allocation of jurisdiction among the courts in

---

[131] Convention of Accession of 9 October 1978 of the Kingdom of Denmark, of Ireland and of the United Kingdom of Great Britain and Northern Ireland to the Convention on jurisdiction and enforcement of judgments in civil and commercial matters and to the Protocol on its interpretation by the Court of Justice, OJ L 304 of 30 October 1978, 1.

[132] *Owusu*, note 108 above, paras 71 and 81.

the EU. Furthermore, the ECJ was worried that permitting the application of *forum non conveniens* in the context of the Brussels Convention would have the result that the Convention would no longer be applied uniformly in all EU Member States, because the rule only exists in a few of the Member States. The Court did not consider the reasons defendants might have to request a stay on the basis of *forum non conveniens*. Neither did it pay attention to the fact that a defendant in no way harmed the guarantee of legal certainty (or deprived another of it) if he was the one requesting the stay. The second question remained unanswered, for the reasons given by the Advocate General.

The outcome of this case is a shame. No other EU Member State was **5.98** involved. The mere fact that one of the defendants was domiciled in England in an international dispute brought the case under Brussels I, while it really should have been outside the European judicial area.[133] The result is that all the other defendants, who had no connection with the European judicial area, were dragged into rules that were not created for them and are not concerned with their interests.

Some authors argue that the distinction between attributing jurisdiction **5.99** and declining jurisdiction should receive more attention.[134] They disagree with the assertion that, because jurisdiction is mandatory, it cannot be declined. There are examples where Article 2 jurisdiction can be declined, such as where a court in another EU Member State has exclusive jurisdiction, or is appointed by a forum clause, or has been seised of the matter first (*lis pendens*). Instead, the question is whether declining jurisdiction (which the court clearly has) falls within the scope of the Regulation when the other court is in a third State. Then the resulting judgment would never influence other EU Member States: there would be no EU judgment that could circulate freely. If recognition and enforcement is necessary in other EU Member States, this will have to be achieved under their national law.

The issue of protecting litigating parties does not provide a sound argu- **5.100** ment for eliminating *forum non conveniens*. The plaintiff has a chance to sue the defendant at his own domicile, but this is not a right that can never be detracted from. The Regulation itself provides exceptions and alternatives

---

[133] As Fentiman, 'Jurisdiction, discretion and the Brussels Convention', note 115 above, 72 stated: '[a] court need not, so to speak, switch exclusively into Convention mode simply because it has jurisdiction under Article 2'. He ventures further to argue how the doctrine of *forum non conveniens* is compatible with the Brussels Convention.

[134] Fentiman, '*Owusu* and after', note 127 above, 714–716; Cuniberti, note 126 above, 974–976.

to this rule. The defendant, on the other hand, is protected by the existence of the rule: he asks for the stay.[135] If he himself applies for a stay so that another court can hear the case, he probably does not need protection against his own choices.

5.101 The European Court of Justice's formulation was general. Maybe the English courts wanted the doubts solved once and for all. However, this case cannot and should not be the authority for disallowing the application of the rule of *forum non conveniens* to decline jurisdiction in situations where a court in a third State has exclusive jurisdiction or has been prorogated by the choice of the parties. The Court specifically refrained from answering the more general question by the Court of Appeal on when *forum non conveniens* might be permitted, since the answer would have been hypothetical.[136] Hopefully the concise answer by the European Court of Justice will not prevent the use of the doctrine in matters where it can be of real value.[137]

5.102 However, the European Court of Justice's *Lugano* opinion is more worrying.[138] In this case the court found that Article 2 jurisdiction is always compulsory, including when the jurisdiction of a third State court is exclusive, or based on a forum clause. The ECJ came to this conclusion in an analysis of the nature of the Regulation's jurisdiction rules in order to determine whether the European Community had exclusive external competence to conclude the updated version of the Lugano Convention with Iceland, Norway, and Switzerland.[139] In this process, the ECJ examined how the Lugano Convention would change the rules of Brussels I. The response is obiter: the case did not deal with the exact question of the clash between Article 2 jurisdiction and exclusive jurisdiction in, or a forum clause for, a court in a third State. Hopefully the ECJ will receive a preliminary question on the point and reconsider. The result for third States and for party autonomy is shocking: will forum clauses for third State courts never be respected if the defendant lives in the EU? How can

---

[135] Hartley, 'The EU and systematic dismantling', note 126 above, 827; Harris, note 126 above, 937.

[136] *Owusu*, note 108 above, para 50–52.

[137] Such as in cases of exclusive jurisdiction of a third State court (chapter 3, paras 3.10 and following, especially para 3.16) and of prorogation of a third State court (chapter 4, paras 4.51 and following).

[138] Opinion 1/03 *Competence of the Community to conclude the new Lugano Convention on jurisdiction and the recognition and enforcement of judgments in civil and commercial matters* [2006] ECR I–1145.

[139] This issue is discussed in more detail in chapter 7.

such an approach exist in a world of international litigation? It is submitted that this result should be amended in the text of the Regulation.

NATIONAL RULES ON JURISDICTION (INCORPORATED INTO BRUSSELS I)

General

If the defendant is not domiciled in the EU, Brussels I refers the EU Member **5.103** State courts back to the national rules on jurisdiction.[140] As explained, this provision has been interpreted by the European Court of Justice as part of the scheme of the Regulation. Thus, those national rules are drawn into the Regulation by the reference to them. This is an important point of departure. If those rules are part of the Regulation, is *forum non conveniens* excluded when they apply? Obviously the case is different where jurisdiction is based on the domicile of the defendant rather than on service on the defendant when he was present in the country. Should that second rule now also become mandatory if the defendant is domiciled in a third State? The result is far-reaching, since a judgment can be recognized and enforced in all EU Member States.

The other variable is whether the court in favour of which a stay is granted, **5.104** is an EU Member State court or not. That may bring about a clash between the rules on *forum non conveniens* and *lis pendens*. An analysis of the English case law is once again necessary.

Other court in EU while jurisdiction based on national rules

The 'Xin Yang' and the 'An Kang Jiang' concerned a collision between two **5.105** ships at Vlaardingen in the Netherlands.[141] The vessel 'Jo Aspen' was moored at the Van Ommeren Tank Terminal and was loading when struck by the 'Xin Yang', which had a Chinese crew and a Dutch pilot. The 'Xin Yang' was arrested to secure Van Ommeren's claim for damages to the jetty. Two days later, the plaintiffs brought proceedings in the Queens Bench Division (Admiralty Court) in England and arrested the 'An Kang Jiang', sister ship to the 'Xin Yang'. Two days later the defendants (the ship-owners) submitted a petition to the District Court in Rotterdam

---

[140] Art 4 of Brussels I.
[141] [1996] 2 Lloyd's Rep 217. On this judgment, see also JJ Newton, '*Forum non conveniens* in Europe (again)' [1997] LMCLQ 337–344. Prior to the judgment, Verheul, note 85 above, 422 agreed that this would be the correct solution.

(the Netherlands) to limit their liability. They also applied to the English court to stay its jurisdiction on the basis of *forum non conveniens*, stating that the District Court of Rotterdam was better placed to hear the dispute. It was clear that both courts would apply the same law, namely the Convention on Limitation of Liability for Marine Claims.[142] The case, unlike *Berisford, Arkwright, Re Harrods, Lubbe* and *Owusu*, concerned the jurisdiction of two EU Member States.

5.106 The English court found that where jurisdiction was based on Article 4, the court retained discretion to stay the action on the basis of *forum non conveniens*.[143] This was true whether the more convenient forum was one in an EU Member State or in a third State.[144] The judge then considered the combined effect of the rules of *forum non conveniens* and *lis pendens:* if the court first seised (in this case the English court) were to stay the proceedings on the basis of *forum non conveniens*, it would not be a case 'where the jurisdiction of the court first seised is established'.[145] By this comment, the judge made it clear that the staying of an action on the basis of *forum non conveniens* was part of the establishment of jurisdiction, therefore a jurisdiction rule. If, however, the foreign court viewed the matter differently, and declined to hear the case on the basis of *lis pendens,* or for another reason, the stay in the English proceedings could be lifted.[146] Therefore the stay on the basis of *forum non conveniens* was granted.

5.107 This view of the relationship between *lis pendens* and *forum non conveniens* has been criticized.[147] The argument is that, if the court first seised stays an action, it remains the court first seised so that a court in the EU later seised will be bound to decline jurisdiction by the *lis pendens* rule. This is probably correct, upon an interpretation of the current wording of the

---

[142] Concluded in London in 1976.

[143] However, Newton, note 141 above, states that viewing the jurisdiction as based on Article 4 was not entirely correct. The jurisdiction was based on the International Convention for the Unification of Certain Rules relating to the Arrest of Seagoing Ships (Brussels, 1952). According to the Schlosser Report (note 84 above, para 240, p 140), and according to Advocate General in Case C-406/92 *The owners of the cargo lately laden on board the ship 'Tatry' v the owners of the ship 'Maciej Rataj'* [1994] ECR I–5439 (at para 9), the jurisdiction rules of the specific Convention (in this case the Arrest Convention) are to be regarded as if they were provisions of the Brussels Convention. This was also the conclusion of the European Court of Justice in Case C–148/03 *Nürnberger Allgemeine Versicherungs AG v Portbridge Transport International BV* [2004] ECR I–10327. This view is in line with the approach that Art 4 is part of the system of the Regulation.

[144] *The 'Xin Yang' and the 'An Kang Jiang'*, note 141 above, 222.

[145] Ibid, 222 of the judgment; Art 27(2) of Brussels I.

[146] *The 'Xin Yang' and the 'An Kang Jiang'*, note 141 above, 222.

[147] For example by Newton, note 141 above, 341.

lis pendens rule. The rule does not refer to assuming and declining jurisdiction, but merely to being seised. A foreign court would probably have difficulty in making a distinction that the Regulation itself does not make.

Sarrio SA v Kuwait Investment Authority, a later case, falls in the same **5.108** category.[148] Sarrio, a Spanish company, sold its paper business to Torraspapel. The Kuwait Investment Authority (KIA), through its London-based Kuwait Investment Office (KIO), controlled Grupo Torras (GT), of which Torraspapel was a subsidiary. The KIA was the investment arm of the government of Kuwait and therefore clearly not domiciled in the EU. As part of the transfer, Sarrio had a 'put and call' option in the contract, entitling it to transfer the shares in Torraspapel back to GT in three tranches. GT made the first payment, but not the second and third, having been placed in receivership.

Sarrio commenced proceedings in Madrid to hold KIA liable for the sums **5.109** that GT was supposed to pay. A year later Sarrio brought two actions in England claiming damages for mis-statements by or on behalf of KIA (regarding the books of the companies), which had induced Sarrio to enter into the sales contract. Since KIA was not domiciled in the EU, jurisdiction could have been based on a national ground of jurisdiction. However, the Kuwait Investment Office was its London-based branch.

KIA applied for a stay of the actions in the English courts, relying on **5.110** *lis pendens* or related actions. The court of first instance (Queen's Bench, commercial court) held that the provision on *lis pendens* could not apply since the causes of action were not the same.[149] The Queen's Bench then stayed the proceedings on the basis of the provision on related actions. Sarrio appealed that decision, and KIA cross-appealed against the refusal of the court to stay proceedings on the basis of *lis pendens*.

The Court of Appeal reversed the judgment of the court of first instance. **5.111** It reached the same conclusion regarding *lis pendens*.[150] However, it found that the actions were not related as the court of first instance had found.[151] The court then considered whether the proceedings could be stayed on the ground of *forum non conveniens*. It found that if jurisdiction were based on a national rule, nothing in the Convention would prevent a stay. In this

---

[148] [1997] 1 Lloyd's Rep 113. This case was reversed on appeal, but on the related actions point; *forum non conveniens* was not considered by the House of Lords; [1998] 1 Lloyd's Rep 129. See the discussion below, para 5.143.

[149] [1996] 1 Lloyd's Rep 650.

[150] Note 148 above, 120.

[151] Ibid, 121–122. On this point the House of Lords ruled differently (see para 5.143 below), and then did not consider *forum non conveniens*.

case the defendants requested a stay in favour of the Spanish courts, where they were going to bring proceedings. The fact that the other court was in an EU Member State, did not exclude the possibility of applying the doctrine of *forum non conveniens*. [152] On the facts the Court of Appeal refused to exercise its discretion in favour of a stay. One of the considerations was the delay that would be caused by the nature of the proceedings in Spain (where the two actions would have to be accumulated).[153]

5.112 This case highlights the difficult interaction between *forum non conveniens* and the EU rules. The difficulty with *lis pendens* could also arise here. If the stay had been granted and the parties subsequently instituted proceedings in a Spanish court, that court would probably have considered the English court to be 'first seised', but it would also have noted that the jurisdiction of the court first seised was not 'established'. (Technically the court first seised would have had jurisdiction but had declined to exercise it, with the result that the jurisdiction had not been 'established'.) Furthermore, the nature and time of proceedings in other EU Member State courts may never be taken in consideration in *the club of friends*.[154] If one were to apply the EU rules of *lis pendens* or related actions, that mutual trust and loyalty would be inbuilt. However, when applying *forum non conveniens* an English court still has a tool to express its limited trust in other EU legal systems, because of the element of discretion contained in this rule. It is also worth noticing that there may be a different test for related actions than for *forum non conveniens*. [155]

5.113 In *Haji-Ioannou and Others v Frangos and Others* [156] the question of Article 4 in relation to other EU courts arose only obiter. Mr Haji-Ioannou was the father-in-law of Mr Frangos. They were both in the shipping business and Mr Haji-Iaonnou gave sums of money to Mr Frangos to enable him and his various companies to buy vessels. Mr Frangos also worked for Mr Haji-Ioannou. After the marriage between Mr Frangos and Mr Haji-Ioannou's daughter broke down, Mr Haji-Ioannou and a number of companies belonging to him brought proceedings against Mr Frangos for embezzlement. Mr Frangos's domicile was in dispute.[157] The Court of Appeal found that Mr Frangos was in fact domiciled in Greece according to the Greek rule on special domicile, which meant that Mr Frangos would have to be served in Greece, the state of his domicile, and the English court

---

[152] Ibid, 122–123.
[153] Ibid, 126.
[154] Case C–116/02 *Erich Gasser GmbH v MISAT Srl* [2003] ECR I–14693, para 73.
[155] These two rules will be compared below, para 5.141 and following.
[156] [1999] 2 Lloyd's Rep 337 (CA).
[157] This issue in this case has been discussed in chapter 2 above, para 2.16.

lacked jurisdiction. In the event that this conclusion was wrong, the Court of Appeal also considered the hypothesis of the defendant being domiciled in a third State, namely Monaco (Article 4). In that scenario the court confirmed the judgment in *Sarrio*, stating that, when jurisdiction is based on Article 4, a court may stay proceedings in favour of a court in another EU Member State:

if in a case such as the present a Court such as this defers to the Court of another Contracting State which in its considered judgment is significantly better placed, for whatever reason, to administer true justice between the parties, such deference involves not jurisdictional imperialism or chauvinism nor any clash or competition between jurisdictions but the truest comity between Courts of Contracting States.[158]

The Court admitted that a question should be posed to the European Court of Justice regarding this matter, but stated that it could not do so in the present case because of the conclusion it had reached regarding Article 2 and the domicile of the defendant.[159]

The application of the *forum non conveniens* rule poses difficulties with **5.114** regard to the relations between EU Member States, as has also been pointed out in the previous paragraphs. The doctrine in itself is not contrary to the loyalty that is expected between EU Member State courts. Quite to the contrary, declining to hear a case so that another court can do so is a sign of trust and respect. It is the consideration of the qualities of the other legal system that might pose difficulties in EU law. It should be possible to allow the rule, while keeping the requirement of mutual trust in mind.

The application of the *forum non conveniens* rule to cases where jurisdiction **5.115** had been based on national law is different to where jurisdiction had been based on Article 2. Therefore it is submitted that *Owusu* is not directly transposable. True, the European Court of Justice found that the national bases for jurisdiction have been incorporated into the system of Brussels I. However, it has not (yet) ruled that those rules are compulsory. It would amount to great unfairness if they became so. They have been classified as exorbitant, and can only be used against defendants domiciled in third States. The resulting judgments can be recognized and enforced in all EU Member States. It is submitted that the rules should then at least be confined to their natural limits. These defendants should not be further disadvantaged. Where an English rule can be pushed back on the facts of a case,

---

[158] Note 156 above, 346.
[159] Ibid, 348. A question before the European Court of Justice may not be of mere theoretical importance. See Lenaerts & Arts, note 116 above, 77–82.

so that serving the defendant will not always lead to an English judgment, Brussels I cannot reasonably take that limitation away.[160]

Other court in third State while jurisdiction based on national rules

5.116 The argument that to disallow a stay of proceedings on the basis of *forum non conveniens* would widen the traditional bases for jurisdiction too far, would be true whether the other court is a third State court or an EU Member State court. Therefore, if the conclusion in the previous paragraph has been that the rule should be retained, the conclusion here is all the stronger: no EU principles are concerned; the issue of mutual trust is not at stake.

EXCLUSIVE JURISDICTION IN A THIRD STATE

5.117 According to Brussels I, if a defendant is domiciled in an EU Member State, the courts of that state have jurisdiction. The jurisdiction is mandatory.[161] If a court has jurisdiction, there is nothing in the Regulation to permit it to consider the fact that a court in a third State has exclusive jurisdiction on a head of jurisdiction similar to one that exists in Brussels I, for instance immovable property. The result, however, could lead to unfair results. Accordingly Droz developed the theory of the reflexive effect.[162] This theory states that, where an EU Member State court has jurisdiction, but a third State court has exclusive jurisdiction, the Member State must refuse to accept jurisdiction on the basis of a reflexive effect: the situation mirrors that of an EU Member State having exclusive jurisdiction and therefore the exclusive jurisdiction of the third State court must be respected. Except for the discretion element, the effect of this theory is very similar to *forum non conveniens*. [163] A court that has jurisdiction declines to

---

[160] See also Collins, note 70 above, vol I, 469–470; Briggs, *The Conflict of Laws*, note 97 above, 86–87; Stone, note 96 above, 496–297; Huber, *'Forum non conveniens* und EuGVÜ', note 72 above, 982.

[161] Schlosser Report, note 84 above, para 22, p 81; *Owusu*, note 108 above.

[162] GAL Droz, *Pratique de la convention de Bruxelles du 27 septembre 1968* (Paris: Librairie Dalloz 1973) 34; GAL Droz, 'La Convention de San Sebastian alignant la Convention de Bruxelles sur la Convention de Lugano' [1990] *Revue critique de droit international privé* 1–21, 14; P Gothot & D Holleaux, *La convention de Bruxelles du 27.9.1968* (Paris: Jupiter, 1985) 84; Gaudemet-Tallon, 'Les frontières extérieures', note 72 above, 95–97; discussed in more detail in chapter 3 above, para 3.10 and following.

[163] See A Nuyts, 'La théorie de l'effet réflexe', in M Storme & G de Leval (eds), *Le droit processuel & judiciaire européen* (Bruges: die Keure, 2003) 73–89 at 84; see also Stone, note 96 above, 297 stating that the *forum non conveniens* doctrine can be applied in this case.

exercise that jurisdiction in favour of another court which has jurisdiction and is better placed to hear the action.

However, the European Court of Justice brought this pragmatic solution **5.118** to disarray when it was considering the external competences of the European Community to conclude the updated Lugano Convention.[164] It implicitly stated that it was impossible under Brussels I to decline jurisdiction in favour of a court in a third State that has exclusive jurisdiction. The argumentation was formalistic and this conclusion was incidental, since the case did not deal with a matter specifically at point.

It is submitted that either the reflexive effect, or rules of national law like **5.119** *forum non conveniens* should be permitted to safeguard the exclusive jurisdiction of third States. Possibly this will have to be done in an explicit provision of Brussels I.

FORUM CLAUSE IN FAVOUR OF A THIRD STATE

As with the problem above, there is no rule requiring courts to refuse to **5.120** hear a case when there is a forum clause in favour of a third State court. Droz would have applied the reflexive effect in this situation: respect the forum clause. The situation is similar to that of an exclusive head of jurisdiction in a third State.[165] The European Court of Justice has, however, caused difficulty in the recent *Lugano* opinion.[166] It implicitly stated that the EU Member State courts could not decline regulation-based jurisdiction for the reason that a court in a third State had been chosen in a forum clause.

A peek into English case law indicates the use that the *forum non conven-* **5.121** *iens* rule can have in situations where courts in third States had been chosen in forum agreements. *Ace Insurance* [167] was based on the Lugano Convention, but turns on the same question as would have been the case under the Brussels Convention.[168] The contract between Zurich Insurance Company (ZIC), established in Switzerland, and its reinsurer, Ace Insurance, contained a 'service of suit' clause to the effect that ZIC would accept the jurisdiction of any court in the United States of America

---

[164] *Lugano* Opinion, note 138 above.

[165] See also Stone, note 96 above, 297 stating that the *forum non conveniens* doctrine can be applied in this case, just as to the case of exclusive jurisdiction in a third State.

[166] *Lugano* Opinion, note 138 above.

[167] *Ace Insurance SA–NV (Formerly Cigna Insurance Co of Europe SA–NV) v Zurich Insurance Co and Zurich American Insurance Co* [2001] 1 Lloyd's Rep 618.

[168] It was not possible, of course, to refer a preliminary question to the European Court of Justice since this possibility only exists in the framework of the European Union.

of competent jurisdiction. When an accident occurred, Ace instituted proceedings in England against ZIC and Zurich American Insurance Company (ZAIC), its new US branch, for a declaration of non-liability. By English or US law, the choice of the American court would not be seen as excluding other fora, such as is the case under Brussels I and Lugano Convention. Nevertheless, the American court would have jurisdiction and this is sufficient for the application of *forum non conveniens*. ZIC and ZAIC applied for a stay in favour of proceedings in Texas on the grounds of *forum non conveniens*. The judge at first instance granted the stay, upon which Ace Insurance appealed to the Court of Appeal.

5.122   The main question was whether the stay would be incompatible with the Lugano Convention. The English court had jurisdiction since ZIC submitted to the English court (with a reservation regarding its *forum non conveniens* argument).[169] The Court of Appeal, relying on the *Re Harrods* judgment, found that it could grant a stay in favour of a third State where there was a forum clause, similar to those provided for by the Convention itself, but in favour of that third State.[170]

5.123   Even after *Owusu* an English court found that *forum non conveniens* could be used when there was a forum clause in favour of a court in a third State (in this case Zambia). The court finally lifted the stay, because of the specific facts of the case and the other parties involved.[171] It is uncertain whether the court could have come to this conclusion after the *Lugano* opinion.

5.124   The *forum non conveniens* rule seems a good solution for the gap in Brussels I: a facility to decline Regulation-based jurisdiction in favour of a third State court which has been appointed in a forum clause. If the European Court of Justice genuinely meant to annul this possibility, then permission to decline jurisdiction in favour of a third State court chosen in a forum clause should be inserted in the text of the Regulation. At present, it seems that the only way for third States to safeguard forum clauses in favour of their courts against EU courts, is by ratifying the Hague Choice of Court Convention in the hope that the EC does the same.[172] That Convention

---

[169]   Art 18 Lugano and Brussels Conventions; Art 24 of Brussels I.

[170]   Note 167 above, 626.

[171]   *Konkola Copper Mines Plc v Coromin* [2005] EWHC 898 (Comm); Fentiman, '*Owusu* and after', note 127 above.

[172]   Hague Convention of 30 June 2005 on Choice of Court Agreements; available at <http://www.hcch.net>.

will impose an obligation on courts in EU Member States to decline jurisdiction if the courts in another Contracting State had been chosen.[173]

FORUM NON CONVENIENS IN THE EU CIVIL JURISDICTION REGULATIONS?

The revision and elaboration of Brussels II, the so-called Brussels II *bis*,   **5.125**
contained a surprise: a form of *forum non conveniens*? An EU court may
transfer a case to a court that is better placed to hear it.[174] The rule only
applies in cases of parental responsibility, and not in claims for divorce,
legal separation, or annulment of marriages. It attempts to take the reality
of moving children into account, and acknowledges the need for flexibility. The large number of possible courts with jurisdiction may of course
result in more than one court having jurisdiction to hear a specific case.
The Regulation does not allow courts under such circumstances to decline
their own jurisdiction. Rather, it encourages dialogue between the courts
to ensure that the court that is best placed to hear a case, in fact does so.

A court may transfer a case upon application by a party, of its own motion,   **5.126**
or upon application by a court in another EU Member State with which
the child has a particular connection. The initiative by one of the courts is
only possible if at least one of the parties accepts the transfer. The provision explicitly states that this type of transfer is an exception.

Since it is not based on the declining of jurisdiction as a unilateral act, one   **5.127**
cannot really speak of a *forum non conveniens* rule. The principle present
here is acceptable in the civil law systems because the discretion is subjected to guidelines; the Regulation lays down the following elements to
be considered when determining whether a child has a particular connection to a state: the new or former habitual residence of the child, the child's
nationality, the habitual residence of a holder of parental responsibility, or
the place where property of the child is situated if the case concerns that
property. An additional safety net is that the referring EU court sets a time
limit for seising the other court (to which the case was referred). If the
court is not seised within the time limit, the first court may continue with
the case.

All the same, it is enlightening to see that the strict EU rules can be   **5.128**
softened and that there is a real concern for justice, and for finding the

---

[173] Art 6 of the Hague Choice of Court Convention.

[174] Art 15 of Brussels II *bis*. See also the Hague Convention of 19 October 1996 on
Jurisdiction, Applicable Law, Recognition, Enforcement and Co-operation in respect of
Parental Responsibility and Measures for the Protection of Children, which contains a simi-
lar rule in Arts 8 and 9.

appropriate forum. This rule seems to acknowledge that the jurisdictional grounds in the Regulation do not in all circumstances appoint the court best placed to hear the case.[175]

ASSESSMENT: FORUM NON CONVENIENS VERSUS LIS PENDENS

5.129 The analysis has indicated where *forum non conveniens* originated and why it was necessary in the places where it developed. The rule is often misunderstood and unappreciated, especially on the European continent, where legal rules tend to be more precise and to allow less discretion.

5.130 On the other hand, *forum non conveniens* can be useful in international litigation as it responds to the reality that even just rules do not always lead to the most just result in all circumstances. It can provide a solution for the situations in which an EU Member State court has jurisdiction, while a basis of exclusive jurisdiction exists in a third State. Likewise, it can prove useful when an EU Member State court has jurisdiction, while the parties had concluded a forum clause in favour of a third State court.

5.131 Both *lis pendens* and *forum non conveniens* attempt to limit parallel proceedings, to avoid conflicting judgments and to promote procedural economy. The biggest difference is the fact that the *lis pendens* rule is strictly based on priority, and has the underlying notion of mutual trust, while *forum non conveniens* seeks the most appropriate forum to hear a dispute, not only on the basis of abstract jurisdiction rules, but considering the facts of each case. In a perfect world, one can imagine a perfect combination between the strict and predictable *lis pendens* approach and the discretion-based *forum non conveniens*. Such a perfect rule was sought by the negotiators of the draft Hague convention on jurisdiction and foreign judgments in civil and commercial matters.[176] The general rule of *lis pendens* seemed acceptable, so that a court second seised would be obliged to stay proceedings in favour of a court first seised in the same action. As regards negative declarations, the *lis pendens* rule would be reversed: it would not be the court asked first for a negative declaration, but the court second seised of the true action that will have the ability to hear the case.[177] This would be a

---

[175] Advocating this view: Huber, '*Forum non conveniens* und EuGVÜ', note 72 above, 980.

[176] This large project was exchanged in 2001 for the negotiation of a more limited convention, which led to the conclusion of the Hague Choice of Court Convention in 2005. For more information see <http://www.hcch.net>, especially 'Summary of the Outcome of the Discussion in Commission II of the First Part of the Diplomatic Conference (2001),' Arts 21 and 22.

[177] See also AF Lowenfeld, 'Forum Shopping, Anti-Suit Injunctions, Negative Declarations, and Related Tools of International Litigation' [1997] AJIL 314–324; J Bomhoff, 'Het negatief declaratoir in de EEX-Verordening' [2004] *Nederlands Internationaal Privaatrecht* 1–8.

welcome limitation of the blind *lis pendens* rule, since it would take into account that the true defendant should not be permitted to pre-empt and trump the plaintiff's election of a forum. It would also counter the race to the court that the *lis pendens* rule sometimes encourages. A natural defendant would now have to wait until he or she is sued and would lose interest to go to court first. In exceptional circumstances, if a court were clearly inappropriate to exercise jurisdiction, and a court in another state were obviously more suitable, a court seised might suspend proceedings. The court would only be able to do so on an application by one of the parties and not of its own motion. Under which circumstances the possibility to decline would exist was not resolved (for instance when the case concerned a protective basis for jurisdiction for a weaker party). It seems a good compromise, but there was lack of consensus on the extent to which *forum non conveniens* should be permitted under the Convention and how far under national law. The difficulties of parallel proceedings was the main reason that the Hague Convention on Choice of Court Agreements is in general restricted to exclusive choice of court agreements: the negotiators did not want to reopen the debates on what to do when various courts are seised, and on whether a court might decline jurisdiction in favour of another court, also chosen. The Convention now contains a rule eliminating the application of *forum non conveniens*.[178] This makes sense if the Convention is only applied to cases where a single court had been chosen.

Returning to Brussels I, the judgment of the European Court of Justice in **5.132** *Owusu* has seriously restricted *forum non conveniens*, even in favour of third State courts. However, the effects of the judgment should not be permitted to spill over to fields that were not considered by the European Court of Justice. Moreover, a true application of the law of precedent would not allow the judgment to have such effects. The European Court of Justice's ruling in the *Lugano* opinion that it is impossible to decline Regulation-based jurisdiction, even if such jurisdiction is exclusive or based on a forum clause, was incidental. Hopefully a question specifically on the issue of such jurisdiction in a third State court would be considered by the European Court of Justice in the light of comity and the requirements of international trade. If *forum non conveniens* is ruled out for these circumstances, then the Regulation itself must be amended to permit declining jurisdiction in favour of third State courts in certain cases.

---

[178] Art 5(2).

D. RELATED ACTIONS

Article 28 of Brussels I:

1. *Where related actions are pending in the courts of different Member States, any court other than the court first seised may stay its proceedings.*
2. *Where these actions are pending at first instance, any court other than the court first seised may also, on the application of one of the parties, decline jurisdiction if the court first seised has jurisdiction over the actions in question and its law permits the consolidation thereof.*
3. *For the purposes of this Article, actions are deemed to be related where they are so closely connected that it is expedient to hear and determine them together to avoid the risk of irreconcilable judgments resulting from separate proceedings.*

GENERAL

5.133 Brussels I states that when related cases are pending in courts of two different EU Member States, the court second seised may decline jurisdiction if the court first seised has jurisdiction. The test is that the cases are so closely connected that there is a risk of irreconcilable judgments.[179] The proposed Maintenance Regulation contains an identical provision.[180] The rule has the same objective as that of *lis pendens,* namely to avoid conflicting judgments and to facilitate the proper administration of justice in the European Community.[181] However, it differs from the *lis pendens* rule in two important respects: the initiative must come from one of the parties (not the court of its own motion), and the court has discretion whether or not to decline jurisdiction. Brussels II *bis* does not contain a similar rule. Its *lis pendens* rule is broader, and contains a possibility for cases to be transferred from one court to another.[182] The criteria for related actions to lead to a stay by one court in favour of another include the assessment that there must be a danger of irreconcilable judgments. This factor makes the test stricter than that for *forum non conveniens.*[183] It is not permitted, as is sometimes done when applying the *forum non conveniens*

---

[179] Art 28.

[180] Proposal for a Council Regulation on Jurisdiction, Applicable law, Recognition and Enforcement of Decisions and Cooperation in Matters relating to Maintenance Obligations of 15 December 2005, COM(2005) 649 final, available at <http://eur-lex.europa.eu>, Art 8.

[181] Jenard Report on the 1968 version of the Brussels Convention; OJ C 59, 5 March 1979 (Jenard Report), 41.

[182] Art 15; above paras 5.125 and following.

[183] P North & JJ Fawcett, *Cheshire and North's Private International Law* (13th edn, London: Butterworths, 1999) 258.

rule, to take into account the way in which, or the speed by which the other court will do justice.

The domiciles of the parties are irrelevant for the application of the rule on **5.134** related actions. It comes into play if the courts of two different EU Member States are concerned. This is the same as for *lis pendens* and for recognition and enforcement. It is irrelevant whether jurisdiction is based on Brussels I, national rules, or a (bilateral or multilateral) convention.[184]

In this short section, the relationship this rule has with, respectively, exclu- **5.135** sive jurisdiction and forum clauses, will briefly be discussed. Since the rule is similar to that on *lis pendens,* but an element of discretion is added, the bases for jurisdiction will not be reconsidered in great detail. In conclusion, a comparison will be made between the rule and *forum non conveniens.*

RELATED ACTIONS AND EXCLUSIVE JURISDICTION

The European Court of Justice has stated (obiter*)* that if the court seised **5.136** second has exclusive jurisdiction, an exception to *lis pendens* exists.[185] If this is so for *lis pendens,* it seems logical that the discretion in the rule on related actions could be exercised in such a way that the court second seised might refuse to decline its exclusive jurisdiction.

RELATED ACTIONS AND FORUM CLAUSES

English law again provides us with examples of the interaction between **5.137** different rules. In *IP Metal Ltd v Ruote OZ SpA,*[186] the parties had concluded several agreements containing forum choices for London. The validity of the clauses was in dispute. Proceedings ensued, first in the court at Padua in Italy and then in London. The proceedings in the two courts did not involve the same contracts and therefore, according to the

---

[184] Y Donzallaz, *La Convention de Lugano du 16 septembre 1988 concernant la compétence judiciaire et l'exécution des décisions en matière civile et commerciale* (Berne: Editions Stæmpfli + Cie SA Berne, 1996) vol 1, 601; H Gaudemet-Tallon, *Compétence et exécution des jugements en Europe* (3rd edn, Paris: LGDJ, 2002) 276; H Gaudemet-Tallon, 'Les frontières extérieures de l'espace judiciaire européen: quelques repères' in A Borrás, A Bucher, AVM Struycken, M Verwilghen (eds), *E Pluribus unum. Liber Amicorum Georges AL Droz* (The Hague: Martinus Nijhoff Publishers, 1996) 85–104 at 91.

[185] Case C–351/89 *Overseas Union Insurance v New Hampshire Insurance* [1991] ECR I–3317, para 26.

[186] [1993] 2 Lloyd's Rep 60 QB (Comm Ct).

English court, could not fall within the ambit of the strict *lis pendens* rule.[187] The question then was whether a stay could be granted on the basis of related actions brought earlier in the Italian court.

5.138 The English court found that there was a valid choice of court agreement on the basis of the Brussels Convention.[188] For that reason it would not be in accordance with justice to stay the action because of the related action that was pending in Italy. The court was of the opinion that the Italian court should reach the same conclusion as the English court when testing the validity of the forum clause according to the Brussels Convention. However, the defendants pointed out that the Italian court would find the forum clause invalid and hear the action. The English court, however, refused to grant a stay since it found the clause to be valid.

5.139 This judgment differs from the later *Gasser* judgment by the European Court Justice.[189] The European Court of Justice made it clear that the *lis pendens* rule has precedence over a forum clause. The court seised second is under an obligation to stay its action in favour of the court first seised even if there is a forum clause in favour of the court seised second. Indeed, the important difference between the provision on *lis pendens* and that on related actions is that the provision on related actions allows discretion. The fact that there is a forum clause in favour of the court second seised is surely an important, if not decisive, factor in considering whether or not to grant a stay.

5.140 In interpreting European civil jurisdiction rules, it seems that a forum clause would receive the same relative importance in cases of *lis pendens* and related actions. The fiction that all courts within the European Union will reach the same conclusion on the validity of a forum clause still seems relevant. However, as *Gasser* received deserved criticism, the rule it established should be interpreted in a limited way.[190] When considering declining jurisdiction on the basis of the related actions rule, courts have discretion. It seems that the chosen court, if seised second, would use the discretion to refuse to decline jurisdiction in favour of a non-chosen, but

---

[187] Ibid, 61.

[188] Ibid, 67.

[189] Case C–116/02 *Erich Gasser GmbH v MISAT Srl* [2003] ECR I–14693, para 73.

[190] R Fentiman, 'Access to Justice and Parallel Proceedings in Europe' [2004] CLJ 312–314; J Mance, 'Exclusive Jurisdiction Agreements and European Ideals' [2004] LQR 357–365; A Wittwer, 'Auch bei italienischer Prozessdauer gilt Art. 21 EuGVÜ' [2004] *European Law Reporter* 49–50; case notes: H Muir Watt [2004] *Revue critique de droit international privé* 459–464; R Fentiman [2005] CML Rev 241–259; M-L Niboyet, 'La globalisation du procès civil international dans l'éspace judiciaire européen et mondial' [2006] *Journal de droit international* 937–954 at 944–945.

first seised court. The approach of the English court in *IP Metal* is probably still tenable after *Gasser*.

ASSESSMENT: RELATED ACTIONS *VERSUS FORUM NON CONVENIENS*

Von Mehren likened the rule on related actions to a broad form of *forum* **5.141** *non conveniens*.[191] There is in fact a great similarity: a court has discretion to decline to hear a case over which it has jurisdiction. There are, however, differences as well: for the rule on related actions it is required that the two cases must be pending, while this is not a requirement for *forum non conveniens*. Under the rule on related actions, only the second court can decline to hear the case, while the *forum non conveniens* rule does not contain such a restriction. The extent of the discretion may be different as well. For related actions, a court must consider whether there is a risk of irreconcilable judgments. This may be a consideration in a *forum non conveniens* plea, but the court is not obliged to consider that factor. However, if the court does consider that factor, it is not decisive.

In *The 'Linda'* Sheen J found that the doctrine of *forum non conveniens* could **5.142** not have any relevance in cases to which the rules on *lis pendens* or related actions applied; according to him the Articles raised the simple question of which court was first seised over a matter.[192]

In later cases, the English courts on several occasions distinguished **5.143** between the two rules. Saville LJ stated in *Sarrio*[193] that the objective of the rule on related actions did not call for an over-sophisticated analysis.[194] Being sure of this conclusion, he did not regard it necessary to pose a preliminary question to the European Court of Justice. He declined jurisdiction in favour of the Spanish court. Interestingly, in this case the House of Lords stayed the case on the basis of a related action in Spain while the Court of Appeal did so on the basis of *forum non conveniens*. This indicates that the English courts do make a distinction between the rules, but one might forgive them for not being certain exactly what that distinction is.

---

[191] AT von Mehren, 'Theory and Practice of Adjudicatory Authority in Private International Law: a comparative study of the doctrine, policies and practices of common- and civil-law systems. General course on Private International Law' in (2002) 295 Collected Courses of the Hague Academy of International Law 369.

[192] The 'Linda' [1988] 1 QB (Adm Ct) 175.

[193] *Sarrio SA v Kuwait Investment Authority* [1998] 1 Lloyd's Rep 129 (HL); JJ Newton, 'Forum non conveniens in Europe (again)' [1997] LMCLQ 337–344; the decision of the Court of Appeal, dealing mainly with *forum non conveniens*, is discussed above at paras 5.108 and following.

[194] Ibid, 135.

5.144 In *Haji-Ioannou and Others v Frangos and Others*[195] the English Court of Appeal found that the proceedings in the Greek court and the proceedings in the English court were not related in the sense of the Brussels Convention since the Greek proceedings were 'an appendage' to criminal proceedings. That, according to the Court of Appeal, made the application of the rule on related actions inappropriate.[196] One cannot help but be surprised by this stringent application made by an English court, from which one would expect more flexible interpretations and wider discretions, such as those of *forum non conveniens*. Interestingly, the Court of Appeal reached the opposite conclusion on applying the *forum non conveniens* doctrine to the case. The Court thus saw *forum non conveniens* as being more flexible than the provision on related actions. It is not clear on what basis it held this view.

5.145 It may be relevant that in some civil law systems, civil proceedings can be hooked onto criminal proceedings. The European Court of Justice has not seen this as an obstacle for the normal application of the Brussels regime to the civil part of those actions. The nature of the tribunal is irrelevant.[197] The civil part of the judgment would be recognizable under Brussels I.[198]

5.146 Whatever the case, the differences between the rules and their effect in practice are not clear. Now that the European Court of Justice has found that the rule on *forum non conveniens* could not be applied if the defendant was domiciled in the EU, the English courts may be able to reach the same result of international comity through the rule on related actions. The problem is that parties would have to go to the trouble and expense of instituting both actions, and furthermore that the rule on related actions can only be applied if the other court is in an EU Member State, and that other court was seised first.

E. ANTI-SUIT INJUNCTIONS

Definition

5.147 Anti-suit injunctions are the most aggressive way of dealing with, or avoiding, parallel proceedings. The effect of such injunctions is that parties are prohibited from bringing suit in a different court. Courts that have

---

[195] [1999] 2 Lloyd's Rep 337 CA.
[196] Ibid, 352.
[197] Art 1(1) of Brussels I.
[198] Case C–172/91 *Sonntag v Waidmann* [1993] ECR I–1963, para 19; Case C–7/98 *Krombach v Bamberski* [2000] ECR I–1935, para 30.

jurisdiction grant such an order to prevent the occurrence of parallel proceedings or, if there are already parallel proceedings, to prevent conflicting judgments.[199] The conditions for the granting of such injunctions are that there must be jurisdiction *in personam* over the party against whom the order is asked and the court should consider that the applicant is entitled to such an injunction.[200] Consequently the court has discretion.

The anti-suit injunction emerged from case law: it originated in the English **5.148** Court of Chancery, but is now based in statute.[201] The House of Lords summarized the essential features of an anti-suit injunction as follows:

(a) The applicant is a party to existing legal proceedings in the country;
(b) The defendants have in bad faith commenced and propose to prosecute proceedings against the applicant in another jurisdiction for the purpose of frustrating or obstructing the proceedings in this country;
(c) The court considers that it is necessary in order to protect the legitimate interest of the applicant in the English proceedings to grant the applicant a restraining order against the defendants. [202]

An anti-suit injunction can only be granted if the case has a relation to an **5.149** English court. *Airbus Industrie GIE v Patel and Others*[203] concerned a domestic flight of Indian Airlines from Bombay to Bangalore. When it landed, the aircraft was damaged and caught fire, resulting in many passengers dying or sustaining injury. The aircraft had been assembled by Airbus (registered in France) in Toulouse. Four English passengers were killed and four were injured. The English claimants commenced proceedings against Airbus in Texas. The Texan court had jurisdiction on the basis that Airbus had previously done business there and that jurisdiction could not be stayed since Texan law did not know an exception like *forum non conveniens* (at that time). Airbus sought an anti-suit injunction in England. The judge in the court of first instance considered the advantages of the claimants litigating in Texas and the prejudice to Airbus and held that it would not be appropriate to grant an anti-suit injunction. Airbus appealed.

---

[199] W Kennett, 'Les injonctions *anti-suit*' in M-T Caupain & G De Leval, *L'efficacité de la justice civile en Europe* (Brussels: Larcier, 2000) 133–144; P Wautelet, *Les conflits de procédures. Etude de droit international privé comparé* (unpublished doctoral thesis, Katholieke Universiteit Leuven, 2002) 237–347.

[200] A Briggs & P Rees, *Civil Jurisdiction and Judgments* (4th edn, London: LLP, 2005) 416–417.

[201] Supreme Court Act 1981, s 37(1). For a description of the history of anti-suit injunctions: TC Hartley, 'Comity and the Use of Anti-suit Injunctions in International Litigation' [1987] AJCL 487–511 at 489–490.

[202] *Turner v Grovit and others* [2001] UKHL 65.

[203] [1999] 1 AC 119.

On appeal the anti-suit injunction was granted on the ground that the action of the claimants was oppressive. The claimants appealed to the House of Lords, which allowed the appeal on the basis that the English court did not have a sufficient interest in or connection with the case. The House of Lords considered it inconsistent with comity for the English courts to interfere in this case.

5.150 Anti-suit injunctions raise serious objections with regard to comity.[204] The Institute of International Law stated in a resolution:[205]

[c]ourts which grant anti-suit injunctions should be sensitive to the demands of comity, and in particular should refrain from granting such injunctions in cases other than (a) a breach of a choice of court agreement or arbitration agreement; (b) unreasonable or oppressive conduct by a plaintiff in a foreign jurisdiction; or (c) the protection of their own jurisdiction in such matters as the administration of estates and insolvency.[206]

5.151 The defenders of the anti-suit injunction state that it does not violate rules of comity since it does not interfere with the sovereignty of the foreign court. It gives an order to the proceeding parties and not to the foreign court itself. However, Hartley points out that this is a false argument.[207] In practice, a court can only exercise its sovereignty (at least in civil matters) if the parties initiate procedures. By prohibiting parties from doing so, the sovereignty and independence of the foreign court is necessarily affected. This point was also made by the Oberlandesgericht (District Court of Appeal) Düsseldorf concerning the enforcement of an English anti-suit injunction:[208] the court refused to recognize the injunction, stating that it interfered with the sovereignty of the German courts by preventing it from carrying out its tasks, since parties had been prohibited to take steps in the proceedings. Similarly, the Rechtbank van eerste aanleg (Court of First Instance) of Brussels refused to give effect to an anti-suit injunction of the District Court of the State of Nevada, Second Judicial District.[209] The Brussels

---

[204] On comity in general, see HE Yntema, 'The Comity Doctrine' [1966–1967] *Michigan Law Review* 1–32 including the introduction by K Nadelman at 1–8.

[205] At their session in Bruges, Belgium in 2003; [2004] Institute of International Law. Yearbook, Part II, 81–112; available at <http://www.idi-iil.org>.

[206] Art 5.

[207] Hartley, 'Comity and Anti-suit Injunctions', note 201 above, 506; see also J Wilson, 'Anti-suit injunctions' [1997] *Journal of Business Law* 424–437, 426 stating that anti-suit injunctions have an indirect effect on foreign courts, even though they are granted against a litigant and not against a foreign court.

[208] Judgment of 10 January 1996 [1997] ILPr 320.

[209] Judgment of 18 December 1989 [1990–1991] *Rechtskundig Weekblad* 676–680.

court found that the injunction was contrary to fundamental principles of access to justice. It barred the defendant in the Brussels proceedings (applicant for the anti-suit injunction) from in any way negating the procedural rights of the plaintiff and imposed a fine if he tried to do so.

In this section, after a general introduction of the relation between anti-suit injunctions and Brussels I, the situation with respect to courts in the EU and courts in third States will be considered. Thereafter, the discussion will turn to the utility of anti-suit injunctions to protect forum clauses in favour of EU Member State courts and exclusive bases for jurisdiction in EU Member State courts. In conclusion, there will be a brief assessment of the anti-suit injunction. **5.152**

Anti-suit Injunctions and Brussels I

Just as for *forum non conveniens*, Brussels I does not contain any explicit reference to anti-suit injunctions.[210] Probably other EU Member States would regard the injunction as infringing on their sovereignty and would not recognize it on the basis that it is contrary to public policy.[211] The problem is one of the mutual trust that should exist between the courts of the EU Member States. Mutual trust goes further than comity: it is the implication that the EU Member States not only have respect for, but also blind trust in each other's courts. A recent example of that mutual trust is found in the judgment of the European Court of Justice in *Gasser*,[212] where the Court refused to take into account the argument that the judicial systems of some Member States function slower than those of others, since it was said that the Member States have to trust each other's legal systems.[213] **5.153**

In line with this view, the European Court of Justice has ruled that the anti-suit injunction is incompatible with the Brussels Convention and the ideas underlying the European judicial area.[214] The nature of anti-suit injunctions, being aggressive and intrusive, does not have as close a link with jurisdiction as the doctrine of *forum non conveniens*. Anti-suit injunctions will first be considered as against EU Member States and then as against third States. **5.154**

---

[210] Nor did the Brussels Convention.

[211] Briggs & Rees, note 200 above, 41.

[212] Case C–116/02 *Erich Gasser GmbH v MISAT Srl* [2003] ECR I–14693, para 73.

[213] Ibid, para 72.

[214] Case C–159/02 *Turner v Grovit* [2004] ECR I–3565; discussed below, para 5.164 and following.

5.155 Although the anti-suit injunction is seen as contrary to the comity of Brussels I, and the underlying idea that the Member States trust each other's legal systems, some authors still plead in favour of its utility.[215] The argument is that the anti-suit injunction can prevent abuse of the rules contained in the Regulation and so protect weaker parties against unscrupulous litigants. It could be a useful tool to prevent abuse of the *lis pendens* rule by bringing proceedings in an EU Member State where the judicial system works slower than in the other EU Member States, so that the other party is blocked from bringing proceedings elsewhere in the EU. This tactic has been nicknamed the Italian Torpedo and is often used in intellectual property cases. Hartley suggests that the anti-suit injunction should be used in order to do justice by refusing to hear cases brought in bad faith. However, he adds that the use of the injunction should be limited, so as not to harm the comity between Member States.[216]

Anti-suit Injunction as Against EU Member State Courts

5.156 The English courts, in a number of cases, granted anti-suit injunctions to restrain proceedings in other EU Member State courts. The European Court of Justice has now overturned this practice in the *Turner* judgment.[217] The English courts can no longer grant anti-suit injunctions in cases that fall within the scope of application of Brussels I and where the other court is in another EU Member State.

5.157 There will be a brief overview of the cases where anti-suit injunctions had been given in the past, before turning to the European Court of Justice's judgment prohibiting anti-suit injunctions. The House of Lords has referred another preliminary question to the European Court of Justice regarding an anti-suit injunction against proceedings in an EU Member State.[218]

---

[215] See TC Hartley, 'How to abuse the law and (maybe) come out on top: Bad-faith proceedings under the Brussels Jurisdiction and Judgments Convention' in JAR Nafziger & SC Symeonides (eds), *Law and Justice in a Multistate World. Essays in Honour of Arthur T von Mehren* (Ardsley: Transnational Publishers Inc, 2002) 73–81 at 81; TC Hartley, 'Brussels Jurisdiction and Judgments Convention: Jurisdiction agreement and *lis alibi pendens*' [1994] ELR 549–552 at 552: '[i]f the Court of Justice were to rule that the position taken by the English Courts is incorrect, the result would probably be that bankers and other businessmen would insert a New York jurisdiction clause into their contracts in place of an English one. This would be good news for New York lawyers, but it would not promote the interests of the Community.'

[216] Hartley, 'How to abuse the law', ibid, 77–78 and 81.

[217] *Turner v Grovit*, note 214 above.

[218] Case C–185/07 *Ras Riunione Adriatica di Sicurta Spa v West Tankers Inc*, reference to ECJ on 2 April 2007, still pending; referring judgment [2007] UKHL 4.

In that case there was a breach of an arbitration clause (for arbitration in London).

In the *Continental Bank* case[219] the forum clause between Continental Bank **5.158** (domiciled in the United States of America, but having a Greek branch) and the borrowers (one-ship companies registered in Panama and Liberia and managed by Aegis Shipping Co Ltd of Athens) was drafted as follows:

Each of the Borrowers. . . hereby irrevocably submits to the jurisdiction of the English Courts. . . but the Bank reserves the right to proceed under this Agreement in the Courts of any other country claiming or having jurisdiction in respect thereof.[220]

A dispute arose regarding the loans and the borrowers sued the bank in **5.159** the Multi-Membered First Instance Court of Athens, claiming damages and a declaration that the guarantors had been released. The action was based on a provision in Greek law that whoever causes damage to another, intentionally and in a manner that violates the commands of morality, is bound to make reparation.[221] The borrowers argued that the bank had acted contrary to business morality. Subsequently the bank requested the English court to grant an anti-suit injunction to restrain the Greek proceedings, which were in contravention of the forum clause. The borrowers applied for the bank's writ and points of claim to be struck from the roll, or that the action be stayed on the basis of the *lis pendens* or related actions rules of the Brussels Convention. The first question was whether the borrowers had breached the contract by suing in Greece. The Court of Appeal found that there had been a clear intention that the borrowers, but not the

---

[219] *Continental Bank NA v Aeakos Compania Naviera SA and others* [1994] 1 WLR 588. See also Hartley, 'Jurisdiction agreement and *lis alibi pendens*', note 215 above; M McKee, 'Case Comment. Jurisdiction Clauses' (1994) 9(4) *Journal of International Banking Law* N85–N86; C Chatterjee, 'The legal effect of the exclusive jurisdiction clause in the Brussels Convention in relation to banking matters' (1995) 10(8) *Journal of International Banking Law* 334–340; M Mildred, 'The use of the Brussels Convention in group actions' [1996] *Journal of Personal Injury Litigation* 121–134 at 130; PM North & JJ Fawcett, *Cheshire and North's Private International Law* (13th edn, London: Butterworths, 1999) 256 and 270; TC Hartley, 'Anti-suit injunctions and the Brussels Jurisdiction and Judgments Convention' [2000] ICLQ 166–171 at 170–171; Briggs & Rees, note 200 above, 40–42.

[220] The clause provides an example of an asymmetric choice of court agreement, frequently used in the banking sector. These clauses do not fall within the scope of the Hague Convention of 30 June 2005 on Choice of Court Agreements (although states may make declarations in order to include them according to Art 22); Explanatory Report to the Convention of 30 June 2005 on Choice of Court Agreements by TC Hartley and M Dogauchi, 39, available at <http://www.hcch.net>.

[221] Art 919 Greek Civil Code.

bank, be obliged to submit disputes to the English courts, and in this sense the borrowers were not permitted to bring proceedings in Greece, as they had done.

5.160 The Court ruled that the *lis pendens* rule was not applicable since the proceedings in Greece and the request for an anti-suit injunction in England did not concern the same causes of action. The fact that jurisdiction was at issue in both cases was not sufficient to bring the matter within the scope of the rule. The Court of Appeal further found that the two actions were not at all 'related' in the sense of the Brussels Convention.

5.161 The lawyer for the borrowers did not contest the English courts' inherent power to grant an anti-suit injunction, but argued that the English court ought to trust the Greek court. She stated that such interference with the jurisdiction of another EU Member State court could only be justified if the proceedings in the foreign court were vexatious and oppressive, and that was not the case. According to her, the English court had to allow the Greek court to decide on the jurisdiction issue. However, expert evidence on Greek law had pointed out that the Greek court would assume jurisdiction in the case because of the bank's cooperation at an early stage of the proceedings. The decisive argument for the Court of Appeal was that the injunction would be the only remedy for the breach of contract (i.e. the forum clause) committed by the borrowers. Therefore the Court of Appeal upheld the injunction and rejected the appeal.

5.162 In *The Eras EIL Actions* no anti-suit injunction was granted since it had not been proved that the actions in Illinois were vexatious or oppressive.[222] The actions were also pending in England, so that the English court had an interest in the matter. However, the court did not consider the granting of an anti-suit injunction impossible under the Brussels Convention.

5.163 *OT Africa Line Ltd v Hijazy and Others, (The 'Kribi')* concerned a Liberian businessman, Mr Hijazy, who imported and exported goods between Europe and Liberia.[223] He exported sweets and coffee from the port of Antwerp to Liberia on board the 'Kribi', but there was a shortage of both upon delivery. In both cases Mr Hijazi and one of his companies brought proceedings against the ship owners in Antwerp.[224] In the coffee actions, the receivers (Belgian companies) and their insurers were also involved. However, the bills of lading contained forum clauses in favour of London. The ship owners therefore subsequently brought proceedings in London

---

[222] [1995] 1 Lloyd's Rep 64 QBD (Comm Ct).
[223] [2001] 1 Lloyd's Rep 76.
[224] Case AR 99/12538.

and requested anti-suit injunctions restraining the other parties from continuing the actions in Antwerp. The court held that the Brussels Convention did not exclude the possibility of granting an anti-suit injunction. The Civil Jurisdiction and Judgments Act 1991 did not prohibit anti-suit injunctions and therefore English common law applied. The court discarded the argument that the Belgian court would be offended by the anti-suit injunction.[225] Therefore the court granted the anti-suit injunction. The Belgian proceedings were not pursued further and the parties applied to the Commercial Court of Antwerp to have the case removed from the roll.[226] Strictly speaking the Belgian court was not offended; however, it was hampered in its functioning. The parties stopped taking steps in the proceedings and they died quietly. The anti-suit injunction was effective and served its purpose. The result is probably equitable, if one for a moment forgets a possible insult to the Belgian court. In the search of procedural fairness, the issue is not the sovereignty of another state, but forcing the parties to play by the rules of the game.

Turner v Grovit

The European Court of Justice had the opportunity to consider anti-suit **5.164** injunctions in *Turner v Grovit*.[227] Mr Turner was a British lawyer domiciled in the United Kingdom. He had been employed in 1990 by the Chequepoint Group, a group of companies directed by Mr Grovit, as 'Group Solicitor'. The group of companies operated various *bureaux de change*. Mr Turner's contract had initially been with China Security Ltd, but was taken over by the end of 1990 by Chequepoint UK Ltd, both member companies of the Chequepoint Group. Mr Turner performed his work in London and sometimes had to travel. In May 1997 he asked for a transfer to Madrid and in November 1997 started working there at the premises of Changepoint, a Spanish company in the Chequepoint Group. Chequepoint UK Ltd was taken over by another company in the group, Harada, on 31 December 1997. On 16 February 1998 Mr Turner gave notice of his

---

[225] Note 223 above, 93.

[226] Judgment of 30 January 2001 (AR 99/12538).

[227] Note 214 above; case notes: A Nuyts [2005] *Journal des tribunaux* 32–35; XE Kramer, 'De harmoniserende werking van het Europees procesrecht: de disqualificatioe van de anti-suit injunction' [2005] *Nederlands Internationaal Privaatrecht* 130–137; T Kruger, 'The Anti-suit injunction in the European Judicial Space: *Turner v Grovit*' [2004] ICLQ 1030–1040. Also TC Hartley, 'The EU and the systematic dismantling of the common law conflict of laws' [2005] ICLQ 813–828 at 821–823; M-L Niboyet, 'La globalisation du procès civil international dans l'éspace judiciaire européen et mondial' [2006] *Journal de droit international* 937–954 at 944–945.

resignation to Harada. He did not return to the office in Madrid, having worked in Spain for only 35 days.

5.165 Back in London, on 2 March 1998, Mr Turner brought an action against Harada before the Employment Tribunal. He argued that they had tried to implicate him in illegal conduct and that this amounted to unfair dismissal.

5.166 In July 1998 Changepoint and Harada started conciliation proceedings against Mr Turner in Spain. This was a requirement under Spanish law before legal proceedings could be initiated.

5.167 In the meantime, Harada contested the jurisdiction of the Employment Tribunal. It stated that it was incorporated in Ireland and Mr Grovit was resident in Belgium. The argument was dismissed. On 10 September 1998 the Tribunal found that it had jurisdiction, based on Harada's domicile in the United Kingdom. Harada appealed that judgment to the Employment Appeal Tribunal on 14 October 1998.

5.168 On 21 October 1998, after the attempted conciliation, Changepoint brought proceedings for damages for losses resulting from his professional conduct against Mr Turner in the court of First Instance of Madrid.

5.169 The appeal to the Employment Appeal Tribunal was dismissed. Mr Turner was awarded damages.

5.170 The summons to the Spanish proceedings was served on Mr Turner in London around 15 December 1998. Mr Turner contested the jurisdiction of the Spanish court and did not take any steps in that proceeding, but sought an anti-suit injunction from the High Court of Justice of England and Wales on 18 December 1998. The purpose of the injunction was to restrain both Changepoint from continuing, and Mr Grovit and Harada from commencing, proceedings in Spain. An interlocutory injunction was issued on 22 December 1998, but the High Court refused to extend that injunction on 24 February 1999.

5.171 Mr Turner appealed to the Court of Appeal (England and Wales).[228] That Court issued an injunction forbidding the defendants to continue the proceedings commenced in Spain and from commencing other proceedings in Spain or elsewhere against Mr Turner regarding his contract of employment (on 28 May 1999). The reasons given for the judgment stated that the proceedings in Spain had been brought in bad faith and to vex Mr Turner's application before the Employment Tribunal in London.

---

[228] *Turner v Grovit* [1999] ILPr 656.

The Court of Appeal was aware of the possible relevance of the Brussels **5.172**
Convention:

> were the English court to find that the proceedings had been launched in another
> Brussels Convention jurisdiction for no purpose other than to harass and oppress
> a party who is already a litigant here, the English court possesses the power to
> prohibit by injunction the plaintiff in the other jurisdiction from continuing the
> foreign process.[229]

Upon the facts the Court found that the proceedings in Spain were merely **5.173**
abusive and vexatious. It thought that the parties had to be restrained
from acting further in a way that abused the proceedings in the Employment
Tribunal. The Court was of the view that, by granting the injunction,
it was not being disrespectful to the Spanish court, but rather protecting
the proper application of the Brussels Convention.[230]

On 28 June 1999 Changepoint discontinued the proceedings pending **5.174**
before the Spanish court. This was done by way of a *desistimiento,* meaning
that there was no prejudice to their rights and no waiver of the cause of
action or of the right to bring a further action.

Subsequently, Mr Grovit, Harada, and Changepoint appealed to the House **5.175**
of Lords on the ground that the English courts did not have the power to
make restraining orders preventing the continuation of proceedings in
other states bound by the Brussels Convention.

The House of Lords considered the interpretation of European Union law **5.176**
important in the case before them. For this reason they referred a preliminary question to the European Court of Justice:

> Is it inconsistent with the Convention on Jurisdiction and the Enforcement of
> Judgments in Civil and Commercial Matters signed at Brussels on 27 September
> 1968 (subsequently acceded to by the United Kingdom) to grant restraining orders
> against defendants who are threatening to commence or continue legal proceedings
> in another Convention country when those defendants are acting in bad faith with
> the intent and purpose of frustrating or obstructing proceedings properly before
> the English courts?

The House of Lords added a word of explanation. An anti-suit injunction
was based on the presumption that the English courts had *in personam*
jurisdiction over parties to proceedings pending before it. Therefore the
English courts had the right to prescribe a code of conduct to them, and
this code of conduct could include its actions towards other courts: parties

---

[229] Ibid, 666.
[230] Ibid, 674.

could be prohibited from bringing or continuing proceedings before other courts. This prohibition, as viewed by the English courts, did not interfere with the sovereignty of other courts, but only told the parties how to act while under the auspices of the English courts. The injunction did not in any way comment on the jurisdiction of the foreign court. In that sense, the terminology 'anti-suit' injunction was misleading, the House of Lords explained. The House of Lords was conscious of the comity problems that anti-suit injunctions could bring about. For that reason the English courts were reluctant to take upon themselves the decision of whether the foreign forum was an inappropriate one. In the sphere of application of the Brussels Convention, an English court would not venture that decision. According to the House of Lords there was nothing in the Brussels Convention that prohibited anti-suit injunctions. Furthermore, the anti-suit injunction was an effective mechanism for preventing irreconcilable judgments, which was one of the purposes of the Brussels Convention. In the case under discussion, irreconcilable judgments would be prevented by the anti-suit injunction. The Law Lords added that, if they had to interpret the question, they would have had no problem with finding the anti-suit injunction compatible with the Brussels Convention.

5.177 The Advocate General emphasized the importance of reciprocal trust between the various national legal systems of the EU Member States. The English anti-suit injunction seemed to place doubt on this structure of mutual trust. This mutual trust meant that each State recognized the capacity of the other legal systems to contribute to the objectives of integration. No superior control authorities had been appointed, except for the European Court of Justice. He added:

> still less has authority been given to the authorities of a particular State to arrogate to themselves the power to resolve the difficulties which the European initiative itself seeks to deal with.[231]

Courts should not be permitted to influence the jurisdiction of other EU Member States, even if the influence would be only indirect. Furthermore, only legal systems of the common law tradition knew this mechanism and allowing the anti-suit injunction would create an imbalance. This fact was not problematic according to the House of Lords since the purpose of the Brussels Convention was not uniformity, but the creation of clear rules on jurisdiction.[232]

---

[231] Note 214 above, para 31.
[232] [2001] UKHL 65, para 37.

Responding to the assertion by the House of Lords that the injunction was **5.178**
given against parties and not against foreign courts, the Advocate General
stated that if a party were prohibited, under threat of penalty, from bringing an action in a foreign court, the result would be the deprivation of the
foreign court's jurisdiction. The firm opinion of the Advocate General was
therefore that the anti-suit injunction in relations with other EU Member
States could not be tolerated.

The European Court of Justice, like the Advocate General, emphasized the **5.179**
mutual trust that should exist between the courts of the EU Member States.
This was what enabled the system of jurisdiction and a simplified procedure for recognition and enforcement of judgments. Prohibiting a party
from going to a foreign court interfered with that court's jurisdiction. That
interference was incompatible with the system of the Brussels Convention.
The argument that there was no direct interference, since the injunction
is directed at the parties and not at the foreign court, did not convince
the European Court of Justice. Even an indirect interference would be
too much.

The Court did not accept the argument that an anti-suit injunction could **5.180**
help to reach one of the goals of the Convention—to reduce irreconcilable
judgments. The Convention had its own rules to deal with that situation:
lis alibi pendens. The anti-suit injunction did not fit in with the rest of the
Convention: there are no rules on the situation that a foreign court gives a
judgment despite an injunction and there were no rules to regulate the
existence of two contradictory injunctions.

This judgment has given a long-awaited response. But the simplicity with **5.181**
which the European Court of Justice has seen and addressed the problem
is disappointing. If so many wondered about this for so long, surely there
was more to it.[233] There must have been more to consider.

The Court found that the anti-suit injunction could not be tolerated in the **5.182**
light of the mutual trust that should exist between the EU Member States.
The point here is not that the anti-suit injunction in itself breaks the rules

---

[233] Wilson, note 207 above; North & Fawcett, note 219 above, 268–272; J O'Brien, *Smith's Conflict of Laws* (2nd edn, London: Cavendish Publishing, 1999) 218–220; L Collins, *Dicey and Morris on the Conflict of Laws* vol I, 419–420; Hartley, 'Anti-suit injunctions and Brussels', note 219 above; D McClean, *Morris: The Conflict of Laws* (5th edn, London: Sweet & Maxwell, 2000) 130; CMV Clarkson & J Hill, *Jaffey on the Conflict of Laws* (2nd edn, London: Butterworths, 2002) 147–149; Wautelet, note 199 above, 294 and 298–299; A Briggs & P Rees, *Civil Jurisdiction and Judgments* (3rd edn, London: LLP, 2002) 366–368. For a more general reflection on anti-suit injunctions from a continental point of view, see JP Verheul, 'Waait de *antisuit injunction* naar het continent over?' [1989] *Nederlands Internationaal Privaatrecht* 221–224.

of the Brussels Convention, but that the value underlying it fundamentally opposes that of the European judicial area.[234] In this sisterly union, how can one court think itself superior to the extent of telling another court what its job is?

5.183 This crucial argument of mutual trust has overshadowed any argument that could be brought in favour of anti-suit injunctions. They can help to fill a gap in the Convention without negating its existence. In the absence of an anti-suit injunction the present case might fall into the gap. It does not completely fall within the scope of the *lis pendens* rule. The provision on related actions might be relevant, but that Article merely gives discretion to the judge to join two actions and it is up to him to decide whether they are related. At the same time, it was clear to the English judges that the proceedings in Spain had been brought with the sole purpose of vexing Mr Turner. Changepoint, the plaintiff in Spain, was not the employer of Mr Turner and the amount of damages they claimed was beyond all reasonable proportion; if they had suffered any damage in the first place. If the anti-suit injunction could not be issued and the Spanish judge decided that the proceedings were not adequately related, Mr Turner would have had no protection and would have been vexed and harassed by the Spanish proceedings.

5.184 Anti-suit injunctions protect English proceedings, but not necessarily only English litigants. Any litigant would be eligible for the protection. Anti-suit injunctions might also be useful in the protection of arbitration clauses (for instance for arbitration in London). The House of Lords has referred a preliminary question to the European Court of Justice on this issue.[235] In that case the ECJ will have to consider how far the arbitration exclusion reaches; furthermore, where there has been a breach of an arbitration clause, whether an anti-suit injunction against proceedings in a court in another EU Member State is in conflict with Brussels I.

Anti-suit Injunctions as Against Third State Courts

5.185 It is also possible that an English court has jurisdiction under Brussels I and the plaintiff seeks an injunction to restrain proceedings in a third State. Here the injunction is not inconsistent with the Regulation, since it will probably uphold the jurisdiction granted under it.[236] Thus such an

---

[234] See Hartley, 'Anti-suit injunctions and Brussels', note 219 above, 166 and 168.
[235] *Ras Riunione Adriatica*, note 218 above.
[236] See North & Fawcett, note 219 above, 272–273.

injunction might be granted if the English courts have exclusive jurisdiction based on a forum clause.

The House of Lords formulated their question in *Turner v Grovit* to the **5.186** European Court of Justice carefully. The question related only to anti-suit injunctions when the other court was situated in an EU Member State. Nothing was discussed relating to third States.

The question whether an English court can grant an anti-suit injunction **5.187** restraining the parties from commencing or continuing actions in third State courts remains open. Jurisdiction might be based on Brussels I, for example, because the defendant is domiciled in England while the plaintiff is domiciled in Canada. At the same time, a Canadian court might have jurisdiction. Can an English court issue an anti-suit injunction to keep the litigants out of the Canadian court? According to purely internal English law, this would be possible since the English courts have *in personam* jurisdiction. Such an injunction would protect Brussels I. It would ensure compliance with its rules on jurisdiction. Furthermore, it would prevent contradictory judgments and thus facilitate automatic recognition within the EU: a court could refuse recognition if there were an earlier irreconcilable judgment from a third State, involving the same parties and the same cause of action and which could be recognized in that state.[237] An anti-suit injunction could help to prevent the occurrence of irreconcilable judgments.

The argument that there should be mutual trust between the EU Member **5.188** States is not relevant in this case. The fact that an English court prevents a party from bringing proceedings in a third State court, has no bearing on the functioning of the European judicial area.

Another case would be where a third State court is involved while juris- **5.189** diction is based on a rule of English domestic law, permitted by Article 4 of Brussels I. Such will be the case if the defendant is domiciled in a third State. In this case the anti-suit injunction would have the same effect as described above. No mutual trust would be in question.

ANTI-SUIT INJUNCTIONS IN PROTECTION OF A FORUM CLAUSE IN FAVOUR
OF AN EU MEMBER STATE COURT

Anti-suit injunctions can be used to safeguard a forum clause that the par- **5.190** ties had agreed to in favour of an EU Member State court. An example in this regard is *Ultisol Transport Contractors Ltd v Bouygues Offshore SA*

---

[237] Art 34(4) of Brussels I.

and another.[238] Ultisol, a Bermudan company managed from the Netherlands, and Bouygues, a French company, contracted for the lease of a tug for towing Bouygues's barge from the Congo to Cape Town. The contract contained a forum clause for the High Court of Justice in London and a choice for English law. Upon arrival in Cape Town, in stormy weather, the towline parted and the barge was lost. Bouygues instituted proceedings in South Africa against Ultisol, Caspion the (Russian or Azerbaijani) owners of the tug, and Portnet the South African port authority, which allowed the vessels to enter despite the bad weather conditions.

5.191 Ultisol applied for an anti-suit injunction in England on the basis of the forum clause between it and Bouygues. The court granted the anti-suit injunction, finding that the forum clause was valid under the Brussels Convention. It further found that the Brussels Convention did not exclude the court's discretion to grant an anti-suit injunction 'in circumstances such as these'.[239] The anti-suit injunction only restrained Bouygues's proceedings against Ultisol and not against the other parties. Even though leave to appeal was subsequently granted, the point made about the Brussels Convention was not put in question.

5.192 The case shows a situation where an anti-suit injunction was used against a third State court without in any way harming the European judicial area. On the contrary—the anti-suit injunction protected the proceedings on the basis of a Brussels Convention forum clause in England.

5.193 For example, parties conclude a non-exclusive choice of court agreement for the High Court in London and a court in Australia.[240] If at least one of the parties is domiciled in the EU, the case may fall within the scope of the Regulation.[241] The English court might issue an anti-suit injunction

---

[238] *Ultisol v Bouygues* [1996] 2 Lloyd's Rep 140; the later application *Bouygues Offshore SA v Caspian Shipping Co and Others (No 5) Ultisol Transport Contractors Ltd v Bouygues Offshore SA and Another* [1997] 2 Lloyd's Rep 533; and decision on appeal: *Bouygues Offshore SA v Caspian Shipping Co (Nos 1, 3, 4 and 5)* [1998] 2 Lloyd's Rep 461.

[239] Ibid, 147.

[240] Compare the agreement concluded between the parties in *Continental Bank*, note 55 and paragraph 5.158 above: the borrowers had to bring proceedings in England while the bank retained the right to bring proceedings in any country that had jurisdiction. The Court of Appeal found that there had been a clear intention that the borrowers, but not the bank, be obliged to submit disputes to the English courts and in this sense the borrowers were not permitted to bring proceedings in Greece, as they had done.

[241] Art 23 of Brussels I provides for choice of court clauses in favour of courts in the EU between two parties at least one of which is domiciled in the EU. These clauses are exclusive unless the parties have agreed otherwise. In the example mentioned, the application of the Regulation would in fact depend on the court seised: if it is an EU court, the Regulation will be applied. Note that the Hague Convention of 30 June 2005 on Choice of Court Agreements

restraining the parties from instituting proceedings in Australia. That injunction, as in the examples above, will protect the scheme of Brussels I without denying the mutual trust between the EU Member States. However, it would not demonstrate comity towards the third State court.

In an even more aggressive fashion, but less frequently, the English court **5.194** might grant an anti-suit injunction despite the existence of a choice of court clause in favour of a third State, because the court was of the opinion that the clause is invalid, or because an exclusive basis for jurisdiction existed for the courts in England. The injunction, whether tolerable on grounds of comity or not, has nothing to do with Brussels I and the European judicial area.[242]

ANTI-SUIT INJUNCTIONS IN PROTECTION OF AN EXCLUSIVE BASIS FOR JURISDICTION IN AN EU MEMBER STATE COURT

Whether or not an anti-suit injunction could protect the exclusive bases **5.195** for jurisdiction of Brussels I is unclear. Perhaps the English courts do not have the same strict view on exclusive jurisdiction as the civil law systems, while the examples of anti-suit injunctions come mostly from English law. Just as is the case for forum clauses in favour of EU Member State courts, the anti-suit injunction might be a useful tool.

ASSESSMENT: ANTI-SUIT INJUNCTIONS *VERSUS LIS PENDENS*

It might be appropriate at this stage to consider the advantages and dis- **5.196** advantages of the application of the anti-suit injunction in comparison to the plea of *lis pendens*. That can be done by considering the applicability of the *lis pendens* rule to the case of *Turner v Grovit*. First, would the courts have viewed the parties as the same? The plaintiff in London was

---

generally does not apply if the forum election is not exclusive, but it presumes it to be exclusive; it permits a state to declare that it will also apply the Convention (at the recognition stage) on non-exclusive choice of court agreements (Art 22); see <http://www.hcch.net>.

[242] One can make reference here to the *effet réflexe*, the doctrine of GAL Droz, stating that the courts of EU Member States should decline jurisdiction if there is a forum clause in favour of a third State court; GAL Droz, *Pratique de la convention de Bruxelles du 27 septembre 1968* (Paris: Librairie Dalloz, 1973) 34; GAL Droz, 'La Convention de San Sebastian alignant la Convention de Bruxelles sur la Convention de Lugano' [1990] *Revue critique de droit international privé* 1–21 at 14; P Gothot & D Holleaux, *La convention de Bruxelles du 27.9.1968* (Paris: Jupiter, 1985) 84; H Gaudemet-Tallon, 'Les frontières extérieures de l'espace judiciaire européen: quelques repères' in A Borrás, A Bucher, A VM Struycken, M Verwilghen (eds), *E Pluribus unum. Liber Amicorum Georges AL Droz* (The Hague: Martinus Nijhoff Publishers, 1996) 85–104 at 95–97.

Mr Turner, while the defendant was Harada. Changepoint brought the proceedings in Madrid against Mr Turner. Therefore, strictly speaking, the *lis pendens* rule would not apply since the parties were not identical.[243] However, both Harada and Changepoint belonged to the same group, which could have been an argument in favour of a more liberal application of the *lis pendens* rule. If the *lis pendens* rule were not applicable here, the only possible solution would be the application of the rule on related actions, bearing in mind that this rests on discretion exercised by the judges. The identical nature of the causes of action is not beyond doubt. The English proceedings concerned wrongful dismissal while the Spanish proceedings related to damages for unprofessional conduct. It was not clear to the English Court of Appeal that the plaintiff in the Spanish actions was even the true employer of Mr Turner.[244] That moves the causes of action for the two matters even further apart.

5.197 The priority rule of the *lis pendens* plea is a strict time-based one and does not always ensure the most just outcome.[245] However, that is probably a shortcoming the EU Member States have grown accustomed to. The anti-suit injunction, on the other hand, is flexible in that it takes the more natural forum into account while the strict priority and race to the court does not exist.[246]

5.198 Another advantage of the anti-suit injunction is that it can be granted before actions are initiated. One need not have two pending cases before a solution can be sought.

5.199 In international civil litigation, the anti-suit injunction is not a phenomenon that should be promoted in all circumstances. It raises problems of comity, as has been explained above. Therefore the European Court of Justice has eliminated it in the European judicial area. Since *Turner*, anti-suit injunctions are no longer possible against EU Member State courts, but are probably still available against third State courts. When foreign proceedings are truly vexatious and the basis for jurisdiction of the forum

---

[243] On this requirement with respect to the *lis pendens* rule, see Case C–406/92 *The owners of the cargo lately laden on board the ship 'Tatry' v the owners of the ship 'Maciej Rataj'* [1994] ECR I–5439.

[244] *Turner v Grovit*, note 228 above, 632.

[245] *Gasser*, note 212 above, where the strict priority rule was confirmed. The Brussels Convention required reference to national law for the time of seizure of the court: Case 129/83 *Zelger v Salinitri* [1984] ECR 2397. Brussels I has instituted a unified rule in Art 30: H Gaudemet-Tallon, *Compétence et exécution des jugements en Europe* (3rd edn, Paris: LGDJ, 2002) 267–269.

[246] McClean, note 233 above, 126 and following; Briggs & Rees, note 200 above, 252, state that Brussels I provides a high degree of uniformity, but a low degree of discretion.

court is beyond doubt, the injunction can in some instances be a useful tool. It could even in some instances safeguard Brussels I.

F. CONCLUSION

This chapter has examined rules on declining jurisdiction and mechanisms **5.200** that courts posess to resolve the problem of parallel proceedings and to avoid conflicting judgments. The legal traditions of civil and common law legal systems differ greatly in this respect. The lack of understanding is at times huge. However, each of these mechanisms has something positive to offer, whilst at the same time having certain drawbacks.

In the EU civil jurisdiction regulations one finds only the rules on *lis pen-* **5.201** *dens* and related actions. The other rules, *forum non conveniens* and anti-suit injunctions, have, at least partially, been outlawed by the European Court of Justice in the context of Brussels I. It has been argued that anti-suit injunctions may in some instances be useful in obtaining the very goals of that Regulation. However, in the European judicial area, the mutual trust between the EU Member State courts is of great importance.

The manner in which *forum non conveniens* was outlawed is more trouble- **5.202** some. The European Court of Justice has stated that Brussels I's Article 2 is mandatory and that a court in an EU Member State that has jurisdiction on such basis, may not decline it. The ECJ seems to maintain this view, even if a court in a third State has exclusive jurisdiction or if it had been appointed in a forum clause. If this is what the court meant, the civil law courts of the European continent are not permitted to decline jurisdiction on the basis of the *lis pendens* rules in their national laws either. The result is far-reaching for third States. It is submitted that the text of the Regulation should be amended to rectify the current state of affairs.

6

Provisional and protective measures

Article 31 of Brussels I:

Application may be made to the courts of a Member State for such provisional, including protective, measures as may be available under the law of that State, even if, under this Regulation, the courts of another Member State have jurisdiction as to the substance of the matter.

Article 47 of Brussels I:

1. *When a judgment must be recognised in accordance with this Regulation, nothing shall prevent the applicant from availing himself of provisional, including protective, measures in accordance with the law of the Member State requested without a declaration of enforceability under Article 41 being required.*
2. *The declaration of enforceability shall carry with it the power to proceed to any protective measures.*
3. *During the time specified for an appeal pursuant to Article 43(5) against the declaration of enforceability and until any such appeal has been determined, no measures of enforcement may be taken other than protective measures against the property of the party against whom enforcement is sought.*

Article 20 of Brussels II *bis*:

In urgent cases, the provisions of this Regulation shall not prevent the courts of a Member State from taking such provisional, including protective, measures in respect of persons or assets in that State as may be available under the law of that

Member State, even if, under this Regulation, the court of another Member State has jurisdiction as to the substance of the matter.

The measures referred to in paragraph 1 shall cease to apply when the court of the Member State having jurisdiction under this Regulation as to the substance of the matter has taken the measures it considers appropriate.

Recital 16 of the Insolvency Regulation:

The court having jurisdiction to open the main insolvency proceedings should be enabled to order provisional and protective measures from the time of the request to open proceedings. Preservation measures both prior to and after the commencement of the insolvency proceedings are very important to guarantee the effectiveness of the insolvency proceedings. In that connection this Regulation should afford different possibilities. On the one hand, the court competent for the main insolvency proceedings should be able to order provisional protective measures covering assets situated in the territory of other Member States. On the other hand, a liquidator temporarily appointed prior to the opening of the main insolvency proceedings should be able, in the Member States in which an establishment belonging to the debtor is to be found, to apply for the preservation measures which are possible under the law of those States.

Article 25(1) of the Insolvency Regulation:

Judgments handed down by a court whose judgment concerning the opening of proceedings is recognised in accordance with Article 16 and which concern the course and closure of insolvency proceedings, and compositions approved by that court shall also be recognised with no further formalities . . .

The first subparagraph shall also apply to judgments deriving directly from the insolvency proceedings and which are closely linked with them, even if they were handed down by another court.

The first subparagraph shall also apply to judgments relating to preservation measures taken after the request for the opening of insolvency proceedings.

Article 38 of the Insolvency Regulation:

Where a court of a Member State which has jurisdiction pursuant to Article 3(1) appoints a temporary administrator in order to ensure the preservation of the debtor's assets, that temporary administrator shall be empowered to request any measures to secure and preserve any of the debtor's assets situated in another Member State, provided for under the law of that State, for the period between the request for the opening of insolvency proceedings and the judgment opening the proceedings.

A. INTRODUCTION

Chapters 2, 3, and 4 have explained the circumstances under which the **6.01** jurisdiction rules of the civil jurisdiction regulations apply. Chapter 5 examined other procedural rules linked to jurisdiction. Therefore the question of provisional and protective measures still remains. The main issue is whether the rules on such measures provide an exception to what has already been discussed: that is, do they contain an autonomous rule as to their application or conversely, do the rules on provisional and protective measures follow those already laid out?

Provisional and protective measures are aimed at protecting rights, parties, **6.02** proceedings or judgments. They can take many forms and can be granted at different stages of the proceedings.

A court that has jurisdiction under the Brussels I, Brussels II *bis*, or Insolvency **6.03** Regulations, or under the proposed Maintenance Regulation[1] has jurisdiction to grant provisional measures before the judgment.[2] It seems logical that the court that has jurisdiction over the substance of a case can not only grant final relief, but also interim where necessary.

The provisions discussed in this chapter concern jurisdiction of EU Member **6.04** State courts other than the court that has jurisdiction over the substance of the matter. These provisions are therefore aimed to give jurisdiction to courts that do not have jurisdiction under any of the other provisions of the Regulation.

Brussels I and II *bis* are the main focus of this chapter. The proposed Main- **6.05** tenance Regulation will occasionally be referred to, but its rule is identical to that of Brussels I and hence a separate discussion is not necessary. Provisional and protective measures have a different nature under the Insolvency Regulation, which deals only with one branch of law (a very specific branch on the border between procedure and substantive law). The possible provisional and protective measures seen in different legal

---

[1] Proposal for a Council Regulation on Jurisdiction, Applicable law, Recognition and Enforcement of Decisions and Cooperation in Matters relating to Maintenance Obligations, COM(2005) 649 final of 15 December 2005; available at <http://eur-lex.europa.eu>. Note that this Regulation, like the other regulations on civil and commercial matters, will not apply in Denmark (see rec 27 and Art 1). The United Kingdom has indicated that it would not opt in, while Ireland has indicated that it would opt in.

[2] This was confirmed in Case C–391/95 *Van Uden Maritime BV, trading as Van Uden Africa Line v Kommanditgesellschaft in Firma Deco-Line and Another* [1998] ECR I–7091, para 22.

systems cannot vary significantly in this field. In fact, the opening of an insolvency proceeding is one huge protective measure.[3] This measure aims at protecting the insolvent debtor's assets in order to safeguard the orderly distribution of the remaining assets.

6.06 This chapter starts by attempting to define provisional measures. In this chapter, 'provisional measures' includes protective measures. Not all possible provisional measures under the different national laws of the EU Member States will be fully discussed.[4] A brief examination of the material scope of provisional measures under the regulations will follow. The main body of the chapter will be devoted to an examination of the nature of the jurisdictional basis for provisional measures and how these rules fit into the scheme of the Regulations. Thereafter, the time at which provisional measures can be granted and the recognition and enforcement of such measures will be examined.

B. DEFINITION

General

6.07 Provisional measures are difficult to define; they are something less than a full judgment. In some legal systems they might be seen as a fast-track way to get the same result as through a proper judgment.[5] They form a strange and hybrid part of the law. One enters a domain where it is difficult to draw the line between procedural and substantive law.[6]

---

[3] K Vandekerckhove, 'Voorlopige en bewarende maatregelen in de EEX-Verordening, in EEX-II en in de Insolventieverordening,' in M Storme & G de Leval (eds), *Le droit processuel et judiciaire européen* (Bruges: La Charte, 2003) 119–151, 141.

[4] For a survey of national legal systems: C Kessedjian 'Note on Provisional and Protective Measures in Private International Law and Comparative Law' (Choice of Court Convention's Preliminary Document No 10 of October 1998), available at <http://www.hcch.net>; A Verbeke & M-T Caupain, *Transparence Patrimoniale. Condition nécessaire et insuffisante du titre conservatoire européen?* (Paris: Les Éditions Juridiques et Techniques, 2001); A Briggs & P Rees, *Civil Jurisdiction and Judgments* (4th edn, London: LLP, 2005), 459–464; F Gerhard, 'La compétence du juge d'appui pour prononcer des mesures provisoires extraterritoriales. A propos du prononcé d'une *worldwide Mareva injunction* anglaise à l'appui d'une procédure au fond suisse et de la jurisprudence *van Uden* de la Cour de Justice des Communautés européennes' [1999] *Revue suisse de droit international et de droit européen* 97–141.

[5] This has specifically become the case under the French *référé-provision* and the Dutch and Belgian *kort geding*. See also P de Vareilles-Sommières, 'La compétence internationale des tribunaux français en matière de mesures provisoires' [1996] *Revue critique de droit international privé* 397–437, 398–399.

[6] See GA Berman, 'Provisional Relief in Transnational Litigation' [1997] *Columbia Journal of Transnational Law* 553–617.

The Regulations do not contain definitions of provisional measures.[7] **6.08**
However, clear definitions of provisional measures under the Regulations
are important for parties from third States. It will inform them where
to request such measures and what their legal basis is in a specific case;
either through domestic law or the Regulations. It will also inform defendants from third States what the likely outcome will be. The Regulations'
rules on provisional measures provide an exception to the normal rules
of jurisdiction, taking away the defendant's protection.[8] Therefore the
provisions should be given a limited interpretation.[9]

The concepts of the Regulations need to be interpreted autonomously. This **6.09**
is a difficult task, especially since Brussels I (Article 31), Brussels II *bis*
(Article 20), and the proposed Maintenance Regulation (Article 10) explicitly
refer to national law, instead of providing such an autonomous definition.[10]
Brussels II *bis* goes furthest in providing some form of autonomous definition. It explicitly states the requirement of urgency, and specifies that the
measures would lapse when the court that has jurisdiction as to the substance takes the required measures. This approach contains some of the
characteristics of the rules in the 1996 Hague Convention on the Protection
of Children, which grants jurisdiction to order provisional measures, and
at the same time sets the conditions for the use of such jurisdiction.[11] Some
authors favoured such an autonomous definition at the time of the review-
ing of the Brussels Convention (and its conversion into Brussels I).[12] Their
hope that the Article would be modified did not materialize. The wording

---

[7] For the revision of the Brussels Convention that was underway in 1998, the European
Commission suggested such an autonomous definition, Art 18a(2): '[f]or the purposes of this
Convention, provisional, including protective measures means urgent measures for the
examination of a dispute, for the preservation of evidence or of property pending judgment
or enforcement, or for the preservation or settlement of a situation of fact or of law for the
purpose of safeguarding rights which the courts hearing the substantive issues are, or may
be, asked to recognise'; OJ C 33 of 31 January 1998, 20.

[8] H Gaudemet-Tallon, *Compétence et exécution des jugements en Europe* (3rd edn, Paris:
LGDJ, 2002) 246.

[9] G Maher & BJ Rodger, 'Provisional and Protective Remedies: The British experience of
the Brussels Convention' [1999] ICLQ 302–339, 302.

[10] It is interesting to note that also the Helsinki Principles (67th Conference of the International Law Association, 1996) expressly stated that they did not seek to confine the existing
bases of national jurisdiction; see P Nygh, 'Provisional and Protective Measures in
International Litigation. The Helsinki Principles' [1998] *Rabels Zeitschrift für Ausländisches
und Internationales Privatrecht* 115–122, 121.

[11] Hague Convention of 19 October 1996 on Jurisdiction, Applicable Law, Recognition,
Enforcement and Co-Operation in respect of Parental Responsibility and Measures for the
Protection of Children, Arts 11 and 12, available at <http://www.hcch.net>.

[12] See H Gaudemet-Tallon, case note on *Van Uden* [1999] *Revue de l'arbitrage* 152–166, 165.

of the provision of Brussels I (and that of the proposed Maintenance Regulation) is identical to that of the Brussels Convention.

6.10 Although the judgments of the European Court of Justice do not go all the way in providing definitions, it has offered some guidance. Not all measures that are seen as 'provisional' or 'protective' in national legal systems can be so regarded for purposes of the regulations.[13] The ECJ stated in *Reichert II* that regard should be had not to the measure itself but to the rights it aimed to protect.[14] This case dealt with the French *action paulienne*, which does not seek to preserve a factual or legal situation pending a decision of the court having jurisdiction as to the substance of the matter, but could alter legal positions.[15] It could not be seen, therefore, as a provisional or protective measure under the Brussels Convention.[16]

6.11 Consequently, it is difficult to find an exact definition of provisional measures under the civil jurisdiction regulations, ingredients of national law, and limitations imposed by the European Court of Justice. These elements will be discussed in the following paragraphs. It is argued that the definitions, to the extent that they can be made, apply only when the Regulations apply, and not every time an EU Member State's court seeks to grant provisional measures.

Urgency

6.12 Not all provisional measures that exist in national systems strictly require that the relief sought must be urgent. Nor is the requirement of urgency explicitly stated in Brussels I.[17] Brussels II *bis*, on the other hand, does contain an explicit reference to urgency.[18] This has led some authors to conclude

---

[13] L Pålsson, 'Interim Relief under the Brussels and Lugano Conventions' in *Liber amicorum Kurt Siehr: Private Law in the International Arena. From National Conflict Rules Towards Harmonization and Unification* (The Hague: TMC Asser Press, 2000), 621–638, 625.

[14] Case C–261/90, *Mario Reichert, Hans-Heinz Reichert and Ingeborg Kockler v Dresdner Bank AG (No 2)* [1992] ECR I–2149. See case notes by B Ancel [1992] *Revue critique de droit international privé* 720–726 and P Vlas [1993] *Nederlands Internationaal Privaatrecht* 499–501. A Huet, in his case note [1993] *Journal de droit international* 461–465, 464–465 expresses doubts about the definition adopted by the European Court of Justice.

[15] This action can be used by a creditor of an insolvent debtor to invalidate a disposal of assets in fraud of the creditor's rights.

[16] This view had also been pronounced, with view to the material scope of provisional measures, in Case 143/78 *Jacques de Cavel v Louise de Cavel (Cavel I)* [1979] ECR 1055; see below, para 6.22.

[17] Art 31 of Brussels I.

[18] See Art 20 Brussels II *bis* . See also B Ancel & H Muir Watt, 'La désunion européeenne: le Règlement dit "Bruxelles II"' [2001] *Revue critique de droit international privé* 403–457, 427.

(the reference being absent from Brussels I) that such urgency requirement does not exist.[19] Others argue to the contrary: the mention of urgency is said to be an incorporation of the judgments of the European Court of Justice.[20] This argument is plausible and a narrow interpretation of the measures seems to be in favour of the requirement for urgency.[21] Urgency would be a part of the justification for extending jurisdiction to courts other than those that would normally have such jurisdiction. However, if one sees the rule in Brussels II *bis* as the more modern and correct one, it is unclear why the proposed Maintenance Regulation uses the exact wording of Brussels I, again with no reference to urgency.

The requirement for urgency should probably be sought in national law. **6.13** Analysis of the *Italian Leather* judgment provides support for such assertion.[22] In this case Italian Leather sought interim relief (an order restraining the defendant to use a specific brand name) in a German court. The relief was unavailable under German law since the judge found that there was no urgency under the German law interpretation of the requirement: Italian Leather had not proved that there was a risk of irreparable damage or of a definitive loss of rights. Italian Leather then tried obtaining the same interim relief in Italy. There, upon a different view of the requirement for urgency, the relief was granted. The European Court of Justice recognized these different interpretations without choosing one or giving an autonomous interpretation of urgency.

Territoriality

The rule in Brussels II *bis* on provisional measures contains an express limi- **6.14** tation to 'persons or assets in that State'. This is in line with the 1996 Hague Child Protection Convention that states that provisional measures have a territorial effect.[23] Brussels I and the proposed Maintenance Regulation, on the other hand, do not explicitly restrict provisional measures in this way. Thus, it is unclear under these provisions whether defendants and assets

By way of comparison, note that the Hague Protection of Children Convention, note 11 above, also contains a reference to urgency.

[19] See Vandekerckhove, note 3 above, 121.

[20] See N Watté & H Boularbah, 'Les nouvelles règles de conflits de juridictions en matière de désunion des époux. Le règlement communautaire "Bruxelles II"', [2001] *Journal des tribunaux* 369–378, 375.

[21] See Gaudemet-Tallon, *Compétence et exécution*, note 8 above, 249–250.

[22] Case C–80/00, *Italian Leather Spa v WECO Polstermöbel GmbH & Co* [2002] ECR I–4995. See also Vandekerckhove, note 3 above, 122.

[23] Note 11 above, Arts 11 and 12.

not present in the Member State granting provisional measures can be affected.[24]

6.15 In the English case *Haiti v Duvalier*[25] a Mareva injunction (aimed at freezing the assets of the defendants all over the world) was granted to the plaintiff, the Republic of Haiti. Of the 11 defendants, only one was domiciled in England. The main proceedings were pending in France since most of the defendants were domiciled there. It was clear that the English court did not have jurisdiction to do more than grant interim measures. The English judge found it reasonable to grant this order because of the unusual nature of the case. The link with England was tenuous: one bank was situated in England and the lawyers dealing with some of the assets (who were not defendants) were domiciled in England.

6.16 In its judgments the European Court of Justice has not imposed a requirement of territoriality, but of a 'real connecting link,' which will be discussed below.

Real connecting link

6.17 The European Court of Justice introduced this important limitation in the *Van Uden* judgment:

> It follows that the granting of a provisional or protective measure on the basis of Article 24 is conditional on, *inter alia*, the existence of a real connecting link between the subject matter of the measures sought and the territorial jurisdiction of the Contracting State of the court before which those measures are sought.[26]

Many pages have been written on this case, but the uncertainty remains.[27] What is a 'real connecting link'? Does this refer to the territory on which

---

[24] See B Audit, *Droit international privé* (3rd edn, Paris: Economica, 2000) 437.
[25] [1990] 1 QB 202.
[26] Note 2 above, para 40.
[27] See, for instance, case notes by XE Kramer [1999] *Nederlands Tijdschrift voor Burgerlijk Recht* 74–79; JJ van Haersolte-van Hof [1999] *Nederlands Tijdschrift voor Europees recht* 66–67; Gaudemet-Tallon, note 12 above; P Vlas [1999] *Netherlands International Law Review* 106–109; A Huet [1999] *Journal de droit international* 613–625; H Boularbah, 'Les measures provisoires en droit commercial international: développements récents au regard des Conventions de Bruxelles et de Lugano' [1999] *Revue de droit commercial belge* 604–610; AVM Struycken [2000] *Ars Aequi* 579–586. See also L Demeyere, 'Voorlopige en bewarende maatregelen (Art 24 EEX) na het arrest *Van Uden* en het arrest *Mietz* ' [1999–2000] *Rechtskundig Weekblad* 1353–1363; P Beaumont, 'Interplay of Private International Law and European Community Law' in C Kilpatrick, T Novitz & P Skidmore (eds), *The future of remedies in Europe* (Oxford: Hart Publishing, 2000) 137–190, 173–177; A Schulz, 'Einstweilige Maßnahmen nach dem Brüsseler Gerichtsstands- und Vollstreckungsübereinkommen in der Rechtsprechung des Gerichtshofs der Europäischen Gemeinschaften (EuGH)' [2001] *Zeitschrift für Europäisches*

the measure will be executed? The German Government stated, in its arguments before the Court on *Van Uden*, that the condition of the real connecting link is satisfied when the provisional measure can be enforced in that state.[28] However, that cannot be the only possible link. Does the 'real connecting link' refer to the presence of some or all of the assets concerned in the main action? Does it refer to business interests in the territory?[29] Probably a balance of the different interests would have to be made and the establishment of a real link would be a question of fact.

This rule seems to limit measures that would go too far under national law. **6.18** The criterion, as it is formulated, can be used to impose a degree of territoriality, or even an extent of urgency.

One might ask whether the rule of the real connecting link may be used in **6.19** cases where the protection of assets situated in third States is at stake. However, it seems that the answer lies at a different point. These limitations imposed by the European Court of Justice can only be triggered once it has been established that the Regulation provides jurisdiction to an EU Member State court. If an EU Member State court has jurisdiction then assets in a third State would also fall under the limitations. That would be the case for the worldwide injunction given in *Haiti v Duvalier* (where the French court had jurisdiction), since the test of the real connecting link could prevent measures going too far.[30] If not, the EU Member State court is free to apply its national rules to their full extent.

Provisional nature

Brussels II *bis* has introduced a sell-by date for provisional measures: they **6.20** will cease to apply when the Member State court with jurisdiction over the substance of the matter has taken the necessary measures.[31] The 1996 Hague Child Protection Convention (concerning situations where children or their property are present in a Contracting State) distinguishes between measures in urgent cases and measures of a provisional nature. It expressly provides for these measures to lapse when the court in a Contracting State with jurisdiction on the substance takes the necessary steps. If the child is

---

Privatrecht 805–836; M Pertegás Sender, *Cross-Border Enforcement of Patent Rights* (Oxford: Oxford University Press, 2002) 129–131 and 136–140; Briggs & Rees, note 4 above, 467–468.

[28] *Van Uden* , note 2 above, para 36 of the judgment.

[29] Boularbah, note 27 above, 604.

[30] See also CMV Clarkson & J Hill, *Jaffey on the Conflict of Laws* (2nd edn, London: Butterworths, 2002) 143.

[31] Art 20(2) Brussels II *bis*. This rule was not contained in Brussels II. The Helsinki Principles also contained a time limit for provisional measures; Nygh, note 10 above, 120.

habitually resident in a non-Contracting State, the measures shall lapse when the necessary measures have been taken in another state and are recognized in the Contracting State that granted the urgent or provisional measures.[32]

6.21 Regarding Brussels I, the European Court of Justice in *Van Uden* emphasized that the measure granted must not be final:

> Depending on each case and commercial practices in particular, the court must be able to place a time-limit on its order or, as regards the nature of the assets or goods subject to the measures contemplated, require bank guarantees or nominate a sequester and generally make its authorisation subject to all conditions guaranteeing the provisional or protective character of the measure ordered.[33]

This requirement, as with that of the real connecting link, creates the possibility of limiting measures that could go too far. Measures that are not truly temporary, but in fact grant substantive relief to the plaintiff (possibly to the detriment of the defendant), will not pass this test if it is not certain that the measure will be reversible if the plaintiff is unsuccessful in the main action.

C. THE REACH OF PROVISIONAL MEASURES: MATERIAL SCOPE

Limitation to the material scope of the Regulation: Brussels I

6.22 The starting point is that the rule on provisional measures has the same scope as the other provisions of Brussels I. Only when a matter (civil or commercial) is already within the scope of the Regulation, can provisional measures be taken on the basis of the Regulation. If the matter falls outside the scope of the Regulation, so will the provisional measures in that case. Accordingly the European Court of Justice ruled that an order by a French court pending a divorce, that the wife's furniture be put under seal and assets and accounts be frozen, could not be enforced in Germany under

---

[32] Arts 11 and 12; Report by P Lagarde on the (1996) Hague Convention on jurisdiction, applicable law, recognition, enforcement and co-operation in respect of parental responsibility and measures for the protection of children, [1996] Hague Conference on Private International Law. Proceedings of the Eighteenth Session, vol II, *Protection of children* , 535–604 at 565–571, available at <http://www.hcch.net>.

[33] *Van Uden* , note 2 above, para 38. See also Case C–99/96, *Hans-Hermann Mietz v Intership Yachting Sneek BV* [1999] ECR I–2277, para 42 and Case C–104/03, *St Paul Dairy Industries NV v Unibel Exser BVBA* [2005] ECR I–34814, para 14.

the Brussels Convention.[34] Divorce was not within the scope of the Convention (or the Regulation) and the fact that the measures were provisional could not draw them into the scope. In another preliminary question in the same dispute a French judge in divorce proceedings granted an interlocutory maintenance order.[35] The question was whether this was a 'civil matter' and whether enforcement could thus take place under the Brussels Convention. Rights in property arising out of a matrimonial relationship fell outside the scope of the Brussels Convention (according to Article 1(2)), but maintenance fell within its ambit (Article 5(2)).[36] The European Court of Justice found that the provisions of the French code civil (Civil Code) on which the order was based dealt with all financial obligations between former spouses after divorce. They therefore amounted to civil matters and fell within the scope of the Brussels Convention. This line of reasoning was followed in the judgment of *CHW v GJH*, a case dealing with the delivery of a codicil, claimed to allow an exemption from liabilities resulting from a spouse's management of property.[37] The European Court of Justice held that the issue was closely connected to a matrimonial relationship and therefore outside the scope of the Brussels Convention.

The particularity of arbitration

Brussels I does not apply to arbitration.[38] It may therefore seem logical **6.23** that the matter is also excluded for the purposes of provisional measures. However, the existence of an arbitration clause will not preclude the possibility of granting provisional measures under Brussels I, according to the much-discussed *Van Uden* case.[39] Under the slot/space charter agreement between Van Uden, a Dutch company, and Deco-Line, a German company,

---

[34] See *Cavel I* , note 16 above. See case notes by A Huet, [1979] *Journal de droit international* 681–691; T Hartley, [1979] ELR 222–224; GAL Droz, [1980] *Revue critique de droit international privé* 621–629.

[35] Case 120/79, *Louise de Cavel v Jacques de Cavel (Cavel II)* [1980] ECR 731. See case notes by Droz, ibid; A Huet, [1980] *Journal de droit international* 442–448; R Hausmann [1981] *Praxis des internationalen Privat- und Verfahrensrechts* 5–7.

[36] These provisions on the scope have not changed under Brussels I.

[37] Case 25/81, *CHW v GJH* [1982] ECR 1189. See case notes by A Huet, [1982] *Journal de droit international* 942–948; JG Sauveplanne, [1983] *Praxis des internationalen Privat- und Verfahrensrechts* 65–67; GAL Droz, [1984] *Revue critique de droit international privé* 354–361.

[38] See Art 1(4). The extent of the exclusion will be put to the test in a case referred to the ECJ by the House of Lords: Case C–185/07 *Ras Riunione Adriatica di Sicurta Spa v West Tankers Inc*, reference to ECJ on 2 April 2007; referring judgment [2007] UKHL 4. In that case the House of Lords is asking whether granting an anti-suit injunction against a court in an EU Member State to protect an arbitration clause is in conflict with the Convention.

[39] *Van Uden*, note 2 above. For the case notes on this decision, see note 27 above.

Van Uden undertook to make available to Deco-Line cargo space on board a vessel operated by it. The contract contained an arbitration clause. Van Uden instituted arbitration proceedings in the Netherlands and also sought interim relief there, by way of *kort geding* proceedings. Deco-Line contested the jurisdiction of the court in the Netherlands, arguing that the German courts, the place of its seat, had jurisdiction. The European Court of Justice found that, in situations where the parties had concluded an arbitration clause, jurisdiction could not be based on the other jurisdiction rules of the Regulation, but only on its provisional measures rule. The only test for the applicability of the rule on provisional measures was that the dispute should fall within the material scope of the Convention, i.e. civil and commercial matters. The Court stated that provisional measures should not be seen as ancillary to arbitration proceedings but parallel to them, intended as measures of support.

6.24 Drawing this matter within the scope of Brussels I (then Convention) was advantageous for the defendant. He could then rely on that instrument to limit jurisdiction, while under Dutch law such a limitation did not exist.

6.25 The dispute was clearly one within the ambit of 'civil and commercial' matters and the fact that the agreement contained an arbitration clause did not alter its civil and commercial nature. Arbitration, as an excluded matter, is *sui generis:* it does not define a branch of substantive law like the status or capacity of natural persons, rights in property arising out of a matrimonial relationship, wills and succession, bankruptcy, or social security.[40] Arbitration can be distinguished from those exceptions by the fact that it only refers to a chosen procedure. One should distinguish between the material scope of the Regulation regarding the substance of legal relations on the one hand, and procedural matters on the other. The arbitration exception refers to the fact that Brussels I does not regulate the recognition of arbitral awards.[41] This matter is left to the efficient and widely accepted New York Convention.[42] All EU Member States are party, and it would

---

[40] These exceptions to the material scope of Brussels I are contained in Art 1.

[41] The question whether a decision to annul or invalidate arbitration proceedings should be recognized in another EU Member State under Brussels I falls outside the scope of this book. The Advocate General in his opinion on *Van Uden* , note 2 above, stated that the recognition of such proceedings was not excluded from the Brussels Convention (para 55). According to Audit, note 24 above, 433, the matter is excluded from the regime of Brussels I. See also H Van Houtte, 'May court judgments that disregard arbitration clauses and awards be enforced under the Brussels and Lugano Conventions?' [1997] *Arbitration International* 85–92 especially 88.

[42] Convention on the Recognition and Enforcement of Foreign Arbitral Awards (New York, 1958). This Convention has 142 States Party. All the Member States of EFTA are also States Party to this Convention, so that the same argument for exclusion of arbitration from the Lugano Convention applies. It should be noted, however, that Art 220 of the Rome Treaty,

therefore have been superfluous to regulate the matter; it would not have been a good idea to create a conflict of Conventions.[43] Thus, while parties respect any arbitration clause, civil and commercial provisional measures sought in a court will remain of a civil and commercial nature and will fall under Brussels I.

Beyond the material scope of the Regulation: Brussels II *bis*

Provisional and protective measures operate differently under Brussels II *bis*. **6.26** Such measures that fall outside the scope of the Regulation may also be granted under it. This rule refers to assets; but the scope of Brussels II *bis* does not include assets.[44] From an EU point of view such a rule makes sense. Some excluded matters are so closely related that their implication might be essential to safeguard the rights of a party under the Regulation. An example is the law concerning matrimonial property. This extension is probably only temporary in nature as the European Commission has published a Green Paper on matrimonial property, and thus the matter will soon be regulated by EC legislation.[45]

D. THE NATURE OF THE JURISDICTIONAL BASIS FOR PROVISIONAL MEASURES

The rule on provisional measures does not entail an autonomous basis of jurisdiction

According to some authors the rule on provisional measures provides an **6.27** independent basis for jurisdiction.[46] No subsequent reliance on a national

---

the basis of the Brussels Convention, expressly provided for the recognition of arbitral awards. See also the opinion of the Advocate General in *Van Uden*, note 2 above, paras 50–53.

[43] See Audit, note 24 above, 433.

[44] See Art 20 of Brussels II *bis*. See also Borrás Report on the Convention, drawn up on the basis of Article K.3 of the Treaty on the European Union, on Jurisdiction and the Recognition and Enforcement of Judgments in Matrimonial Matters; OJ C 221, 16 July 1998, 27, para 59. See also V Van den Eeckhout, "Europees' echtscheiden. Bevoegdheid en erkenning van beslissingen op basis van de EG Verordening 1347/2000 van 29 mei 2000' in H Van Houtte & M Pertegás Sender (eds), *Het nieuwe Europese IPR: van verdrag naar verordening* (Antwerpen: Intersentia, 2001) 69–101, 93–94.

[45] Green Paper on Conflict of Laws in Matters Concerning Matrimonial Property Regimes, including the Question of Jurisdiction and Mutual Recognition of 17 July 2006, COM(2006) 400 final; available at <http://eur-lex.europa.eu>. A Green Paper is the initiation of a consultation round, and does not yet contain proposed text for EC legislation.

[46] Pertegás Sender, note 27 above, 130; M Claeys, 'Het international kortgeding en artikel 24 EEX', case note on Hof van Beroep, Gent, 8 December 1994 [1995–96] *Algemeen Juridisch*

basis for jurisdiction is necessary. This argument states that the reference to national law in the Article points only at the kind of measure available and not at any jurisdiction rule. This means that a court that does not have jurisdiction under Brussels I can acquire jurisdiction if it is in a position to grant a provisional measure. Jurisdiction is based on the fact that the purported measure will only be provisional. The only limitations to the basis for jurisdiction are those imposed by the European Court of Justice (mainly the requirement of a real connecting link).

Jurisdiction for provisional measures is dependent on a basis for jurisdiction in national law

6.28 It is submitted that the interpretation that the rule on provisional measures provides an autonomous basis for jurisdiction goes too far, and that the existence of a basis for jurisdiction in national law is essential.[47] If one took away this requirement, the rule would grant jurisdiction to any court in an EU Member State. If a court lacked jurisdiction, it could still acquire jurisdiction for provisional measures if a certain number of requirements, set by the European Court of Justice in the interpretation of the provision, were met.

6.29 The Jenard Report does not clarify the meaning of the reference to national law. It merely states that application may be made to the competent courts for provisional and protective measures. As regards the measures that may be granted, the report states that reference should be made to the internal law of the country concerned. Nothing is said about the basis for jurisdiction and it is not clear whether the reference to national law includes the issue of jurisdiction or merely the availability of a remedy.[48]

Tijdschrift 151–154 at 152–153; see also the judgment of the Rechtbank van Eerste Aanleg (District court) of Brussels of 22 September 2000 [2000] *Revue de la propriété intellectuel* 292–302.

[47] See, in support of this theory, Briggs & Rees, note 4 above, 464–465 and 467–468; Gaudemet-Tallon, *Compétence et exécution*, note 8 above, 250; J Kropholler, *Europäisches Zivilprozeßrecht. Kommentar zu EuGVO und Lugano-Übereinkommen* (7th edn, Heidelberg: Verlag Recht und Wirtschaft GmbH, 2002) 356; Boularbah, note 27 above, 604; G Cuniberti, *Les mesures conservatoires portant sur des biens situés à l'étranger* (Paris: LGDJ, 2000) 320–321, stating '[i]l nous semble tout simplement inconcevable qu'une telle règle de compétence ait été imaginée. Nous ne l'avons jamais rencontrée en droit comparé. Même si elle devait exister, elle serait très certainement considérée comme exorbitante.' See also *Mietz* , note 33 above, para 46.

[48] P Jenard, 'Rapport du Comité restreint sur la bilateralisation' [1969] Hague Conference on Private International Law. Proceedings of the Extraordinary Session 11, 145–151 (Jenard Report), 42.

Van Uden confirms that jurisdiction may be based on national law. In this **6.30**
case, jurisdiction in interim proceedings (*kort geding*) in the Netherlands
was based on the domicile of the plaintiff, according to Article 126(3) of
the Dutch Wetboek van Burgerlijke Rechtsvordering (Code of Civil Procedure). Not surprisingly, this basis for jurisdiction had been seen as exorbitant and outlawed by Brussels I.[49] One of the preliminary questions
referred to the European Court of Justice was whether, in the case of provisional and protective measures, the jurisdiction of the court could be
based on such an exorbitant ground of jurisdiction. The European Court
of Justice ruled that it could. This conclusion came about in a very formalistic
way: the first subparagraph of Article 3 states that a defendant domiciled
in a Member State can only be sued in the courts of another Member State
by virtue of the rules set out in sections 2 to 6 of the Convention (2 to 7 of
the Regulation). These sections contain the rules on special jurisdiction
(e.g. for contract and tort), jurisdiction over parties that deserve protection
(insured parties, consumers and employees), exclusive jurisdiction (e.g.
concerning immovable property), and prorogation of jurisdiction. Other
procedural matters like *lis pendens* and related actions are dealt with next
in the scheme of the Regulation. Only in section 9 of the Convention (10 of
the Regulation), the last section of the chapter on jurisdiction, does the rule
on provisional and protective measures get its turn. Therefore the Court
concluded that this rule is not affected by the limitation in Article 3.

Jurisdictional nature of provisional measures

The civil jurisdiction regulations in fact do no more than permit courts in **6.31**
EU Member states to assume jurisdiction to grant provisional and protective measures. They do not create a new basis for jurisdiction. The negative formulation of the rule in Brussels II *bis* seems clearer in this respect:
'the provisions of this Regulation shall not prevent the courts of a Member
State from taking such provisional, including protective, measures . . .'.[50]
This wording makes it clear that no jurisdiction is granted by the Regulation; the Regulation merely leaves in place the rules that already exist.
The true basis of those rules is to be found in national law. The European

---

[49] See Art 3 & Annex I of Brussels I. In the meantime, this basis for jurisdiction has been
deleted from Dutch law and subsequently also the reference to it in Brussels I. See Commission
Regulation (EC) No 1496/2002 of 21 August 2002 amending Annex I (the rules of jurisdiction
referred to in Article 3(2) and Article 4(2)) and Annex II (the list of competent courts
and authorities) to Council Regulation (EC) No 44/2001 on jurisdiction and the recognition
and enforcement of judgments in civil and commercial matters, OJ L 225 of 22 August 2002,
p 13, Art 1.
[50] See Art 20 of Brussels II *bis* .

Commission states, in its practice guide on the application of Brussels II *bis*, that the rule 'is not a rule which confers jurisdiction'.[51]

6.32 The inclusion of the rules in the Regulations makes it possible for the European Court of Justice to provide limitations to the use of national bases for jurisdiction. Furthermore, their explicit mention in the EC instruments forces EU Member State courts to make available those measures that exist under national law to parties from other EU Member States.[52] Such a rationale seems perfectly in line with the aim of extending the EU's internal market, while respecting its borders. The fact that the Regulations mention provisional and protective measures also safeguards them from the defence of *lis pendens*. In the absence of an explicit reference to provisional measures, the *lis pendens* rule would make it impossible for a court second seised to grant any ruling in the case; such court would have to stay its proceedings and declare that it has no jurisdiction if the court first seised has jurisdiction.

E. PROVISIONAL MEASURES IN THE SCHEME OF THE OTHER JURISDICTION RULES

The complete system of the jurisdiction rules

6.33 The question of whether Brussels I contains a complete system of jurisdiction rules has been examined in chapter 1.[53] The European Court of Justice's view is that the Regulation does create such a complete system.[54] Thus the national rules on jurisdiction can only be applied when expressly authorized by the Regulation (such as in Article 4). Regarding provisional measures, the Regulation contains such express authorization in Article 31. This rule permits national jurisdiction rules to be used and limits them to a certain extent.

6.34 It is submitted that, as is the case regarding the material scope, the rules on provisional measures can only be triggered once the Regulation in question is already applicable. This assertion is supported by the UK's Civil

---

[51] Practice guide for the application of the Regulation, drawn up by the European Commission in consultation with the European Judicial Network in civil and commercial matters; available at <http://ec.europa.eu/civiljustice/divorce/divorce_int_en.htm>, p 11.

[52] See Struycken, note 27 above, 581–582.

[53] Paras 1.52 and following.

[54] Opinion C–1/03 *Competence of the Community to conclude the new Lugano Convention on jurisdiction and the recognition and enforcement of judgments in civil and commercial matters* [2006] ECR I–1145.

Jurisdiction and Judgments Act 1982, which incorporated the Brussels Convention into the law of the UK:

(1) The High Court in England and Wales or Northern Ireland shall have power to grant interim relief where—
   (a) proceedings have been or are to be commenced in a Brussels or Lugano Contracting State or a Regulation State other than the United Kingdom or in a part of the United Kingdom other than that in which the High Court in question exercises jurisdiction; and
   (b) they are or will be proceedings whose subject-matter is within the scope of the Regulation as determined by Article 1 of the Regulation (whether or not the Regulation has effect in relation to the proceedings).[55]

The rule, and its limitations established by the European Court of Justice, can only be invoked once it is clear that the Regulation provides a basis for the jurisdiction of an EU Member State court. The words 'under this Regulation' make it clear that the Regulation's applicability must be ascertained *before* Article 31 can be applied.

On the other hand, some are of the view that the mere fact that a party **6.35** requests provisional measures from a court in the EU triggers the application of the Regulations' rules. The limitations set down by *Van Uden* would always apply. The advocates of this interpretation base their argument partly on *Van Uden*, where the European Court of Justice stated that the limitation in Article 3 does not apply to provisional measures. Therefore (so the argument goes) Articles 2 and 4 do not apply to provisional measures either and the rule on provisional measures has a scope of its own. Thus, if a court in the EU were requested to grant provisional measures, the court would necessarily base its jurisdiction on Article 31 if the case were not purely domestic. However, the finding in *Van Uden* that exorbitant bases for jurisdiction may be used, is more a consequence of the reference to national law than due to the separate nature of the rules on provisional measures. To extend the rules on provisional measures that far would be unreasonable to parties from third States. Furthermore it would not comply with the principle of subsidiarity in European Union law. There is no reason for European Union law to regulate all possible provisional measures any court within the EU might grant as soon as it has an international element. Furthermore, not all jurisdiction rules in the EU are harmonized, even though all EU judgments can be recognized and

---

[55] Civil Jurisdiction and Judgments Act 1982, s 25(1). See, in support of the view that the general rule on the scope of the Regulation applies: XE Kramer, *Het kort geding in internationaal perspectief. Een rechtsvergelijkende studie naar de voorlopige voorziening in het internationaal privaatrecht* (Deventer: Kluwer, 2001) 121–122; Kropholler, note 47 above, 356.

enforced throughout the EU. The need to recognize and enforce provisional measures would not arise as often as the need to recognize other judgments.[56] It therefore seems unnecessary that all provisional measures granted by EU Member State courts in civil and commercial matters should be based on Brussels I.

Defendants domiciled in the EU and in third States

6.36 As has been explained, whenever a defendant is domiciled in the EU, Brussels I provides the bases for jurisdiction: the place of domicile, or the place of performance of a contract, or of commission of a tort, etc. Then any other court in an EU Member State may grant provisional measures. Brussels II *bis* contains a number of alternative bases for jurisdiction, based on habitual residence, nationality, etc. If a court in the EU has jurisdiction on the basis of those rules, courts in other EU Member States are *not prevented* from granting provisional measures: they may do so, but within the limitations of the Regulation.

6.37 If the defendant is domiciled in a third State Brussels I refers to the national bases for jurisdiction. This reference has the effect of bringing those national bases for jurisdiction into the scheme of the Regulation. Similarly, Brussels II *bis* provides a number of bases for jurisdiction and if these appoint no competent court in an EU Member State, reference is made to national bases for jurisdiction. By this reference those bases for jurisdiction are incorporated into the scheme of the Regulation. Thus, if a court in an EU Member State has jurisdiction, then courts in other EU Member States may grant provisional measures.

Exclusive jurisdiction and provisional measures

6.38 In stating the rule that provisional measures may be granted, even if the courts of another EU Member State have jurisdiction as to the substance of the matter, Article 31 is silent on the bases for exclusive jurisdiction. The question might arise whether a court in an EU Member State (other than the one with exclusive jurisdiction) may grant provisional measures. This might be necessary if a lessor wants to freeze assets, or request a bank guarantee to secure unpaid rent he has claimed or intends to claim from the lessee. The matter as to the substance will have to be brought at the court where the immovable property is situated, but one can imagine that the lessee/debtor might not have any assets there, and might not even live there. The same type of problem could arise as to intellectual property rights.

---

[56] On the enforcement of provisional measures, see below, paras 6.61–6.63.

The validity must be contested in the courts of the place of registration. However, a party might wish to request provisional measures in another court. Although it has been explained that the rules on provisional measures should be interpreted restrictively, a literal interpretation of Article 31 seems to permit provisional measures when the substance of the dispute is subject to an exclusive jurisdiction rule.[57]

Forum clauses and provisional measures

If a court in the EU has (exclusive) jurisdiction on the basis of a forum clause, any court within the EU may grant provisional measures, if it has a basis for doing so in its national law, and subject to the limitations imposed by the ECJ. The European Court of Justice accepted this in the *Italian Leather* case.[58] The courts of Bari (Italy) had been chosen. Italian Leather applied to the Landgericht (Regional Court) Koblenz, the domicile of the defendant, WECO, for an order restraining WECO from using a brand name. The European Court of Justice, without going into the question, stated: **6.39**

> [b]y way of preliminary point, the Court proceeds on the assumption that, the court competent to adjudicate on the substance being the Tribunale di Bari, the Landgericht Koblenz did not by its judgment of 17 November 1998 exceed the limits, as interpreted by the Court, of the jurisdiction which it derived from Article 24 of the Brussels Convention [Article 31 of the Regulation].

Thus, choosing a court in the EU will trigger the applicability of Brussels I's rule on provisional measures, and its limitations. Note that it does not matter whether the parties that concluded the forum clause, or one of them, is domiciled in the EU; the fact that a court in an EU Member State has jurisdiction suffices. Some authors are of the opinion that, when a judge resorts to Article 31 in spite of the existence of a forum clause, the requirements of the real connecting link and speed are more stringent.[59] Although this argument might seem plausible, it is hard to uphold in light of the recent judgments of the European Court of Justice. **6.40**

However, the fact that a court outside the EU has been chosen is irrelevant. A court where provisional measures are requested would look only at possible jurisdiction in the EU. If the defendant is domiciled in the EU, **6.41**

---

[57] On this debate: M Pertegás Sender, 'Handhaving van intellectuele rechten in internationaal perspectief. Welke rechter is bevoegd voor voorlopige maatregelen?' in Storme & de Leval, note 3 above, 160; Kramer, note 55 above, 139–143.

[58] Note 22 above, para 39; case note by XE Kramer [2003] CML Rev 953–964. See also Pres. Arnhem 22 December 1999, KG 2000, 58.

[59] Kramer, note 55 above, 143.

the rule will be applied. The court will only be able to apply its national measures in an unfettered way if there is no basis for jurisdiction in the EU.

Arbitration clauses and provisional measures

6.42 The European Court of Justice accepted in *Van Uden* that an EU court could grant provisional measures despite the existence of an arbitration clause. The criteria for such an application are unclear: are the domiciles of the parties relevant? Should one take into account the fact that there would have been jurisdiction in the EU had there not been an arbitration clause? Is the seat of the arbitration relevant?

Voluntary appearance and provisional measures

6.43 If a court in an EU Member State has jurisdiction on the basis that the defendant has appeared before it without contesting jurisdiction, a court in another EU Member State may grant provisional measures.

6.44 The European Court of Justice found in *Mietz* that the voluntary appearance of the defendant in the interim proceedings cannot provide unlimited jurisdiction to grant any provisional measures that the court might consider appropriate if it had jurisdiction under Brussels I as to the substance of the matter.[60]

No court in an EU Member State has jurisdiction as to the substance of the matter

6.45 After examining all the bases for jurisdiction under Brussels I or Brussels II *bis* (the direct rules of the Regulation and the national rules which they refer to), it could appear that no court in an EU Member State has jurisdiction. In such a case, the Regulations' rules on provisional measures will not be triggered. This is similar to a situation that does not fall within the material scope of a regulation. The national court will then revert to its national bases of provisional measures, without the limitations imposed by the European Court of Justice. If there will not be a judgment as to the substance in an EU Member State, there is no reason for the limitations to apply. However, as will be explained, measures that did not adhere to the ECJ's limitations might encounter difficulties when recognition or enforcement is sought in other EU Member States.[61] This will rarely pose

---

[60] *Mietz*, note 33 above, para 52.
[61] Para 6.61 below.

a problem: if substantive proceedings are in a third State and there is a connection only to one EU Member State, the granting of measures valid in that State should be sufficient and the plaintiff probably will not need to have the measures recognized and enforced in other EU Member States.

Before the institution of proceedings as to the substance

A plaintiff may request provisional measures prior to the main action. The **6.46** same criterion then applies: if a court of another EU Member State has jurisdiction under the Regulation, the court may grant provisional measures. The difficulty that the court faces in this case is that it is not yet certain which courts would have jurisdiction as to the substance. According to Briggs and Rees, the court should assume that it does not have jurisdiction and not exercise broader powers than it would have under Article 31.[62] This is probably the best practical approach. Theoretically, the court could attempt to identify all the courts that could have jurisdiction and then decide whether or not to apply Article 31. However, the additional question might then arise whether courts in other EU Member States are bound by that court's findings on jurisdiction over the substance, for instance its interpretation of where a natural or legal person is domiciled.

Lis pendens and provisional measures

The civil jurisdiction regulations contain a simple and clear rule to solve **6.47** the problem of *lis pendens:* the court at which the action had been instituted second stays the proceedings until the first court has ruled on its own jurisdiction. If the first court has jurisdiction, the second court declares that it lacks jurisdiction. The second court may proceed only if the first court does not have jurisdiction.[63] This rule is rigid and elements such as the existence of a forum clause, or proceedings taking longer in some countries than in others, are not taken into consideration.[64]

The rules on provisional measures in fact establish exceptions to the rule of **6.48** *lis pendens.* So, even if a court in an EU Member State has been seised and has jurisdiction, a court in another EU Member State may still grant provisional measures. In most cases, what is asked for in the two courts will not be exactly the same and thus the provision on *lis pendens* will not apply.[65]

---

[62] Briggs & Rees, note 4 above, 472.

[63] See Art 27 of Brussels I.

[64] Case C–116/02, *Erich Gasser GmbH v MISAT Srl* [2003] ECR I–14693. See also A Wittwer, 'Auch bei italienischer Prozessdauer gilt Art. 21 EuGVÜ', [2004] *European Law Reporter*, 48–50.

[65] See Kramer, note 55 above, 145.

6.49 It is also possible that a party tries to obtain interim relief in various courts. The cause of action will seldom be exactly the same since there are as many different provisional measures as legal systems. The nature of provisional measures is such that one usually requests measures relating to property situated in an EU Member State in the courts of that particular State in order to remedy a situation quickly or avoid irreversible damage. Therefore, the occurrence of *lis pendens* becomes rare.[66] However, it is possible that an applicant fears that his (presumed) debtor might move assets quickly from one EU Member State to the next, and then to the next, and so on. In such a case, one could imagine the applicant requesting identical provisional measures in different States at the same time, but such measures will probably only concern the territory of each State. It is submitted that, where such identical measures regarding exactly the same assets are requested in the courts of two different EU Member States, the *lis pendens* rule is not applicable. At the stage of provisional measures, the main object is speedy action. There would be no sense in waiting for another court. At that point, the court will also be less concerned with possible later recognition and enforcement. Furthermore, based on the structure of the Regulations and the place where the rules of provisional measures are found, this rule should be seen as an exception to the *lis pendens* rule. If there are conflicting judgments in the strict sense of the Regulations, the issue can probably only be solved at the time of recognition or enforcement.[67]

6.50 Brussels II *bis* clearly states that the provisional measures lose their effect once there is a judgment on the substance of the case. Thus there could be proceedings in two different courts at the same time. However, once there is a judgment on the substance, the provisional measures cease to apply, whether these were requested before or after the main action was instituted.

The reflexive effect and provisional measures

6.51 The theory of the reflexive effect, and its existence after the European Court of Justice's recent judgments, has been discussed in the previous chapters.[68] One might wonder what the position would be with regard to provisional measures in cases where the defendant is domiciled in the EU, while a court in a third State has been chosen in an exclusive choice of

---

[66] Ibid, 147 on the different views that exist on this point.
[67] See C Wolf & S Lange, 'Das Europäisches System des einstweiligen Rechtsschutzes— doch noch kein System?' [2003] *Recht der Internationalen Wirtschaft* 55–63 at 56.
[68] In particular, paras 3.10 and following.

court agreement, and the plaintiff requests provisional measures in an EU Member State other than that of the domicile of the defendant. Following the judgments of the European Court of Justice, the courts of the Member State where the defendant is domiciled still have jurisdiction.[69] The theory of the reflexive effect, if accepted, would provide a basis for declining such jurisdiction. However, since there is jurisdiction in the EU (even if it has been declined), Article 31 on provisional measures comes into play, and such measures can be granted by a court in another EU Member State (if there is a basis for jurisdiction in national law), and the limitations imposed by the European Court of Justice apply. Following this logic, whether or not the reflexive effect is used is irrelevant for the application of the rule on provisional measures. As soon as there is jurisdiction somewhere in the EU, the provision is triggered.

F. TIME WHEN PROVISIONAL MEASURES CAN BE GRANTED

Provisional measures before institution of the main proceedings

Provisional measures may be granted before the institution of main proceedings. In some cases, after provisional measures have been granted, main proceedings do not follow, or are discontinued. The request for provisional measures is often used as part of the litigation tactic, attempting to force a party into settlement.[70] In some areas of the law, speedy action is necessary and disputes often come to an end after a provisional measure is granted by a court. This is especially frequent in intellectual property cases.[71]   **6.52**

The Insolvency Regulation foresees the possibility of appointing a temporary administrator.[72] He or she may request any measures to secure and preserve any of the debtor's assets situated in another EU Member State, according to that Member State's law. This provision provides a bridge for the period between the request and the opening of the insolvency proceedings. This differs from Brussels I and Brussels II *bis* in the sense that not just any court can grant them; they have to be linked to the court that has jurisdiction to open the main insolvency proceeding. Also, the measures   **6.53**

---

[69] *Lugano* Opinion, note 54 above, para 153.
[70] Maher & Rodger, note 9 above, 302.
[71] See M Pertegás Sender, note 27 above, 127; Rechtbank van Eerste Aanleg (District court) of Brussels, 14 September 2001, AR 00/1456/C.
[72] Art 38.

may only be granted after the opening of the proceeding has been requested. This provision is not very far-reaching and it is hard to imagine that it could be applicable with regard to assets in third States. To reach those assets, national rules of private international law would have to be applied.

Provisional measures after the institution of proceedings, but before judgment

6.54 Provisional measures can also be granted after the institution of proceedings but before judgment.[73] This is the situation when a case is pending in the court of an EU Member State, but the courts of other EU Member States may grant provisional measures. This occurrence of provisional measures entails an exception to the *lis pendens* rule: despite the pending proceedings in an EU Member State, a court in another Member State may go ahead and grant such measures.

6.55 The Brussels II *bis* explicitly foresees that such measures will lapse at the time when the court that has jurisdiction as to the substance grants appropriate measures. Brussels I does not explicitly set a similar deadline, but the European Court of Justice has reaffirmed that it is crucial that the measures are temporary.[74]

6.56 Also, the Insolvency Regulation explicitly states that protective measures taken by the court which has jurisdiction over the main proceedings will be recognized without formality, as are all other judgments.[75] This fits into the court's universal jurisdiction, which is the object of the Insolvency Regulation, at least for main insolvency proceedings.[76] The position is

---

[73] See Briggs & Rees, note 4 above, 459–460; Vandekerckhove, note 3 above, 124. Clarkson & Hill, note 30 above, 142, state that in English law, extraterritorial injunctions are more likely to be granted after judgment than before.

[74] Para 6.21 above.

[75] Art 25.

[76] See, *inter alia* P Wautelet, 'De Europese Insolventieverordening' in Van Houtte & Pertegás Sender, note 44 above, 136–140; H-C Duursma-Kepplinger, D Duursma & E Chalupsky, *Europäische Insolvenzverordnung: Kommentar* (Vienna: Springer–Verlag, 2002) p 137; PLC Torremans, *Cross Border Insolvencies in EU, English and Belgian Law* (The Hague: Kluwer Law International, 2002) 150–155; P Hameau & M Raimon, 'Les Faillites internationales. Approche européenne' [2003] *International Business Law Journal* 645–665, 655–656; E Dirix & V Sagaert, 'Verhaalsrechten en zekerheidsposities van schuldeisers onder de Europese Insolventieverordening' [2001] *Revue de droit commercial belge* 580–600, 582; SCJJ Kortmann & PM Veder, 'De Europese Insolventieverordening' [2000] *Weekblad voor Privaatrecht, Notariaat en Registratie* 764–774, 765; N Watté & V Marquette, 'Le règlement communautaire, du 29 mai 2000, relatif aux procédures d'insolvabilité' [2001] *Revue de droit commercial belge* 565–579, 572;

different to that of Brussels I and II *bis*, where separate jurisdictional grounds exist for provisional and protective measures. Article 25 of the Insolvency Regulation is merely a confirmation of the fact that the judge that has jurisdiction may also grant provisional measures. The possible influence on third States is therefore the same as for other judgments. This influence depends, to a large extent, on the interpretation of the words of the Virgos/Schmit Report:

Main insolvency proceedings have universal scope. They aim at encompassing all the debtor's assets on a world-wide basis and at affecting all creditors, wherever located. [77]

According to some authors the word 'worldwide' implies that even assets in third States can be subjected to insolvency proceedings in an EU Member State.[78] Therefore assets in third States could also be subjected to provisional measures that a Member State judge grants (such as freezing injunctions). Most often, these measures would not be automatically recognized in third States, due to their lack of legal basis for such recognition. Recognition or enforcement proceedings would have to be started. Whether a judgment would be recognized or enforced would depend on the views that the third State holds on universality and territoriality of insolvencies, i.e. whether insolvency proceedings in one state encompass only the assets in that state, or all the assets of the debtor wherever they are.[79] It seems more plausible to admit that the European Union simply cannot govern all assets of a debtor *worldwide*.[80] The principle of subsidiarity seems to warrant limitation to the EU; the assets in third States should be left out of reach of the Insolvency Regulation.[81] Whether or not those assets form part of the insolvent estate should be left to the national private international law of the EU Member State where the insolvency proceeding has been opened.

T Bosly, 'La faillite internationale. Une ère nouvelle s'est-elle ouverte avec le règlement du Conseil du 29 mai 2000?' [2001] *Journal des tribunaux* 689–696, 690–691.

[77] Virgos/Schmit Report on the Convention on Insolvency Proceedings (unpublished), no 73.

[78] See Wautelet, note 76 above, 136.

[79] See, on this distinction, Wautelet, ibid, 103–110.

[80] See, for support of this view, Watté & Marquette, note 76 above, 572; Kortmann & Veder, note 78 above, 765.

[81] However, Torremans, note 76 above, does not agree. He states at 172–173 '[t]his limitation may make sense for those that see subsidiarity as a sacred cow of EU law, but it is unfortunate from both an insolvency law and a private international law point of view. From a private international law point of view the co-existence of two divergent regimes is undesirable . . .'.

6.57 In any event, provisional measures in territorial or secondary proceedings will not be able to take effect outside the Member State where they were granted. These proceedings, whether opened before or after main insolvency proceedings, are based on territoriality.[82] They only take account of assets situated within the Member State of the territorial or secondary proceeding.

Provisional measures after judgment in the main proceedings

6.58 Provisional measures can also be granted after judgment. This is possible at various stages. After judgment, but before a declaration of enforceability, an applicant may request provisional measures in the Member State where recognition is sought.[83] At a later stage, if there is an appeal against the declaration of enforceability, provisional measures may also be granted.

6.59 Brussels II *bis* does not foresee the possibility of provisional measures at the recognition and enforcement stage. The nature of the matters covered by that Regulation is different: money is not key and there should be no concern that a debtor removes his assets in order to evade a foreign judgment. In matters of divorce it is hard to see where provisional and protective measures at the time of recognition could be useful. On the other hand, when it comes to disputes concerning custody over children, quick action might be required in some cases. The Regulation, supported by the 1980 Hague Child Abduction Convention, makes such quick action possible by way of cooperation between central authorities and the mechanism of enforcement without a declaration of enforceability.[84]

6.60 The procedural nature of insolvency proceedings means that measures are taken continuously throughout the process and therefore the reference to 'after judgment' cannot correctly be made.

G. ENFORCEMENT OF PROVISIONAL MEASURES

General

6.61 First of all it must be noted that the need to recognize or enforce provisional measures may not often arise. In a matter where time is of the essence,

---

[82] See, *inter alia* Wautelet, 140; Torremans, 155; Hameau & Raimon, 656; Dirix & Sagaert, 582; Kortmann & Veder, 765–766; Watté & Marquette, 573; Bosly, 691; all cited at note 76 above.

[83] Art 47(1) of Brussels I. See Vandekerckhove, note 3 above, 120.

[84] Hague Convention of 25 October 1980 on the Civil Aspects of International Child Abduction, available at <http://www.hcch.net>.

an applicant would probably first go to the court where enforcement is to take place. However, the European Court of Justice has affirmed the fact that enforcement is possible.[85] Of course the exceptions provided by the Regulations, such as public policy and non-service on the defendant, will also apply.[86] The ECJ has, however, introduced an additional difficulty in *Mietz*.[87] Provisional measures must fall under the definition of the rules in Brussels I, including the limitations introduced by ECJ judgments. In this case the order made in interim (*kort geding*) proceedings could not be enforced, since the national court had not explicitly based its jurisdiction on the rule in the Brussels Convention.[88] This leads to a strange result: normally judgments by EU Member States can circulate freely to all other EU Member States, but now some checks have to be carried out by the enforcing court. Briggs and Rees argue that the enforcing court should not check the jurisdiction of the first court, but rather whether the order is 'an Article 31 order'.[89] Even so, the enforcing court is permitted to second-guess the first court. This judgment indicates unease at the imperfect double nature of the civil jurisdiction regulations: not all jurisdiction rules are harmonized, but enforcement should always be possible.

The rule of Brussels II *bis* seems to exclude recognition and enforcement; under it, measures have to be requested where the relevant persons or assets are situated.[90]   **6.62**

As pointed out in the previous paragraphs, the Insolvency Regulation has a specific regime and in relation to provisional measures it is hard to compare it to Brussels I and II *bis*. The enforcement of provisional measures in   **6.63**

---

[85] Case 125/79 *Bernhard Denilauler v SNC Couchet Frères* [1980] ECR 1553 and case notes by A Huet, [1980] *Journal de droit international* 939–948; T Hartley [1981] ELR 59–61; R Hausmann [1981] *Praxis des internationalen Privat- und Verfahrensrechts* 79–82, all agreeing that enforcement is possible; *Cavel II* , note 35 above. See also *Mietz* , note 33 above, where the principle of the recognition and enforcement of provisional measures was accepted, and the Opinion of Advocate General Léger in *Van Uden*, note 2 above, para 138. On the recognition and enforcement of provisional measures in general: Cuniberti, note 47 above, especially at 189–195.

[86] *Denilauler*, ibid, where the European Court of Justice stated that a provisional measure was not enforceable in another EU Member State if the defendant had not been served. See also Briggs & Rees, note 4 above, 461, making the practical remark that a Mareva injunction is likely to be effective only if applied for without notice. For criticism of *Denilauler*, mostly because of the loss of the surprise effect: Cuniberti, ibid, 190–195.

[87] *Mietz*, note 33 above.

[88] Ibid, para 55.

[89] Briggs & Rees, note 4 above, 478–479.

[90] Watté & Boularbah, note 20 above, 376, state that the rule should be interpreted reasonably, and for instance must allow the enforcement of provisional measures if the person or assets have (been) moved to another Member State.

insolvency proceedings is part of the entire process and cannot be subjected to a separate regime.

H. CONCLUSION

6.64 International trade needs a mechanism such as provisional measures to prevent denial of justice in some instances, either by maintaining the status quo, or by providing satisfaction in anticipation.

6.65 The civil jurisdiction regulations had to permit these rules. Instead of creating a separate autonomous rule, the drafters have chosen to refer to national law and the bases for jurisdiction available there. The reference to national law, however, is limited. Brussels II *bis* contains the limitation in the rule itself. For the limitations on the rules in Brussels I and the proposed Maintenance Regulation, one has to refer to the judgments of the European Court of Justice.

6.66 The existence of the limitations, however, cannot lead to the conclusion that the rules contain an autonomous basis for jurisdiction. A court is not able to grant provisional measures if there is no basis to do so in its national law.

6.67 The rules on provisional measures do not extend the scope of the Regulations. Only if the Regulations are applicable, due to some basis for jurisdiction in the EU, can the rules apply. If the matter is in no way connected to the EU, there is no reason why a court cannot apply its national law in an unfettered way.

6.68 On the enforcement issue, one must establish whether the measures are 'Article 31' measures (for Brussels I). If not, enforcement in other Member States will not be possible.

6.69 The difficulties in defining, classifying, and examining the effect of provisional measures once again emphasize the ambiguity of the Regulations; they are of a double nature, but not completely so. It seems that it would be more just for the EU to choose between two approaches: either provisional measures become an EU matter, are autonomously defined in the Regulations, and enforcement in other EU Member States is possible; or the reference to national law remains, but with the result that such orders are always territorial and cannot be enforced in other EU Member States.

7

The European Union and beyond:
external relations

A. INTRODUCTION

In some areas the European Community has external competence: that is,   **7.01**
competence to act on the international stage. The EC then speaks in its
own right (sometimes alongside the Member States) concerning the outside world.[1]

---

[1] See, in general, PJG Kapteyn, 'Het advies 1/76 van het Europese Hof van Justitie,
de externe bevoegdheid van de Gemeenschap en haar deelneming aan een Europees
oplegfonds voor de binnenscheepvaart' [1978] *Sociaal-economische wetgewing: tijdschrift voor
Europees en economisch recht* 276–288; JHJ Bourgeois, 'External relations powers of the
European Community' [1998–1999] *Fordham International Law Journal* S149–S173;
A Dashwood, 'External relations provisions of the Amsterdam Treaty' [1998] CML Rev 1019–
1045; RA Wessel, 'The inside looking out: consistency and delimitation in EU external rela-
tions' [2000] CML Rev 1135–1171; A Mignolli, 'The EU's Powers of External Relations' [2002]
The International Spectator 101–114; F Dehousse & C Maczkovics, 'Les arrêts *open skies* de la
Cour de justice: l'abandon de la compétence externe implicite de la Communauté?' [2003]
Journal des tribunaux 225–236; K Takahashi, 'External competence implications of the
EC Regulations on jurisdiction and judgments' [2003] ICLQ 529–534; CA Joustra, 'Naar een

7.02 In this chapter, the sources and types of external competence will be discussed first, followed by exclusive and shared external competence. The third issue will be the specific problems relating to judicial cooperation in civil matters. Denmark deserves a separate discussion. Thereafter the general transparency for third States and the practical approach to the matter will be considered. There will not be a detailed analysis of procedures of concluding agreements and the required majorities to do so.[2]

B. WHERE DOES EXTERNAL COMPETENCE COME FROM?

7.03 The necessary starting point is noting that the European Community has legal personality.[3] This means that when EC law permits, the EC may act externally in its own right.

7.04 At this stage of EU integration, external powers are a reality that can no longer be contested. Private international law was transposed by the Treaty of Amsterdam from the third to the first pillar (i.e. into Community competence generally).[4] The EC used its newly gained competence on the

communautair internationaal privaatrecht!' in CJ Joustra & MV Polak, *Internationaal, communautair en nationaal IPR* (The Hague: TMC Asser Press, 2002) 35–47; M Wilderspin & A-M Rouchaud Joët, 'La compétence externe de la Communauté européenne en droit international privé' [2004] *Revue critique de droit international privé* 3–48; A Borrás, 'The effect of the adoption of Brussels I and Rome I on the external competences of the EC and the Member States' in J Meeusen, M Pertegás Sender & G Straetmans (eds), *Enforcement of International Contracts in the European Union. Convergence and Divergence between Brussels I and Rome I* (Antwerp: Intersentia, 2004) 99–125; A Borrás, 'The frontiers and the institutional constitutional questions' in A Nuyts & N Watté (eds), *International civil litigation in Europe and relations with third States* (Brussels: Bruylant, 2005) 27–54; C Gonzalez Beilfuss, 'EC legislation in matters of parental responsibility and third States' in the same book, 493–507; P Eeckhout, *External Relations of the European Union* (Oxford: Oxford University Press, 2004) 58–100 and 135; TC Hartley, *The Foundations of European Community Law* (5th edn, Oxford: Oxford University Press, 2003) 160–193; K Lenaerts & P Van Nuffel, *Constitutional Law of the European Union* (2nd edn, London: Sweet & Maxwell, 2005) 828–895; P Pustorino, 'Observation sur les principes généraux opérant dans le droit international privé et procédural communautaire' [2005] *Revue du droit de l'Union européenne* 113–158, 142–148; N Lavranos, Case note on Opinion 1/03 [2006] CML Rev 1087–1100; K Boele-Woelki & R H van Ooik, 'Exclusieve externe bevoegdheden van de EG inzake het Internationaal Privaatrecht' [2006] *Nederlands Tijdschrift voor Europees Recht* 194–201.

[2] For these details, see Hartley, ibid, 160–162; Lenaerts & Van Nuffel, ibid, 882–897.

[3] Art 266 EC Treaty (Nice version). Art I-7 Constitution would grant the EU legal personality.

[4] See Art 65 EC Treaty (which is the same in the Amsterdam and Nice versions); chapter 1 above, para 1.12 and following.

internal level by adopting legislation (the civil jurisdiction regulations). By this exercise of its internal competence, the EC also obtained external competence in the field.

C. EXCLUSIVE *VERSUS* SHARED EXTERNAL COMPETENCE

What was heavily contested, though, was the extent of these powers: how **7.05** far have the Member States' powers to act towards the outside world been pushed back? The Member States, as sovereign states, have legal personality as well and in principle can also act on the international stage. It is the co-existence of these powers of the EC on the one hand and the Member States on the other that gives rise to confusion.

If the competence is shared, both the EC and the Member States may act **7.06** towards the outside world. This means that the EC has competence in a field, but that this competence has not (yet) become exclusive, while the Member States have not (yet) lost their external competence. When the EC alone may act internationally and the Member States have lost that competence, one refers to exclusive external competence of the EC.

In order to find the border between exclusive and shared external compe- **7.07** tence, one has to look at how and when exclusive external competence arises. Where the EC has exercised its competence, and thus has external competence, and that external competence is not (yet) exclusive, it remains shared.

The arising of exclusive external competence

Exclusive external competence can arise in three ways: explicitly, by neces- **7.08** sity, and implicitly.

First, the EC Treaty explicitly grants exclusive external competence for a **7.09** number of matters, for instance, certain agreements to implement the EC's commercial policy worldwide (such as tariff and trade agreements), and association agreements.[5] This field of expressly granted external competence is limited: it does not include private international law.

---

[5] Arts 133 & 310 EC Treaty (Nice version). The Euratom Treaty, dealing with nuclear energy, also gave such explicit external powers: Ruling 1/78 *Ruling delivered pursuant to the third paragraph of Article 103 of the EAEC Treaty. International Agreement on Natural Rubber* [1978] ECR 2151.

7.10 Second, exclusive external competence can arise because the external actions are necessary for the proper functioning of the internal market.[6] For example, in the *Inland waterway navigation* case, the EC had to negotiate with Switzerland in order to exercise its internal competence, because Swiss vessels used the same rivers and were part of the same navigational network.[7] This basis of exclusive external competence is very limited. Even the example of the inland waterway case shows that this kind of situation will not occur frequently. It does not seem at the moment that this source of exclusive external competence would be relevant to private international law, and in particular civil jurisdiction, although one cannot exclude that it could become relevant in future. [8]

7.11 It is the third occurrence of exclusive external competence that is important for the subject of civil jurisdiction: the EC can implicitly obtain exclusive external competences by reason of its internal actions. Reference is sometimes made to the 'pre-emption' of exclusive external competence. In other words, by acting internally, the EC triggers its exclusive external competence. For implicit external competence to arise, the EC must have exhaustively exercised its internal competence, or have largely covered the area concerned.[9] The Member States then can no longer be permitted to act externally and thus may not influence the internal legislation. This doctrine has been developed, and is still being refined, by the judgments of the European Court of Justice. A starting point is the *ERTA* case:[10]

In particular, each time the Community, with a view to implementing a common policy envisaged by the Treaty, adopts provisions laying down common rules,

---

[6] See Art I–13(2) of the Constitution, codifying the rule.

[7] Opinion 1/76 *Draft Agreement establishing a European laying-up fund for inland waterway vessels* [1977] ECR 741, especially para 4. This opinion concerned inland waterway transport, a matter in which relations with Switzerland were involved. In this case, there had not yet been internal action, as negotiations with Switzerland were necessary in order to take internal measures. Whether or not the factor of necessity can be invoked even if no internal measure has been taken, will not be discussed here; for our topic of civil jurisdiction regulations have been enacted, as I have indicated, so that the point becomes irrelevant for this study. For more information, see Hartley, note 1 above, 167–173.

[8] Wilderspin & Rouchaud Joët, note 1 above, 61.

[9] Opinion 1/94 *Competence of the Community to conclude international agreements concerning services and the protection of intellectual property—Article 228 (6) of the EC Treaty* [1994] ECR I–5267, especially para 77, and Opinion 2/91, *Opinion of the Court of 19 March 1993—Opinion delivered pursuant to the second subparagraph of Article 228 (1) of the EEC Treaty—Convention Nº 170 of the International Labour Organization concerning safety in the use of chemicals at work* [1993] ECR I–1061, especially para 25. See also Lenaerts & Van Nuffel, note 1 above, 862.

[10] Case 22/70 *Commission v Council* [1971] ECR 263. ERTA stands for the European Agreement on Road Transport, with which the case was concerned. The French abbreviation, AETR ('Accord européen sur les transport routiers') is sometimes used to refer to this case. See also Dehousse & Maczkovics, note 1 above, 226; Hartley, note 1 above, 162.

whatever form these may take, the Member States no longer have the right, acting individually or even collectively, to undertake obligations with third States which affect those rules.[11]

The theory is based on parallelism of internal and external competence.[12] **7.12** Thus, when the EC can act internally, it is also able to act externally to safeguard measures already taken, or the interests of the EC more generally. The justification for the parallel nature of internal and external competence of the EC lies in the need for a uniform and consistent application of Community rules, their proper functioning, and the preservation of the full effectiveness of Community law.[13] Once a specific field of law has been regulated internally, the Member States should not be permitted to bring the system into disequilibrium by undertaking international obligations towards third States.

In the field of civil jurisdiction, the EC has enacted a number of regula- **7.13** tions. Whether or not these enactments have led to the EC obtaining exclusive external competence depends on whether the internal power has been exercised exhaustively, and whether the envisaged external action might affect the internal legislation. To find the answer to these questions, one must scrutinize the rules of the envisaged convention with third States and the regulation in question, which will be done later in this chapter.

How far does exclusive external competence go?

If exclusive competence arises implicitly, for example through the com- **7.14** plete harmonization of a specific field of the law, one might wonder what the situation is before such harmonization takes place. The answer is that competence remains shared for that period of time.[14] Exclusive external competence cannot be triggered unless there has been complete harmonization in that field. In other words, in any period when the EC has power to legislate in a particular domain (and thus also has external powers), but has not yet legislated, those external powers remain shared with the Member States. This shared competence is only temporary in nature and disappears when the EC adopts a Community legislative instrument that fully covers the area.[15] This might have the result that the Member States begin negotiation with third States, subsequently losing their capacity to continue the negotiations or to conclude the envisaged treaty.

---

[11] Ibid, para 17.

[12] See Kapteyn, note 1 above, 284.

[13] Opinion 1/03 *Competence of the Community to conclude the new Lugano Convention on jurisdiction and the recognition and enforcement of judgments in civil and commercial matters* [2006] ECRI-1145.

[14] Opinion 2/00 *Cartagena Protocol—Conclusion* [2001] ECR I–9713, especially para 46–47.

[15] Dehousse & Maczkovics, note 1 above, 226 and 227.

7.15 Competence may also be shared where the envisaged international treaty will deal with matters that fall in the EC's sphere of exclusive competence and matters over which the EC does not have (exclusive) external competence.

7.16 This division of powers causes confusion, especially for third States. Negotiators might have difficulty working out with whom they are in fact talking, and with whom they will be concluding a treaty. If there is a dispute between the EC and its Member States on who has competence, or on whether competence is shared or exclusively belongs to the EC, matters are made worse for third States. This is the situation regarding civil jurisdiction, as will be explained in the following paragraphs.

7.17 When the EC has obtained exclusive external competence on a matter, the EU Member States may not act in that particular matter. This is a peculiar situation in which sovereign states, with full legal personality, may not exercise their legal personality because of their integration in the EC.[16] If in any event, despite the fact that they are not permitted to do so, the Member States exercise their legal personality to negotiate and conclude treaties with third States, problems occur. This happened in the events leading to the *Open Skies* judgments.

7.18 Moreover, whether competence is shared or exclusive, Member States can no longer have the authority to affect harmonization adversely by contracting with third States. Affecting internal harmonization is interpreted extensively, and one does not look merely at formal conflicts.[17] The Member States must act in good faith and always with the interests of the European Community at heart.

Exclusive external competence in practice

7.19 With regard to implicit exclusive external competence, the first practical concern is the exact moment at which that competence arises. The relevant moment is that of the adoption of the instrument, and not of its entry into force.[18] It is of course difficult for third States to be aware of an instrument from the moment of its adoption, even before it is published.

---

[16] This is different to federal States, where the component units can only act internationally to the extent that they are authorized to do so by the constitution of the federal State in question; see I Brownlie, *Principles of Public International Law* (6th edn, Oxford: Oxford University Press, 2003) 58–59.

[17] See G Middeldrop & RH van Ooik, 'Van verdeelde *Open Skies* naar een uniform Europees extern luchtvaartbeleid' [2003] *Nederlands Tijdschrift voor Europees Recht* 1–10, 5.

[18] Wilderspin & Rouchaud Joët, note 1 above, 9. *ERTA* note 10 above, also refers (in paras 17 and 28) to the adoption of the instrument.

Another practical difficulty arises when an international organization **7.20** does not permit the EC to negotiate or an international convention does not permit the EC to sign an agreement. In this case the Member States must participate, but as representatives of the Community.[19] The structure and rules of the international organization do not influence the division of competences within the EU.[20]

If it is known at the time an international agreement is negotiated that the **7.21** EC wishes to sign and ratify it, a so-called REIO clause may be inserted. Such a clause states that Regional Economic Integration Organizations (hereafter, REIO) may sign the agreement if they are competent for all or some of the matters regulated in the convention. The REIO is then a single Contracting State for purposes of certain parts of the convention, or, in the absence of specification, where the context so requires.[21] Often such a clause is inserted to accommodate the EC, and some agreements refer explicitly to the EC.[22] The advantage for third States of more general clauses is that other international organizations, which might in the future have external competences, will be able to use them.[23] On the other hand, if a convention contains no REIO clause, and the EC has external competence over the matter dealt with in the convention, the Member States may be authorized to sign the convention in the interest of the EC.[24]

---

[19] This was the case at the Hague Conference on Private International Law, but the situation has changed with the entry into force of the new Statute on 1 January 2007, which allowed the EC to become a Member of the Conference, and the subsequent admission of the EC as a Member on 3 April 2007. At the time of becoming a Member, the European Community made a declaration concerning its competence. The Hague Conference's Statute (Art 3(4)) obliges the EC to inform it of any changes in the competence.

[20] Wilderspin & Rouchaud Joët, note 1 above, 9.

[21] For example, Art 53(2) of the Convention for the Unification of Certain Rules for International Carriage by Air (Montreal, 1999), available at <http://www.lexmercatoria.org>; Art 48 of the Convention on International Interests in Mobile Equipment (Cape Town, 2001), available at <http://unidroit.org>; Art 18 of the Hague Convention of 5 July 2006 on the Law Applicable to Certain Rights in respect of Securities held with an Intermediary; Art 29 of the Hague Convention of 30 June 2005 on Choice of Court Agreements, both the last two available at <http://www.hcch.net>.

[22] For example, Art 22(1) of the Convention on Contact concerning Children (Strasbourg, 2003).

[23] The role of the Hague Conference for Private International Law has been highlighted in chapter 1 above, paras 1.78 and following.

[24] For example, Council Decision 2002/762/EC of 19 September 2002 authorizing the Member States, in the interest of the Community, to sign, ratify or accede to the International Convention on Civil Liability for Bunker Oil Pollution Damage, 2001 (the Bunkers Convention), OJ L 256 of 25 September 2002, p 7; Council Decision 2002/971/EC of 18 November 2002 authorizing the Member States, in the interest of the Community, to ratify or accede to the International Convention on Liability and Compensation for Damage in

7.22 If a Member State is responsible for the external relations of a territory that is not part of the EU, that Member State may negotiate and sign the treaty, but only as a representative.[25] This is not influenced by the existence of the EC's external competence.

Shared external competence in practice and mixed agreements

7.23 As has been stated above, if the EC has external competence, this remains shared until it becomes exclusive by the complete harmonization of law in the field, or by the fact that the external action will affect internal legislation. The exact point of complete harmonization is unclear. Similarly, it might be difficult to determine the extent to which the external instrument will affect internal legislation. As for the outside world, bilateral or multilateral agreements often encapsulate several issues; it might happen that some of these have been regulated within the Community. For these issues the Community, according to the ERTA doctrine, has obtained exclusive external competence. For others, the Community might have external competence, but not exclusive external competence (yet). For a third group of issues, the EC might have no external competence, and the Member States might be able to act externally. In other words, the EC is competent for some of the issues and the Member States are competent for others. The EC and the Member States must cooperate closely in these matters, so as to prevent contradictions. This requirement is even stricter if the negotiations take place in a forum of which the EC as such is not a Member.[26]

7.24 Mixed agreements are born when the EC has competence for some issues in the instrument, while the Member States have competence for others. In practice, the Member States and the EC all have a place at the negotiation table; the Commission usually negotiates for the EC. At the end of negotiations both the EC and the Member States sign the agreement. For third States it might seem strange that the EU Member States are in fact

---

Connection with the Carriage of Hazardous and Noxious Substances by Sea, 1996 (the HNS Convention), OJ L 337 of 13 December 2002, p 55; Council Decision 2003/93/EC of 19 December 2002 authorising the Member States in the interest of the European Community, to sign the 1996 Hague Convention on jurisdiction, applicable law, recognition, enforcement and cooperation in respect of parental responsibility and measures for the protection of children, OJ L 48 of 21 February 2003, p 1; see also Gonzalez Beilfuss, note 1 above, 495.

[25] See Wilderspin & Rouchaud Joët, note 1 above, 8–9 and 12.

[26] Opinion 2/91 *Convention N° 170 of the International Labour Organization concerning safety in the use of chemicals at work* [1993] ECR I–1061, especially paras 12 and 37. This case dealt with negotiations at the International Labour Organization, where the EC had observer status.

twice party to a convention: once because of their own signatures and once by virtue of the EC's signature that binds them. A further practical implication is that either the entire EU will become party to a treaty, or no EU Member State at all. It is impossible for some Member States to sign a treaty without the EC and without the sister Member States. This, despite the initial confusion, might be positive for third States: all EU Member States being party to a treaty already gives it a large scope. On the other hand, if there is a problem in some of the Member States, or a political problem within the EU, the signing or ratification of the treaty could be delayed for all the Member States. This has been the case for the Hague Convention for the Protection of Children.[27]

In theory the Member States are signing the specific provisions for which **7.25** they have competence and the EC is signing the specific provisions for which it has exclusive external competence. However, it is often extremely difficult to draw an exact line. At face value the border does not seem important: the Member States are bound to the entire treaty. However, for the EC competences, the European Court of Justice will also have competence. Furthermore, where a dispute arises with third States as to the non-performance of treaty obligations, a third State will have difficulty knowing which is the violator in law: the particular Member State or the EC.

A further problem arises with respect to the definition of 'Contracting **7.26** State' in treaties: sometimes 'Contracting State' refers to the EC and sometimes to every Member State, depending on whether the EC or the Member States had competence over the matter. This issue gave rise to many discussions at the negotiations of the Hague Convention on Choice of Court Agreements. It was deemed impossible to provide a precise indication of whether it is the EC or Member States that are meant when the convention refers to a 'Contracting State'. The Convention finally states that a reference to 'Contracting State' applies equally to a REIO, 'where appropriate'.[28]

---

[27] Hague Convention of 19 October 1996 on Jurisdiction, Applicable Law, Recognition, Enforcement and Co-operation in Respect of Parental Responsibility and Measures for the Protection of Children. This Convention has been signed or acceded to by all EU Member States except Malta, but has been ratified only by Bulgaria, the Czech Republic, Estonia, Hungary, Latvia, Lithuania, the Slovak Republic, and Slovenia. For the 15 old Member States a dispute concerning Gibraltar has delayed ratification; A Schulz, 'Haager Kinderschutzüber einkommen von 1996: Im Westen nichts neues' [2006] *Zeitschrift für das gesamte Familienrecht* 1309–1311.

[28] Hague Choice of Court Convention, note 21 above, Art 29(4).

In mixed conventions, the EC may be required to notify the depositary of the exact division of competence between the EC and the Member States. This obligation may also entail the notification of changes in those competences.[29]

D. THE DISPUTE BETWEEN THE EC AND THE MEMBER STATES OVER CIVIL JURISDICTION

7.27 The fact that the EC has acquired external competence in the matters covered by Brussels I has far-reaching consequences. Many conventions on specific matters include some rule on civil jurisdiction, for instance that private parties can or cannot conclude forum clauses, or that exclusive or non-exclusive jurisdiction exists in a particular matter.[30] Instead of investigating each of these convention provisions separately, a thorough analysis of the dispute that has arisen between the European Commission and the Member States concerning the negotiation of the new Lugano Convention will point out the issues.

7.28 During negotiations to update the Lugano Convention in order to bring it into line with the changes to Brussels I, a dispute soon arose as to who had the power to negotiate with third States Iceland, Norway, and Switzerland. The existence of the Community's external competence in the field of jurisdiction and the recognition and enforcement of judgments was not questioned. The dispute only concerned whether this competence was exclusive or shared with the Member States. The Commission stated that the EC had exclusive competence to negotiate the Convention, whereas some of the Member States were of the opinion that the competence was shared between the EC and themselves so that they were permitted to

---

[29] For instance, Art 18 of the Hague Securities Convention, note 21 above, (not yet in force); explanatory report by R Goode, H Kanda & K Kreuzer (with the assistance of C Bernasconi), p 149–150; available at <http://www.hcch.net>. Another (very similar) example is found in Art 48 of the Convention on International Interests in Mobile Equipment, note 21 above.

[30] Fr example, Arts 38–40 of the International Convention on Liability and Compensation for Damage in connection with the Carriage of Hazardous and Noxious Substances by Sea (London, 1996); Arts 9 and 10 of the International Convention on Civil Liability for Bunker Oil Pollution Damage (London, 2001). See also Wilderspin & Rouchaud Joët, note 1 above, 28–32 and Borrás, 'The Frontiers and the Institutional Constitutional Question', note 1 above, 41–48, discussing various conventions.

negotiate with the third States alongside the Commission. Therefore the Council requested the European Court of Justice to give an opinion:

Does conclusion of the new Lugano Convention on jurisdiction and the recognition and enforcement of judgments in civil and commercial matters . . . fall entirely within the Community's exclusive competence or is competence shared between the Community and the Member States?[31]

The hearing in this case took place on 19 October 2004 under the auspices of a full bench and all the Advocates General.

The rules on external relations that have been developed in the sphere of **7.29** economic law could not merely be transposed to private international law.[32] At the same time, the *Open skies* judgments (in the economic sector) had indicated the approach that was also relevant for the Lugano dispute: one had to examine the future convention's provisions one by one and examine whether they affect the European Community law (in the case under discussion Brussels I).[33] In the *Open skies* cases a dispute also arose between the Council and Commission regarding the EC's external competence and whether the EC or the Member States had the power to update old bilateral agreements (facilitating alliances between US and European airlines, free access to routes, route and traffic rights, code sharing possibilities, etc)[34] and conclude new ones with third State the United States of America. In this case the European Court of Justice found that some aspects had been regulated exhaustively (such as the use of computerized reservation systems). Therefore the EC had exclusive external competence in that area and the EU Member States could no longer conclude agreements with third States. That was not so for every aspect of the bilateral agreements. In this sense, the operating licences of air carriers of third States were not regulated by the EC so that the Member States retained

---

[31] *Lugano* Opinion, note 13 above. Comments on this Opinion: Lavranos, note 1 above; Boele-Woelki & van Ooik, note 1 above; A Capik, 'Zuständigkeit der Gemeinschaft für den Abschluss des neuen Übereinkommens von Lugano' [2006] *European Law Reporter* 225–229.

[32] Borrás, 'The Frontiers and the Institutional Constitutional Question', note 1 above, 33.

[33] Case C–466/98 *Commission v The United Kingdom* [2002] ECR I–9427; Case C–467/98 *Commission v Denmark* [2002] ECR I–9519; Case C–468/98 *Commission v Sweden* [2002] ECR I–9575; Case C–469/98 *Commission v Finland* [2002] ECR I–9627; Case C–471/98 *Commission v Belgium* [2002] ECR I–9681; Case C–472/98 *Commission v Luxembourg* [2002] ECR I–9741; Case C–475/98 *Commission v Austria* [2002] ECR I–9797; Case C–476/98 *Commission v Germany* [2002] ECR I–9855. Note that these cases were not opinions by the European Court of Justice as the Lugano case is, but proceedings in which the Member States were found to have failed to fulfil their obligations under EU law.

[34] Case C–467/98, ibid, para 24.

their competence to conclude agreements on this aspect with third States. The judgments made it clear that exclusive external competence arises only where the EC has regulated the specific aspect completely. Some authors criticize this tentative approach, stating that it would lead to legal uncertainty.[35] Quite to the contrary, it seems correct to interpret the acquisition of external competence strictly so as not to create uncertainty for third States: where the EC has regulated and where the envisaged agreement would affect the EC legislation, there is external competence.

7.30 Accordingly, a detailed analysis of the provisions of the future Lugano Convention had to be made. The opinion of the European Court of Justice will be discussed critically. The most logical structure is to follow the order of the four cornerstones discussed in the previous chapters and then refer briefly to provisional measures and the enforcement of judgments. Finally, the provisions in Brussels I itself on bilateral conventions with third States should be examined.

Defendants domiciled in third States

7.31 The Lugano Convention would provide rules of jurisdiction over defendants domiciled in third States Iceland, Norway, and Switzerland. To examine whether or not such rules would affect Brussels I, one has to turn to the Regulation itself, in particular Article 4:

> If the defendant is not domiciled in a Member State, the jurisdiction of the courts of each Member State shall, subject to Articles 22 and 23, be determined by the law of that Member State. . .

7.32 It was pointed out in chapter 1 that there are two possible interpretations of this provision.[36] First, one might say that the national rules on jurisdiction only apply because Article 4 of Brussels I permits them. Second, one might see Article 4 as doing no more than admitting that Brussels I does not regulate cases where the defendant is domiciled in a third State (except in cases of exclusive jurisdiction or forum clauses). The choice between these two approaches is crucial as a starting point.

7.33 The European Court of Justice chose the first view when faced with the question whether Article 4 meant that the field had not been completely taken over by EC legislation. It found that the provision had the effect of incorporating the national bases of jurisdiction into the Regulation. Thus those national rules became part of the Brussels I system and should not

---

[35] Dehousse & Maczkovics, note 1 above, 231–232.
[36] Chapter 1 above, paras 1.52 and following.

be seen as an exception.[37] This point of view was important in arguing external competence. The Lugano Convention would indeed deal with defendants domiciled in third States, namely in Iceland, Norway, and Switzerland. If the situation of defendants domiciled in third States were left to the EU Member States, then the Member States would still have competence in the area and the EC's competence would not be exclusive. However, following the first line of argument, the court ruled the EC's competence to be exclusive.

This conclusion, however, is not free from criticism. Even following the **7.34** first line of argument, one would have to admit that Brussels I did not harmonize civil jurisdiction for all defendants. Article 4 in fact acknowledges this, whichever way one interprets it. The national rules have been retained with regard to defendants from outside the EU. If a Member State has a rule in its domestic civil procedure that states that a defendant that has property on its territory is subject to the jurisdiction of its courts, that rule will be valid with regard to defendants from outside the EU. A Member State may also change its code of civil procedure, including the provisions that refer to international jurisdiction and are applied to defendants from third States. For example, the Netherlands altered some of its rules, which required the amendment of Brussels I as regards its reference to Dutch law.[38] Similarly, when adopting its new Code de droit international privé (Private International Law Code), Belgium deleted the provision in the code civil (civil code) granting jurisdiction based on the Belgian nationality of the defendant. That provision was listed in Brussels I as outlawed for defendants domiciled in EU Member States. These changes of domestic law are accepted even though a change in the code of civil procedure of the Netherlands or of the civil code of Belgium might have consequences in other Member States: no matter where the defendant is from, Member States have committed themselves to recognize and enforce a judgment coming from another Member State. The German Bundesgerichtshof (Federal Supreme Court) stated in 1991 that the rule granting jurisdiction on the basis of the defendant owning property within Germany[39] must be

---

[37] *Lugano* Opinion, note 13 above, para 148.

[38] Commission Regulation (EC) No 1496/2002 of 21 August 2002 amending Annex I (the rules of jurisdiction referred to in Article 3(2) and Article 4(2)) and Annex II (the list of competent courts and authorities) to Council Regulation (EC) No 44/2001 on jurisdiction and the recognition and enforcement of judgments in civil and commercial matters, OJ L 225 of 22 August 2002, 13.

[39] §23 Zivilprozessordnung (Code of Civil Procedure). This rule has always been listed as exorbitant in the Brussels Convention and Brussels I Regulation.

interpreted restrictively.[40] It added that the reference to the rule in Brussels I (with regard to defendants domiciled in third States) could not bring about a general application of that rule without considering the points that the Court made in that case (e.g. compatibility with international law).[41] If the Netherlands and Belgium were permitted to change their codes, and Germany was permitted to change the interpretation of the rules, they may as well decide to write into that code a specific rule relating to domiciliaries of third State X. Therefore, if one looks at the substance, there is no objection to a rule dealing with jurisdiction over defendants from third States. If the Netherlands or Belgium could make a new rule regarding defendants from third States, it seems that they can also conclude a bilateral treaty with third State X to the same effect. The same applies to Germany and its ability to change the interpretation of its rule. If the Member States have the right to change the rules relating to defendants from outside the EU, it would appear the competence must be shared.

7.35 Let us now turn to Brussels II *bis*. This Regulation states that if no EU Member State has jurisdiction under its rules, then one may fall back on the national rules of the Member States. Thus national rules on jurisdiction have also survived to a certain extent under Brussels II *bis*. Also, possibly, they might only be used when explicitly authorized by the Regulation. It seems that the same dispute between the Commission and the Member States could arise with regard to Brussels II *bis*: does the Commission have exclusive competence to negotiate a similar convention with third States? To answer this question on the current version of Brussels II *bis*, the provision referring to national law would also have to be analysed. The same difficulties arise as with Brussels I. The national rules still exist, and may be changed. However, the proposal to change this Regulation will delete reference to national rules.[42]

Exclusive jurisdiction

7.36 The next jurisdiction rule under investigation is exclusive jurisdiction. Brussels I gives exclusive jurisdiction to EU Member State courts on the basis of certain connections, such as the situation of immovable property,

---

[40] Judgment of 2 July 1991 (1992) 115 *Entscheidungen des Bundesgerichtshofes in Zivilsachen* 90–99.

[41] Ibid, 96.

[42] Proposal for a Council Regulation amending Regulation (EC) No 2201/2003 as regards jurisdiction and introducing rules concerning applicable law in matrimonial matters of 17 July 2006, COM(2006) 399 final, available at <http://eur-lex.europa.eu>.

the place of registration of a company (if its validity, nullity, or dissolution is concerned), and the place of registration of an intellectual property right (if its registration or validity is concerned).[43]

The Regulation is silent on the question of exclusive bases for jurisdiction **7.37** that courts of third States might have. The Lugano Convention would import such rules. The courts of Iceland, Norway, and Switzerland would have exclusive jurisdiction over immovable property situated there, over companies registered there, and over intellectual property rights registered there (if the dispute concerned the validity of the company or the intellectual property right). In some of these cases an EU Member State court would have had jurisdiction, for instance on the basis of the domicile of the defendant (Brussels I Article 2) or on the basis of the place of performance of the contract (Brussels I Article 5(1)). The Lugano Convention would remove such jurisdiction.

It has been pointed out in Chapter 3 that the Regulation does not contain **7.38** a basis for the Member States to refuse jurisdiction in these situations if the defendant is domiciled in the EU.[44] For example, a dispute arises between a company domiciled in Canada and a company domiciled in the Netherlands regarding immovable property situated in Canada. If the party from Canada brings suit in the Netherlands, where the defendant is domiciled, the court will have jurisdiction, without investigating possible jurisdiction in Canada. Authors have suggested that, in such a case, the court in the Netherlands would have to be able to refuse its jurisdiction in favour of the courts in Canada, on the basis of what they called the reflexive effect of the jurisdictional rules.[45] This means that EU Member State courts have to respect jurisdiction rules of third States in cases where, if the reverse or the reflex situation occurred, the EU Member State courts would assume their jurisdiction as exclusive. Uncertainty has long existed about this reflexive effect and whether it is compatible with Brussels I.

The European Court of Justice had to consider this question in the course **7.39** of its investigation of the Regulation's jurisdiction rules. The Lugano

---

[43] Art 22 of Brussels I.

[44] Paras 3.07 and following.

[45] For more detail see the discussion in chapter 3 above, paras 3.10 and following; GAL Droz, 'Entrée en vigueur de la Convention de Bruxelles révisée sur la compétence judiciaire et l'exécution des jugements' [1987] *Revue critique de droit international privé* 251–303, 260–261; GAL Droz, 'La Convention de San Sebastian alignant la Convention de Bruxelles sur la Convention de Lugano' [1990] *Revue critique de droit international privé* 1–21, 14. See also P Gothot & D Holleaux, *La Convention de Bruxelles du 27.9.1968* (Paris: Jupiter, 1985) 84; A Nuyts, 'La théorie de l'effet réflexe' in M Storme & G de Leval (eds), *Le droit processuel et judiciaire européen* (Bruges: die Keure, 2003) 73–89.

Convention would grant exclusive jurisdiction to third States Iceland, Norway, and Switzerland, including in cases where the defendant was domiciled in one of the EU Member States. The European Court of Justice thus had to consider whether third State courts could have such exclusive jurisdiction in the absence of the Lugano Convention. Its conclusion was that they could not.[46] The European Court of Justice seems to have denied the existence of the reflexive effect by implication. Thus the Court stated that the Lugano Convention would influence the operation of Brussels I: it could take away the jurisdiction of an EU Member State court (for instance on the basis of the domicile of the defendant) while such jurisdiction could not be taken away if the Lugano Convention did not exist.

7.40 This finding has far-reaching results for third States: there is no possibility under Brussels I to decline jurisdiction on the basis that a third State court has exclusive jurisdiction. Whether this conclusion will survive later preliminary questions on exactly that point remains to be seen. If it does, hopefully the Regulation will be amended on this point. It is submitted that the Regulations should be consistent: either they are not perfect double instruments and national rules have survived, among others those on declining jurisdiction; or they are true double instruments, containing all jurisdiction rules, in which case they must also contain rules for declining jurisdiction.

Forum clauses

7.41 The European Court of Justice also considered the jurisdiction rule on forum clauses. The issue is similar to the one described above, and sometimes even more surprising from a commercial or contractual point of view. If the parties had contractually agreed that a forum within the European Union should hear their disputes, their agreement would be respected.[47] However, if the parties agreed to a forum in a third State, the position is uncertain. What if the defendant is domiciled in an EU Member State and the plaintiff brings suit in the court of the defendant's domicile? It is in this situation that the advocates of the reflexive effect revert to their theory. The reflexive effect prescribes that the EU Member State courts would have to respect the forum choice made for the courts of a third State, just as they would assume jurisdiction if their own courts had been chosen.

---

[46] *Lugano* Opinion, note 13 above, para 153.
[47] Art 23 of Brussels I.

The argument by the European Court of Justice was the same as explained **7.42** above, regarding exclusive bases of jurisdiction. The Court stated that, in the situation described in the previous paragraph, the EU Member State court would have jurisdiction on the basis of the domicile of the defendant. Again, the European Court of Justice implicitly denied the existence of any reflexive effect. For third States Iceland, Norway, and Switzerland the Lugano Convention would change the situation. EU Member State courts would now have to yield to the jurisdiction of courts in those third States if such jurisdiction were based on a forum agreement, even if the EU Member State court would have had jurisdiction according to Brussels I on the basis of the defendant's domicile.[48] In the absence of this provision of the Lugano Convention, the rules of Brussels I might have led to an EU Member State court having jurisdiction, for instance, because the defendant was domiciled there.

One can only hope that this conclusion of the ECJ will be remedied soon. **7.43** This might be done by admitting that the Regulation is not a perfect double instrument and that national rules declining jurisdiction should be permitted (for instance, in a response to a preliminary question). In the alternative the text of the Regulation itself could be amended to the effect that it becomes a true double instrument containing its own rules on declining jurisdiction in favour of third States. Finding that courts in EU Member States will not respect forum agreements if defendants are domiciled in the territory of those courts is plainly unreasonable. The argument is unduly formalistic, clinging only to the wording of the Regulation and not taking previous judgments[49] or reports[50] into account.

Furthermore, the Member States (whether as judiciary or legislator) do **7.44** not seem to have shared the ECJ's opinion on this matter. In the recent case *Konkola*, the English court found that it could grant a stay on the basis that the parties had agreed that the courts of Zambia would have jurisdiction to hear their dispute.[51] The Belgian Code de droit international privé (Private International Law Code), enacted after Brussels I stipulates that the Belgian courts will respect forum clauses in favour of

---

[48] *Lugano* Opinion, note 13 above, para 153.

[49] Case C–387/98 *Coreck Maritime GmbH v Handelsveem BV and others* [2000] ECR I–9337

[50] Schlosser Report on the 1978 version of the Brussels Convention; OJ C 59, 5 March 1979, 71, para 176.

[51] [2005] EWHC 898 (Comm); R Fentiman, 'Civil jurisdiction and third States: *Owusu* and after' [2006] CML Rev 705–734. The principle behind this conclusion was not contested before the Court of Appeal: [2006] 1 Loyd's Rep 410.

foreign courts.[52] One could imagine a Canadian and a Belgian party concluding a contract to the effect that a judge in Ontario has jurisdiction. The parties, knowing both Ontarian and Belgian law, might feel confident that their forum clause will be respected. If in a later dispute the party from Ontario is the claimant and the Belgian party the defendant, Brussels I in fact provides that the Belgian court has jurisdiction. The Belgian court would decline this jurisdiction according to its own law.

7.45 In this examination, it is also relevant to refer to the Hague Convention on Choice of Court Agreements, adopted in 2005. While negotiating this Convention, the EC and the Member States all sat at the negotiation table to coordinate their viewpoints. However, whether just the EC or both the EC and the Member States would sign the Convention, was unclear as the negotiators awaited the *Lugano* Opinion. Two situations treated by the Hague Convention must be distinguished. To explain this, the example of the Belgian and Canadian parties will again be taken, on the assumption that both those states will be bound by the Hague Convention.

7.46 First, those two parties can conclude a choice of court agreement in favour of a Canadian court. That is the situation that would not have been covered by Brussels I. Jurisdiction would have been declined on the basis of the Belgian code, or on the basis of the reflexive effect, at least before the *Lugano* Opinion. However, in future the Hague Convention would govern this situation. The Convention would require the Belgian court to decline jurisdiction in favour of the chosen Canadian court. Whether this effect of the Hague Convention would influence Brussels I (in the sense of taking away jurisdiction of an EU court on the basis of the domicile of the defendant) or national law, was uncertain at the time the Hague Convention was negotiated. The situation seems comparable with that of the Lugano Convention. Thus the conclusion that the European Court of Justice reached also affects external competence to sign and ratify the Hague Convention.

7.47 Second, those two parties can conclude their choice of forum agreement in favour of the Belgian rather than the Canadian courts. At present Brussels I would cover that situation. However, in that instance the Hague Convention will replace Brussels I.[53] This is in the interests of all involved

---

[52] Code de droit international privé (Private International Law Code), Act of 16 July 2004, *Belgisch Staatsblad*, 27 July 2004, Art 7.
[53] Hague Choice of Court Convention, note 21 above, Art 26(6).

so that not only other EU Member State courts, but all states bound by the Hague Convention, would decline jurisdiction.[54]

Parallel proceedings

The European Court of Justice did not go into the issue of parallel pro- **7.48** ceedings at length, but only in the context of discussing the disconnection clause.[55] It stated that the provision in the Lugano Convention on parallel proceedings would affect the operation of Brussels I. The view of the Court is that, if an EU Member State has jurisdiction based on the domicile of the defendant, and a court in a third State is seised first, then subsequently a court in an EU Member State, the EU Member State would not decline jurisdiction. The Lugano Convention would change this situation: if a court in a Lugano Convention State is seised first, the EU Member State court must stay jurisdiction to allow the first court to examine its jurisdiction.

The European Court of Justice should have discussed this point more **7.49** fully. Brussels I indeed contains rules on parallel proceedings for the situation where the same case is pending in the courts of two EU Member State courts. Whether or not an EU Member State court that has jurisdiction may decline that jurisdiction in favour of a third State court first seised, was somewhat unclear. As has been discussed in chapter 5, the effect of the *Owusu* judgment on this situation was uncertain.[56] The ECJ said that an EU Member State court may not decline jurisdiction in favour of a third State court where the third State court is deemed more appropriate to hear the case. However, the ECJ did not go into the issue of whether jurisdiction based on the domicile of the defendant is also compulsory if a court in a third State had been seised first. If the result of the *Owusu* judgment is that jurisdiction in the EU based on the domicile of the defendant is compulsory and cannot be declined, even if the same action had first been brought in the court of a third State, then the EU rules are all-encompassing in this area and the EC has exclusive external competence to negotiate the

---

[54] The Lugano Convention is different in this respect: a party domiciled in Belgium and one domiciled in Switzerland conclude a forum clause in favour of the courts of Belgium. That situation would remain under Brussels I and would not fall under the Lugano Convention; see Art 54B of the current version of the Lugano Convention; Art 64 of the subsequently concluded Lugano Convention (2007).

[55] *Lugano* Opinion, note 13 above, para 158.

[56] Case C–281/02 *Owusu v Jackson and others* [2005] ECR I–1383. See chapter 5, para 5.26.

provision in the Lugano Convention on parallel proceedings. If, on the other hand, the EU Member State courts can use their national law to decline jurisdiction because an action had previously been brought in a third State court, then Brussels I does not contain all the rules in this area. The Court should at least have considered this point.

Provisional Measures

7.50 The European Court of Justice did not examine the issue of provisional and protective measures. The Lugano Convention will also contain rules permitting third State courts to grant such measures when EU Member State courts have jurisdiction as to the substance of a case. However, these provisional measures will in no way influence the jurisdiction of the EU Member State court. That court will maintain its jurisdiction over the substance of the matter. As has been pointed out, in any event Brussels I refers to national law on this matter, but curtails the national rules. It seems, therefore, that the Member States remain competent in this matter, even if such competence is not unfettered.

The disconnection clause of the Lugano Convention

7.51 The fact that the Lugano Convention would contain a so-called disconnection clause did not alter the European Court of Justice's conclusions. It explained that a disconnection clause would merely regulate, in a consistent manner, the relationship between Brussels I and the Convention. It would not ensure that the Convention does not influence Brussels I's rules.[57] Furthermore, the disconnection clause contained exceptions: for instance, it covered exclusive jurisdiction, forum clauses, and parallel proceedings. According to the ECJ, these exceptions had the result of affecting Brussels I.

7.52 The difficulty of this argument is that it can be turned both ways: does a disconnection clause explain the situation, or does it remedy the situation? Is the clause necessary in order to regulate which instrument will apply, or is it merely explaining which instrument will apply? The response to this question depends on the analysis of each of the jurisdiction rules, as set out above. Thus the disconnection argument does not stand alone, but rather follows the previous arguments.

---

[57] *Lugano* Opinion, note 13 above, paras 155–158.

Enforcement of judgments

The European Court of Justice also analysed the rules that the Lugano **7.53**
Convention would contain on the recognition and enforcement of foreign
judgments. At first the Court explained that the jurisdiction rules on the
one hand, and the recognition and enforcement rules on the other, could
not be separated. The system of easy recognition and enforcement between
EU Member States is only possible because of the existence of common
jurisdiction rules.[58] Furthermore, Brussels I contains certain rules on the
recognition and enforcement of judgments from third States, notably when
such judgments date from before an EU Member State court judgment in
the same matter and between the same parties. In such a situation, the recognition or enforcement of the Member State judgment can be refused if
the earlier third State judgment can be recognized and enforced.[59] The recognition and enforcement of judgments from third States Iceland, Norway,
and Switzerland will be treated more favourably under the Lugano
Convention: they will necessarily be capable of being recognized and
enforced and thus the Brussels system will be affected.[60] The ECJ also stated
that the rules on recognition and enforcement were indissociable from
those on jurisdiction: easy recognition and enforcement could only be
achieved because of uniform jurisdiction rules. Therefore a Convention
such as the envisaged Lugano Convention would affect Brussels I's rules,
whether it just contained provisions on jurisdiction, or also on recognition
and enforcement.

Of course, the rationale behind the Lugano Convention is that the judg- **7.54**
ments of third States Iceland, Norway, and Switzerland should easily be
recognized and enforced in those states in the EU Member States. However,
that purpose of the Convention with those third States does not strictly
speaking 'affect' the EU rules. Whether or not a convention exists with the
outside world, a request may be made to have a third State judgment
enforced in an EU Member State. That EU Member State will either apply
its national law or a convention (such as the Lugano Convention).
Recognition and enforcement under the Lugano Convention might be
easier and quicker than under national law, but this does not seem to harm
the European Judicial Area. The enforcement will only be effective in the

---

[58] Ibid, para 163.
[59] Ibid, para 165.
[60] In support of this argument: F Pocar, 'The Drafting of a world-wide convention on jurisdiction and the enforcement of judgments: which format for the negotiations in The Hague?'
in JAR Nafziger & SC Symeonides (eds), *Law and Justice in a Multistate World. Essays in Honour
of Arthur T von Mehren* (Ardsley: Transnational Publishers Inc, 2002) 191–197, 195–196.

EU Member State where it had been granted. An enforcement order cannot be given in another EU Member State based on the first enforcement order (*exequatur sur exequatur ne vaut*).[61] If enforcement were sought in another EU Member State, that Member State would have to apply its national law or a convention. Therefore it seems that the European Court of Justice came to its conclusion too quickly, and that competence on these provisions may have remained shared between the EC and the Member States.

Other provisions in Brussels I on conventions with third States

7.55 The European Court of Justice pointed out only briefly the existence of the provisions in Brussels I and their predecessors in the Brussels Convention on existing and future conventions with third States.[62] These provisions, and the changes they have undergone, merit a more thorough examination.

7.56 One might have sought an answer in Articles 71 and 72 of Brussels I. These provisions replace Articles 57 and 59 respectively of the Brussels Convention, but have been modified. Examining the provisions, it will be indicated that their changes should not be seen as decisive for the external competence of the EC. Article 57 of the Brussels Convention and Article 71 of Brussels I deal with conventions on particular matters. As has been pointed out in chapter 1, jurisdictional provisions are often taken up in conventions on particular matters, for instance transport. Article 57(1) of the Brussels Convention states:

This Convention shall not affect any conventions to which the Contracting States **are or will be** parties and which in relation to particular matters, govern jurisdiction or the recognition or enforcement of judgments.

Article 71(1) of Brussels I states:

This Regulation shall not affect any conventions to which the Member States **are** parties and which in relation to particular matters, govern jurisdiction or the recognition or enforcement of judgments. (emphasis added)

Article 59 of the Brussels Convention and Article 72 of Brussels I deal with recognition and enforcement conventions. Article 59 of the Brussels Convention states:

This Convention shall not prevent a Contracting State from assuming, in a convention on the recognition and enforcement of judgments, an obligation towards a

---

[61] Case C–129/92 *Owens Bank Ltd v Fulvio Bracco and Bracco Industria Chemica SpA* [1994] ECR I–117; chapter 5, paras 5.29 and following.

[62] *Lugano* Opinion, note 13 above, para 147.

third State not to recognize judgments given in other Contracting States against defendants domiciled or habitually resident in the third State where, in cases provided for in Article 4, the judgment could only be founded on a ground of jurisdiction specified in the second paragraph of Article 3. . .

Article 72 of Brussels I states:

This Regulation shall not affect agreements by which Member States undertook, prior to the entry into force of this Regulation pursuant to Article 59 of the Brussels Convention, not to recognise judgments given, in particular in other Contracting States to that Convention, against defendants domiciled or habitually resident in a third country where, in cases provided for in Article 4 of that Convention, the judgment could only be founded on a ground of jurisdiction specified in the second paragraph of Article 3 of that Convention.

While Article 57 of the Brussels Convention referred to existing and future **7.57** instruments, Article 71 of Brussels I refers only to existing instruments. Similarly, while Article 59 of the Brussels Convention retained the possibility of the Member States concluding recognition and enforcement conventions with third States, Article 72 of Brussels I merely permits EU Member States to respect international law obligations under already existing recognition and enforcement conventions with third States. These textual amendments seem to support the argument that the authority to conclude any jurisdiction provision in a convention is now vested exclusively in the EC and that the Member States no longer have competence to do so.[63] However, the silence on future instruments should not be interpreted as taking away from Member States powers that they have under international law as sovereign states. External competence is not conferred on the EC by such a silence in the specific EU legislation, but only by one of the ways discussed.

One also has to take into account that Article 59 of the Brussels Convention **7.58** had been inserted to reply to accusations of EEC chauvinism due to the negative situation of defendants domiciled in third States: an EEC judgment based on an exorbitant basis of jurisdiction could be recognized and enforced against them throughout the EEC. It merely confirmed in an explicit way the position under international law: Member States can conclude conventions with third States. At the conclusion of the first version of the Brussels Convention, a convention on the recognition and enforcement

---

[63] In support of this argument: Proposal for a Council Regulation (EC) on jurisdiction and the recognition and enforcement of judgments in civil and commercial matters (including an explanatory memorandum); OJ C 376E of 28 December 1999, p 1; M Traest, *De verhouding van de Europese Gemeenschap tot de Conferentie van Den Haag voor het Internationaal Privaatrecht* (Antwerp: Maklu, 2003) 260–261.

of civil judgments was being negotiated at the Hague Conference on Private International Law. The message of Article 59 was that those negotiations would continue and the possibility of other conventions would remain open. Although the deletion of the message can be criticized as unfriendly towards third States, it does not mean that the Member States have lost their external competence.[64]

7.59 In fact these provisions can be compared to Article 307 of the EC Treaty, which states that agreements with third States dating from before the establishment of the European Community, or before a specific Member State's accession, will remain valid. Such a rule seems inevitable under international law: existing international obligations must be respected.[65]

7.60 Furthermore, Article 67 of Brussels I states that the Regulation shall not prejudice the application of relevant provisions of Community instruments. This provision does not refer explicitly to future Community instruments, but one can hardly imagine that it was the intention of the drafters to freeze Community law at the phase where it was at the time of the adoption of the Regulation.[66]

Consequences of the Lugano Opinion for future instruments

7.61 By stating that the European Community now has exclusive external competence in the field covered by Brussels I, the European Court of Justice has closed the door for Member States to individually conclude international conventions with third States. As a matter of practice, this is a pity. Some EU Member States might have specific reasons to conclude bilateral conventions with a specific third State, for instance a neighbour, or a state many of whose nationals live in the Member State. However, from now on the EU Member States will have to ask the EC to negotiate and conclude these bilateral agreements for them, or will have to ask for a Council decision

---

[64] See, *inter alia* the reaction of GAL Droz & H Gaudemet-Tallon, 'La transformation de la convention de Bruxelles du 27 septembre 1968 en Règlement du Conseil concernant la compétence judiciaire, la reconnaissance et l'exécution des décisions en matière civile et commerciale' [2001] *Revue critique de droit international privé* 602–652, 621–625.

[65] Arts 26, 27, 30 and 46 of the Vienna Convention on the Law of Treaties (Vienna, 1969). See also Middeldrop & van Ooik, note 17 above, 8, where they discuss the consequences of the *Open Skies* judgments, stating that these judgments cannot negate the obligations that the Member States have taken up towards third States. See also A Schulz, 'The relationship between the judgments project and other international instruments' (Choice of Court Convention's Preliminary Document No 24), available at <http://www.hcch.net>.

[66] A Nuyts, 'La communautarisation de la convention de Bruxelles. Le règlement 44/2001 sur la compétence judiciaire et l'effet des décisions en matière civile et commerciale' [2001] *Journal des tribunaux* 913–922.

on proposal by the Commission, authorizing them to conclude bilateral agreements. This seems inefficient: not all Member States might have the same interests in concluding bilateral conventions with specific third States; some third States might not be interested in a convention with the entire EU, since they might have friends and foes in the same European club. Furthermore, an enforcement convention with one Member State does not affect Brussels I, as has been explained above.[67] A bilateral convention would facilitate enforcement in one Member State. Apart from that Member State, the judgment from the particular third State would not have ready access to the entire EU. Judgments given by the EU Member State in question against a defendant domiciled in the third State would be enforceable in the other EU Member States, but that would have been the case no matter what the basis of jurisdiction was, even if jurisdiction were based on a (exorbitant) national ground. Thus, there should be no objection against such bilateral conventions. In practice Member States still conclude this type of convention. Borrás refers to bilateral agreements Spain has recently concluded with El Salvador and Tunisia, and states that one has to admit that the conclusion of these conventions is still possible, though one might imagine that there is a duty on Member States to inform the Community, on the basis of the principle of loyalty.[68] This can be compared to the situation where an EU Member State informs the Community that one of its bases of exorbitant jurisdiction (in national law) has been altered.

Regarding multilateral conventions, the same limitations arise. From now on the EC will have to negotiate and conclude them. This issue has arisen particularly in the work of the Hague Conference on Private International Law. The Hague Choice of Court Convention was concluded while the *Lugano* Opinion was pending at the European Court of Justice.[69] Representatives and delegates from the EU Member States and the EC sat at the negotiation table, often explaining to the delegations of other states why they wanted to have their cake and eat it: they were not sure whether the external competence of the EC was exclusive or shared with the Member States and therefore they wanted to leave the possibilities open. The Convention provides for signature by a Regional Economic Integration Organization (such as the EC), on its own or as well as the Member States of that Organization.[70] After the European Court of Justice **7.62**

---

[67] Para 7.54 above.

[68] Borrás, 'The effect of the adoption of Brussels I', note 1 above, 117.

[69] Hague Choice of Court Convention, note 21 above.

[70] Arts 29 and 30 of the Choice of Court Convention, ibid; TC Hartley & M Dogauchi, Explanatory Report to the Convention of 30 June 2005 on Choice of Court Agreements, 81; available at <http://www.hcch.net>.

gave its Opinion, it seems that only the EC will have to sign and ratify that Hague Convention, and not the EU Member States. While this might be positive in some respects and could speed up the process of ratification, the risk is that political issues between some EU Member States may spill over to the other Member States, and thus postpone ratification for all. This has been the case regarding the Hague Child Protection Convention.[71] A part of the field covered by this Convention falls within the sphere of the exclusive external competence of the EC, while another part falls under the ambit of shared external competence. Thus the Convention has to be ratified both by the EC and by the Member States. However, the entire process is held up by a dispute between Spain and the United Kingdom regarding the application of the Convention to Gibraltar. Under normal circumstances such a dispute might delay the ratification for those two states only. However, currently, its effects are much further-reaching. Similarly, an unfortunate factor has delayed the signing by the EC and the EU Member States of the Hague Securities Convention.[72] Because of issues in one EU Member State, the signatures not only of that Member State, but of the EC and all the other Member States are held up.

E. DENMARK

7.63 As explained, Denmark does not participate in the EU's Regulations on civil jurisdiction. Furthermore, Ireland and the United Kingdom only participate in the private international law regulations if they explicitly opt in.[73] After the adoption of Brussels I, the Brussels Convention was still in force between Denmark and the EU Member States. These rules were similar, but older than the ones contained in Brussels I. Denmark noted the utility of Brussels I and decided they wanted to join. A way of circumventing the Protocol had to be found: the EC would have to conclude an agreement with Denmark to extend the application of the rules of Brussels I to that Member State.

7.64 It seems that the only solution to the lack of clarity over relations with Denmark is to liken it to a third State for civil jurisdiction (and all private international law) instruments.[74] The same will hold true for the United

---

[71] Hague Child Protection Convention, note 27 above.

[72] Hague Securities Convention, note 21 above.

[73] Chapter 1 above, para 1.23.

[74] *Contra:* Borrás, 'The effect of the adoption of Brussels I', note 1 above, 108, states that the situation with Denmark is not one of external competence, but of necessarily concluding an international agreement, which will have the same content as a Community instrument.

Kingdom and Ireland regarding instruments to which they have not opted in.[75] The European Community must then be seen as if composed of all the Member States except those that opted out. Therefore the Commission, in matters over which the EC has competence, speaks for everyone except them. This line of reasoning is supported by the Council Decision that authorized the EU Member States to sign the 1996 Hague Child Protection Convention, stating that it does not bind Denmark, and that 'Member State' in the decision means all Member States except Denmark.[76]

If the above analysis were not followed, the EU would find itself tied in **7.65** a Gordian knot: the EU and the Member States wanted to conclude a new convention with Denmark, as successor to the Brussels Convention but updated in line with Brussels I. But if the fiction of non-Membership were not applied, Denmark would be concluding a convention with itself: once as part of the EU and once as counterparty. This is a legal and factual impossibility.

The Council of the European Union authorized the Commission to negoti- **7.66** ate with Denmark for the extension of the rules of Brussels I to Denmark. Thereafter, in September 2005, the Council adopted a decision on the signing of an Agreement between the European Community and Denmark and this Agreement was signed in October 2005.[77] It was approved for the European Community and by Denmark, and entered into force on 1 July 2007.[78] This Agreement contains rules on the interpretational powers of the European Court of Justice.[79] Furthermore, it unambiguously

---

[75] Although neither the UK nor Ireland has opted out of any of the instruments currently in force, they will probably opt out of the proposed amendment to Brussels II *bis* (17 July 2006, COM(2006) 399final, available at <http://eur-lex.europa.eu>) and the UK will probably opt out of the Proposed Council Regulation on Jurisdiction, Applicable Law, Recognition and Enforcement of Decisions and Cooperation in Matters relating to Maintenance Obligations of 15 December 2005, COM(2005) 649 final, available at <http://eur-lex.europa.eu>.

[76] Council Decision of 19 December 2002, note 24 above, especially rec 9 and Art 1(3).

[77] Council Decision 2005/790/EC of 20 September 2005 on the signing, on behalf of the Community, of the Agreement between the European Community and the Kingdom of Denmark on jurisdiction and the recognition and enforcement of judgments in civil and commercial matters, OJ L 299 of 16 November 2005, 61 and Agreement between the European Community and the Kingdom of Denmark on jurisdiction and the recognition and enforcement of judgments in civil and commercial matters (Brussels, 19 October 2005), OJ L 299 of 16 November 2005, 62–70.

[78] Council Decision 2006/325/EC of 27 April 2006 concerning the conclusion of the Agreement between the European Community and the Kingdom of Denmark on jurisdiction and the recognition and enforcement of judgments in civil and commercial matters, OJ L 120 of 5 May 2006, 22.

[79] Art 6.

states that international agreements entered into by the EC will not bind Denmark. However, Denmark will have to abstain from entering into international conventions that might affect or alter the scope of Brussels I, unless the EC has been consulted and arrangements are made with respect to the relationship between the convention and Brussels I rules. In negotiating international agreements Denmark must coordinate its position with that of the EC.[80]

7.67 This way of proceeding, while the *Lugano* Opinion was still pending at the European Court of Justice, was rather strange. The Council and (some of) the Member States seemed to be contradicting themselves. On one hand they waited for more than two years for an opinion from the European Court of Justice on the external competence of the Community to negotiate and conclude a convention in this field with Iceland, Norway, and Switzerland. On the other hand, shortly before receiving that opinion, they let the European Community conclude an agreement with Denmark without even signing it alongside the Community. Authorizing the Commission to negotiate this Agreement might have been the most practical way to proceed, especially since the Agreement is short and only concerns technical issues, while the substance lies in the annexed Brussels I Regulation. However, signing the Agreement is not merely a practical issue. It is now the Community that is the international contracting party and not the Member States. By this fact, it seems that the Member States acknowledged they did not have external competence in this matter. Probably this was not their intention and their vision might have been blurred by the fact that Denmark is in principle an EU Member State. However, as has been explained, Denmark should be seen as a third State with respect to this chapter of EU law. Ironically, the Council Decisions themselves confirm this point of view: the considerations state that Denmark is not taking part in the adoption of the decision.[81] It is thus not part of the EC in this matter.

F. THE DIFFICULTIES FOR THIRD STATES

7.68 It appears to be an impossible task for third States to determine when the conclusion of an international agreement will *affect* or *alter the scope of* internal rules of the EU. Furthermore, as European Union law is in constant evolution and the position is not always clear, the EU and the Member States

---

[80] Art 5.
[81] Rec 5 of both the decisions on signing and conclusion of the Agreement.

may differ as to the external competence of the EU in certain cases. External competence could even arise in a way that was unintended as a result of some actions of the EU institutions.[82] If negotiations are already under way and external competence of the EC then arises, it is not fair towards third States to change the negotiator. In such instances the Commission and Council should attempt to find a political solution.[83] This was the case in The Hague. While an international jurisdiction convention was being negotiated, the European Community obtained external powers by the advent of the Treaty of Amsterdam. It would not have been fair to tell the other states that the Member States would no longer be negotiating, but only the European Community.

A simple way of creating clarity is through the use of a disconnection **7.69** clause.[84] Such a clause indicates that another instrument exists for internal relations in the EU. By virtue of the principles of EU law, international law, and the Vienna Convention, one might be able to find which convention takes precedence. However, disconnection clauses have two functions: they indicate prevalence of older instruments (such as the Lugano Convention, or the old Brussels Convention, which still applies for Denmark), which would not have such prevalence in the absence of an explicit rule in the treaty, and they make life much easier for all involved. In this second sense a disconnection clause can be seen as a lesson in international and European Union law. It explains when the Convention has to defer to European Union law, without in itself establishing that result. This means that in some cases a disconnection clause is, strictly legally speaking, unnecessary, since it might achieve the same result as would have been the case if no clause were inserted. The problem with disconnection clauses is that it seems very difficult to explain the situation in a simple, straightforward way. There are always exceptions. The disconnection for jurisdiction rules is different to that for rules on recognition and enforcement. Furthermore, as has been indicated, the EC and the Member States might be in dispute, or be unsure of the situation themselves.

---

[82] See Middeldrop & van Ooik, note 17 above, 4.

[83] Hartley, note 1 above, 166.

[84] On disconnection clauses in general: A Borrás, 'Les clauses de déconnexion et le droit international privé communautaire' in H-P Mansel, T Pfeiffer, H Kronke, C Kohler & R Hausmann (eds), *Festschrift für Erik Jayme* (Munich: Sellier. European Law Publishers, 2004) vol 1, 57–72; see also Schulz, 'The judgments project and other international instruments', note 65 above.

G. A PRACTICAL INTERIM APPROACH: THE EXAMPLE OF THE HAGUE CONFERENCE ON PRIVATE INTERNATIONAL LAW

7.70 In 1992 negotiations started at the Hague Conference on Private International Law to attempt to establish a worldwide convention on jurisdiction and foreign judgments in civil and commercial matters.[85] In 1999 came the Amsterdam Treaty and in 2001 the European Community enacted Brussels I, a Community instrument on the same subject matter. Uncertainty arose as to the external competences. In 2003 an opinion on the matter was asked of the European Court of Justice concerning the Lugano Convention. The problem of competence with regard to the Lugano Convention is largely the same as that for the Hague Convention and the judgment would probably also be relevant for the Hague negotiations. While waiting for the judgment, negotiations went ahead and the EU Member States and European Commission had to find a way of continuing their participation. According to the old Statute of the Hague Conference only states could be Members and have the right to vote during negotiations.[86] However it was possible for organizations to attend the negotiations as observers.[87] In that capacity the representatives from the European Commission, the Council, and the Parliament could attend the negotiations. The voice of these institutions, especially that of the Commission, grew in importance although the EC could not vote formally.

7.71 In the meantime, negotiations on the jurisdiction convention carried on, but no voting took place. The Member States negotiated as members and the Commission as observer. This made the negotiations very difficult in light of the fact that quasi-consensus had to be reached on each point. The Commission and Member States also had so-called coordination meetings before every session. At those meetings they aligned their views so that they would negotiate from the same position. This action was not only to help the negotiations, but it encompassed an obligation on EU Member States

---

[85] For a detailed discussion of the EU's relationship with the Hague Conference, see Traest, note 63 above.

[86] That Statute was amended in June 2005 in order to permit the EC (and other Regional Economic Integration Organizations that meet certain requirements) to become a Member of the Hague Conference on Private International Law, and to set up a new voting mechanism. The new Statute entered into force on 1 January 2007. The EC became a Member on 3 April 2007.

[87] For a similar situation, see Opinion 2/91, note 26 above (the EC also had observer status at the International Labour Organization).

in fields where competence is shared. If every EU Member State were permitted to take its own stance at the negotiations this would jeopardize the EC's part of the competence.[88] When well coordinated these efforts helped the negotiations: a number of states already had the same stance. On the other hand, some negotiating states experienced these efforts as a block vote against which it was very difficult to raise their own concerns. The only state that really had equal bargaining power was the USA. If compromises could be struck between these two blocks, it became very difficult for other states to intervene. At a certain point this seriously threatened the work at the Hague Conference.[89]

While negotiating the Hague Choice of Court Convention, the EC and the **7.72** Member States were still in dispute as to whether the Convention was within the exclusive external competence of the EC, or entailed shared competence between the EC and the Member States.[90] The case on the similar Lugano dispute was pending at the European Court of Justice. The EC and the Member States wanted to leave both options open; both had to be written into the text of the Convention. The EC tried to justify this by saying that the clause would apply not only to the EC, but to all REIOs that might exist and have extended powers in the future. At the time of the negotiations, however, it was clear that the EC was the only REIO that would need the option at that moment, and for the near future. Also, they were the only ones that needed two options. Of course this was not only confusing for third States, but it also seemed that the EC and the Member States wanted to have their cake and eat it.

In the end the Convention contains both a disconnection clause (attempt- **7.73** ing to explain when the EU instruments will enjoy precedence),[91] and a clause stating that a Regional Economic Integration Organization (REIO) may sign the Convention if it has competence over all or some of the matters governed by the Convention.[92] The wording 'some or all' left open the question whether the EC was exclusively competent or shared competence with its Member States. At the time of signature, the REIO must

---

[88] Ibid, especially paras 12 and 37–38.
[89] Pocar, note 60 above, 191: '[s]hould the negotiations be regarded by States as unduly unbalanced, their outcome would have little chance of success'. AVM Struycken, 'Het Verdrag van Amsterdam en de Haagse Conferentie voor international privaatrecht. Brusselse schaduwen over Den Haag' [2000] *Weekblad voor Privaatrecht, Notariaat en Registratie* 735–745.
[90] Hague Choice of Court Convention, note 21 above.
[91] Art 26; Hartley and Dogauchi, Explanatory Report, note 70 above, 70–80.
[92] Art 29; Hartley and Dogauchi, ibid, 81. This clause has been inspired by Art 18 of the Hague Securities Convention.

inform the depositary of the exact scope of its competence. If this competence changes in future, the REIO is also under an obligation to notify the depositary of this.

7.74 The *Lugano* Opinion brought clarity to the external competence of the EC. Henceforth, signature and ratification of the Hague Convention on Choice of Court Agreements will be a matter for the EC and not for its Member States. Note that Denmark is once again excluded: the EC signature and ratification will not bind it. However, being an EU Member State and having an agreement on the same matter as Brussels I with the EC, it is bound by the general loyalty duty under the EC Treaty.[93] Accordingly, Denmark will probably join the Convention at the same time as the rest of the EU.

H. INTERNATIONAL COOPERATION INSTEAD OF HIERARCHY?

7.75 These discussions concerned Brussels I primarily, but this does not mean that the same problems do not arise with respect to Brussels II *bis*. An interesting interaction took place between the Brussels II Convention (predecessor of Brussels II *bis*) and the 1996 Hague Convention on parental responsibility. This different approach merits a short discussion at this point, by way of comparison and to indicate another approach to dealing with third States. The Hague Conference and the European Union seemed to have been entwined in a love–hate relationship. They wanted to work together, but the EU also wanted to create a closer collaboration than the Hague Conference was able to establish.

7.76 The 1996 Hague Child Protection Convention does not contain a Regional Economic Integration Organization (REIO) clause. This can be explained by the fact that this Hague Convention was signed before the great changes of the Treaty of Amsterdam. Only after the completion of the Hague Convention did family law become an EU matter. The solution was that all the EU Member States signed the Hague Convention in two capacities: first for themselves and second in the interest of the European Community. Before signing, there was a Council Decision to authorize the Member States (except Denmark) to sign in the EC's interest.[94] This way the European

---

[93] Art 10.

[94] Council Decision 2003/93/EC, note 24 above, 1–2. At that stage the Netherlands had already signed the Convention. On the compromise needed for this Council act, see A Schulz, 'Die Zeichnung des Haager Kinderschutz-Übereinkommens von 1996 und der Kompromiss zur Brüssel IIa-Verordnung' [2003] *Zeitschrift für das gesamte Familienrecht* 1351–1354, 1352.

Community became involved in the Hague Convention. In this development the duality of the relationship between the EU and the Hague Conference can be felt. On one hand, it is positive for the Hague Conference that the Convention is guaranteed at least 26 States Party.[95] Additionally, the Convention will benefit from the interpretation by the European Court of Justice of a similar instrument. Furthermore Brussels II *bis* gives a slight incentive to third States to become party to the Hague Convention by inserting presumptions of the best interests of a child that is habitually resident in a third State which is not party to the Hague Convention, and thus drawing the child into the sphere of application of Brussels II *bis*.[96] While this approach of the EU might be criticized, if the children are going to be subjected to EU rules in any event, a third State might as well become party to the Hague Convention and at least have reciprocity. On the other hand, working with the EU as a whole, the Hague Conference could be dragged into EU politics. For example, disputes about Gibraltar can delay the extension of the Convention.

I. FUTURE INSTRUMENTS ON MAINTENANCE

The existing Regulations have raised questions on the external competence **7.77** of the EC. As EC legislation increases, the issues concerning external competence may arise more frequently. Currently both the Hague Conference on Private International Law and the European Community are working on legal instruments on maintenance. The European Commission has proposed a Council Regulation on Jurisdiction, Applicable law, Recognition and Enforcement of Decisions and Cooperation in Matters relating to Maintenance Obligations.[97] As the name indicates, this will be a broad instrument dealing with various aspects of maintenance claims. It will replace Article 5(2) of Brussels I, which presently contains the EU's jurisdiction rule on the topic. At the Hague Conference a future Convention on maintenance obligations is being negotiated.[98] This Convention will not be as broad as the EU's proposed Regulation. It will only deal with authorities able to aid in the recovery of maintenance, and with the recognition

---

[95] Denmark falls outside the EU's competence in this matter. However, a convention between Denmark and the rest of the EU will be created. In practice it can be established with near certainty that Denmark will also become party to the Hague Convention along with the other EU Member States.

[96] Art 12(4) of Brussels II *bis* ; chapter 2 above, para 2.109.

[97] COM(2005) 649 final, note 74 above.

[98] See <http://www.hcch.net>.

and enforcement of maintenance decisions. The Convention will not contain jurisdiction rules, but it has a draft protocol on applicable law.[99] The EU's Regulation will also deal with this form of administrative aid by authorities in different states and will also contain rules on applicable law, and the recognition and enforcement of maintenance decisions. Thus the two instruments will overlap to an extent. The European Commission has acknowledged this and stated in the Explanatory Memorandum attached to the Proposal:

> The relationships between the negotiations undertaken in The Hague and Community work should be seen in terms of the search for possible synergies between them; these two exercises are not contradictory, but consistent and complementary. . .

7.78 By adopting legislation in this field, and since the Hague Convention might affect such legislation, the European Community is gaining exclusive external competence, following the *Lugano* Opinion. It will therefore be responsible for signing and ratifying the Hague Convention. The Convention will contain a provision permitting REIOs to sign, accept, approve, or accede to it, and a provision stating that REIOs may declare that they have exclusive competence on the matters treated by the Convention.

J. CONCLUSION

7.79 This chapter has examined the external relations of the EU; currently a hot issue in European private international law. The *Lugano* Opinion by the European Court of Justice has explained that the EC now has exclusive external competence on the matters treated in Brussels I. Therefore negotiations with Iceland, Norway, and Switzerland, and the conclusion of the amended Lugano Convention, would be the task of the European Community and not its Member States. This finding was based on the fact that the Lugano Convention would affect the operation of the Regulation. In reaching this conclusion, the European Court of Justice analysed the provisions of the envisaged Lugano Convention and of Brussels I. However, it has been pointed out in this chapter that the analysis was very formalistic and the ECJ did not consider all relevant points.

7.80 The effects of this conclusion are broad. The European Community is rapidly increasing its competences. Internal competence brings along

---

[99] Available at <http://www.hcch.net>.

external competence. The influence of this development on third States should not be underestimated. Third States would increasingly be negotiating with the EC instead of individual states, or with the EC alongside its individual Member States. Furthermore, third States would have to bear in mind that the Council would have to approve any treaty negotiated by the Commission before it can be ratified by the EC. The effect could be more dramatic where a single third State and a single EU Member State have an interest in cooperation in a specific field. If the EC has exclusive external competence in the field at issue, the Member States will no longer be able to assume individual international obligations. An EU Member State wishing to enter international agreements would have to ask the EC to do the job for it, or would have to seek authorization.

It should be emphasized that other negotiation tables, such as that of the Hague Conference on Private International Law, should not be seen as a threat to the EU, but rather as an opportunity to work together with third States in a world of international trade and cross-border families. **7.81**

8

Conclusion and recommended amendments to the Regulations

A. THE OUTSIDE WORLD

Coming to the end, one sees a building constructed upon a quadrangle, and **8.01**
one has to admire what the EU has achieved in the area of civil jurisdiction. However, this building does not seem to have enough windows and doors to the outside world. It appears that the rules were drawn up from the inside, for the inside. It is a pity that the drafters paid little attention to the outside world. In its judgments on civil jurisdiction, one sometimes finds that the European Court of Justice attaches more weight to the functioning of the European judicial area than to considerations of international trade more generally and to the interests of third States.

B. DOUBLE INSTRUMENTS?

At the outset the idea was that the Brussels Convention should be a dou- **8.02**
ble convention, meaning that it would contain not only rules on the recognition and enforcement of judgments, but also on jurisdiction. The argument was that, if jurisdiction rules were unified, then recognition and enforcement should be much easier, because there would be no need for any examination of the basis for the court's jurisdiction. This proved to be a good idea, and the Convention worked well. The system was followed in the subsequent civil jurisdiction regulations of the EU.

8.03 However, there was a flaw: the double nature was imperfect (and still is in some of the regulations). The Brussels Convention, and subsequently the Brussels I and II *bis* Regulations are not completely double: in some instances they refer back to the national rules on jurisdiction. The European Court of Justice has stated that such reference means that those national bases for jurisdiction have been incorporated into the complete system of the Regulations. The *Lugano* Opinion specifically considered Brussels I and its complete system, but the argument can be transposed to Brussels II *bis*. A pure double system would mean that jurisdiction rules are unified and recognition and enforcement are made easy. But the EU's unification is not complete: some rules of national law can still enter the system.

8.04 At this point it seems that a choice will have to be made. The first option is admitting that the system is not completely double; then recognition and enforcement of judgments based on the (exorbitant) national bases of jurisdiction should not be included. The second option is eliminating the (exorbitant) national bases of jurisdiction, so that they would no longer exist. This would be true unification of jurisdiction rules: the same jurisdiction rules would apply throughout the EU, no matter if the defendant is domiciled in the EU or in a third State. Then having easy recognition would not be to anyone's detriment.

8.05 After the recent judgments of the European Court of Justice, the first option has become less viable. The ECJ has repeatedly emphasized the mutual trust that should exist between the courts of EU Member States. It has also argued that there is a single system of jurisdiction rules and that the national bases for jurisdiction are part of that system. Asking the EU's legislator and judiciary to go back and insert conditions for certain cases, so that the bases for jurisdiction have to be examined before a judgment can be recognized or enforced, would be contrary to the European judicial area's goals and would undermine the strength of the instruments, namely blind trust by the recognizing or enforcing court that the basis for jurisdiction was correct.

8.06 The second option is contrary neither to the European ideal nor to the principle of mutual trust. It would also be fair towards third State courts and parties domiciled in third States. It should be borne in mind that the permissible national bases for jurisdiction are only applied if the defendant is domiciled in a third State (in the case of Brussels I) or if no court in the EU has jurisdiction on the basis of the Regulation's direct jurisdiction rules (in the case of Brussels II *bis*). These national rules are the dangerous ones; they have not been included among the EU's direct jurisdiction rules in the first place because of their exorbitant nature. The question is why they are necessary at all. There are sufficient bases for jurisdiction to supply plaintiffs with ample possibilities. The outlawed bases for jurisdiction might as well disappear from the face of the earth. The second option seems to have been chosen for the Insolvency and proposed Maintenance Regulations. These instruments do not refer to national bases for jurisdiction, but create their own rules, which are universal across the EU.

C. RECOMMENDED AMENDMENTS TO BRUSSELS I

In the following paragraphs amendments are proposed on the basis of the second option. If the first option can still be chosen, the text itself will need fewer amendments. However, space should be left for the operation of national rules to decline jurisdiction; recognition and enforcement of judgments that have been based on exorbitant grounds for jurisdiction should not be covered by the Regulation. **8.07**

Article 3 of Brussels I should be broadened. At present it reads: **8.08**

1. Persons domiciled in a Member State may be sued in the courts of another Member State only by virtue of the rules set out in Sections 2 to 7 of this Chapter.
2. In particular the rules of national jurisdiction set out in Annex I shall not be applicable as against them.

The reference to 'persons domiciled in a Member State' should be taken out. This rule should apply to all people, no matter where they are domiciled. Thus the rule should read:

A defendant may be sued in the courts of another Member State only by virtue of the rules set out in Sections 2 to 7 of this Chapter.

Or:

1. Jurisdiction may be based only on the rules set out in Sections 2 to 7 of this Chapter.

Paragraph 2 of Article 3 would then be unnecessary and could be deleted, together with the list in Annex I. If the legislator wanted to include it for purposes of clarity (and to draw attention to the amendment of such an old provision), it should be modified in the following way:

2. In particular the rules of national jurisdiction set out in Annex I may never be applied.

Subsequently, Article 4 of the Regulation should be deleted. It reads: **8.09**

1. If the defendant is not domiciled in a Member State, the jurisdiction of the courts of each Member State shall, subject to Articles 22 and 23, be determined by the law of that Member State.

2. As against such a defendant, any person domiciled in a Member State may, whatever his nationality, avail himself in that State of the rules of jurisdiction there in force, and in particular those specified in Annex I, in the same way as the nationals of that State.

The result of the new rule in Article 3 would be that the national rules could never be used any more. Therefore Article 4 should be deleted.

8.10 These amendments would have to be reflected in Article 26(1), on the examination of jurisdiction, which at present reads as follows:

Where a defendant domiciled in one Member State is sued in a court of another Member State and does not enter an appearance, the court shall declare of its own motion that it has no jurisdiction unless its jurisdiction is derived from the provisions of this Regulation.

In this Article the reference to the domicile of the defendant should be taken out. It should in future apply to all defendants and not just to those domiciled in the Member States:

Where a defendant is sued in a court of a Member State and does not enter an appearance, the court shall declare of its own motion that it has no jurisdiction unless its jurisdiction is derived from the provisions of this Regulation.

This modification is a logical consequence of the changes to Articles 3 and 4. The reason why the current provision distinguishes between defendants domiciled in the EU and those domiciled in third States, is the existence of exorbitant jurisdictional grounds that may be employed in cases against the latter group. Currently, a court could revert to its national law against defendants domiciled in third States. If the national rules of jurisdiction are disallowed, this possibility will no longer exist, and a court will have to decline to hear a case if it cannot base its jurisdiction on the Regulation itself.

8.11 In Articles 5 and 6 the references to 'domiciled in a Member State' could be deleted. The content of these articles should be carefully reconsidered to ensure that they are not too far-reaching.

8.12 The Regulation's provision on *lis pendens* should be altered in order to provide explicitly for certain exceptions. At present Article 27 states:

1. Where proceedings involving the same cause of action and between the same parties are brought in the courts of different Member States, any court other than the court first seised shall of its own motion stay its proceedings until such time as the jurisdiction of the court first seised is established.

2. Where the jurisdiction of the court first seised is established, any court other than the court first seised shall decline jurisdiction in favour of that court.

The rule should be extended to include the following:

3. Notwithstanding points 1 and 2, a court will not have to stay its proceedings if:
   — it has exclusive jurisdiction pursuant to Article 22 of this Regulation;
   — it has jurisdiction pursuant to an agreement between the parties in accordance with Article 23 of this Regulation;
   — it is exercising its jurisdiction to grant provisional or protective measures and such jurisdiction is in accordance with Article 31 of this Regulation.

Probably one of the most important alterations that should be made to **8.13** Brussels I is that it should provide explicit rules for declining jurisdiction in favour of the courts of third States. The European Court of Justice is taking the line that the Regulation contains a complete system of rules. It is also of the opinion that these rules are compulsory. A court in an EU Member State may not decline its Regulation-based jurisdiction if there is no basis for declining in the Regulation itself. The only bases for declining one finds in the Regulation are in favour of courts in other EU Member States. However, if the Regulation purports to be a complete system, it should be truly complete, and not half-complete. Thus there must be ways to decline jurisdiction in favour of third State courts if the ends of justice so require.

Such a provision could form part of the section on *'Lis pendens—related* **8.14** *actions'* (Section 9), or could form a separate section. If the first option is chosen, the section should be renamed *'Declining jurisdiction'*. If a separate section is inserted, it could be called *'Declining jurisdiction in favour of courts in third States'*. The starting point of the rule should be the reflexive effect. In other words, if the Regulation grants exclusive jurisdiction to a court in an EU Member State regarding disputes on immovable property situated in that State, the Regulation should also permit a court in an EU Member State to decline jurisdiction in favour of the third State court of the place where a disputed immovable property is situated. The same applies to forum clauses. The Regulation respects forum clauses in favour of the courts of EU Member States. Thus, it should also respect forum clauses in favour of the courts of third States. This basic rule of comity should be inserted in the Regulation so that it will apply to forum clauses for all third States, and not just for the Contracting States of the Hague Choice of Court Convention (on the assumption that the EC will ratify that Convention). It is in the interest of legal certainty that contracting parties are held to their promises, and are sent to the courts to which they had agreed, no matter where those courts are situated. Furthermore, when a court in a third State had been seised first, and subsequently a court in an EU Member State, the Regulation should at least foresee the possibility of declining jurisdiction in favour of the third State court first seised. Declining jurisdiction in favour of a third State court on this basis is of course different from declining jurisdiction in favour of a court of another EU Member State: in the latter case, one knows that the same jurisdiction rules will be applied, and that the subsequent judgment will be recognized and enforced throughout the EU. Therefore the rule should not make declining jurisdiction compulsory, but possible. Preferably the rule should also contain some guidelines for the EU courts. For example:

Article A

1. Notwithstanding Articles 2–21 of this Regulation, where one of the parties claims that the courts of a third State have exclusive jurisdiction to hear the case, a court in a Member State shall stay its proceedings in order to give that party the opportunity to introduce proceedings in a court in that third State.

2. Where the exclusive jurisdiction of the court in the third State is established, a court in a Member State shall decline its jurisdiction in favour of that court.

Article B

1. Notwithstanding Articles 2–21 of this Regulation, where one of the parties brings to the attention of a court in a Member State that the parties had agreed that a court or the courts of a third State are to have exclusive jurisdiction to settle any disputes which have arisen or which may arise in connection with a particular legal relationship, a court in a Member State shall stay its proceedings in order to give that party the opportunity to introduce proceedings in a court in that third State.

2. Where the jurisdiction of the court in the third State is established on the basis of the agreement between the parties, a court in a Member State shall decline its jurisdiction in favour of that court.

Article C

1. Notwithstanding Articles 2–21 of this Regulation, where one of the parties claims that a protective basis of jurisdiction exists in a third State (in the form of a mandatory rule), a court in a Member State shall stay its proceedings in order to give the parties the opportunity to introduce proceedings in a court in that third State.

2. Where the jurisdiction of the court in the third State is established on the basis of the protection of the weaker party, a court in a Member State shall decline its jurisdiction in favour of that court.

Article D

1. Notwithstanding Articles 2–21 and 24 of this Regulation, where proceedings involving the same cause of action and between the same parties are brought first in a court in a third State and subsequently in a court in a Member State, the court in the Member State may stay its proceedings until such time as the jurisdiction of the court first seised is established.

2. Where the jurisdiction of the third State court first seised is established, a court in a Member State may decline jurisdiction in favour of that court. In considering whether to decline its jurisdiction, the court shall take the following in consideration:
   — whether the judgment will be capable of being recognized in its own State;
   — whether the third State court considers its jurisdiction to be exclusive;
   — whether there is a (non-exclusive) forum clause in favour of the third State court;
   — whether the jurisdiction of the third State court is not based only on the nationality of one of the parties, or only on the presence of property of the defendant in that State, or only on the temporary presence of the defendant on the territory of that State.

Article E

1. Notwithstanding Articles 2–21 of this Regulation, where the defendant submits that there is a court in a third State that also has jurisdiction and that is clearly in a better position to adjudicate the case, a court in a Member State may stay its proceedings until such time as the jurisdiction of the court in the third State is established.

2. Where the jurisdiction of the court in a third State is established, a court in a Member State may decline jurisdiction in favour of that court. In considering whether to decline its jurisdiction, the court shall take the following in consideration:
   — whether the judgment will be capable of being recognized in its own State;
   — whether there is a (non-exclusive) forum clause in favour of the third State court;
   — whether the jurisdiction of the third State court is not based only on the nationality of one of the parties, or only on the presence of property of the defendant in that State, or only on the temporary presence of the defendant in the territory of that State;
   — whether the case has a close connection to the court of the third State;
   — whether the evidence necessary for the case can be accessed more easily by the court in the third State.

Article F

1. Notwithstanding Article 22 of this Regulation and upon request by a defendant domiciled in a third State, a court in a Member State may stay its proceedings in favour of a court in a third State if such proceedings have as their object tenancies of immovable property concluded for a maximum period of six consecutive months, if the tenant is a natural person, and if the landlord and tenant are domiciled in the same third State.

2. Where the jurisdiction of the court in a third State is established, a court in a Member State may decline jurisdiction in favour of that court. In considering whether to decline its jurisdiction, the court shall take the following in consideration:
   — whether the judgment will be capable of being recognized in its own State;

— whether there is a (non-exclusive) forum clause in favour of the third State court;

— whether the jurisdiction of the third State court is not based only on the nationality of one of the parties, or only on the presence of property of the defendant in that State, or only on the temporary presence of the defendant in the territory of that State;

— whether the case has a close connection to the court of the third State;

— whether the evidence necessary for the case can be accessed more easily by the court in the third State.

D. RECOMMENDED AMENDMENTS TO BRUSSELS II *BIS*

8.15 Article 6 of Brussels II *bis* states:

A spouse who:

(a) is habitually resident in the territory of a Member State; or
(b) is a national of a Member State, or, in the case of the United Kingdom and Ireland, has his or her 'domicile' in the territory of one of the latter Member States,

may be sued in another Member State only in accordance with Articles 3, 4 and 5.

As pointed out, the provision has caused much confusion. Furthermore, the distinction between defendants based on their habitual residence and nationality should be removed from the Regulation. The Commission's proposed amendments to Brussels II *bis* purport to delete this provision.

8.16 It is proposed that Article 7 of that Regulation should also be deleted. At present this Article reads:

1. Where no court of a Member State has jurisdiction pursuant to Articles 3, 4 and 5, jurisdiction shall be determined, in each Member State, by the laws of that State.
2. As against a respondent who is not habitually resident and is not either a national of a Member State or, in the case of the United Kingdom and Ireland, does not have his 'domicile' within the territory of one of the latter Member States, any national of a Member State who is habitually resident within the territory of another Member State may, like the nationals of that State, avail himself of the rules of jurisdiction applicable in that State.

This provision makes it possible to revert to (exorbitant) national bases for jurisdiction if no court in the EU has jurisdiction under the other rules of the Regulation. The other rules are broad (as pointed out in chapter 2). If no court in the EU has jurisdiction under those rules, it is probably because the case has no link or a very tenuous link with the EU. The better approach to such a case would be to acknowledge that there simply is no jurisdiction in the EU. A spouse returning to his or her home country after having lived in the US for twenty years can institute a divorce action after six months. Surely that is reasonable enough. The second paragraph of this provision enlarges the exorbitant bases of jurisdiction to those that exist in EU Member States' national law. If such rules are based on nationality, they are also being made available to persons having another EU nationality, but habitually resident in that state. This in fact means that any EU national can move back from a third State and go to France, establish a habitual residence, and institute divorce proceedings against his or her spouse, no matter where in the world that spouse is. This is obviously too far-reaching. It is also unnecessary. Going back to one's state of nationality, divorce is possible after six months. In the alternative, if the person wanting to divorce lives for one year in the EU and not in a third State, the court of habitual residence has jurisdiction.

The proposal to amend Brussels II *bis* contains the following replacement **8.17** for the current Article 7:

Where none of the spouses is habitually resident in the territory of a Member State and does not have a common nationality of a Member State, or, in the case of the United Kingdom and Ireland do not have their 'domicile' within the territory of one of the latter Member States, the courts of a Member State are competent by virtue of the fact that:

    (a) the spouses had their common previous habitual residence in the territory of that Member State for at least three years; or

    (b) one of the spouses has the nationality of that Member State, or, in the case of United Kingdom and Ireland has his or her 'domicile' in the territory of one of the latter Member States.

In so far as this provision repairs the double nature of the Regulation, it should be welcomed. The national bases for jurisdiction are deleted. However, the proposed Article still distinguishes between defendants on the basis of habitual residence and nationality. Paragraph (a) grants jurisdiction on the basis of a previous habitual residence of at least three years, without any limit to how long ago this habitual residence might have existed. If a German and a Canadian lived in France for three years directly after their marriage and then moved to Canada to live there for twenty years, the French court will forever retain its jurisdiction. At that stage the parties might have no connection whatsoever with France. It is not clear why the already broad bases for jurisdiction should be broadened further. Paragraph (b) grants jurisdiction to the courts of the nationality of one spouse. This is similar to the exorbitant basis for jurisdiction in French law. It is unclear why this basis for jurisdiction has to re-enter the Regulation. As explained, the existing rules seem broad enough: a spouse can return to the state of his or her domicile and institute proceedings after a habitual residence there of six months. The Commission states in its Explanatory Report that, under the current rule, there might be situations where no court in an EU Member State or in a third State has jurisdiction. It does not give any examples and I must admit that I have difficulty in finding them. In most legal systems an action is possible at the place of the residence of the defendant.

8.18 Article 14 of Brussels II *bis* is similar to Article 7 and should also be deleted:

> Where no court of a Member State has jurisdiction pursuant to Articles 8 to 13, jurisdiction shall be determined, in each Member State, by the laws of that State.

This rule should be deleted for the same reasons as Article 7, discussed above. However, the arguments here are even stronger. Article 14 deals with parental responsibility—a delicate area of the law where the interests of children must be safeguarded. The general basis for jurisdiction in this field is the habitual residence of the child. This provides a form of protection for the child. It enables social workers and psychologists to survey the child's situation in his or her natural environment and report to the court. The Regulation does foresee exceptions, for instance to hear a divorce and parental responsibility case together. It also foresees possibilities to transfer a case to a court in another EU Member State. This should suffice. A reference to other (possibly exorbitant) bases for jurisdiction of national law seems unnecessary and unwarranted.

8.19 Articles 6, 7, and 14 would not need to be replaced. The fact that the Regulations contain a complete system of rules would make it clear that courts in EU Member States can never revert to national law. Those national law provisions will not exist any more. For the sake of clarity, Article 17 should be amended. This provision is similar to Article 26(1) of Brussels I (discussed above) and at present it states:

> Where a court of a Member State is seised of a case over which it has no jurisdiction under this Regulation and over which a court of another Member State has jurisdiction by virtue of this Regulation, it shall declare of its own motion that it has no jurisdiction.

It is proposed that the reference to the jurisdiction of a court of another Member State should be deleted. The provision then would read:

> Where a court of a Member State is seised of a case over which it has no jurisdiction under this Regulation, it shall declare of its own motion that it has no jurisdiction.

A court in an EU Member State would then have to examine its jurisdiction according to the Regulation's rules. If it has jurisdiction, it will exercise such jurisdiction. If it does not have jurisdiction, it will plainly find that it cannot hear the case. National judges then will not have to go to the effort of checking the jurisdiction of the courts in other EU Member States. This step, as explained in chapter 2, was only necessary in order to determine whether the court might revert to its national bases for jurisdiction. If there are no national bases for jurisdiction any more, the need for such examination falls away.

E. CONCLUSION

Although it is not an easy task, this book modestly hopes to have shed **8.20** some light on the sphere of application of the EU civil jurisdiction rules for litigants and contracting parties from third States. Its conclusion is that the system is imperfect, but that rectification is possible and should be pursued. Jurisdiction rules can contribute to the goals of the EU's internal market. However, this should never be done at the expense of litigating parties or children domiciled in other parts of the world, of courts in third States, or of comity and justice.

Bibliography

BOOKS

B Audit, *Droit international privé* (3rd edn, Paris: Economica, 2000)

C Barnard & J Scott (eds), *The Law of the Single European Market* (Oxford: Hart Publishing, 2002)

J Basedow, I Meier, AK Schnyder, T Einhorn & D Girsberger (eds), *Private Law in the International Arena. Liber Amicorum Kurt Siehr* (The Hague: TMC Asser Press, 2000)

PR Beaumont & PE McEleavy, *The Hague Convention on International Child Abduction* (Oxford: Oxford University Press, 1999)

J-S Bergé & M-L Niboyet, *La réception du droit communautaire en droit privé des Etats membres* (Brussels: Bruylant, 2003)

H Born, M Fallon & J-L Van Boxstael, *Droit judiciaire international. Chronique de jurisprudence 1991–1998* (Brussels: Larcier, 2001)

GB Born & D Westin, *International Civil Litigation in United States Courts* (Deventer/ Boston: Kluwer, 1989)

A Borrás, A Bucher, AVM Struycken & M Verwilghen (eds), *E Pluribus unum. Liber Amicorum Georges AL Droz* (The Hague: Martinus Nijhoff Publishers, 1996)

P Bourel, U Drobnig, GAL Droz, B Goldman, O Lando, K Lipstein, C Morse, J Pipkorn & F Pocar, *The Influence of the European Community upon Private International Law of the Member States* (Brussels: Larcier, 1981)

A Briggs, *The Conflict of Laws (Clarendon Law Series)* (Oxford: Oxford University Press, 2002)

A Briggs & P Rees, *Civil Jurisdiction and Judgments* (2nd edn, London: LLP, 1997)

—— *Civil Jurisdiction and Judgments* (3rd edn, London: LLP, 2002)

—— *Civil Jurisdiction and Judgments* (4th edn, London: LLP, 2005)

I Brownlie, *Principles of Public International Law* (6th edn, Oxford: Oxford University Press, 2003)

M-T Caupain & G de Leval, *L'efficacité de la justice civile en Europe* (Brussels: Larcier, 2000)

Centre for International Legal Studies, *Serving process and obtaining evidence abroad* (London: Kluwer, 1998)

CMV Clarkson & J Hill, *Jaffey on the Conflict of Laws* (2nd edn, London: Butterworths, 2002)

L Collins (ed), *Dicey and Morris on the Conflict of Laws* (13th edn, London: Sweet & Maxwell, 2000)

—— *Dicey, Morris and Collins on the Conflict of Laws* (14th edn, London: Sweet & Maxwell, 2006)

Court of Justice of the European Communities, *Civil Jurisdiction and Judgments in Europe* (London: Butterworths, 1992)

P Craig & G De Búrca, *EU Law* (3rd edn, Oxford: Oxford University Press, 2003)

G Cuniberti, *Les mesures conservatoires portant sur des biens situées à l'étranger* (Paris: LGDJ, 2000)

F Delpérée, *Le principe de subsidiarité* (Brussels: Bruylant, 2002)

Y Donzallaz, *La Convention de Lugano du 16 septembre 1988 concernant la compétence judiciaire et l'exécution des décisions en matière civile et commerciale* (Berne: Editions Stæmpfli + Cie SA Berne, 1996)

GAL Droz, *Pratique de la convention de Bruxelles du 27 septembre 1968* (Paris: Dalloz, 1973)

H-C Duursma-Kepplinger, D Duursma & E Chalupsky, *Europäische Insolvenzverordnung: Kommentar* (Vienna: Springer–Verlag, 2002)

P Eeckhout, *External Relations of the European Union* (Oxford: Oxford University Press, 2004)

J Erauw & M Fallon, *De nieuwe wet op het internationaal privaatrecht* (Mechelen: Kluwer, 2004)

European Commission, Practice guide for the application of the Regulation, drawn up by the European Commission in consultation with the European Judicial Network in civil and commercial matters; available at <http://www.europa.eu.int/comm/justice_home/ejn>

JJ Fawcett, *Declining Jurisdiction in Private International Law* (Oxford: Clarendon Press, 1995)

JJ Fawcett, JM Harris & M Bridge, *International sale of goods in the conflict of laws* (Oxford: Oxford University Press, 2005)

JJ Fawcett & P Torremans, *Intellectual Property and Private International Law*(Oxford: Clarendon Press, 1998)

R Fentiman, A Nuyts, H Tagaras & N Watté (eds), *The European Judicial Area in Civil and Commercial Matters* (Brussels: Bruylant, 1999)

CF Forsyth, *Private International Law* (4th edn, Lansdowne, South Africa: Juta, 2003)

S Francq, *L'applicabilité du droit communautaire dérivé au regard des méthodes du droit international privé* (Brussels: Bruylant & Paris: LGDJ, 2005)

H Gaudemet-Tallon, *Les Conventions de Bruxelles et de Lugano* (2nd edn, Paris: Montchrestien, 1996)

—— *Compétence et exécution des jugements en Europe* (3rd edn, Paris: LGDJ, 2002)

R Geimer, R Greger, R Gummer, K Herget, H-J Heßler, P Philippi, K Stöber & M Vollkommer, *Zöller Zivilprozessordnung* (24th edn, Cologne: Verlag Dr Otto Schmidt, 2004)

R Geimer, *Internationales Zivilprozeßrecht* (Cologne: Verlag Dr Otto Schmidt, 2005)

P Gothot & D Holleaux, *La Convention de Bruxelles du 27.9.1968. Compétence judiciaire et effets des jugements dans la CEE* (Paris: Editions Jupiter, 1985)

P Grolimund, *Drittstaatenproblematik des europäischen Zivilverfahrensrechts* (Tübingen: Mohr Siebeck, 2000)

TC Hartley, *Civil Jurisdiction and Judgments* (London: Sweet & Maxwell, 1984)

—— *The Foundations of European Community Law* (5th edn, Oxford: Oxford University Press, 2003)

P Hay, RJ Weintraub & PJ Borchers, *Conflict of Laws Cases and Materials* (11th edn, New York: Foundation Press, 2000)

K Hertz, *Jurisdiction in Contract and Tort under the Brussels Convention* (Copenhagen: DJØF Publishing, 1998)

CA Joustra & MV Polak, *Internationaal, communautair en nationaal IPR* (The Hague: TMC Asser Press, 2002)

PJG Kapteyn and P VerLoren van Themaat, *Introduction to the law of the European Communities* (London: Kluwer Law International, 1998)

P Kaye, *Law of the European Judgments Convention* (Chichester: Barry Rose, 1999)

XE Kramer, *Het kort geding in internationaal perspectief. Een rechtsvergelijkende studie naar de voorlopige voorziening in het internationaal privaatrecht* (Deventer: Kluwer, 2001)

J Kropholler, *Europäisches Zivilprozeßrecht. Kommentar zu EuGVO und Lugano-Übereinkommen* (7th edn, Heidelberg: Verlag Recht und Wirtschaft GmbH, 2002)

D Lasok & PA Stone, *Conflict of Laws in the European Community* (Abingdon, Oxon: Professional Books Limited, 1987)

P-O Lapie, *Les trois communautés* (Paris: Librairie Arthême Fayard, 1960)

A Layton & H Mercer, *European Civil Practice* (2nd edn, London: Sweet & Maxwell, 2004)

K Lenaerts & D Arts, *Europees Procesrecht* (3rd edn, Antwerp: Maklu, 2003)

K Lenaerts & P Van Nuffel (ed R Bray), *Constitutional Law of the European Union* (2nd edn, London: Sweet & Maxwell, 2005)

AF Lowenfeld & LJ Silberman (eds), *The Hague Convention on Jurisdiction and Judgments* (USA: Juris Publishing, 2001)

D McClean, *Morris: The Conflict of Laws* (5th edn, London: Sweet & Maxwell, 2000)

J Meeusen, M Pertegás Sender & G Straetmans (eds), *Enforcement of International Contracts in the European Union. Convergence and Divergence between Brussels I and Rome I* (Antwerp: Intersentia, 2004)

PAM Meijknecht & H Duintjer Tebbens, *Europees bevoegdheids- en executierecht op weg naar de 21ste eeuw* (Deventer: Kluwer, 1992)

G Moss & IF Fletcher, *The EC Regulation on Insolvency Proceedings* (Oxford: Oxford University Press, 2002)

JAR Nafziger & SC Symeonides (eds), *Law and Justice in a Multistate World. Essays in Honour of Arthur T von Mehren* (Ardsley: Transnational Publishers Inc, 2002)

P North & JJ Fawcett, *Cheshire and North's Private International Law* (13th edn, London: Butterworths, 1999)

A Nuyts, *L'exception de* forum non conveniens. *Etude de droit international privé comparé* (Brussels: Bruylant & Paris: LGDJ, 2003)

A Nuyts & N Watté (eds), *International Civil Litigation in Europe and Relations with Third States* (Brussels: Bruylant, 2005)

P Nygh, *Autonomy in international contracts* (Oxford: Clarendon Press, 1999)

J O'Brien, *Smith's Conflict of Laws* (2nd edn, London: Cavendish Publishing, 1999)

P-E Partsch, *Le droit international privé européen: De Rome à Nice* (Brussels: Larcier, 2003)

M Pertegás Sender, *Cross-border Enforcement of Patent Rights* (Oxford: Oxford University Press, 2002)

F Rigaux & M Fallon, *Droit internatonal privé* (2nd edn, Brussels: Larcier, 1987 & 1993)

—— *Droit internatonal privé* (3rd edn, Brussels: Larcier, 2005)

M Storme (ed), *Approximation of judiciary law in the European Union* (Dordrecht: Kluwer Rechtswetenschappen, 1994)

T Taylor & N Cooper, *European Litigation Handbook* (London: Sweet & Maxwell, 1995)

PLC Torremans, *Cross Border Insolvencies in EU, English and Belgian Law* (The Hague: Kluwer Law International, 2002)

M Traest, *De verhouding van de Europese Gemeenschap tot de Conferentie van Den Haag voor het internationaal privaatrecht* (Antwerp: Maklu, 2003)

J Vanhamme, *Volkenrechtelijke beginselen in het Europees recht* (Groningen: Europa Law Publishing, 2001)

H Van Houtte & M Pertegás Sender (eds), *Europese IPR-Verdragen*, (Leuven: Acco, 1997)

—— *Het nieuwe Europese IPR: van verdrag naar verordening* (Antwerp: Intersentia Rechtswetenschappen, 2001)

H Van Houtte (ed), *Themis vormingsonderdeel 10: Internationaal handelsrecht en arbitrage* (Bruges: die Keure, 2001)

H Van Houtte, *The Law of International Trade* (2nd edn, London: Sweet & Maxwell, 2002)

H Van Houtte (ed), *Internationaal Privaatrecht, Themis vormingsonderdeel 28* (Bruges: die Keure, 2005)

CJJC van Nispen, AIM van Mierlo & MV Polak, *Burgerlijke rechtsvordering. Tekst & Commentaar* (Deventer: Kluwer, 2002)

JP Vanheul & MWC Feteris, *Rechtsmacht in het Nederlandse internationaal privaatrecht deel 2* (TMC Asser Instituut, Apeldoorn: Maklu, 1986)

A Verbeke & M-T Caupain (eds), *Transparence Patrimoniale. Condition nécessaire et insuffisante du titre conservatoir européen?* (Paris: Les Éditions Juridiques et Techniques, 2001)

R Verstraeten, *Handboek Strafvordering* (Antwerp: Maklu, 1999)

B von Hoffmann (ed), *European Private International Law* (Nijmegen: Ars Aequi Libri, 1998)

G Walter & SP Baumgartner (eds), *Recognition and Enforcement of Foreign Judgments Outside the Scope of the Brussels and Lugano Conventions* (The Hague: Kluwer Law International, 2000)

P Wautelet, *Les conflits de procédures. Etude de droit international privé comparé* (unpublished doctoral thesis, Katholieke Universiteit Leuven, 2002)

ARTICLES AND CASE NOTES

D Alexandres, *Encycl. Dalloz, Droit communautaire*, 'Convention de Bruxelles (Compétence)' no 239

A Albors-Llorens, 'Changes in the jurisdiction of the European Court of Justice under the Treaty of Amsterdam' [1998] CML Rev 1273–1294

R Amoussou-Guénou, 'Perspectives des principes ASEAN (ou Asiatiques) du droit des contrats' [2005] *Revue de droit des affaires* 573–591

B Ancel, case note on *Reichert II* [1992] *Revue critique de droit international privé* 720–726

B Ancel & H Muir Watt, 'La désunion européeenne: le Règlement dit "Bruxelles II"' [2001] *Revue critique de droit international privé* 403–457

Ph Antonmattei, case note on *Rutten* [1997] *La Semaine juridique*—ed enterprise II, no. 659

S Armstrong, 'L'articulation du règlement "Bruxelles II *bis*" et des Conventions de La Haye de 1980 et 1996' (2005) 139 *Droit & Patrimoine* 46–51

B Audit, case note on Cour d'appel of Paris, 18 February 1994 [1994] Recueil Dalloz 351

Y Baatz, 'Who Decides on Jurisdiction Clauses?' [2004] LMCLQ 25–29

T Bachner, 'The Battle over Jurisdiction in European Insolvency Law' [2006] *European Company and Financial Law Review* 310–329

J Basedow, 'The Communitarization of the Conflict of Laws under the Treaty of Amsterdam' [2000] CML Rev 687–708

P Beaumont, 'European Court of Justice and jurisdiction and enforcement of judgments in civil and commercial matters' [1999] ICLQ 223–229

—— 'Interplay of private international law and the European Community' in C Kilpatrick, T Novitz & P Skidmore (eds), *The future of remedies in Europe* (Oxford: Hart Publishing, 2000) 137–190

P Beaumont & G Moir, 'Brussels Convention II: A New Private International Law Instrument in Family Matters for the European Union or the European Community?' [1995] ELR 268–288

AJ Berends, 'The *Eurofood* Case: One Company, Two Main Insolvency Proceedings: Which One is the Real One?' [2006] *Netherlands International Law Review* 331–361

GA Berman, 'Provisional Relief in Transnational Litigation' [1997] *Columbia Journal of Transnational Law* 553–617

F Bernard-Fertier, case note on *Coreck* [2001] *Revue critique de droit international privé* 367–375

C Bernasconi & A Gerber, 'La théorie du *forum non conveniens*—un regard suisse' [1994] *Praxis des internationalen Privat- und Verfahrensrechts* 3–10

J-M Bischoff, case note on *Coreck* [2001] *Journal de droit international* 701–704

Blume, 'Place of trial of civil cases' [1949] *Michigan Law Review*

K Boele-Woelki, 'Kodifikation des niederländischen Internationalen Privat- und Verfahrensrechts' in [1995] *Praxis des internationalen Privat- und Verfahrensrechts* 264–271

K Boele-Woelki & RH van Ooik, 'Exclusieve externe bevoegdhededn van de EG inzake het Internationaal Privaatrecht' [2006] *Nederlands Tijdschrift voor Europees Recht* 194–201.

J Bomhoff, 'Het negatief declaratoir in de EEX-Verordening' [2004] *Nederlands Internationaal Privaatrecht* 1–8

G Bonet, case note on *Duijnstee* [1984] *Revue critique de droit international privé* 366–372

PJ Borchers, 'Comparing Personal Jurisdiction in the US and the EC: Lessons for American Reform' [1992] AJCL 121–157

—— 'Tort and Contract Jurisdiction via the Internet: The "Minimum Contacts Test" and the Brussels Regulation Compared' [2003] *Netherlands International Law Review* 401–418.

GB Born, 'Reflections on judicial jurisdiction in international cases' [1987] *Georgia Journal of International and Comparative Law* 1–43

A Borrás, 'Les clauses de déconnexion et le droit international privé communautaire' in H-P Mansel, T Pfeiffer, H Kronke, C Kohler & R Hausmann (eds), *Festschrift für Erik Jayme* (Munich: Sellier. Europa Law Publishers, 2004) vol I, 57–72

T Bosly, 'La faillite internationale. Une ére nouvelle s'est-elle ouverte avec le règlement du Conseil du 29 mai 2000?' [2001] *Journal des tribunaux* 689–696

H Boularbah, 'Les measures provisoires en droit commercial international: développements récents au regard des Conventions de Bruxelles et de Lugano' [1999] *Revue de droit commercial belge* 604–610

JHJ Bourgeois, 'External relations powers of the European Community' [1998–1999] *Fordham International Law Journal* S149-S173

RA Brand, 'Introductory Note to the 2005 Hague Convention on Choice of Court Agreements' (2005) 44 ILM 1291.

A Briggs, case note on *Six Constructions* [1989] *Yearbook of European Law* 323–328

—— 'Spiliada and the Brussels Convention' [1991] LMCLQ 10–15

—— 'Forum non conveniens and the Brussels Convention Again [1991] LQR 180–182

—— case note on *Mulox* [1993] *Yearbook of European Law* 520–525

—— case note on *Hutton* [1993] *Yearbook of European Law* 511–517

—— 'Anti-European teeth for choice of court clauses' [1994] LMCLQ 158–163

—— 'Forum non conveniens and ideal Europeans' [2005] LMCLQ 378–382

—— 'The Death of Harrods: *forum non conveniens* and the European Court' [2005] LQR 535–540

—— 'Jurisdiction over defences and connected claims' [2006] LMCLQ 447–452

L Brilmayer, 'Related contacts and personal jurisdiction' [1988] *Harvard Law Review* 1444

L Brilmayer, J Haverkamp, B Logan, L Lynch, S Neuwirth & J O'Brien, 'A general look at general jurisdiction' [1988] *Texas Law Review* 721–783

K Broeckx, 'Wat voor nieuws brengt de EEX-verordening?' [2003] *Nieuw Juridisch Weekblad* 186–196

C Bruneau, 'Les règles européennes de compétence en matière civile et commerciale [2001] *La Semaine juridique* 533–541

—— 'La reconnaissance et l'exécution des décisions rendues dans l'union européenne' [2001] *La Semaine juridique* 801–808

A Bucher, 'Vers une convention mondiale sur la compétence et les jugements étrangers' [2000] *La Semaine juridique* 77–133

A Capik, 'Zuständigkeit der Gemeinschaft für den Abschluss des neuen Übereinkommens von Lugano' [2006] *European Law Reporter* 225–229

E Caracciolo di Torella & A Masselot, 'Under Construction: EU Family Law,' [2004] ELR 32–51

J-Y Carlier, 'La libre circulation des personnes dans l'Union europeenne,' [2004] *Journal des tribunaux* 74–80

J-Y Carlier, S Francq & J-L Van Boxstael, 'Le règlement de Bruxelles II. Compétence, reconnaissance et exécution en matière matrimoniale et en matière de responsabilité parentale' [2001] *Journal des tribunaux* 73–90

ME Carranza, 'Mercosur, the Free Trade Area of the Americas, and the future of US hegemony in America' [2003–2004] *Fordham International Law Journal* 1029–1065

C Chalas, case note on *Owusu* [2005] *Revue critique de droit international privé* 708–722

C Chatterjee, 'The legal effect of the exclusive jurisdiction clause in the Brussels Convention in relation to banking matters' (1995) 10(8) *Journal of International Banking Law* 334–340

M Claeys, 'Het international kortgeding en artikel 24 EEX,' case note to Hof van Beroep, Gent, 8 December 1994 [1995–96] *Algemeen Juridisch Tijdschrift* 151–154

L Collins, '*Forum non conveniens* and the Brussels Convention' [1990] LQR 535–539

E Cornut, '*Forum shopping* et abus du choix de for en droit international privé' [2007] *Journal de droit international* 27–55

I Couwenberg, case note on *Owens Bank* [1993–94] *Rechtskundig Weekblad* 1403

G Cuniberti, '*Forum non conveniens* and the Brussels Convention' [2006] ICLQ 973–981

A Dashwood, 'External relations provisions of the Amsterdam Treaty' [1998] CML Rev 1019–1045

ThM de Boer, 'Jurisdiction and Enforcement in International Family Law: A Labyrinth of European and International Legislation' [2002] *Netherlands International Law Review* 307–345

G-R de Groot & S Rutten, 'Op weg naar een Europees IPR op het gebied van het personen- en familierecht' [2004] *Nederlands Internationaal Privaatrecht* 273–282

P de Vareilles-Sommières, 'La compétence internationale des tribunaux français en matière de mesures provisoires' [1996] *Revue critique de droit international privé* 397–437

LI De Winter, 'Excessive Jurisdiction in Private International Law' [1968] ICLQ 706–720

RE Degnan & MK Kane, 'The Exercise of Jurisdiction over and Enforcement of Judgments against Alien Defendants' [1987–1988] *The Hastings Law Journal* 799–855

F Dehousse & C Maczkovics, 'Les arrêts *open skies* de la Cour de justice: l'abandon de la competence externe implicite de la Communauté?' [2003] *Journal des tribunaux* 225–236

L Demeyere, 'Voorlopige en bewarende maatregelen [Art 24 EEX] na het arrest *Van Uden* en het arrest *Mietz*' [1999–2000] *Rechtskundig Weekblad* 1353–1363

A Dickinson, 'European private international law: embracing new horizons or mourning the past?' [2005] *Journal of Private International Law* 197–236

E Dirix & V Sagaert, 'Verhaalsrechten en zekerheidsposities van schuldeisers onder de Europese Insolventieverordening' [2001] *Revue de droit commercial belge* 580–600

Documents, Conférence de la Haye de Droit international privé, les 2 avant-projets [1996] *Netherlands International Law Review* 327–336

M Dogauchi, 'The Hague Draft Convention from the Perspective of Japan' Seminar on the Draft Convention on Jurisdiction and Foreign Judgments in Civil and Commercial Matters, UIA (Union International des Avocats), Edinburgh, 20–21 April 2001

S Drouet, 'La communautarisation de "Bruxelles II". Chronique d'une mutation juridique' [2001] *Revue du Marché commun et de l'Union européenne* 247–257

GAL Droz, 'La récent projet de Convention de La Haye sur la reconnaissance et l'exécution des jugements étrangers en matière civile et commerciale' [1966] *Netherlands International Law Review* 225–242

GAL Droz, case note on *Cavel I* and *Cavel II* [1980] *Revue critique de droit international privé* 621–629

—— case note on *CHW* [1984] *Revue critique de droit international privé* 354–361

—— case note on *Rösler* [1986] *Revue critique de droit international privé* 135–142

—— 'Entrée en vigueur de la Convention de Bruxelles révisée sur la compétence judiciaire et l'exécution des jugements' [1987] *Revue critique de droit international privé* 251–303

—— 'La convention de Lugano parallèle à la convention de Bruxelles concernant la compétence judiciaire et l'exécution des décisions en matière civile et commerciale' [1989] *Revue critique de droit international privé* 1–51

—— 'La Convention de San Sebastian alignant la Convention de Bruxelles sur la Convention de Lugano' [1990] *Revue critique de droit international privé* 1–21

—— 'Le récent projet de Convention de La Haye sur la reconnaissance et l'exécution des jugements étrangers en matière civile et commerciale' [1996] *Netherlands International Law Review* 225–242

GAL Droz & H Gaudemet-Tallon, 'La transformation de la convention de Bruxelles du 27 septembre 1968 en Règlement du Conseil concernant la compétence judiciaire, la reconnaissance et l'exécution des décisions en matière civile et commerciale' [2001] *Revue critique de droit international privé* 601–652

H Duintjer Tebbens, 'From Jamaica with pain' in P van der Grinten & T Heukels (eds), *Cross Borders. Essays in European and Private International Law, Nationality Law and Islamic Law in honour of Frans van der Velden* (Deventer: Kluwer, 2006) 95–103

AA Ehrenzweig, 'The Transient Rule of Personal Jurisdiction. The 'Power Myth' and *forum non conveniens*' [1955–1956] *The Yale Law Journal* 289–314

J Erauw, 'De verdragen van Brussel en Lugano uitmekaar houden' [1996] *Revue de droit commercial belge* 772–782

M Fallon, case note on *Mulox* [1993] *Journal des tribunaux*. Droit européen 37

M Fallon & S Francq, 'La coopération judiciaire civile et le droit international privé. Vers un droit proprement communautaire des conflits de lois ou de juridiction' in O de Schutter & P Nihoul, *Une constitution pour l'Europe. Réflexions sur les transformations du droit de l'Union européenne* (Brussels: Larcier, 2004)

JJ Fawcett, 'A new Approach to Jurisdiction over Companies in Private International law' [1988] ICLQ 645–667

—— 'Multi-party litigation in private international law' [1995] ICLQ 744–770

—— 'Non-exclusive jurisdiction agreements in private international law' [2001] LMCLQ 234–260

R Fentiman, 'Jurisdiction, discretion and the Brussels Convention' [1993] *Cornell International Law Journal* 59–99

—— case note on *Owens Bank* [1994] CLJ 239–241

—— 'Access to Justice and Parallel Proceedings in Europe' [2004] CLJ 312–314

—— case note on *Gasser* [2005] CML Rev 241–259

—— 'Civil jurisdiction and third States: *Owusu* and after' [2006] CML Rev 705–734

H Gaudemet-Tallon, case note on *Elefanten Schuh* [1982] *Revue critique de droit international privé* 152–161

—— case note on *Spitzley* [1985] *Revue critique de droit international privé* 687–688

—— 'Le *forum non conveniens*, une menace pour la convention de Bruxelles? [A propos de trois arrêts anglais récents]' [1991] *Revue critique de droit international privé* 491–524

—— case note on *Overseas Union* [1991] *Revue critique de droit international privé* 769–777

—— case note on Cour d'appel of Versailles, 26 September 1991 [1992] *Revue critique de droit international privé* 336–340

—— case note on *Hutton* [1993] *Revue critique de droit international privé* 325–332

—— case note on Paris 17 November 1993 [1994] *Revue critique de droit international privé* 117–120

—— 'Les régimes relatifs au refus d'exercer la compétence juridictionelle en matière civile et commerciale: *forum non conveniens, lis pendens*' [1994] *Revue critique de droit international privé* 423–435

—— case note on *Owens Bank* [1994] *Revue critique de droit international privé* 382–387

—— case note on *Rutten* [1997] *Revue critique de droit international privé* 341–346

—— case note on *Réunion européenne* [1999] *Revue critique de droit international privé* 333–340

—— case note on *Van Uden* [1999] *Revue de l'arbitrage* 152–166

—— 'Le Règlement no. 1347/2000 du Conseil du 29 mai 2000: "Compétence, reconnaissance et exécution des decisions en matière matrimoniale et en matière de responsabilité parentale des enfants communs"' [2001] *Journal de droit international* 381–430

R Geimer, case note on Bundesgerichtshof, 20 January 1986 [1986] *Neue Juristische Wochenschrift* 1439–1440

R Geimer, 'Ungeschriebene Anwendungsgrenzen des EuGVÜ: Müssen Berührungspunkte zu mehreren Vertragsstaaten bestehen?' [1991] *Praxis des internationalen Privat- und Verfahrensrechts* 31–35.

F Gerhard, 'La compétence du juge d'appui pour prononcer des mesures provisoires extraterritoriales. A propos du prononcé d'une worldwide Mareva injunction anglaise à l'appui d'une procédure au fond suisse et de la jurisprudence *van Uden* de la Cour de Justice des Communautés européennes' [1999] *Schweizerische Zeitschrift für internationals und europäisches Recht* 97–141

D Gwynn Morgan, 'Discretion to stay jurisdiction' [1982] ICLQ 582–587

P Hameau & M Raimon, 'Les Faillites internationales. Approche européenne' [2003] *International Business Law Journal* 645–665

JM Harris, 'Stays of proceedings and the Brussels Convention' [2005] ICLQ 933–950

TC Hartley, case note on *Cavel I* [1979] ELR 222–224

—— case note on *Denilauler* [1981] ELR 59–61

—— case note on *Elefanten Schuh* [1982] ELR 237–239

—— case note on *Duijnstee* [1984] ELR 64–66

—— case note on *Rösler* [1985] ELR 361–363

—— case note on *Spitzley* [1986] ELR 98

—— 'Comity and the Use of Anti-suit Injunctions in International Litigation' [1987] AJCL 487–511

—— case note on *Six Constructions* [1989] ELR 236–238

—— 'The Brussels Convention and *forum non conveniens*' [1992] ELR 553–555

—— case note on *Hutton* [1994] ELR 537–538

—— case note on *Mulox* [1994] ELR 540–545

—— case note on *Owens Bank* [1994] ELR 545–547

—— 'Brussels Jurisdiction and Judgments Convention: Jurisdiction agreement and *lis alibi pendens*' [1994] ELR 549–552

—— 'Anti-suit injunctions and the Brussels Jurisdiction and Judgments Convention' [2000] ICLQ 166–171

—— 'International Law and the Law of the European Union—A Reassessment,' [2001] *British Yearbook of International Law* 1–35

—— 'The EU and the systematic dismantling of the common law conflict of laws' [2005] ICLQ 813–828

P Hay, 'The Common Market Preliminary Draft on the Recognition and Enforcement of Judgments—Some Considerations of Policy and Interpretation' [1968] AJCL 149–174

R Hausmann, case note on *Cavel II* [1981] *Praxis des internationalen Privat- und Verfahrensrechts* 5–7

—— case note on *Denilauler* [1981] *Praxis des internationalen Privat- und Verfahrensrechts* 79–82

J Hill, 'Jurisdiction in Matters relating to a Contract under the Brussels Convention' [1995] ICLQ 591–619

G Hogan, 'The Brussels Convention, *forum non conveniens* and the Connecting Factors Problem' [1995] ELR 471–493

A Homburger, 'Recognition and enforcement of foreign judgments. A New Yorker reflects on uniform acts' [1970] AJCL 367–405

P Huber, '*Forum non conveniens* und EuGVÜ' [1993] *Recht der Internationalen Wirtschaft* 977–983

—— '*Forum non conveniens*—The Other Way Round' [1996] *Praxis des internationalen Privat- und Verfahrensrechts* 48–52

A Huet, case note on Cour de cassation, 19 December [1979] *Revue critique de droit international privé* 617–624

—— case note on *Cavel I* [1979] *Journal de droit international* 681–691

—— case note on *Cavel II* [1980] *Journal de droit international* 442–448

—— case note on *Denilauler* [1980] *Journal de droit international* 939–948

—— case note on *CHW* [1982] *Journal de droit international* 942–948

—— case note on Cour d'appel of Paris, 27 March 1987 [1988] *Journal de droit international* 140–143

—— case note on *Gubisch* [1988] *Journal de droit international* 537–544

—— case note on Paris, 17 November 1987 [1989] *Journal de droit international* 96

—— case note on *Six Constructions* [1989] *Journal de droit international* 461–465

—— case note on Cour d'appel of Paris, 30 November 1990 [1992] *Journal de droit international* 192–195

—— case note on Cour d'appel of Versailles, 26 September 1991 [1993] *Journal de droit international* 51–53

—— case note on Cour de cassation civ 1re ch, 14 May 1992 [1993] *Journal de droit international* 151–152

—— case note on *Reichert II* [1993] *Journal de droit international* 461–465
—— case note on *Mulox* [1994] *Journal de droit international* 539–546
—— case note on *Owens Bank* [1994] *Journal de droit international* 546–550
—— case note on Paris 17 November 1993 [1994] *Journal de droit international* 676–678
—— case note on *Van Uden* [1999] *Journal de droit international* 613–625
—— 'Chronique de jurisprudence du Tribunal et de la Cour de justice des Communautés européennes' [2004] *Journal de droit international* 641–645
Institute of International Law, Resolution recognizing that the doctrine of *forum non conveniens* can sometimes be in the interests of justice, [2004] Institute of International Law Yearbook, Part II, 81–112
M Jänterä-Jareborg, 'Marriage dissolution in an integrated Europe: The 1998 European Union Convention on Jurisdiction and the Recognition and Enforcement of Judgments in Matrimonial Matters [Brussels II Convention]' [1999] *Yearbook for Private International Law* 1–36
E Jayme, 'Zum Jahrtausendwechsel: Das Kollisionsrecht zwischen Postmoderne und Futurismus' [2000] *Praxis des internationalen Privat- und Verfahrensrechts* 165–171
FK Juenger, 'Jurisdiction as an evolutionary process: the development of quasi *in rem* and *in personam* principles' [1978] *Duke Law Journal* 1157–1161
—— 'Supreme Court Intervention in Jurisdiction and Choice of Law: A Dismal Prospect' [1980–1981] *UC Davis Law Review* 907–917
—— 'La Convention de Bruxelles du 27 septembre 1968 et la courtoisie internationale, Réflexions d'un américain' [1983] *Revue critique de droit international privé* 37–51
—— 'Judicial Jurisdiction in the United States and in the European Communities: a comparison' [1984] *Michigan Law Review* 1195–1212
—— 'A Shoe Unfit for Globetrotting' [1995] *UC Davis Law Review* 1027–1045
PJG Kapteyn, 'Het advise 1/76 van het Europese Hof van Justitie, de externe bevoegdheid van de Gemeenschap en haar deelneming aan een Europees oplegfonds voor de binnenscheepvaart' [1978] *Sociaal-economische wetgewing: tijdschrift voor Europees en economisch recht* 276–288
G Kaufmann-Kohler, 'Internet: mondialisation de la communication—mondialisation de la résolution des litiges?' in K Boele-Woulki & C Kessedjian (eds), *Internet. Which Court Decides? Which Law Applies?* (The Hague: Kluwer, 1998)
P Kaye 'The Meaning of domicile under United Kingdom Law for the Purposes of the 1968 Brussels Convention on Jurisdiction and the enforcement of Judgments in Civil and Commercial Matters' [1988] *Netherlands International Law Review* 181–195.
—— case note on *Owens Bank* [1995] *Praxis des internationalen Privat- und Verfahrensrechts* 214–217
—— 'The EEC Judgments Convention and the Outer World: Goodbye to *forum non conveniens*?' [1992] *Journal of Business Law* 47–76
Z Kembayev, 'Integration processes in South America and in the Post-Soviet area: a comparative analysis,' [2005] *Southwestern Journal of Law and Trade in the Americas* 25–44
W Kennett, 'Place of Performance and Predictability' [1995] *Yearbook of European Law* 193–218

W Kennett (ed), 'Current developments: Private International Law. The Brussels I Regulation' [2001] ICLQ 725–737

KD Kerameus, 'A civilian lawyer looks at common law procedure' [1986–1987] *Louisiana Law Review* 493–509

C Kessedjian, 'La Convention de La Haye du 30 juin 2005 sur l'élection de for' [2006] *Journal de droit international* 813–850

A Kohl, case note on *Mulox* [1994] *Jurisprudence de Liège, Mons et Bruxelles* 463–465

—— case note on *Hutton* [1994] *Jurisprudence de Liège, Mons et Bruxelles* 457–459

ME Koppenhol-Laforce & I van Rooij, 'Nieuw Europees bevoegdheids- en tenuitvoerleggingsrecht' [2002] *Advocatenblad* 410–427

SCJJ Kortmann & PM Veder, 'De Europese Insolventieverordening' [2000] *Weekblad voor Privaatrecht, Notariaat en Registratie* 764–774

XE Kramer, case note on *Van Uden* [1999] *Nederlands Tijdschrift voor Burgerlijk Recht* 74–79

—— case note on *Italian Leather* [2003] CML Rev 953–964

—— 'De harmoniserende werking van het Europees procesrecht: de disqualificatioe van de anti-suit injunction' [2005] *Nederlands Internationaal Privaatrecht*, 130–137.

K Kreuzer, case note on *Rösler* [1986] *Praxis des internationalen Privat- und Verfahrensrechts* 75–80

T Kruger, case note on *Ingmar* [2002] *Columbia Journal of European Law* 85–91

—— 'Reactie: Antwoord op de annotatie "IPR-aspecten met betrekking tot de betaling van de koopprijs—art 5, 1° b] EEX-Verordening"' [2002–2003] *Rechtskundig Weekblad* 1636–1637

—— case note on Rechtbank van koophandel of Tongeren, 20 February 2003, [2004] *Revue de droit commercial belge* 71–74

—— 'The Anti-suit injunction in the European Judicial Space: *Turner v Grovit*' [2004] ICLQ 1030–1040

—— 'Letter from The Hague: Global choice of forum clauses?' [2004] *South African Law Journal* 752–757

—— case note on *Warbecq* [2004–2005] *Columbia Journal of European Law* 203–206

—— 'The 20th Session of the Hague Conference: a New Choice of Court Convention and the Issue of EC Membership' [2006] ICLQ 447–455

—— 'Opinion 1/03, competence of the Community to conclude the new Lugano Convention on the Jurisdiction and the Recognition and Enforcement of Judgments in Civil and Commercial Matters' [2006] *Columbia Journal of European Law* 189–199

P Lagarde, case note on *Mulox* [1994] *Revue critique de droit international privé* 574–577

—— case note on *Garcia Avello* [2004] *Revue critique de droit international privé* 192–202

BM Landay, 'Another look at the EEC Judgments Convention: should outsiders be worried?' [1987–1988] *Dickenson Journal of International Law* 25–44

N Lavranos, Case note on Opinion 1/03 [2006] CML Rev 1087–1100

F Leclerc, case note on *Josi* [2002] *Journal de droit international* 623–628

K Lenaerts, 'The principle of subsidiarity and the environment in the European Union: keeping the balance of federalism' [1993–1994] *Fordham International Law Journal* 846–895

—— 'De Europese Unie: doel of middel' [1998–1999] *Rechtskundig Weekblad* 689–710

N Levy Jr, 'Mesne process in personal actions at common law and the power doctrine' [1968–1969] *The Yale Law Journal* 52–98

HS Lewis Jr, 'A brave new world for personal jurisdiction: flexible tests under uniform standards' [1984] *Vanderbilt Law Review* 1–66

R Libschaber, case note on *Brenner & Noller* [1995] *Revue critique de droit international privé* 758–769

M Looyens, case note on *Owens Bank* [1994] *Tijdschrift voor het Notariaat* 343–347

V Lowe, 'Overlapping Jurisdiction in International Tribunals' [1999] *Australian Yearbook of International Law* 191–204

AF Lowenfeld, 'Thoughts about a Multinational Judgments Convention: A Reaction to the Von Mehren Report' [1994] *Law and Contemporary Problems* 289–303

—— 'Forum Shopping, Anti-Suit Injunctions, Negative Declarations, and Related Tools of International Litigation,' [1997] AJIL 314–324;

G Maher & BJ Rodger, 'Provisional and Protective Remedies: The British experience of the Brussels Convention' [1999] ICLQ 302–339

J Mance, 'Exclusive Jurisdiction Agreements and European Ideals' [2004] LQR 357–365

FA Mann, case note on *Rösler* [1985] LQR 329–330

V Marquette & C Barbé, 'Les procédures d'insolvabilité extracommunautaire' [2006] *Journal de droit international* 511–562

P McEleavy, 'The Brussels II Regulation: How the European Community has moved into Family Law' [2002] ICLQ 883–908

—— 'The Communitarization of Divorce Rules: What Impact for English and Scottish Law?' [2004] ICLQ 605–642

—— 'The New Child Abduction regime in the European Union: Symbiotic Relationship or Forced Partnership?' [2005] *Journal of Private International Law* 5–34

C McLachlan, 'Transnational applications of Mareva injunctions and Anton Piller orders' [1987] ICLQ 669–679

M McKee, 'Case Comment. Jurisdiction Clauses' (1994) 9(4) *Journal of International Banking Law* N85-N86

J Meeusen, 'Nieuw internationaal procesrecht op komst in Europa: het EEX II-verdrag' [1998–1999] *Rechtskundig Weekblad* 755–758

—— 'De werkelijke zetel-leer en de communautaire vestigingsvrijheid van vennootschappen' [2003] *Tijdschrift voor rechtspersoon en vennootschap* 95–127

P Mercier, 'Le projet de convention du marché commun sur la procedure civile internationale et les etats tiers' [1967] *Cahier de droit européen* 367–387 & 513–531

G Middeldrop & RH van Ooik, 'Van verdeelde *Open Skies* naar een uniform Europees extern luchtvaartbeleid' [2003] *Nederlands Tijdschrift voor Europees Recht* 1–10

A Mignolli, 'The EU's Powers of External Relations' [2002] *The International Spectator* 101–114

M Mildred, 'The use of the Brussels Convention in group actions' [1996] *Journal of Personal Injury Litigation* 121–134

PMM Mostermans, 'Nieuw Europees scheidingsprocesrecht onder de loep. De rechtsmacht bij echtscheiding' [2001] *Nederlands Internationaal Privaatrecht* 293–305

A Mourre, 'Thirty years later: current problems and perspectives with the application of the Brussels and Lugano Conventions provisions concerning jurisdiction in contractual matters' [1999] *International Business Law Journal* 385–409

H Muir Watt, case note on *Gasser* [2004] *Revue critique de droit international privé* 459–464

—— case note on *Konkola* [2005] *Revue critique de droit international privé* 725–731

KH Nadelmann, 'Jurisdictionally improper fora in treaties on recognition and enforcement of judgments. The Common Market draft' [1967] *Columbia Law Review* 995–1023

KH Nadelmann & WLM Reese, 'The Tenth Session of the Hague Conference on Private International Law' [1964] AJCL 612–615

KH Nadelmann & AT von Mehren, 'Equivalences in treaties in the conflicts field' [1966–1967] AJCL 195–203

KH Nadelmann & AT von Mehren, 'The extraordinary session of the Hague Conference on Private International Law' [1966] AJIL 803–806

B Nascimbene, 'Community courts in the area of judicial cooperation' [2005] ICLQ 489–497

JJ Newton, '*Forum non conveniens* in Europa [again]' [1997] LMCLQ 337–344

M-L Niboyet, 'La globalisation du procès civil international dans l'éspace judiciaire européen et mondial' [2006] *Journal de droit international* 937–954

A Nuyts, 'La communautarisation de la convention de Bruxelles. Le règlement 44/2001 sur la compétence judiciaire et l'effet des décisions en matière civile et commerciale' [2001] *Journal des tribunaux* 913–922

—— 'La théorie de l'effet réflexe,' in M Storme & G de Leval, *Le droit processuel & judiciaire européen* (Bruges: die Keure, 2003) 73–89

—— '*Forum shopping* et abus du *forum shopping* dans l'espace judiciaire européen,' in *Mélanges John Kirkpatrick* (Brussels: Bruylant, 2004) 745–790

—— case note on *Turner* [2005] *Journal des tribunaux* 32–35

P Nygh, 'Provisional and Protective Measures in International Litigation. The Helsinki Principles' [1998] *Rabels Zeitschrift für Ausländisches und Internationales Privatrecht* 115–122

E Peel, case note on *Owens Bank* [1994] LQR 386–390

—— '*Forum non conveniens* and European ideals' [2005] LMCLQ 363–377

M Pertegás Sender, case note on *Rutten* [1997] *Columbia Journal of European Law* 292–298

—— 'Handhaving van intellectuele rechten in internationaal perspectief. Welke rechter is bevoegd voor voorlopige maatregelen?' in M Storme & G de Leval, *Het Europees Gerechtelijk Recht & Procesrecht* (Bruges: die Keure, 2003)

—— 'De EEX-Verordening in de praktijk: enkele knelpunten' in Orde van Advocaten van de Balie te Kortrijk, *Internationale aspecten in de verschillende takken van het recht* (Brussels: Larcier, 2005)

—— news item on the *GAT* and *Roche* judgments [2006] EIPR N193–194

M Pertegás Sender & B Strowel, 'Grensoverschrijdende octrooigeschillen: Spannend afwachten op de arresten van het Europees Hof van Justitie' [2004] *Revue de droit commercial belge* 755–763

B Piltz, 'Die Zuständigkeitsordnung nach dem EWG-Gerichtsstands- und Vollstreckungsübereinkommen' [1979] *Neue Juristische Wochenschrift* 1071–1075

RA Porrata-Doria Jr, 'MERCOSUR: The Common Market of the Twenty-first century?' [2004] *Georgia Journal of International and Comparative Law* 1–72

P Pustorino, 'Observation sur les principes généraux opérant dans le droit international privé et procédural communautaire' [2005] *Revue du droit de l'Union européenne* 113–158

T Rauscher, case note on *Six Constructions* [1990] *Praxis des internationalen Privat- und Verfahrensrechts* 152–157

O Remien, 'European Private International Law, the European Community and its emerging area of freedom, security and justice' [2001] CML Rev 53–86

WM Richman, 'Review Essay. Part I: Casad's jurisdiction in civil actions. Part II: A sliding scale to supplement the distinction between general and specific jurisdiction' [1984] *California Law Review* 1328–1346

BJ Rodger, '*Forum non conveniens* Post-*Owusu*' [2006] *Journal of Private International Law* 71–97

P Rodière, case note on *Six Constructions* [1989] *Revue critique de droit international privé* 560–567

P Rogerson, 'Habitual residence: the new domicile?' [2000] ICLQ, 86–107

C Rommelaere, 'Het EVO in EVO-lutie' [2004] *Tijdschrift@ipr.be* Vol 2, 91–94

S Rutten, 'IPR-aspecten met betrekking tot de betaling van de koopprijs—art 5, 1° b) EEX-Verordening,' noot onder Hb Gent 31 januari 2002 [2002–2003] *Rechtskundig Weekblad* 664–669

S Rutten, 'Wederantwoord' [2002–2003] *Rechtskundig Weekblad* 1637–1639

JG Sauveplanne, case note on *CHW* [1983] *Praxis des internationalen Privat- und Verfahrensrechts* 65–67

JC Schultsz, case note on *Owens Bank* [1994] *Nederlandse jurisprudentie. Uitspraken in burgerlijke en strafzaken* n° 351, 1627–1646

A Schulz, 'Einstweilige Maßnahmen nach dem Brüsseler Gerichtsstands- und Vollstreckungsübereinkommen in der Rechtsprechung des Gerichtshofs der Europäischen Gemeinschaften [EuGH]' [2001] *Zeitschrift für Europäisches Privatrecht* 805–836

—— 'Internationale Regelungen zum Sorge- und Umgangsrecht' [2003] *Zeitschrift für das gesamte Familienrecht* 336–348

—— 'Die Zeichnung des Haager Kinderschutz-Übereinkommens von 1996 und der Kompromiss zur Brüssel-II a Verordnung' [2003] *Zeitschrift für das gesamte Familienrecht* 1351–1354

—— 'International Organizations: The Global Playing Field for US–EU Cooperation in Private law Instruments,' in RA Brand (ed), *Private Law, Private International Law, & Judicial Cooperation in the EU–US Relationship*, CILE Studies Vol 2 (St Paul: Thomson West, 2005) 237–262

—— 'The Hague Convention of 30 June 2005 on Choice of Courts Agreements including Appendix Hague Conference on PIL 20th Session' [2006] *Journal of Private International Law* 243–269

—— 'Haager Kinderschützbereinkommen von 1996: Im Westen nichts Neues' [2006] *Zeitschrift für das gesamte Familienrecht* 1309–1311

AR Schwartz, '*In Re Harrods Ltd*: The Brussels Convention and the Proper Application of *forum non conveniens* to Non-Contracting States [1991–1992] *Fordham International Law Journal* 174–206

SR Shackleton, 'Global warming: milder still in England: Part 2' [1999] *International Arbitration Law Review* 117–136

LJ Silberman, 'Comparative Jurisdiction in the International Context: will the Proposed Hague Judgments Convention be Stalled?' [2002] *DePaul Law Review* 319–349

AG Slater, '*Forum non conveniens*, a View from the Shopfloor' [1988] LQR 554–575

A Staudinger, case note on *Josi* [2000] *Praxis des internationalen Privat- und Verfahrensrechts* 483–488

D Staunder, case note on *Duijnstee* [1985] *Praxis des internationalen Privat- und Verfahrensrechts* 76–79

AR Stein, 'Styles of argument and interstate federalism in the law of personal jurisdiction' [1987] *Texas Law Review* 689–765

PA Stone, 'The Civil Jurisdiction and Judgments Acts 1982: Some comments' [1983] ICLQ 477–499

H Storme & S Bouzoumita, 'Arbeidsovereenkomsten in internationaal privaatrecht' [2005] *Nieuw Juridisch Weekblad* 290–314

AVM Struycken, 'Les consequences de l'intégration européenne sur le développe-ment du droit international privé' (1992) 232 Collected Courses of the Hague Academy of International Law (I), 257–379

—— case note on *Van Uden* [2000] *Ars Aequi* 579–586

—— 'Het Verdrag van Amsterdam en de Haagse Conferentie voor international privaatrecht. Brusselse schaduwen over Den Haag' [2000] *Weekblad voor Privaatrecht, Notariaat en Registratie* 735–745

ER Sunderland, 'The provisions relating to trial practice in the new Illinois Civil Practice Act' [1933–1934] *University of Chicago Law Review* 188–223

K Swerts, 'Internationale bevoegdheidsregels' [2003] *Nieuw Juridisch Weekblad* 47–54

H Tagaras, case note on *Six Constructions* [1990] *Cahiers de droit européen* 676–681

—— case note on *Owens Bank* [1995] *Cahiers de droit européen* 195–199

—— case note on *Mulox* [1995] *Cahiers de droit européen* 188–191

—— 'Chronique de jurisprudence de la Cour de justice relative à la Convention de Bruxelles' [2006] *Cahiers de droit européen* 483–553

K Takahashi, 'External competence implications of the EC Regulations on jurisdiction and judgments' [2003] ICLQ 529–534

O Tell, 'Tentative Draft on the Jurisdiction and the Enforcement of Foreign Judgments: Can a Mixed Convention Work?', in JJ Barcelo & KM Clermont (eds), *A Global Law of Jurisdiction and Judgments: Lessons from The Hague*, (The Hague: Kluwer 2002) 37–46

C Thiele, '*Forum non conveniens* im Lichte europäischen Gemeinschaftsrechts' [2002] *Recht der Internationalen Wirtschaft* 696–700

M Twitchell, 'The Myth of General Jurisdiction' [1988] *Harvard Law Review* 610–681

ML Ultsch, 'Die Forum-non-Conveniens-Lehre im recht der USA (inbesondere Floridas)' [1997] *Recht der Internationalen Wirtschaft* 26–31

A-M van den Bossche, 'L'espace européen de justice et le (rapprochement du) droit judiciaire' in M Storme & G de Leval (eds), *Het Europees gerechtelijk recht & proces-recht* (Bruges: die Keure, 2003) 1–23

V Van den Eeckhout, 'Communitarization of Private International Law: Tendencies to "liberalise" European Family Law' [2004] *Tijdschrift@ipr.be* Vol 3, 52–70

JJ van Haersolte-van Hof, case note on *Van Uden* [1999] *Nederlands Tijdschrift voor Europees Recht* 66–67

—— 'EEX-verordening treedt in werking per 1 maart 2002' [2001] *Nederlands Internationaal Privaatrecht* 244–248

—— case note on *Besix* [2002] *Nederlands Tijdschrift voor Europees Recht* 226–229

AAH Van Hoek, case note on *Ingmar* [2001] *Sociaal-economische wetgewing: tijdschrift voor Europees en economisch recht* 195

H Van Houtte, case note on *Hutton* [1993] *Tijdschrift voor Rechtsdocumentatie* 153–154

—— 'May Court Judgments that Disregard Arbitration Clauses and Awards be Enforced under the Brussels and Lugano Conventions?' [1997] *Arbitration International* 85–92

C Van Schoubroeck, case note on *Josi* [2001] *Revue de droit commercial belge* 146–148

K Vandekerckhove, 'Voorlopige en bewarende maatregelen in de EEX-Verordening, in EEX-II en in de Insolventieverordening,' in M Storme & G de Leval (eds), *Het Europees Gerechtelijk Recht & Procesrecht* (Bruges: die Keure, 2003) 119–151

P Vlas, case note on *Reichert II* [1993] *Netherlands International Law Review* 499–501

—— case note on *Owens Bank* [1994] *Netherlands International Law Review* 355–359

—— case note on *Van Uden* [1999] *Netherlands International Law Review* 106–109

—— 'Herziening EEX: van verdrag naar verordening' [2000] *Weekblad voor Privaatrecht, Notariaat en Registratie* 745–753

—— case note on *Coreck* [2001] *Nederlandse jurisprudentie. Uitspraken in burgerlijke en strafzaken* no. 599, 4442–4445

—— 'Stoeien met verbintenissen, worstelen met art 5 sub 1 EEX-Verordening' [2002] *Weekblad voor Privaatrecht, Notariaat en Registratie* 301–302

—— case note on *Josi* [2003] *Nederlandse jurisprudentie. Uitspraken in burgerlijke en strafzaken* no. 597, 4584–4586

—— case note on *Besix* [2004] *Nederlandse jurisprudentie. Uitspraken in burgerlijke en strafzaken* 1283–1297

JP Verheul, 'The *forum (non) conveniens* in English and Dutch law and under some international conventions' [1986] ICLQ 413–423

—— 'Waait de *antisuit injunction* naar het continent over?' [1989] *Nederlands Internationaal Privaatrecht* 221–224

J Verlinden, case note on *Besix* [2002] *Columbia Journal of European Law* 493–497

P Volken, case note on Handelsgericht (Commercial Court) Zurich, judgment of 9 January 1996 [1997] *Schweizerische Zeitschrift für internationals und europäisches Recht* 384–386

AT von Mehren, 'Recognition and enforcement of sister-state judgments: reflection on general theory and current practice in the European Economic Community and the United States' [1981] *Columbia Law Review* 1044–1060

—— 'Adjudicatory Jurisdiction: General theories compared and evaluated' [1983] *Boston University Law Review* 279–340

—— 'Recognition and Enforcement of Foreign Judgments: a new approach for the Hague Conference?' [1994] *Law and Contemporary Problems* 271–287

—— 'Theory and Practice of Adjudicatory Authority in Private International Law: a comparative study of the doctrine, policies and practices of common- and civil-law systems. General course on Private International Law' (2002) 295 *Collected Courses of the Hague Academy of International Law*

AT von Mehren & DTT Trautman, 'Jurisdiction to Adjudicate: A Suggested Analysis' [1966] *Harvard Law Review* 1121–1179

W von Meibom & J Pitz, 'The reach and limitations of European transborder jurisdiction' [1999] *Journal of World Intellectual Property* 593–605

N Watté, case note on *Mulox* [1993] *Revue de droit commercial belge* 1117

N Watté & H Boularbah, 'Les nouvelles règles de conflit de jurisdictions en matière de désunion des époux. Le règlement dit 'Bruxelles II'' [2001] *Journal des tribunaux* 369–378

N Watté & V Marquette, 'Le règlement communautaire, du 29 mai 2000, relatif aux procédures d'insolvabilité' [2001] *Revue de droit commercial belge* 565–579

P Wautelet, case note on *Gasser* [2004] *Revue de droit commercial belge* 794–799

DJ Werner, 'Dropping the other shoe: *Shaffer v Heitner* and the demise of presence-oriented jurisdiction' [1978–1979] *Brooklyn Law Review* 565–606

RA Wessel, 'The inside looking out: consistency and delimitation in EU external relations' [2000] *CML Rev* 1135–1171

M Wilderspin & A-M Rouchaud Joët, 'La compétence externe de la Communauté européenne en droit international privé' [2004] *Revue critique de droit international privé* 3–48

J Wilson, 'Anti-suit injunctions' [1997] *Journal of Business Law* 424–437

A Wittwer, 'Auch bei italienischer Prozessdauer gilt Art. 21 EuGVÜ,' [2004] *European Law Reporter*, 48–50

—— 'Zuständigkeit, Anerkennung und ordre public im internationalen Insolvenzrecht—ein wegweisendes Urteil' [2006] *European Law Reporter* 221–224

C Wolf & S Lange, 'Das Europäisches System des einstweiligen Rechtsschutzes— doch noch kein System?' [2003] *Recht der Internationalen Wirtschaft* 55–63

HE Yntema, 'The Comity Doctrine' [1966–1967] *Michigan Law Review* 1–32

T Zamudio, 'MERCOSUR: General Ideas' [2004] *International Journal of Legal Information* 627–638

OFFICIAL REPORTS AND PRACTICE GUIDES OF EUROPEAN COMMUNITY INSTRUMENTS

(In Date Order)

Jenard report on the 1968 version of the Brussels Convention; OJ C 59, 5 March 1979, 1

Schlosser Report on the 1978 version of the Brussels Convention; OJ C 59, 5 March 1979, 71

De Almeida Cruz, Desantes Real & Jenard Report on the San Sebastian (1989) version of the Brussels Convention, C 189 of 28 July 1990

Jenard & Möller Report on the Lugano Convention, C 189 of 28 July 1990

Borrás Report on the Convention, drawn up on the basis on Article K.3 of the Treaty on the European Union, on Jurisdiction and the Recognitiion and Enforcement of Judgments in Matrimonial Matters; OJ C 221, 16 July 1998, 27

Virgos/Schmit Report on the Convention on Insolvency Proceedings (unpublished)

Proposal for a Council Regulation (EC) on jurisdiction and the recognition and enforcement of judgements in civil and commercial matters (including an explanatory memorandum); OJ C 376E of 28 December 1999, p 1

Practice guide for the application of the Regulation, drawn up by the European Commission in consultation with the European Judicial Network in civil and commerical matters; available at <http://www,europa.eu/comm/justice_home/ejn>

OFFICIAL DOCUMENTS OF THE HAGUE CONFERENCE ON PRIVATE INTERNATIONAL LAW

(In Date Order)

P Jenard, 'Rapport du Comité restreint sur la bilateralisation' [1969] Hague Conference on Private International Law. Proceedings of the Extraordinary Session 11, 145–151 (Jenard Report)

Report by CN Fragistas on the Special Commission meeting for the (1971) Hague Convention on the recognition and enforcement of foreign judgments in civil and commercial matters [1969] Hague Conference on Private International Law. Proceedings of the Extraordinary Session, 360–388

Explanatory report by GAL Droz on the (1971) Hague Convention on the recognition and enforcement of foreign judgments in civil and commercial matters [1969] Hague Conference on Private International Law. Proceedings of the Extraordinary Session, 498–504

Report by P Lagarde on the (1996) Hague Convention on jurisdiction, applicable law, recognition, enforcement and cooperation in respect of parental responsibility and measures for the protection of children, [1996] Hague Conference on Private International Law. Proceedings of the Eighteenth Session, vol. II, *Protection of children*, 35–604

C Kessedjian, 'International jurisdiction and foreign judgments in civil and commercial matters', Preliminary Document No 7 of the Choice of Court Convention (1997)

C Kessedjian, 'Note on Provisional and Protective Measures in Private International Law and Comparative Law,' Preliminary Document No 10 of the Choice of Court Convention (1998)

Report by P Nygh & F Pocar on the Preliminary Draft Convention on jurisdiction and foreign judgments in civil and commercial matters, Preliminary Document No 11 of the Choice of Court Convention (2000)

C Kessedjian on 'Electronic Commerce and International Jurisdiction', Preliminary Document No 12 of the Choice of Court Convention (2000)

Report of the experts meeting on the intellectual property aspects of the future convention on jurisdiction and foreign judgments in civil and commercial matters, Preliminary Document No 13 of the Choice of Court Convention (2001)

Summary of the Outcome of the Discussion in Commission II of the First Part of the Diplomatic Conference (2001)

A Haines on 'The impact of the internet on the Judgments Project: Thoughts for the Future', Preliminary Document No 17 of the Choice of Court Convention (2002)

A Schulz 'Reflection paper to assist in the preparation of a convention on jurisdiction and recognition and enforcement of foreign judgments in civil and commercial matter', Preliminary Document No 19 of the Choice of Court Convention (2002)

A Schulz, 'The relationship between the judgments project and other international instruments', Preliminary Document No 24 of the Choice of Court Convention (2003)

Report by TC Hartley & M Dogauchi on the Preliminary Draft Convention on Exclusive Choice of Court Agreements, Preliminary Document No 26 of the Choice of Court Convention (2004)

Explanatory Report to the Convention of 30 June 2005 on Choice of Court Agreements by TC Hartley and M Dogauchi

E Gerasimchuk, 'The relationship between the judgments project and certain regional instruments in the arena of the Commonwealth of Independent States', Preliminary Document No 27 of the Choice of Court Convention (2005)

A Schulz, Report on the meeting of the Drafting Committee of April 2005, Preliminary Document No 28 of the Choice of Court Convention (2005)

Index